7E Cases in Management,
Organizational Behavior
and Human Resource Management

Managing
ORGANIZATIONS

Paul F. Buller and Randall S. Schuler

and People

SOUTH-WESTERN
CENGAGE Learning

Australia · Brazil · Japan · Korea · Mexico · Singapore · Spain · United Kingdom · United States

SOUTH-WESTERN
CENGAGE Learning™

**Managing Organizations and People,
Seventh Edition**
Paul F. Buller, Randall S. Schuler

VP/Editorial Director: Jack W. Calhoun

VP/Editor-in-Chief: Dave Shaut

Sr. Publisher: Melissa S. Acuña

Executive Editor: John Szilagyi

Marketing Manager: Jacquelyn Carrillo

Production Editor: Starratt E. Alexander

Manager of Technology, Editorial: Vicki True

Technology Project Editor: Kristen Meere

Web Coordinator: Karen L. Schaffer

Sr. First Print Buyer: Doug Wilke

Production House: Off Center Concept
House, Inc.

Art Director: Anne-Marie Rekow

Internal Designer: Bethany Casey

Cover Designer: Anne-Marie Rekow

Cover Images: © Photodisc

For product information and technology assistance, contact us at
Cengage Learning Customer & Sales Support, 1-800-354-9706

For permission to use material from this text or product,
submit all requests online at **www.cengage.com/permissions**
Further permissions questions can be emailed to
permissionrequest@cengage.com

Library of Congress Control Number: 2004117304

ISBN-13: 978-0-324-31457-1

ISBN-10: 0-324-31457-4

South-Western
5191 Natorp Boulevard
Mason, OH 45040
USA

Cengage Learning is a leading provider of customized learning solutions with
office locations around the globe, including Singapore, the United Kingdom,
Australia, Mexico, Brazil, and Japan. Locate your local office at
www.cengage.com/global

Cengage Learning products are represented in Canada by Nelson Education, Ltd.

To learn more about South-Western, visit **www.cengage.com/southwestern**

Purchase any of our products at your local college store or at our preferred
online store **www.ichapters.com**

Printed in the United States of America
3 4 5 6 7   14 13 12 11 10

ED364

Contents

MODULE V—HUMAN RESOURCE MANAGEMENT

MODULE VI—MANAGING DIVERSITY

MODULE VII—MOTIVATION AND PERFORMANCE

MODULE VIII—COMMUNICATION AND GROUP DYNAMICS

MODULE IX—ORGANIZATIONAL CHANGE AND TRANSFORMATION

Management and Leadership

Cases Outline

BULLER | SCHULER

Managing Organizations and People

A Resource for Cases in Management, Organizational Behavior, and Human Resource Management

Abstract

The Custom Chip, Inc. case provides students with an opportunity to understand and explore the complexity of a manager's job. The case, set in the semiconductor industry, describes a middle level engineering manager's activities over the course of a day. Students see that this manager—Frank Questin—is faced with a never-ending stream of organizational situations and opportunities to which he can respond. The primary issue in this case is Frank Questin's effectiveness as a manager. The interplay of his personality, job requirements, and environment make the assessment of his effectiveness a challenging task for the students.

Custom Chip, Inc.

Introduction

It was 7:50 on Monday morning. Frank Questin, Product Engineering Manager at Custom Chip, Inc. was sitting in his office making a TO DO list for the day. From 8:00 to 9:30 A.M. he would have his weekly meeting with his staff of engineers. After the meeting, Frank thought he would begin developing a proposal for solving what he called "Custom Chip's manufacturing documentation problem"—inadequate technical information regarding the steps to manufacture many of the company's products. Before he could finish his TO DO list, he answered a phone call from Custom Chip's human resource manager, who asked him about the status of two overdue performance appraisals and reminded him that this day marked Bill Lazarus' fifth year anniversary with the company. Following this call, Frank hurried off to the Monday morning meeting with his staff.

Frank had been Product Engineering Manager at Custom Chip for 14 months. This was his first management position, and he sometimes questioned his effectiveness as a manager. Often he could not complete the tasks he set out for himself due to interruptions and problems brought to his attention by others. Even though he had not been told exactly what results he was supposed to accomplish, he had a nagging feeling that he should have achieved more after these 14 months. On the other hand, he thought maybe he was functioning pretty well in some of his areas of responsibility given the complexity of the problems his group handled and the unpredictable changes in the semiconductor industry—changes caused not only by rapid advances in technology, but also by increased foreign competition and a recent downturn in demand.

Company Background

Custom Chip, Inc. was a semiconductor manufacturer specializing in custom chips and components used in radars, satellite transmitters, and other radio frequency devices. The company had been founded in 1977 and had grown rapidly with sales exceeding $25 million in 1986. Most of the company's 300 employees were located in the main plant in Silicon Valley, but overseas manufacturing facilities in Europe and the Far East were growing in size and importance. These overseas facilities assembled the less complex, higher volume products. New products and the more complex ones were assembled in the main plant. Approximately one-third of the assembly employees were in overseas facilities.

While the specialized products and markets of Custom Chip provided a market niche that had thus far shielded the company from the major downturn in the semiconductor industry, growth had come to a standstill. Because of this, cost reduction had become a high priority.

The Manufacturing Process

Manufacturers of standard chips have long production runs of a few products. Their cost per unit is low and cost control is a primary determinant of success. In contrast, manufacturers of custom chips have extensive product lines and produce small production runs for special applications. Custom Chip, Inc., for example, manufactured over 2000 different products in the last five years. In any one quarter the company might schedule 300 production runs for different products, as many as one-third of which might be new or modified products which the company had not made before. Because they must be efficient in designing and manufacturing many product lines, all custom chip manufacturers are highly dependent on their engineers. Customers are often first concerned with whether Custom Chip can design and manufacture the needed product *at all*, secondly with whether they can deliver it on time, and only thirdly with cost.

After designing a product, there are two phases to the manufacturing process. (See Figure 1.) The first is wafer fabrication. This is a complex process in which circuits are etched onto the various layers added to a silicon wafer. The number of steps that the wafer goes through plus inherent problems in controlling various chemical processes make it very difficult to meet the exacting specifications required for the final wafer. The wafers, which are typically "just a few" inches in diameter when the fabrication process is complete, contain hundreds, sometimes thousands of tiny identical die. Once the wafer has been tested and sliced up to produce these die, each die will be used as a circuit component.

If the completed wafer passes the various quality tests, it moves on to the assembly phase. In assembly, the die from the wafers, very small wires and other components are attached to a circuit in a series of precise operations. This finished circuit is the final product of Custom Chip, Inc.

Each product goes through many independent and delicate operations, and each step is subject to operator or machine error. Due to the number of steps and tests involved, the wafer fabrication takes 8 to 12 weeks and the assembly process takes 4 to 6 weeks. Because of the exacting specifications, products are rejected for the slightest flaw. The likelihood that every product starting the run will make it through all of the processes and still meet specifications is often quite low. For some products, average yield[1] is as low as 40 percent, and actual yields can vary considerably from one run to another. At Custom Chip, the average yield for all products is in the 60 to 70 percent range.

Because it takes so long to make a custom chip, it is especially important to have some control of these yields. For example, if a customer orders one thousand units of a product and typical yields for that product average 50 percent, Custom Chip will schedule a starting batch of 2200 units. With this approach, even if the yield falls as low as 45.4 percent (45.4% of 2200 is 1000) the company can still meet the order. If the actual yield falls below 45.4 percent, the order will not be completed in that run, and a very small, costly run of the item will be needed to complete the order. The only way the company can effectively control these yields and stay on schedule is for the engineering groups and operations to cooperate and coordinate their efforts efficiently.

FIGURE 1
Manufacturing
Process

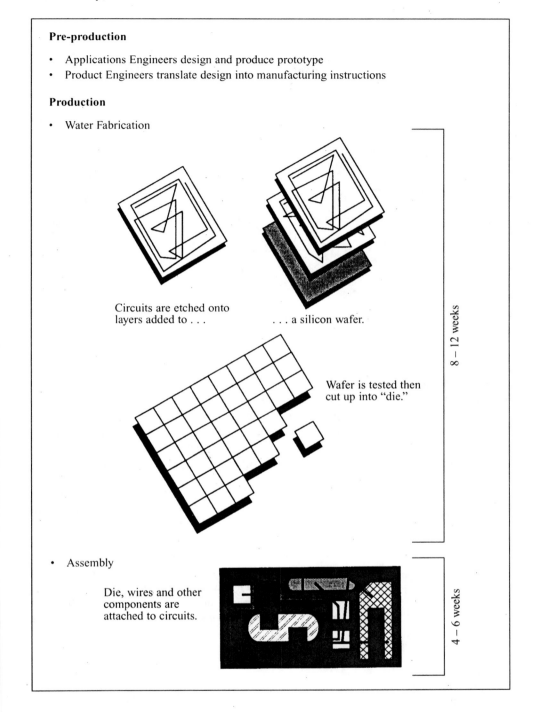

Pre-production

- Applications Engineers design and produce prototype
- Product Engineers translate design into manufacturing instructions

Production

- Water Fabrication

Circuits are etched onto
layers added to . . .   . . . a silicon wafer.

Wafer is tested then
cut up into "die."

- Assembly

Die, wires and other
components are
attached to circuits.

8 – 12 weeks

4 – 6 weeks

Role of the Product Engineer

The product engineer's job is defined by its relationship to application engineering and operations. The applications engineers are responsible for designing and developing prototypes when incoming orders are for new or modified products. The product engineer's role is to translate the application engineering group's design into a set of manufacturing instructions, then to work alongside manufacturing to make sure that engineering related problems get solved. The product engineers' effectiveness is ultimately measured by their ability to control yields on their assigned products. The organization chart in Figure 2 shows the engineering and operations departments. Figure 3 summarizes the roles and objectives of manufacturing, application engineering, and product engineering.

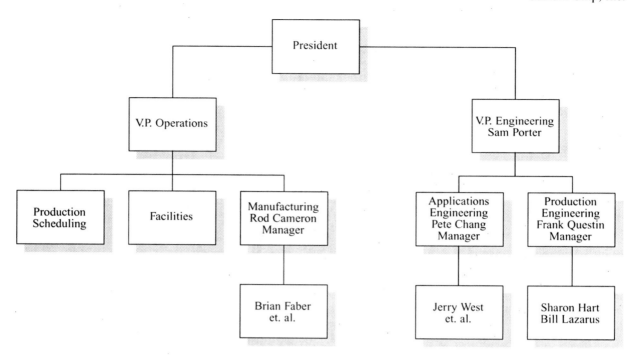

FIGURE 2
Custom Chip, Inc.
Partial Organization
Chart

The product engineers estimate that 70 to 80 percent of their time is spent in solving day-to-day manufacturing problems. The product engineers have cubicles in a room directly across the hall from the manufacturing facility. If a manufacturing supervisor has a question regarding how to build a product during a run, that supervisor will call the engineer assigned to that product. If the engineer is available, he or she will go to the manufacturing floor to help answer the question. If the engineer is not available, the production run may be stopped and the product put aside so that other orders can be manufactured. This results in delays and added costs. One reason that product engineers are consulted is that documentation—the instructions for manufacturing the product—is unclear or incomplete.

The product engineer will also be called if a product is tested and fails to meet specifications. If a product fails to meet test specifications, production stops, and the engineer must diagnose the problem and attempt to find a solution. Otherwise, the order for that product may be only partially met. Test failures are a very serious problem, which can result in considerable cost increases and schedule delays for customers. Products do not test properly for many reasons, including operator errors, poor materials, a design that

FIGURE 3
Departmental Roles
and Objectives

Department	Role	Primary Objective
Applications Engineering	Design and develop prototypes for new or modified products	Satisfy customer needs through innovative designs
Product Engineering	Translates designs into manufacturing instructions and works alongside manufacturing to solve "engineering related" problems	Maintain and control yields on assigned products
Manufacturing	Executes designs	Meet productivity standards and time schedules

is very difficult to manufacture, a design that provides too little margin for error, or a combination of these.

On a typical day, the product engineer may respond to half a dozen questions from the manufacturing floor, and two to four calls to the testing stations. When interviewed, the engineers expressed a frustration with this situation. They thought they spent too much time solving short-term problems, and consequently they were neglecting other important parts of their jobs. In particular, they felt they had little time in which to:

- **Coordinate with applications engineers during the design phase.** The product engineers stated that their knowledge of manufacturing could provide valuable input to the applications engineer. Together they could improve the manufacturability and thus, the yields, of the new or modified product.
- **Engage in yield improvement projects.** This would involve an in-depth study of the existing process for a specific product in conjunction with an analysis of past product failures.
- **Accurately document the manufacturing steps for their assigned products, especially for those which tend to have large or repeat orders.** They said that the current state of the documentation is very poor. Operators often have to build products using only a drawing showing the final circuit, along with a few notes scribbled in the margins. While experienced operators and supervisors may be able to work with this information, they often make incorrect guesses and assumptions. Inexperienced operators may not be able to proceed with certain products because of this poor documentation.

Weekly Meeting

As manager of the product engineering group, Frank Questin had eight engineers reporting to him, each responsible for a different set of Custom Chip products. According to Frank:

When I took over as manager, the product engineers were not spending much time together as a group. They were required to handle operation problems on short notice. This made it difficult for the entire group to meet due to constant requests for assistance from the manufacturing area.

I thought that my engineers could be of more assistance and support to each other if they all spent more time together as a group, so one of my first actions as a manager was to institute a regularly scheduled weekly meeting. I let the manufacturing people know that my staff would not respond to requests for assistance during the meeting.

The meeting on this particular Monday morning followed the usual pattern. Frank talked about upcoming company plans, projects and other news that might be of interest to the group. He then provided data about current yields for each product and commended those engineers who had maintained or improved yields on most of their products. This initial phase of the meeting lasted until about 8:30 A.M. The remainder of the meeting was a meandering discussion of a variety of topics. Since there was no agenda, engineers felt comfortable in raising issues of concern to them.

The discussion started with one of the engineers describing a technical problem in the assembly of one of his products. He was asked a number of questions and given some advice. Another engineer raised the topic of a need for new testing equipment and described a test unit he had seen at a recent demonstration. He claimed the savings in labor and improved yields from this machine would allow it to pay for itself in less than nine months. Frank immediately replied that budget limitations made such a purchase unfeasible, and the discussion moved into another area. They briefly discussed the increasing inaccessibility of the application engineers, then talked about a few other topics.

In general, the engineers valued these meetings. One commented that:

The Monday meetings give me a chance to hear what's on everyone's mind and to find out about and discuss company wide news. It's hard to reach any conclusions because the meeting is a freewheeling discussion. But I really appreciate the friendly atmosphere with my peers.

Coordination with Applications Engineers

Following the meeting that morning, an event occurred that highlighted the issue of the inaccessibility of the applications engineers. An order of 300 units of custom chip 1210A for a major customer was already overdue. Because the projected yield of this product was 70 percent, they had started with a run of 500 units. A sample tested at one of the early assembly points indicated a major performance problem that could drop the yield to below 50 percent. Bill Lazarus, the product engineer assigned to the 1210A, examined the sample and determined that the problem could be solved by redesigning the writing. Jerry West, the application engineer assigned to that product category was responsible for revising the design. Bill tried to contact Jerry, but he was not immediately available, and didn't get back to Bill until later in the day. Jerry explained that he was on a tight schedule trying to finish a design for a customer who was coming into town in two days, and could not get to "Bill's problem" for a while.

Jerry's attitude that the problem belonged to product engineering was typical of the applications engineers. From their point of view there were a number of reasons for making the product engineers needs for assistance a lower priority. In the first place, applications engineers were rewarded and acknowledged primarily for satisfying customer needs through designing new and modified products. They got little recognition for solving manufacturing problems. Secondly, applications engineering was perceived to be more glamorous than product engineering because of opportunities to be credited with innovative and ground breaking designs. Finally, the size of the applications engineering group had declined over the past year, causing the workload on each engineer to increase considerably. Now they had even less time to respond to the product engineer's requests.

When Bill Lazarus told Frank about the situation, Frank acted quickly. He wanted this order to be in process again by tomorrow and he knew manufacturing was also trying to meet this goal. He walked over to see Pete Chang, head of applications engineering (see Organization Chart in Figure 2). Meetings like this with Pete to discuss and resolve interdepartmental issues were common.

Frank found Pete at a workbench talking with one of his engineers. He asked Pete if he could talk to him in private and they walked to Pete's office.

Frank: We've got a problem in manufacturing in getting out an order of 1210A's. Bill Lazarus is getting little or no assistance from Jerry West. I'm hoping you can get Jerry to pitch in and help Bill. It should take no more than a few hours of his time.

Pete: I do have Jerry on a short leash trying to keep him focused on getting out a design for Teletronics. We can't afford to show up empty handed at our meeting with them in two days.

Frank: Well, we are going to end up losing one customer in trying to please another. Can't we satisfy everyone here?

Pete: Do you have an idea?

Frank: Can't you give Jerry some additional support on the Teletronics design?

Pete: Let's get Jerry in here to see what we can do.

Pete brought Jerry back to the office, and together they discussed the issues and possible solutions. When Pete made it clear to Jerry that he considered the problem with the 1210A's a priority, Jerry offered to work on the 1210A problem with Bill. He said, "This will mean I'll have to stay a few hours past 5:00 this evening, but I'll do what's required to get the job done."

Frank was glad he had developed a collaborative relationship with Pete. He had always made it a point to keep Pete informed about activities in the Product Engineering group that might affect the applications engineers. In addition, he would often chat with Pete informally over coffee or lunch in the company cafeteria. This relationship with Pete made Frank's job easier. He wished he had the same rapport with Rod Cameron, the Manufacturing Manager.

Coordination with Manufacturing

The product engineers worked closely on a day-to-day basis with the manufacturing supervisors and workers. The problems between these two groups stemmed from an inherent conflict between their objectives (see Figure 3). The objective of the product engineers was to maintain and improve yields. They had the authority to stop production of any run that did not test properly. Manufacturing, on the other hand, was trying to meet productivity standards and time schedules. When a product engineer stopped a manufacturing run, he was possibly preventing the manufacturing group from reaching its objectives.

Rod Cameron, the current manufacturing manager, had been promoted from his position as a manufacturing supervisor a year ago. His views on the product engineers:

The product engineers are perfectionists. The minute a test result looks a little suspicious they want to shut down the factory. I'm under a lot of pressure to get products out the door. If they pull a few $50,000 orders off the line when they are within a few days of reaching shipping, I'm liable to miss my numbers by $100,000 that month.

Besides that, they are doing a lousy job of documenting the manufacturing steps. I've got a lot of turnover, and my new operators need to be told or shown exactly what to do for each product. The instructions for a lot of our products are a joke.

At first, Frank found Rod very difficult to deal with. Rod found fault with the product engineers for many problems and sometimes seemed rude to Frank when they talked. For example, Rod might tell Frank to "make it quick, I haven't got much time." Frank tried not to take Rod's actions personally, and through persistence was able to develop a more amicable relationship with him. According to Frank:

Sometimes, my people will stop work on a product because it doesn't meet test results at that stage of manufacturing. If we study the situation, we might be able to maintain yields or even save an entire run by adjusting the manufacturing procedures. Rod tries to bully me into changing my engineers' decisions. He yells at me or criticizes the competence of my people, but I don't allow his temper or ravings to influence my best judgment in a situation. My strategy in dealing with Rod is to try not to respond defensively to him. Eventually he cools down, and we can have a reasonable discussion of the situation.

Despite this strategy, Frank could not always resolve his problems with Rod. On these occasions, Frank took the issue to his own boss, Sam Porter, the Vice President in charge of engineering. However, Frank was not satisfied with the support he got from Sam. Frank said:

Sam avoids confrontations with the Operations VP. He doesn't have the influence or clout with the other VPs or the president to do justice to engineering's needs in the organization.

Early that afternoon, Frank again found himself trying to resolve a conflict between engineering and manufacturing. Sharon Hart, one of his most effective product engineers was responsible for a series of products used in radars—the 3805A–3808A series. Today she had stopped a large run of 3806A's. The manufacturing supervisor, Brian Faber, went to Rod Cameron to complain about the impact of this stoppage on his group's productivity. Brian felt that yields were low on that particular product because the production instructions were confusing to his operators, and that even with clearer instructions, his operators would need additional training to build it satisfactorily. He stressed that the product engineer's responsibility was to adequately document the production instructions and provide training. For these reasons, Brian asserted that product engineering, and not manufacturing, should be accountable for the productivity loss in the case of these 3806A's.

Rod called Frank to his office, where he joined the discussion with Sharon, Brian and Rod. After listening to the issues, Frank conceded that product engineering had responsibility for documenting and training. He also explained, even though everyone was aware of it, that the product engineering group had been operating with reduced staff for over a year now, so training and documentation were lower priorities. Because of this staffing situation, Frank suggested that manufacturing and product engineering work together and pool their limited resources to solve the documentation and training problem. He was especially interested in using a few of the long-term experienced workers to assist in training newer workers. Rod and Brian opposed his suggestion. They did not want to take experienced operators off of the line because it would decrease productivity. The meeting ended when Brian stormed out, saying that Sharon had better get the 3806A's up and running again that morning.

Frank was particularly frustrated by this episode with manufacturing. He knew perfectly well that his group had primary responsibility for documenting the manufacturing steps for each product. A year ago he told Sam Porter that the product engineers needed to update and standardize all of the documentation for manufacturing products. At that time, Sam told Frank that he would support his efforts to develop the documentation, but would not increase his staff. In fact, Sam had withheld authorization to fill a recently vacated product engineering slot. Frank was reluctant to push the staffing issue because of Sam's adamance about reducing costs. "Perhaps," Frank thought, "if I develop a proposal clearly showing the benefits of a documentation program in manufacturing and detailing the steps and resources required to implement the program, I might be able to convince Sam to provide us with more resources." But Frank could never find the time to develop that proposal. And so he remained frustrated.

Later in the Day

Frank was reflecting on the complexity of his job when Sharon came to the doorway to see if he had a few moments. Before he could say "come in," the phone rang. He looked at the clock. It was 4:10 P.M. Pete was on the other end of the line with an idea he wanted to try out on Frank, so Frank said he could call him back shortly. Sharon was upset, and told him that she was thinking of quitting because the job was not satisfying for her.

Sharon said that although she very much enjoyed working on yield improvement projects, she could find no time for them. She was tired of the application engineers acting like "prima donnas," too busy to help her solve what they seemed to think were mundane day-to-day manufacturing problems. She also thought that many of the day-to-day problems she handled wouldn't exist if there was enough time to document manufacturing procedures to begin with.

Frank didn't want to lose Sharon, so he tried to get into a frame of mind where he could be empathetic to her. He listened to her and told her that he could understand her frustration in this situation. He told her the situation would change as industry conditions improved. He told her that he was pleased that she felt comfortable in venting her frustrations with him, and he hoped she would stay with Custom Chip.

After Sharon left, Frank realized that he had told Pete that he would call back. He glanced at the TO DO list he had never completed, and realized that he hadn't spent time on his top priority—developing a proposal relating to solving the documentation problem in manufacturing. Then, he remembered that he had forgotten to acknowledge Bill Lazarus' fifth year anniversary with the company. He thought to himself that his job felt like a roller coaster ride, and once again he pondered his effectiveness as a manager.

Endnote

1. Yield refers to the ratio of finished products that meet specifications relative to the number that initially entered the manufacturing process.

BULLER | SCHULER

Managing Organizations and People

A Resource for Cases in Management, Organizational Behavior, and Human Resource Management

Abstract

This case shows the problems in trying to get others to change, especially old established work habits, and the costs involved in making career changes in an organization. Dick Spencer has made many career changes and has been successful, but the changes haven't been without personal costs and problems.

Dick Spencer

After the usual banter when old friends meet for cocktails, the conversation between a couple of University professors and Dick Spencer, who was now a successful businessman, turned to Dick's life as a vice-president of a large manufacturing firm.

"I've made a lot of mistakes, most of which I could live with, but this one series of incidents was so frustrating that I could have cried at the time," Dick said in response to a question. "I really have to laugh at how ridiculous it is now, but at the time I blew my cork."

Spencer was plant manager of Modrow Company, a Canadian branch of the Tri-American Corporation. Tri-American was a major producer of primary aluminum with integrated operations ranging from the mining of bauxite through the processing to fabrication of aluminum into a variety of products. The company had also made and sold refractories and industrial chemicals. The parent company had wholly-owned subsidiaries in five separate United States locations and had foreign affiliates in fifteen different countries.

Tri-American mined bauxite in the Jamaican West Indies and shipped the raw material by commercial vessels to two plants in Louisiana where it was processed into alumina. The alumina was then shipped to reduction plants in one of three locations for conversion into primary aluminum. Most of the primary aluminum was then moved to the companies' fabricating plants for further processing. Fabricated aluminum items included sheet, flat, coil, and corrugated products; siding; and roofing.

Tri-American employed approximately 22,000 employees in the total organization. The company was governed by a board of directors which included the chairman, vice-chairman, president, and twelve vice-presidents. However, each of the subsidiaries and branches functioned as independent units. The board set general policy, which was then

■ This case was developed and prepared by Professor Margaret E. Fenn, Graduate School of Business Administration, University of Washington. Reprinted by permission.

1

interpreted and applied by the various plant managers. In a sense, the various plants competed with one another as though they were independent companies. This decentralization in organizational structure increased the freedom and authority of the plant managers, but increased the pressure for profitability.

The Modrow branch was located in a border town in Canada. The total work force in Modrow was 1,000. This Canadian subsidiary was primarily a fabricating unit. Its main products were foil and building products such as roofing and siding. Aluminum products were gaining in importance in architectural plans, and increased sales were predicted for this branch. Its location and its stable work force were the most important advantages it possessed.

In anticipation of estimated increases in building product sales, Modrow had recently completed a modernization and expansion project. At the same time, their research and art departments combined talents in developing a series of twelve new patterns of siding which were being introduced to the market. Modernization and pattern development had been costly undertakings, but the expected return on investment made the project feasible. However, the plant manager, who was a Tri-American vice-president, had instituted a campaign to cut expenses wherever possible. In this introductory notice of the campaign, he emphasized that cost reduction would be the personal aim of every employee at Modrow.

Salesman

The plant manager of Modrow, Dick Spencer, was an American who had been transferred to this Canadian branch two years previously, after the start of the modernization plan. Dick had been with the Tri-American Company for fourteen years, and his progress within the organization was considered spectacular by those who knew him well. Dick had received a Master's degree in Business Administration from a well-known university at the age of twenty-two. Upon graduation he had accepted a job as salesman for Tri-American. During his first year as a salesman, he succeeded in landing a single, large contract which put him near the top of the sales-volume leaders. In discussing this phenomenal rise in the sales volume, several of his fellow salesmen concluded that his looks, charm, and ability on the golf course contributed as much to his success as his knowledge of the business or his ability to sell the products.

The second year of his sales career, he continued to set a fast pace. Although his record set difficult goals for the other salesmen, he was considered a "regular guy" by them, and both he and they seemed to enjoy the few occasions when they socialized. However, by the end of the second year of constant traveling and selling, Dick began to experience some doubt about his future.

His constant involvement in business affairs disrupted his marital life, and his wife divorced him during the second year with Tri-American. Dick resented her action at first, but gradually seemed to recognize that his career at present depended on his freedom to travel unencumbered. During that second year, he ranged far and wide in his sales territory, and successfully closed several large contracts. None of them was as large as his first year's major sale, but in total volume he again was well up near the top of salesmen for the year. Dick's name became well known in the corporate headquarters, and he was spoken of as "the boy to watch."

Dick had met the president of Tri-American during his first year as a salesman at a company conference. After three days of golfing and socializing they developed a relaxed camraderie considered unusual by those who observed the developing friendship. Although their contacts were infrequent after the conference, their easy relationship seemed to blossom the few times they did meet. Dick's friends kidded him about his ability to make use of his new friendship to promote himself in the company, but Dick brushed aside their jibes and insisted that he'd make it on his own abilities, not someone's coattails.

By the time he was twenty-five, Dick began to suspect that he did not look forward to a life as a salesman for the rest of his career. He talked about his unrest with his friends, and they suggested that he groom himself for sales manager. "You won't make the kind of money you're making from commissions," he was told, "but you will have a foot in the door from an administrative standpoint, and you won't have to travel quite as much as you do now." Dick took their suggestions lightly, and continued to sell the product, but was aware that he felt dissatisfied and did not seem to get the satisfaction out of his job that he had once enjoyed.

By the end of his third year with the company Dick was convinced that he wanted a change in direction. As usual, he and the president spent quite a bit of time on the golf course during the annual company sales conference. After their match one day, the president kidded Dick about his game. The conversation drifted back to business, and the president, who seemed to be in a jovial mood, started to kid Dick about his sales ability. In a joking way, he implied that anyone could sell a product as good as Tri-American's, but that it took real "guts and know-how" to make the products. The conversation drifted to other things, but the remark stuck with Dick.

Sometime later, Dick approached the president formally with a request for a transfer out of the sales division. The president was surprised and hesitant about this change in career direction for Dick. He recognized the superior sales ability that Dick seemed to possess, but was unsure that Dick was willing or able to assume responsibilities in any other division of the organization. Dick sensed the hesitancy, but continued to push his request. He later remarked that it seemed that the initial hesitancy of the president convinced Dick that he needed an opportunity to prove himself in a field other than sales.

Trouble Shooter

Dick was finally transferred back to the home office of the organization and indoctrinated into production and administrative roles in the company as a special assistant to the senior vice-president of production. As a special assistant, Dick was assigned several trouble-shooting jobs. He acquitted himself well in this role, but in the process succeeded in gaining a reputation as a ruthless head hunter among the branches where he had performed a series of amputations. His reputation as an amiable, genial, easygoing guy from the sales department was the antithesis of the reputation of a cold, calculating head hunter which he earned in his troubleshooting role. The vice-president, who was Dick's boss, was aware of the reputation which Dick had earned but was pleased with the results that were obtained. The faltering departments that Dick had worked in seemed to bloom with new life and energy after Dick's recommended amputations. As a result, the vice-president began to sing Dick's praises, and the president began to accept Dick in his new role in the company.

Management Responsibility

About three years after Dick's switch from sales, he was given an assignment as assistant plant manager of an English branch of the company. Dick, who had remarried, moved his wife and family to London, and they attempted to adapt to their new routine. The plant manager was English, as were most of the other employees. Dick and his family were accepted with reservations into the community life as well as into the plant life. The difference between British and American philosophy and performance within the plant was marked for Dick who was imbued with modern managerial concepts and methods. Dick's directives from headquarters were to update and upgrade performance in this branch. However, his power and authority were less than those of his superiors, so he constantly found himself in the position of having to soft pedal or withhold suggestions that he would have liked to make, or innovations that he would have liked to introduce. After a frustrating year and a half, Dick was suddenly made plant manager of an old British company which had just been purchased by Tri-American. He left his first English assignment with mixed feelings and moved from London to Birmingham.

As the new plant manager, Dick operated much as he had in his troubleshooting job for the first couple of years of his change from sales to administration. Training and re-education programs were instituted for all supervisors and managers who survived the initial purge. Methods were studied and simplified or redesigned whenever possible, and new attention was directed toward production which better met the needs of the sales organization. A strong controller helped to straighten out the profit picture through stringent cost control; and by the end of the third year, the company showed a small profit for the first time in many years. Because he felt that this battle was won, Dick requested transfer back to the United States. The request was partially granted when nine months later he was awarded a junior vice-president title, and was made manager of a subsidiary Canadian plant, Modrow.

Modrow Manager

Prior to Dick's appointment as plant manager at Modrow, extensive plans for plant expansion and improvement had been approved and started. Although he had not been in on the original discussions and plans, he inherited all the problems that accompany large-scale changes in any organization. Construction was slower in completion than originally planned, equipment arrived before the building was finished, employees were upset about the extent of change expected in their work routines with the installation of additional machinery, and, in general, morale was at a low ebb.

Various versions of Dick's former activities had preceded him, and on his arrival he was viewed with dubious eyes. The first few months after his arrival were spent in a frenzy of catching up. This entailed constant conferences and meetings, volumes of reading of past reports, becoming acquainted with the civic leaders of the area, and a plethora of dispatches to and from the home office. Costs continued to climb unabated.

By the end of his first year at Modrow, the building program had been completed, although behind schedule, the new equipment had been installed, and some revamping of cost procedures had been incorporated. The financial picture at this time showed a substantial loss, but since it had been budgeted as a loss, this was not surprising. All managers of the various divisions had worked closely with their supervisors and accountants in planning the budget for the following year, and Dick began to emphasize his personal interest in cost reduction.

As he worked through his first year as plant manager, Dick developed the habit of strolling around the organization. He was apt to leave his office and appear anywhere on the plant floor, in the design offices, at the desk of a purchasing agent or accountant, in the plant cafeteria rather than the executive dining room, or wherever there was activity concerned with Modrow. During his strolls he looked, listened, and became acquainted. If he observed activities which he wanted to talk about, or heard remarks that gave him clues to future action, he did not reveal these at the time. Rather he had a nod, a wave, a smile, for the people near him, but a mental note to talk to his supervisors, managers, and foremen in the future. At first his presence disturbed those who noted him coming and going, but after several exposures to him without any noticeable effect, the workers came to accept his presence and continue their usual activities. Supervisors, managers, and foremen, however, did not feel as comfortable when they saw him in the area.

Their feelings were aptly expressed by the manager of the siding department one day when he was talking to one of his foremen: "I wish to hell he'd stay up in the front office where he belongs. Whoever heard of a plant manager who has time to wander around the plant all the time? Why doesn't he tend to his paper work and let us tend to our business?"

"Don't let him get you down," joked the foreman. "Nothing ever comes of his visits. Maybe he's just lonesome and looking for a friend. You know how these Americans are."

"Well, you may feel that nothing ever comes of his visits, but I don't. I've been called into his office three separate times within the last two months. The heat must really be on from the head office. You know these conferences we have every month where he reviews our financial progress, our building progress, our design progress, etc.? Well, we're not really progressing as fast as we should be. If you ask me we're in for continuing trouble."

In recalling his first year at Modrow, Dick had felt constantly pressured and badgered. He always sensed that the Canadians he worked with resented his presence since he was brought in over the heads of the operating staff. At the same time he felt this subtle resistance from his Canadian work force, he believed that the president and his friends in the home office were constantly on the alert, waiting for Dick to prove himself or fall flat on his face. Because of the constant pressures and demands of the work, he had literally dumped his family into a new community and had withdrawn into the plant. In the process, he built up a wall of resistance toward the demands of his wife and children who, in turn, felt as though he was abandoning them.

During the course of the conversation with his University friends, he began to recall a series of incidents that probably had resulted from the conflicting pressures. When describing some of these incidents, he continued to emphasize the fact that his attempt to be relaxed and casual had backfired. Laughingly, Dick said, "As you know, both human relations and accounting were my weakest subjects during the Master's program, and yet they are two fields I felt I needed the most at Modrow at this time." He described some of the cost procedures that he would have liked to incorporate. However, without the support and knowledge furnished by his former controller, he busied himself with details that were unnecessary. One day, as he describes it, he overheard a conversation between two of the accounting staff members with whom he had been working very closely. One of them commented to the other, "For a guy who's a vice-president, he sure spends a lot of time breathing down our necks. Why doesn't he simply tell us the kind of systems he would like to try, and let us do the experimenting and work out the budget?" Without commenting on the conversation he overheard, Dick then described himself as attempting to spend less time and be less directive in the accounting department.

Another incident he described which apparently had real meaning for him was one in which he had called a staff conference with his top-level managers. They had been going "hammer and tongs" for better than an hour in his private office, and in the process of heated conversation had loosened ties, taken off coats, and really rolled up their sleeves. Dick himself had slipped out of his shoes. In the midst of this, his secretary reminded him of an appointment with public officials. Dick had rapidly finished up his conference with his managers, straightened his tie, donned his coat, and had wandered out into the main office in his stocking feet.

Dick fully described several incidents when he had disappointed, frustrated, or confused his wife and family by forgetting birthdays, appointments, dinner engagements, etc. He seemed to be describing a pattern of behavior which resulted from continuing pressure and frustration. He was setting the scene to describe his baffling and humiliating position in the siding department. In looking back and recalling his activities during this first year, Dick commented on the fact that his frequent wanderings throughout the plant had resulted in a nodding acquaintance with the workers, but probably had also resulted in foremen and supervisors spending more time getting ready for his visits and reading meaning into them afterwards than attending to their specific duties. His attempts to know in detail the accounting procedures being used required long hours of concentration and detailed conversations with the accounting staff, which were time-consuming and very frustrating for him, as well as for them. His lack of attention to his family life resulted in continued pressure from both wife and family.

The Siding Department Incident

Siding was the product which had been budgeted as a large profit item of Modrow. Aluminum siding was gaining in popularity among both architects and builders, because of its possibilities in both decorative and practical uses. Panel sheets of siding were shipped in standard sizes to order; large sheets of the coated siding were cut to specifications in the trim department, packed, and shipped. The trim shop was located near the loading platforms, and Dick often cut through the trim shop on his wanderings through the plant. On one of his frequent trips through the area, he suddenly became aware of the fact that several workers responsible for the disposal function were spending countless hours at high-speed saws cutting scraps into specified lengths to fit into scrap barrels. The narrow bands of scrap which resulted from the trim process varied in length from seven to twenty-seven feet and had to be reduced in size to fit into disposal barrels. Dick, in his concentration on cost reduction, picked up one of the thin strips, bent it several times and fitted it into the barrel. He tried this with another piece, and it bent very easily. After assuring himself that bending was possible, he walked over to a worker at the saw and asked why he was using the saw when material could easily be bent and fitted into the barrels, resulting in saving time and equipment. The worker's response was, "We've never done it that way, sir. We've always cut it."

Following his plan of not commenting or discussing matters on the floor, but distressed by the reply, Dick returned to his office and asked the manager of the siding department if he could speak to the foreman in the scrap division. The manager said, "Of course, I'll send him up to you in just a minute."

After a short time, the foreman, very agitated at being called to the plant manager's office, appeared. Dick began questioning him about the scrap disposal process and received the standard answer: "We've always done it that way." Dick then proceeded to review cost-cutting objectives. He talked about the pliability of the strips of scrap. He called for a few pieces of scrap to demonstrate the ease with which it could be bent, and ended what he thought was a satisfactory conversation by requesting the foreman to order heavy duty gloves for his workers and use the bending process for a trial period of two weeks to check the cost savings possible.

The foreman listened throughout most of this hour's conference, offered several reasons why it wouldn't work, raised some questions about the record keeping process for cost purposes, and finally left the office with the forced agreement to try the suggested new method of bending, rather than cutting, for disposal. Although he was immersed in many other problems, his request was forcibly brought home one day as he cut through the scrap area. The workers were using power saws to cut scraps. He called the manager of the siding department and questioned him about the process. The manager explained that each foreman was responsible for his own processes, and since Dick had already talked to the foreman, perhaps he had better talk to him again. When the foreman arrived, Dick began to question him. He received a series of excuses, and some explanations of the kinds of problems they were meeting by attempting to bend the scrap material. "I don't care what the problems are," Dick nearly shouted, "when I request a cost-reduction program instituted, I want to see it carried through."

Dick was furious. When the foreman left, he phoned the maintenance department and ordered the removal of the power saws from the scrap area immediately. A short time later the foreman of the scrap department knocked on Dick's door reporting his astonishment at having maintenance men step into his area and physically remove the saws. Dick reminded the foreman of his request for a trial at cost reduction to no avail, and ended the conversation by saying that the power saws were gone and would not be returned, and the foreman had damned well better learn to get along without them. After a stormy exit by the foreman, Dick congratulated himself on having solved a problem and turned his attention to other matters.

A few days later Dick cut through the trim department and literally stopped to stare. As he described it, he was completely nonplussed to discover gloved workmen using hand shears to cut each strip of scrap.

BULLER | SCHULER

Managing Organizations and People
A Resource for Cases in Management, Organizational Behavior, and Human Resource Management

Abstract

Jim Wallace, the Vice President of Sales at ChemCorp, is being faced with a difficult situation. His boss has just asked him to market a product line that is likely to be banned because of its link with cancer. Jim's boss, Art Jackson, tells Jim that he has to market the product and present him with a marketing plan by the next morning. Because Jim is in the Midwest, it is likely that his customers will not know about the harmful effects of Agri-Coat, a product produced by another West Coast subsidiary. The firm's real intent is to unload the inventory before the federal ban is official and known to customers.

The Marketing Campaign at ChemCorp

Jim Wallace stood at the window of his 8th floor office looking out over a city about to be engulfed by dusk. He had just come back from a meeting with Art Jackson, President of ChemCorp, an agricultural chemical and fertilizer company. Unlike other meetings with Art, this one left Jim with a feeling of uneasiness.

Art had proposed that Jim, in his position as Vice President of Sales, develop a sales campaign for AgriCoat, a pesticide to be shipped from Western Fertilizers and Chemicals, a California company. The President had asked that this project be given top priority because of its importance to both ChemCorp and its parent company, CCA. But the circumstances surrounding the request made it difficult for Jim to start designing the campaign right away. He struggled to find the reasons for his reluctance.

Background of ChemCorp
ChemCorp was founded in the early 1920s by two chemical engineers as a small chemical company with a focus on the market in the southeastern part of the United States. With a limited product line but a reputation for quality and service, it became a very successful company, weathering both the Great Depression and World War II. The booming post-war economy found ChemCorp poised for expansion within the emerging agricultural industry in the Southeast. Agricultural cooperatives and larger farmers became the primary customers who fueled its growth as they came to rely on ChemCorp to meet their needs.

The small core of managers who had guided the company through its early period gave way to a new group of managers in the 1950s who brought new sophistication to both

---

■ This case was written by D. Jeffrey Lenn, School of Business and Public Management at The George Washington University. While it portrays an actual situation, names and places have been changed to maintain confidentiality for the managers involved. Reprinted by permission.

production and marketing. ChemCorp expanded its production capacity by building new plants in a number of small towns in the Southeast. An aggressive marketing strategy was inaugurated through a well-trained sales force, an expanded product line, and a substantial research and development program designed to create products suited to the needs of farmers. Growth never clouded ChemCorp's fundamental mission of retaining a reputation for product quality and customer service.

Art Jackson became president 10 years ago, the first outsider to take over the reins of the company. Well-established in the industry as a divisional vice president of a major chemical company, Art found a new home at ChemCorp. He quickly surrounded himself with a new executive group and set his sights on consolidating the position of ChemCorp as a regional leader in the agricultural chemical industry.

Four years ago, ChemCorp was taken over by CCA, a diversified conglomerate headquartered in the Northeast. CCA was searching to expand its portfolio of small and medium companies with excellent cash flow and established market share in the agricultural industry. ChemCorp was a prime candidate to round out a new CCA division which already included two other small chemical and several agricultural product companies. While reluctant initially to sell, the ChemCorp board took Art's advice that the price was right. CCA's promise to maintain an arms-length management relationship while providing capital infusion was important also in the board's decision. They sold to CCA with the understanding that top management would stay and the thrust of the business would be maintained.

Jackson's forecast had been correct. CCA was liberal in its capital expenditure policy as it approved a large initial capital budget proposed by the President. This led to a full revamping of the ChemCorp plants with the latest in technology built into the production process. The inclusion of ChemCorp in a national division provided the basis for further integration into a broader marketing strategy in which ChemCorp was expected to play a major role over the next few years.

Jim Wallace's Career at ChemCorp

Jim started as a chemical engineer with ChemCorp right out of college. He worked in the production side for nearly 7 years but became a little frustrated with the highly technical aspects of his job. When an opening in the sales department came up, he jumped at it. His first two years were rocky ones as he just met his sales quota each year. He found that his engineering training had not equipped him very well to handle the day-to-day contacts with customers. While he could help them understand the technical characteristics of the products, he was not always sure just how to convince them to buy these products.

But he worked hard, and with the help of an excellent regional sales manager, began to learn how to couple his product knowledge with customer knowledge to become a highly successful salesman. When a regional manager's position opened up, his own manager recommended him highly. Jim proved his ability in this new position because of his sales expertise and his management experience. An earlier stint as an engineering manager had helped set the stage for this success.

Five years ago, when Art Jackson had reorganized, he had chosen Jim as his new Vice President of Sales. The CEO saw in Jim someone with executive talent. He had fine experience in the field and an excellent reputation with key customers and the sales force. He had acquired good product knowledge through his years in engineering. And most of all, he had developed a good sense of the importance of overall corporate objectives with his exposure to both sales and production. Art recognized that the informal grooming process for executive talent in ChemCorp had produced a fine candidate for this position.

Jim took to the position nicely. Sales volume increased as well as the customer base during his tenure. He worked hard to shape the sales force into a cohesive unit through his hiring practices, a new incentive program, and a personal touch, where he was in touch with top producers on a quarterly basis. His department developed a new sense of pride which led to even greater productivity.

Jim fostered a good working relationship with the engineering department. He worked closely with them to develop new products which were responsive to farmers' needs for fertilizers and pesticides. One of these new products, Gro-Go, was developed nearly three years ago in response to growers' concerns about environmentally safe products. Gro-Go was a breakthrough in a market which was now demanding pesticides which could both control insects and not be harmful to the ultimate consumer. In its first two full years on the market, Gro-Go established itself as a strong product with an excellent future.

At 42, Jim recognized that he had become a successful executive. His relationship with Art made him a key member of the ChemCorp executive team. His hard work and full commitment to his staff had increased his stature within the sales department as well as within other departments. He was pleased with his ability to forge a career which incorporated both production and sales skills rather than simply being defined as a narrow advocate of one or the other of the corporate functions. He was optimistic about his future career.

The Meeting with Art Jackson

Jim was puzzled by the hastily arranged meeting with Art Jackson. He was disturbed by the CEO's manner as they sat across the large oak desk in Art's office. Art's words seemed to be more carefully chosen than usual as he explained that the CCA Group Vice President had called yesterday with a proposal for ChemCorp.

The proposal detailed that ChemCorp would add AgriCoat, a pesticide produced by Western Fertilizers and Chemicals, another subsidiary of CCA on the West Coast, to its product line. The CCA Vice President indicated that the full inventory of AgriCoat would be shipped within the next two weeks and ChemCorp should be prepared to sell it to its customers over the next six months. It suggested that AgriCoat might be heavily discounted or coupled with other promotions to move it quickly into the market in light of such a short time horizon.

While Art was covering some of the financial details, Jim sifted through his knowledge of AgriCoat. He originally had considered adding it to the ChemCorp line but decided that another pesticide would be better suited to his market. His decision to develop Gro-Go had been prompted by customer interest in the environmental aspect. Art had been supportive of this decision even though he recognized that the research and development costs would be higher. Jim's strategy had paid off in terms of the sales figures for Gro-Go. Thus, Art's acceptance of the current CCA proposal was all the more surprising because it appeared that AgriCoat would be in direct competition with Gro-Go.

As Jackson started to outline some of his own ideas about a sales campaign, Wallace interrupted: "But Art, why the big push for AgriCoat now? Sales for Gro-Go are excellent, and we are just beginning to see the early signs of our campaign to build its image as a pesticide which is effective while safe. Introducing AgriCoat would work at cross purposes with what my sales force is doing right now."

Art stumbled a little as he explained the importance of the AgriCoat campaign. Then he paused and looked Jim in the eye: "I wasn't supposed to tell you this, but we have worked together too long not to be honest with each other. CCA staff has found out from inside sources that the U.S. Government has decided from confidential studies that a number of pesticides should be banned from the market. These studies show a direct link between these pesticides and cancer in laboratory animals. The implication is that they also cause cancer in human beings. AgriCoat is one of these pesticides."

"CCA will join with other chemical companies to appeal the ban but expects that it will be unsuccessful. Western is already in shaky financial condition with a heavy inventory of AgriCoat. A California newspaper has leaked a state environmental agency report which questions the safety of this product in particular. Sales have begun to drop off, so CCA has decided that Western will discontinue production of AgriCoat in a week and ship their full inventory to us for marketing here. The Group Vice President estimates that the federal ban will finally take effect in six months. In the meantime, there is little likelihood of much controversy here in our market as nobody knows anything about AgriCoat."

The CEO moved quickly to the point of the meeting: "Jim, I know that the arms-length relationship with CCA has been beneficial to ChemCorp. Now it is time that we begin to see ourselves as part of the larger company by assuming some of the burden from another subsidiary. You are in charge of this operation and I have full confidence that you will be successful.

"We need tell nobody else about the real reason for taking on AgriCoat. Let's just position it as part of our product line. I can understand your difficulties in light of the strength of Gro-Go, but this is only temporary. We really have no choice on this one, as it comes from the top. Your work on this campaign will be important to me and to CCA. This is a big one for your career as well. Those guys at headquarters will be watching us on this one.

"Remember, Jim, we have to move it! In fact, that might be a good start on your campaign with the sales force—'Move it!' I will need a general outline of your campaign by tomorrow morning so I can call CCA. We can finalize the details by the end of the week."

The Decision on the AgriCoat Campaign

Having called home to say he would be working late, Jim settled down to review the CCA proposal. He began to think through a strategy for the campaign with Art's words of "Move it!" echoing in his ears. He realized that marketing in a highly competitive industry took a lot of creativity. But there was something which nagged at him on this campaign. He had always been able to overcome his uncertain feelings in the past and work out a successful strategy. But there was some deep uncertainty about this one, something which he could not put a label on.

BULLER | SCHULER

Managing Organizations and People

A Resource for Cases in Management, Organizational Behavior, and Human Resource Management

Abstract

Many small- and medium-sized firms experience growth problems due to the absence or dearth of professional supervisors/managers. This is the nub of the Traveler Import Cars case. The company, a car dealership, was started by a capable and ambitious married couple. The dealership experienced immediate fast growth due to its location, the quality of its products, and the customer-oriented climate in the company. However, fast growth of the dealership, and several related acquisitions, created a number of problems in the company. Randy and Beryl hired new managers to help them gain control, and the organization structure became more complex. The case illustrates some of the problems of growth—such as a lack of clear goals, poor communication, and lack of control—that are largely caused by lack of skilled management.

Traveler Import Cars, Incorporated

Background

Randy Traveler had been a partner in Capitol Imports, one of the most prosperous foreign car dealerships in greater Columbus, Ohio, selling expensive European automobiles. His wife, Beryl, a holder of an MBA degree from a respected private university, was a consultant specializing in automobile dealerships.

In 1979, Randy and Beryl decided to go into business for themselves. Since between the two of them they had four decades of automobile dealership experience, they elected to acquire their own dealership. With some luck, they obtained a dealership selling a brand of Japanese cars that had become known in the United States for its very high quality. Randy became president and Beryl executive vice-president.

Evolution of the Firm

Stage 1. After obtaining the Japanese dealership, Randy and Beryl decided to locate it approximately two miles from Capitol Imports. The decision was made on the basis of immediate availability of a suitable facility. This location, however, was several miles from a major shopping area of any kind, and the closest automobile dealership was Capitol Imports. Furthermore, the location was approximately three miles from the nearest interchange of a major interstate highway. Nonetheless, the dealership was located on a busy street within easy access to half a dozen upper-middle-class-to-affluent neighborhoods with residents predisposed to purchasing foreign automobiles with a high-quality image.

A number of key employees were enticed by Randy and Beryl to leave Capitol Imports and join Traveler Import Cars. Stuart Graham, who was in charge of Finance and Insurance at Capitol Imports, became general manager at Traveler Import Cars. Before specializing in finance and insurance, Graham was a car salesman. Several mechanics and car salesmen also left Capitol Imports to join Traveler Import Cars. As a rule, the policies and procedures that pertained at Capitol Imports were relied on at Traveler Import Cars, Inc. for the first five years of operations.

No one at Traveler Import Cars was unionized, but the mechanics were given everything that unionized mechanics received at other dealerships in order to remove the incentive to unionize. By everything, it is meant direct compensation, indirect compensation (fringe benefits), and work rules.

Randy and Beryl viewed their dealership as a family. This was in some measure due to the fact that the dealership was part of a Japanese Corporation (which viewed its employees as family), and partly due to the beliefs that Randy and Beryl shared about organizations. Randy and Beryl made every effort to involve subordinates in day-to-day decision-making. As tangible evidence of her commitment to democratic leadership, Beryl decided to introduce a quality circle into Traveler Import Cars, Incorporated. This was done by selecting five non-supervisory employees (one from each part of the organization) to meet once a month with Beryl and Stuart Graham in order to discuss problems, possible solutions, and implementation strategies. No training whatsoever regarding quality circles was provided anyone involved with the so-called "quality circle," and this includes Beryl and Stuart.

Stuart Graham, on the other hand, was a benevolent autocrat, although he tried to create the facade of a democratic leader because he understood well Randy and Beryl's leadership preferences. Most employees agreed with Randy and Beryl that Traveler Import Cars was a family. Furthermore, most employees felt free to voice an opinion on anything to Randy, Beryl, and Graham, or to any other supervisor or manager, for that matter.

Stage 2. As long as the dealership was small everything went well, largely because Randy and Beryl made all key decisions, provided daily direction to supervisors and managers (including the general manager—Stuart Graham, who should have been running the dealership on a day-to-day basis), and resolved problems through face-to-face communications with the involved individuals. As the dealership grew and prospered, it generated enough money for growth. Expanding the dealership rapidly was impractical because of the limited allotment of cars due in large measure to the so-called "voluntary" import quotas by the Japanese car manufacturers. The demand for these cars was so great that cars were even sold from the showroom floor, leaving at times few models for new customers to view.

The first acquisition that Randy and Beryl made was a car leasing company, which they located next to the dealership. Randy elected to spend most of his time building up the car leasing company, leaving the operations of the dealership to Beryl. The second acquisition consisted of another car dealership located approximately ten miles from the original one. The new dealership sold another make of Japanese cars and an expensive European make. The newly acquired dealership was located in the midst of automobile dealerships on a main road, but was housed in inadequate facilities and beset by many problems. Beryl became the chief operating officer of the second dealership as well. Soon after acquiring the second dealership, Randy and Beryl decided to construct new facilities adjacent to the existing ones.

Stage 3. The newly acquired dealership created a great deal of additional work for Beryl, but she understood and accepted that reality because she and Randy knowingly acquired a business that had been plagued by problems prior to acquisition. What bewildered and frustrated Beryl was the fact that the operation of Traveler Import Cars, Inc. took so much of her time as well as physical and psychic energies. After all, it had been five years since she and Randy purchased that dealership. Many key supervisory and managerial personnel now have five years of experience with the dealership, yet the task of running Traveler Import Cars is just as consuming at this time as it was when the dealership was new. Frequently, Beryl would tell one of the managers to do something, but it wouldn't get done. Decisions were reached at management meetings, but they did not get implemented. Programs were initiated, but were frequently permitted to drift and disappear. Important deadlines were being missed with increasing frequency. Mechanics and salesmen were coming to work late and taking excessive lunch breaks with greater frequency. Beryl knew that these problems were not due to insubordination or lack of motivation. Yet, if she did not directly oversee implementation of an important decision, it did not get implemented.

In order to relieve herself of some of the work load, Beryl hired two experienced managers. In order to justify their salaries, however, they spent half of their time at Traveler Import Cars and the other half at the newly acquired dealership. The newly hired managers had good ideas, yet Beryl was working just as hard as ever, and the problems that motivated Beryl to hire two experienced managers remained practically unchanged. In spite of the problems, the dealership grew as rapidly as the increase in the quota of cars that was allotted to the dealership by the manufacturer permitted. In addition, Traveler Import Cars began wholesaling parts to service stations and car repair shops, and started to lease cars in direct competition with the leasing operation managed by Randy. Although an organizational chart did not exist, it would look like Figure 1, if Randy and Beryl bothered to construct one.

About this time, Randy and Beryl's marriage had come undone, and Randy remarried a lady considerably his junior. Even so, Beryl and Randy maintained their business relationship, and were able to work together professionally without visible acrimony. Beryl now had more money than she knew what to do with, and was about to make much more because the newly acquired dealership was being turned around rapidly, largely due to Beryl's considerable talents, the new facility, and the rapidly recovering economy. Yet Beryl no longer wanted to work as hard as she had in the past.

Beryl understood that Stuart Graham lacked the right stuff to be general manager of a car dealership in a metropolitan area, and she approached Randy on the matter. His response was: "Stuart Graham is too valuable of an asset because Traveler Import Cars, Inc. had generated a $500,000 after tax profit last year. He must be doing something right."

Even though Beryl had been a consultant to automobile dealerships for twenty years, she decided nonetheless to retain a consultant. Beryl was fortunate to contact a particularly astute consultant by the name of J.P. Muzak. Her request was that Muzak straighten out the quality circle, which she felt wasn't living up to her expectations. Muzak, however, was reluctant to get involved unless he was permitted to conduct a thorough needs analysis before selecting any kind of intervention strategy. Beryl, after thinking the matter through, assented to Muzak's proposal. The organizational needs analysis relied on confidential structured interviews with all the managers, supervisors, and select non-supervisory personnel. The summary of Muzak's organization needs analysis follows.

Possible Problem Areas

Goals. Although general goals (such as providing the best customer service possible) exist at the organizational level, many individuals report that what is expected of them, in terms of specific and measurable objectives, isn't clearly defined. It is difficult to make a superior happy if the subordinate isn't sure just what it is that the boss wants.

Also, there does not appear to be a philosophy for setting goals. For example, should goals and objectives be imposed unilaterally by the superior on the subordinate, or should the goals and objectives be set jointly between the superior and subordinate?

Organizational Structure. The organizational structure in a number of instances appears to be confusing. Specifically, a number of individuals appear to be reporting to two or more superiors. Irma Krupp reports to David Chapel and Stuart Graham. Tom Tucker reports to Sam Carney and Stuart Graham. Charles Spikes reports to Tom Tucker, Sam

FIGURE 1
Organizational
Chart of Traveler
Import Cars, Inc.

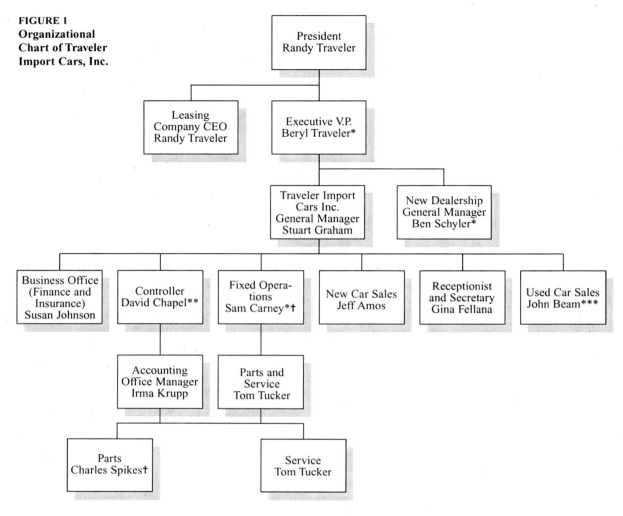

* These individuals spent approximately one-half of their time at Traveler Import Cars and one-half at the new dealership.

** David Chapel is the controller for Traveler Import Cars, the new dealership, and the leasing company. He spends about one-half of his time at Traveler Import Cars and one-half at the new dealership.

*** John Beam frequently is asked by Randy Traveler to assist with matters pertaining to the leasing company.

† Sam Carney owned and operated his own small business prior to joining Traveler Import Cars, Inc. Charles Spikes was a supervisor at a local office of a national automobile parts distributor before coming to work for Traveler Import Cars, Inc.

Carney, and Stuart Graham. John Beam had Susan Johnson's jobs before he became manager of used cars. David Chapel believes that he reports to the two general managers, to Beryl, and to Randy. Gina Fellana appears to report to everyone.

There is the perception that few managers know what they can do on their own authority and what they must get approved and by whom.

Communications. There appear to be too many meetings and they do not seem to be as productive as they could be. On this point there is a consensus.

A paper flow problem exists in several areas. The Accounting Office at times does not receive properly filled out forms from the Business Office. It appears that Susan Johnson does not have the time to fill out carefully and on a timely basis all the forms and attend to her other finance and insurance duties. The Accounting Office at times does not receive the necessary paper work from New Car Sales. The Parts Department at times doesn't receive on a timely basis the necessary information from New Car Sales.

Some individuals complain that their superiors do not keep them informed. Everything is a secret.

Training and Development.   A number of individuals have risen through the ranks into supervisory and managerial positions. Since these individuals have never received formal managerial training, the void must be filled by coaching. In a number of cases, the void has not been filled by coaching, and these persons are learning through trial and error—an expensive and time-consuming way of learning, indeed.

The consensus is that the computer equipment is adequate to the task, but the operators need additional training to realize the potential of the equipment. The mechanics receive the latest training from the manufacturer.

Performance Appraisal.   Many people reported that they do not receive a periodic formal appraisal. Thus, their need for performance feedback is frustrated.

Wage and Salary Administration.   Numerous individuals have reported that it is the subordinate who has to initiate a wage or salary increase. Most individuals report that they would like to see the superior initiate wage and salary action at least annually. Moreover, a number of individuals are not sure on what basis they are remunerated. The absence of a systematic periodic performance appraisal is responsible, in part, for this perception.

Discipline.   In a number of instances, individuals arrive late, take extended lunch breaks, and violate rules with impunity. This creates a demoralizing effect on others.

Control System.   The financial control system at the top of the organization appears to be satisfactory. The operational control systems in the rest of the organization are problematic.

Morale.   While there is still the feeling that the organization is a family and the best place the employees have ever worked, the feeling is starting to diminish.

Sundry Problems.

1.   Quality circle may need restructuring along traditional lines.
2.   The time it takes to make decisions should be shortened.
3.   The organization has difficulty implementing decisions that have been made.
4.   Lack of follow-up presents serious problems.
5.   Policies and programs are permitted to drift and disappear (motivator board is an example).
6.   Managers may not be delegating enough.
7.   New car salesmen do not always turn customers over to the Business Office, resulting in loss of revenue to the dealership.
8.   Service desk is crucial and it has been a revolving door.

At a meeting, Muzak presented the findings of his needs analysis to the management team of Traveler Import Cars, Inc., and a discussion ensued regarding each of the possible problem areas. Randy Traveler did not attend since he relegated the operation of the dealership to Beryl. At the end of the discussion, the management team agreed that all the problems uncovered by Muzak were real and, if anything, understated.

Muzak did not present at the meeting his assessment of the potential of the key managers. This he did in a private discussion with Beryl. In summary, Muzak concluded that Stuart Graham was too set in his ways to change. Moreover, he displayed too much emotion publicly, and lacked the respect of his subordinates. Jeff Amos was considered by his subordinates to be a nice guy, but was indecisive, lacked firmness, was manipulated by subordinates, and did not enjoy the respect of his subordinates. Tom Tucker was probably in over his head in his present position. He was only a high school graduate, he was not a mechanic, was unsure of himself, and lacked the confidence of his subordinates. Lastly, he was quite impulsive. His previous experience was as a service desk writer (the person to whom the customer explains the car problems and who writes the work order). All the other managers and supervisors were thought to possess the necessary potential which could be realized through training and experience.

BULLER | SCHULER

Managing Organizations and People

A Resource for Cases in Management, Organizational Behavior, and Human Resource Management

Abstract

International Medical Laboratories (IML) is a U.S. multinational corporation with subsidiaries in Western Europe. The German general manager, an American expatriate, is eager to promote the IML products through product endorsements by prominent European physicians. His opportunity comes soon enough, but is accompanied by a request for a research contribution which sounds a lot like a bribe. IML has a clear policy regarding such requests—Just say no. But is this really a request for a bribe? The general manager must decide how to deal with it.

The Prominent Dr. Rombach

John had settled comfortably into the soft, leather passenger seat. The big, black Mercedes slipped silently onto the autobahn on the outskirts of Munich. In a few moments the driver, Klaus Ehrwald, was expertly guiding the car at over 120 miles per hour. They were heading for Salzburg, Austria, for a meeting with Dr. Hans Rombach, a prominent cardiovascular surgeon. At this speed it wouldn't take them long to get there.

John Cannon was an American expatriate managing the German subsidiary of International Medical Laboratories (IML), a large American biomedical equipment company specializing in expensive, high-quality heart/lung machines used in open heart surgery. John was a graduate of a prestigious American west coast university where he majored in international business and had been a very successful biotechnology market analyst early in his career. When he joined IML as their marketing product line manager for cardiovascular instrumentation, he was charged with the responsibility of taking the system into the international market. He immediately targeted Western Europe.

The system proved to be an instant success, with Germany the strongest market. It wasn't long until John was appointed the subsidiary manager for Germany and became a quick learner of local business practices. He was determined to successfully promote the

IML system to surgeons in all the clinics and hospitals in the German sales region. He had been living in Munich for over a year now.

He spoke casually about the upcoming meeting with Dr. Rombach to Klaus, his general sales manager. Klaus was a Bavarian native and understood the "Teutonic character" very well.

John: *I've been wanting to meet Dr. Rombach for a long time, Klaus. He has quite a reputation among his peers. What sort of a man is he?*

Klaus: *Pretty typical for a successful European surgeon: arrogant, confident and with a very great opinion of himself. He did one of the very first heart transplants in Austria, and now people come from everywhere to him for routine cardiovascular surgery. He does four or five surgeries a week and makes a fortune. He has really pioneered some new, successful procedures and publishes the results of his work in the very best medical journals. He has an international reputation as both a brilliant surgeon and a very successful entrepreneur at his private clinic.*

John: *What kind of equipment is he using now?*

Klaus: *He's using a Freznus system, German of course. It's not as good as ours, but the company has been around for a long time and he's been using their equipment for years. Like most surgeons, he doesn't like to change equipment once he gets used to it.*

John: *As I recall, we can be very price-competitive with Freznus. Our system sells for about $25,000, and theirs typically sells for over $30,000 when you compare all the same features. Besides, we have a much more stable temperature control system (for controlling blood temperatures during bypass surgery) plus the very latest technology in the new pump systems. Our overall system is based on U.S. technology, and one of the main subsystems now includes new Swiss-designed pumps which are generally thought to be the most reliable in the world.*

Klaus: *Tell it to Dr. Rombach. I've been trying to sell him on our system for a long time, but he continues to use the German system in spite of the price difference and the high-tech image of our equipment. He's very concerned about quality and reliability. I guess he regards the German equipment as being more reliable, or maybe he's just nationalistic.*

As they moved smoothly and swiftly along the autobahn, John thought about the nationalism issue for a while. It was true that many citizens of Europe actively sought out nationally produced products—the French, Germans, and the British in particular. In some cases it was a subconscious sort of thing. In other cases it was very specific. In order to sell capital equipment to the public hospitals and clinics in France, for example, you had to be named on the French-approved supplier list. The only companies which appeared on this list were French companies or perhaps a few foreign firms that had no French competitor.

The Austrians were not quite so tough on foreigners, but they typically favored the German products. John hoped that the current attempt to unify Europe would help to remove some of the traditional barriers to foreign products. He thought carefully about how to approach this issue with Dr. Rombach and decided to let the product speak for itself. After all, the IML system was in use in the most prestigious heart hospitals in the United States, and that fact would not be lost on the prominent doctor.

After a brief conversation with Klaus on sales strategy and a technical comparison of the competing systems, they exited the autobahn onto a long sweeping curve, gearing down smoothly, and soon arrived at the outskirts of Salzburg. Dr. Rombach's clinic was only a few kilometers from the exit. As they approached the clinic, John could not help but admire the gracious old building with its Greek columns. Upon entering, they were struck by the transition from the dusty marble entryway with its classic style of architecture to a modern, gleaming, state-of-the-art medical facility. There was no mistaking the detailed attention to high quality everywhere. Dr. Rombach's office was on the third floor, overlooking the river and the woods beyond. The secretary greeted them efficiently and confirmed their appointment. Yes . . . the doctor was in and expecting them. As they were being ushered into the office, Dr. Rombach swiveled around in his huge chair and rose to welcome them.

Klaus: *Good morning Dr. Rombach. I'd like to introduce my colleague, Herr Cannon.*

Dr. Rombach: *Ah, good morning Herr Ehrwald and Herr Cannon. I suppose you have come to tell me of your new and wonderful American equipment.*

Klaus: *Of course. As always, we wish you to have the very best equipment for your work.*

Dr. Rombach: *Fine, fine . . . Let us have some coffee while we chat, and then I shall take you for a tour of our facility and show you our new operating theaters and recovery wing, just finished last month.*

As they began to make conversation, both John and Klaus were careful to avoid any direct mention of their purpose for the visit. All parties knew that they were there to talk about the American equipment, but it could wait until the proper moment. The tour was impressive. State-of-the-art equipment was everywhere; the facilities and laboratories were the most modern John had ever seen. He had recently been in Los Angeles, Houston, and Minneapolis to see the best of the U.S. facilities, as well as the new hospital in Rotterdam, but this clinic was truly incredible. He noted the Freznus equipment in the operating theaters. It seemed oddly dated among all the other high-tech equipment.

Dr. Rombach: *We have been able to reduce the stay in our clinic to only four or five days following open heart surgery. Most of the best hospitals around the world require two or three weeks. It's due to our new surgical techniques and postoperative care. We have the highest success rate and the best recovery time in the world. I've just published an article in the European Medical Review describing our successful program.*

John: *This is really incredible, Dr. Rombach. To what do you owe your success?*

Dr. Rombach: *Good people, good technology, and good care. There's nothing mystical about good medicine. The technology helps you make good diagnoses and safe surgeries. The people provide the skill, the support, and the care necessary for success. We have also developed some new low-trauma techniques that seem to work very well.*

John's mind was racing. If they could convince Dr. Rombach to use their equipment, they could be a part of every medical advance he reported. Every one would want to use the same equipment and follow the same techniques pioneered here. John quietly wondered why Klaus had not yet been able to sell him on the IML system. They returned to Dr. Rombach's office for some earnest conversation.

John: *I know you're very busy, Dr. Rombach, so I won't waste your time with a lengthy sales pitch about the IML system. But I did want to be sure that you knew about our recent advances in temperature controls and our new pumping system that uses the Friedreich pumps from Switzerland.*

Dr. Rombach: *Yes, yes . . . I know all about them. I was in the Friedreich factory in Zurich just a few months ago. You see, Karl Friedreich is an old friend of mine. I even gave him some ideas on the best way to design the perfusionist's cart.*

John: *Then you know that the IML system has the most reliable pumps in the world.*

Dr. Rombach: *Of course. That's why I'm willing to talk to you about your system.*

John: *I guess you also know that Drs. Shumway, Barnard, and DeBaky also use the IML system. (John was banking on the use of these prominent surgeons' names to impress Dr. Rombach. While they had not specifically endorsed IML, they did indeed use the system.)*

Dr. Rombach: *Yes, I spoke with DeBaky in Houston last year. He seemed satisfied enough with the system. But, he's sort of retired now and is not as active as he once was.*

John: *We would very much like to see you using the IML system, too. It's really more cost-effective than your present Freznus system, and with the Friedreich pumps, perhaps even more reliable.*

Dr. Rombach: *Perhaps. I am impressed with your system and may be willing to give it a try, especially if it can help my research. You know, conducting our research is very expensive. Our research methods must use real patients to be of any practical value to other surgeons. This means not only developing new techniques but advising patients, obtaining consents, explaining methods, publishing results, etc. Would your company, IML, be willing to make a contribution to my research fund? This would make my decision to purchase your equipment much easier.*

John: *Um . . . contribution to your research fund? Well, I don't know. How much did you have in mind?*

Dr. Rombach: *Well any amount would be helpful, but $25,000 or so would be particularly helpful.*

John's memory flashed to a recent meeting at corporate headquarters. The subject was the various forms of international bribery and the interpretation of the Foreign Corrupt Practices Act as passed by Congress after the Lockheed scandal in Japan. The company was very specific about adherence to the letter of the law of this act and maintained a corporate position of steadfastly refusing to participate in any questionable actions, no matter how they might be presented. Being a leader in the life-saving medical equipment business meant that the company should also be perceived as a leader in maintaining absolute trust in the public eye and unquestioned ethical behavior. Their reputation meant everything, and even the appearance of inappropriate behavior could be disastrous. They had included in their corporate mission the statement "The company does not engage in any sort of activity which might be construed as unethical." Their consistent advice was to "just say no" to any questionable request. But still, John hesitated. Was this really a request for a bribe? After all, Dr. Rombach was the most prominent cardiovascular surgeon in Europe. Everyone knew him—he certainly published a lot of his research. Surely a $25,000 contribution could be made up in future sales of the IML system once the medical community knew that Dr. Rombach was using the IML system in his work. After all, the system produced a 10-percent pre-tax margin so they would only have to sell an extra ten systems to break even. Rombach might even buy three or four himself!

John: *Well, I guess I'll have to think about that. Perhaps I can discuss this with our management and we can get back to you.*

Dr. Rombach: *Of course. My secretary will show you out. Have a safe trip back to Munich.*

Having said that, Dr. Rombach smiled, punched a button on his telephone, and turned his attention to his work on the desk. His secretary appeared immediately and courteously showed them the way to their car.

As Klaus eased the Mercedes back onto the autobahn, John thought about the possibilities. He knew that if he contacted the corporate management, they would never approve such an expenditure. In fact, it might be risky to even ask. They might see him as a questionable representative of IML with regard to ethical issues. He knew that several other Austrian cardiovascular surgeons had purchased the IML system without any requests for research funds. Still, John was sure that it made some good business sense to consider it. There was almost $100,000 available in the budget for discretionary spending. It was supposed to be used to promote IML products in whatever way he thought was most effective. He knew he would receive lots of recognition if he could get Dr. Rombach as an IML system customer. He also knew everyone would want to know exactly how he had pulled off such a coup.

John: *Klaus, do you think Freznus makes contributions to Dr. Rombach's research fund?*

Klaus: *Well, I suspect they might. What do you think?*

John: *I don't know what to think. What should we do?*

BULLER | SCHULER

Managing Organizations and People

A Resource for Cases in Management, Organizational Behavior, and Human Resource Management

Abstract

The United States Supreme Court decision affirming the right of the Scouts to determine its membership and exclude gays has caused controversy in some American communities, including the Portland, Oregon area. The local United Way director, Larry Norvell, met with a great deal of resistance with his initial plan of directing the United Way allocations to the Boy Scout program that did not discriminate—Learning for Life. His board overwhelmingly supported allocating funds to the Scouts, without making them provisional on accepting the United Way anti-discrimination policy that included sexual orientation. The local Scout leader, Larry Otto, had no trouble presenting a great deal of information that showed the positive impact of Scouting. Norvell wondered how to proceed and if he should try and make future funding contingent on the Scouts' adoption of a non-discrimination policy.

The United Way and the Boy Scouts: Controversy in Portland, Oregon

James Dale spent 12 years of his life working with the Boy Scouts of America (BSA). As an assistant Scoutmaster, he was proud of the work he was doing and the organization itself. But in 1990, the Scouts learned he was gay and expelled him from the organization. In an interview with *The Advocate*, Dale was quoted as saying, "I think what the scouting program teaches is self-reliance and leadership. Giving your best to society. Leaving things better than you found them. Standing up for what's right. That's one of the ironies of this whole story—that when they found out that I was gay, suddenly I wasn't good enough anymore."[1]

Searching for vindication, Dale's journey through the courts began with an initial loss in a New Jersey court. However, a state appeals court ruled that the BSA's restriction was illegal and Dale should be allowed to serve as a Scoutmaster. This was the first time any court had ruled against the Boy Scouts' policy of not permitting avowed gays to be members. The court further concluded that there was no evidence that a gay Scoutmaster could not care for or impart the BSA's values to his Scouts. When the BSA appealed this decision, the New Jersey supreme court upheld the appeal court's decision.

Despite his earlier victories, on June 28, 2000, the United States Supreme Court reversed the state supreme court's decision and ruled against Dale and for the Boy Scouts of

■ Howard Feldman, University of Portland, and Asbjorn Osland, San Jose State University.

America (BSA).[2] In essence, the decision allowed the BSA to continue to be able to determine who could or could not join their organization. This decision was the springboard for deliberations held around the country at local United Way agencies, who realized their anti-discrimination policies were in conflict with the national BSA policy allowing discrimination against avowed gays. The national United Way organization, in anticipation of these deliberations, issued a statement emphasizing that local United Way chapters determined their own anti-discrimination policies.[3]

As the case wound its way through the courts, several independent United Way agencies had already taken action. From 1992 through June 2000, eight local United Ways in San Francisco, CA; Santa Clara, CA; Santa Cruz, CA; New Haven, CT; Branford, CT; Santa Fe, NM; Portland, ME; and Somerset County, NJ adopted anti-discrimination policies that affected their funding relationship with the Boy Scouts. These local United Way organizations had funding policies requiring agencies wishing to receive funds over which the United Way has discretion to agree to provide services without discriminating on the basis of age, gender, race, religion, sexual orientation, ethnicity, national origin, or disability. These actions were taken independently by each United Way after extensive study and review of their local situations and conditions. Directly following the U.S. Supreme Court decision, several other United Way agencies took similar steps.

United Way of the Columbia-Willamette (Portland, Oregon)

About six months had passed since the Supreme Court decision on James Dale. Larry Norvell, the local head of the United Way of the Columbia-Willamette (UWCW), knew that the time had come for the agency to face the issue of allocations to the local BSA organization, the Cascade Pacific Council of the Boy Scouts of America (CPCBSA). In the previous six months, the stage was set for a decision. In September, the UWCW had communicated with the local Boy Scout headquarters asking them to clarify a number of issues related to their operations and policies.[4] In October, three board members had spoken to the media accusing the BSA of teaching hatred and intolerance. Shortly afterward, the UWCW board announced plans to review their relationship with the Boy Scouts. One day later, CPCBSA leaders met with 30 corporate leaders to discuss BSA policy and United Way support.

As Norvell saw it, his board would likely not support a confrontation with donors, who generally supported the CPCBSA. Still, Norvell had to work with other stakeholders (such as agency heads, UWCW personnel, donors, board members, community people, etc.) who strongly felt that the agency's anti-discrimination policy should be applied to the local Boy Scout organization. Norvell experienced his own personal struggles over the matter. He realized that as the head of the local United Way his task was to obtain donations for the numerous agencies in the Portland area that served the needy. It was not to pursue a personal agenda or one that could be construed as divisive.

United Way of the Columbia-Willamette: Community Services

The UWCW assisted 93 agencies in four counties in Northwest Oregon and Southwest Washington states. In 1999, its revenues were $18.2 million. For fiscal years 1998 through 2000 (i.e., July 1, 1997 through June 30, 2001), the top beneficiaries (listed in order of magnitude for fiscal year 2000) of United Way assistance were the following agencies:

Allocation and Grants	7/1/99–6/30/00	7/1/98–6/30/99	7/1/97–6/30/98
American Red Cross—Oregon Trail	$1,664,460	$1,800,000	$1,800,000
American Cancer Society	$400,000	$400,000	$400,000
Metropolitan Family Service	$309,690	$379,068	$379,068
Salvation Army—Cascade Division	$301,210	$367,610	$367,610
Volunteers of America	$286,736	$353,291	$353,291
Boys and Girls Clubs of Portland	$253,304	$315,304	$315,304
Boy Scouts—Cascade Pacific Council	$252,387	$335,892	$335,892

For fiscal year ending June 30, 2001, the CPCBSA had received essentially the same amount as the previous year. However, in the past year, there had been a major increase in designated gifts to the CPCBSA: $182,000. Eleven hundred donors had designated their

United Way gifts be given directly to the Boy Scouts rather than going into the agency's general fund and subsequently being allocated to all of the agencies designated to receive funds from the UWCW. The previous year had seen only 400 donors and $62,000 designated specifically to the Boy Scouts. Not only were these donors not critical of the BSA's discrimination against avowed gays as members, in fact, they supported it by specifically designating donations for the Boy Scouts.

Larry Norvell's Perspective

In an interview with the casewriters, Norvell recalled:

"Long before the Dale case, our allocation volunteers had raised questions about the Scouts' outreach to minorities and gays. We have an anti-discrimination policy within the United Way but don't impose it on agencies. It originated in 1984 when one of our board members became very concerned about the Boy Scouts and the gay issue. In addition, several of our allocations volunteers raised questions about the Scouts. I wasn't here at the time, but I was told that the board didn't want lots of negative publicity during the campaign. Apparently, they really tussled with the issue and eventually decided against weighing in on a moral issue. Instead, they came up with a policy statement strongly encouraging agencies to have policies of anti-discrimination, including sexual orientation.

"When the Dale story broke in the paper last summer (2000), my board chair told me to get on it. One board member, in particular, was very concerned. Other board members were equally concerned about the possibility of negative publicity occurring during our campaign.

"We know the Scouts are unlikely to change their views. Three large church groups who are in sympathy with their stance heavily support them. However, I have heard that behind the scenes, there's a lot of pressure to make this a local decision within the Scouts. I don't think it'll happen anytime soon.

"There are a couple of board members who are particularly conflicted about this issue. I know it is going to be a difficult decision for them as well as the other board members, but I am convinced everyone will go into this with an open mind and make the best decision for us. We have to put aside any personal agendas. The central issue is, 'How can the United Way best serve the community?' We have to look beyond the immediate situation. We can decide to not fund the Scouts because of our policy against any kind of discrimination, but we have to weigh the consequences for all of our stakeholders.

"We have to consider the future implications of any decision that we make. If we adopt a policy that precludes allocation of United Way funds to any agency that discriminates, we might lose $2 million in contributions, which is about 10 percent of our total campaign.

"A bigger issue is future controversy; how does a decision today set us up for the next controversial issue to affect our community, for example, euthanasia? Several years ago we had a controversy over allocations to Planned Parenthood. Catholic Charities withdrew from the United Way in opposition to Planned Parenthood's stance on abortion. Should we take stances on community issues and run the risk of losing agencies, funding, and other types of support? And yet, these are exactly the types of agencies we are pledged to help.

"Others argue that we represent 83,000 contributors in this community and those contributors do not speak with one voice. People make contributions to the United Way without advocating a particular moral set or philosophy. They're saying we want the United Way to be the big umbrella that makes decisions based on where the dollars can have the greatest impact. One line I heard from another community was, 'How do you expect the United Way to resolve issues that the community is divided on and can't resolve?'

"Another thing to consider is that we have one of the most progressive donor-directed giving programs in the nation. Donors have the ability to direct their gifts to a specific agency or away from a specific agency. We administer that with 100 percent integrity. If you say you don't want one penny of your dollars to go to Planned Parenthood, we have a system in place that absolutely and unequivocally assures that not one penny of your gift goes there. It's the same way with the Boy Scouts. If you say that you want your dollars to go to Planned Parenthood or the Salvation Army, we absolutely and unequivocally send your dollars there. And that's on top of the amount they would normally get. If people feel an agency is unacceptable to them, they can send their gift where they choose. Since the

Boy Scouts have become a major issue in our community, a few corporate donors have asked to keep their company's donations from the Boy Scouts, but their individual employees were free to give however they chose.

"Ironically, the controversy has resulted in a windfall for the Scouts. To understand how, you have to understand the concept of donor-designated funds. This is where a donor can specify funds either go directly to a specific agency or they negatively designate their funds, i.e., they ask that their funds not go to a specific agency. This past year we only had 11 agencies that were negatively designated and the Scouts were one. I believe they were negatively designated to the tune of about $380,000, most of which were corporate funds. In particular, Wells Fargo Bank and Portland General Electric asked us to withhold funds from the local BSA because of their companies' anti-discrimination policies. When donors direct their funds either toward or away from specific agencies, those funds are pulled out of our general pool. That means there are fewer dollars available to the general pool used to allocate funds to all of our beneficiary agencies. In past years the negative designation was only $13,000 and this year it was $400,000. While the Scouts lost some funds, they are still going to make out like bandits because of donor-directed giving.

"Since some people thought we were dumping the Scouts, they directed their contributions specifically to the organization. In addition, we had 140 companies that told us they would not conduct their United Way campaigns until we resolve this Scout issue. We met with 30–40 key business leaders who told us, 'United Way, why are you into this mess? We are not supporting you to weigh in on political or controversial issues. If you're going to do so, we'll give our money to agencies directly.' I think, if I remember correctly, the Scouts actually ended up with about $500,000 more than they normally get, which is a substantial sum of money. It also means that our other beneficiary agencies were deprived of that money since it didn't go into the general pool.

"Looking backward, in the 1960s, the United Way wasn't a leader in the civil rights movement. Would our weight have made a difference? Would we have simply been on one side of the fence lobbing hand grenades at the other side?

"Personally I don't want anyone discriminated against. I believe that people don't choose to be gay. I spoke with several ethicists about our situation. Does discrimination against gays fall in the context of a moral issue? Both said it did. But one told me that at least half of the energy devoted to the gay issue would be feelings-oriented rather than rational. He said I wouldn't be likely to persuade people with reason. I also spoke with African-American leaders and several Jewish leaders and asked for their advice.

"One advisor told me to look at how the United Way can serve the greater good. If the United Way weighed in for gays, who would be helped? Who would be hurt? Would it change the public's feelings about gays? What about the poor elderly lady who lives in isolation and needs assistance? If donor-designated giving continues to favor the Scouts, our general pool decreases. What if she isn't able to receive help from an agency because our contributions fall? Is taking a moral stance worth it? Can we really change the Scouts? And what of our ability to leverage the Scouts behind the scenes to try to make change happen?

"One of the most frustrating issues in this whole debacle is the dilemma posed by some of our member agencies; they want us to raise as much money as we can yet there are 10 to 15 smaller agencies that are outraged that we don't throw the Scouts out. Some of the directors feel we should hold the Scouts to a higher standard. I told them, 'Do we raise funds or focus on morals?'

"Another option the board can consider is to follow Seattle's model. They shifted to Learning for Life, which is a school-based BSA subsidiary that does not discriminate against gays and lesbians. Learning for Life just celebrated its 25th year in the Portland and Clark County areas. It serves over 4,500 boys and girls and also over 6,000 junior high and high school students. If we choose this route, it means we will be weighing in on this as a moral issue and taking a stance.

"One other option available is to consider changing our allocation process for June 2002. We could take at least 40 percent of our funds and free them up for all agencies, including non-member agencies. Agencies could compete for these funds based on their ability to address one of the four target areas we focus on—helping kids succeed in school, keeping people safe and healthy, getting citizens involved in their neighborhoods and communities, and helping people live independently and with dignity—and reporting outcomes. These funds could be tied to a higher standard of ethics that could include anti-discrimination in terms of sexual orientation. There's a better than even chance that we'll change but it won't happen for another year and a half. I'd be one of the champions internally but I don't know what the board will do with this model. If they choose to adopt it, it could potentially eliminate the Scouts, if they continue to discriminate. However, the Boy Scouts still have a lot of support. What if people and organizations begin to donate directly to the CPCBSA rather than continuing to support the United Way? The 40 percent might be a way of easing into a more equitable system.

"By the way, only 12 local United Ways out of over 1,400 nationally have chosen to not fund the Scouts, which is a very small number."

Larry Otto's Perspective

The local press had interviewed Larry Otto, the Executive Director of the CPCBSA, on a number of occasions regarding the controversy with the United Way. He said his organization relied more on families for funds than corporate donors. "Our values aren't for sale," he said after learning that PGE and Wells Fargo restricted their funds. "We aren't going to be trumped by anyone's dollars." He continuously defended the Scouts' national policy, saying that sexual orientation had nothing to do with Scouting.[5]

Otto also met with one of the case authors and provided numerous insights on the Boy Scouts' position. "I worry about the 30-year-old mother who may not send her son to Cub Scouts because of this controversy. I don't want her to keep her son out of Scouting. We're not homophobic. We don't sit around making cracks about gays. In fact, many of our people disagree with the BSA's national policy. We don't ask people about their sexual preference—it's inappropriate.

"There was one individual—a young man who was registered in Scouting as an adult volunteer. When he insisted on presenting me with his document declaring his homosexuality, I was required by BSA policy to deny his volunteer status with the BSA and sent him a letter stating this. He wasn't in our employ so we didn't fire him but simply denied him registration.

"We don't discuss the matter with children because it would be inappropriate. We want them to be children and not concern themselves with sexual orientation.

"I'm Catholic. For decades Catholics have been told about approved birth control methods, which some follow and some ignore. The fact that someone uses pills doesn't mean that they're going to leave the church. We can't let specific issues blow communities apart. Look at the agencies that have strong ties to religious denominations—they don't welcome gays either yet they haven't been singled out for media attention or pressure from the United Way.

"Look at all the positive things the Scouts do. For example, we annually serve more than 53,000 youth, operate nine summer camps that served nearly 13,000 boys in the summer of 2000, and operate three winter lodges serving 6,000 youth and a Sea Scout base serving 200 young men and women. Our outreach programs served 16,000 boys and girls in "at-risk" neighborhoods. Our members contributed more than 1.3 million hours of service to the local communities in the Cascade Pacific Council. We planted more than two million trees and collected 500,000 pounds of usable clothing and household goods for Goodwill Industries and more than 361,000 pounds of food for local relief agencies.

"We're a large organization with diverse membership—look at these figures (see Appendix D).

"Also look at our financial data for the CPCBSA:

Category[6]	2000	1999	1998	1997
Total revenue—Line 12	$6,403,343	$7,917,096	$8,128,592	$7,743,155
Total expenses—Line 17	$6,919,192	$5,984,250	$5,627,608	$6,505,794
Excess revenues—Line 18	$(515,849)	$1,932,846	$2,500,984	$1,237,361
Net assets at the end of the Year—Line 21	$20,854,759	$21,370,608	$19,478,460	$16,975,790

"In 2000, the endowment was $14.4 million. The annual United Way contribution to the Scouts has been around 3 to 4 percent of the Scouts' total revenues of late, depending on the year. To date (May 24, 2001), the CPCBSA has raised $17,780,946, of its current $40 million capital campaign. It's destined for camp facilities ($12 million), endowment ($15 million), and Special Initiatives ($13 million).

"What we're most proud of is that the Scouts have clearly had a positive impact on the lives of so many young people. Take a look at the data from a 1998 Lou Harris study on national program outcomes (see Appendix E). Furthermore, our supporters are strongly behind us on this gay issue. We just had a national opinion survey taken using telephone interviews of 2,400 parents, almost two-thirds of who were non-Scout households. The results provide powerful support for our position. And other opinion polls agree (see Appendix F).

"The Scouts have the right to decide who is a member, which is ultimately what the Supreme Court confirmed (see Appendix G). Our national headquarters has made clear policy statements on diversity, access to schools, and the United Way (see Appendix H). The Scouts helped found the United Way. It was to raise money, not weigh in on moral issues. Our beliefs are clearly spelled out (see Appendix I). We're here to help kids grow up to be good citizens.

"You know, this all began when a *New York Times* article that was full of errors came out after the Supreme Court decision. We continue to deal with it and talk to people but it's quite a distraction from our work. We had to answer an extensive list of questions asked by the United Way, which we were happy to do. It defined our position and clarified it for the United Way.

"The gay issue just doesn't play in Middle America. Only a dozen or so United Way agencies, out of 1,400, have pressured the Scouts. And as the Lou Harris survey shows, only around 30 percent of the public question what we did.

"The Mormons clearly line up behind us. Some of the other church groups are ambivalent but generally supportive. It's unfair to single the Scouts out. Other agencies like the Salvation Army would also have trouble with gay employees, I believe.

"I try not to make a big deal out of this pressure we're getting and I certainly don't play it to raise money. Yet, we get a lot of donations from people who are concerned that the Scouts are suffering because of the PC climate. If you would like to take a look at the tremendous variety of opinions regarding this issue, take a look at some of these websites (see Appendix J). Their views are all over the map."

Larry Norvell's Dilemma

Larry Norvell was faced with a difficult dilemma. He needed to bring a recommendation to his board regarding the funding/defunding of the CPCBSA. He realized that the annual UWCW contribution to the CPCBSA had been around 3 to 4 percent of the Scouts' total revenues of late, depending on the year. But even that amount made the Boy Scouts one of the UWCW's largest recipients of funds in the Portland metropolitan area. Still, it was a small part of the Boy Scouts' annual funding. How influential could he and his agency be in persuading the BSA to change its policy that discriminated against gays?

Norvell knew the local chapter had to follow the national BSA policy. Clearly the Scouts contributed greatly to the young people in the area. However, he questioned whether their approach to gays was going to stand the test of time. Perhaps the Scouts needed to be nudged into a more tolerant mindset? Could the United Way do it?

He understood how the leadership of the Scouts were well meaning and effective people. However, one could wonder how capable they were of change, given that nearly all of them came from Scouting.

This would be the first time in his career that he had to make a specific recommendation to the board and he wanted to be sure that he knew what was at stake. There were a lot of things to consider: the Boy Scouts and the good they did for the community; the conflict between their discrimination policy and the United Way's policy on discrimination; the loss of potential financial contributions to the United Way and the impacts of this on their beneficiary agencies; the agency's history, in particular their decision on funding Planned Parenthood several years ago; the expressed concerns of 10–15 of the UWCW's beneficiary agencies who vigorously opposed the BSA's policies; the corporate community and their financial decisions; the individuals who had called, e-mailed, and faxed remarks to the agency in support of the Boy Scouts; and all the other myriad issues related to this situation that had managed to occupy his time over the last six months.

While trying to balance the pros and cons, Norvell remembered what Martin Luther King, Jr., once said, "The hottest place in hell won't be for those who opposed us but rather for those who stood by and said nothing and were neutral."

Appendix A

***Boy Scouts of America and Monmouth Council, et al. v. James Dale*. No. 99–699. Supreme Court of the United States. Argued—April 26, 2000. Decided—June 28, 2000.**

"In an opinion by Rehnquist, Chief Justice, joined by O'Connor, Scalia, Kennedy, and Thomas, J.J., it was held that the application of New Jersey's public accommodations law to require the Boy Scouts to admit the assistant scoutmaster violated the Boy Scouts First Amendment right of expressive association, as, among other matters, (1) the Boy Scouts (a) engaged in expressive activity, and (b) sincerely asserted the view that homosexual conduct was inconsistent with the Boy Scouts' values; (2) requiring the Boy Scouts to accept the assistant scoutmaster would significantly affect the Boy Scouts' expression, by interfering with the Boy Scouts' choice not to propound a point of view contrary to the Boy Scouts' beliefs; and (3) the state interests embodied in the public accommodations law did not justify such a severe intrusion." (pp. 1–2)[7] In his opinion, Chief Justice Rehnquist stated the following:

James Dale entered scouting in 1978 at the age of eight by joining Monmouth Council's Cub Scout Pack 142. Dale became a Boy Scout in 1981 and remained a Scout until he turned 18. By all accounts, Dale was an exemplary Scout. In 1988, he achieved the rank of Eagle Scout, one of Scouting's highest honors.

Dale applied for adult membership in the Boy Scouts in 1989. The Boy Scouts approved his application for the position of assistant scoutmaster of Troop 73. Around the same time, Dale left home to attend Rutgers University. After arriving at Rutgers, Dale first acknowledged to himself and others that he is gay. He quickly became involved with, and eventually became the co-president of the Rutgers University Lesbian/Gay Alliance. In 1990, Dale attended a seminar addressing the psychological and health needs of lesbian and gay teenagers. A newspaper covering the event interviewed Dale about his advocacy of homosexual teenagers' need for gay role models. In early July 1990, the newspaper published the interview and Dale's photograph over a caption identifying him as the co-president of the Lesbian/Gay Alliance.

Later that month, Dale received a letter from Monmouth Council Executive James Kay revoking his adult membership. Dale wrote to Kay requesting the reason for Monmouth Council's decision. Kay responded by letter that the Boy Scouts "specifically forbid membership to homosexuals." (pp. 6–7)

Appendix B

United Way Funding of Boy Scouts[8]
United Way organizations have a long history of support for non-profit organizations that provide services to young people, including local chapters of the Boy Scouts of America. United Way of America's research indicates that United Way organizations distributed $83,743,000 in funding in 1996 to Boy Scouts of America nationwide.

- Action taken by the volunteer board of any local United Way has no bearing on any other United Way or Boy Scout Council across the country. United Way of America as the national membership service and training organization for local United Way organizations, does not dictate policy or funding decisions to local United Ways except to the extent that funding decisions must be consistent with applicable laws . . .
- . . . Withdrawing donor support for a United Way in any one community has no bearing upon the policy set by another local United Way. Withholding donations in response to any allocations decision ultimately hurts the people in the donor's community.

Over the years, there have been several legal challenges to Boy Scout policies concerning atheists, homosexuals, and girls who have been denied participation in various Boy Scout programs. Today's decision addressed the issue of whether the Boy Scouts, a private membership organization, can exclude homosexuals from serving as troop leaders. The Court ruled that the First Amendment freedom of expression and association allowed the Boy Scouts to exclude homosexuals from serving as troop leaders.

United Way is a system of 1,400 separately incorporated, independent organizations. Each raises money in an annual fund-raising campaign and allocates funds to local health and human service agencies.

United Way of America is the national service organization providing training, resources, and technical assistance to 1,400 member United Ways. Together, they raised $3.77 billion in their 1998–99 campaigns, supporting over 45,000 agencies delivering programs and services for millions of people from all walks of life.

Appendix C

Questions and Answers between the United Way of the Columbia-Willamette and the Cascade Pacific Council of the Boy Scouts of America[9]

Q: *Who sets the national Boy Scouts of America policy?*

A: The National Council Executive Board of the BSA.[10]

Q: *What role, if any, does Cascade Pacific Council play in determining national policy and to what extent is the Council permitted to adopt policies and interpretations different from the national Boy Scouts of America?*

A: The Cascade Pacific Council plays no role in determining national policy. The Cascade Pacific Council is chartered by the Boy Scouts of America and, as a chartered organization is obligated to adhere to National BSA policy.

Q: *What is the actual wording of the national policy regarding discrimination? Does it apply to volunteer leaders, employees, and the Scouts themselves?*

A: The Non-Discrimination Policy of the Boy Scouts of America prohibits discrimination based on color, race, religion, ethnic background, economic status, or physical disability for volunteers, employees, and Scouts. Membership in Scouting is open to all boys who meet basic requirements for membership and who agree to live by the Scout Oath and Law. The National Council Executive Board has adopted a policy that homosexual conduct is inconsistent with the requirements of the Scout Oath and Law. Based on this policy, the BSA does not accept avowed homosexuals as leaders or members.

Q: *What rationale/circumstances led the Boy Scouts of America to adopt its policy regarding discrimination?*

A: The National Council Executive Board's policy prohibiting avowed homosexuals from membership in the BSA was adopted without input from local councils. This policy has never been published and is not in any Boy Scout reference materials, manuals, charters, or other publications. We believe that the issue of sexual preference has no place in Scouting. We do not ask prospective members about their sexual preference, nor do we investigate the sexual orientation of boys or adult leaders who are already Scouts or Scout leaders. We allow youth to live as children and enjoy Scouting without involving them in issues that are adult in nature. Scout leaders as proper role models, should keep private matters, such as their sexual orientation, private.

Q: *What steps have been taken to implement the policy by the Cascade Pacific Council?*

A: The Cascade Pacific Council vigorously pursues the non-discrimination policy. The Cascade Pacific Council is justifiably proud of our efforts and success at delivering the Scouting program to the poor, people of color, children of all faiths, ethnic minorities, and disability challenged. Frankly, the matter of sexual orientation never comes up in the normal course of Scouting activity.

Q: *Does the local council make any effort to determine sexual orientation of its Scouts, volunteer leaders, or employees prior to their association with the Scouts?*
A: Absolutely not.

Q: *What is the national Boy Scouts of America policy regarding religious discrimination?*
A: The BSA does not discriminate against any religion. Since its founding in 1910, the Boy Scouts of America has had an ongoing commitment to encouraging moral, ethical, and spiritual growth. The BSA believes that spirituality plays an important role in a young person's development. The basic values are defined in the Cub Scout Promise, Scout Oath, and Venturing Code. All members whether youth or adult, must agree to abide by these principles in order to belong to the organization. However, the BSA doesn't interpret God or the practice of any religion. That is the role of the Scout's family and religious leaders.

Q: *What is the Learning for Life program? Is there an explicit written policy for this program addressing discrimination? If so, please provide a copy of the policy. If this policy is different from the national Boy Scouts of America policy, why?*
A: Learning for Life/Exploring are school-based/career-based programs that are part of Learning for Life, a BSA subsidiary corporation that is not governed by the principles of the traditional BSA movement and programs. These programs are directed and run by school leadership/government and business leaders. The chartered community organizations and schools select leadership. Participants do not have to meet traditional Scouting standards for leadership and membership. They are participants (not members) in the Learning for Life/Exploring program. The Learning for Life subsidiary corporation nondiscrimination policy prohibits discrimination based on color, race, religion, sexual orientation, ethnic background, economic status, citizenship, or physical disability.

Q: *How are employers in other communities, e.g., Seattle, continuing support of Scouts while staying true to their own corporate policies of anti-discrimination?*
A: In 1998, Catholic Charities and the Columbia-Willamette United Way were in debate over funding to Planned Parenthood. At the core of the discussion was the issue of abortion. In force at that time was a policy on Differences of Opinion.[11] Two sentences stand out in that policy and find relevance in the current discussions: "Because the United Way does draw its support from the entire community, and because there are few matters with respect to which there are not differences of opinion in the community, it is not desirable or feasible for the United Way to support only those activities which are approved by all members of the community. . . . While the United Way will support no agency that engages in an activity that is illegal . . . it cannot assume the responsibility of attempting to resolve differences of opinion as to the moral standards of the community."[12]

Q: *What options does the local Boy Scouts of America council believe are available for United Way that would enable United Way to continue funding Boy Scouts of America and be true to an anti-discrimination policy that includes sexual orientation?*
A: Possible options include: Our understanding of the United Way policy assures the Cascade Pacific Council that, as long as our activities continue to be legal, the Columbia-Willamette United Way will not assume the responsibility of resolving differences of opinion as to the moral standards of our community. . . . To the extent that the issue of discrimination against homosexual conduct is one of moral standards, the Cascade Pacific Council expects that the United Way would continue to fund the Cascade Pacific Council and "strongly encourage" the BSA to adopt policies as defined by Columbia-Willamette United Way. As an alternative, the Columbia-Willamette United Way could elect to fund Boy Scout programs that meet CWUW recommended policies, such as the Cascade Pacific Council's "Learning for Life" programs.

Appendix D

**Top 20 Chartered Organizations for 2000 by
Numbers of Youths, at the National Level[13]**

Top 20 Organizations	1999 Youth	2000 Youth	% Change
United Methodist Churches	424,198	417,425	–1.6%
LDS Churches	410,814	411,367	0.1%
Public Schools, Board of Education	378,229	360,782	–4.8%
Roman Catholic Churches	353,794	351,296	0.7%
Parent Clubs in Schools	180,687	171,605	–5.3%
Lutheran Churches	150,051	147,824	–1.5%
Presbyterian Churches	144,716	144,206	–0.4%
Baptist Churches	118,001	117,644	–0.3%
Lions International	103,519	99,923	–3.6%
Parent Teachers Associations	93,007	85,663	–8.6%
American Legion	77,067	74,893	–2.9%
Business/Industry	55,686	69,689	20.1%
Fire Services	53,057	51,477	–3.1%
Episcopal Church	51,378	51,031	–0.7%
United Church of Christ	51,695	50,339	–2.7%
Rotary International	51,058	48,964	–4.3%
Kiwanis International	44,705	42,847	–4.3%
Private Schools	37,292	42,147	11.5%
Veterans of Foreign Wars	39,452	38,030	–3.7%
Christian Church	37,824	37,168	–1.8%

Cascade Pacific Council's (CPCBSA) Distribution of Scouting Units[14]

Churches	59.09%
Schools	13.50%
Fraternal	7.84%
Service Clubs	6.39%
Government	5.86%
Businesses	2.37%
Social Clubs	2.11%
Other	<2.00%

Appendix E

Examples of Findings from Louis Harris Research on BSA[15]

- Overall, boys who are currently members of Scouting and have five or more years of membership tenure indicate attitudes and behaviors distinct from those of non-Scouts on a variety of issues. They include being more likely to assume a leadership role in clubs or school organizations, more likely to put the needs of others before themselves, more likely to make the most honest, not easiest, decisions, and more likely to value education and the environment.
- When boys who are in Scouting are directly asked what Scouting has taught them, almost nine of ten indicate that Scouting has taught them to take better care of the environment, get along with others, always give your best effort, have confidence in yourself, set goals for yourself, care for other people, and treat others with respect.
- 70 percent of men who are former Scouts feel that Scouting has been a positive influence. 90 percent feel Scouting has been a benefit to disadvantaged kids. 94 percent feel Scouting helps character development.
- Ethical/moral perspectives of Scouts are higher than non-Scouts, on some dimensions.
- 40 percent of men who were Scouts for five or more years graduated from college, in comparison to 16 percent who were never in Scouting.
- 33 percent of men who were Scouts for five or more years have annual household incomes of more than $50,000, compared to 17 percent of non-Scouts.

- 96 percent of parents/guardians identified "learning moral/ethical values" as an "important" reason for involving their boys in Cub Scouting.
- 95 percent of parents agree that Cub Scouting encourages parent and son interaction.
- 95–96 percent of parents agreed that Cub Scouting encouraged how to get along with others, respect for feelings of others, and social skills.
- Regarding reasons to join Boy Scouting, 90–95 percent of parents valued learning self-reliance, learning moral values, and involvement in community service; 88 percent of parents rated positive role models and making new friends as important; and 94 percent rated a friendly, safe environment as important.
- 65 percent of Boy Scouts reported receiving help from peers during outings/activities.
- 60–62 percent of Boy Scouts at typical troop meetings reported new learning from skill instruction or expert/professional instruction.
- 80 percent of Scouts said the reason to join Boy Scouting was that they liked the Scout activities and liked going on hikes, trips, or outings. 96 percent of parents of Boy Scouts said they felt the opportunities for fun and adventure were important reasons for joining Scouting. 90 percent mentioned Community Service Projects as important.

Appendix F

National Opinion Surveys on Scouting's Rejection of Gay Leaders[16]

- Telephone interviews, conducted by the BSA (1/24/2001) among 2,400 parents, across the nation, in households with boys between the ages of 6 and 16. Non-Scout households surveyed = 1,573; Scout households surveyed = 827. Findings include:
  - Overall, 60.3 percent of parents were aware of the U.S. Supreme Court issue regarding the BSA. 71.3 percent of Scout parents were aware versus 54.3 percent of non-Scout parents.
  - More than seven of 10 parents (72.0 percent) agree with the U.S. Supreme Court's decision that gives the Boy Scouts of America the right to set volunteer leadership standards that do not allow avowed homosexuals to be Scout leaders. Scout parents were more likely than non-Scout parents to agree with the Supreme Court's decision.
  - 65.4 percent of American parents agree with the BSA's belief that homosexuals are not appropriate role models for Scouts. Notably, among fathers, 73.5 percent agree that homosexuals are not appropriate role models for Scouts, compared to 60.4 percent of mothers.
- The Gallup Poll (June 22–25, 2000) asked: "Do you think the Boy Scouts of America should or should not be required to allow openly gay adults to serve as Boy Scout leaders?" 64 percent of the respondents said the BSA should not be required to do so. (http://www.gallup.com/poll/surveys/2000/topline000622/q21t24.asp)
- 61 percent agree that the Boy Scouts can ban gays from adult membership (July 6, 2000) (http://www.portraitofamerica.com/html/poll-1041.html)
- 68 percent of likely voters agree that the BSA should have the right to set their own rules and dismiss Scout leaders for being avowed homosexuals or other rights violations (Zogby International American Values Poll, January 8, 2001).
- 56 percent of adults agree with the Supreme Court decision that "the Boy Scouts of America have a constitutional right to block gay men from becoming troop leaders."

Appendix G

CPCBSA Position Statement[17]

What the Supreme Court Said   Whose right and whose obligation is it to teach values to our children? The Supreme Court of the United States said it is not the government's role to decide, but a constitutional right of individuals to join groups that reflect their own ideals.

Sexuality and the BSA   The issue of sexual preference has no place in Scouting. We do not ask prospective members about their sexual preference, nor do we investigate the sexual orientation of boys who are already Scouts. We allow youth to live as children and enjoy Scouting without involving them in issues that are adult in nature. Scout leaders, as proper role models, should keep private matters private.

United Way   The United Way has been an important partner of Scouting and many other outstanding service agencies for years. We encourage everyone to continue their generous support of the United Way and its agencies. If you must, you may designate toward or away from a particular agency, but we encourage you to help maintain the spirit that makes us all a community, which cares for each other despite our differences.

Respecting Each Other's Right to Disagree   For over 90 years, parents have trusted the BSA to help develop traditional values and qualities of character in their children. Not everyone agrees with those values, and we respect their right to disagree. In fact we teach Scouts to respect the differences of others.

Appendix H   **BSA Position Statements[18]**

Diversity   More than 90 years ago, the Boy Scouts of America (BSA) was founded on the premise of teaching boys moral and ethical values through an outdoor program that challenges them and teaches them respect for nature, one another, and themselves. Scouting has always represented the best in community, leadership, and service.

The Boy Scouts of America has selected its leaders using the highest standards because strong leaders and positive role models are so important to the healthy development of youth. Today, the organization still stands firm that their leaders exemplify the values outlined in the Scout Oath and Law.

On June 28, 2000, the United States Supreme Court reaffirmed the Boy Scouts of America's standing as a private organization with the right to set its own membership and leadership standards.

The BSA respects the rights of people and groups who hold values that differ from those encompassed in the Scout Oath and Law, and the BSA makes no effort to deny the rights of those whose views differ to hold their attitudes or opinions.

Scouts come from all walks of life and are exposed to diversity in Scouting that they may not otherwise experience. The Boy Scouts of America aims to allow youth to live and learn as children and enjoy Scouting without immersing them in the politics of the day.

We hope that our supporters will continue to value the Boy Scouts of America's respect for diversity and the positive impact Scouting has on young people's lives. We realize that not every individual nor organization prescribes to the same beliefs that the BSA does, but we hope that all Americans can be as respectful of our beliefs as we are of theirs and support the overall good Scouting does in American communities.

United Way   As a founding agency of the United Way, the Boy Scouts of America greatly appreciates the support that has been extended to Boy Scout councils across the country. For many decades, United Way funding has helped the BSA bring the Scouting programs to underprivileged youth, introduce new programs, and broaden the existing program.

In our pluralistic society, the strength of local United Ways has been their ability to bring together and support a mosaic of community needs. These needs are best met through a comprehensive mix of agencies, many of which serve exclusive constituencies.

The United Way does not implement a specific policy of nondiscrimination for individual charities so as to avoid conflict with charities that serve only specific segments of the population, including all-women's shelters, programs for persons of a certain age group, or programs for persons of specific cultural communities.

In its more than 90-year history, the Boy Scouts of America has served more than 100 million members and their families as a consistent platform for the values upon which America was built. We remain committed to providing these values to future generations.

A core value of the BSA is respect. Scouting respects those with ideas and customs that are different from our own and expects the same respect from those who may disagree with Scouting's position. Tolerance for a diversity of values and ideals does not require abdication of one's own values.

As a values-based educational movement, the Boy Scouts of America asks its members to subscribe to the tenets of the Scout Oath and Scout Law. Inculcating moral and religious values in young people benefits all of society.

Scouts are at work in our communities, everyday—collecting food, recycling, visiting nursing homes and hospitals, and in thousands of other ways living out the Scout Oath and Law.

The BSA aims for the United Way to realize Scouting's value to the potential, dignity, and worth of all people, regardless of their background.

School Access   For more than 90 years, the Boy Scouts of America (BSA) has complemented youth education with a program that teaches boys skills and values that will help them throughout their lifetimes.

Scouting has become an American institution, a natural element in most communities. Scouts exemplify the values outlined in the Scout Oath and Law and dedicate themselves to serving their communities.

On June 28, 2000, the United States Supreme Court reaffirmed the Boy Scouts of America's standing as a private organization with the right to set its own membership and leadership standards.

The BSA respects the rights of people and groups who hold values that differ from those encompassed in the Scout Oath and Laws, and the BSA makes no effort to deny the rights of those whose views differ to hold their attitudes or opinions.

The Boy Scouts of America aims to allow youth to live and to learn as children and enjoy Scouting without immersing them in the politics of the day. However, people dissatisfied with the Boy Scouts of America's membership policies and the moral views on which they are based have suggested that the BSA not have the privilege of meeting in public schools or distributing recruitment information at public schools.

Just as other student or community groups are permitted to have access to public school facilities, the Boy Scouts of America aims to have the same access.

Appendix I

Central Beliefs of the BSA[19]

BSA Mission Statement: It is the mission of the Boy Scouts of America to serve others by helping to instill values in young people and in other ways prepare them to make ethical choices over their lifetime in achieving their full potential.

Scout Oath: On my honor I will do my best to do my duty to God and my country and to the obey the Scout Law; To help other people at all times; To keep myself physically strong, mentally awake, and morally straight.

Scout Law: A Scout is: trustworthy, loyal, helpful, friendly, courteous, kind, obedient, cheerful, thrifty, brave, clean, reverent.

Purpose of the Boy Scouts of America: The purpose of the Boy Scouts of America is to promote, through cooperation with other agencies, the ability of youth to do things for themselves and others, and to teach youth patriotism, courage, self-reliance, and kindred virtues. In achieving this purpose, emphasis is placed upon the Boy Scouts of America's educational program and its oaths, promises, and codes for character development, citizenship training, and mental and physical fitness.[20]

Declaration of Religious Principle: The Boy Scouts of America maintains that no member can grow into the best kind of citizen without recognizing an obligation to God and, therefore, recognizes the religious element in the training of the member, but is absolutely nonsectarian in its attitude toward that religious training. The Boy Scouts of America's policy is that the home and the organization or group with which the member is connected shall give definite attention to religious life. Only persons willing to subscribe to this Declaration of Religious Principle and to the Bylaws of the Boy Scouts of America shall be entitled to certificates of leadership.

Leadership Requirements: The applicant must possess the moral, educational, and emotional qualities that the Boy Scouts of America deem necessary to afford positive leadership to youth. The applicants must also be the correct age, be a citizen of the United States of America (or satisfy one of the approved alternatives), and subscribe to the Declaration of Religious Principles, the Scout Oath or Promise, and the Scout Law.

Appendix J   **Websites for Further Reference:**

http://www.saveourscouts.com

> Those who maintain this site strive to maintain status quo of the Scouts. Quote from the site: "Why would a radical feminist, a practicing homosexual or a dedicated atheist demand the 'right' to join an organization that was founded to teach them to become a God fearing 'husband and father'"?

http://www.traditionalvalues.org

> This site supports conversion efforts for homosexuals. The BSA logo is displayed. Quote from the site: "For additional information on therapy, counseling, and prayer resources for struggling homosexuals, TVC recommends NARTH (www.narth.com) and Exodus International (www.exodusnorthamerica.org)."

http://www.grassfire.net

> This site lists perceived threats to the Scouts and urges action in support of the Scouts. Quote from the site: "The pressure is mounting against the Boy Scouts. Let's join together and take a stand! Sign the petition today and help us meet our goal of exceeding the 55,000 anti-Scout petitions gathered by Scout opponents. We can do it if everyone adds their spark to the grassfire!"

http://www.family.org/cforum/feature/A0012664.html

> James Dobson, on August 24, 2000, called on listeners to express their support for the BSA. He provided specific addresses of United Ways and urged people to express their concern that some United Ways were reviewing allocations to the BSA.

http://www.scoutingforall.org

> This links to an alternative Scouting organization established by the father of a boy who quit the Scouts in protest of its anti-gay position. The mission of the organization is to provide Scouting experiences for all without discrimination regarding sexual orientation.

http://www.claremont.org/1_naturallaw.cfm

> The Claremont Institute filed a brief in support of the Scouts. Insert "Scouts" in search space.

http://www.advocate.com/html/news/newssubjects/scouts.asp

> This is a magazine for gays with links to news stories.

http://www.reclaimamerica.org/PAGES/BoyScouts/BSAnew.asp

> This is a religiously oriented website that has articles in support of the Scouts.

http://www.scouting.org

> Official BSA site.

http://national.unitedway.org/boyscouts.cfm

> Discusses actions local United Ways have taken in relation to the Boy Scouts and impact of withdrawing donor support.

Endnotes

1. Erik Meers, "The Model Boy Scout," *The Advocate*, April 14, 1998.
2. See Appendix A: *Boy Scouts of America and Monmouth Council, et al. v. James Dale*. No. 99–699. Supreme Court of the United States.
3. See Appendix B: United Way Funding of Boy Scouts.
4. See Appendix C: Questions and Answers between the United Way of the Columbia-Willamette and the Cascade Pacific Council of the Boy Scouts of America.
5. David Austin, "Wells Fargo & PGE Divert Funds from Scouts," *The Oregonian*, December 11, 2000.
6. Information provided by CPCBSA or copied from IRS form 990.
7. Lexis-Nexis Academic Universe. *Boy Scouts of America and Monmouth Council, et al. v. James Dale*. No. 99–699. Supreme Court of the United States. 530 U.S. 640; 120 S. Ct. 2446; 2000 U.S. LEXIS 4487; 147 L. Ed. 2d 554; 13 Fla. L. Weekly Fed. S 520. Argued—April 26, 2000. Decided—June 28, 2000.
8. http://national.unitedway.org/boyscouts.cfm
9. The questions were attached to a letter dated September 18, 2000, from the United Way president to the Scout executive. The Scout executive provided the answers on September 27, 2000.
10. An attachment, not included here, lists the members of the BSA governing groups.
11. The policy is not included but is from the United Way of the Columbia-Willamette policy manual and is dated October 1, 1984.
12. The attached document #2, not included here because of its length, contains a number of statements from United Way chapters in other parts of the country where they expressed support for the work of Scouting and a reluctance to attempt to influence BSA policy.
13. Source: The Boys Scouts of America, Relationships Division, May 4, 2001.
14. Source: CPCBSA (undated but received May 22, 2001).
15. Information contained in BSA document on the national program outcomes study (1998).
16. Princeton Survey Research Associates, July 1, 2000. Information provided by Larry Otto of the CPCBSA.
17. Quoted from CPCBSA document dated November 7, 2000.
18. Copied from official BSA website (http://www.scouting.org).
19. Taken from a flyer provided by the CPCBSA.
20. The purpose is taken from the application form for Volunteer Leaders. The Scout Executive must approve all applications.

Strategy, Planning, and Organizational Culture

Cases Outline

BULLER | SCHULER

Managing Organizations and People

A Resource for Cases in Management, Organizational Behavior, and Human Resource Management

Abstract

This case traces the strategic moves that made American Express one of the most formidable competitors in the financial services industry. It describes the vision and strategy of American Express's executives such as James Robinson and Lou Gerstner. The case provides an "inside" look at the personal values and skills that influence strategic decision making. It also demonstrates how the strong personal ambition of some individual leaders can lead them to poor judgment and unethical behavior.

American Express

It was 1977 when James D. Robinson III became chairman and CEO of the profitable charge card, travelers checks and finance company, American Express Corporation (Amex). For 30 years Amex had maintained a string of increased earnings, "The Record" as it was called.[1] This record was considered so significant that maintaining it became a primary goal of the company. This was not a simple task. Amex's three core businesses were experiencing problems. The company ". . . managed to maintain 'the Record' into the mid-1970's only by resorting to fancy accounting."[2] The earnings of Amex's property/casualty insurance company, Fireman's Fund, were volatile. Amex's second core business, American Express International Bank, suffered losses in 1977 when it experienced a significant reduction in its return on assets.[3] Also, several major loans to Third-World countries made the threat of loan defaults a serious concern. Amex's largest sector, Travel Related Services (TRS) was prospering. However, its business of credit cards and travelers checks was mature and did not seem to offer much growth potential. Furthermore, its rivals, Visa and Master Charge, were applying competitive pressure by entering into the business travel market. Citicorp's recent purchase of Carte Blanche, another credit card company, was also threatening.

1

Jimmy Threesticks

Robinson had gained a reputation for hard work and fast solutions in his early years on Wall Street. "Jimmy was a white-shoe (version of) what makes Sammy run," said Abram Claude Jr., who supervised him for a time at Morgan Guaranty Trust Co. "He just ate up problems and spit them back at you. He became almost a chore for me as a manager."

Adds Paul Hallingby Jr., who oversaw Robinson at the investment bank White, Weld & Co., "I've never, ever seen someone work so hard."[4] In 1970, Howard Clark Sr., Amex's chairman at the time, wanted Robinson at Amex. Clark knew all about Robinson. "Everybody in town wanted to hire him when he came out of Harvard (Business School),"[5] said Clark, who also knew Robinson's father. The 54-year-old Clark approached Robinson and said he planned to retire at 60 and that Jim would have a chance to succeed him.[6]

True to his word, when Clark retired in 1977, he left Robinson in charge. Yet, despite Robinson's achievements, the nickname, Jimmy Threesticks, still stuck with him. It derived from James III and the prevalent conception that his success was predetermined by his father's wealth and influence. His great-grandfather and grandfather had been bankers in Atlanta and the family was wealthy, prestigious and aristocratic. Although Robinson clearly benefitted from some powerful family friends, he did not like to be thought of as one whose success was handed to him on a platter as if it was a birthright.[7] Consequently, he continued to struggle to prove his management abilities. Now that he was responsible for managing Amex, he had the opportunity. What was he going to do?

Lou Gerstner and TRS

Robinson devised two strategies to stimulate growth. "Plan A was to find a major new line of businesses . . . and plan B (was to) . . . hire Lou Gerstner to revive the TRS business."[8]

Amex's core business, TRS, comprised of the American Express card, travelers checks and a variety of products and services sold to cardholders. Before Robinson became CEO of Amex, he ran TRS and Lou Gerstner was hired as his younger advisor. Gerstner graduated from Dartmouth, with an engineering degree, and Harvard Business School. People who knew Gerstner referred to him as serious and driven, "a guy in a hurry."[9] In a cover story, the Institutional Investor described him as having ". . . the methodical, research and planning approach consistent with his Harvard MBA and ten years as a McKinsey and Co. consultant."[10]

Gerstner performed a variety of studies for Robinson. Robinson explained that Gerstner ". . . moved into the position of kind of (a) . . . spiritual as well as (a) . . . professional sounding board . . . Lou was someone in whom I had confidence to brainstorm with. He is insightful, excellent at summarizing things and laying out the key alternatives or issues."[11] In 1978, when Robinson was promoted to CEO, he placed Gerstner in charge of TRS.

"Gerstner quickly transformed the card business, which was overwhelmingly based on the U.S. green card, into a rainbow of different products around the world. He created a successful corporate product by combining the card with Amex's money-losing travel-agency business to offer companies a unified system to monitor and control travel expenses . . . (He) . . . also expanded the overseas card business changing the focus from serving international travelers to going after purely domestic business in other countries. Perhaps most important, . . . (he). . . fundamentally redefined the green card, positioning it for use not merely for business travel but for any purchase its customers wanted to make. This allowed dramatic expansion on two fronts: new sorts of card members (such as women and graduating college students) and new merchants (boutiques and department stores at first and now practically everything from gas stations to hardware stores).

(Gerstner) . . . codified the TRS business proposition into eight principles, generally management platitudes such as staying close to the customer and valuing employees. But also on the list are the key ideas that differentiate American Express from the pack: that it will offer premium, top-of-the-line products and that quality service will be its principal competitive weapon. It's no accident that his principles resemble the Ten Commandments. Like a missionary, Gerstner has had them translated into fourteen languages, and he has just mailed desk cards with the principles to the homes of all 44,000 TRS employees."[12]

McGraw-Hill

Robinson's Plan B, to hire Lou Gerstner at TRS, proved successful. His Plan A, to find a new line of business, was more complicated. Robinson had to consider what kind of company Amex should become. Some possible business areas were travel, financial services, insurance or communications. Still uncertain what future direction was appropriate for Amex, Robinson decided that he would diversify the company and transform it into what he called a "broadly defined service company."[13] He began this diversification using what *Fortune* called a "classic acquisition strategy."[14] He considered several different types of diversifications including companies in the entertainment, communications, financial, and insurance businesses. Attempts were made to buy the Walt Disney and Philadelphia Life Insurance Companies, but they were not successful. To help guide the process, Amex developed a new department, the Office of Strategic Program Development (OSPD), "to act as a catalyst and to develop and evaluate opportunities for new and important sources of earnings."[15]

In 1979, Robinson and the OSPD considered McGraw-Hill, the publishing and information services company, for their next acquisition attempt. Amex had developed its own highly sophisticated data and communications services in its recent tie with Warner Communications. McGraw-Hill, better known for its publishing of educational texts, was also profitably involved in selling specialized information through magazines and financial and data base services.

The acquisition never took place. Harold McGraw-Hill, the company's chairman, declined Amex's offer. Amex did not take no for an answer and continued to pursue the company, announcing a tender offer. McGraw was angered and went on the offensive publishing an open letter in major newspapers throughout the country questioning "the morality of the travelers cheque because Amex didn't pay any interest on their funds" and questioning whether it was appropriate for Amex to own *Business Week*, that published articles on the company, and Standard and Poor, which rated its bonds.[16] Amex threatened to sue McGraw-Hill for libel. These hostilities brought a quick end to Amex's takeover attempts, leaving the company publicly embarrassed. President Roger H. Morley resigned, taking the brunt of the blame. Robinson remained unscarred and Amex managed to maintain its "Record."

A Vision

Robinson liked to surround himself with brilliant people—visionaries. He worked best as a catalyst for innovative ideas, translating them into practical strategies. When his longtime friend, Salim Lewis, an investment banker, described the future financial services industry as being dominated by large companies able to offer a wide range of financial services—stock brokerage, real estate, insurance, lending, etc., Robinson's vision of Amex changed. He realized that Amex's move into a major new line of business meant an expansion into financial services. His "broadly defined service company" became a financial service company. Lewis suggested that the acquisition of Shearson Loeb Rhoades, a large, profitable brokerage firm, could make Amex one of the first of these large financial service institutions.[17]

Shearson

Shearson was one of the most profitable brokerage houses in the nation. Under the leadership of Sanford Weill, Shearson had grown through a process of numerous acquisitions during the seventies. Connie Bruck of *The New Yorker* described the company as having ". . . scavenged up Wall Street for weakened firms, swallowing up one after another"[18] and as a ". . . paradigm of cost consciousness (acquiring each of its firms) at a bargain-basement price, disbanding the firm's back office, and stripping away other redundant employees."[19] One longtime Shearson employee commented that "The genius of Shearson was that one and one always equalled one and a half, never two."[20]

Robinson and the OSPD began to explore the possibility of acquiring Shearson. There were several issues to consider. One was whether the two companies' customers were compatible. Amex's travelers checks and credit card customers were essentially buying security and convenience. Would the same customers be interested in the risky buying and trading of securities? Would Amex customers buy a wider variety of financial services if the company acquired Shearson? Robinson and the OSPD reasoned that because Amex provided financial services primarily through their credit cards, and 70% of the financial assets in the country were held by card holders, Shearson's products and services could be sold to Amex card holders and Amex's cards could be sold to Shearson's clientele.[21]

Another consideration was the apparent cultural and operational differences between the two companies. Shearson was a younger and smaller company that concentrated on efficiencies in its back office operations. It was also entrepreneurial with open lines of communications to the environment. It was "sharp toothed"[22] with a "hard-sell hustle."[23] Conversely, Amex was mature, conservative and formal. Connie Bruck described Amex as "the imperial corporation" as exemplified by its ". . . concerns with titles and lines of authority, its intensely political atmosphere, its formidable public relations apparatus, its endless deluge of memos, and its readiness to convene numerous meetings for almost any reason, no matter how trivial."[24] A Shearson executive remarked, "We always thought of the American Express people as overly planned, overly staged, overly bureaucratic. We saw ourselves, on the other hand, as the tough guys, very smart who were marching to our own drummer, who made decisions by the seat of our pants."[25] Shearson was involved in the volatile brokerage business, very different from the more stable credit services business central to Amex. The company's profit swings could mar Amex's steady growth record. Also, Shearson's salaries and bonuses were far greater than Amex's corporate pay scale.

Despite these differences, expectations and events in the financial services industry finally led Amex to make the acquisition. Financial market activity was expected to increase significantly following the Reagan administration's loosening of regulations controlling financial institutions, and its encouragement of investment activity in general. Also, in March of 1981, Prudential Insurance Co. purchased Bache Securities forming the large, wide-ranged financial services company Lewis had envisioned and setting an example for Amex. A move into Shearson's brokerage business became that much more appealing and important. Robinson was emphatic with respect to the merger and the OSPD agreed. That following June, Amex purchased Shearson Loeb Rhoades Inc. for $930 million, and with it, acquired Sandy Weill and Peter A. Cohen.[26]

Sandy Weill was the quintessential self-made entrepreneur, Brooklyn-born, cigar smoking, charming, yet ruthless and tenacious. Peter Cohen was Weill's sidekick, his detail man and number cruncher. Weill took over Roger H. Morley's position as president of Amex and he and Robinson placed Cohen in charge of Shearson. Weill, however, had difficulty conforming to Amex's structured management regimen. Robinson had given him ". . . a three-page memo defining the limits of his authority . . . (Yet) Weill was unable or unwilling to alter his free-wheeling style and instead of working through organizational channels to get something done, he tended to just go and do it."[27] Despite these conflicts, Amex's merger with Shearson proved to be profitable. In 1983, Shearson's profits rose a spectacular 40% and revenues 37% over the previous year.[28]

A Changing Wall Street

In the mid-eighties, the expectations of increased financial activity were realized. Deregulation gave many financial institutions the opportunity to involve themselves in additional financial activities. Baby boomers began to spend and invest their substantial mid-life incomes. Wall Street entered a bull market and financial service institutions began to experience rapid growth and profitability.

Cohen's Vision

In 1981, when Robinson made Cohen CEO of Shearson, at 36, he was the youngest head of a major Wall Street firm. He continued to operate as he had while working for Weill. He was methodical, fastidious and pragmatic. Cohen's friends had thought of him as short of the imagination and vision needed to create a great institution. As CEO of Shearson, however, Cohen now had a vision. He wanted Shearson to become an investment banking powerhouse. In order to realize his vision, Cohen tried to build an investment banking arm, but with little success. Then Cohen discovered what he called "a once-in-a-lifetime opportunity": Lehman Brothers.[29]

Lehman Brothers Kuhn Loeb

Lehman Brothers had been an influential investment banking house since its founding in 1850. However, internal conflicts between its traders and investment bankers had weakened the company. Cohen saw a promising connection between Shearson and Lehman. He recognized the value of the Lehman partners. Having been reared in the old school of "relationship banking," they had developed a network of longtime clients who were worth a wealth of business.[30] Lehman had managed to maintain many of these blue-chip clients. A merger with Lehman could bring its partners' clients and trading expertise to Shearson, but only if its partnership remained intact. Cohen asked that the majority of partners sign a contract preventing them from working for a competitor in the three years following the merger. Fifty-seven agreed to sign and Shearson acquired Lehman for $360 million in 1984.[31]

Wall Street was skeptical. Lehman Brothers had a reputation of elegance, old-line tradition, and hauteur. In comparison, Shearson was considered a "tacky wire house," parochial and homely.[32] Lehman's dining room was a virtual display of grandiosity, with everything from the finest Havana cigars for partners and their guests to Renoirs and Picassos hanging on the walls. By contrast, Shearson occupied a thrifty space at the World Trade Center. The companies' cultures differed as well. Lehman was an investment banking house driven by big deals and egos. Shearson was a retail securities brokerage—tightfisted and controlled. Still Cohen, with Robinson's blessing, set out to show Wall Street that despite the differences, the two companies were compatible.

Cohen and the Shearson Lehman contingent put together a long-term strategic plan. Under the plan, the company would "try to regain the ground Lehman Brothers had lost by concentrating on areas in which Lehman and Shearson had excelled as separate firms. They would also solicit business from giant corporations instead of smaller companies that had been a Lehman specialty."[33] To Cohen's dismay, however, the Lehman investment bankers had little idea how to go after new clients. They had been accustomed to waiting for longtime clients to bring in business. Said Sherman Lewis, who Cohen had placed in charge of Lehman, "For all that's been made of the difference between the Shearson and Lehman cultures, this was the one real difference."[34]

Cohen worked hard to motivate the Lehman partners to adapt to Shearson's aggressive culture. He awarded bonuses for the pursuit of new business. When the Lehman partners were reluctant to lure customers from other Wall Street houses, the response they received was "This is our plan. Do it." Within six months, his efforts began to pay off. Despite Wall Street's skepticism, Cohen had his investment bankers out hustling for business and getting it. Thomas W. Strauss, a managing director of rival Salomon Brothers, said of Shearson, "They have demonstrated that the merger worked."[35]

The Financial Supermarket

The acquisition of Lehman Brothers represented a uniting of Robinson and Cohen's vision for Amex. They both believed that the global marketplace had arrived and that within the next decade it would be dominated by a handful of giant firms offering the gamut of financial services to a wide range of customers.[36] In other words, a financial supermarket. Lehman Brothers was vital to their shared vision. The acquisition expanded Amex's financial offerings by bringing Shearson into the business of primary securities.

Robinson looked to Shearson as a primary vehicle for fulfilling his financial supermarket vision. Shearson was Amex's main connection to the burgeoning activities on Wall Street. However, he also moved Amex toward this vision through the company's acquisition of Swiss-based Trade Development Bank (TDB) founded by Edmond Safra, well known for his financial connections and reputation among the very wealthy.

Safra, TDB's chairman, was a legend—a reclusive Lebanese-born banker who had brought in close to $5 billion in deposits for TDB.[37] He specialized in personal banking and was highly respected by immensely wealthy people who trusted him to handle their money. "Edmond is a guy who sits in an office all day alone and who has always controlled his own destiny," said Cohen, who had once worked for Safra. Cohen assisted in the TDB deal by bringing Safra to American Express for negotiations. Robinson sought TDB for its exclusive, wealthy niche and Safra for his elite clientele, international connections and personal banking expertise. According to the *Institutional Investor*, the deal ". . . was supposed to marry Safra's private banking savvy to Amex's then-wobbly international banking arm (its American Express Bank) and give the then Shearson Lehman Brother's asset managers access to a rich market."[38]

Robinson had other goals for Amex as well. He wanted to build on the company's existing strengths. He followed the TDB acquisition by another of Investors Diversified Services (IDS) of Minneapolis in 1984, a mass-market financial planning and investment company. IDS marketed an array of annuities, life insurance and mutual funds to middle America and was attractive to Robinson because it would, as he said, ". . . open up the savings and investment side of the equation, where we correctly anticipated growth. Whether consumers spent with the card or saved with IDS, American Express had a chance to win."[39] One security analyst acclaimed the acquisition a "masterstroke" for it got "Amexco's toe, if not their entire foot into the middle-income market."[40]

Robinson also worked to develop synergies. He had Shearson bankers approach TDB clients for business, TDB bankers approach Shearson clients for business, Shearson securities sold to investors who were customers of other Amex divisions, and American Express Cards and life insurance sold to everyone. From 1982 to 1987, billions of dollars in life policies were sold to American Express cardholders and customers of Shearson, TDB and IDS.[41] Pretax profits on life insurance sales to card members alone were $45 million in 1985.[42] Robinson implemented a synergy plan he called "One Enterprise."

"Amex, he (Robinson) said, is 'one enterprise,' a collection of companies that sell different brands to different consumers but are united in the same goal of making money for the same shareholders. (He required) senior executives to identify two or three promising One Enterprise synergy projects in their annual strategic plans and work on them during the year. He made it a corporate policy to evaluate every manager and professional employee on their contributions to One Enterprise, and then handed out extra bonuses to senior executives who did their bit for the cause."[43]

Robinson supervised middle managers to make sure that they too cooperated. He had a monthly report developed on the status of each "One Enterprise" project, which was circulated among the company's top 100 executives. His measures proved successful, for roughly 10% of Amex's net income in 1986 came from capitalizing on synergistic opportunities.[44] One analyst from Paine Webber commented that "American Express management is better at finding new pockets of growth and exploiting them than any financial company I'm aware of."[45]

Robinson contributed to the success of TRS by, as he describes, "accelerating the focus on quality."[46] During Gerstner's development of the 8 commandments, Robinson was emphasizing service. As described by John Paul Newport, Jr., of *Fortune* magazine, "Service has two components at American Express. The first is quality. While it may sound like a cliche, management really does insist that the company (TRS) strive to deliver the highest quality of service possible. The second and more daring element has to do with change. Robinson demands that employees not merely anticipate change but also reach out to embrace it before it overpowers them."[47] Said Robinson, "Change is going to happen, and we should be excited by that. We should be out there helping change to happen so that we can be the first to take advantage of it."[48]

TRS earnings grew 17% a year compounded and return on equity increased to 28% in 1988. With $800 million in profits, TRS would have been the third largest financial services company in the U.S. if it were an independent firm.[49] Said Paine-Webber analyst, Rodney Schwartz, "TRS has been more profitable by a mile than any other large financial services company I can think of."[50]

Gerstner's success in running TRS had made him a likely candidate for the number 2 spot under Robinson. In 1983, however, Weill was made president. Friends described Gerstner as frustrated during this period, that he began to consider seriously some of the job offers he was getting as his success became known.[51] "He talked to some of us quietly and privately about frustrations and aspirations," a friend recalled. Despite his frustrations, however, "He hunkered down. He knew that the core business he was running was still the family jewel."[52]

The Loss of Safra

All of American Express was not doing as well as TRS. In late 1983, Fireman's Fund suffered combined losses of $452 million, forcing Amex to pump in $230 million in fresh capital which ended their 35-year unbroken string of earnings gains.[53] Robinson fired the subsidiary's top management, and with his blessing, ". . . the Amex board sent Weill to San Francisco to fix Fireman's Fund. The assignment removed Weill from the mainstream of management."[54]

Safra, who was Amex's largest shareholder, was infuriated. *Institutional Investor* remarked that (he) ". . . felt deceived about the woes of Amex's Fireman's Fund subsidiary which sorely damaged the value of the stock he had accepted at TDB's sale."[55]

Safra also was having difficulties adjusting to Amex's style of management. He was unable to function within the rigid framework of a multinational conglomerate. "American Express officials found Safra remote; he was reluctant to leave Geneva for forays to American Express headquarters in New York and was disinclined to adjust to the firm's memo-and-meeting style of business."[56] Cohen tried to mediate the clash in styles between Robinson and Safra. He explains,

"I used to say to Jim, 'If you understand what Edmond is and you create the environment for him to be himself here, it can work. But if we impose upon him the bureaucracy and surround him with all the things that are alien to him, it will never work.'. . . And unfortunately, I don't think Jim fully understood what I meant when I said that. And visa versa, I said to Edmond, 'You know, you're going to have to come to board meetings occasionally, you're going to have to play the game a little bit.' But it turned out to be, 'I don't want to play the game.'"[57]

In December, 1984, Safra resigned as chairman of the TDB-American Express Bank.

A Plan for Ames

Amex continued to experience difficulties.

"It was still digesting its acquisition of Lehman, TDB and IDS, and Fireman's Fund was still reeling from unexpected losses. . . . The board asked for a review of the company's strategy, and Robinson assigned the task to Weill. Weill organized a presentation of the plans for each of the divisions, but the board wasn't satisfied. It wanted an overall strategy for the corporation. 'Sandy just gulped,' recalls a participant. It was back to the drawing board, and a series of meetings were held at the Plaza hotel in New York attended by Weill, Gerstner, Cohen, IDS chief Harvey Golub and William McCormick, who at the time was running Fireman's Fund along with Weill, and other executives. They debated organization, marketing and financial goals as they tried to hammer out a single coherent mission for American Express. Robinson wasn't there for most of the meetings but would join them for dinner later."[58]

As head of corporate planning, Gerstner presented the results of the brainstorming to the board in the spring of 1985. His plan was a success. It included specific criteria, however, that excluded Fireman's Fund.

"As Gerstner saw things, Amex should aim to be first, second or third in market share in any business it was to be in and control its own distribution channels. That way the company could differentiate its own products from the competition. Fireman's Fund did not meet these criteria. It was eighth in the property/casualty market, it had only a 1 percent market share, and it worked entirely through independent agents. Institutional business such as Fireman's did was seen as less attractive than efforts aimed at individuals, in which there is more opportunity for cross-marketing different products. And most important, Gerstner set out a target of 18 to 20 percent return on equity and 12 to 15 percent average annual earnings growth for each division. Even in good years, Fireman's Fund fell far below these targets, and Amex shortly decided to sell."[59]

The Loss of Weill

Weill had been unhappy with Amex's management style. "Moreover, he plainly (had) . . . not (been) satisfied with just being president and (had) pressed for the additional post of chief operating officer."[60] Robinson was not responsive. So, ". . . Weill carefully remained within the bounds of his job, (but) he openly chafed under Robinson's direction."[61]

When Weill was assigned to Fireman's Fund, he immersed himself in the project of turning the company around. He became ". . . enamored of (the company's). . . prospects (and) . . . was itching to run his own company again."[62] Upon hearing that Amex was planning to sell the troubled company, Weill made a bid to buy it. The board rejected his bid and Weill resigned. In October, 1985, Amex sold 58% of Fireman's Fund to the public, which turned out to be the largest public stock offering ever made on Wall Street. It sold an additional 15% in May of 1986.[63]

The Financial Supermarket and Shearson

Shearson's acquisition of Lehman Brothers in 1984 significantly changed the company's nature. "Now, with Lehman's investment-banking franchise and inestimable cachet, Shearson was making a bid to break into the elite Wall Street club—the 'bulge bracket,' or first-tier securities firms."[64] Cohen set out to prove that Shearson Lehman could live up to the style of Lehman Brothers. Shearson moved to the World Financial Center in New York and built its own Shearson Lehman executive dining room that "rivalled its Lehman forerunner in elegance."[65] Cohen too began to change. He no longer managed Shearson with "compulsive vigilance."[66] He now began to ". . . (give) himself over to the far more chimerical high-profile and high-margin world of investment banking."[67] Robinson supported Cohen's transition. He said that he "encouraged Peter to establish his contacts around the world in banking, in government and in business."[68]

Both Robinson and Cohen believed that a global presence was necessary and that it should be sizable. Shearson began its international expansion before acquiring Lehman. It acquired L. Messel, a middle-sized securities firm in London. By the end of 1989, Shearson had opened branches in 9 countries across Europe, Asia, the Far East and Australia. Expansion occurred, domestically as well. In late 1987, Shearson acquired E.F. Hutton Group Inc., one of the nation's largest retail brokers that was experiencing severe organizational problems.

"It was a perfect strategic move, inasmuch as it would enable Shearson to go from third place as a retail power to a spot where it could vie with Merrill Lynch for No. 1. Of all the expansions Shearson was undertaking, this was the most justifiable, since it involved the firm's core, historic business. There were no dissenters, or even doubters, on the American Express board, and Robinson was strong in his support."[69]

Shearson also moved into the business of merchant banking. It took substantial equity positions in deals, such as leveraged buyouts (when public shares of a company are bought in an acquisition financed largely by debt and collateralized by the company's assets) and bridge loans (loans that span the interval between a deal's closing and the placement of its debt with buyers). Thus Shearson

"moved from a traditional role as an intermediary to the far more dramatic one of principal. Shearson and its Boston Company private-banking and asset-management subsidiary both invested hundreds of millions of dollars in junk bonds. Shearson also acquired twenty-eight per cent of a high-flying Los Angeles life-insurance company, First Capital, which maintained an enormous junk-bond portfolio. And Shearson's primary real-estate subsidiary, Balcor was now moving aggressively into construction lending—a somewhat anomalous business for a Wall Street securities firm, even in the freewheeling, improvisational eighties."[70]

Cohen's vistas were widening as rapidly as Shearson's. Cohen had been frugal. He had continued to drive a Buick station wagon long after he became a multimillionaire. However, by 1989, through Shearson, he owned three Gulfstream jets, one lined with ultrasuede in a style created by Ralph Lauren's interior designer. Flight attendants were asked to regularly brush the lining. Under Cohen's direction, Shearson built a conference center at the ski resort town of Beaver Creek, Colorado. When Karen, Cohen's wife, noticed that other neighboring chalets could be seen from the conference center's windows, she directed that full-grown evergreen trees be planted. The center ended up costing Shearson $25 million.

Cohen built Shearson toward his vision of "a securities-industry titan—the biggest in retail brokerage and one of the foremost in investment banking and capital markets, here and abroad."[71] His reign at Shearson was characterized by "an ethos of limitlessness: that there was, and should be, no limit to resources, no limit to businesses in which to invest, no limit to the sublime market conditions of the mid-eighties. 'The view was that you had to be in every market doing everything with every product, because you didn't want to miss the pot of gold,'" said J. Tomilson, the co-head of investment banking at Shearson.[72] A Shearson executive remarked that "Peter was always saying, 'Here is the opportunity—let's take it.' Shearson did not miss one opportunity—some opportunities were related to our core businesses, and some not."[73] Another Shearson executive said, "The question that most would ask was not 'What is in the best interests of the firm?' but 'What does Peter want?'"[74]

Gerstner's Vision

The success of Gerstner's strategic plan for Amex guaranteed him presidency in 1985 following Weill's resignation. Gerstner had finally achieved the number 2 spot he had long hoped for. He still held the chairman position at TRS and was also officially responsible for the corporate finance and planning functions and IDS. Shearson and American Express Bank reported to Robinson. Robinson began to turn his attention to outside policy issues such as trade and international debt. There were even rumors that he was angling for a job in Washington.[75] This left Gerstner in charge of more of the daily operations of the company.

During this time, Gerstner developed his own unique vision for the Amex Corporation that did not place Shearson at the center of a financial supermarket. Gerstner believed that computer services was destined to be Amex's core business. He visualized high-priced, high-quality service, and computer services fit that vision better than financial services. "In the data-processing area, Amex (was) . . . already the fifth-largest provider of computer services in the country. 'It is a high-profit, high-cash-flow, rapidly growing business,' said Gerstner, 'And it is a business that relies on a couple of things we know very well: customer service and technology.'"[76] Gerstner considered First Data Resources to be the company at the center of computer services at Amex. He developed a clear strategy for FDR that aimed to capitalize on its strengths. "The company wants to take its expertise in billing and customer-record keeping and move into other industries. . . . If Amex makes another large acquisition, (Gerstner said) . . . it will most likely be a computer company."[77]

Symbiosis or Autonomy

In the mid-eighties, Robinson emphasized service and "One Enterprise." Yet he focused most of his energy toward global issues like solving the Third World debt crisis which had cost Amex in lost reserves from bad Latin American loans. He was chairman of the United Way of America and the New York City Partnership, a prominent corporate sponsor of minority housing and employment projects. During this time, Gerstner was emphasizing synergy and information management. He concentrated on developing Amex's computer services. Cohen, on the other hand, was trying to build Shearson into the biggest, most powerful financial firm on Wall Street. And, according to Bruck, he wasn't building Shearson for the greater glory of the American Express empire, but "qua Shearson" and was glad to have resources of American Express behind him. He had resisted Robinson's entreaties for synergy ". . . and Shearson had remained stubbornly isolationist. His desire was not for symbiosis but for even-greater autonomy, . . . to pursue his vision . . . with a minimum of interference."[78] Cohen was required to participate in Amex's strategic planning sessions. One participant in these planning sessions recalls Cohen as "blasé, bored, just not interested. His attitude was that you could not plan for a securities firm as you would for other industries. Peter would say, 'You guys, don't give me that crap. This (Shearson) is a real industry, this is a *tough* industry, this isn't selling traveller's checks.'"[79]

Gerstner was growing more frustrated with Cohen and Shearson as time went on. Shearson's erratic earnings were obscuring TRS's enormous success. Said Henry Duques, the president and CEO of Information Services Corporation, "While earnings at TRS, under Lou, were growing at fifteen per cent, year after year, Shearson's earnings were up one quarter, down another, and it was disturbing when the market valuation of American Express stock was so affected by Shearson's ups and downs. So Lou would ask Peter for numbers, and ask him some probing questions. But Peter's response was 'Don't try to pin me down. I can't manage it (Shearson) the way you do—it's a different business. The market goes up and the market goes down. And if it goes up next month I could make a hundred million.'"[80]

Gerstner argued to Robinson that Shearson's strategy should be subjected to the kind of rigorous review experienced by other parts of Amex. Robinson treated Shearson differently than Amex's other divisions. He did not supervise the company's activities as intently and allowed Cohen significant leeway. Bruck describes Robinson's light supervision of Cohen as "attributable to his belief in decentralization, and to his 'hands-off' style."[81] Robinson, himself, acknowledges that he may have sometimes given subordinates what looked like too much latitude. But, he said, "if that's what their personalities require to be the most turned-on, dynamic contributors to American Express, that's an easy price to pay."[82]

Robinson considered Cohen to be one such dynamic contributor. Bruck describes Robinson as having "believed so intensely in Cohen's prowess that he willingly suspended disbelief. Even today, . . . Robinson speaks about Cohen (with) . . . the echo of thrall."[83] Some believed that Cohen had become overzealous, too confident to the point of being condescending and abrasive. But Robinson seemed to overlook these quirks. One Robinson associate said that although many people, including Robinson's wife, Linda, criticized Peter, ". . . Jim really was his booster, I think he was mesmerized by him."[84]

Under Cohen's direction, Shearson had provided Amex a significant boost. The company's record earnings in 1986, $341 million, were a blessing to Amex during its recovery from its Fireman's Fund's losses.[85] With Shearson, Amex was sharing in the money that everyone was making on Wall Street. A Robinson associate commented that "Jim wanted to build a great financial-services company that would be the biggest or one of the biggest in the world, and Shearson was critical to that strategy."[86]

Fortune and Fame

Despite the rising tensions between Cohen and Gerstner, the company was doing extremely well. Amex had tripled its revenues between the years of 1979 and 1987[87] and earned an average return on shareholders' equity of better than 15% a year.[88] It was the first to top $1 billion a year in income in 1986 and was responsible for more than $298 billion in other people's money.[89] The press surrounding Robinson, Cohen and the Shearson-Amex empire was equally as glowing. In January of 1988, a *Business Week* cover story on Robinson declared that he had ". . . transformed the company. . . (into) . . . the unrivalled colossus of financial services . . . (having led) . . . what is widely considered the most successful financial services diversification drive of the 1980's."[90] Cohen's press was also stunning. There were few publications that had not glorified him as a "wunderkind" or a "legend."[91] In 1987, *Euromoney* named him Banker of the Year. In 1988, following the E.F. Hutton acquisition, *Institutional Investor* released a cover story on him. Its title read, "Today Hutton, tomorrow . . ." The article compared Cohen to such Wall Street legends as "Andre Meyer, Sidney Weinberg and Robert Lehman."

The Safra Affair

When Edmond Safra resigned as chairman of the TDB and American Express Bank, he agreed, at the request of Amex, to not found a new Swiss bank until March 1988. Months later, Amex suspected that Safra was hiring away TDB employees in preparation for his re-entry into Swiss banking. Amex feared that when Safra returned to Swiss banking, he would reclaim his former customers. The company considered Safra's activities as unfair competition and tried to protect itself through legal action. Despite these efforts, in the summer of 1988, Safra opened a new bank at the site of his old one in Geneva.

Only two weeks later, Safra was upset to find several published articles linking him to the Mafia, South American drug traffickers, the CIA, the Iran Contra scandal and drug money laundering. These articles attacked Safra's reputation and threatened his business.

Safra conducted his own investigation and determined that Amex was behind the smear campaign. Eventually, he confronted Robinson on the telephone and later at a meeting in Safra's Manhattan apartment. Robinson claimed that he would be "dumbfounded" if he found out his people had anything to do with the smear and that he would check into the matter.[92]

Several links suggested that Harry L. Freeman, Executive Vice President of Amex, likely was in charge of the scandal. He had hired Susan Cantor and Antonio Greco to investigate Safra's dark side and was alleged to have trumped up the illegal connections. A month later, in the summer of 1988, Amex admitted to the campaign to ruin Safra's reputation and made a public apology for what Robinson called "an unauthorized and shameful effort to use media to malign . . . (Safra) . . ."[93] Amex paid $8 million to Safra and charities he selected as penance.[94]

Robinson received little criticism for the scandal. He was able to escape the blame partly because Freeman retired after the company's public apology and became the scapegoat. Robinson's reputation of escaping blame for his company's errors has earned him the description "slicker than teflon."[95] Public relations people like Robinson's wife, Linda, who owns her own public relations firm, call this "damage control."[96]

"An Albatross Named Shearson"[97]

The 1987 stockmarket crash brought the end of the Bull Market and Shearson's earnings reflected this change, dropping severely in 1988. Securities analysts contended that Shearson was spread too thin to excel in any one area of its highly cyclical industry. "All of a sudden, they've got more businesses than they can handle."[98] It seemed that Cohen had overreached. Some believe that he had inflated a highly profitable retail brokerage outfit into a full-service investment house that did absolutely everything but excelled in nothing. As the financier, Michael David-Weill described it, "We are only as good as the times we are in."[99] The glory years were over and Cohen and Shearson's glory would end with them.

A string of devastating setbacks befell Shearson. The company's net worth had been severely diminished by the E.F. Hutton acquisition and the "junk-bond" market collapsed. These and other losses destroyed Shearson's financial profile. The company's losses began to affect Amex's balance sheet and Robinson took notice.

First, Shearson damaged its own and Amex's reputation by representing a British firm, Beazer P.L.C., in its hostile bid for Pittsburgh's Koppers Company in the spring of 1988. Although Beazer and Shearson eventually won control of Koppers, the battle was a rough one. Pittsburgh residents, including the mayor and civic leaders, were incensed. Wall Street disapproved. It was not appropriate for a reputable investment bank to be a principal in a hostile takeover. Residents were televised burning and cutting their American Express cards in half. Remnants were mailed to Robinson, who had a difficult time handling the public ridicule, especially since Shearson, and not Amex, was to blame. The incident infuriated Robinson, who began to question his trust in Cohen's management capabilities.[100] He forbade Shearson from backing any more hostile deals.

Shearson also failed to back F. Ross Johnson's attempt to acquire RJR Nabisco from its shareholders in late 1988. This incident was detailed in the best-selling book by Burrough and Helyar called *Barbarians at the Gate*.[101] Shearson made an embarrassingly low first bid, and was easily beaten out by Kohlberg Kravis Roberts and Company. The defeat cost Shearson more than $200 million in potential fees and led to a loss of credibility. Shearson had been out-classed. Robinson was, again, furious. Johnson was one of Robinson's closest friends and Cohen had fumbled the merger out of Johnson's hands. Shearson was humiliated and was labeled inept by the press.

Other embarrassments occurred. Shearson's Boston Company, a monetary management subsidiary, was caught having overstated its 1988 earnings by $30 million. Cohen had to fire Boston Company president, James N. VonGermeten, for the scandal, and Chief Financial Officer, Joseph F. Murphy, resigned. Amex's earnings were subsequently reduced by $30 million as the company admitted to the blunder.

In *Barbarians*, Burrough and Helyar blamed Cohen for the failed RJR deal and described him as having flawed judgement and bad demeanor.[102] Shearson had become a liability to Amex, and Cohen, an embarrassment. On January 29, 1990, Robinson fired

Cohen. Amex absorbed the rest of Shearson and discovered the company to be a patchwork of dozens of investment houses sloppily stitched together. *Business Week's* cover story titled "The Failed Vision" described its own interpretation of why Robinson's dream never materialized.

"The plans of one-source delivery of various financial services and cross-selling to AmEx's various customers never materialized. In many ways the product mix and clientele became so varied that customers and executives alike were confused."[103]

Robinson spent the next few months cutting the unwieldy Shearson down to a more manageable size.

Total Revenues for American Express Company Divisions 1977 – 1982 (millions of dollars)

	1977	1978	1979	1980	1981	1982	1983	1984	1985	1986	1987	1988	1989
Travel Related Services	792	993	1,239	1,661	2,175	2,516	2,889	3,620	4,226	5,951	5,607	6,854	8,357
International Banking Services American Express Bank '83–'89	381	516	706	930	1,068	1,025	1,437	1,548	1,568	1,685	1,733	1,738	2,100
Insurance Services	2,253	2,556	2,719	2,914	3,104	3,356	601	740	659	—	—	—	—
American Express Information Services	—	—	—	—	—	—	—	—	—	—	384	447	660
Investment Services/Shearson Lehman Brothers '83–'89	—	—	—	922	1,016	1,318	1,826	2,280	3,246	4,600	*6,749	*10,529	*12,501
IDS Financial Services	—	—	—	—	—	—	—	1,576	2,201	2,395	1,360	1,557	1,934
Other and Corporate	27	32	33	35	22	14	(6)	82	166	330	342	108	193
Adjustments and Eliminations	(7)	(21)	(30)	(36)	(94)	(136)	(149)	(204)	(216)	(309)	(213)	(338)	(698)
Consolidated	3,446	4,076	4,667	6,426	7,291	8,093	6,598	9,642	11,850	14,652	15,962	20,895	25,047

*Includes Hutton

Endnotes

1. Saul Hansel, "What's in the Cards for Lou Gerstner?" *Institutional Investor,* December 1988, p. 51.
2. Anthony Bianco, "Do You Know Me? An Intimate Profile of Jim Robinson, CEO of American Express," *Business Week,* January 25, 1988, p. 75.
3. Peter Z. Grossman, "James D. Robinson, III Takes Charge," *Best of Business Quarterly 9,* no. 2 (Summer 1987), p. 90.
4. Anthony Bianco, "Do You Know Me? An Intimate Profile of Jim Robinson, CEO of American Express," *Business Week,* January 25, 1988, p. 75.
5. Ibid.
6. Ibid.
7. Ibid., p. 74.
8. Saul Hansel, "What's in the Cards for Lou Gerstner?" *Institutional Investor,* December 1988, p. 51.
9. Ibid., p. 51.
10. Ibid., p. 50.
11. Ibid., p. 51.
12. Ibid., pp. 52, 55.
13. Peter Z. Grossman, "James D. Robinson, III Takes Charge," *Best of Business Quarterly 9,* no. 2 (Summer 1987), p. 90.
14. John Paul Newport Jr., "American Express: Service that Sells," *Fortune,* November 20, 1989, p. 80.
15. Peter Z. Grossman, "James D. Robinson, III Takes Charge," *Best of Business Quarterly 9,* no. 2 (Summer 1987), p. 90.
16. Ibid., p. 87.
17. Ibid., p. 90.
18. Connie Bruck, "Undoing The Eighties," *The New Yorker,* July 23, 1990, p. 56.
19. Ibid., p. 58.
20. Ibid.
21. Peter Z. Grossman, "James D. Robinson, III Takes Charge," *Best of Business Quarterly 9,* no. 2 (Summer 1987), p. 89.
22. Anthony Bianco, "Do You Know Me? An Intimate Profile of Jim Robinson, CEO of American Express," *Business Week,* January 25, 1988, p. 76.
23. "Not Doing Nicely, American Express and its Broker, Shearson Lehman," *The Economist,* February 3, 1990, p. 84.
24. Connie Bruck, "Undoing The Eighties," *The New Yorker,* July 23, 1990, p. 56.
25. Ibid.
26. *Business Week,* March 19, 1990, p. 110.
27. Anthony Bianco, "Do You Know Me? An Intimate Profile of Jim Robinson, CEO of American Express," *Business Week,* January 25, 1988, p. 76.
28. Connie Bruck, "Undoing The Eighties," *The New Yorker,* July 23, 1990, p. 58.
29. Monci Jo Williams, "Shearson Lehman: The 'Mismatch' May be Working," *Fortune,* March 31, 1986, p. 33.
30. Anthony Bianco, "Do You Know Me? An Intimate Profile of Jim Robinson, CEO of American Express," *Business Week,* January 25, 1988, p. 76.
31. Joe Queenan and Tatiana Pouschine, "The Peter Principle," *Forbes,* July 10, 1989, p. 41.
32. Connie Bruck, "Undoing The Eighties," *The New Yorker,* July 23, 1990, p. 58.
33. Monci Jo Williams, "Shearson Lehman: The 'Mismatch' may be Working," *Fortune,* March 31, 1986, p. 33.
34. Ibid.
35. Ibid.
36. Connie Bruck, "Undoing The Eighties," *The New Yorker,* July 23, 1990, p. 57.
37. Lenny Glynn, "Edmond Safra Targets Geneva," *Institutional Investor,* March 1988, p. 154.
38. Ibid.
39. John Paul Newport Jr., "American Express: Service that Sells," *Fortune,* November 20, 1989, p. 84.
40. Ibid.
41. Monci Jo Williams, "Synergy Works at American Express," *Fortune,* February 16, 1987, p. 79.
42. Ibid.
43. Ibid., p. 80.
44. Ibid., p. 79.
45. Ibid., p. 80.
46. John Paul Newport Jr., "American Express: Service that Sells," *Fortune,* November 20, 1989, p. 80.
47. Ibid., p. 80.
48. Ibid., p. 82.
49. Saul Hansel, "What's in the Cards for Lou Gerstner?" *Institutional Investor,* December 1988, p. 50.
50. Ibid.
51. Ibid.
52. Ibid, pp. 56, 59.
53. Connie Bruck, "Undoing The Eighties," *The New Yorker,* July 23, 1990, p. 62.
54. Anthony Bianco, "Do You Know Me? An Intimate Profile of Jim Robinson, CEO of American Express," *Business Week,* January 25, 1988, p. 77.
55. Lenny Glynn, "Edmond Safra Targets Geneva," *Institutional Investor,* March 1988, p. 154.
56. Ibid.
57. Ibid., pp. 154, 156.
58. Saul Hansel, "What's in the Cards for Lou Gerstner?" *Institutional Investor,* December 1988, p. 59.
59. Ibid.
60. Anthony Bianco, "Do You Know Me? An Intimate Profile of Jim Robinson, CEO of American Express," *Business Week,* January 25, 1988, p. 76.
61. Ibid.
62. Saul Hansel, "What's in the Cards for Lou Gerstner?" *Institutional Investor,* December 1988, p. 59.
63. Jaques Lowe, "Fireman's Fund: Who's in Charge Here?" *Institutional Investor,* August 1986, p. 104.
64. Connie Bruck, "Undoing The Eighties," *The New Yorker,* July 23, 1990, p. 58.
65. Ibid.
66. Ibid., p. 59.
67. Ibid.
68. Ibid.
69. Ibid., p. 60.
70. Ibid., pp. 60–61.
71. Ibid., p. 57.
72. Ibid., p. 62.
73. Ibid., p. 61.
74. Ibid.
75. Saul Hansel, "What's in the Cards for Lou Gerstner?" *Institutional Investor,* December 1988, p. 51.
76. Ibid., pp. 59, 61.
77. Ibid., p. 61.
78. Connie Bruck, "Undoing The Eighties," *The New Yorker,* July 23, 1990, pp. 57, 61.
79. Ibid.
80. Ibid.
81. Ibid., p. 71.
82. John Paul Newport Jr., "American Express: Service that Sells," *Fortune,* November 20, 1989, p. 89.
83. Connie Bruck, "Undoing The Eighties," *The New Yorker,* July 23, 1990, p. 62.
84. Ibid., p. 57.
85. Ibid., p. 62.
86. Ibid.
87. Anthony Bianco, "Do You Know Me? An Intimate Profile of Jim Robinson, CEO of American Express," *Business Week,* January 25, 1988, p. 78.
88. John Paul Newport Jr., "American Express: Service that Sells," *Fortune,* November 20, 1989, p. 80.
89. Anthony Bianco, "Do You Know Me? An Intimate Profile of Jim Robinson, CEO of American Express," *Business Week,* January 25, 1988, p. 72.
90. Ibid.
91. Connie Bruck, "Undoing The Eighties," *The New Yorker,* July 23, 1990, p. 56.

92. Brian Burrough, "The Vendetta: How American Express Orchestrated a Smear of Rival Edmond Safra," *The Wall Street Journal,* September 24, 1990.

93. Connie Bruck, "Undoing The Eighties," *The New Yorker,* July 23, 1990, p. 65.

94. Brian Burrough, "The Vendetta: How American Express Orchestrated a Smear of Rival Edmond Safra," *The Wall Street Journal,* September 24, 1990.

95. Allan Sloan, "Being Slicker Than Teflon at American Express," *Los Angeles Times,* March 5,1990, p. D5.

96. Ibid.

97. Kurt Eichenwald, "An Albatross Named Shearson," *The New York Times,* July 15, 1990, p. F1.

98. Ibid.

99. Connie Bruck, "Undoing The Eighties," *The New Yorker,* July 23, 1990, p. 58.

100. Ibid., pp. 63-65.

101. Ibid., p. 68.

102. Ibid.

103. John Meehan and Jon Friedman with Leah J. Nathans, "The Failed Vision," *Business Week,* March 19, 1990, p. 111.

BULLER | SCHULER

Managing Organizations and People

A Resource for Cases in Management, Organizational Behavior, and Human Resource Management

Abstract

XEL Communications, Inc. designs and manufactures various telecommunications products for a number of companies—primarily large U.S. telephone operating companies. The case traces the formation of XEL, which at one time was a division within GTE. Having been spun off from GTE, President Bill Danko and several key managers were faced with the issue of positioning this stand-alone business in a highly competitive marketplace. The case begins with Bill Danko assessing key developments that could have a significant effect on the future growth and direction of XEL—namely, regulatory changes that may allow these large telephone companies to manufacture their own equipment, emerging alliances between telephone and cable companies, new technologies that could replace their existing products, and the globalization of telecommunications. Key initial steps are the development of a vision statement and the formation of a formal strategic planning process. The case concludes with Bill initiating his annual strategic planning process in which he as well as his key managers must assess key strategic issues facing XEL. At the same time, he must determine how XEL can maintain its entrepreneurial culture while it manages growth. In short, this case provides a unique opportunity for students to understand the linkage between human resource management issues and strategic management issues.

XEL Communications, Inc. (A)

As he was turning into the parkway that curves around his company's plant, Bill Sanko, President of XEL Communications, glanced at a nearby vacant facility that once housed a now-defunct computer manufacturer. Over the next few months, in May 1995, XEL would be moving into this building. While this move was a sign of how far XEL had come in the last ten years, Bill considered that they might have met the same fate as the previous tenant. He also wondered whether they would be able to sustain the same culture that enabled the company to succeed in a rapidly changing, highly competitive industry. At the same time, he realized that change could also create opportunities.

After parking and completing the short walk to his office, Bill grabbed a copy of today's *Wall Street Journal*. One article which caught his attention was entitled, "Baby Bells Lobby Congress for Regulatory Freedom." As one of many suppliers of telecommunications equipment to the Regional Bell Operating Companies (RBOCs), this development posed some interesting issues for XEL Communications. If the RBOCs were allowed to pursue their own manufacturing (which they are currently prohibited from doing), how would this affect XEL's existing contracts? As telephone and cable companies develop more strategic alliances and partnerships, would this provide an opportunity for XEL? At the same time, it appeared that the telecommunications industry was now becoming a global industry in which developing countries are allowing outside companies the ability to establish and maintain telecommunications services. What role could XEL play in this rapidly growing market?

The Telecommunications Industry

A decade after the breakup of the telephone monopoly, the prospect of intense competition driving the telecommunications industry was creating some interesting scenarios.[1] The AT&T of old was the model for the telecommunications company of the future. "You're going to see the re-creation of five or six former AT&Ts—call them 'full-service networks'—over the next five years or more," said Michael Elling, first vice president at Prudential Securities. Marketing and capital-equipment dollars are invested more efficiently if distribution is centralized, he continued. "It could be that US WEST, Time Warner, and Sprint get together. It could be that Bell Atlantic, Nynex and MCI get together. It could be that GTE, AT&T and a few other independents (local providers not affiliated with a regional Bell) get together." The inevitability of such combinations was matched by the uncertainty over what form they would take. A business known for its predictability had suddenly found itself unpredictable. "I think you can't rule anything out in this industry anymore," says Simon Flannery, a vice president at J.P. Morgan Securities. "All the rules of the game are up for review." In most cases, telecommunications systems transmitted information by wire, radio, or space satellite. Wire transmission involved sending electrical signals over various types of wire lines such as open wire, multipair cable, and coaxial cable. These lines could be used to transmit voice frequencies, telegraph messages, computer-processed data, and television programs. Another somewhat related transmission medium that had come into increasingly wider use, especially in telephone communications, was a type of cable composed of optical fibers. Here, electrical signals converted to light signals by a laser-driven transmitter carried both speech and data over bundles of thin glass or plastic filaments. Radio communication systems transmitted electronic signals in relatively narrow frequency bands through the air. They included radio navigation and both amateur and commercial broadcasting. Commercial broadcasting consisted of AM, FM, and TV broadcasting for general public use. Satellite communications allowed the exchange of television or telephone signals between widely separated locations by means of microwaves—that is, very short radio waves with wavelengths from 4 inches to 0.4 inches, which corresponded to a frequency range of 3 to 30 gigahertz (GHz), or 3 to 30 billion cycles per second. Since satellite systems did not require the construction of intermediate relay or repeater stations, as did ground-based microwave systems, they could be put into service much more rapidly.

Not only had the mode of delivery changed, but also the content. Modern telecommunications networks not only sent the traditional voice communications of telephones and the printed messages of telegraphs and telexes, they also carried images—the still images of facsimile machines or the moving images of video in video conferences in which the participants could see as well as hear each other. Additionally, they carried encoded data ranging from the business accounts of a multinational corporation to medical data relayed by physicians thousands of miles from a patient.

The U.S. telecommunications services industry was expected to continue to expand in 1994.[2] Revenues were expected to rise about 7.7 percent, compared with a 6 percent increase in 1993. In 1994, revenues generated by international services increased about 20 percent, and local exchange telephone service was expected to rise by 3 percent. Sales of domestic long distance services were expected to grow more than 6 percent in 1994, depending on overall growth in the economy. Value-added network and information services were to climb an estimated 15 percent in 1994. Revenues from cellular mobile telephone services were to increase 39 percent in 1994; satellite service revenues in 1994 were to grow nearly 25 percent.

Local telephone services were provided by about 1,325 local telephone companies (telcos), including 7 Regional Bell Operating Companies (RBOCs), telcos owned by GTE, Sprint (United Telecom and Centel franchises), and independent local telephone companies. Many of these small, local companies operated as rural telephone cooperatives. Long distance service was provided by AT&T, MCI, Sprint, WilTel, Metromedia Communications, Litel Telecommunications, Allnet, and more than 475 smaller companies.

In 1993, the local exchange telephone companies were confronted with increasing competitive pressures in certain local services they had monopolized for decades. In response to these pressures, and to possible future competition from cable TV companies and others for local exchange telephone service itself, the RBOCs stepped up their campaign to obtain authority to enter the long distance and telecommunications equipment manufacturing businesses, and to offer video programming services.

The major long distance carriers, meanwhile, focused their attention on wireless technologies and made plans to work with or acquire companies in the wireless market. This would enable them to provide long distance services to cellular users and possibly to develop a more economical local access network to reach their own subscribers. Internationally, the large service providers continued to make alliances and seek out partners in efforts to put together global telecommunications networks and offer the international equivalent of the advanced telecommunications services available in the U.S. domestic market.

In terms of policy developments that affect the telecommunications industry, the Clinton Administration had focused its attention on the national telecommunications infrastructure, or the "information superhighway." Bills were introduced in both houses of Congress that addressed this and other key telecommunications policy issues. There was broad consensus that the Federal Government should not finance the construction of a national network. Rather, the Government was being urged to help promote competition in network access, advance interconnection and interoperability standards, see that customers would have access to new services provided over the digital infrastructure at reasonable rates, and support pilot projects for applications in education and health care. Under proposed legislation, the digital infrastructure would be extended to tap information resources at libraries, research centers, and government facilities. Congress was to consider major telecommunications legislation in the future and would then face how it would resolve the contentious issues involved that concerned so many large and powerful interests. There were also signs that some states would also open up their exchange and local service markets to competition.

Cable TV companies were likely to become another group of competitors the local telephone companies would face in the near future. Cable companies already had connections with 60 percent of U.S. households, and cable facilities extended into areas where another 30 percent of the households were located. New digital and fiber optic technologies would allow them to provide telephone services over their networks, something cable companies already were doing in Britain.

XEL Communications: The Beginning

XEL Communications was born not only with an opportunity but with a challenge as well. Bill Sanko started with General Telephone and Electronics (GTE) as a product manager after spending six years in the U.S. Army.[3] He was chosen in 1972 to help establish the GTE Satellite Corporation. After he was successful with this enterprise, GTE then selected Bill for another startup business called Special Service Products in 1980.

The Special Service Products Division (SSPD) was established to manufacture certain telecommunications products to compete with small companies who were making inroads into GTE's market. These products ranged from voice and data transmission products to switches customized to specific business needs. After two previous failures, it was GTE's third (and perhaps final) try at starting such a division. Company officials granted Sanko almost full autonomy to build the division, including recruiting all key executives, establishing a location in Aurora, Colorado, a rapidly growing region east of Denver, and in designing the division's overall operating philosophy.

By 1984, the division realized its first year of break-even operations, but it wasn't enough to win over GTE executives. Despite its initial success and the prospect of a fast-growing market, SSPD found itself heading toward orphan status in GTE's long-range plans.[4] After divestiture in telecommunications, GTE opted to concentrate primarily on providing telephone service rather than hardware. (GTE has subsequently divested all of its manufacturing divisions.) "Even though we were doing the job expected of us in building the business," Sanko said, "GTE's and SSPD's strategic plans were taking different directions." They opted to close the division. Sanko lobbied and ultimately persuaded GTE to sell the division.

The result was an action as unlikely as it was logical. On July 3, 1984, appropriately one day before Independence Day, Sanko and fellow managers from SSPD signed a letter of intent to buy the division from GTE. Two months later, the bill of sale was signed and XEL Communications Inc. became an independent company. Sanko gathered a group of managers and raised the money—some through second mortgages on homes. GTE loaned Sanko and his colleagues money, and the rest was supplied by venture capitalists. In fact, just before the new company was scheduled to begin operations, one of the banks backed out of the arrangement. According to Julie Rich, one of the co-founders and Vice President for Human Resources, "we didn't have any money lined up from September to December of 1984. Making the first payroll for a company of 180 employees was one of the major challenges. Christmas that first year was particularly lean."

The financing was eventually arranged, and XEL was underway. Sanko reflected on the perils and rewards of leaving the corporate nest to seek one's fortune: "In the end, it was the right thing to do, but it wasn't an easy decision to make. After 17 years with GTE, I had achieved vice president status; and I was more than a little nervous about leaving the corporation."[5]

Early Years

One of the more interesting exercises in starting any new company is what to name it. John Puckett, Vice President for Manufacturing and also one of the original founders, recalled: "We did a lot of brainstorming about what to call this new company—including taking initials from the original founders' names and seeing what combinations we could come up with. Usually, they didn't make a whole lot of sense. We finally decided on XEL which is a shortened version of excellence."

More than simply naming the company, one of the key concerns for XEL Communications was whether their customers would stay with them once they were no longer part of GTE. Not that XEL has ever exactly been an abandoned child. GTE may have kicked XEL out the door in 1984, but it remains XEL's biggest customer, with GTE Telephone Operations accounting for about 35 percent of the company's total business. In fact, the relationship between the two companies continues to be close and mutually beneficial. Ever the proud parent, GTE recognized XEL as its Quality Vendor of the Year in both 1987 and 1988, and as a Vendor of Excellence in subsequent years.

At first, all XEL produced was a handful of products for GTE. Even so, the company showed a profit in its first year of independent operation. "We were off to a better start than you might expect, just because we had always had a certain independence," says Sanko. "We had our own engineers, we were a non-union shop (unlike most of the other divisions of GTE at the time), we had installed our own computer systems, and we were out here in Colorado, on our own. We were doing things differently from the start, and so we just continued."

Weaning itself from GTE was a corporate goal entirely dependent on new product development, and XEL spent over 10 percent of its revenues on R&D. That focus on development would not likely change: The XEL product line is custom manufactured and therefore constantly evolved and changed as customers' needs changed. "Running a small company has a lot of challenges," Sanko says. "But one of the major advantages is being able to respond to the market and get things done quickly. Here we can respond to a customer requirement."

XEL's Products and Markets

For example, XEL sold products that facilitated the transmission of data and information over phone lines. Driving the need for XEL's products was the fact that "businesses are more and more dependent on the transfer of information," as Bill Sanko noted. In addition, more businesses, including XEL, were operating by taking and filling orders, for example, through electronic data exchanges. Instead of dialing into inside salespeople, businesses often accessed databases directly.

XEL's products performed a number of functions that allowed businesses to incorporate their specific telecommunications needs into the existing telephone "network" functions such as data exchanges. XEL had a diverse product line of over 300 products that it manufactures. Some of its major products included:

- Fibre Optic Terminal Products
- Coaxial Business Access
- Analog Voice Products
- Analog Data Products
- Digital Data Products
- Digital Transmission
- Telecom Maintenance Products

XEL's products would, for example, translate analog information into digital transmissions. Adapting electronic information for fiber optic networks was another area of emphasis for XEL, as was adapting equipment to international standards for foreign customers.

One of XEL's strengths was its ability to adapt one manufacturer's equipment to another's. Often, it was the bits and pieces of telecommunications equipment that XEL provided to the "network," that allowed the smooth integration of disparate transmission pieces. XEL also sold central office transmission equipment and a full range of mechanical housings, specialty devices, power supplies and shelves.

"Business customers and their changing telecommunications needs drive the demand for XEL's products. That, in turn, presents a challenge to the company," said Sanko. Sanko cited the constant stream of new products developed by XEL—approximately two per month—as the driving force behind its growth. Industry-wide, product life cycle times were getting ever shorter. Before the breakup of the Bell System in 1984, transmission switches and other telecommunications devices enjoyed a 30-to-40 year life. In 1995, with technology moving so fast, XEL's products had about a three-to-five year life.

In terms of its customers, XEL sold to all of the Regional Bell Operating Companies as well as such companies as GTE and Centel. Railroads, with their own telephone networks, were also customers. XEL's field salespeople worked with engineers to satisfy client requests for specific services. Over a period of time, a rapport was built up with these engineers, providing XEL with new product leads.

With all the consolidations and ventures in telecommunications, one may suspect that the overall market would become more difficult, but Sanko believed "out of change comes opportunity. The worst-case scenario would be a static situation. Thus, a small company, fast to respond to customer needs and able to capitalize on small market niches, will be successful. Often, a large company like AT&T will forsake a smaller market and XEL will move in. Also, XEL's size allows it to design a product in a very short time."

Interestingly, Sanko was watching pending federal legislation proposing to open up local telephone services to companies other than the regional Baby Bells. Consequently, said Sanko, "we need to expand our market and be prepared to sell to others as the regulatory environment changes." Sanko believed legislation would be signed in the near future that would set the groundwork and time tables to open local telephone monopolies to competition. The recent joint venture between Time Warner and US WEST also signalled that telephone and cable companies would be pooling their resources to provide a broader array of information services.

As for the future, Sanko saw "a lot of opportunities we can't even now imagine."

The XEL Vision

In addition to the issue of developing products and maintaining customer loyalty, XEL also had to deal with a number of important "people" issues. "We had good, sound management practices right from the beginning," Sanko said. "We were competing with small companies who did not have the control systems, discipline and planning experience that we had gained as part of GTE. Coming from a large arena, we could start from the top down and tailor the procedures to our needs, rather than, as many small businesses do, have to start developing controls from the bottom and then apply them—hopefully in time."[6]

Yet, while bringing such experiences from GTE proved to be quite valuable, there were also a number of thorny issues which emerged. The first one involved people. As with any transition, there were those people that the owners wished to bring on to the new team and those whose future, for whatever reasons, was not with this new organization. "We were fortunate that personnel from GTE worked in tandem with us in this people transition phase," noted Julie Rich. "We spent a great deal of time talking people through it."

There were other critical human resource issues as well. One of the first ones was the design of the benefits package for the people. Under GTE, XEL had a traditional benefits package with little employee selection. To be competitive as well as cost effective, Julie needed to design a package that had to be reduced from 42 percent of overall payroll costs to 30 percent. She also wanted to create a package that was flexible and allowed the individual some latitude. "One approach we instituted was to allow individuals to have an allowance for total time off as opposed to so many days for sick leave, vacation, and the like. Its primary purpose was to bring down costs. And while it did succeed in this regard, we did have occasions in which people were coming to work sick rather than use this time."

Another approach was to institute a cafeteria plan of benefits in which the individual would select the specific benefits they would like to receive as part of an overall package. "The cafeteria approach was just beginning to be discussed by organizations at this time (1984)," noted Julie. "We felt there were a great deal of pluses to this approach; and it allowed the employee some discretion."

One critical issue that XEL wanted to address was developing a culture that would distinguish them from others and would also demonstrate that they were no longer a division of a large corporation. So, beginning in 1985 and carrying over into 1986, Julie Rich did a lot of reading and research on changing culture. By 1986, a first draft of these ideas and principles were developed (Exhibit 1). Julie reflected on this initial effort: "Once we developed 'XEL's Commitment to XEL-ENCE,' we printed up a bunch and hung them on the walls. However, nothing changed. You also have to realize that this company is largely comprised of engineers and technicians; and for them, a lot of this visioning was foreign."

By late 1986 and early 1987, the senior management team felt that a change agent was needed to help them deal with the issue of managing culture. An outside party was brought in; and his philosophy was that corporate vision should be strategically driven. This approach was warmly received by Bill Sanko; and through a series of monthly meetings, he worked with senior management.

His first effort was directed at getting the team to determine what their core values were and what they would like the company to look like in five years. Bill made an effort to develop a first draft of such a statement. In addition, other members of the senior team made similar efforts. "It was interesting," Julie notes, "Even though we each had a different orientation and background, there was a lot of consistency among the group." The team then went off-site for several days and was able to finalize the XEL Vision statement (Exhibit 2). By the summer of 1987, the statement was signed by members of the senior team and was hung up by the bulletin board. Again, Julie reflects: "The other employees were not required to sign the Vision statement. We felt that once they could really buy into it then they were free to sign it or not."

Julie then described their approach to getting the rest of the organization to understand as well as become comfortable with the XEL Vision: "Frequently, organizations tend

EXHIBIT 1
XEL's Commitment
to XEL-ENCE

XEL Communications, Inc. is a customer oriented supplier of high quality transmission system products and services to telecommunications service providers with emphasis on the effective application of emerging digital technologies.

XEL provides its customers with products which allow them to offer competitive special service features to the end users while improving system operating efficiencies.

To achieve our commitment to XEL-ENCE:

Our customers needs shall always come first.

Profitability ensures a return to our investors, company growth, and team member rewards.

High ethical standards are maintained in all corporate relationships.

On time individual commitments are a personal pledge.

Superior performance through teamwork achieves rewards and advancement.

Customers, employees, and suppliers are team members to be treated with respect and dignity at all times.

to take a combination top-down/bottom-up approach in instituting cultural change. That is, the top level will develop a statement about values and overall vision. They will then communicate it down to the bottom level and hope that results will percolate upward through the middle levels. Yet it is often the middle level of management which is most skeptical, and they will block it or resist change. We decided to take a "cascade" approach in which the process begins at the top and gradually cascades from one level to the next so that the

EXHIBIT 2
The XEL Vision

XEL will become the leader in our selected telecommunications markets through innovation in products and services. Every XEL product and service will be rated Number One by our customers.

XEL will set the standards by which our competitors are judged. We will be the best, most innovative, responsive designer, manufacturer and provider of quality products and services as seen by customers, employees, competitors, and suppliers.*

We will insist upon the highest quality from everyone in every task.

We will be an organization where each of us is a self-manager who will:
· initiate action, commit to, and act responsibly in achieving objectives
· be responsible for XEL's performance
· be responsible for the quality of individual and team output
· invite team members to contribute based on experience, knowledge and ability

We will:
· be ethical and honest in all relationships
· build an environment where creativity and risk taking is promoted
· provide challenging and satisfying work
· ensure a climate of dignity and respect for all
· rely on interdepartmental teamwork, communications and cooperative problem solving to attain common goals**
· offer opportunities for professional and personal growth
· recognize and reward individual contribution and achievement
· provide tools and services to enhance productivity
· maintain a safe and healthy work environment

XEL will be profitable and will grow in order to provide both a return to our investors and rewards to our team members.

XEL will be an exciting and enjoyable place to work while we achieve success.

* Responsiveness to customers' new product needs as well as responding to customers' requirements for emergency delivery requirements has been identified as a key strategic strength. Therefore, the vision statement has been updated to recognize this important element.

** The importance of cooperation and communication was emphasized with this update of the Vision Statement.

critical players are slowly acclimated to the process. We also did a number of other things—including sending a copy of the vision to the homes of the employees and dedicating a section of the company newspaper to communicate what key sections of the vision mean from the viewpoint of managers and employees."

Unlike the first vision statement which was hung on the wall but not really followed, this new vision statement has sustained and reinforced a corporate culture. Julie believed that employee involvement in fashioning and building the statement made the real difference, as well as the fact that XEL made significant use of teams in all facets of its business, including decision making. For example, in 1990, XEL was experiencing some economic difficulties. The employees were brought into meetings and were told the business was in trouble, and were asked for ideas on how to deal with the downturn. The employees discussed the problem and decided to try a four-day work week rather than lay off anyone. After a few months, the economic difficulties continued and the employees reluctantly decided to lay off 40 percent of the workforce. The work teams were asked if they wanted to be involved in deciding who would be laid off. They declined to participate in these tough decisions, but were still clearly concerned about the decisions themselves. In fact, Julie recalls being visited by a number of production workers during this time. "There was one particular fellow who knew that a coworker had a family, and that he would suffer a great deal of hardship if he was to be laid off," Julie remembers, "This fellow came in to my office and asked that he be laid off instead of his coworker. That's when I knew the employees believed in and shared our vision." Eventually, virtually all of the laid off production workers were hired back.

In a strange way, the business crisis of 1990 moved the teams along more quickly than they might have developed in times of profit. Like many businesses using work teams and facing downsizing, XEL laid off a number of middle managers who were not brought back when business improved. When tough decisions needed to be made, the work teams no longer had managers to fall back on.

When teams, or managers, are making decisions, it is routine for the XEL Vision statement to be physically brought into the discussion, and for workers to consult various parts of the statement to help guide and direct decisions. According to Julie, the statement has been used to help evaluate new products, to emphasize quality (a specific XEL strategic objective is to be the top quality vendor for each product), to support teams, and to drive the performance appraisal process.

The XEL Vision was successfully implemented as a key first step; but it was far from being a static document. Key XEL managers continually re-visited the statement to ensure that it became a reflection of where they want to go, not where they have been. Julie believed this was a large factor in the success of the vision. "Our values are the key," Julie explains, "They are strong, they are truly core values, and they are deeply held." Along with the buy-in process, the workers also see that the statement is experimented with. This reflected the strong entrepreneurial nature of XEL's founders—a common bond that they all share. They were not afraid of risk, or of failure, and this spirit was reinforced in all employees through the vision itself, as well as through the yearly process of revisiting the statement. Once a year, Bill Sanko sat with all employees and directly challenged (and listened to direct challenges) on the XEL Vision. Since 1987, only two relatively minor additions have altered the original statement (see Exhibit 2).

Human Resource Management at XEL

Julie Rich was pleased as she scanned the recent article in *Business Week* which mentioned XEL's efforts to use team-based compensation.[7] It mentioned that, once they instituted this system, average production time has been slashed from 30 days to 3, and waste as a percentage of sales has been cut in half. "We have certainly come a long way."

Julie was heavily involved in the development of XEL's first vision statement, and she chuckled about the reaction from others: "Being the non-engineer in an outfit that is predominantly made up of technical people, they looked at me like they thought I was crazy. This 'touchy-feely' vision and values statement was about as foreign to them as it could get. Yet, once they saw the linkage to XEL's strategy and direction, it began to catch on." In many ways, Julie was an unusual HR manager. Not only did Julie believe HR to be a strategic issue for XEL, Julie herself was one of the owners of the business. Where HR was often relegated to a "staff" function, Julie was clearly a "line" manager at XEL. Julie felt very comfortable working closely with technical managers, and carried the entrepreneurial spirit as strongly as her colleagues.

Once the vision statement had been finally developed, Julie and others soon turned their attention to the issue of managing the new culture within XEL. A key ingredient of this process was changing the mindset of the employees. In the GTE days, individuals had discrete jobs and responsibilities which were governed by specific policies and procedures. "We wanted to instill a sense of ownership on the part of employees," Julie noted. When asked when she knew that the culture was working, she replied, "One day, a work team was having a meeting. The team leader was agitated, and was speaking harshly to one of the team members. One of the other workers stood up and confronted the team leader, saying that his treatment of the worker was not consistent with The XEL Vision." The worker, and her team leader, still work on the same team at XEL.

The HR system at XEL was unusually well-integrated. The team-based work system created a great deal of intrinsic motivation, and opportunities for employee voice and influence were in abundance. The workers participated in hiring decisions, and XEL used a 360 degree performance appraisal system. Production workers were appraised by peers and also appraised themselves. The compensation system used a three-pronged approach: profit-sharing to encourage teamwork, individual and team-based merit to encourage quantity and quality of performance, and skill-based pay to encourage continuous improvement. In one quarter in 1994, the 300 production workers were paid an average of $500 each in profit-sharing. When workers mastered a new task, they had the opportunity to earn an additional 50 cents per hour. Finally, each unit shared a bonus based on meeting a quarterly goal, such as improving on-time delivery. The average reward was 4.5 percent of payroll, with top teams earning up to 10 percent and lagging groups getting nothing. Employee response to the compensation system was generally positive. "The pay system doesn't stand alone," said Julie. "It's only in support of the teams."[8]

Julie did a lot of background reading in the management literature as well as exploring what other companies were doing. Unfortunately, she found that there was little to go on. "That is when, in working with John Puckett, vice-president for manufacturing, we began to see that self-directed work teams could give them a distinct competitive advantage—resulting in better quality products that could be delivered in a timely manner."

A key step in the development of self-directed teams was to create an open organization. The first step was to take a look at the physical layout of the work environment. One experience remains vivid for Julie: "I remember that on one particular Friday, John was toying with the idea of how to better organize the plant. One worker approached John and told him to take the weekend off and go fishing. John, initially hesitant, decided to do so; and over one weekend, the workers came in and, on their own, redesigned the entire floor. On Monday, John returned and found that they had organized themselves in various work cells—each devoted to a particular product group. Teams were then organized around this cellular production and began to set their own production goals and quality procedures."

XEL's Strategic Planning Process

The business telecommunications market was rapidly changing and evolving in 1995—creating an ideal business climate for XEL.[9] Working with local telephone companies and others, XEL designed and manufactured equipment that "conditioned" existing lines to make them acceptable for business use.

As a means of positioning themselves for products and markets in a rapidly changing environment, XEL engaged in a strategic planning process on an annual basis. Exhibit 3 provides an overview of this process. As Bill Sanko noted: "Since there are such rapid changes taking place and new products being constantly introduced, we needed to tie what we're doing back to the strategic elements—quality, responsiveness, cost."

The strategic planning process began in August of each year with the senior management team listing strategic issues and taking on key assignments. For Bill, his key assignment began with assessing key external factors. Taking on such an assignment provided him an opportunity to step back and look at the bigger picture.

EXHIBIT 3
XEL Planning Cycle

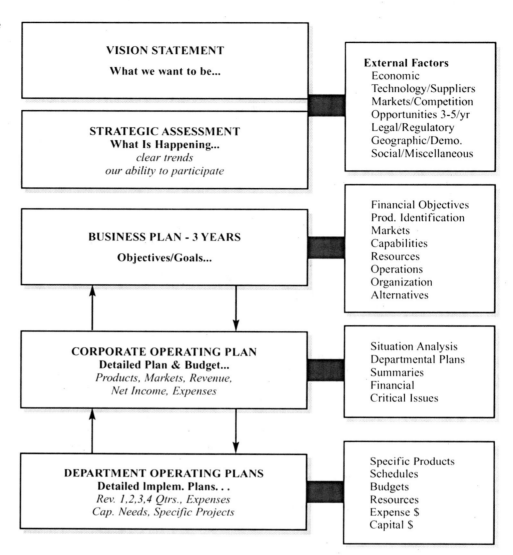

"I hope that legislation pending will deregulate local telephone companies. This will open up local telephone services to companies other than the regional Baby Bell. At present, AT&T has almost 60 percent hold in the market with respect to long distance but deregulation will allow the local companies to enter the global market. Major telephone companies have been downsizing in the recent past to cut down on costs by developing products and installing services that require less maintenance and, therefore, less people to maintain them. With this trend, we hope to get business from our present customers seeking help to develop such products for them."

Another key industry trend which was constantly monitored is technology. The pace at which the technology was moving had reduced the product life cycle from 40 years to less than 5 years. Bill noted the example of fiber optic products, which is a very hot area in today's market; XEL was trying to compete with other companies with respect to building fiber optic products. Other areas in which it was trying to find opportunities for a small company was the emerging personal communications systems market.

With the industry trend data as a beginning, the senior team then spent the ensuing months in developing plans around the key strategic issues. This would then entail capturing data on key competitors and assessing their strengths and weaknesses relative to XEL. "Some of these data are available due to public disclosure requirements," according to Bill Sanko," but data on private competitors are particularly difficult to get—due to the competitive nature of the business; we get a lot of information through trade show contacts."

Throughout this entire process, the XEL team needed to keep a focus on those critical success factors that would determine their performance. Essentially, they involved: innovativeness, skilled sales force, quality, investing in automation, effective pricing, and, above all, responsiveness.

Another key goal was to achieve a 20 percent improvement in margin by year end 1994 and to strive to reach 25 percent by December 1995 and 30 percent by December 1997. This goal is one that was particularly sensitive among the senior management team since it involved two critical variables: pricing coupled with achieving economies of scale in the manufacturing plant. Previously, achieving such a goal was parceled out among the respective groups: marketing and sales, operations, finance and the like. Unfortunately, this activity was frequently tabled in the face of day-to-day activities. It was then decided that a cost reduction team needed to be formally structured to address this goal. As such, XEL decided to hire an engineer, a technician, and a buyer from outside the organization to constitute the team. Its primary responsibility was to examine the pricing of products and costs, and to target core products for the purpose of achieving 25 percent improvement in margin by December of 1995. The team reported primarily to the vice president of manufacturing, John Puckett.

In terms of overall financial performance, XEL has been profitable. Its revenues increased from $16.8 million in 1992 to $23.6 million in 1993 and $52.3 million in 1994—over a three-fold increase in three years.

Another key issue that was identified in the strategic planning process was how much to invest in R&D—given the rapid pace of technology development that is taking place in this industry. XEL's goal was to invest 10 percent of its sales in R&D. "We have come to realize that we grew faster than last year's plan," according to Bill Sanko, "and we need to invest more in engineering as a means of keeping pace. Our goal is to have one-third of our revenue in any given year come from products introduced in the past two years." This would also involve investing its R&D efforts into new technologies as cable TV converges with telecommunications.

Aside from investment in new technologies, the other key strategic issue that was identified in the planning process was penetration into international markets. XEL was seeking to do business in Mexico in order to build data networks that are critical in upgrading Mexico's infrastructure. It has also looked for business opportunities in countries such as Brazil, Chile, Argentina, Puerto Rico, and the Far East. As a means of focusing responsibility for this effort, XEL tapped Malcom Shaw, a new hire of XEL who is fluent in Spanish and has prior marketing experience in South America, to lead this international expansion effort.

As all of the above issues indicate, the formal strategic planning process was a critical ingredient of XEL's way of doing business. "Strategic planning makes you think about how to invest for the future," Bill emphasized. "The role of the CEO is really to keep a viewpoint of the big picture—not to micro-manage the operation." To reinforce this last point, it should be noted that Bill Sanko had a personal tragedy in June of 1992, in which he was involved in a serious auto accident—the car in which he was traveling was broadsided by another auto. "Even while I was out of the office for an extended period of time," noted Bill, "the fact that we had a formal strategic plan and an annual operating plan gave us the guidance to continue business as usual." As the planning process moved forward, Bill's goal was to have their 1995 strategic plan ready for the November meeting of the Board of Directors. As Julie noted, "We don't just look for 'programs,' but for ideas for the long-term."

XEL's Markets

The marketing and sales functions for XEL closely reinforced the earlier emphasis on being responsive and oriented to customer's needs. Don Bise, vice president of marketing, came to XEL with diverse experience, having moved around in nine previous firms. "The culture here at XEL is much less structured than some other organizations where I worked before," Don reflected, "I feel much more comfortable in a stand-alone company as opposed to being a branch or subsidiary of a large firm."

Unlike many companies in which the marketing approach is to have product managers dedicated to certain product segments or accounts, XEL's sales managers worked closely with the engineers in addressing customer needs. "The difficulty with having the sales manager or the engineer working solely with the customer is that their particular perspectives may differ," noted Don. "By having both the engineer and the sales manager working with the customer, we have cut down on the communications difficulties and have been able to develop a more realistic pricing and delivery schedule. At the same time, by having the engineer present, he is able to understand their specific needs or can steer them towards a reasonable solution to what they are trying to achieve. This has gone a long way to create great customer loyalty and repeat business. In addition, we have been able to manage our overall costs better. Our marketing expenses are typically 6–7 percent of sales which is low compared to a number of companies."

In terms of XEL's marketing strategy, a number of external developments have reshaped its approach. "Traditionally, in a market as concentrated as the telecommunications industry, the customer has tremendous buying potential and tries to leverage this as much as possible. With more players coming into this market, coupled with downsizing on the part of the Regional Bell Operating Companies, we are trying to develop a portfolio approach to make us less dependent on a few key accounts. As a result, XEL must introduce new products for traditional as well as new accounts. This means that XEL must pay a great deal of attention to technology."

To meet this goal, marketing worked closely with the engineering group—not only in the sales area but also in new product development. Specific market opportunities included the convergence of telephony with cable, personal communication services based on radio expertise, and business access in developing countries. To reach these market segments, Don Bise noted that XEL was exploring several avenues.

One approach was the OEM (Original Equipment Manufacturer) market in which XEL built the product according to another's specification. GTE's Airfone, which allowed airline passengers to place calls and receive calls, was a three-way venture in which XEL manufactured the electronics for the phone and did final assembly and test. This venture was quite profitable for XEL; they shipped about 300 Airfones a day out of their plant in 1995. A second approach was to build customized units for voice and data transmission in the industrial market. Exhibit 4 provides an example of XEL's approach to this market.

EXHIBIT 4
An Overview
of Our Products
and Services

XEL Communications offers complete product selection for voice and data applications. Products include a complete line of both voice and data channel units for D4, 9004, D448, and DE-4 channel banks. We have expanded our product line to include intelligent DSTs, 11 equipment, and 2B1Q systems.

XEL pioneered the development of the multifunctional, modular approach to transmission card design—the XCard. This concept uses a basic board (such as a line amplifier) and through modular "build-ons," adds specific functions resulting in a custom-performance card. Customers specify their requirements and XEL assembles, tests, and ships the solution on a single board.

In 1990, XEL introduced a new line of channel units to address the needs of customers who use D448 T-Carrier Systems. These channel units incorporate our years of special service design experience to provide many unique units that reduce installation time and eliminate the needs for external equipment and units.

As part of XEL's product family, our 2B1Q system provides service for two 4-wire customers on a single pair of wires (3 pair gain) while still providing unique (patent pending) testing features.

A third avenue, one that offered a great deal of future potential is the international market. This is an area that Don was particularly excited about: "Clearly the growth path is international as developing regions are looking to upgrade their telecommunications infrastructure to spur economic growth. To do this, both voice and data transmission are key. What XEL can do is take something that we are familiar with and use it in areas they aren't familiar with. For example, in one particular country, we found that we can take one of our channel units and plug it into their system—providing an instant upgrade to their current capabilities." Yet going international was not without its risks. "We would prefer to begin by developing a niche in international markets with our existing equipment. This would minimize some of the up-front risks. As the international side of the business begins to take off, we realize we will need to have a local in country partner and will need to have some local manufacturing content."

To successfully compete in the future, Don felt that XEL should "go where they ain't." XEL needed to seek out niches where there was very little or no competition, keep its cost low, and price accordingly. He felt that their traditionally strong customer base, the major telephone companies, was using its buying power to telegraph the prices they would accept. At the same time, they were cutting down their list of vendors quite extensively.

Financial Considerations

Turning from the ever-present spreadsheet on his desktop computer, Jim Collins, vice-president of finance, reflected on the key financial considerations facing XEL. "Coming from another company to XEL, I soon found out that the culture here is quite different. There is indeed a sense of empowerment and teamwork. People set their own goals; and the engineers make a serious commitment to the customer."

In addition to the formal strategic planning process, financial planning at XEL involved a three-year top-down plan with input from the bottom-up. According to Jim, "I interface a great deal with marketing and sales and develop costs. My goal is to ensure that there aren't a lot of surprises. We also tend to manage by percentages." Jim was asked whether XEL was experimenting with implementing some form of activity-based accounting. He noted that they reviewed it in 1993 and decided that they weren't ready. Yet, they do plan to implement a modified activity-based accounting system in 1995. "We tend to look at the major drivers of cost in this business. There is an overall operations review once a month among the senior management team in which there is open dialogue; and we explore a number of key operational issues."

Yet the financial picture for XEL has not always been rosy. "In addition to the costs associated with the separation from GTE, there were three years where we lost money—part of this was due to our dependency on GTE as it was going through its own consolidation as well as a new product introduction which didn't fly." Again, Jim Collins remarked: "those two setbacks were a bitter pill to swallow. We now try to make our financial projections more realistic—even somewhat on the conservative side. We also set targets by market segments."

Although there was pressure to raise cash by going public, Jim felt that this wasn't realistic for XEL. "We really don't want analysts setting constraints for our business—rather we tend to look for cash infusions from strategic partnerships and alliances." Both Bill Sanko and Jim Collins were actively involved in negotiating these partnerships, particularly in the international arena. "Above all," Jim commented, "we need to stay focused, develop a plan, and get realistic input."

Quality Management at XEL

One of the critical success factors that was identified in the strategic planning process and was imbedded throughout XEL was the focus on responsiveness to customers. When XEL was in its initial stages, cycle time—the period from start of production to finished goods—was about six weeks. That left customers disgruntled and tied up money in inventory.[10] XEL's chain of command, moreover, had scarcely changed since the GTE days. Line workers reported to supervisors, who reported to unit or departmental managers, who reported on up the ladder to Sanko and a crew of top executives. Every rung in the ladder added time and expense. "If a hardware engineer needed some software help, he'd go to his manager," Sanko says. "The manager would say, 'Go write it up.' Then the hardware manager would take the software manager to lunch and talk about it. We needed everybody in the building thinking and contributing about how we could better satisfy our customers, how we could improve quality, how we could reduce costs."

Soon after XEL drafted its vision statement, John Puckett, vice president for manufacturing, redesigned the plant for cellular production, with groups of workers building whole families of circuit boards. Eventually, Sanko and Puckett decided to set up the entire plant with self-managing teams. By 1988, the teams had been established; and the supervisory and support staff was reduced by 30 percent.

The RIF (Reduction in Force) was achieved by a number of avenues. In 1990, there was a downturn in business and workers went to a four-day work week in order to avoid layoffs. Unfortunately, the downturn continued and production workers, supervisors, and support staff were laid off. Workers were asked for cost-saving ideas. Some workers moved to trainer roles. One worker was moved to Industrial Engineering while another became the manager of facilities.

Unlike other plans where workers are incented to provide cost saving ideas and suggestions, there was no such direct financial incentive at XEL. As Julie recalled, "We were in a total survival mode—the only payoff was that the doors stayed open." Eventually, the teams and the quality strategy took hold and a turnaround was achieved. Virtually all laid-off production workers were rehired. The supervisory and support staff were not. This is a testament to the strength of the team system at XEL.

XEL rebuilt itself around those teams so thoroughly and effectively that the Association for Manufacturing Excellence chose the company as one of four to be featured in a video on team-based management. Dozens of visitors, from companies such as Hewlett-Packard, have toured through their facility in search of ideas for using teams effectively.

On the shop floor, colorful banners hung from the plant's high ceiling to mark each team's work area. Charts on the wall tracked attendance, on-time deliveries and the other variables by which the teams gauge their performance. Diagrams indicated who on a team was responsible for key tasks such as scheduling.

Every week, the schedulers met with Production Control to review what needed to be built as well as what changes needed to be made. The teams met daily, almost always without a manager, to plan their part in that agenda. Longer meetings, called as necessary, took up topics such as vacation planning or recurring production problems. Once a quarter, each team made a formal presentation to management on what it had and hadn't accomplished.

As for results, XEL's cost of direct assembly dropped 25 percent. Inventory had been cut by half; quality levels rose 30 percent (Exhibits 5 and 6). The company's cycle time went from six weeks to four days and was still decreasing (Exhibit 7, page 16). Sales also grew to $52 million in 1994, up from $17 million in 1992. Above all, according to John Puckett, these self-directed work teams must be guided by customer focus (Exhibit 8, page 16). In order to facilitate this, customers frequently came in and visited with the team. By clearly understanding their customers' needs the teams were able to respond rapidly with a highquality product. At the same time, XEL team members went and visited with their key suppliers.

Another key issue for manufacturing involved establishing certain procedures while retaining a certain degree of flexibility. Part of this involved the strategic issue of entering global markets. As firms go global, meeting ISO 9000 standards for quality becomes critical. "To meet these standards, several things have to take place," John noted. "We have to have a structure that defines the process; then we need to document and have solid procedures in place." In addition, John felt that manufacturing for international markets would also mean building manufacturing capabilities closer to those markets, which entailed a whole host of environmental issues and labor laws. Developing alliances would also be critical since XEL could not afford to run it all.

In terms of integration with other parts of XEL, John briefly sketched out the overall process. "Basically, most of manufacturing is driven off of the financial and market plan. We start with a three-year plan which is converted in terms of the demands on facilities. My staff then develops models which reflect product development and product mix. The

**EXHIBIT 5
XEL
Communications, Inc.
Process Solder
Defects**

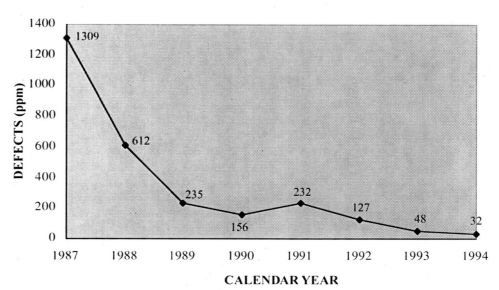

budget then sets the baseline for new product development. Here, at XEL, we tend to plan on the low side and are fairly conservative. Currently, we target two new products per month and produce in low volume for beta testing. This allows us to carefully manage costs."

As for future issues, John was struggling with the XEL goal of improving margins by 25 percent by December of 1995. "This is going to be a real challenge for my operation since we have to maintain a short cycle time as the business grows without a lot of excess inventory. We instituted a just-in-time (JIT) system several years ago, and we are currently turning our inventory about 7 or 8 times, which is close to our benchmarks relative to the best in our business (Exhibit 9, page 17). Supply chain management is really critical for us."

Another issue John faced was maintaining the culture which had been instituted through the team-based training. "While the current teams have pretty much gelled in terms of feeling comfortable with setting their targets and self-managing, orienting new members becomes a challenge. We are exploring some form of built-in orientation which would involve two weeks of internal training."

**EXHIBIT 6
XEL
Communications, Inc.
Scrap/Rework
(in $Thousands)**

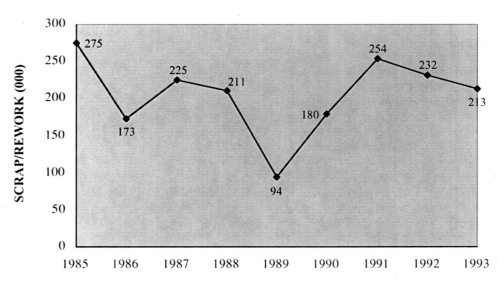

**EXHIBIT 7
XEL
Communications, Inc.
Cycle Time
Reduction, 1984-94**

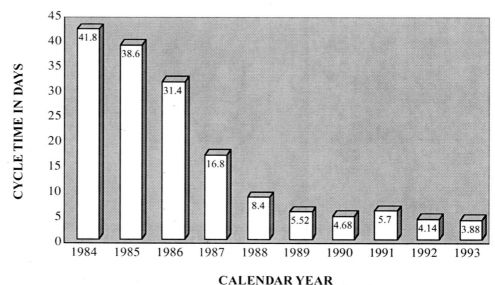

John also faced an even greater concern: skilled workers. "I think one of the serious deficiencies in our current U.S. educational system is vocational and occupational education. People have simply not been prepared. There is a misconception that there is a shortage of jobs in this business. They are dead wrong. One of my difficulties is finding qualified workers. As a basic assembler, you aren't going to become rich and put down a deposit on a BMW. But it provides a nice steady income—particularly for two wage earning families." John felt that there needed to be a stronger work ethic for those entering the labor force. "We need to understand how to transfer those hard skills that are needed as well as the concept of holding a job. Part of this should involve more industry-level involvement in changing the overall mind-set of what is needed for today's workers. I would like to create an environment in which people really enjoy working here."

The strategic need for skilled workers drove XEL's involvement in a Work Place Learning Skills program, funded by the Department of Education. When XEL began training workers in quality tools, managers noticed that the training was not having as great an effect as it might have. Upon further investigation, the managers discovered that some workers were having difficulty not only in making calculations, but also in reading the

**EXHIBIT 8
XEL
Communications, Inc.
Customer Returns,
Compoment Level,
All Causes**

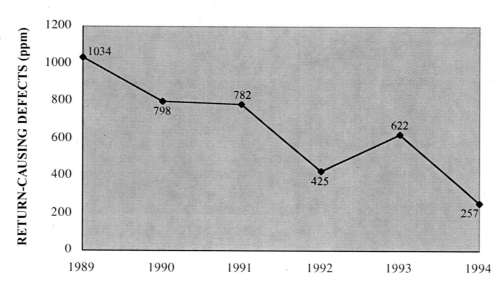

**EXHIBIT 9
XEL
Communications,
Inc. WIP Annual
Inventory Turns
1985–94**

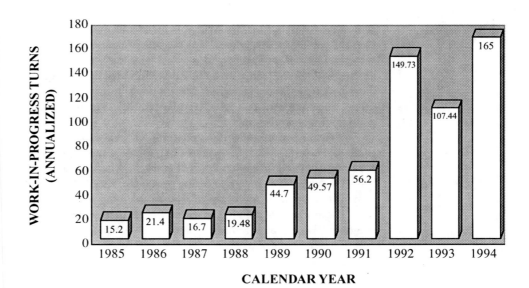

training materials. Using the DOE grant, and working with Aurora Community College, which is located near the plant, XEL developed a basic skills training program which is now used as a template by DOE for worker training across the United States. The program, not surprisingly, was designed by an employee task force made up of managers and workers. The task force used a questionnaire to ask employees which courses they would be interested in taking. Participation in the program was not mandatory, but a measure of its success is that 50 percent of employees participated in the program on their own time. Courses were offered on site for convenience, and included "soft" skills such as communication and stress management. On December 1, 1994, XEL was awarded a three-year DOE grant to expand and continue the training, and to scientifically evaluate the effects of the training on such outcomes as productivity and ROI. Julie believed that these training programs were consistent with other Human Resource policies of XEL, such as skill-based pay. More than that, Julie stated, "The Work Place Learning Skills program is consistent with our XEL vision." As further testament to these efforts, XEL's overall work force productivity continues to improve (Exhibit 10).

**EXHIBIT 10
XEL
Communications, Inc.
Productivity, 1989–94**

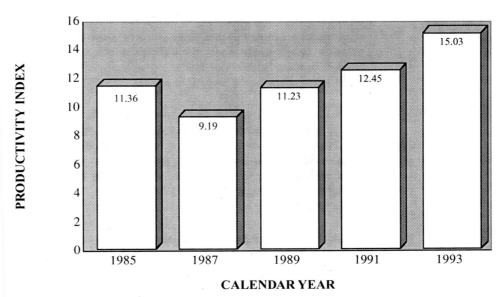

Maintaining Innovation

In a climate that is constantly undergoing rapid change, staying ahead of the competition is the name of the game. For XEL, this meant that cross-functional relationships were key. One critical link in this process was the role of new product development. Terry Bolinger, vice-president of engineering, described how this process worked: "Here at XEL, engineering is involved from start to finish. Rather than have a large marketing staff that is out there making calls or picking up new pieces of information, we deliberately have a small group. The engineers do a lot of traveling at XEL—going out in the field and working directly with the customers."

As for its commitment to innovation, XEL allocated approximately 10 percent to 12 percent of sales to R&D. Terry noted that, for the current year, he spent below this amount. When pressed why, he commented: "I guess I am hesitant to spend up to this amount since I don't want to grow my engineering group too fast. A few years back, we went through some cutbacks due to a number of factors; and I am somewhat gun-shy about that experience. I know we are running at about the 10 percent level; and Bill keeps pressing me about this. But I would rather proceed somewhat cautiously."

In order to create a climate to allow his people to innovate, Terry noted that he was careful not to create a management system that bogged everything down. "Our process of setting priorities is fairly free-form. While we are typically running 50 projects at one time, we don't do much formal scheduling. We went through a time in which a lot of formal planning and presentations were done. Unfortunately, we spent too much time in meetings and too little in what I considered the search and discovery process." While Terry was comfortable with this loose form of management, he laughed that others were not so at ease. "I see Bill Sanko stroll the office periodically; and I know that he is often perplexed with how this works—coming from his engineering background. I just say 'trust me' and he is pretty good at accepting it."

In addition to this loose form of project management, Terry tried to motivate his engineers in other ways. "I also try to give them interesting assignments which will challenge them. They are also allowed to work at odd hours—many come to work on weekends or at night. In a number of cases, I will simply send them to work at home where they can be relaxed. If they need some particular equipment, I will get it for them with little or no questions asked. Also, they periodically like to travel just to get out of the office; and field calls to customers or potential customers is a way of getting them charged up." There were also periodic in-house seminars with professors from various universities who would come and brief them on new technological advances. In a sense, Terry was trying to recreate the college environment within XEL.

As XEL continued to grow, Terry saw several issues that were critical for his group: "First is the issue of how do I improve time to market without sacrificing quality; second, how do I speed up product development; and third, how do I respond extremely fast to new technology developments?" As he prepared his departmental plan for the strategic planning meeting, he also shared some concern about the opening of the second building. While he clearly needed more space for his people, the ease with which an engineer could go over to manufacturing or marketing and sales if he or she had a question or needed some information would be hard to replace.

XEL's Future

Ironically, the most serious current issue for XEL came from its own success, namely growth. XEL had increased its labor force by 50 percent and had doubled its revenues in the last year, and was experiencing some associated growing pains. Hiring sufficient workers was difficult, and assuring that the new workers will "fit" the XEL culture was hindered because of the pressures to add staff. The teams, who normally hired their own replacement workers, were less able to participate in the hiring process since they were under great pressure to produce and satisfy their customers.

Another example of the pressures of growth occurred in the skills training program. Originally, team members were scheduled to teach the classes. Unfortunately, as pressures for production increased, more and more team members canceled their training classes. As a solution, trainers were hired from local community colleges, and the team members acted as their partners to assure the course content was job-related.

Growth increased pressure to satisfy customer demands, increased pressure on the culture via the increased size and complexity, and created additional financial pressures. As a high-technology company, XEL faced the challenge of using technology to help the company be more effective. XEL would use its annual strategic planning process to determine its priorities, what measures it will use to assess its results, and which feet to hold to the fire.

Having finished reading the *Wall Street Journal* article, Bill Sanko made a note to have a copy made for the next managers' meeting, which was scheduled for every other Thursday. He also wondered what the new session of Congress would bring—now that the Republicans appeared to be in solid control.

Since XEL was in the process of beginning its annual strategic planning process, Bill thought that a useful exercise for the next managers' meeting would be to have everyone list and prioritize the key strategic issues facing XEL over the next three to five years. At the same time, he wondered whether it would be possible for XEL to maintain its entrepreneurial culture while it managed rapid growth.

Endnotes

1. *Financial World,* October 11, 1994.
2. 1994 University of Michigan Economic Forecast.
3. *Denver Business Journal,* June 17, 1994, p. 12.
4. *Rocky Mountain Business Journal,* July 1, 1985.
5. *Colorado Business,* July 1990.
6. *Rocky Mountain Business Journal,* July 1, 1985.
7. *Business Week,* November 14, 1994, p. 62.
8. Ibid., p. 62.
9. *Denver Business Journal,* April 15, 1994.
10. *Inc.,* September 1993, p. 66.

BULLER | SCHULER

Managing Organizations and People

A Resource for Cases in Management, Organizational Behavior, and Human Resource Management

Abstract

This case describes the consequences of XEL's success and the decision to sell. XEL Communications, Inc., designs and manufactures various telecommunications products for a number of companies—primarily large U.S. telephone operating companies. As a spin-off of GTE, XEL was acquired by a group of managers who had worked together for a number of years. XEL had a business strategy that complemented the company's human resource management (HRM) approach. The previous case, "XEL Communications, Inc.," provides detail on the fit between HRM and business strategy for the company. In this case students can make some judgments about the results of that system and on XEL's current practices. After providing background information about XEL, the case examines the three alternatives that XEL's management team has outlined for managing growth and developing the resource base: (1) staying the course, (2) initiating a public offering, and (3) finding a strategic partner. After a review of each option, we learn that XEL decided to pursue a strategic partnership. The case describes the process by which XEL searched for and screened potential candidates for partnership, and the firm's subsequent decision to be acquired by Gilbert Associates, a Pennsylvania-based holding company that was seeking to enter the telecommunications industry. We also describe the process by which the management team informs XEL employees about the acquisition.

XEL Communications, Inc. (C): Forming a Strategic Partnership

In the fall of 1995, Bill Sanko, president of XEL Communications, Inc., strolled around the new 115,000 square foot facility with its spacious conference rooms and computer-based skills training center, into which the company had just moved. Their former facility had been a 53,000 square foot building that just could not accommodate XEL's growth. During the upcoming round of strategic planning sessions, Bill wondered how XEL and its management team would decide to grapple with the two-edged sword of rapid growth. Would it be possible for XEL to maintain its entrepreneurial culture while it experienced rapid growth? Would they find the resources necessary to sustain their growth without harming their culture? From where?

■ This case was prepared by Professors Robert P. McGowan and Cynthia V. Fukami, Daniels College of Business, as a basis for classroom discussion rather than to illustrate either effective or ineffective handling of an administrative situation. Copyright © 1995 by the authors; Copyright © 1997 by the Case Center, Daniels College of Business, University of Denver. Published by South-Western, Cengage Learning.

1

XEL Communi- cations, Inc.[1]

XEL Communications, Inc.—located in the outskirts of Denver, Colorado—designed and manufactured various telecommunications products for a number of companies— primarily large U.S. telephone operating companies. Originally a division within GTE headed by Bill Sanko, it was in the process of being closed when Bill and a few key managers persuaded GTE to sell the division to them. In July 1984, Sanko and fellow managers signed a letter of intent to buy the division from GTE. Two months later, the bill of sale was signed, and XEL Communications, Inc., became an independent company. Ironically, GTE remained as one of XEL's major customer accounts.

In terms of overall financial performance, XEL was profitable. Its revenues increased from $16.8 million in 1992 to $23.6 million in 1993 and $52.3 million in 1994—over a three-fold increase in three years. In 1996, XEL employed approximately 300 people.

XEL designed and manufactured more than 300 individual products that enabled network operators to upgrade existing infrastructures and cost-effectively enhance the speed and functionality of their networks while reducing operating expenses and overhead costs. The firm's products provided access to telecommunications services and automated monitoring and maintenance of network performance, and extended the distance over which network operators were able to offer their services.[2] For example, XEL produced equipment that "conditioned" existing lines to make them acceptable for business use and sold products that facilitated the transmission of data and information over phone lines. Driving the need for XEL's products was the keen interest in electronic data transference: "Businesses are more and more dependent on the transfer of information," Bill Sanko noted. In addition, more businesses, including XEL, were operating by taking and filling orders through electronic data exchanges. Instead of dialing into inside salespeople, businesses often accessed databases directly.

One of XEL's strengths was its ability to adapt one manufacturer's equipment to another's. XEL provided the bits and pieces of telecommunications equipment to the "network," allowing the smooth integration of disparate transmission pieces. XEL also sold central office transmission equipment and a full range of mechanical housings, specialty devices, power supplies, and shelves.

In 1995, XEL began developing a hybrid fiber/cable broadband modem for use by cable television firms seeking to provide enhanced data communication services over their network facilities. Cable modems were one of the hottest new products in telecommunications. The devices would enable computers to send and receive information about one hundred times faster than standard modems used with phone lines. Given that 34 million homes had personal computers, cable modems were seen as a surefire way to exploit the personal computer (PC) boom and the continuing convergence of computers and television. Media analysts estimated that cable modem users would rise to 11.8 million by the end of 2005 from a handful in 1996.[3]

"Business customers and their changing telecommunications needs drive the demand for XEL's products. That, in turn, presents a challenge to the company," said Sanko. Sanko cited the constant stream of new products developed by XEL—approximately two per month—as the driving force behind the growth. Throughout the industry, product life-cycle times were getting even shorter. Before the breakup of the Bell System in 1984, transmission switches and other telecommunications devices enjoyed a 30 to 40 year life. In 1995, with technology moving so fast, XEL's products had about a three-year to five-year life.

XEL sold products to all of the Regional Bell Operating Companies (RBOCs), as well as such companies as GTE and Centel. Railroads, with their own telephone networks, were also customers. In addition to its domestic business, products were sold in Canada, Mexico, and Central and South America.[4] XEL's field salespeople worked with engineers to satisfy client requests for specific services. Over a period of time, the salespeople developed a rapport with these engineers, providing XEL with new product leads.

With all the consolidations and ventures in telecommunications, those who watched the industry often concluded that the overall market would become more difficult. Sanko believed, however, that "out of change comes opportunity. The worst-case scenario would be a static situation. Thus, a small company, fast to respond to customer needs and able to capitalize on small market niches, will be successful. Often, a large company like AT&T will forsake a smaller market and XEL will move in. Also, XEL's size allows it to design a product in a very short time."

Sanko watched federal legislation keenly. The recently signed Telecommunications Act of 1996, which removed numerous barriers to competition, had clearly changed the rules of the game. Consequently, said Sanko, "we need to expand our market and be prepared to sell to others as the regulatory environment changes." The recent joint venture between Time-Warner and US West also signaled that telephone and cable companies would be pooling their resources to provide a broader array of information services. As for the future, Sanko saw "a lot of opportunities we can't even now imagine."

The XEL Vision

A feature that set XEL apart from other companies was its strong, healthy corporate culture. Developing a culture of innovation and team decision making was instrumental in providing the results XEL prided itself on.[5] An early attempt to define culture in a top-down fashion was less successful than the management team had hoped,[6] so the team had embarked on a second journey to determine what their core values were and what they would like the company to look like in five years. The team had then gone off-site for several days and finalized the XEL Vision Statement (Exhibit 1). By the summer of 1987, the statement had been signed by members of the senior team and been hung up by the bulletin board. Employees were not required to sign the statement, but were free to do so when each was ready.

Julie Rich, vice-president of human resources, described the management team's approach to getting the rest of the organization to understand as well as become comfortable

EXHIBIT 1
The XEL Vision

XEL will become the leader in our selected telecommunications markets through innovation in products and services. Every XEL product and service will be rated Number One by our customers.

XEL will set the standards by which our competitors are judged. We will be the best, most innovative, responsive designer, manufacturer and provider of quality products and services as seen by customers, employees, competitors, and suppliers.*

We will insist upon the highest quality from everyone in every task.

We will be an organization where each of us is a self-manager who will:
- initiate action, commit to, and act responsibly in achieving objectives
- be responsible for XEL's performance
- be responsible for the quality of individual and team output
- invite team members to contribute based on experience, knowledge and ability

We will:
- be ethical and honest in all relationships
- build an environment where creativity and risk taking is promoted
- provide challenging and satisfying work
- ensure a climate of dignity and respect for all
- rely on interdepartmental teamwork, communications and cooperative problem solving to attain common goals**
- offer opportunities for professional and personal growth
- recognize and reward individual contribution and achievement
- provide tools and services to enhance productivity
- maintain a safe and healthy work environment

XEL will be profitable and will grow in order to provide both a return to our investors and rewards to our team members.

XEL will be an exciting and enjoyable place to work while we achieve success.

* Responsiveness to customers' new product needs as well as responding to customers' requirements for emergency delivery requirements has been identified as a key strategic strength. Therefore, the vision statement has been updated to recognize this important element.

** The importance of cooperation and communication was emphasized with this update of the Vision Statement.

with the XEL Vision: "Frequently, organizations tend to take a combination top-down/ bottom-up approach in instituting cultural change. That is, the top level will develop a statement about values and overall vision. They will then communicate it down to the bottom level and hope that results will percolate upward through the middle levels. Yet it is often the middle level of management which is most skeptical, and they will block it or resist change. We decided to take a 'cascade' approach in which the process begins at the top and gradually cascades from one level to the next so that the critical players are slowly acclimated to the process. We also did a number of other things—including sending a copy of the vision statement to the homes of the employees and dedicating a section of the company newspaper to communicate what key sections of the vision mean from the viewpoint of managers and employees."

The vision statement became a living symbol of the XEL culture and the degree to which XEL embraced and empowered its employees. When teams or managers made decisions, they routinely brought out the XEL Vision document so workers might consult various parts of the statement to help guide and direct decisions. According to Julie, the statement was used to help evaluate new products, emphasize quality (a specific XEL strategic objective was to be the top quality vendor for each product), support teams, and drive the performance-appraisal process.

The XEL Vision was successfully implemented as a key first step; but it was far from being a static document. Key XEL managers continually revisited the statement to ensure that it became a reflection of where they wanted to go, not where they had been. Julie believed this regular appraisal was a large factor in the success of the vision. "Our values are the key," Julie explained. "They are strong, they are truly core values, and they are deeply held." Along with the buy-in process, the workers also saw that the managers experimented with the statement, which reflected the strong entrepreneurial nature of XEL's founders—a common bond that they all shared. They were not afraid of risk, or of failure, and this spirit was reinforced in all employees through the vision itself, as well as through the yearly process of revisiting the statement. Once a year, Bill Sanko sat with all employees and directly challenged (and listened to direct challenges to) the XEL Vision. From 1987 to 1995, only two relatively minor additions had altered the original statement.

Which Path to Choose

When the 1995 annual strategic planning process got underway, XEL was in good shape on any one of a number of indicators. Profits were growing, new products were being developed, the culture and vision of the company were strong, employee morale was high, and the self-directed work teams were achieving exceptional quality.[7] Rapid growth, however, was also presenting a challenge. Would it be possible for XEL to maintain its entrepreneurial culture in the face of rapid growth? Could they sustain their growth without harming their culture? Would they find the resources necessary to sustain the growth? From where?

As the strategic planning retreat progressed, three options seemed apparent to the team. First, they could stay the course and remain privately held. Second, they could initiate a public offering of stock. Third, they could seek a strategic partnership. Which would be the right choice for XEL?

Staying the Course

The most obvious option was to do nothing. Bill Sanko indicated that the management team did not favor staying the course and remaining privately held. "We had a venture capitalist involved who, after being with us for 10 years, wanted out. In addition, the founders—ourselves—also wanted out from a financial standpoint. You also have to understand that one of the original founders, Don Donnelly, had passed away; and his estate was looking to make his investment more liquid. So, there were a lot of things that converged at the same time."

Once they determined they would not remain privately held, Bill mentioned that the decision boiled down to two main avenues: XEL would do an initial public offering and go public, or it would find a strategic partner. "To guide us in this process, we decided to retain the services of an outside party; we talked to about a dozen investment houses. In October 1994, we decided to hire Alex Brown, a long-time investment house out of

Baltimore. What we liked about this firm was that they had experience with doing both options—going public or finding a partner."

Going Public

One avenue open to XEL was initiating a public offering of stock. Alex Brown advised them of the pluses and minuses of this option. Sanko reviewed their recommendations:

The plus side for XEL doing an initial public offering was that technology was really hot about this time [October 1994]. In addition, we felt that XEL would be valued pretty highly in the market. The downside of going public was that XEL was really not a big firm, and institutional investors usually like doing offerings of firms that generate revenues of over $100 million. Another downside was that you had to deal with analysts, and their projections become your plan, which really turned me off. Also, shareholders want a steady and predictable rate of return. Technology stocks are not steady—there are frequent ups and downs in this marketplace—caused by a number of factors, such as a major telecommunications company deciding not to upgrade at the last minute or Congress considering sweeping regulatory changes. Finally, Alex Brown felt that the stock would have traded thinly. This, coupled with SEC restrictions on trading, made the option of going public less desirable.

Strategic Partnership

After taking these factors into account, Sanko said,

". . . we decided to take the third path and look for a potential partner. But you have to also note that there was always the first option available as a safety valve. We could not do anything and stay the way we were. That's the nice thing about all of this. We were not under any pressure to go public or seek a partner. We could also wait and do one of these things later on. So, we had the luxury of taking our time.

In terms of finding a potential partner, there were certain key items that we wanted Alex Brown to consider in helping us in this process. The first was that we, management, wanted to remain with XEL. We had really grown XEL as a business and were not interested in going off and doing something else. The second key item was that we were not interested in being acquired by someone who was interested in consolidating our operations with theirs, closing this facility and moving functions from here to there. To us, this would destroy the essence of XEL. The third item was that we wanted a partner that would bring something to the table but would not try to micromanage our business."

The Case Against Strategic Partnership

In the 1990s, "merger mania" swept the United States. In the first nine months of 1995, the value of all announced mergers and acquisitions reached $248.5 billion, surpassing the record full year volume of $246.9 billion reached in 1988. This volume occurred in the face of strong evidence that over the past 35 years, mergers and acquisitions had hurt organizations more than they had helped.[8] Among the reasons for failure in mergers and acquisitions were the following:

- Inadequate due diligence
- Lack of a strategic rationale
- Unrealistic expectations of possible synergies
- Paying too much
- Conflicting corporate cultures
- Failure to move quickly to meld the two companies

Nevertheless, there had been successful mergers and acquisitions. Most notably, small and mid-sized deals had been found to have a better chance for success. Michael Porter argued that the best acquisitions were "gap-filling," that is, a deal in which one company bought another to strengthen its product line or expand its territory, including globally. Anslinger and Copeland argued that successful acquisitions were more likely when preacquisition managers were kept in their positions, big incentives were offered to top-level executives so that their net worths were on the line, and the holding company was kept flat (that is, the business was kept separate from other operating units and retained a high degree of autonomy).[9]

More often than not, however, the deal was won or lost after it was done. Bad post-merger planning and integration could doom the acquisition. "While there is clearly a role for thoughtful and well-conceived mergers in American business, all too many don't meet that description."[10]

Choosing a Partner

"With these issues in mind, Alex Brown was able to screen out possible candidates," said Sanko. "In January 1995, this plan was presented to our board of directors for approval, and by February, we had developed the 'book' about XEL that was to be presented to these candidates. We then had a series of meetings with the candidates in the conference room at our new facility. The interesting aside on these meetings was that, often, senior management from some of these firms didn't know what pieces of their business that they still had or had gotten rid of. We did not see this as a good sign."

One of the firms with which XEL met was Gilbert Associates, based in Reading, Pennsylvania. Gilbert Associates was founded in the 1940s as an engineering and construction firm, primarily in the area of power plants. They embarked on a strategy of reinventing themselves by divesting their energy-related companies and becoming a holding company whose subsidiaries operated in the high-growth markets of telecommunications and technical services. Gilbert also owned a real estate management-and-development subsidiary. After due diligence and due deliberation, Gilbert was chosen by the management team as XEL's strategic partner. The letter of intent was signed on October 5, 1995, and the deal was closed on October 27, 1995. Gilbert paid $30 million in cash.[11]

Why was Gilbert chosen as the partner from among six or seven suitors? Not because they made the highest bid. XEL was attracted to Gilbert by three factors: (1) Gilbert's long-term strategy to enter the telecommunications industry, (2) its intention of keeping XEL as a separate, autonomous company, and (3) its willingness to pay cash (as opposed to stock or debt). "It was a clean deal," said Sanko.

The deal was also attractive because it was structured with upside potential. XEL was given realistic performance targets for the next three years. If these targets were achieved, and Sanko had every expectation that they would be, approximately $6–$8 million would be earned. Gilbert did not place a cap on the upside.

In spite of the attractive financial package, more was necessary to seal the deal. "At the end of the day," said Sanko, "culture, comfort, and trust—those were more important than money." It was important to XEL's board that Gilbert presented a good fit. Sanko was encouraged because he felt comfortable with Gilbert's chief executive officer. Vice president of Human Resources, Julie Rich, also noted, "The management team was to remain intact. Gilbert recognized that the XEL Vision was part of our success and our strength. They wanted to keep it going."

As one way of gaining confidence in Gilbert, Bill Sanko personally spoke with the CEOs of other companies Gilbert had recently acquired. In these conversations, Sanko was assured that Gilbert would keep its promises.

Timothy S. Cobb, chair, president, and CEO of Gilbert Associates, commented at the time of the acquisition: "This transaction represented the first clear step toward the attainment of our long-term strategy of focusing on the higher margin areas of telecommunications and technical services. XEL's superior reputation for quality throughout the industry, its innovative design and manufacturing capabilities, and its focus on products aimed at the emerging information highway markets, will serve us well as we seek to further penetrate this important segment of the vast communications market."[12]

Mr. Cobb continued, "We see long-term growth opportunities worldwide for XEL's current proprietary and Original Equipment Manufacturer [OEM] products as well as for the powerful new products being developed. These products fall into two families: (1) fiber-optic network interfaces designed specifically to meet the needs of telephone companies, interexchange carriers (e.g., AT&T, Sprint, MCI), and specialized network carriers installing fiber-optic facilities, and (2) a hybrid fiber/cable broadband modem for use by cable television firms seeking to provide enhanced data communications services over their network facilities. Going forward, we expect to leverage Gilbert's knowledge and relationships with the RBOCs to significantly increase sales to those important customers, while also utilizing our GAI-Tronics subsidiary's established international sales organization to further penetrate the vast global opportunities which exist. As a result, revenues from Gilbert Associates' growing telecommunications segment could represent over half of our total revenues by the end of 1996."

Timothy Cobb had come to Gilbert from Ameritech, an RBOC which covered the midwestern United States. He had been president of GAI-Tronics Corporation, an international supplier of industrial communication equipment, a subsidiary of Gilbert, prior to his appointment as Gilbert's CEO.

Bill Sanko offered, "When all the dust had settled, the one firm that we really felt good about was Gilbert. . . . Gilbert is an interesting story in itself. Ironically, they had contacted us in August 1994, based on the advice of their consultant who had read about us in an *Inc.* Magazine article. Unfortunately, at the time, they did not have the cash to acquire us since they were in the process of selling off one of their divisions. In the intervening period, Gilbert Associates divested itself of one of its companies, Gilbert/Commonwealth. This sale provided needed funds for the acquisition of XEL."

Once Sanko was confident that the deal would go, but before the letter of intent was signed, the pending acquisition was announced to the management team, and a general meeting was held with all employees. SEC regulations prohibited sharing particular information (and common sense seconded this directive), but Sanko and his associates felt it was important to keep employees informed before the letter was signed.

During the meeting, Sanko told the employees that the board was "seriously considering" an offer. Sanko assured the employees that the suitor was not a competitor, and that he felt that the suitor was a good fit in culture and values. Sanko reiterated that this partnership would give XEL the resources it needed to grow. Questions were not allowed because of SEC regulations. Employees left the meeting concerned and somewhat nervous, but members of the management team and Julie Rich were positioned in the audience and made themselves available to talk.

During the closing of the deal, Sanko held another general meeting, attended by Timothy Cobb, where more detailed information was shared with employees. Managers had been informed in a premeeting so that they would be prepared to meet with their teams directly following the general meeting.

Employees wanted to know about Gilbert. They wanted to know simple information, such as where Gilbert was located and what businesses it was in. They also wanted to know strategic plans, such as whether Gilbert had plans to consolidate manufacturing operations. Finally, they wanted to know about the near future of XEL—they wanted to know if their benefits would change, if they would still have profit sharing, and if the management team would stay in place. "We have a track record of being open," says Sanko. "Good news or bad is always shared. This history stemmed much of the rumor mill."

In the next few weeks, Tim Cobb returned to hold a series of meetings with the management team and with a focus group of thirty employees representing a cross-section of the organization. Cobb also met with managers and their spouses at an informal reception. Sanko wanted to ease the management team into the realization that they were now part of a larger whole in Gilbert. He asked Cobb to make the same presentation to XEL that he was currently making to stockholders throughout the country—a presentation that emphasized the role XEL would play in the long-term strategy of Gilbert.

Going Forward

The human resource systems remained in place with no changes. The management bonus system would change slightly because it included stock options, which were no longer available. XEL's internal advisory board, the "management team," remained intact, but XEL's external advisory board was disbanded. Bill Sanko reported to Gilbert's chairman.

XEL's strategic plan was to follow the process it already had in place, and which was not unlike Gilbert's. The cycle did not change; Gilbert expected XEL's next strategic plan in early November 1996.

XEL's strategic objectives also remained the same. Nothing was put on hold. Plans were still in place to penetrate Brazil, Mexico, and South America.[13] Sanko hoped to capitalize on the synergies of Gilbert's existing international distribution network. XEL met with Gilbert's international representatives to see if this was an avenue for XEL to gain a more rapid presence in South America. Finally, XEL was planning to move into Radio Frequency (RF) engineering and manufacturing, potentially opening the door for wireless support.

Whether XEL would grow depended on the success of these new ventures. In 1996, slight growth was forecasted. But if these new markets really took off, Julie Rich was concerned about hiring enough people in Colorado when the labor market was approaching full employment. Julie considered more creative ways of attracting new hires: for example, by offering more flexible scheduling, or by hiring unskilled workers and training them internally. A new U.S. Department of Education grant to test computer-based training systems was being implemented. Nevertheless, employment was strong in the Denver metro area in 1996, and migration to Colorado had slowed. It would be a challenge to staff XEL if high growth became the business strategy.

Approximately six weeks after the acquisition, Sanko noted that few changes had taken place. Now that they were a publicly held company, there was a great deal more interest in meeting quarterly numbers. "If there has been a change," said Sanko, "it is that there is more attention to numbers." Julie Rich noted that there had been no turnover in the six-week period following the acquisition. She took this calm in the work force as a sign that things were going well so far.

One reason things went well was that the management team had all worked for GTE prior to the spin-off of XEL. Having all worked for a large public company, they did not experience a terrible culture shock when the Gilbert acquisition took place. Time would tell if the remaining XEL employees would feel the same way.

As Sanko awaited Cobb's upcoming visit, he wondered how to prepare for the event, and for the year ahead. He wondered whether XEL would attempt new ventures into RF technology, or how the planned fiber/cable broadband modem would progress. He wondered whether Gilbert's experience in selling in South America would prove valuable for XEL's international strategy. In addition, he wondered how he could encourage XEL and its employees to become members of Gilbert's "team." Would XEL's vision survive the new partnership?

Finally, according to one study of CEO turnover after acquisition, 80% of acquired CEOs left their companies by the sixth year after the acquisition, but 87% of those who did leave, did so within two years. The key factor in their turnover was post-acquisition autonomy.[14] After nearly 12 years as the captain of his own ship, Sanko wondered what his own future, and the future of the XEL management team, would hold.

Endnotes

1. For additional information on XEL Communications, Inc., and the key strategic issues facing XEL, see "XEL Communications, Inc. (A)" by McGowan and Fukami, 1995.
2. *PR Newsletter*, October 5, 1995.
3. Menezes, Bill, "Modem Times," *Rocky Mountain News*, April 28, 1996.
4. *PR Newswire*, October 5, 1995.
5. Sheridan, John, "America's Best Plants: XEL Communications," *Industry Week*, October 16, 1995.
6. See McGowan and Fukami, XEL Communications, Inc. (A) for a larger discussion of corporate culture at XEL.
7. Sheridan, John, "America's Best Plants: XEL Communications," *Industry Week*, October 16, 1995.
8. Zweig, Philip, "The Case Against Mergers," *Business Week*, October 30, 1995.
9. Anslinger, Patricia and Thomas Copeland, "Growth Through Acquisitions: A Fresh Look," *Harvard Business Review*, January–February 1996.
10. Zweig, Philip, "The Case Against Mergers," *Business Week*, October 30, 1995.
11. Bunn, Dina, "XEL to be Sold in $30 Million Deal," *Rocky Mountain News*, October 27, 1995.
12. *PR Newswire*, October 5, 1995.
13. For more information on XEL's global penetration, see McGowan and Allen, "XEL Communications (B): Going Global."
14. Stewart, Kim A. "After the Acquisition: A Study of Turnover of Chief Executives of Target Companies," Doctoral Dissertation, University of Houston, 1992.

BULLER | SCHULER

Managing Organizations and People

A Resource for Cases in Management, Organizational Behavior,
and Human Resource Management

Abstract

This case deals with a new business that was launched in Czechoslovakia in 1991 by two men, Pavel Jisa and Dalibor Dusek, to supply information to the public on companies that sold goods and services the consumers needed. The company furnished information to the public primarily over the telephone via a toll-free number, but it also utilized the internet and compact disks. The primary question raised in the case is "How can Europska Databanka use marketing research to improve its operations?" Two secondary questions are: "How can the company deliver a high-quality service that runs counter to the culture established by a command economy?" and "How can the company secure the type of workers they need when the unemployment rate is so low and a cap has been placed on wages by the government?"

Europska Databanka

Pavel Jisa, co-owner of Europska Databanka, shifted his weight and leaned forward in his chair as he contemplated the question that his friend Richard, the 84th Duke of Siebenlugner, had just asked him and his partner, Dalibor Dusek. "Are there any ways that you two might use marketing research to improve the operations of your company?" had been Richard's query. The Europska Databanka office in Prague, Czech Republic, had been launched in 1991. It was now May of 1997. The company had been so successful that the question of marketing research had never been raised. But perhaps now was the time to determine whether engaging in some research on the effectiveness of their organization might allow the partners to be even more efficient in their operations.

Background on Europska Databanka

Pavel let his mind race back to the launching of the company. The Velvet Revolution which had occurred in Czechoslovakia in November of 1989 had presented unique opportunities to latent entrepreneurs in the country. Not in 50 years had the possibility of beginning their own businesses existed for citizens of Czechoslovakia. The Revolution was ushered in by hundreds of thousands of citizens jingling their keys in the streets of Prague around the popular Wenceslas Square and shouting, "Closing time," or "We shall overcome." The mood at that time in history was that of an endless carnival.

■ Written by Marlene Mints Reed and Edward L. Felton, Jr., Samford University. Reprinted with permission.

1

Before the Revolution, Pavel and Dalibor had worked for a transit company that shipped goods transported in containers on the company's trucks and scheduled the containers for shipment on railway cars when needed. Pavel was a computer technician and had the responsibility of working with the logistics of using the company's trucks in the most efficient manner. Dalibor was the Supervisor of the Computer Department on one of the three shifts of the day and was Pavel's Supervisor. After the Velvet Revolution, Pavel and Dalibor began thinking about their business options. Dalibor had suggested: "It seems to me that there will be a great need for information about new companies that are producing specific goods and services that customers may need. The *Yellow Page* Directory published by the telephone company is only distributed once a year, and new businesses are starting every day." Pavel had responded, "Since we've both been involved in getting goods on containers to the right place at the right time and keeping accurate records about the transportation of these goods, we should be able to use those skills to start a company that delivers information to people in a timely manner about companies that provide the goods and services that they desire."

Someone had told Pavel and Dalibor about a man named Schwanzen who had started a business in Brno, Czechoslovakia, similar to the one they were thinking about launching. They contacted him, talked about their desire to start a similar company, and discovered that he was franchising his business throughout the Czech Republic and Slovakia.

They learned from Schwanzen that the company operated in the following manner:

1. Salespeople from Europska Databanka contacted businesses that offered goods or services to the public and agreed to represent them and refer callers inquiring about such products or services to their offerings. They charged the companies that they represented a fee which could range from 5,000 korunas[1] to 30,000 korunas per year based on the size of the company and the number of their products. Not only did they handle goods and services of companies but also offered travel services and accommodations for travelers. Some of the companies that had signed contracts with them were Skoda, VW Group, IBM, Hewlett Packard, Credit Management, British Petrol Oil, Nissan, Citibank, and Dun and Bradstreet. Detailed information about the client firms was stored in the company's databank in Germany and made available to all of their foreign clients.
2. The company publicized its services to consumers through ads in various *Yellow Pages*, billboard messages along the highways, sponsoring a television show on aerobics, and advertising on the sides of buses and trams. (See Exhibit 1 for illustrations of the company's advertising.)
3. The company distributed information to consumers regarding the availability of products and services they were interested in through the use of the following means of communication: a bank of telephone receptionists who were available from 7:00 A.M. until 7:00 P.M. to take calls for information; a web site on the internet to offer the same information; and compact disks also bearing information about the companies and their products. (See Exhibits 2, 3, 4 and 5 [pages 4–7, respectively] for the content of flyers distributed by the company explaining its products and services.)

Unlike the 1-900 numbers in the United States that received revenues by charging the caller a fee, this company secured their revenues from the companies they represented. The contracts from the companies were renegotiated each year.

Pavel and Dalibor were even more interested in the business after their conversation with Schwanzen. They knew that beginning a new business could be risky, so they decided to put together a business plan to test the feasibility of such a franchise in Prague. After working on the business plan for three months, they decided that there was a market for such a company in Prague; and they entered into an agreement with Schwanzen for exclusive franchise rights in the city. (See Exhibit 6 for a map of locations of Europska Databanka in the Czech Republic and in Slovakia.)

The first step Pavel and Dalibor took was to raise the needed 100,000 Czech korunas that it would take to launch the business. Since the newly-formed private banks were not lending money to anyone, they raised their start-up capital from friends and relatives. They decided to borrow the money rather than bring in additional owners of the company.

EXHIBIT 1
Europska
Databanka

EUROPEAN DATABANK

EVERYBODY'S INFORMATION

E D B   I S   W E L L   K N O W N ...

... for instance at several places of the D1 motorway...

... in TV the EDB sponsors the TV 3 × 5 aerobics gymnastics...

...and also in the streets of Prague, where you can see a tram in the colours of the European databank...

Excerpt from company brochure, courtesy of Europska Databanka.

After the money had been raised, Pavel and Dalibor applied for a concession (certificate or business license) with the Concession Office in Prague. They had to pay 1,000 Czech korunas to pay for the concession. In addition to filling out the form for the concession and paying the 1,000 koruna fee, they also had to bring with them a certificate from the court stating that neither of the partners had ever been convicted of a criminal

**EXHIBIT 2
Europska
Databanka
Who We Are**

WHO WE ARE

- We would like to introduce to you one of the most important and most widely used information services in the Czech and Slovak Republics:
- You can reach our public telephone information service, the "EDB Service phone", at number 185 in 62 towns and cities throughout the Czech and Slovak Republics.
- Every day we answer more than 9500 calls on our EDB service phone, providing information about products, services, firms, travel agency offers and accommodation capacities.
- We were the first and today are still the only information service that helps Czech firms make almost 50,000 business contacts daily, with other Czech firms and also with foreign companies.
- We are the first company able to ensure the presentation of your firm in all modern ways; i.e. through our telephone information service, in on-line information services, on compact discs, through written profiles or in our membership journal.
- We are contract partners with over 18,000 firms from both republics, from small to medium size business companies to industry giants.
- Our main job is to ensure a complex information service for all our clients' business activities. Starting October 1995 we are implementing into the entire EDB the "New marketing system", thus expanding the range of information services we offer.
- We are direct contract partners with the European Union Commission. Signed contracts enable us for entry into the world's largest business contact databases and on the other hand we enable our clients presentation in these databases.
- Also from the turn-over point of view we are amongst the largest information services in the republic. The total turn-over exceeds 100 million Kc with a steadily growing trend.
- Since September 1996 we have been providing information also on the Internet system therefore anyone may find our databases at the address: **www.edb.cz**

Excerpt from company promotional documents, courtesy of Europska Databanka.

offense. In one week, they received their certificate from the Concession Office. The next step they had to take was to present the business certificate to the Taxation Department and receive a tax number. Finally, they located a site for the business at # 15 Husitska in the heart of the Prague business district.

Pavel had read in a publication for entrepreneurs that in the first six years since the Velvet Revolution, 1.5 million certificates to begin a business had been issued by the government. It had been estimated by the government that for only 150,000 of these business certificate recipients would the business be their primary jobs. For the rest, the ventures would merely be a way to supplement their full-time jobs.

Most businesses that were begun in 1990 had been launched by former Communist leaders because they had the right contacts and sufficient money to begin a business. A popular saying in the United States, "It's not what you know, but who you know," applied also to the burgeoning new Czech economy. However, by 1991 other people were finding ways to raise money to begin their own businesses.

Privatization of Czechoslovakia

Before the revolutions that shook the countries of Eastern Europe in 1989, there were basically two kinds of firms in operation: state-owned and cooperatives. Whereas Poland had a rather strong private sector with many cooperatives, Czechoslovakia did not. In fact, in 1986, 96.7% of Czechoslovakia's net national product was produced by the state-owned firms. East Germany, the Soviet Union and Czechoslovakia had the highest percentage of state production of all of the Communist countries.

Czechoslovakia had several advantages as it moved toward a free market economy. The country's annual inflation rate never exceeded 5% throughout the decade of the 1980s; the external debt of Czechoslovakia was low by international standards; and the country had a well educated and skilled labor force. However, the country also had some major disadvantages. It had no private sector and all prices had been centrally controlled. Also, Czech exports had been aimed at the countries of the Soviet Union and Eastern

**EXHIBIT 3
Europska
Databanka
What Do We Offer?**

WHAT DO WE OFFER?

FIRM PRESENTATION:

- Through 185 - our service phone number
- On INFOSERVIS EDB compact disc
- On the Internet
- In the European Union databases
- In EDB-REVIEW - our membership journal
- In on-line information services

INFORMATION SERVICES FOR YOUR BUSINESS
from the Czech Republic:

- Business and contact information on Czech and Slovak firms
- Through 185 - our service phone number
- Written summaries from EDB databases
- Detailed profiles on Czech and Slovak firms
- INFOSERVIS EDB compact discs
- EDB-REVIEW membership journal
- "Annual reports of companies" compact disc
- Information on state administrative subjects and important institutions in the ČR
- From on-line systems

from abroad:

- Basic profiles on firms throughout Europe
- Detailed profiles on foreign firms
- Advice on business contacts to foreign firms
- Information on business contacts from the European Union databases

Excerpt from company promotional documents, courtesy of Europska Databanka.

Europe. In fact, 40% of their exports had been to the Soviet Union. Most of their products were not saleable in Western markets because of their poor quality.

By the Spring of 1997, there was another problem that bothered economists, economic journalists and politicians: the fraudulent activities which had recently surfaced in the economy. It was apparent that shady speculators were destroying small investment funds by selling off their assets and "tunneling" the money out of the country. Thomas Jezek, a godfather of speedy privatization, used to cry that, "We must be faster than the lawyers" to keep the process (of privatization) from bogging down in needless controls. By 1997, the same Mr. Jezek, as Chairman of the Prague Stock Exchange, spoke in horror of the lack of controls on business in the new Czech Republic.

Emergence of the Czech Republic Economy

After the 1993 split between the northwestern, primarily Bohemian, section of Czechoslovakia into the Czech Republic and the southeastern, mostly Moravian, section of the country into Slovakia, the economy of the Czech Republic initially held up quite well. Although the Czech Gross Domestic Product (GDP) fell precipitously in 1991–92 because of economic problems in the eastern markets that were formerly their primary customers and a fall in domestic demand as a result of rising prices, there were still many bright spots in the economy.

Most encouraging was the very low unemployment rate and the growth of the private sector. A Czech economist named Kamil Janacek speculated:

One can infer that faster progress of the private sector in the Czech Republic is one of the reasons for the less adverse impact of transformation there. In the Czech Republic, private sector's share of the GDP was almost 10% in 1991 compared to 4% in Slovakia.

However, as the months turned into years since the Revolution, the Czech Republic found itself in the Spring of 1997 facing serious economic problems. To begin with, there had been very little restructuring in the older, recently-privatized Czech companies. This

**EXHIBIT 4
Europska
Databanka**

Service phone on number 185

Traditional service of the EUROPEAN DATABANK, which guarantees its customers that anyone calling 185 in the Czech and Slovak Republics and looking for their firm, products or offered service will find out about their firm.

Every day 270 operators are working at more than 60 places in the Czech and Slovak Republics to mediate 50,000 contacts for businessmen and other customers.

One of the great advantages of the EUROPEAN DATABANK programs is the ability to update information on every client at any EDB contact office.

Regular, 3 times a week, information transfers between branch-offices create a permanent flow of fresh information on EUROPEAN DATABANK clients at all branch-offices. Practically every day clients of the EDB may change information on their firm and the newest information is available for our customers.

A separate EDB database is the accommodation facilities and travel agencies database. Firms providing accommodation services can specify in detail in the appendix the number of beds and the amenities offered.

Through the EUROPEAN DATABANK these firms can also publicize the up-to-date list of tours offered by their travel agencies.

Every client of the EUROPEAN DATABANK has the opportunity to publicize information on all his branch outlets to the same extent as he does on his mother firm at advantageous rates.

Presentation on the Internet

The EDB server has been accessible on the Internet from the October 1997 (the address is http://www.edb.cz). From this moment all information about our clients has been accessible within the framework of EDB Product Database.

Moreover every client has an opportunity to create his own www pages on the EDB server.

Those pages will be accessible on the address http://www.edb.cz/name of the company shortened into 8 characters. So stored presentation will be accessible either from EDB Product Database by entering a short address, or from special directory placed on the WWW EDB client page.

For our clients already having their own WWW pages, EDB offers a possibility to create a link directly from the record in the EDB Product Database.

Presentation in on-line information services

In the Czech Republic the databases of the EUROPEAN DATABANK are displayed in the EOTEL and Videotex on-line systems and in the database centre of the National Information Centre.

Information about your organization is thus available to all users of these on-line information services daily around the clock.

Excerpt from company promotional documents, courtesy of Europska Databanka.

situation was responsible for the low unemployment rate in the country. The country's trade deficit had also grown. This was coupled with a concern about some underhanded dealings in the Czech capital markets and a compromised position at some of the big banks. In January and February of 1997, industrial production slumped 4%, wages soared 16%, and the budget deficit hit 8.5 billion korunas.

In response to the shocking financial news, an emergency economic package was unveiled by Prime Minister Vaclav Klaus in late Spring of 1997. The most striking provisions were for large budget cuts through cuts in investment and welfare spending, a public sector wage growth limited to 7.3% with pressure on the private sector to follow suit, the immediate introduction of 20% import deposits on foodstuffs and consumer goods (to stop the hemorrhage in the balance of payments), and the completion of privatization of government-owned businesses and sales to foreign strategic partners or managerial groups.

INFOSERVIS EDB Compact disc

EDB's hit for 1995 was publishing the compact disc (CD-ROM) INFOSERVIS EDB. This compact disc is chiefly meant for people working often with verified information - it enables them to look at information from different points of view and selective criteria, to use alternative approaches and logical data analysis. The system is built as a permanent partner for working with information. Searching for information in the INFORSERVIS EDB system is possible by indexes (SKP, SIC, EDB), filters and the fulltext method.

A new feature is built into the INFOSERVIS EDB compact disc imaging; which extends the EDB clients' selection to include the conveying of information by means of graphics (advertisements, price-lists, schemes, products, etc.). Besides minor graphics manipulation (enlarging, minimalizing, cutting, turning) it enables the INFOSERVIS EDB user to print out the graphics information.

The INFOSERVIS EDB information is brought up-to-date 4 times a year and offers not just contact addresses but also detailed information on the activity of the desired subject and what is more, the imaging technology enables our clients to publish extensive information about themselves. Publishing the INFOSERVIS EDB compact disc was activated by the growing demand for information among businessmen. Therefore all data on EUROPEAN DATABANK clients is now accessible daily around the clock.

Written summaries from EDB databases

The option of obtaining summaries from the EDB databases has been provided by the EUROPEAN DATABANK since its creation. Summaries are obtainable as print-outs or in electronic form on discettes. EDB non-clients can obtain only information summaries on EUROPEAN DATABANK clients, for our clients we offer information from a list of one hundred thousand firms active on our market. It is enough to specify the desired product or service and locality.

Excerpt from company promotional documents, courtesy of Europska Databanka.

One resource that had not been sufficiently utilized in solving many of the economic problems of the new economy was the brain power of the local schools of higher learning. Within Prague, there was the prestigious Charles University which was well known for its programs in medicine, law, puppetry and economics. Another school that drew many foreign students to study was the University of Economics in Prague. There were also technical schools which had business programs.

The Challenges for Europska Databanka

The early months of Europska Databanka had been more successful than Pavel and Dalibor could have imagined. They had paid off all of their loans to friends and family within the first six months of operation. The company continued to grow, but they wondered if there were ways of making it grow faster.

Pavel and Dalibor had not been able to open a bank account initially because the banks told them they would have to have 50,000 korunas before they could open an account. And even if they had that much cash, the bank suggested they did not have an account number to give them. They were instructed to come back in a year and a half and perhaps then they would allow the company to open a checking account. Most people in the Czech Republic paid cash in all of their transactions, so a bank account was not a necessity. However, there were those who realized that a cash economy has very few controls for violating the tax laws.

There were other challenges for entrepreneurs in the new Czech Republic. Although in the early years of the Czech free market economy sole proprietorships and partnerships had limited liability, in 1996 the law had changed and proprietorships and partnerships now had unlimited liability. Pavel and Dalibor realized they could lose all of the money they had invested in the company plus anything else of value that they owned if the business went under and they were sued by their creditors. The partners knew unlimited liability made sense for an economy that was attempting to establish sufficient ground rules to keep the possibility of fraud out, but it did make their position much riskier.

EXHIBIT 6
Europska
Databanka

EUROPEAN DATABANK
EVERYBODY'S INFORMATION

We are at your disposal in the following towns on the telephone number 185:

ČR

Beroun, Břeclav, České Budějovice, Domažlice, Frýdek-Místek, Hodonín, Hradec Krá-lové, Chomutov, Jablonec n/N., Jičín, Jihlava, Jindřichův Hradec, Karlovy Vary, Kar-viná, Kladno, Kolín, Kroměříž, Kutná Hora, Liberec, Mělník, Mladá Boleslav, Nymburk, Olomouc, Opava, Ostrava, Pardubice, Plzeň, Prostějov, Přerov, Příbram, Rožnov p/R., Svitavy, Šumperk, Tábor, Teplice, Trutnov, Třebíč, Třinec, Uherské Hradiště, Ústí n/L., Vlašim, Vyškov, Zlín, Znojmo, Žamberk, Žďár n/Sázavou.

SR

Banská Bystrica, Bratislava, Dunajská Streda, Košice, Liptovský Mikuláš, Nitra, Nové Zámky, Prešov, Prievidza, Rožňava, Rimavská Sobota, Trenčín, Trnava, Žilina.

Excerpt from company brochure, courtesy of Europska Databanka.

By May of 1997, the company had 10 women working on the telephones supplying information on goods and services to callers and 10 people working in the field as sales-people. The sales force called on prospective companies and attempted to get them to agree to sign a contract with Europska Databanka. One of the primary problems of the business was the difficulty of hiring good employees. Because the unemployment rate in the Czech Republic was so low, it was almost impossible to find qualified employees. In fact, the company had recently run an advertisement in the newspaper for new salespeo-ple and had received 50 inquiries about the position. However, only 4 people showed up for an interview, and only 1 of the 4 people was qualified for the job. The low unemploy-ment rate also meant that workers were not afraid to lose their jobs because of low pro-ductivity; they knew they could always get another job.

There were a few employment search agencies in Prague; however, they were not utilized by the companies because the idea of search agencies was completely new. The primary customers of these agencies were foreigners seeking jobs in the Czech Republic.

As to competition, Pavel and Dalibor believed at the present time the only competition was from the *Yellow Pages* printed by the telephone company. However, they also knew there were few barriers to entry into the industry. Another entrepreneur could simply observe what they were doing and copy their operations. The primary barrier to entry was the massive task of organizing all of the information about the companies that they represented. They wondered if there were other barriers to entry that they could construct. Richard had suggested to them that if they could offer superior customer service, this might prove to be a barrier to entry. Pavel liked the idea of customer service but had to laugh when he thought of the lack of customer service that existed under the former command economy. He remembered that customers were treated as slaves who had to beg for products from the government-owned businesses. He wondered how they could implement customer service in their operations.

Pavel reflected on a question that a young American named Suzanna Pierce had asked him yesterday. Susanna was a student at the University of Economics in Prague and was keenly interested in the economic changes that were taking place in the economy. Her question had been, "What do you consider to be the greatest challenges for new businesses in a country that has recently moved from a command economy to a free market economy?" He thought about the state of the former and present Czech economy and began in his mind to formulate a response to that intriguing question.

Pavel's thoughts came back to the present when Richard rose from the desk on the mezzanine at #15 Husitska where the two of them and Dalibor had been sitting. As Richard put his wide-brimmed black hat on his head and moved toward the door, he suggested again that they consider utilizing market research to improve the performance of the company. There must be some way, he urged, to find out if consumers are actually taking the firm's advice and buying the products that it had recommended to them. Also, there must be a way of determining how the callers found out about the company so that the company could be assured that it had used the most effective method of advertising. Pavel wondered how they would accomplish these things.

Endnote

1. $1.00 is equal to 25 korunas.

BULLER | SCHULER

Managing Organizations and People

A Resource for Cases in Management, Organizational Behavior, and Human Resource Management

Abstract

The Boston YWCA was originally formed over 100 years ago by a group of affluent women to provide women and children who had come to work in the city factories with clean, safe, and healthy living conditions. It also offered an employment training and referral network, as well as the first YWCA gymnasium. This was the beginning of its mission "to employ women through fitness, health care, and independent employment opportunities." During the next 50 years, the YWCA evolved from being a charitable organization to becoming an organization of women helping other women to achieve the goal of becoming economically independent. Over the years, the YWCA changed its focus from private funding to government funding. It began to implement more social service programs, which enabled it to secure government funds and grants that were available in the 1960s and 1970s. These funds allowed the YWCA growth in physical locations as well as services.

As the political and economic environment changed, the YWCA became one of many organizations competing for shrinking social service government funds. The change in focus from government funding to private support funds had also left the YWCA alienated from wealthy women who had been the base of its earlier sources of support. The decrease in support funding has left the YWCA's directors faced with the hard choice of allocating funds to provide programs and services or using the scarce resources for upkeep and improvement of the facilities. The YWCA's directors chose to fund the programs and attempted to obtain bank loans to fund renovations. Due to its lack of a strong strategic plan and the suffering economy, the YWCA's requests for loans were not looked upon favorably by the Boston banking establishment. At present, the YWCA's directors are confronted with the task of determining how to raise funds for renovations and continue to provide services needed by the women of Boston.

The Boston YWCA: 1991

In the summer of 1991 Mary Kinsell, Controller and Chief Financial Officer for the Boston YWCA, briefed her successor, Carolyn Rosen, and Marti Wilson-Taylor, the YWCA's new Executive Director. Deeply aware of the organization's financial crisis, Kinsell noted that the past 20 years had created many difficulties for the once-predominant

Boston YWCA. Especially pressing was the need to seek out new sources of funding because of significant cuts in federal funding to non-profits, increased demand and competition in the fitness and day-care industries, and increased real estate costs. In addition, the YWCA faced questions about how to deal with several aging YWCA buildings, located in prime neighborhoods of Boston but unmodernized and slowly deteriorating. Ms. Kinsell warned, "The Boston YWCA is like a dowager from an old Boston family that has seen better days: it is 'building rich' and 'cash poor.' Leveraging equity from its buildings is difficult and making operations generate enough cash flow to maintain the buildings seems almost impossible." The YWCA must now meet these challenges or it will be forced to cut back its activities, and may even face bankruptcy.

The First 100 Years

The Young Women's Christian Association (YWCA) is a non-profit organization whose original mission was "To provide for the physical, moral, and spiritual welfare of young women in Boston." For more than 12 decades it has done just that: meeting the changing needs of women in the community by providing services, opportunities, and support in an environment of shared sisterhood.

In 1866, a group of affluent women formed the Boston Young Women's Christian Association to rent rooms to women and children whom the Industrial Revolution had forced to leave their failing farms for work in city factories. Not only were their working conditions deplorable, but their living conditions consisted almost entirely of unsafe slums and unsanitary tenements. The Boston YWCA offered a clean, safe alternative to these living conditions, as well as recreation, companionship, and an employment referral network for women. The success of the facility led to the opening of the Berkeley Residence (40 Berkeley Street, Boston) in 1884, with accommodations for 200 residents and an employment and training bureau. It also housed the first YWCA gymnasium in America, a crucial part of its mission to "empower women through fitness, health care, and independent employment opportunities." At this early date in the YWCA's history, most of the funding for the YWCA's facilities and services was raised by wealthy women patrons both through their family connections and from among their friends and acquaintances. From its inception, the YWCA, unlike the larger, more well-known, and more aggressive YMCA, which easily garnered bank loans and donations, had to struggle to fund its projects.

In the ensuing decades, the Boston YWCA opened The School of Domestic Science to train women as institutional housekeepers and managers, and started a secretarial training program, and other training and educational programs for women. In 1911, the Boston YWCA became affiliated with the other YWCAs in the United States. By this time, the YWCA was no longer merely a philanthropic association run by upper-class women for women of a lower class, but an association of working women meeting the needs of other working women in the home and in the marketplace. Nevertheless, the continued support of wealthy patrons was crucial to the YWCA's viability as a community resource.

In the early 1920s, the "Y" initiated a capital campaign under the slogan "Every Girl Needs the YWCA" to raise funds for another building. Over one million dollars in contributions was received by subscription from donors of both the middle and upper classes, and in 1927 ground was broken at the corner of Clarendon and Stuart Streets for the Boston YWCA's new headquarters. The new building, including recreational facilities, a swimming pool, class rooms, meeting rooms, and offices for the staff, was dedicated in 1929 and has served as headquarters for the association ever since.

During World War II, the YWCA contributed to the war effort by sponsoring educational lectures and forums such as "Fix-It-Yourself" for the wives of servicemen, offering housing to women doing war work, and providing recreation and entertainment to men and women in the armed services. During this time the YWCA continued to be managed and funded primarily by women, for women.

After the war, YWCA administrators made a concerted effort to reach out to immigrant women. An interracial charter was adopted at the national convention which called for the integration and participation of minority groups in every aspect of the association, the community, and the nation. In addition, rapid postwar population growth in the suburbs west of Boston led to the opening in 1964 of the West Suburban Branch of the "Y" in Natick, Massachusetts, 20 miles west of Boston. The Natick "Y" focused its energies on the needs and wants of suburban women and their children. Additionally, advocates formed a lobbying group, the YWCA Public Affairs Committee, to focus on the areas of housing and family planning, and to call attention to the needs of those women, especially mothers, who were not being met by traditional social service organizations.

Throughout its first 100 years, the Boston YWCA, staffed and funded almost entirely by women, worked to empower women by helping them take charge of their lives, plan for their futures, and become economically independent and self-supporting.

Recent History

In 1866, the Boston YWCA became the first YWCA in the nation. Today we are part of the oldest and largest women's organization in the world, serving all people regardless of sex, race, religion, or income. Our One Imperative is the elimination of racism.

Mary L. Reed—Former Executive Director, 1986

The 1960s were a time of social and cultural upheaval, especially with regard to civil rights, the movement whose goal was equality for all races. In support of the civil rights movement, the YWCA made a commitment to fight racism and integrate its programs and services at every level, initiating a special two-year action plan in 1963. The operating budget for the plan provided for two staff members and support services to become more involved with other community groups working in the areas of fair housing, voter registration, and literacy programs. In 1967, the YWCA's first black President, Mrs. Robert W. Clayton, was elected at the National Convention. In 1968 the Boston YWCA opened Aswalos House in Dorchester, Massachusetts, especially to meet the needs of women in the inner city. As a fitting ending to the 1960s, the One Imperative "to eliminate racism wherever it exists and by any means necessary" was adopted and added to the statement of purpose as the philosophical basis for the YWCA in coming years.

Although fighting racism remained important, in the 1970s the YWCA shifted its attention to issues raised by the changing roles of women in American society. The 1960s and 1970s were decades of the revival and growth of the feminist movement in the United States and throughout the world. The social and political arena in which the Boston and other YWCAs were operating was changing rapidly. More and more women were working outside the home while raising children. The number of women living at or near the poverty level was on the rise. Classes and programs at the YWCA had to be redesigned to meet changing demands. For instance, the "Y" offered instruction in survival skills for urban living; but more radically, because non-traditional jobs for women were on the rise, in 1977 the "Y" launched its first non-traditional training program, funded by the federal government, to train women to work in the construction industry. Thus, in the 1970s, federal, state, and local governments became increasingly involved in social welfare, whereas in the past these needs had been met by private charitable and voluntary organizations. At the same time that the YWCA began to rely more on government funding and less on private donations, the YWCA's Board of Directors in the 1960s and 1970s changed to reflect the racial and class diversity of the women in the communities the YWCA served. While the new Board members helped the YWCA respond effectively to the immediate needs of the inner city community, they lost touch with the monied constituency that had formerly been the YWCA's base of support, and that monied constituency in turn shifted its attention and support to other causes. See Exhibit 1 for the YWCA's organization chart.

The Changing Environment

The late 1970s saw a dramatic rise in the number of unwed mothers, teen pregnancies, and teen parents. At the same time, more and more state and federal funds became available for social programs, and many non-profits directed their energies to establishing themselves as vendors or service providers to win government contracts. The Boston YWCA became a major vendor in the areas of child care, employment training, teen services, and domestic abuse programming. As a result of the YWCA's strong advocacy efforts, major federal and state contracts were awarded to the YWCA for further study of issues related to teen pregnancy. However, the YWCA's redirecting of its efforts toward securing government funding significantly eroded its base of private support, especially among those

EXHIBIT 1

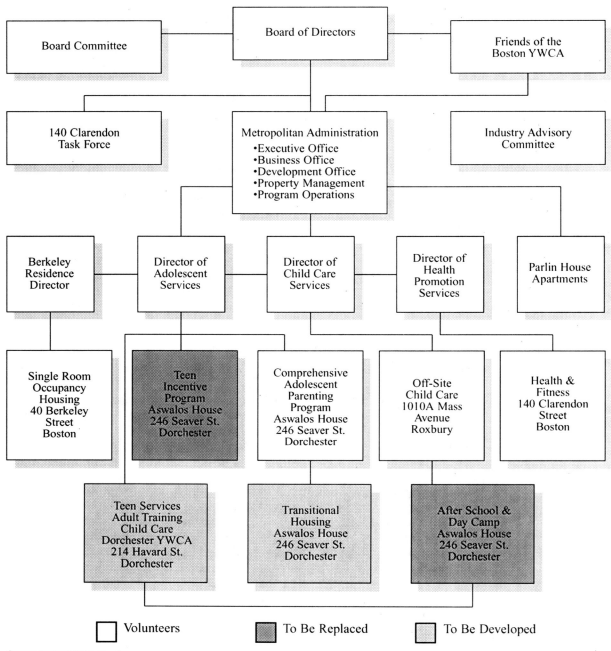

Source: Boston YWCA records.

upper crust women who had, for generations, been the primary source of funds for the YWCA in Boston, and the YWCA, which had for a long time been one of a few non-profits, became one of many contending for the same funds.

As the decade came to a close, the outlook for the Boston YWCA began to shift. Given the community's growing need for services and their own aging facilities, the management team of the Boston YWCA realized they would have to make some tough decisions about allocating funds that were beginning to get more scarce. If they were to decide that a major outlay of cash or large loans for facilities were necessary, they would have to pull funds from the programs and services the association provided to the community at a time when the need for community services was greater than ever and funds for these services were scarcer than they had been for some time. However, if the YWCA's management team continued to allocate funds for services and programs while making only minimal allocations for facility maintenance, they risked incurring the cost either of major repairs further down the line, or the serious deterioration of their major assets. Though the management team did not want to lose sight of the YWCA's commitment to the women and children in the community, the "Y's" financial crisis would require foresight, careful planning, and some hard choices.

The Economic Crunch

In the early 1980s the need for social services grew, increasing the number of non-profit organizations competing for the same funds. At the same time the Reagan Administration cut back federal funding, and non-profits were forced to go back to raising funds through private donations, grants, bequests, and the United Way. The mid-1980s, however, were prosperous years, especially in the Boston area. Individuals and companies gave more generously than in past years to non-profits, and in response to the limited availability of federal funds for social services during the Reagan era, non-profits increasingly directed their resources to funding everything from homeless shelters and food pantries to drug and alcohol rehabilitation centers.

However, the economic downturn in late 1987 immediately cut into the funding flow for non-profits. Corporations and the general public became more discerning about where they directed their charitable contributions. Many people lost their jobs; a high-debt lifestyle caught up with others: in short, people's disposable income dropped off. It became increasingly difficult to raise the funds necessary to keep up the facilities and to provide the services the community continued to demand. As the economy worsened, the need for services increased proportionately and at a more rapid rate than the Boston YWCA had ever witnessed. At the same time, the YWCA had to contend both with its old "mainstream" image in the face of the proliferation of more "chic" non-profits such as homeless shelters, battered women's shelters, or "safe houses," and with the growing misperception of the YWCA as an organization run primarily by women of color for women of color.

The climate for the banking industry in Boston during the late 1980s also altered dramatically. Many banks were in financial trouble and those that had lent freely in the mid-1980s now scrutinized every loan request and rejected a large majority of those they received. Funds for capital improvements and construction were not looked upon favorably by most Boston area banks; and money to fund new projects and large renovations became nearly impossible to obtain. These negative trends have only worsened so far in the 1990s, as the YWCA faces the absolute necessity of making some hard decisions regarding the allocation of its shrinking resources.

Sources of Funding

Revenue for the Boston YWCA comes from three sources:

1. **Support Funds**—funds from the United Way of Massachusetts Bay, contributions, grants, legacies, and bequests.
2. **Operating Revenue**—money from program fees, government-sponsored programs, membership dues, housing and food services.
3. **Non-Operating Revenue**—income from leasing of office space to outside concerns, investment income, and net realized gain on investments.

Exhibit 2 shows the percentage each has contributed to total revenue for the past five years. From 1985 to 1989 the United Way accounted for 70–80% of the support funds revenue. But like all non-profit organizations in the late-1980s, the United Way was under fire for its operational procedures and found itself in a fiercely competitive fundraising environment. The United Way anticipated a 30% drop in fundraising for 1991, which would affect all the agencies it funded, including the Boston YWCA (see Exhibit 3). At the same time, operating revenues for the YWCA dropped off in 1990 as well, so that more, rather than less support funding was needed to operate. Since support funding is expected to continue to decrease in the next three to five years, the Boston YWCA must discover new sources of funding to maintain its services and meet its operational expenses. The financial statements for the Boston YWCA are shown in Exhibits 4 and 5 (pages 7–9).

**EXHIBIT 2
Percentage
Breakdown—
Sources of Funding:
Boston YWCA**

	Years					
	1990	1989	1988	1987	1986	1985
Source of funding						
Support funds	33%	24%	21%	23%	22%	22%
Operating revenue	54%	63%	67%	65%	66%	67%
Non-operating revenue	13%	13%	12%	12%	12%	11%

Facilities

In 1987, the Boston YWCA was operating from four facilities in neighborhoods of Boston and one in a Natick, a western suburb of the city. During 1987, the Boston Redevelopment Authority, a commission that oversees all real estate development in the city, awarded a parcel of land to the YWCA for $1.00 on which to build a new facility as part of the city's redevelopment plan. The new facility would replace the old Dorchester YWCA, Aswalos House, which a grant would then convert to transitional housing for unwed mothers and their children. Since the YWCA now had a new parcel of land, and other existing facilities in need of maintenance records and repair, the management team embarked on a three-year study to analyze its programs and services, and its properties. Most importantly, they decided to implement an aggressive renovation schedule designed to modernize all facilities, to protect the value of the YWCA's major assets, its buildings.

As part of this renovation, repair, and maintenance program, the association's management team had to perform a thorough review of its programs and services. The programs most beneficial to the agency in terms of revenue and those the community had the greatest need for had to be assessed for future expectations of growth and space requirements. New programs would have to be accommodated and those programs that were no longer financially feasible or in demand would have to be eliminated. The management team planned to complete their research and decision making prior to implementing any expansion or renovation of the buildings.

West Suburban Program Center

When the YWCA expanded, and opened a branch in Natick, Massachusetts, a suburb located 20 miles west of Boston in 1964, it bought a building which quickly became inadequate to the YWCA's needs, and in 1981 the center moved to a new facility. The resources for women at this branch were designed to serve its suburban constituency, and included programs for women re-entering the job market after years of parenting, training programs for displaced workers, spousal and family abuse programs, divorce support groups, and counseling for women suffering from breast cancer. However, in 1988, after

**EXHIBIT 3
Detailed Analysis of
YWCA Funding
Revenues 1991:
Boston YWCA**

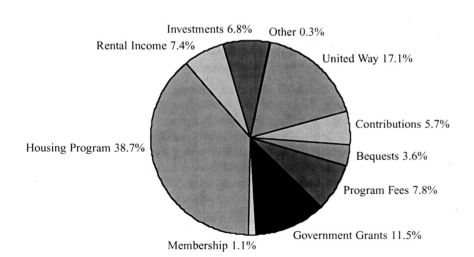

EXHIBIT 4
Statement of Support and Revenue, Expenses, Capital Additions,
and Changes in Fund Balances: Boston YWCA (June 30, 1991)

Years Ending June 30	Current Fund	Plant Fund	Endowment Fund	1991 Totals	1990 Totals
Support and Revenue					
Support					
United Way	$ 703,643	—	—	$ 703,643	$ 713,500
Contributions and grants	233,624	—	—	233,264	197,700
Legacies and bequests	150,386	—	—	150,386	537,540
	1,087,293	—	—	1,087,293	1,488,740
Operating revenue					
Program fees	320,611	—	—	320,611	355,170
Government-sponsored programs	471,615	—	—	471,615	411,050
Membership	45,674	—	—	45,674	71,579
Housing and food service	1,589,587	—	—	1,589,587	1,586,553
	2,427,487	—	—	2,427,487	2,424,352
Non-operating revenue					
Rental income	302,641	—	—	302,641	298,036
Investment income	278,982	—	—	278,982	244,244
Net realized gain on investments	41,392	—	—	41,392	2,308
Other revenue	7,967	—	—	7,967	43,790
	630,982	—	—	630,982	588,358
Total support and revenue	4,145,762	—	—	4,145,762	4,461,450
Expenses					
Program services					
Aswalos House	250,621	14,782	—	265,403	384,776
Berkeley Residence	1,053,131	86,465	—	1,139,596	1,054,106
Cass Branch	1,216,544	128,673	—	1,345,217	1,394,075
Child Care	422,411	2,030	—	424,411	344,011
Harvard	6,132	—	—	6,132	—
	2,948,839	231,950	—	3,180,789	3,176,968
Supporting services					
General and administration	632,657	15,364	—	648,021	793,861
Fundraising	287,449	6,981	—	294,429	135,978
	920,105	22,345	—	924,450	929,839
Total expenses	3,868,944	254,295	—	4,123,239	4,106,807

(continued)

much research and years of restructuring the services offered at the West Suburban Program Center, its inability to support itself financially through its operations led to a decision to close down the facility.

Aswalos House

Aswalos House, located in Dorchester, Massachusetts, an urban center within the jurisdiction of the City of Boston, was originally opened in 1968. Until 1989, it housed an After School Enrichment Program and a Teen Development Program that offered training for word processing and clerical work, and GED preparation courses. Later, Aswalos House added a program for teen mothers.

In 1989, the receipt of a $100,000 Department of Housing and Urban Development (HUD) grant transformed Aswalos House into transitional housing for teenage mothers and their children, and existing programs were transferred to other facilities. Originally

EXHIBIT 4
Statement of Support and Revenue, Expenses, Capital Additions,
and Changes in Fund Balances: Boston YWCA (June 30, 1991)—*continued*

Years Ending June 30	Current Fund	Plant Fund	Endowment Fund	1991 Totals	1990 Totals
Excess (deficiency) of support and revenue over expenses before capital additions	$ 276,818	(254,295)	—	22,523	354,643
Capital Additions					
Grants106,495	38,985	—	145,480	314,798	
Investment income	—	5,529	65,598	71,127	68,018
Net realized gain on investment transactions	—	—	72,577	72,577	63,874
Write-off of deferred charges	—	—	—	—	(305,312)
Loss on sale of asset	—	—	—	—	(11,856)
Total capital additions	106,495	44,514	138,175	289,184	129,522
Excess (deficiency) of support and revenue over expenses after capital additions	$ 383,313	$ (209,781)	$ 128,175	$ 311,707	$ 484,165
Fund balances, beginning of year	$1,379,040	$1,486,053	$3,042,128	$5,907,221	$5,423,056
Transfers between funds					
Plant acquisition	(274,155)	274,155	—	—	—
Principle repayment on loan payable to endowment fund	(143,841)	143,841	—	—	—
Permanent fund transfer	346,908	(346,908)	—	—	—
	(71,088)	71,088	—	—	—
Fund balances, end of year	**$1,691,265**	**$ 1,347,360**	**$3,180,303**	**$6,218,928**	**$5,907,221**

the programs were to be transferred to the new Dorchester Branch planned for the parcel acquired from the City of Boston. However, that parcel was never developed because development costs were estimated at $1.5–$2 million, but the YWCA was only able to raise $300,000. Consequently, the parcel of land was returned to the City of Boston.

The new Aswalos House for teen mothers opened in October 1990, and provided transitional housing for ten mothers and their children. Prospective occupants have to be between 16 and 20 and demonstrate severe financial need. Counseling services are provided, and a staff case worker arranges for schooling and job training for the teenagers. In addition, a staff housing advocate coordinates permanent housing for the mothers and their children.

Half the expense of running the facility is covered by a federal grant to the Boston YWCA. The remaining half is made up by fees paid by the teen mothers from their welfare income, and by contributions from the United Way and private donations.

YWCA Child Care Center

The YWCA Child Care Center is rather inconveniently located in downtown Boston on the fringe of the commercial district, and is rented rather than owned by the YWCA. To be licensed as a day-care center in the Commonwealth of Massachusetts, it had to undergo extensive renovations. The owner of the property contributed a substantial portion of the cost of the renovation work, and the balance of the expense was covered by a private grant so that no loans were necessary to complete the project.

The center, a licensed pre-school, provides day care for 50 children at fees of $110 a week per toddler and $150 a week per child for children under 3. Some scholarships are available for families who are unable to pay. When the center first opened, many of its

EXHIBIT 5
Balance Sheet: Boston YWCA (June 30, 1991)

Years Ending June 30	Current Fund	Plant Fund	Endowment Fund	1991 Totals	1990 Totals
Assets					
Current assets					
Cash	$ 137,469	66,292	—	203,761	110,684
Cash in escrow and security deposits	40,642	—	—	40,642	37,932
Accounts receivable (less allowance for doubtful accounts of $3,500 in 1991 and $2,687 in 1990)	102,334	—	—	102,334	166,245
Supplies and prepaid expenses	54,452	—	—	54,452	73,613
Total current assets	334,897	66,292	—	401,189	388,474
Pooled investments	1,793,198	—	3,180,303	4,973,501	4,755,252
Land, buildings, and equipment, net	—	2,147,155	—	2,147,155	1,869,963
Deferred charges	—	349,638	—	349,638	349,638
	1,793,198	2,496,793	3,180,303	7,470,294	6,994,853
Total assets	**$2,128,095**	**2,563,085**	**3,180,303**	**7,871,483**	**7,383,327**
Liabilities and Fund Balances (Deficit)					
Current liabilities					
Current maturities of long-term notes payable	—	18,979	—	18,979	17,524
Accounts payable and accrued expenses	254,757	—	—	254,757	201,581
Deferred revenue	182,073	—	—	182,073	202,717
Total current liabilities	436,830	18,979	—	455,809	421,822
Long-term notes payable, less current maturities	—	1,196,746	—	1,196,746	910,443
Loan payable to endowment fund	—	—	—	—	143,841
Total liabilities	436,830	1,215,725	—	1,652,555	1,476,106
Fund balances (deficit)					
Unrestricted					
Designated by governing board to function as endowment	1,507,135	—	—	1,507,135	1,453,867
Undesignated	(101,933)	—	—	(101,933)	(354,084)
Total unrestricted	1,405,202	—	—	1,405,202	1,099,783
Restricted—nonexpendable	286,063	223,798	3,180,303	3,690,164	3,545,183
Net investment in plant	—	1,123,562	—	1,123,562	1,262,255
Total fund balances	1,691,265	1,347,360	3,180,303	6,218,928	5,907,221
Total liabilities and fund balances (deficit)	**$2,128,095**	**2,563,085**	**3,180,303**	**7,871,483**	**7,383,327**

clients were on state-funded day-care vouchers. Participation has now dropped considerably, however, because a significant percentage of state-funded day-care vouchers were cut from the state budget. To compensate for the loss of clients, the center went into the infant care business, caring for children from 6 months to 2 years, but it continues to run at less than capacity.

The Berkeley House

The Berkeley Residence was opened in 1884 in downtown Boston to serve as housing for women of all ages. Originally there was housing for 100 residents, an employment and training bureau, and a gymnasium, the first in the country for women. In 1907, 35 rooms and a meeting hall were added to the facility.

In 1985 the Berkeley Residence was cited by Boston's Building Code Department because it did not meet current safety and fire codes of the city or the Commonwealth. Major repairs and renovations estimated at $1 million were necessary to bring the building up to health, safety, and legal standards. In 1986, a construction loan for the full amount was secured at 10% interest amortized over 25 years. Once the project was completed, payments would come to approximately $100,000 annually. Work began in 1988. Repairs were needed to the infrastructure of the building, and included a conversion from oil heat to gas, a sprinkler system and smoke detector system wired throughout the building, new elevators, as well as many other repairs and maintenance work of a less costly nature. Tenants were not displaced during construction, a major concern at the beginning of the project's planning stage.

After completion of the renovation work in the spring of 1991, the facility now rents 215 rooms, which provide long-term and short-term housing for women of all ages. The Berkeley Residence offers inexpensive rent and meals, an answering service, and maid service. Other services located at the facility include a referral network for jobs and services, social services, tourist information, and emergency services. The building is open and staffed 24 hours a day, 7 days a week, providing safe, secure housing at reasonable rates for single women in the city.

Boston YWCA Headquarters at 140 Clarendon Street

Constructed between 1927 and 1929, the headquarters for the Boston YWCA is advantageously located at the corner of Clarendon and Stuart Streets, on the edge of one of the city's most prestigious retail districts, Newbury and Boylston Streets and Copley Place, in the heart of Boston's Back Bay business district. The area offers the finest in upscale retail stores and desirable office space, including the John Hancock Building and the Prudential Center. The Clarendon Headquarters, a 13-story brick and steel building, sits on approximately 13,860 square feet of land and includes approximately 167,400 square feet of space. It currently houses the YWCA administration offices, the Parlin House Apartments, the Melnea Cass Branch of the YWCA, and several commercial tenants. The Melnea Cass Branch operates health and fitness facilities, which include a swimming pool, and employment training programs. The Parlin House Apartments occupy floors 9–13 and comprise studio, one-, and two-bedroom apartments rented at market rates.

The building has not been significantly renovated since its completion in 1929, and no longer complies with city and state building codes. In 1987, the building elevators desperately needed repairs at an estimated cost of $270,000. The building also now needs a new sprinkler system to ensure the safety of its residents and tenants and to bring the building up to code. The Parlin House Apartments also require major renovations to achieve an acceptable standard of safety, appearance, and comfort. The Apartments currently use common electric meters, and need to be rewired so tenants can control the electricity to their individual units, and pay accordingly. The YWCA's administrative offices also require improvements and repairs.

The health and fitness facilities also require significant repairs, updating, and renovation. Old, dreary locker rooms are unattractive to current and potential members, and a larger men's locker room is needed to accommodate male members. In addition, to keep up with new trends in the fitness industry, the YWCA needs to refurbish its space for aerobics classes and purchase new weight training equipment. During this time, the YWCA has also been forced to close the pool for repairs, and the pool building itself needs significant exterior work. Cost estimates for the work on the pool and pool building are in excess of $200,000. At the same time, a decrease in demand for health and fitness clubs and an increase in competition in both the day-care and health and fitness industries has had a negative impact on revenues for this facility.

Because the YWCA's Clarendon headquarters is in such a state of disrepair, it has become very costly to maintain and operate the building. In years past, the Board of Directors has chosen to funnel their scarce available resources into their programs rather than into general repairs and maintenance of the facilities, with the result that the building at 140 Clarendon Street is currently running at a net loss in excess of $200,000 a year.

In 1988 a certified appraiser valued the Clarendon property at $16 million dollars. (However, the real estate market in the Boston area has since declined significantly.) The Boston YWCA's Board of Directors then sought a $7 million loan for the proposed renovations from several major Boston area banking and financial institutions, but most of these institutions did not respond favorably to the loan request. While there were a number of valid reasons for the banks' refusing to loan the YWCA the funds necessary for the renovations, including the YWCA's own uncertainty about how the changes would impact revenues, the fact that the YWCA is a women's organization without connections in the "old-boy" network of the banking establishment contributed to the YWCA's lack of financial credibility. Finally, although the Clarendon building's excess value would cover the loan-to-value ratio, the banks raised serious questions about whether the YWCA's existing and potential cash flow could meet the debt service obligation.

The executive committee of the Boston YWCA is now faced with a serious dilemma. It must decide what to do with a deteriorating facility that not only serves as its headquarters, but also as a flagship of services offered by all the area YWCAs. After several years of study, review, and debate they are considering the following options for the Clarendon headquarters.

1. Sell the building with a guaranteed leaseback for its facilities and offices.
2. Sell the building to an interested local insurance company and rent space for the administrative offices in a nearby office building.
3. Bring in an equity partner to fund the renovations for a percentage of ownership in the facility.
4. Continue with minimal renovations and operate as they have in the past.

Increasing Competition in Fitness Services

In 1989, the management team of the Boston YWCA hired a consulting firm to review their Health Promotion Services division, housed at 140 Clarendon Street, one of the YWCA's primary sources of both operating revenue and expense, and to assist them in finding ways to enhance this branch of their services. The consultants surveyed current, former, and potential members about the strengths and weaknesses of the YWCA's Health Promotion Services including appearance, cleanliness, scheduling, products (i.e., equipment, classes, swimming pool, etc.), and overall management of the facility. This study also noted that there is considerable competition from the following vendors in the area of health and fitness:

- Bally's Holiday Fitness Centers
- Healthworks
- Fitcorp
- Boston Sports
- SkyClub
- The Mount Auburn Club
- Nautilus Plus
- Fitness International
- Fitness First
- The Club at Charles River Park
- Mike's Gym
- Fitness Unlimited
- Gold's Gym

The health club marketplace is, for the most part, a standardized industry in terms of the products and services offered at the various facilities. Most clubs offer free weights, weight equipment, exercise and aerobics classes, locker rooms, and showers with towels available. During the 1980s many new health clubs opened and the health club market became increasingly competitive. These clubs went to great expense to promote elaborate grand openings and fund extensive advertising campaigns to attract new members. The consultants' study found that 15 other health and fitness facilities within the city are in direct competition with the YWCA. However, the YWCA does fill a unique niche because it is affordable, strongly emphasizes fitness in a non-competitive and non-commercial environment, appeals to a diverse cross-section of people, and is conveniently located. Other clubs are perceived as more commercial and competitive than the YWCA, with a greater emphasis on social interaction and frills such as saunas, racquetball and squash courts, eating facilities, etc. A comparison of the YWCA's Health Promotion Services to other health clubs in the city shows the YWCA to be in a price range somewhere between the commercial clubs and the no-frills gymnasiums. The commercial clubs range from $800–$1200 a year, plus a one-time initiation fee of from $100–$1200; the no-frills gymnasiums range from $300–$400 per year; and the YWCA costs between $420 and $600 a year, plus an annual membership fee of $35.

The YWCA is comparable in size to the competition, but its space is not as well laid out as at other clubs. Most of the other clubs are air-conditioned but the YWCA isn't and its membership drops significantly during the summer months, while for other clubs summer is the peak season. The YWCA also ranks behind the top four clubs in cleanliness, and members note that its dreary atmosphere contributes to their sense of its uncleanliness. The YWCA's weight-lifting equipment and weight machines are not quite up to the standards of the competition and the YWCA lacks the staffing and supervision other clubs provide. On the other hand, the YWCA can boast a swimming pool, an indoor track, and day care. Only one other club has a pool that comes close in size to the YWCA's, and only two other clubs offer indoor tracks or day care.

According to the consultants' study, current users of the YWCA's Health Promotion Services joined because the YWCA is convenient, provides a caring environment that promotes interaction, and is relatively inexpensive. A current user profile revealed that members are generally seeking a health and fitness experience for themselves as individuals rather than a social atmosphere, and that what mattered to them additionally were sensible class schedules, adequate staffing, staff communication with the members, timely information, affordable pricing, an atmosphere without pressure, and an open, caring, and diverse environment. The complaint most often cited among current users was the lack of communication with members with regard to scheduling changes for classes, changes in the hours of operation, class cancellations, pool closings, and changes in procedures and policies of the club. Other factors that concerned current members were: the lack of cleanliness, dreary appearance, small men's locker room, poor management of the staff, poor management of class capacity, inadequate maintenance of equipment, poor scheduling, poor layout of the facility, and the lack of public relations and advertising to attract new members.

Former members were also surveyed to determine why they did not renew. Their reasons mirrored the complaints of current members:

- Poor communication with members
- Equipment breakdowns
- Untimely equipment repairs
- Poor upkeep/cleanliness
- Poor ventilation
- Dreary appearance
- Dissatisfaction with staff (no personal attention)
- Rigid schedules
- Lack of air conditioning
- Overall deterioration of the facility

The study also concluded that marketing and promotion of the Health Promotion Services are minimal, with little effort put into attracting new members, making it nearly invisible in the community.

Marti Wilson-Taylor, the new Executive Director, and Carolyn Rosen, the new Chief Financial Officer, quickly realized as they took control of the Boston YWCA in 1991 that several major decisions concerning the YWCA's physical facilities and programs and services had to be made. However, first and foremost, it was necessary for them to determine the strategic direction of the YWCA for the remainder of the decade. In an environment of increasing competition and shrinking resources, the challenge facing them is great.

BULLER | SCHULER

Managing Organizations and People

A Resource for Cases in Management, Organizational Behavior, and Human Resource Management

Abstract

The BCH TeleCommunications case opens with the realization by Jeff Welker, one of the founders of the company, that his trusted partner and friend has left the Czech Republic (where the company is based) and has taken all of the company's liquid assets and legal documents with him. As Jeff attempts to deal with these problems, the reader is led through a series of events in Jeff's life that have led him from the beaches of California to the Czech Republic and a successful telecommunications business. The enumerable problems encountered in attempting to establish a restaurant and bar in Prague and finally giving up on the project because of the ineffectiveness of the country's contract law are unfolded as well as the events that led to the establishment of BCH TeleCommunications, a company that represented WorldLink, a callback service provider. Jeff also speculates about the product life cycle of the company's primary product—callback services—in light of the growing number of substitute products that are less costly than traditional international telephone calls and the possibility that the domestic telephone companies in Eastern Europe may soon lower their long-distance calling rates to compete with callback services.

BCH TeleCommunications

As the Prague Police car pulled away from the curb in front of 156 Sokolovska, 32-year-old Jeff Welker bit his lip to hold back the tears. It was bad enough that his partner had left the country and taken all of the $150,000 in cash they had in the BCH TeleCommunications checking account, but to compound matters, this was one of his oldest and dearest friends. In addition to the money, his partner had also taken some important legal documents that were necessary for running the company. It was July of 1996 and the business was just beginning to take off.

Jeff's partner had simply left a letter on his desk telling Jeff that he was leaving because the partnership had caused him great frustration, and he was going to Poland and taking the money with him. As he left his spartan office on the second floor of an older building in the northeast section of Prague, Jeff reflected on the fact that the course of his life semed to have been shaped by disappointing letters. Walking along Sokolovska in a westerly direction, he lifted his eyes to the beautiful Czech skyline with the imposing fortress of Prazsky Hrad (Prague Castle) dominating the city and the maze of red-tiled roofs on the lovely old buildings stretched out before him. How many times he had strolled

■ Marlene Mints Reed, Samford University and Rochelle Reed Brunson, Alvin Community College.

through the narrow, cobblestone streets of Mala Strana (the Lesser Quarter) or paused to admire murals on the baroque buildings that surround Staromestske namesti (Old Town Square) and thought what a long way this was from the beaches of sunny Southern California. His mind raced back to the events that had eventually led him here.

Preparation for Prague

For as long as he could remember, Jeff had wanted to go into hospitality management. It was quite natural, then, that when he completed high school in Glendale, California, he entered Glendale Community College and ultimately completed an Associate Degree in Business Management with a concentration in Food Management.

After researching a number of schools that offered bachelor's degrees in Hospitality Management, Jeff decided to enter the program at the University of Nevada at Las Vegas. During his time at the University, he established many close relationships—including friendships with managers and directors of hotels in Las Vegas.

With the conclusion of his work at UNLV, Jeff interviewed with a number of companies and ultimately accepted a job as Assistant Convention Director at a Sheraton Hotel located in the Los Angeles area. Within the next 3 years, Jeff was promoted several times. He reflected, "Part of it was being in the right place at the right time, and part of it was giving 120 percent of myself. I had the people skills, the work ethic, morals, flexibility, and ability to change when that was needed."

Early Entrepreneurial Speculations

Jeff's family had some wealthy friends in California who said, "If you are ever going to be involved in some venture, come and talk with us. We would like to help with the financing." He filed this away in the back of his mind just in case something interesting did come along. After a couple of years, Jeff was transferred to the Sheraton Hotel in San Diego. He soon became friends with an older man who was a real estate developer in Los Angeles and Hawaii.

Perhaps because of discussions with this man about opportunities in Hawaii, Jeff began contemplating putting together a project for a hotel there. For the next two years, he worked concertedly on this plan. He even selected a parcel of land in Hawaii, talked to the owner of the land about his interest in putting a hotel there, and developed an aerial shot video of the land to show to potential investors. In addition, he had a graphic artist overlay a sketch of the proposed hotel onto a photograph of the land. Jeff was now 26 years old, had enough pledges to build a hotel in Hawaii and envisioned that his lifelong dream was about to become a reality.

However, this dream was not to be. He had made friends with a young lawyer from New York named Charles, and Charles was tired of the grueling hours in the large law firm that he worked for and planned to quit his job and start a business of his own. Jeff was understandably startled when Charles asked him one day, "Have you ever thought of building the hotel somewhere else for about 100 times less money?" He continued, "Do you know anything about the Riviera—the Yugoslavian Riviera?" Jeff admitted that he knew almost nothing about Yugoslavia, and he certainly didn't know it had a Riviera. However, by a strange twist of fate, the travel section of the local newspaper had a 12-page article on the Yugoslavian Riviera the following weekend. Jeff read each word carefully and began doing some research on this part of the world. He went back to his investors and told them about this new opportunity, and they became as excited as he was. Charles and Jeff began applying for visas, but, unfortunately, it was late 1990 and early 1991 and war broke out in the country before they could get there. This forced them to scrap the whole idea and begin all over.

Four months later, Charles suggested that they continue to concentrate on Eastern Europe where doors of opportunity were beginning to open for entrepreneurs. He proposed that they consider starting a bar and grill in Prague, Czechoslovakia, which was the gateway between Eastern and Western Europe. Jeff knew a bit more about Czechoslovakia although he had never been there. Other circumstances in his life at the time caused him to rethink the future. He had left Sheraton and gone with Marriott Hotels, and Marriott was in the process of restructuring. Jeff became uncomfortable with the changes he saw taking place and decided Charles's idea was not so bad after all. He quit his job and began serious research on the new project. It was now April of 1992.

Research for the Venture in Prague

Although a formal business plan was never developed, Jeff and Charles did spend some time researching the proposed project in Czechoslovakia. Charles had decided that in addition to the bar and grill that Jeff would run, he would like to start an import-export business in Prague because he had always been enamored by this type of operation and had a hunch that such a business might work in this country newly opened to Western goods.

One thing he needed to know was the type of goods not presently available in that country. First, they did some research at home in the library of the University of California at San Diego on Czechoslovakia and visited the Czech Consulate in Los Angeles. Then they flew to Washington, D.C. and talked to the Czech Embassy, the United States Commerce Department, the EXIM (Export-Import) Bank, the IMF (International Monetary Fund), and searched anywhere else they could get information on the country and the economic climate there. The Czech Consulate and Embassy told them there was a great need for used blue jeans and used computers in the country at that time. This was before the time of the Internet, so much of the research had to be done in libraries and people's offices. Charles's law firm had a one-person office in Prague, and that lawyer also assisted them in understanding the country.

Jeff and Charles began exploring names for their embryonic company and decided to use an acronym for the company title. After brainstorming for days, they finally arrived at the acronym BCH which was an abbreviation for "beach"—a place where Jeff had spent some of the best years of his life. In November of 1992, Jeff and Charles arrived in Prague to launch their business operations. Jeff secretly wondered just where BCH Enterprises would take these two entrepreneurial friends.

Economic Developments in Czechoslovakia

In November of 1989, Czechoslovakia experienced what would later be referred to as the "Velvet Revolution." In response to the pleas of students and nurses, the Socialist government finally stepped down and handed the country over to the people. Great social, political, and economic changes subsequently occurred in the newly freed nation. The disintegration of the former Council for Mutual Economic Cooperation (Comecon) was one of the most significant factors for change. The National Assembly elected Vaclav Havel as President of Czechoslovakia on December 29, 1989. Havel came from a family that had a long history of business and cultural activity. In spite of major difficulties under the former Socialist government, Havel became one of the most celebrated of all Czech contemporary playwrights.

The primary constraint to any reform efforts on the part of Vaclav Havel and his new government was the fact that all industrial and agricultural production was owned by the state or state-dependent collective farms. The new Minister of Finance, Vaclav Klaus, proposed in February of 1990 a coupon privatization project. By paying only a small administration fee, all Czechoslovakian citizens were given the opportunity to obtain a coupon book that could be used to purchase shares in certain privatized concerns. The first coupon books were sold on May 18, 1992, with the result that 70 percent of the population became shareholders. Following this, there was a project entitled "Small Privatization" that singled out smaller service and trade premises from state property and sold them at auction.

Another constraint to reform was the less-than-rapid integration of Czechoslovakia into the community of Western European states. Exporters in the Western European countries were delighted with the new opportunity to sell their goods in Czech markets, but they were reticent to buy Czech goods. The former Socialist economy was strongly oriented towards Comecon (a planned economy) and the Soviet Union. This had a negative effect on domestic production and caused the country to be non-competitive in world markets. The central planning commission stressed heavy industry and neglected the service sector entirely. Because of this, the Czech economy suffered a decrease in exports when Comecon was dissolved, and there was a loss of Eastern markets for their goods.[1]

Somehow the Czechoslovakian economy survived the breakup into the Czech Republic and Slovakia on January 1, 1993, and the collapse of markets in Eastern Europe. The country began to develop a greater orientation toward the markets of Western Europe, and more foreign firms began to enter the domestic Czech market.[2] (See Exhibit 1.)

According to *The Economist* magazine, by the end of 1994 65 percent of the gross domestic product in the Czech Republic was from contributions of private sector business

**EXHIBIT 1
Direct Foreign
Investments in the
Czech Republic**

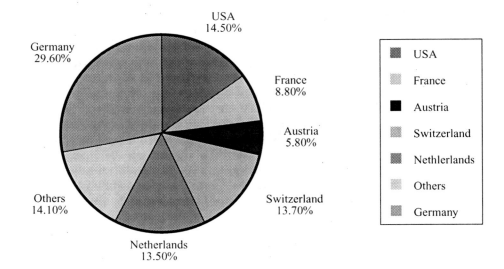

activities (both domestic and foreign). However, even though a whole range of laws and decrees had been promulgated that purported to encourage the formation of small business, a proper legal system to defend private property and enterprise and enforce contracts had not been implemented.[3]

For one thing, the government bureaucracy had become a major barrier to the creation of new enterprises. The former state-owned banks were very slowly being privatized and new banks from other countries were beginning to enter the country. However, the experience of one company in what was once Russia is very similar to experiences of entrepreneurs in the Czech Republic. This new small business received the required 27 documents—many requiring notarizations—after a loan approval and before the money could be disbursed.[4]

Two separate Czech economies appeared to be developing by the middle 1990s. One was the economy in which new Czech entrepreneurs were attempting to start up new ventures and having great difficulty getting a loan from the bank (except at 30 percent interest) and breaking through the old-boy network that was a residual of the Socialist state. And the other sector, which represented companies from Western countries that had access to banks outside the Czech Republic and well-skilled lawyers to assist with the bureaucracy, was experiencing great success.[5] It was within this economic climate that Jeff and Charles hoped to start a business.

Hurdles for the New Business

Many foreign companies that made investments in the Czech Republic became frustrated with the difficulty of getting things taken care of in a timely manner. Every contract or piece of paper needed a stamp by someone to make it official. Sometimes the stamps were paper stamps that could be purchased at a post office, and sometimes they were the imprint of a rubber stamp.

Jeff decided very early that he would not be daunted by such hurdles. He said to himself, "Look at yourself. You're no longer in America. You must do everything on your own and accept that." He believed that philosophy had saved him from many hours of anxiety fretting over the difficulty of moving processes along in his new country.

However, there were the hurdles that became insurmountable. With the import-export business, the hurdle was the incorrect information they had received from sources with whom they had consulted before entering the Czech Republic. Although they had been told by Czech sources that there was a great need for used computers in the Czech Republic, when they arrived they found that most people who wanted a computer already had one. In addition, although there was a great demand for used blue jeans as had been suggested, any jeans that were imported were either stolen at the border, or if they made it past the border, were burdened with a heavy duty being placed upon them by the Czech government. Therefore, BCH could not make a profit with prohibitive duties on their products.

With the restaurant business, there were insurmountable hurdles with the renovation of the building to house the eating and drinking establishment. Jeff and Charles signed a contract for a stated amount with one construction company only to have them come back later and suggest, "We forgot to put doors and windows in our contract, and also there is water damage in the walls, and we have to fix that." They let this company go and signed a contract with another construction company who later said to them, "Oh, we must add an additional $80,000 to the contract for electrical wiring, elevators, and stairs."

Jeff and Charles began to understand that the signing of contracts meant nothing, and the project would go well beyond their budget. They knew they could not continue to ask their investors to pour money into a black hole, so they gave up on the whole project. Jeff and Charles lost more than $40,000 on this project. Their deal with investors was that the investors would put $250,000 into the project, but they wanted Jeff and Charles to invest (and be willing to lose) the first $50,000. Jeff wondered if part of their problem might have sprung from the fact that neither of them spoke the Czech language and depended upon translators for all transactions.

An Introduction to Callback Services

Jeff began doing some hospitality management consulting in Eastern Europe since tourism had become a big business after the demise of Communism. One of the biggest expenses of the business was the telephone bill. The Czech Republic had a metered charge for local as well as long-distance calls, and the long-distance calling fee at the time was $3.50 a minute. Jeff first used AT&T, then Sprint, then another carrier, but the costs were still quite high.

On a trip back to the United States, Jeff read in a magazine about a "Callback Service for International Calling." As soon as he landed, he called a representative of the company, WorldLink Callback, and asked him to explain the meaning of "Callback Services." The representative explained the process to him in the following way: "You call from Prague to our computer in New York to a specially assigned telephone number, and you hang up before our computer answers. After this, the computer calls you back and offers you a dial tone, and then you dial as if you were in the United States." The representative's explanation was, "International rates in the United States are so much cheaper than the rest of the world, that they give you discounted rates."

Of course, when Jeff tried the process, it didn't work exactly as the representative had said. In Czechoslovakia in 1992, only 1 out of 10 phone calls worked. In addition, 99 percent of telephones in Czechoslovakia had rotary dials. When Jeff and Charles signed up for the service, they needed a touch-tone phone, but they had to bring one with them from the United States. Then they had to get an adaptor to make it work.

One day the CEO of the company that offered callback services called them and asked if they would like the license for the company for Eastern Europe. Jeff immediately responded that they wouldn't be interested because, "Your service doesn't work, and if you want to know why, I will be glad to tell you." Then the CEO responded, "Would you be interested if we got the service working?" Jeff said they might be interested, and the president got an engineer on the phone to listen to their complaints.

When Jeff hung up the phone, he said to Charles, "When people call you peddling a service, it turns you off. I have never liked selling, and I certainly didn't come to Prague to be a salesman." However, Jeff also realized that although he was doing hospitality consulting, his partner was not doing any consulting work and this new venture might bring some money into the company. Also, since they would primarily be speaking with representatives of Western companies, the lack of fluency in the Czech language would not be a hindrance. The growing number of Western companies doing business in the Czech Republic provided an excellent customer base for this service.

As much as Jeff hated the idea of calling people and convincing them that they needed to buy their product, he and Charles reluctantly accepted this licensing and marketing agreement for the callback services in Eastern Europe. WorldLink Callback would be the first company to offer such services in Eastern Europe.

Charles began immediately working on the project in May of 1993, and within four months, he had signed up 60 people. When Charles went back to the United States for two weeks, he asked Jeff if he would follow up with some companies that he had sent information to and see if they were interested in the callback services.

One afternoon from his apartment, Jeff decided to make the calls that Charles had asked him to make. First, he called people who had recently signed up for their service and asked, "How is the service doing?" Although the service from Czech Telecom (the former Czech monopoly) was so bad at the time that it took 10 tries to get 1 call through, the people Jeff called who were using their service said they got their calls through 7 out of 10 times. As one might imagine, they were very pleased with the service. In addition, all of the companies that Charles had sent information to wanted to sign up for the service. All of this happened within 30 minutes, and Jeff was astounded.

After completing the calls, Jeff picked up the English-language newspaper named the *The Prague Post* that gives a synopsis of what is going on in Prague at the time. In the newspaper he saw some ads placed by large multinational companies that were doing business in the Czech Republic. On a whim, Jeff picked some of the companies at random and called them to explain their callback services, and the common reply was, "How fast can you send information and have a meeting with us?" Jeff hurriedly sent the information to the companies, met with them soon afterward and very quickly signed them up for the service.

He was doing so well with the large companies that when Charles returned he suggested he would continue to work with the multinationals and Charles could stay with the smaller companies. Charles concurred with this suggestion. At this juncture of the operations, they decided that it would be appropriate to name the portion of the business dealing with callback services as "BCH TeleCommunications." (See Exhibit 2.)

Competition for BCH

The biggest competitor for BCH TeleCommunications was the state-owned telephone company Czech Telecom. In the former centrally planned economy of Czechoslovakia, the government had a monopoly in all industries. There was no private enterprise. Therefore, unlike the situation in the United States where a Consent Agreement was signed by AT&T in the early 1980s agreeing to break up their company that held a monopoly into a number of smaller regional local calling companies and allowing competition for the long distance calling market, the transition in Czechoslovakia was slow because the legal and economic infrastructure necessary to move to a free market system was slow and cumbersome. Czech Telecom refused to believe that it would be possible for another company to compete with them.

Soon after BCH TeleCommunications began offering callback services, the Czech government and Czech Telecom came to Jeff and Charles and threatened to kick them out of the country. They presented the young men with official documents with the required number of stamps on them and said, "You must leave the country in 60 days." Jeff and Charles consulted with their Czech lawyer who said, "They may make your life more difficult, but you have done nothing wrong." These two relatively naive young Americans soon discovered that competition may come in a thousand different disguises, and some may actually threaten your well being or your life. Jeff mulled over the truth that every entrepreneur must know his or her competition well and understand how to survive in the midst of competition.

Often when Jeff would give information about their company to potential customers, the potential customers would ask, "This is great. Does it break any laws?" Jeff would assure them that it did not, however, when they called Czech Telecom, they would assure them it did. Therefore, some people thought this was an illegal operation.

Jeff became aware later that other countries—including the United States—did not always view this new process as enthusiastically as he did. Often the established operator community in a country publicly and legally took a dim view, claiming in various ways that the services actually constituted a wire fraud. They were especially troubled by revenues they were unable to collect on the use of their assets, and they also suggested that it

EXHIBIT 2
Direct Dial Services

BCH TeleCommunications

DirectDial Services

BCHDirect Dial services are international telephone services that can save up to 42% on your international calls.

There are many added values when using *BCH DirectDial* **Services:**

- Best Rates
- No monthly fees
- Direct dialing to all countries worldwide
- 24 hour unbeatable customer service
- Many different kind of connections to fit the needs of customers
- Detailed call record every month for free
- Easy billing in CZK, USD or by major credit card

Joining *BCH DirectDial* Service is easy. We will need only this information:
- Where the client wishes his billing information to be sent.
- The currency the client wishes to pay with.
- The local numbers to be connected.

This routing creates two legs for each call:
- the first is charged by the local telecom
- the second charged by BCH at tremendous discounts.

BCH DirectDial Service is one of many top-quality services offered by BCH TeleCommunications. Please call us for more information about *DirectDial* and the many other attractive products and services available from Central Europe's leader in discount international telecommunications.

BCH Corporate Business Center * Sokolovska 156 * 180 00 Praha 8 * Czech Republic
Tel. (420 2) 683 1310 * Fax (420 2) 683 5052 * E-mail: bch-tel@ini.cz

circumnavigated their international conventions for settlement. Argentina and several African states had attempted to block the switching techniques that enable callback hardware to capture identification codes and re-route calls.[6]

He was also aware that there was a growing interest—even in the Czech Republic—in substitute products such as e-mail and fax messages. These were both low-cost alternatives to long-distance calling and competitors for callback services. It occurred to him that the telephone companies themselves seemed to have a bright future because they were not tied to the one product for long-distance communications that he was. The very fact that communications in general were rapidly increasing boded well for telephone companies. In 1995, the world spent 60 billion minutes communicating by phone, fax, and data, four times the amount spent just a decade ago.[7]

An issue raised with this type of operation was international comity. International comity is based on the principle of respect. "Comity is implicated where domestic and foreign laws conflict. When a conflict occurs, a country must decide whether to respect the foreign law or to enforce its own domestic law. In making such a decision, the domestic body balances domestic public interests against international considerations. The domestic body is under no obligation to abide by the foreign law; the decision of whether to respect foreign law is entirely discretionary."[8] Jeff reasoned that these potential problems might put a constraint on callback services.

The Company Grows and Takes on More Staff

BCH soon began to represent other telecommunications companies such as Sprint, Direct Net, Axcom, and Dial International (DIT) that did not have representatives in Eastern Europe. They also expanded the operations of BCH TeleCommunications into Poland, Slovakia, and Hungary in July of 1993. Jeff meanwhile expanded his hospitality management consulting into Slovakia and Hungary. The company was doing so well that the Office of the Ministry of Finance identified BCH as one of the top new companies in the country and sought Jeff's advice on ways to help Czech entrepreneurs succeed. (See Exhibit 3.)

Jeff speculated that their company did well not only because of the cheaper telephone services that they offered, but also because of the good technical support they provided their customers. The company hired an engineer just to work on technical problems and help with plans for future expansion of the business. Jeff found it interesting that over 50 percent of their new business came from referrals by satisfied customers.

EXHIBIT 3
Financial
History
of BCH

(Numbers are rounded off to the nearest thousandth)

1992

Revenues from restaurant	-0-
Revenues from consulting	-0-
Total revenues	-0-
Expenses of restaurant	$ 15,000
Profit (loss)	$(15,000)

Note:

Restaurant—There never was any money generated from the restaurant because contract disputes prevented the building from being completed. The owners spent much of this year finding a place to build-out (location, architect, contractor, etc.).

General—In addition, they used most of their time getting themselves established in the business community (networking and getting involved in the expatriate community).

1993

Revenues from consulting	$10,000
Revenues from telecom	50,000
Total revenues	$60,000
Expenses of restaurant	$35,000
Expenses of telecom	12,000
Expenses of consulting	1,000
Profit (loss)	$12,000

Note:

Consulting—Company established a Hospitality & Communications consulting arm of the firm. The primary targets were the hospitality industry and the service industry (real estate, law firms, and grocery stores).

Telecom—At the beginning of this year, the company broke into the telecom market offering discount callback services. BCH was the first to offer such services in the region, and they gained about 100 customers in their first year. They worked out of Jeff's apartment and began a full advertising/marketing campaign.

1994

Revenues from consulting	$ 25,000
Revenues from telecom	105,000
Total revenues	$130,000
Expenses of consulting	$ 3,000
Expenses of telecom	154,000
Profit (loss)	$(27,000)

Note:

Consulting—This part of the business grew well and kept Jeff busy all of the time. The company expanded its activities into Slovakia and Hungary (for specific clients). Much of

(continued)

**EXHIBIT 3
Financial
History
of BCH**—*continued*

this revenue (which was almost pure profit) was supporting and paying many of the company's past bills and financing the marketing efforts of the telecom division.

Telecom—This project continued to grow very rapidly. At the end of the year, the partners decided to work on their own. Instead of making a commission for another firm, BCH would actually buy and sell their own international time from large telecom carriers. In addition, they took on a third partner for additional expansion. He was an expatriate who had lived in Prague for two years. They added four full-time sales staff and moved into a large office complex. They added one post graduate (from graduate school) on a one-year internship to assist with the think-tank process of expanding. They were actively marketing their services in Hungary.

1995

Revenue from consulting	$ 31,000
Revenue from telecom	175,000
Total revenues	$206,000
Expenses of consulting	$ 3,000
Expenses of telecom	217,000
Profit (loss)	$(14,000)

Note:

Consulting—This continued to generate revenue that was used to support the expansion efforts of the telecom division. The partners had decided that it was not necessary to continue to grow this division but to maintain it and use it as a networking effort to further support the telecom division.

Telecom—The company moved to a private office from the office complex where they got more space at a cheaper rental cost. BCH added two more post graduates (from graduate school) who were on one-year internships. They expanded their services portfolio to include an international calling card. This proved to be successful for the next two to three years. The sales team grew by an additional two staff, and then they added two full-time customer service staff. At the end of the year, their third partner was asked to leave the firm, and this added a large financial burden to the bottom line in order to pay his severance costs. The company expanded into Poland and established a full office. One of the partners was stationed in Poland 85 percent of the time. BCH began working with a total of three telecom service providers. These were firms through which they bought and sold telecom time. This allowed BCH to add more services to its portfolio.

1996

Revenues from consulting	$ 17,000
Revenues from telecom	180,000
Revenues from glass/crystal	3,000
Total revenues	$200,000
Expenses of consulting	$ 1,000
Expenses of telecom	39,000
Expenses of glass/crystal	70,000
Profit (loss)	$ 90,000

Note:

This was a year of much change.

Consulting—This division basically was winding down its activities, and the company began to concentrate all of its efforts on the telecom division. This had been very enjoyable for Jeff and a good money maker, but he no longer had enough time for all of its activities.

Telecom—There was much unrest in this division as it continued to grow. All three interns left the firm because they were disgruntled with the overall direction and management of BCH. One of the primary partners—Charles—decided to depart BCH on a permanent basis, and as he did, he removed all of the financial assets of the firm and left the country. This brought on an enormous financial burden to the company operations. At the end of the year, there were only two employees on the payroll. Three additional ones stayed on for four months without pay.

Glass/Crystal—BCH decided to start up a new project of exporting glass and crystal to the USA and Canada.

The company also had an excellent staff of people working with them. One was a young lady named Ivana Svobodova. She had come to work for them in 1994 as a receptionist and within months had worked her way up to sales associate and finally became a director of the company. When Ivana had a free minute, she read everything in the office she could about the operations of the company. When people called the company, Ivana could answer their questions and actually began to sell the company's services over the phone without a meeting. She soon became the person on the staff that Jeff most depended upon to give a realistic assessment of his ideas for the operations in the Czech Republic. She was a native of the country and knew better than he what would work and what would not work there. An added benefit was that Ivana was a native speaker and could assist with Jeff's learning of the Czech language, and she would also constitute a trustworthy translator.

Crisis for Jeff Welker

By January of 1995, Jeff noted that their callback service operations had grown by 150 percent since inception two years ago. He had heard that callback services in general were growing at a rate of 15 percent a month. BCH operations were growing in Poland and Hungary, and Charles wanted to take over the business operations in Poland. However, Charles became increasingly unhappy and frustrated in the business and with his relationship with Jeff, so he left the letter for Jeff telling him he was leaving the business and taking around $150,000 in cash with him. It was now July of 1995, and Jeff felt that the rug had been pulled from underneath him. He normally had a very positive outlook on life, which was reflected in his resume, but this setback seriously discouraged him. (See Exhibit 4.)

With no money in the bank and all of his legal documents gone, Jeff considered filing for bankruptcy. Under the former Socialist state, "bankruptcy" was a word that no one mentioned. Central planning had always provided an easy way out for money-losing enterprises. Under the new government, bankruptcy was beginning to play a role; however, the process was not working well. Usually, for struggling companies, a hint of the possibility of insolvency meant scrambling to hide assets before creditors noticed. The 1991 Bankruptcy Act was based on rules dating back to the Austro-Hungarian Empire. It had already been amended 10 times, and Parliament, bankers, and unions were wrangling over proposed amendments again.[9] The average bankruptcy period in the Czech Republic, from start to finish, was 6 years.[10]

He also had to take a hard look at the future of callback services. Although the offering of these services had been extremely profitable until now, he wondered about the growth of alternative means of communication. He had read that total revenues for callback services in 1994 were $200,000,000; in 1995 $350,000,000; and were projected to grow to $500,000,000 in 1996, $1,000,000,000 in 1997 and to $2,000,000,000 by 1998.[11] A recent article had also suggested a possible saturation of this market. The author had recounted the fact that in 1990 there were only 6 callback operations in North America, and at the present time there were over 200—all offering consumers in dozens of foreign countries cheaper (and even illegal) international phone and fax calls.[12]

In addition, recently the Federal Communications Commission in Washington had taken notice of the disparity in international dialing rates and was considering new pricing rules that would force foreign carriers to lower their rates or face possible punitive measures. They saw competition by the callback services as an additional means of encouraging other nations to comply.[13]

Jeff walked to the Metro station closest to his office and took the train to the Mustek Station and got off. It always cleared his head to stroll from this station at the northern end of Vaclavske namesti (Wenceslas Square) northward along the crooked na Musiku toward Staremestske namisti (Old Town Square). He looked to the left as he passed by the corner of Havelska and Melantricova and saw the wooden stalls with people selling their handmade wooden toys and puppets. As his feet half stumbled along the broken cobblestones on the sidewalk, he looked in the windows of the many little shops along the crooked street selling Bohemian crystal. The smell of klobasy (grilled sausages) and parky (boiled frank-

EXHIBIT 4
Resume of
Jeff Welker

Jeff Welker
Bartakova 34
140 00 Praha 4, Czech Republic
E-mail: bch-tel2@ini.cz

KEY CHARACTERISTICS: Strong leadership and communication skills. More than 7 years working experience in Central/Eastern Europe focusing on sales and marketing in the telecommunications industry.

EXPERIENCE:
9/92 – Present

BCH Enterprises Praha—Prague, Czech Republic
Managing Director (Member of the Board)
Telecommunications Division—Oversee and direct all aspects of marketing, finance, and operations for a cutting-edge firm that offers discount telecommunication services (direct dial, international calling cards, data and frame relay connectivety, and E-commerce). In 1998, generated revenues in excess of 750,000 USD.

EDUCATION:

B.S. Degree from University of Nevada, Las Vegas
May 1985   Major: Hotel Administration
**   Minor: Business Marketing**

A.A. Degree from Glendale Community College
June 1982   Major: Business Administration—
**   Food Management**
Associate Certificate: Food Management—Cooking
**   1 year program**

ADDITIONAL SKILLS: Computer: proficient in on-line/Internet technology, Microsoft Word, Excel, Word Perfect

ACTIVITIES: Active Member in the American Chamber in Commerce, Czech Republic (6 years)

AmCham, Czech Republic—Events Committee Director (2 years)

Foundation Member for TEREZA, Czech Republic

UNLV Mentor Program (1995 to present)

HONORS & AWARDS: TEREZA Environmental Leadership Award (Czech Republic)

UNLV Alumni Achievement Award

Who's Who Among Students in American Colleges (1982–85)

HOBBIES & INTERESTS: Enjoy all sports, traveling and JUST HAVING FUN

furters) cooking at a sidewalk stand filled the air. He heard the strains of Mozart floating from a CD at a music shop nearby, and he thought what a rich cultural town this was and how he would hate to leave it.

He wondered to himself how he could survive and make the business prosper with no money to pay his staff or the creditors that he owed. He also wondered if this would be a good time to move into a related business that would have greater prospects for profitability in the future. Although Czech Telecom was still a monopoly now owned 27 percent by Swiss and Dutch investors, by the year 2000 the monopoly was to be broken up and competition from other companies would be welcomed.

Endnotes

1. Jac, Radomin (1999). "An Overview of the Czech Republic," *Czech Republic Business Guide*, pp. 2–6.
2. Pokorny, Jiri (1994). *The Czech Lands 1918–1997*. Prague, Czech Republic: Prah Press, pp. 41–46.
3. Levitsky, Jacob (1996). *Small Business in Transition Economies*. London: Intermediate Technology Publications, Ltd., pp. XIII–XXV.
4. Wallace, Elizabeth (1996). "Financial Institutional Development—The Case of the Russian Small Business Fund," *Small Business in Transition Economies*. London: Intermediate Technology Publications, Ltd., pp. 76–84.
5. Stacey, Weston, Managing Director of the American Chamber of Commerce in the Czech Republic. Conversation with author April 10, 2000.
6. Liebmann, Lenny (March 1997). "The Siren Song of Callback Services," *International Business*, pp. 37–38.
7. Morton, Peter (October 19, 1996). "Dialing for Dollars: *Callback* Companies Give Consumers Great Long Distance Rates, But They Pluck Revenues from Foreign Phone Systems," *Financial Post*, p. 16.
8. Silber, Seth C. (1996). "The FCC's *Call-Back* Order: Proper Respect for International Comity," *The George Washington Journal of International Law and Economics,* pp. 97–125.
9. "Tunnel Vision," (April 2000). *Business Central Europe*, p. 39.
10. Zivnustkova, Alena (April 24, 2000). "Losing the Bankruptcy Battle," *Prague Business Journal*, p. 1, columns 2–4.
11. McClelland, Stephen (July 1995). "Learning to Love Callback," *Telecommunications*, pp. 40–41.
12. Scheele, Michael J. (March 1995). "You Can't Beat the Price," *Telephony*, pp. 65–70.
13. Shiver, Jube, Jr. (December 13, 1996). "FCC, Phone Firms Take Notice as Callback Industry Expands, *The Los Angeles Times*, p. D-1.

BULLER | SCHULER

Managing Organizations and People

A Resource for Cases in Management, Organizational Behavior, and Human Resource Management

Abstract

This 11-part case follows Chris Johnson, an inventor/entrepreneur who first conceives of a new product while in his early thirties. Chris (1) assesses market demand for the product, (2) determines the market potential for, and patentability of the product, and (3) builds a working prototype, and officially files for U.S. patent protection for the product.

With the patent pending, Chris (4) identifies primary markets and potential demand for the product and (5) approaches several companies about the possibility of their licensing the product. With much positive response from the industry, yet unable to secure commitment from a potential licensor, Chris (6) decides to approach a successful product development/marketing company about helping Chris get his product to market in return for a percentage of future profits. (7) Evan, the company's president, agrees to take on the product and within a few months, approaches Alpha, a major company in one of the three markets Chris has identified.

At this point, the patent is officially awarded. (8) On Chris's behalf, Evan begins to negotiate a licensing contract with Alpha. After a year and a half the contract is signed, but by this point, and despite a huge investment on their part, Alpha's commitment to the product fades. (9) Chris offers to "sell" the product for Alpha. During this time, another company, Beta, approaches Chris with their interest in licensing and selling the product. (10) Chris accepts Beta's offer, but about the time a new contract is to be signed, Beta announces a shift in product focus. Delays ensue as licensing negotiations shift to a new company—a partnership between a Beta subsidiary and a Canadian manufacturing firm. (11) Shortly after a cancelled contract-signing meeting, the Canadian firm declares bankruptcy, the deal is cancelled, and Chris is faced with an important decision. Should he abandon his efforts to license his product or form his own company to manufacture and distribute the product on his own?

Riding the Rollercoaster of Entrepreneurship

I. A Better Mousetrap

Chris Johnson grew up in the automotive industry. Since he was a boy, he worked in all aspects of his father's business, an automotive part manufacturer. After graduating from college with a degree in business and working in a bank for almost a year, he decided to start his own company, an imported automotive parts distribution business. Within three years, annual sales went from $6,000 to over $300,000. While profit margins were healthy (40 percent verses the industry standard of 22 percent), the business was undercapitalized and

■ Suzanne C. de Janasz and Paula S. Daly, James Madison University. Printed with permission.

1

could not support its phenomenal rate of growth. After the demise of his business, Chris went back to work for his father and integrated the remaining inventory and equipment into his father's business.

Chris always had a keen eye for innovation. In his father's business, Chris's idea to computerize manufacturing processes resulted in an 800 percent increase in output. He implemented a just-in-time (JIT) approach to assembly, substantially reducing inventory and related carrying costs, while also improving delivery time for both standard and special orders. Chris also implemented a new packaging system, one commonly used in the prepared foods industry, to resolve complaints about rust forming on their parts. Made out of cast iron, these parts were prone to rust, particularly in high humidity areas in which many customers were located. By sealing parts in plastic instead of wrapping them in paper envelopes, Chris was able to please customers while simultaneously decreasing packing speed and cost by about 80 percent. While he enjoyed innovating and improving his father's business, Chris longed to make it on his own.

Pulling into the driveway of his home one night, Chris fumbled around for his garage door opener transmitter ("clicker"), only to find that the battery had gone dead. After a few minutes of fumbling and muttering, an idea flashed into Chris's head. Why not create a new kind of transmitter that gets integrated into one of many electrical systems in the car? These "clickers," as they're called, have a number of disadvantages and could definitely be improved. Drawbacks of the clicker include: possibly ruined car visors (which can be expensive to replace), dead batteries (at the most inopportune times), theft (thieves can use them to gain entry into your house), and misuse (children playing with them . . . which can be dangerous). Chris went to bed that night thinking he was on to something. . . .

1. Chris sees the opportunity for a new product. What should he do first?

II. To Market, to Market?

Chris mulled his idea over for several weeks before telling anybody. He envisioned a new type of garage door opener transmitter that is mounted under the car's hood and accessed using the car's flash-to-pass (high-beam headlight) feature. He began doing some market research. For starters, he paid close attention to the number of cars he saw that had transmitters clipped to the visor or laying on the seat or console. Encouraged by the preponderance of "clickers," Chris went to the library at a local college of business to gauge the market potential. Data available from government agencies and garage-door manufacturers indicated that there were currently more than 30 million garage door openers in use in private residences in the U.S. alone. The statistics were quite promising.

After sharing his idea with a few close friends and getting a positive reaction, Chris contacted a patent attorney to determine if his product idea was patentable. It was. Bob, the patent attorney, helped Chris find an engineer who could help him finalize the design, and drew up a non-disclosure statement for the engineer to sign. Steve, a mechanical engineer, signed the non-disclosure statement and agreed to provide Chris with an estimate of development costs to create a working prototype of Chris's new product.

1. How thorough was Chris's market research? Where else might he have found relevant information?
2. Was it necessary to apply for patent protection? Why or why not?
3. Do you need to have an attorney file for the patent? Why or why not?
4. What is the purpose of a non-disclosure statement?
5. At this point, does Chris need a business plan? Explain.

III. If You Build It, They Will Come

Within a week, Steve informed Chris that he would develop a working prototype of this new type of "clicker" for $80,000. He said he based his price on market potential! Chris was shocked and outraged, but Steve would not budge on his price. Chris then approached a friend who was knowledgeable about computer hardware to show Chris how to build the basic circuit that was needed. After several attempts, Chris connected this prototype to a spare garage door opener, attached the leads to his car's headlights and tried it. It worked perfectly! He now had a working prototype to patent, and it only cost about $200 to develop.

The working prototype provided Bob, Chris's attorney, with useful information and detail needed for the patent application. After several iterations, and over $5,000 in legal and filing fees, the patent was officially filed. In the interim, Chris hired Allan, an electrical engineer about to be laid off from an aerospace company, to continue refining the device. After Allan signed the non-disclosure agreement, Chris explained how he thought the device's design could be simplified, and therefore cheaper to manufacture. Cost was an issue since Chris knew his product would eventually compete with "traditional" clicker replacement units, which ranged in price from $20 to $40. Allan managed to make it simpler and therefore cheaper to manufacture. Allan charged Chris $800 for his services, but offered Chris the option to not pay him in exchange for a percentage of future profits. (Allan also had some sense of the product's market potential.) The deal was tempting to a cash-strapped Chris, but he decided to pay Allan his fee.

1. Why do you think Chris felt it was necessary to have a working prototype? Could a detailed drawing have sufficed?
2. How should Chris go about establishing a price for his new product?
3. What should Chris do next? Discuss his options at this point.

IV. Decisions, Decisions . . .

With his patent filed and pending and a working prototype in hand, Chris wanted to determine the best way to bring his new "clicker" to the marketplace. One option was to launch the "clicker" business on his own. However, this approach involved obtaining quite a bit of start-up money either through a bank (which came with great personal financial risk should the venture fail) or an investor/venture capitalist (to whom Chris would have to surrender part of product ownership and control). A second option would be to find an existing company to license his product and pay him royalties over the course of the patent, which was to be granted shortly. This route might be the safest, although potentially less profitable, option. After all, now that Chris was married and thinking about having children, he realized that his earlier "bet the house" form of entrepreneurship had to be tempered. He decided to go with the second option.

With the decision to take the licensing route made, Chris thought long and hard about which markets were appropriate for his product and what the demand would be. He identified three primary markets for the product: (1) the mobile electronics market, in which manufacturers (e.g., car stereo, alarm, and radar detector) distributed their products via retail (e.g., Circuit City, Pep Boys) and catalog (e.g., The Sharper Image) outlets; (2) the home improvement/"do-it-yourself" (DIY) market (companies who manufacture products for home improvement stores and discount department stores); and (3) automobile manufacturers, for whom this product could be installed as original equipment (OEM) or at the dealership upon purchase (similar to Lo-Jack®).

1. At this point Chris felt he had two viable options: (1) to manufacture and market the product himself or (2) to find an existing company to license his product. How might Chris evaluate these two alternatives? Discuss which option you would choose.
2. What are other potential markets for Chris's invention that he has not considered?

V. Peddling His Wares

Of the three potential markets identified, Chris selected the consumer electronics market, in particular the mobile electronics market, as his primary target market. This made sense to him for a number of reasons. Even though it might be possible to create higher visibility in the do-it-yourself/home improvement market, there might be many people who feel uncomfortable about installing an electrical device under their car's hood. By licensing his product to manufacturers who sell to mobile electronics retailers that have installation available (e.g., Circuit City), Chris could improve the odds of consumers correctly installing the device while also providing them the option to purchase and install it on their own. Chris was now faced with the decision of which manufacturers to target.

Chris researched several electronics-oriented magazines; some of these targeted end users, others focused on resellers and distributors. Chris approached two firms that manufactured radar detectors about the possibility of licensing his product. He was careful to have each sign non-disclosure agreements. One of these firms said they were interested but "didn't know how to market" his product. The other firm said they would not produce or sell anything that wasn't designed in house. Chris was becoming impatient with the process. . . .

1. Do you think Chris selected the market with the most sales potential for his invention? Why or why not?
2. Despite the protection that the non-disclosure agreement offered, were there any other safeguards Chris could have implemented to ensure that companies selected as potential licensors would not "steal" his idea?
3. What should Chris's next step be?

VI. If at First You Don't Succeed . . .

Several weeks passed. The patent was still pending. Chris was very anxious to get his product to market, especially given his growing mound of debt. At this point, Chris had sunk about $10,000 into legal and design costs for his product. Everyone that knew about Chris's idea thought it was "hot" and that Chris would "make millions." At the moment, however, no one was stepping up to the plate to make it happen.

One day, while reading an industry magazine, Chris learned about a guy named Evan who started a company to help inventors get their products to market. Despite his degree in marketing and experience in the marketing field, it had taken Evan nearly five years to get his invention to market. Chris figured that if someone with a marketing background had this much difficulty, many others were likely to face an even tougher battle, so he decided to enlist Evan's help. Chris contacted Evan, and within a few weeks, they met and talked about working together. Evan explained that numerous inventors had approached him after that article appeared. However, he turned down most of these inventors, focusing only on those projects with a high probability of success. Evan told Chris he thought Chris's product had the potential to be very successful. If Evan agreed to work with Chris, he would do so without requiring any fees in advance. Instead, Evan would be given an agreed-upon percentage of future profits in return for his investment of time, money, and know-how.

1. Evaluate Chris's decision to take on a marketing partner.
2. What kind of partnership arrangement would you offer Evan? Explain.

VII. 50 Percent of Millions Is Better Than 100 Percent of Nothing

Chris struck a deal with Evan. After much deliberation, he accepted Evan's 50 percent fee (50 percent of future profits for the life of the patent), based on his belief that 50 percent of potential millions is worth a lot more than 100 percent of nothing. If this guy were as good as he appeared, and could get Chris's product into the marketplace more quickly and successfully than Chris could without a marketing partner, it would be worth it. In addition, Evan would take whatever steps necessary to get the product to market without any payment for his services. He got paid when he achieved results.

Within a month, Evan told Chris that he was thinking of approaching Alpha, a major manufacturer in the home improvement/do-it-yourself (DIY) market, who happened to be in the same town as Evan. With nothing to lose, Chris agreed, even though Alpha was not in the primary market Chris had originally targeted. In fact, Alpha was in the smallest of the three market segments Chris had previously identified. Upon meeting with Evan, Alpha executives were extremely enthusiastic about, and interested in, a licensing deal. Apparently, garage door openers had remained basically unchanged for the 50+ years they've existed. The executives with whom Evan dealt saw Chris's product as a major innovation—one that could inject new life into a stagnant market. Before signing a licensing agreement, however, Alpha wanted to "test" the patent's strength (could other firms develop legal "knockoffs"?) as well as the market viability. Alpha engineers worked on the first concern while the company's marketing team worked on developing a survey to determine the percentage of the current Alpha garage door opener customers who would switch to the new product and at what price.

1. Evaluate the agreement Chris made with Evan. In what ways would an agreement you negotiated have been similar to/different from Chris's?
2. While Alpha was testing the viability of a licensing deal with Chris, what, if anything, could Evan and Chris have been doing to speed the process?

3.   What factors should be considered when negotiating a licensing agreement of this type?

VIII. Pour the Champagne!

Over the months that followed, Alpha found the patent—which had been officially awarded by the U.S. Patent Office by this time—to be rock solid. In addition, the market research firm they had hired to conduct surveys of current customers found that 30 to 40 percent of those questioned would switch to Chris's product over the current type of garage door opener transmitter. (They were hoping for at least 5 to 10 percent.) At that point, with over 30 million garage door openers currently in use, they estimated the potential for immediate sales was 9 to 12 million units. In addition, another 2.5 million garage door openers were sold each year, either as replacement units or for new construction. Alpha, currently a close second in market share to the industry leader (together, they had about 80 percent of the market), estimated they would easily sell 600,000 units per year. That was without any sales effort, and at a retail price of $50.

Finally, about a year and a half after the initial contact with Alpha was made, the contract was signed. Chris received a substantial initial bonus from Alpha (which was shared with Evan), and was to receive quarterly royalties for the number of units sold. Chris and his wife celebrated, assuming their ship had finally come in. Little did they know that recent turnover in the sales and marketing personnel at Alpha meant that Mark, the sales/marketing manager now in charge of the product, was actually the third person to be assigned to Chris's product. His commitment to the product turned out to be marginal. His lack of interest in and enthusiasm for the product proved to be disastrous. If customers called for the product, he would sell it to them, but he was not going to exert any effort to "market" the product. Later, Mark bluntly informed Chris that he was nonplussed about the product when he first heard about it, and his input was not sought during the time Alpha evaluated and agreed to license the product. At this point, Alpha's investment in the product was at least $2 million, and potential sales from the product could easily double the annual revenues of this division of the company. In addition, the product had won numerous awards from consumer and industry organizations. Those who knew about the product wanted it; unfortunately, many didn't know it existed.

1.   At this point, Chris feels certain that the product is finally on its way to market. How secure should Chris feel? Explain.
2.   If you were the brand or product manager for Chris's product, what would comprise your marketing plan?
3.   If you were Chris, how would you overcome the sales manager's resistance to selling the product?

IX. Rather "Fight" Than Switch?

Chris was frustrated with Alpha. At the same time, he wondered whether the grass would be greener with another firm. Ending the licensing agreement with Alpha and starting the process from scratch with another company could cost him a year or more. What Chris wanted most was to get the product to market. Then he had an idea. If "selling" the product was the issue, what if he could set up a company to market and distribute his product while Alpha continued to manufacture it? When Mark finally returned Chris's calls, he seemed responsive to the idea. Mark gave Chris sales literature and lists of various retailers, and led Chris to believe his idea would work, with the increased sales benefiting both Alpha and Chris. Chris set up a company and started making contacts and sent sell sheets designed by Alpha to manufacturers' representatives ("reps") and "repping" agencies in the mobile electronics industry. The response was tremendous. Many of the reps Chris contacted even offered to cut their commissions (averaging 6 percent) to "get" the product. Chris made arrangements to exhibit his product at the annual Mobile Electronics Show. Just before the show, he got a call from Beta, a major player in the mobile electronics market (e.g., car alarms, radar detectors). Apparently, one of the reps he contacted told Beta of the new product, and Beta was very interested in licensing Chris's device. Chris was particularly excited since Beta was a well-known company in the primary market he had originally targeted. Two months before the show, Chris flew cross country to meet with Beta. All parties were ready to begin negotiating a licensing contract. To do this,

Chris needed to modify his agreement with Alpha and make it non-exclusive. Chris didn't think that Alpha would resist doing this, but knew they would require that he give up the minimum annual royalty he was currently receiving from the company.

Chris was overwhelmed by the response to his product at the Mobile Electronics Show. People were ready to place orders right then and there. It seemed possible to continue marketing Alpha's product to the growing list of interested reps while arranging a second, non-exclusive licensing deal with Beta, assuming his contract with Alpha could be modified. Chris called his contact at Alpha and was surprised to learn that there had been yet another turnover in the sales manager position. The new sales manager was a woman who knew nothing about Chris's arrangement to sell his product for Alpha; she only knew that the project had been shelved. Chris was furious, but grateful that he still had Beta.

1.   How might Chris's plan to sell his product for Alpha change the current situation?
2.   How should Chris respond to Beta's overtures?

X. To Market in 90 Days?

Chris dropped the idea of selling his product for Alpha and focused entirely on negotiating an agreement with Beta. Beta sold Chris on the idea of working with them because, unlike Alpha, Beta saw itself as a young, quick-moving, and "hungry" company. They had recently been bought by a venture capital firm and were looking to substantially increase their growth and revenues. Beta "promised" they could get his product into the market within 90 days. Based on Beta's estimates, the product would probably be introduced in time for the lucrative Father's Day "sales event," and would certainly make it in time for the even more lucrative Christmas season.

As negotiations with Beta continued, licensing contracts were sent back and forth. While most of the contract terms seemed standard, Chris scrutinized every detail. At this point, Chris realized that he hadn't heard from Evan in almost a year. The efforts Evan promised when he agreed to work with Chris seemed to cease once he completed negotiating the licensing contract with Alpha. Once the money started trickling in, communication with Evan was inconsistent and infrequent. According to the terms of Chris's partnership agreement with Evan, Evan would not receive any part of monies gained from a licensing agreement with a new firm.

Chris was expecting the finalized contract from Beta any day. Just as he was thinking things were going very well, Chris was told that Beta's focus had shifted (the bad news), and that his product would be manufactured in Canada by a partnership between a Beta subsidiary and a manufacturer in Canada (the good news). This change involved yet another delay in getting the product to market since this Canadian firm had yet to be brought into the licensing agreement.

1.   Evaluate Beta's promise to get Chris's product to market within 90 days.
2.   How should Chris have responded when Beta initially expressed interest in his product?

XI. Yet Another Curve Ball

Months had passed. Finally, it appeared as if an agreement was reached on all sides represented in the licensing arrangement. The key players in the Beta/Canadian firm partnership invited Chris to visit them at a convention they were attending in order to sign the contract and begin working together. At last! Chris finally saw the light at the end of a long tunnel. He drove four hours to the convention, only to find that the CEO of the Canadian firm was unable to make it to the meeting. Chris was told that the CEO was in his hotel room elevating his foot, which he had injured the previous day. Chris offered to go the Canadian CEO's hotel room to sign the contract, but was assured and reassured that all was ready to go, and that the firm would overnight the signed documents for Chris's signature as soon as they returned from the convention.

It had been a week and the documents still had not arrived. Chris called and was told that everything was fine, reps were in place, and things were moving ahead. More weeks passed. This time Chris was told that there were still a few points in the contract that needed to be ironed out. Chris was getting suspicious, but at the same time, he felt powerless in the process. Several more weeks passed, and still no contract. Months after the convention, Chris was informed that the Canadian firm had filed for bankruptcy, causing Beta to lose over a million dollars in sunk costs and effectively ending the licensing arrangement. In short, the deal was off. At that point Chris had had enough. He felt that he had to decide among four options: (1) give up on the patent idea and get a "real" job, (2) sell the patent, (3) find another company to license his patent and manufacture his product, or (4) raise the necessary capital to start his own business to manufacture and distribute his product.

1. Evaluate the strengths and weaknesses of the four options presented. Which of these options would you suggest and why? Is there another alternative that Chris has not considered? Explain.

Module 3

Organizational Structure and Design

Cases Outline

BULLER | SCHULER

Managing Organizations and People

A Resource for Cases in Management, Organizational Behavior, and Human Resource Management

Abstract

The Plaza Inn is a small, luxury, French-styled "boutique" hotel with two restaurants, located near two office and headquarter areas in one of the nicer suburbs of Kansas City. After briefly describing the origins, ownership, and recent history of the hotel, the case focuses on the front office/reservations department of the business. At the present time, the performance of the front desk is poorly rated by customers and the hotel's association with a French chain is jeopardized. The several recent cost reduction efforts in the department, for example, expanding the front desk position and cutting department management, as well as staff efforts to accommodate these changes are described in some detail. At the end of the case, the general manager is faced with what to do to save the chain affiliation and improve the quality of service in the front desk area.

The Plaza Inn

David Bart, General Manager of the Plaza Inn, had just finished reading a letter from Jean Dumas, President of the prestigious Relais & Chateaux, a French hotel association of which the Plaza Inn was a member. In the formal and polite tone of the French language, the president stated that the last inspection had determined that the service levels of the Plaza Inn did not measure up to the Relais & Chateaux standards. Moreover, the letter noted that the Front Desk and Reservations, two critical guest contact departments, received the worst ratings among all of the Relais & Chateaux member properties. The letter concluded that unless the management of the Plaza Inn could submit a plan for guest service improvement and pass the next inspection scheduled in six months, the Relais & Chateaux would "regrettably be forced to withhold the Plaza Inn's membership."

Background

Located within walking distance of the Country Club Plaza and the Crown Center districts of Kansas City, the Plaza Inn is a 50-room hotel modeled after the boutique hotels of Europe. The Inn's intimate atmosphere and unobtrusive service attract business and leisure travelers alike.

Built in the 1920s in the classic Victorian style and meticulously renovated in 1985, the Inn occupies a place on the National Register of Historic Places. Guest rooms are decorated in the best country manner with antique furnishings and oriental rugs discretely coupled with the most modern leisure and business amenities. Luxurious terry cloth robes and marbled baths, for examples, awaited the weary guest. The Plaza Inn also boasts two gourmet restaurants: the romantic, nationally acclaimed St. Jacques with an award winning wine list, and the more casual Andre's bar and bistro. In addition to its overnight guests, the restaurants have an established local clientele.

Nostalgia prompted Andre Bertrand and Tim Boyle, two successful Kansas City entrepreneurs and real estate developers, to purchase the Plaza Inn in 1983. They entered into a partnership with Antoine Fluri, a Swiss hotelier who soon assumed the position of the Inn's general manager. In addition to the three general partners the Inn is owned by approximately 20 limited partners.

"One of the Ten Best New Inns"

Under the charismatic direction of Antoine Fluri, the Inn quickly established a national reputation. In 1987, *Travel* magazine voted the Plaza Inn among the "ten best new inns." A loyal clientele included such famous people as former French President Valery Giscard D'Estaing, Senator Danforth, and Susan Sontag, to name a few. Antoine Fluri also negotiated the Inn's membership in the prestigious, world-renowned Relais & Chateaux association. The existing hotels in the immediate area: a Marriott, a Holiday Inn, and a Hilton gave the Plaza Inn virtually no competition for the upscale traveler.

Despite the success of the Inn, in early 1989 Antoine Fluri sold his share to the remaining two partners and left the Inn citing, "irreconcilable differences" as the reason. A year later, he opened his own restaurant in the Country Club Plaza District.

To continue to promote the European image of the Inn, the owners hired a French couple from Normandy, Marc and Nicole Duval, to replace Antoine Fluri. However, the Duvals soon proved to lack knowledge about European hospitality practices as well as management expertise. They abused their position and power, and within a short time succeeded in alienating many of the Inn's clientele and most of its staff. Under their management, the Inn rapidly incurred heavy financial losses. Alarmed by the practices of the Duvals, the owners looked for new management for the Inn. In December 1989, David Bart was hired as the new general manager. A native of Missouri, he had a solid hotel management background in the middle west, most recently including several years as controller at the headquarters of a large chain hotel.

As David Bart assumed the direction of the Inn in early 1990, he faced several challenges, including steadily declining hotel occupancy and revenues. Many of the regular clientele complained that the Inn had not been the same since Antoine Fluri left. Moreover, contrary to optimistic expectations, the Inn was also losing business to a 300-room, upscale Ritz-Carlton hotel which had just opened a few blocks down the street, and was offering introductory room rates as low as $75. Finally, toward the end of 1990 demand also declined as a national recession began to set in.

Given the poor performance of the hotel, David Bart immediately proceeded to cut costs, which included the elimination of several staff positions. In the Food and Beverage Department (F&B), two of the three restaurant managers were eliminated. St. Jacques and Andre's were to be run by the F&B director with the assistance of only one restaurant manager. In the Rooms Department, Bart eliminated the position of PBX operator, and transferred the responsibility of answering the phone directly to the front desk. Finally, the front office manager position was eliminated, and the front desk staff came under the supervision of the sales manager. Thus, the Inn began to operate with a lean management and staff group. All operating departments, with the exception of F&B, were headed by one person and with no administrative support. Even Bart himself did not retain a secretary.

The Front Desk

The end of David Bart's first year at the Plaza Inn was marked by the outbreak of the Gulf War. During the first quarter of 1990, occupancy hit an all time low of just 40%. However, business finally began to pick up in April. This increase in demand was especially hard for the front desk. The reception area, consisting of an elegant antique concierge-type desk, was too small to be staffed by more than one person at a time. Consequently, only one front desk receptionist was scheduled per shift. With no PBX operator and no secretarial staff, this meant that the front desk receptionist was responsible for not only providing guest service, but also for answering the telephone, taking messages for the management staff, and booking room and restaurant reservations. Moreover, the sales office was not connected to the computerized Property Management System (PMS), and consequently the sales and catering managers relied on the front desk to check availability and block and update group reservations. Similarly, the housekeeping department was not computerized, and the front desk was charged with the preparation of housekeeping room assignments each morning and evening as well as with the tracking and updating of room status in the PMS. Bart believed that the front desk should perform a central function in the operation of the Inn. Rather than computerize the housekeeping, sales and catering departments, and train the managers to utilize the PMS, Bart preferred the front desk to oversee those activities. This, he believed, allowed for greater consistency and control.

With only one person scheduled per shift, the front desk receptionist had to juggle the telephone, coordinate department activities, and take care of guest needs in the personalized manner that was the trademark of the Inn. On busy days, guests checking in or out were rudely interrupted by the ringing telephone, or alternatively, callers were put on hold for lengthy periods of time while the front desk receptionist helped a guest.

The inability to efficiently expedite phone calls and respond to guest needs became worrisome not only from a guest service perspective, but also from a potential revenue loss standpoint. Room reservation calls usually hung up if they remained on hold for more than two minutes. Moreover, under the pressure to answer the phone and help a guest at the same time, the front desk receptionists frequently underquoted rates, mixed up arrival dates and booked rooms on sold out nights. Cancellation requests were not handled correctly with the consequence that some guests were billed for reservations that they had canceled. One of the front desk receptionists commented: "It's extremely difficult to make a room sale when I constantly have to ask the customer to hold because I'm trying to pick up the other five lines that are ringing. What is more important: making a $130 room reservation for two nights or taking a message for one of the managers?"

Reinstatement of the Front Office Manager

Lost revenues and customer complaints about front office service finally convinced David Bart of the need to reinstate the position of the front office manager. A manager was needed to monitor the rooms inventory and ensure that no revenues were lost due to uncanceled reservations and unreleased room blocks, to coordinate activities between the departments, and to train the front office staff consisting of front desk receptionists and valets/bellhops. However, to minimize costs, Bart decided that the front office manager would also work three shifts per week at the front desk as a receptionist.

In February 1991, Bart offered the position of front office manager to Ms. Claire Ruiz, who had been working as a front desk receptionist since 1989. The promotion worked out well. Claire knew the job thoroughly and was genuinely interested in hotel management. She was able to effectively combine her managerial duties with the three shifts at the front desk.

Cooperation between the departments soon increased significantly. Claire believed that the Inn would never be able to afford the specialized and extensive front office staff of a larger hotel, and thus its ability to deliver high-quality customer service depended on mutual cooperation between all employees. Consequently, when things got busy, she had the front desk ask other departments for support. For example, if the switchboard was busy, reservation calls were transferred from the front desk to accounting or sales. Even the general manager himself got called on to help the valets park cars or assist guests with luggage although he clearly preferred being in his office going over reports and records.

The New PBX Position

While other managers were willing to help out, they also had their own duties to tend to and weren't always available. Since occupancy remained strong, Claire convinced the general manager to reinstate the PBX position. However, Claire's idea was to have the PBX operator function as an extension of the front desk. A PBX station was set up in an unoccupied reception area in the lobby, and with the exception of checking guests in and out, the PBX operator performed the same duties and was compensated at the same rate of pay as the front desk receptionist. This additional support allowed the front desk to provide more efficient and gracious service to the Inn's guests, and improve their room-selling ability. Despite the continuing recession and competition from the Ritz-Carlton, 1991 proved to be a year of record high occupancy and revenues for the Plaza Inn.

In August 1992, Claire left the Plaza Inn to pursue a graduate degree in hotel management at an eastern university. David Bart believed that the situation at the front desk was under control, and did not plan to fill the vacant position of front office manager. The front desk staff once again would be indirectly supervised by the sales manager.

It wasn't long, however, before the same problems Claire had worked so hard to resolve cropped up again. With the start of the school year, the front desk staff were no longer as flexible in terms of scheduling, and the PBX operator was called on to fill vacant shifts at the front desk. More often than not, there was only one person scheduled to work in the front office, and guest service began to suffer again. One day, for example, David Bart discovered that a recently hired front desk receptionist frequently told clients that the hotel was sold out because she was too busy to take a reservation.

Bart believed that there was no one at the front desk capable of being promoted to the position of front office manager. However, he also thought that it would be difficult to hire an outsider who would be willing to work the three shifts at the front desk for the modest salary he was willing to offer (most managers at the Plaza Inn were paid $5,000 to $7,000 less than other Kansas City hotels). Thus, Bart was relieved to learn that Laura Dunbar, who had previously worked at the Plaza Inn as a front desk receptionist, was interested in the position.

A New Front Office Manager

In addition to her experience at the Plaza Inn, Laura had worked as a concierge at one of the convention hotels in downtown Kansas City for several years. She had left the Plaza Inn for a secretarial position that offered more pay than the front desk position at the Inn. However, she missed the excitement and pace of the hospitality industry, and accepted the front office manager position in December 1992 with enthusiasm.

Despite her extensive connections with other Kansas City hotels, as well as the Kansas City Concierge Association, Laura soon found that one of her biggest challenges was the hiring and retaining of the front desk staff. The difficulty of hiring qualified employees forced Laura to work more than three shifts at the front desk. This left her with little time for planning and managing the front office operation. Short-staffed, she sometimes found herself working as much as 30 days in a row without a day off. In addition, the PBX position had not been filled on a regular basis for several months. Laura noticed that the front desk receptionists were not very attentive to the guests and were unable to meet guest expectations of a personalized, concierge-type service. Guest comment cards frequently included negative observations regarding front desk service; in fact, one guest commented that it seemed to him that the front desk receptionists "Were responsible for doing everything with the exception of bartending and bussing the tables in the restaurants."

Laura believed that David Bart was reluctant to hire a full-time PBX operator due to financial constraints. She also felt pressured to meet the front office payroll budget, which had been prepared by Bart and which she felt had been grossly underestimated. In a bi-monthly management staff meeting, Laura suggested to the F&B director that perhaps the restaurant should assume responsibility for managing their own reservations and inquiries, so as to free up the front desk staff to improve guest service and sell more rooms. However, the F&B director was quick to point out that the evening restaurant manager was called on to assist with rooms-related issues on a daily basis, and replaced the evening front desk receptionist so that she could take a break. The restaurants, he asserted, could not afford to create a position just to take reservations and answer inquiries.

Laura felt especially pressured with managing the front desk operation on the weekends. During the week she felt she could call on the other managers for help, whether it was to park a car or take a reservation. On the weekends, however, the only manager on duty was the restaurant manager, and he was often too busy with the restaurant to help with rooms issues. The Manager on Duty (MOD) program (in which all department managers rotated in being at the Inn on call and in charge Friday and Saturday nights) that had been established the prior spring at the initiation of Bart, had been a tremendous help; however, it had been canceled when the Inn had hit the slow summer period. David Bart was not in on the weekends, and Laura felt he somehow forgot that the hotel existed on weekends, not to mention that it usually ran at full occupancy.

By mid-fall, Bart agreed with Laura that there was a definite need to reinstate the MOD program, as well as the PBX position. However, Bart thought that Laura herself had reduced her role of front office manager to that of a front desk receptionist. She seemed to him to surround herself with employees who were either not flexible or not qualified enough, and thus was left to fill a lot of shifts at the front desk herself. This didn't leave her with any time to oversee the operation of the front desk, and to ensure everything was in order. She still hadn't even finished writing up job descriptions for the Inn which he had told her to do two months ago. Bart wondered if the problems at the Front Desk stemmed from Laura's rather shy personality, or perhaps from her lack of management expertise. It appeared that she was unable to articulate her needs to him and other managers. Perhaps he needed to give her more direction, however, this was contradictory to his belief that each manager should assume the responsibility of defining his or her own role consistent with the objectives of the Inn. The weakness he saw in the front office manager was of growing concern to David Bart. Clearly, it was a key position in the operation of the Inn, and required a highly competent, proactive individual.

As he thought back to the ultimatum he had received from the president of Relais & Chateaux, the general manager wondered what he should do. Perhaps he should look for an experienced manager to head the front office, even if it meant paying a much higher salary. Perhaps he just needed to shake Laura up. Perhaps the situation would just straighten itself out. David Bart reached for a copy of the Inn's organization chart (Figure 1), perhaps a major structural change was needed. Perhaps. . . .

**FIGURE 1
Organizational
Chart, The Plaza
Inn—1993**

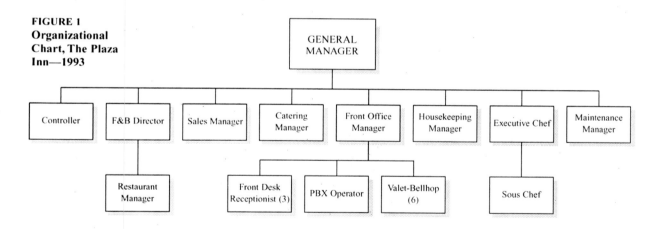

BULLER | SCHULER

Managing Organizations and People

A Resource for Cases in Management, Organizational Behavior, and Human Resource Management

Abstract

Dowling Flexible Metals is an integrative business case that does not contain marketing information or financial data. It does allow an excellent opportunity for students to understand the integrative nature of a seemingly simple business case without getting paranoid over the analysis of financial data. It is a good introductory case demonstrating how an organization must develop internally as sales grow. Implications of sales growth for strategy and changes for internal structure are emphasized. This case also gives the instructor an opportunity to provide the class with a brief synopsis of a capital goods market and direct the students' attention to critical competitive aspects of the industry. In addition, DFM provides for a discussion of more "micro" organizational issues of what different types of people look for in their jobs and how it is possible to fit each group's needs together so that the meeting of those needs maximizes the accomplishment of organizational goals. It also emphasizes the need to change organizational structure to fit strategy.

Dowling Flexible Metals

Background

In 1960, Bill Dowling, a "machine-tool set-up-man" for a large auto firm, became so frustrated with his job that he quit to form his own business. The manufacturing operation consisted of a few general purpose metal working machines that were set up in Dowling's garage. Space was such a constraint that it controlled the work process. For example, if the cutting press was to be used with long stock, the milling machines would have to be pushed back against the wall and remain idle. Production always increased on rain-free, summer days since the garage doors could be opened and a couple of machines moved out onto the drive. Besides Dowling, who acted as salesman, accountant, engineer, president, manufacturing representative, and working foreman, members of the original organization were Eve Sullivan, who began as a part-time secretary and payroll clerk; and Wally Denton, who left the auto firm with Bill. The workforce was composed of part-time "moonlighters," full-time machinists for other firms, who were attracted by the job autonomy which provided experience in setting up jobs and job processes, where a high degree of ingenuity was required.

The first years were touch and go with profits being erratic. Gradually the firm began to gain a reputation for being ingenious at solving unique problems and for producing a quality product on, or before, deadlines. The "product" consisted of fabricating dies for making minor component metal parts for automobiles and a specified quantity of the parts. Having realized that the firm was too dependent on the auto industry and that sudden fluctuations in auto sales could have a drastic effect on the firm's survival, Dowling began marketing their services toward manufacturing firms not connected with the auto industry. Bids were submitted for work that involved legs for vending machines, metal trim for large appliances, clamps and latches for metal windows, and display racks for small power hand tools.

As Dowling Flexible Metals became more diversified, the need for expansion forced the company to borrow building funds from the local bank, which enabled construction of a small factory on the edge of town. As new markets and products created a need for increasingly more versatile equipment and a larger workforce, the plant has since expanded twice until it is now three times its original size.

In 1980, Dowling Flexible Metals hardly resembles the garage operation of the formative years. The firm now employs approximately 30 full-time journeymen and apprentice machinists, a staff of 4 engineers that were hired about three years ago, and a full-time office secretary subordinate to Eve Sullivan, the Office Manager. (See Exhibit 2.) Their rapid growth has created problems that in 1980 have not been resolved. Bill Dowling, realizing his firm is suffering from growing pains, has asked you to "take a look at the operation and make recommendations as to how things could be run better." You begin the consulting project by interviewing Dowling, other key people in the firm, and workers out in the shop who seem willing to express their opinions about the firm.

Bill Dowling, Owner-President

"We sure have come a long way from that first set-up in my garage. On a nice day we would get everything all spread out in the drive and then it would start pouring cats and dogs—so we would have to move back inside. It was just like a one-ring circus. Now it seems like a three-ring circus. You would think that with all that talent we have here and all the experience, things would run smoother. Instead, it seems I am putting in more time than ever and accomplishing a whole lot less in a day's time.

"It's not like the old days. Everything has gotten so complicated and precise in design. When you go to a customer to discuss a job you have to talk to six kids right out of engineering school. Every one of them has a calculator—they don't even carry slide rules anymore—and all they can talk is fancy formulas and how we should do our job. It just seems I spend more time with customers and less time around the shop than I used to. That's why I hired the engineering staff—to interpret specifications, solve engineering problems, and draw blueprints. It still seems all the problems are solved out on the shop floor by guys like Walt and Tom, just like always. Gene and the other engineers are necessary, but they don't seem to be working as smoothly with the guys on the floor as they should.

"One of the things I would like to see us do in the future is to diversify even more. Now that we have the capability, I am starting to bid jobs that require the computerized milling machine process tape. This involves devising a work process for milling a part on a machine and then making a computer process tape of it. We can then sell copies of the tape just like we do dies and parts. These tapes allow less skilled operators to operate complicated milling machines without the long apprenticeship of a tradesman. All they have to do is press buttons and follow the machine's instructions for changing the milling tools. Demand is increasing for the computerized process tapes.

"I would like to see the firm get into things like working with combinations of bonded materials such as plastics, fiberglass, and metals. I am also starting to bid jobs involving the machining of plastics and other materials beside metals."

Wally Denton, Shop Foreman, First Shift

"Life just doesn't seem to be as simple as when we first started in Bill's garage. In those days he would bring a job back and we would all gather 'round and decide how we were going to set it up and who would do it. If one of the 'moonlighters' was to get the job either Bill or I would lay the job out for him when he came in that afternoon. Now, the customers' ideas get processed through the engineers and we, out here in the shop, have to guess just exactly what the customer had in mind.

"What some people around here don't understand is that I am a partner in this business. I've stayed out here in the shop because this is where I like it and it's where I feel most useful. When Bill isn't here, I'm always around to put out fires. Between Eve, Gene, and myself we usually make the right decision.

"With all this diversification and Bill spending a lot of time with customers, I think we need to get somebody else out there to share the load."

Thomas McNull, Shop Foreman, Second Shift

"In general, I agree with Wally that things aren't as simple as they used to be, but I think, given the amount of jobs we are handling at any one time, we run the shop pretty smoothly. When the guys bring problems to me that require major job changes, I get Wally's approval before making the changes. We haven't had any difficulty in that area.

"Where we run into problems is with the engineers. They get the job when Bill brings it back. They decide how the part should be made and by what process, which in turn pretty much restricts what type of dies we have to make. Therein lies the bind. Oftentimes we run into a snag following the engineers' instructions. If it's after five o'clock, the engineers have left for the day. We, on the second shift, either have to let the job sit until the next morning or solve the problem ourselves. This not only creates bad feelings between the shop personnel and the engineers, but it makes extra work for the engineers because they have to draw up new plans.

"I often think we have the whole process backwards around here. What we should be doing is giving the job to the journeymen—after all, these guys have a lot of experience and know-how—then give the finished product to the engineers to draw up. I'll give you an example. Last year we got a job from a vending machine manufacturer. The job consisted of fabricating five sets of dies for making those stubby little legs for vending machines, plus five hundred of the finished legs. Well, the engineers figured the job all out, drew up the plans, and sent it out to us. We made the first die to specs, but when we tried to punch out the leg on the press, the metal tore. We took the problem back to the engineers, and after the preliminary accusations of who was responsible for the screw up, they changed the raw material specifications. We waited two weeks for delivery of the new steel, then tried again. The metal still tore. Finally, after two months of hassle, Charlie Oakes and I worked on the die for two days and finally came up with a solution. The problem was that the shoulders of the die were too steep for forming the leg in just one punch. We had to use two punches (see Exhibit 1). The problem was the production process, not the raw materials. We spent four months on that job and ran over our deadline. Things like that shouldn't happen."

Charlie Oakes, Journeyman Apprentice

"Really, I hate to say anything against this place because it is a pretty good place to work. The pay and benefits are pretty good and because it is a small shop our hours can be somewhat flexible. If you have a doctor's appointment you can either come in late or stay until you get your time in or punch out and come back. You can work as much overtime as you want to.

EXHIBIT 1

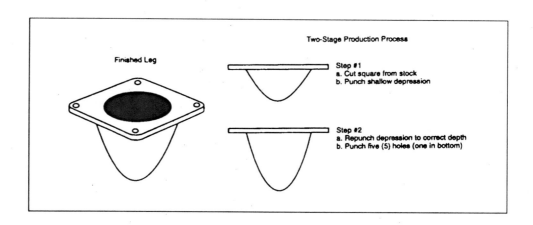

"The thing I'm kind of disappointed about is that I thought the work would be more challenging. I'm just an apprentice, but I've only got a year to go in my program before I can get my journeyman's card, and I think I should be handling more jobs on my own. That's why I came to work here. My Dad was one of the original 'moonlighters' here. He told me about how interesting it was when he was here. I guess I just expected the same thing."

Gene Jenkins, Chief Engineer

"I imagine the guys out in the shop already have told you about 'The Great Vending Machine Fiasco.' They'll never let us forget that. However, it does point out the need for better coordination around here. The engineers were hired as engineers, not as draftsmen, which is just about all we do. I'm not saying we should have the final say on how the job is designed, because there is a lot of practical experience out in that shop; but just as we haven't their expertise neither do they have ours. There is a need for both, the technical skill of the engineers and the practical experience of the shop.

"One thing that would really help is more information from Bill. I realize Bill is spread pretty thin but there are a lot of times he comes back with a job, briefs us, and we still have to call the customer about details because Bill hasn't been specific enough or asked the right questions of the customer. Engineers communicate best with other engineers. Having an engineering function gives us a competitive advantage over our competition. In my opinion, operating as we do now, we are not maximizing that advantage.

"When the plans leave here we have no idea what happens to those plans once they are out in the shop. The next thing we know, we get a die or set of dies back that doesn't even resemble the plans we sent out in the shop. We then have to draw up new plans to fit the dies. Believe me, it is not only discouraging, but it really makes you wonder what your job is around here. It's embarrassing when a customer calls to check on the status of a job and I have to run out in the shop, look up the guy handling the job, and get his best estimate of how the job is going."

Eve Sullivan, Office Manager

"One thing is for sure, life is far from dull around here. It seems Bill is either dragging in a bunch of plans or racing off with the truck to deliver a job to a customer.

"Really, Wally and I make all the day-to-day decisions around here. Of course, I don't get involved in technical matters. Wally and Gene take care of those, but if we are shorthanded or need a new machine, Wally and I start the ball rolling by getting together the necessary information and talking to Bill the first chance we get. I guess you could say that we run things around here by consensus most of the time. If I get a call from a customer asking about the status of a job, I refer the call to Gene because Wally is usually out in the shop.

"I started with Bill and Wally 20 years ago, on a part-time basis, and somehow the excitement has turned into work. Joan, the office secretary, and I handle all correspondence, bookkeeping, payroll, insurance forms, and everything else besides run the office. It's just getting to be too hectic—I just wish the job was more fun, the way it used to be."

Having listened to all concerned, you returned to Bill's office only to find him gone. You tell Eve and Wally that you will return within one week with your recommendations.

EXHIBIT 2
Dowling Flexible
Metals Organiza-
tional Chart

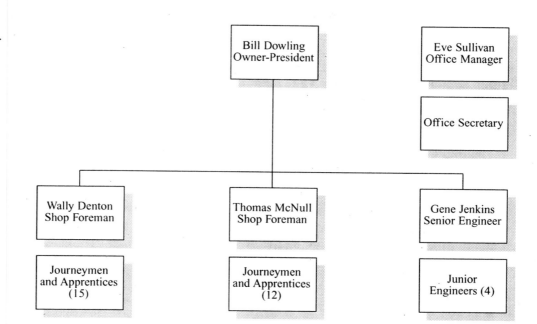

BULLER | SCHULER

Managing Organizations and People

A Resource for Cases in Management, Organizational Behavior, and Human Resource Management

Abstract

The continued rapid growth of Microsoft Corporation has caused a variety of management, structural, and legal challenges for the company. In addition, changing technology, particularly the rise of the Internet, has caused Microsoft to transform its strategy and operations to remain competitive. This case describes how Microsoft has adapted to these challenges by developing an organization that can respond quickly in a dynamic environment.

Microsoft: Adapting to New Challenges

Between 1993 and 1997, Microsoft Corporation continued its historically dramatic growth. Revenue more than quadrupled from $2.75 billion in 1993 to $11.36 billion in 1997, reflecting a compounded annual growth rate over 43%. Net income likewise grew from $708 million to $3.45 billion over the same period.[1] Asset levels rose from $3.8 billion in 1993 to $14.4 billion in 1997, while the number of employees increased to approximately 25,000 worldwide. The company's continuing success in the development and marketing of operating system and personal productivity applications software drove most of this growth. Microsoft's MS/DOS and Windows 3.1 operating systems together with its MS Office Suite of personal productivity applications had commanding market shares in their respective segments.[2]

The rapid growth generated by Microsoft's success, however, began to create coordination, management and legal problems. Coordination problems surfaced in the form of delays in software rewrites and product introductions. Windows 95, for instance, was introduced over one year after the original rollout date.[3] Management of the company's various projects also grew more complex and unwieldy. In fact, between 1982 and 1992, Microsoft went through a series of presidents until Chairman William "Bill" Gates ultimately decided to create an Office of the President in which three senior executives would jointly hold the post.[4] Lastly, legal problems cropped up as government officials from the Antitrust Division of the U.S. Department of Justice began investigating whether or not Microsoft's dominant market position was an impediment to competition in certain segments of the computer software market. In fact, in mid-1995, the Justice Department successfully blocked Microsoft from pursuing its planned acquisition of rival software maker

■ This case was prepared by Richard D. Freedman, Eduardo Olbes, and Sharon Simon, New York University, Leonard N. Stern School of Business. © 1997 by Richard D. Freedman. Reprinted by permission.

Intuit on the grounds that such an action would consolidate too much market power and consequently reduce market competition within the product segment.[5]

In response to these challenges, Gates introduced a number of incremental structural and organizational changes. The coordination problems were partially addressed by continued enhancement of the company's internal communication capabilities. Microsoft used a number of formal and informal methods for facilitating information flows such as frequent project team meetings, internal newsletters, and prodigious E-mail usage. As noted above, on the dismissal of company President Michael Hallman, Gates created the Office of the President to be shared by the three chief operating heads: Michael Maples, who headed the applications systems business; Steve Ballmer, who headed the operating systems business; and Francis Gaudette, Microsoft's chief financial officer.[6] In May of 1995, this group was augmented by Pete Higgins, head of desktop applications, and Nathan Myhrvold, head of advanced technology.[7] By creating the senior committee, Gates freed himself from supervising daily operations in order to focus on broader strategic concerns. Lastly, in terms of the antitrust issues, Microsoft retreated from the proposed merger with Intuit.[8]

Further structural adjustments were made as the three divisions under Maples, Higgins, and Myhrvold were reorganized into two groups. Maples would continue to oversee the Platforms Group, while Higgins and Myhrvold would jointly run the Applications and Content Group. Microsoft's other two divisions were the Sales and Support Group, which continued to manage customer relationships, and the Operations Group, which supervised the manufacturing and delivery of products.[9]

Internet

The Internet is a global network of computer servers providing an alternate communications platform for the private, public, and government sectors. The term "Internet" was coined in the early 1980s as university researchers developed a common computing language to link a loose collection of networks called the Arpanet.[10] The Arpanet, a 1960s product of Department of the Defense, evolved into a research tool to promote data sharing and the remote access of super-computers among researchers in the United States.[11]

The boom in inexpensive personal computers and network-ready servers in the 1980s allowed many companies and universities to join the rapidly growing Internet.[12] By the early 1990s, rapid innovations gave rise to the World Wide Web, which allowed users to navigate the Internet with "point-and-click" ease.[13] In 1993, Mosaic, the first Web browser, provided a user-friendly interface to the Internet.[14]

During this period, the growth in the use of the Internet soared. Between 1987 and 1997, the number of Internet hosts grew from 10,000 to over five million.[15] In 1993, traffic on the Internet expanded at a 341,634% annual rate.[16] By 1996, analysts estimated that over 20 million people used the Internet regularly.[17] Growth has been so rapid that the Internet is believed to have doubled in size every year since 1988.[18] Studies also suggest that over $1.0 billion per year changes hands at Internet shopping malls.[19]

In order to meet this growing demand, a number of companies such as Cisco Systems, Sun Microsystems, Netscape Communications, and Oracle Corporation made significant investments in developing and marketing hardware and software applications for the Internet.[20] Microsoft, on the other hand, initially questioned the Internet's commercial viability and therefore postponed committing significant resources for research and development of Internet-friendly applications.

As the Internet's popularity continued to grow, industry analysts began to forecast the possibility that the Internet could supersede Windows as the de facto operating system for personal computers.[21] The principal concern was the fact that competing firms were developing systems, such as Sun Microsystem's NC computer, that could operate without the industry-standard Windows operating system or other resident applications. Instead, these so-called network computers would be linked to the Internet via high-speed servers in a central location and would operate like PCs.[22] By concentrating computing power and software applications in a central computer, many of the costs and hassles of operating in a PC environment would be significantly reduced.

Development of such a scenario would free consumers from the need to purchase operating systems or software applications. Instead, consumers could rely upon the applications and operating systems resident in the servers of their online service provider. As a result, Microsoft's cash generating capabilities would be severely diminished since the licensing and sale of the company's operating system and personal productivity applications account for the majority of its revenues. Microsoft's principal business of developing operating systems and personal productivity applications would be seriously compromised.[23]

The Response   During the mid-1990s, much of Gates' attention was focused on the development and launch of Windows 95, a new operating system developed to replace Microsoft's popular Windows 3.1 system.[24] With its 15 million lines of computer code, Windows 95 was billed as the operating system that would finally give the PC the ease of use associated with Apple's Macintosh System.[25] Analysts expected Microsoft to take in $1.0 billion on Windows 95 upgrades in year one alone.[26]

In the midst of Windows 95 development, a small band of programmers at Microsoft led by Steven Sinofsky campaigned for the company to articulate a more deliberate strategy for developing Internet-based applications. Sinofsky, one of Gates' technical assistants, sparked an interest in the Internet during a company recruiting visit to Cornell in early 1994. He was surprised to note the popularity of E-mail and the Internet amongst the students and faculty of the university.[27]

Together with programmer J. Allard, Sinofsky began peppering Gates and his technical staff with E-mail messages about the Internet and its potential commercial promise.[28] Both men pointed to the rapidly growing popularity of the Internet with both private and corporate users. In fact, by 1994, analysts estimated that there were some 21,700 commercial Web sites, up from only 9,000 in 1991.[29] Sinofsky and Allard were alarmed at the possibility that Microsoft, which at this point was almost entirely focused on the rewrite of the Windows operating system, might miss the significance of this dramatic development in information technology. Sinofsky was determined to focus management's attention on this issue despite the fact that the technological implications for Microsoft's own operating system and applications software business were still unclear.

After two months of incessant drum beating, senior executives from Microsoft convened for an executive retreat to focus on the Internet. Retreats were commonly used at Microsoft to help executives focus on specific issues and challenges. Gates and his top executives reviewed documents prepared by Sinofsky outlining the critical issues. A second retreat followed during which Gates penned a memo outlining the company's first shades of a formal—albeit tepid—commitment to the Internet. Gates wrote, "We want to and will invest resources to be a leader in Internet support."[30] During the months that followed, however, the intense focus on Windows 95 and Windows NT, which was designed specifically for the corporate market, derailed much of the initial momentum.

By May 1995, with work on Windows 95 rapidly approaching completion, Gates issued a memo declaring the Internet as the "most important single development" since the advent of the personal computer.[31] Benjamin J. Slivka, who was the project leader for Microsoft Explorer, an Internet browser developed to compete with Netscape Communication's Navigator, followed up with his own memo suggesting that an Internet-based platform could potentially supercede Windows as the de facto operating system for the personal computer.[32] This memo was notable because it was one of the first formal, public acknowledgments from Microsoft's senior management of the fundamental threat presented by the Internet. This realization prompted another round of brainstorming sessions for Gates and his colleagues.

On August 24, 1995, after a delay of more than one year, Microsoft officially launched Windows 95. Analysts and industry players alike confirmed the success of the operating system's introduction.[33] While corporate customers generally postponed purchases of the new system in anticipation of the Windows NT operating system, most retail consumers and original equipment manufacturers adopted Windows 95 as the de facto standard.

The success of Windows 95 notwithstanding, on November 16, 1995, Goldman Sachs & Co., the New York investment bank, withdrew Microsoft from its recommended purchase list due to concerns that the company did not have an adequate strategy for coping with the Internet.[34] Despite multiple memos and brainstorming sessions, the company had failed to articulate a comprehensive and convincing response to the threat presented by the Internet.

Subsequent to the ratings downgrade, Steve Ballmer, Microsoft's Executive Vice President, adamantly pushed for the company to solidify its strategic plans. Ultimately, December 7, 1995 was the deadline set for the announcement of Microsoft's wide ranging Internet strategy which called for browsers, Web servers, consumer and content applications, and the Microsoft Network (a new proprietary online service provider), among others. In front of an estimated 300 analysts and reporters, Bill Gates announced that Microsoft was "hard-core about the Internet."[35]

Internet Strategy

Microsoft's vision regarding the Internet extended beyond the immediate competitive threat it presented to the company's virtual monopoly in operating systems and applications software. Gates believed that the Internet would be the principal communications platform of the future, just as the MS/DOS and Windows operating systems are today's dominant platform for personal computing.[36] The Internet offered a cost-effective medium for capturing, analyzing, and transmitting millions of bits of information. Specifically, however, the Internet was a powerful tool for collecting information on consumer practices and behavior. Gates believed that the company that could cost-effectively collect, sift through, and capitalize on information such as purchasing habits, product interests, and hobbies would attain a significant competitive advantage.[37] Consequently, capturing and controlling the key interfaces for the Internet became a critical aspect of the company's overall strategy.[38]

Microsoft announced its intention to develop a broad array of Internet-related applications and software. The company began positioning itself in most of the Web-related market segments by using a variety of tactics from joint ventures and acquisitions to internally funded research and development. As of fiscal year 1996, the company had a cash balance in excess of $8.0 billion that was available to fund their various initiatives.[39] On the hardware segment, Microsoft entered into a joint venture with Intel Corporation, Hewlett Packard, and Compaq in order to develop the NetPC, an Internet PC computer that would be positioned against the NC computer from Sun Microsystems, Oracle, and IBM. The NetPC would make use of both Intel's microprocessor and Microsoft's operating system.[40]

For the software market, Microsoft has allocated significant resources for developing applications for corporate Intranets. An Intranet is similar to the Internet, but it includes networked computers within a single company. Microsoft believes that control of this particular market segment is critical since Intranet applications will effectively act as the de facto operating system for networked computers. The company has also made an effort to transform many of its more popular personal productivity products into Intranet-friendly applications. For example, in 1997 the company introduced Office 97, an upgrade of its widely popular MS Office Suite. Office 97 includes an interface with the World Wide Web.[41]

What Microsoft is unable to create in-house, it attempts to buy. Within a $1^1/_2$ year time frame, Microsoft either acquired or entered into joint ventures with UUNET Technologies Inc., Vermeer Technologies Inc., Colusa Software Inc., eshop Inc., and Electric Gravity Inc.[42] Licensing of software and advanced technology was also frequently used. Notable amongst its recent deals was Microsoft's licensing agreement with chief rival Sun Microsystems for the use of Sun's Java computing language.[43]

For the content segment of the market, Microsoft has embarked on a number of joint ventures with established players in the media, publishing, and telecommunications industry in order to create content for display through a variety of interactive devices. These initiatives included computer equipment, television, and printed publications. For example, to address the needs in the consumer segment of the content market, Microsoft worked with Dreamworks SKG to develop a line of 3-D computer games.[44] Dreamworks provided the creative talent for the venture while Microsoft furnished technical expertise. Microsoft also has allocated a significant portion of its cash reserves to purchase fledgling content development firms. For the business segment of the content market, Microsoft's principal efforts focused on the development of MSNBC, a 24-hour business news channel distributed both via cable networks and the Internet.[45] MSNBC is a joint venture with General Electric's NBC television subsidiary.[46]

While preparing the launch of Windows 95, Microsoft's programmers were also putting the finishing touches on the company's new proprietary online service provider, the Microsoft Network (MSN).[47] The principal business of an online service provider is to provide subscribers access to the Internet. America Online, CompuServe, and Prodigy were among the first companies to actively package and market Internet access.[48] Microsoft began development of MSN in December 1992, in part due to the success of America Online, which rapidly became the world's largest proprietary online service provider.

Results

Jeffrey Katzenberg, principal of Dreamworks SKG, noted, "I cannot think of one corporation that has had this kind of success and after 20 years, just stopped and decided to reinvent itself from the ground up. What they are doing is decisive, quick, breathtaking."[49] A Microsoft employee adds that Bill Gates has taken a booming $11 billion company with 25,000 employees and turned the "battleship around as if it were a PT boat."[50]

Within a one-year period, Gates and his team achieved what many industry analysts said was impossible. Essentially, Microsoft took what was the world's largest and most prolific operating software and personal productivity application developer and transformed it into a dominant Internet-focused company with significant ventures in the hardware, software, and content segments of the market. In fiscal year 1996, total sales revenues grew 46% from $5.96 billion in 1995 to $8.67 billion.[51] Net income grew over 40% from $1.5 billion to $2.2 billion.[52] Perhaps even more telling about the company's future are its plans to dramatically raise its investment in new technologies. Over the next year alone, the company will deploy its financial resources to fund over $2.0 billion worth of research and development, which is almost half of the total $4.4 billion that it has spent over its 22-year history. Employment applications are still flooding in at a rate of 15,000 per month, giving Microsoft the enviable advantage of picking from the best and the brightest.

Government and Competitor Reactions

By packaging MSN together with Windows 95, Microsoft intended to create a system whose features would be seamlessly blended together. While the product was delivered on schedule in November 1995, an antitrust investigation by the Justice Department ultimately forced the company to reassess its approach. The principal issue investigated by the government was whether Microsoft's packaging plan would constitute an unfair advantage over its competitors.[53] While no formal charges were filed during the investigation, Microsoft moved to adjust aspects of its original plan in order to address some of the government's concerns.

In October 1997, Microsoft again came under government scrutiny for tying its Internet browser, known as Internet Explorer (IE), to the upgraded version of Windows 95. The Justice Department sued Microsoft for "trying to use its overwhelming dominance in computer operating systems to compete unfairly in the browser market."[54] Microsoft considers Windows 95 to be an integrated program, which means that a wide variety of features are built into the software. The company was requiring computer manufacturers to install IE as a condition of licensing Windows 95 on new PCs. As such, computers that come with Windows 95 preinstalled would automatically have the IE icon on the desktop. Further,

[s]worn statements from computer manufacturers . . . show exactly how Microsoft ruthlessly used its control over what appears on the PC desktop as the means to displace Netscape's Navigator with its own Internet Explorer browser. Although 'end-users' were free to adapt their desktops, the computer manufacturers had to ensure, as a condition of

their Windows license, that when a machine was switched on for the first time the desktop had every icon on it that Microsoft decreed. Faced with the threat . . . that they would lose their Windows license and thus their business if they removed the IE icon, PC makers all meekly fell into line.[55]

In December 1997, the government ordered Microsoft to offer PC manufacturers the choice of whether or not to include IE on the system. Microsoft responded by offering PC manufacturers two alternatives to the combined Windows and IE system: 1) an outdated version of Windows that predated IE, or 2) a version of Windows with IE disabled. The problem with the second option was that the software would not function properly without IE fully activated. Neither option was accepted by any OEM manufacturers.

The government was outraged by Microsoft's response. Since Windows is the de facto standard for operating systems, the government maintained that Microsoft was "using its near-monopoly in operating system software to restrict competition in the market for Internet browsing software, where its main competitor is Netscape Communications Corporation."[56] Microsoft, on the other hand, maintained that Windows and IE had become a single integrated product. In addition, Microsoft feared that government interference would hamper the company's strategy of blending Internet capabilities into all of its new products.[57]

In addition to complaints from the government and Windows licensees, Microsoft's competitors in the software arena have actively voiced concerns about the company's growing market power. Both Netscape and Sun Microsystems "have suggested that Microsoft's aggressive tactics in the software marketplace border on the tyrannical."[58] Netscape, the current leader for Internet browsers with a 60% market share, has steadily been losing ground, and attributes its losses to Microsoft's policy of bundling IE with the Windows operating system.

Until January 1998, Microsoft continued to insist that IE and Windows were so intricately integrated that Windows simply could not operate without IE. In order to avoid being found in contempt of court, however, Microsoft ultimately gave in to government demands by agreeing to make Windows available with the Internet browser icon hidden or partially removed from the computer desktop. A moderately knowledgeable consumer can easily install the icon on the desktop.

Addressing Government Concerns

Throughout the 1970s and 1980s, while in its infancy, Microsoft had no need to be concerned with government matters. Rapidly increasing market power, however, has caused the government to pay attention to the now large corporation. While Gates maintains that he has done nothing more than remain responsive to consumer demands, the company's ability to influence industry standards has led to intense government scrutiny. Specifically, the Justice Department fears that Microsoft's control of industry standards could impede innovation, leaving competing technologies little chance to survive. Too much government interference, however, could have potentially devastating effects on Microsoft's strategy.

In 1996 Gates began to hire lobbyists, including Washington lawyer Jack Krumholtz, in order to defend his company against government attacks. "We've increased our [political giving] efforts in response to the very concerted campaign by our competitors to use the government against us rather than to compete in the marketplace," says Krumholtz.[59] Until recently, the company made few political contributions and preferred to lobby in Washington through the Business Software Alliance—an industry trade group whose mission is "to advocate free and open world trade for legitimate business software"[60]—and its own law firm, Preston Gates Ellis & Rouvelas Meeds.

Even Gates himself has begun to spend more time in government matters. Although he rarely visits Capitol Hill, Microsoft's chief executive has been inviting more and more politicians to both the company's corporate headquarters and his private home. Microsoft has also increased its campaign contributions. In 1996, for example, the company donated $236,784 to candidates for office, as compared to only $105,484 just two years earlier.[61]

Public Relations

As Microsoft's market power has increased since its humble beginnings, the company's tremendous success has coincided with a shift in Gates's image as a 'quintessential nerd' to one who uses brute force to dominate the marketplace, stifling innovation by controlling industry standards. Indeed, "Microsoft has been able to crush competitors—eliminating competition and perhaps innovation, which could harm consumers."[62] To further promote this negative image, it has been said that Microsoft has taken a "combative stance" in government courtroom confrontations, during which the company, "usually so sure footed, has appeared at times to be throwing a temper tantrum, picking fights with a Federal judge and the Justice Department."[63]

In a campaign beginning in March 1998, Bill Gates became a celebrity endorser for a line of golf clubs. The campaign consisted of a television commercial and print advertisement, and featured Gates as an enthusiastic new golf player. Gates added his role as an endorser to his resume "at a time when he seems to be engaged in a frenetic series of activities intended to change perceptions of him as a rapacious cyber capitalist bent on dominating the information industry."[64] Corporate identity and brand image consultant Clay Timon commended the move, stating, "It will make [Gates] seem human after all."[65] In additional public relations activities, Gates paid tribute to the Wright brothers at *Time* magazine's 75th anniversary party, presented a $640,000 gift to the New York Library, and visited a sixth grade class.

Structure

Microsoft's Internet-focused strategy had dramatic implications for both the company and its employees. New product groups were formed and divisions were reorganized in order to focus on a variety of product initiatives. As previously noted, Microsoft was organized into four main business groups: 1) the Platforms Products Group; 2) the Applications and Content Product Group; 3) the Sales and Support Group; and 4) the Operations Group.[66] In February 1996, both the Platforms Products Group and the Applications and Content Product Group were reorganized in conjunction with company's efforts to enhance its Internet capabilities.

The Platforms Group, headed by Group Vice President Paul Maritz, was organized into three divisions: 1) the Personal and Business Systems Division (which develops and markets applications such as Windows 3.x, Windows 95, Windows NT, and the BackOffice applications, etc.); 2) the Consumer Devices and Public Networks Division (hand-held devices, set-top boxes, etc.); and 3) the Internet Platforms Division (focusing on Web browsers, shell and multimedia technology, developer tools, online service commerce technology, etc.)[67]

The Applications and Content Product Group, run by Group Vice Presidents Nathan Myhrvold and Pete Higgins, was likewise reorganized into three divisions. The Desktop Applications Division focuses on personal productivity and consumer applications (e.g., Microsoft Office).[68] The Interactive Media Division develops online and CD-ROM based versions of consumer and business software while overseeing development of content for MSN. The Advanced Technology and Research Division focuses on emerging technologies such as speech recognition and artificial intelligence.[69]

The Sales and Support Group, headed by EVP Ballmer, is responsible for "building long-term business relationships with customers."[70] This group is structured to focus on three customer types: end users, organizations, and original equipment manufacturers (OEMs).

The Operations Group, headed by EVP and COO Bob Herbold, is responsible for managing business operations. This includes processing, manufacturing, and delivering finished goods, licenses, subscriptions, and overall business planning.[71]

In reorganizing the Platforms Products Group and the Applications and Content Product Group, Microsoft was able to capitalize on its loosely structured team approach to software development. Teams of software developers and marketers frequently are used to develop specific software applications. Because the team concept is so pervasive, management was readily able to reshape both business groups by adding and eliminating product teams according to management's assessment of their strategic value. A variety of new units were created to focus on discrete aspects of the company's overall Internet strategy.

Microsoft was reorganized again in early 1998. The move placed three product groups under Paul Mafitz, Group Vice President for Platforms and Operations. The groups are: 1) Personal and Business Systems, 2) Consumer Platforms, and 3) Applications and Tools. The move also shifted responsibility for Internet Explorer into the Personal and Business Systems Group, which is the unit that develops and markets Windows. David Readerman, a financial analyst at Nationsbanc Montgomery Securities Inc., supports the move, stating that "Internet Explorer is an integrated product. You better integrate the reporting responsibilities." The reorganization came less than one month after the company agreed to make Windows available without the Internet Explorer icon present on the desktop. Due to this timing, it has been said that the move "is certain to raise eyebrows in light of the Microsoft Corporation's antitrust battle with the United States Government."[72]

Conclusion

Now that Microsoft represents the dominant force in the computer software industry, Bill Gates claims to have trouble comprehending the nature of the allegations being thrown at his company. He says that rivals should pay more attention to their own businesses and less time obsessing about Microsoft's competitive position. After all, the technology markets are fast paced, and there are no guarantees that Microsoft will remain the industry leader. In fact, it has been said that the Justice Department "faces an extraordinary challenge in keeping . . . in step with the fast-changing Internet software market and Microsoft's quickly shifting tactics."[73] Gates even cites the emergence of Netscape's Navigator and Sun Microsystem's Java programming language as evidence of the highly competitive and threatening nature of the industry. However, there is little opposition to the point that Microsoft virtually owns the future of computing. In fact, it has been said that if Gates can extend Microsoft's dominance to the Internet browser realm, "the little software company he co-founded in 1975 could come to dominate the nexus of computing and communications well into the 21st century."[74]

Endnotes

1. http://www.microsoft.com
2. Hingorani, Sanjiv G. and Sheela Chandrashekhara, "Microsoft Corporation—The Renaissance at Redmond: From DOS to the Web," Furman Selz LLC, August 1996.
3. Staff, Windows 95, *Business Week*, August 1995.
4. Lohr, Steve, "Three Named to Microsoft's Top Management," *The New York Times*, 5/22/95.
5. Staff, *The New York Times*, 5/7/95.
6. Lohr, Steve, "Three Named to Microsoft's Top Management," *The New York Times*, 5/22/95.
7. Ibid.
8. Staff, *The New York Times*, 5/7/95.
9. Lohr, Steve, "Three Named to Microsoft's Top Management," *The New York Times*, 5/22/95.
10. http://www.PBS.org/internet/history
11. Ibid.
12. Ibid.
13. Ibid.
14. Ibid.
15. http://www.economist.com/surveys/internet/intro.html
16. http://www.PBS.org/internet/history
17. http://www.economist.com/surveys/internet/intro.html
18. Ibid.
19. http://www.PBS.org/internet/history
20. Flynn, Mary Kathleen, "The Battle for the Net," *US News and World Report*, 12/18/95.
21. Cortese, Amy, "Win 95 Lose 96," *Business Week*, 12/18/95.
22. Reinhardt, Andy, "Intel Inside the Net," *Business Week*, 11/18/96.
23. Hingorani, Sanjiv G. and Sheela Chandrashekhara, "Microsoft Corporation—The Renaissance at Redmond: From DOS to the Web," Furman Selz LLC, August 1996.
24. Rebello, Kathy, "Inside Microsoft: The Untold Story of How the Internet Forced Bill Gates to Reverse Course," *Business Week*, 7/15/96.
25. Staff, Windows 95, *Business Week*, August 1995.
26. Ibid.
27. Rebello, Kathy, "Inside Microsoft: The Untold Story of How the Internet Forced Bill Gates to Reverse Course," *Business Week*, 7/15/96.
28. Ibid.
29. Ibid.
30. Ibid.
31. Ibid.
32. Cortese, Amy, "Win 95 Lose 96," *Business Week*, 12/18/95.
33. Hingorani, Sanjiv G. and Sheela Chandrashekhara, "Microsoft Corporation—The Renaissance at Redmond: From DOS to the Web," Furman Selz LLC, August 1996.
34. Rebello, Kathy, "Inside Microsoft: The Untold Story of How the Internet Forced Bill Gates to Reverse Course," *Business Week*, 7/15/96.
35. Flynn, Mary Kathleen, "The Battle for the Net," *US News and World Report*, December 18, 1995.
36. Hafner, Katie, "Microsoft Century," *Newsweek*, 12/2/96.
37. Ibid.
38. Gleick, James, "Making Microsoft Safe for Capitalism," *The New York Times Magazine*, 11/5/95.
39. Annual Report—Fiscal Year 1996, Microsoft Corporation.
40. Reinhardt, Andy, "Intel Inside the Net," *Business Week*, 11/18/96.
41. Rebello, Kathy, "Microsoft's Suite Spot," *Business Week*, 11/25/96.
42. Hingorani, Sanjiv G. and Sheela Chandrashekhara, "Microsoft Corporation—The Renaissance at Redmond: From DOS to the Web," Furman Selz LLC, August 1996.
43. Flynn, Mary Kathleen, "The Battle for the Net," *US News and World Report*, 12/18/95.
44. Hingorani, Sanjiv G. and Sheela Chandrashekhara, "Microsoft Corporation—The Renaissance at Redmond: From DOS to the Web," Furman Selz LLC, August 1996.
45. Ibid.
46. Ibid.

47. Rebello, Kathy, "Inside Microsoft: The Untold Story of How the Internet Forced Bill Gates to Reverse Course," *Business Week*, July 15, 1996.

48. Hingorani, Sanjiv G. and Sheela Chandrashekhara, "Microsoft Corporation—The Renaissance at Redmond: From DOS to the Web," Furman Selz LLC, August 1996.

49. Rebello, Kathy, "Inside Microsoft: The Untold Story of How the Internet Forced Bill Gates to Reverse Course," *Business Week*, 7/15/96.

50. Ibid.

51. Annual Report—Fiscal Year 1996, Microsoft Corporation.

52. Ibid.

53. Markoff, John, "US Won't Challenge Microsoft Network Before Its Debut," *The New York Times*, 8/5/95.

54. Brinkley, Joel, "Microsoft Gives in to a Federal Order on Internet Browser," *The New York Times*, 1/23/98.

55. _____, "Microsoft is Fighting its Competitors and the Justice Department Tooth and Nail. Is it Driven by Strategy or Nature?" *The Economist*, 1/31/98, p. 65.

56. Lohr, Steve and John Markoff, "Why Microsoft is Taking a Hard Line with the Government," *The New York Times*, 1/12/98, p. D1.

57. Hamm, Steve, Amy Cortese and Susan Garland, "Microsoft's Future," *Business Week*, 1/19/98, p. 58.

58. Westneat, Danny and James Grimaldi, "Gates to Testify: Will Star Power Work on Senate? Meek Lessons Suggested for Microsoft Chief," *The Seattle Times*, 3/1/98, p. A1.

59. Yang, Catherine, Amy Borrus, Susan Garland and Steve Hamm, "Microsoft Goes Low-Tech in Washington," *Business Week*, 12/22/97.

60. http://www.bsa.org/info/aboutbsa.html

61. Yang, Catherine, Amy Borrus, Susan Garland and Steve Hamm, "Microsoft Goes Low-Tech in Washington," *Business Week*, 12/22/97.

62. Lohr, Steve and John Markoff, "Why Microsoft is Taking a Hard Line with the Government," *The New York Times*, 1/12/98, p. D1.

63. Ibid.

64. Elliot, Stuart, "Bill Gates is Tiger Woods? Well, He's Doing a Commercial," *The New York Times*, 3/6/98, p. D5.

65. Ibid.

67. Hingorani, Sanjiv G. and Sheela Chandrashekhara, "Microsoft Corporation—The Renaissance at Redmond: From DOS to the Web," Furman Selz LLC, August 1996.

68. Ibid.

69. Ibid.

70. Ibid.

71. Ibid.

72. Markoff, John, "Microsoft Shifts Web Unit to Windows Group," *The New York Times*, 2/6/98, p. D3.

73. Lohr, Steve, "US Facing Lightning Technology Shifts in Microsoft Case," *The New York Times*, 3/30/98, p. D1.

74. Hamm, Steve, Amy Cortese and Susan Garland, "Microsoft's Future," *Business Week*, 1/19/98, p. 58.

BULLER | SCHULER

Managing Organizations and People

A Resource for Cases in Management, Organizational Behavior, and Human Resource Management

Abstract

This case is an "in-basket" problem designed in the usual format to help students deal with the problem of prioritizing a number of conflicting and hierarchical activities. George Hayes, the strategist in the case, is faced with having to take over a division of a moderately large, multiple SBU firm on very short notice. He has a group of 18 open items to deal with in his first week on the job and one day to organize his work schedule for the first critical week. The student is asked to process this "in-basket" and create a schedule for the week.

Sunday at el Tech

**Saturday,
August 14,
1981, 9 p.m.**

George Hayes, Assistant to the President at Star Manufacturing, Inc., was sitting in his motel room in a small city near Chicago with his feet propped up on the bed recalling the events which had prompted his being there. On Thursday, only two days earlier, he had attended a meeting of the top managers at the Star corporate headquarters on the east coast. The day's agenda centered on his analysis of the recent performance of the company's various divisions. One in particular, el Tech, was receiving an unusual amount of attention that day.

George had the numbers on the table next to him. Sales, net income, and return on investment (ROI) for el Tech were down from the previous year and below budgeted performance levels. The results were somewhat understandable given the unexpected severity of the current economic downturn and el Tech's sensitivities to such conditions. Just when George had felt the meeting was about to adjourn, the president asked him for more details concerning el Tech's new expansion and equipment acquisition plans. George knew those numbers all too well. He had reviewed them prior to Star's approval of the project. He had even been sent to the equipment manufacturer for a first-hand look at the technology and accompanying manpower and facilities requirements. George recalled that this had been the trip which had caused him to miss the tenth birthday of his twin daughters.

The meeting had continued with George reporting that the building addition at el Tech was nearing completion and the equipment was scheduled for installation during the month of October. The management group then had briefly discussed el Tech's forecast for

■ Lynda L. Goulet and Peter G. Goulet, Instructor and Associate Professor, respectively, University of Northern Iowa. Reprinted by permission. Copyright © 1983, 1984. All rights reserved. This case describes a hypothetical company based on a composite of several actual experiences in a similar industrial setting.

the year beginning in January 1983, the first full year the new equipment would be operational. Several forecasts had been prepared, each based on different assumptions concerning the utilization of the new technology. The most pessimistic forecast—utilizing less than 50 percent of the new capacity and having no new product lines—still resulted in overall profit performance for the division which was better than that from 1981 or from the current year's adjusted projections.

George had also reported that if the most optimistic forecast were attained, el Tech would become one of the corporation's most profitable divisions. Though marketing new product lines would require development time and the acquisition of experience with the new technology, it was still plausible to expect some sales of new products by the end of the upcoming year.

George's mind wandered. el Tech had been his pet project for the last four years. He had first heard of the company while attending his ten-year college reunion in Illinois over four years ago. George's former fiancee, Julie, who had broken their engagement to marry Ben Brown, introduced him to her husband at the reunion. Ben had just been promoted to Personnel Manager at el Tech. George recalled, however, that Ben wasn't certain how long he would be able to retain that position as the Carter family, who owned the firm, wished to sell it to settle an estate. Only the Vice-President of Sales, Stuart Carter, was a family member. The President, Russell Wainscott, had been hired several years earlier when the founder of the company retired. Following the founder's death, everyone in the family except Stuart wanted the firm to be sold, for cash rather than for stock in another firm. George remembered the many hours of work and travel time he had invested analyzing this potential acquisition for Star Manufacturing. The work had all come to fruition in late 1978 when Star purchased el Tech from the Carter family estate.

A door to a nearby room slammed shut. George was jarred back to thoughts of the last few minutes of last Thursday's meeting at Star. At long last Star's President made it clear why el Tech had been the focus of attention. Russell Wainscott, who had been retained as the General Manager at el Tech after the acquisition, had been severely injured in a car accident and would be hospitalized for an unknown, though substantial, period of time. George was to assume responsibility for the division as its Acting General Manager until Wainscott was able to assume his duties again.

George slipped into bed early, knowing Sunday would be a very long day. He had made arrangements to spend the day at el Tech alone, preparing for his first week as GM. Before going to sleep he felt both apprehension and excitement. Finally he would have the opportunity to get the line management experience he needed to advance his career. However, with line responsibility, especially under these circumstances, comes high visibility. George nervously drifted off to sleep.

**Sunday,
August 15,
8 a.m.**

The keys to the el Tech office building and the GM's office were in the box at the motel desk when George went to breakfast. A note from Wainscott's secretary, Barbara Curtis, was in a manila envelope with the keys. It read:

Mr. Hayes:

As you requested in your Friday telephone call, all the managers prepared memos relating any problems under their responsibility which must be resolved in the near future. Five of the memos are in envelopes on Rusty's [Wainscott] desk. Richard Simcox told me he would slip his memo under the office door as he wasn't able to complete it before I left Friday. In addition, I prepared a summary of Rusty's agenda for next week with some explanations of any meetings to the best of my knowledge. Finally there is a stack of mail on the desk. Some of it is left over from before the accident and some arrived since then. I hope this is satisfactory. I'm looking forward to working for you in Rusty's absence and will arrive early Monday morning to help you begin your first week.

(Signed) Barb Curtis

**Sunday,
August 15,
9 a.m.**

When George arrived at the office he found the following items awaiting his attention:

> Memos from managers (Exhibits 1–6)
> Agenda for the week of the sixteenth (Exhibit 7)
> Correspondence (Exhibits 8–17)

Before he began working George scribbled on a piece of paper and added that to the pile on top of his desk (see Exhibit 18).

Place yourself in George Hayes' position. Plan your activities for the week of August 16. What meetings must be held? When? With whom? What decisions must be made? When? Which decisions can be delegated? To whom? A note on el Tech appears below to provide you with additional background. An organizational chart is also provided as Figure 1.

**A Note on
el Tech**

El Tech is a vertically integrated firm which converts aluminum billets (cylindrical ingots of aluminum) into aluminum extrusions which are then converted into finished products. Aluminum extrusions are produced by hydraulic presses which force billets heated to just below the melting point through profile dies of hardened steel. The hot extrusions run out onto long tables for cooling. These extrusions are cut to length, heat treated, and machined through various operations, typically in punch or brake presses, to produce the constituent parts for numerous products. el Tech makes extrusions for its own lines of windows, storm sash, patio doors, screens, and extension ladders.

The major suppliers for el Tech are companies which provide the aluminum billets, flat glass, and screen cloth. el Tech's customers include nearly 500 firms, though their major source of revenue derives from about twenty manufacturers of recreational vehicles (RVs) and manufactured housing (MH) and two chains of discount retailers who purchase the ladders for sale under private labels.

The major investment to which el Tech recently committed itself is a series of machines which electrostatically paint extrusions. The equipment requires a facility with a forty-foot ceiling as the extrusions are painted while suspended vertically. el Tech's new installation will allow it to paint extrusion lengths among the longest that can be painted in any U.S. facility. Aluminum is very difficult to paint successfully because the paint doesn't adhere to the surface easily. Though painted aluminum also scratches easily, it must still be painted before machining to achieve necessary economies.

There is a great deal of demand for painted aluminum products because painting both colors the surface and prevents the unsightly oxidation of the bare metal characteristic of aluminum. Anodizing also accomplishes these purposes and produces a harder, more durable finish than that achieved with painting. However, the cost of anodizing is so high as to be prohibitive for almost all uses but curtain walls for high-rise office buildings and high-valued decorative products. Painting also offers a greater variety of colors and finish textures than anodizing.

El Tech built its paint facility for internal use. However, with this facility and its extrusion operation, it felt it could develop demand for high-margin custom-extruded, custom-painted parts for current as well as new markets.

EXHIBIT 1

From: Ben Brown
To: George Hayes
Date: August 13, 1982

George:

Looking forward to working with you for a while—too bad it had to be under these circumstances. Barb passed your message along and I guess there are several issues we need to discuss pretty soon.

1. Sam Howarth, one of our designers, has been suspected of the "appropriation" of minor amounts of company materials for a long time. Two weeks ago, Dick Simcox inadvertently caught him piling some obsolete screens into his car. These screens probably would have been sold for scrap. Dick, Rusty, and I decided to let him take some vacation time until we decided what to do about it. We'd have fired him on the spot but the truth is he is a good designer and our designers are underpaid and turnover is terrible. Howarth has been with the firm for over fifteen years and is responsible for a couple of innovations that have been really profitable. His vacation time will run out at the end of the week so some decision must be reached by the 20th.

2. The new paint process equipment is scheduled for delivery and installation during October. I have placed an ad for a supervisor in that department and I have an application in hand for a good man. He used to supervise a line that painted cabinets for TV sets. The problem is that one of our assembly supervisors wants the job. Dick tried to convince her to stay in assembly but she's being a hard-nose about it. She is not qualified for this job from the standpoint of having run a paint room. She probably could be trained eventually but we don't know how good a job she would ever do. It will also delay us for a long time if we go this route. As I see it all she really wants is the money or the prestige associated with the new position. What she doesn't understand, or won't accept, is that the higher wages for the paint room job reflect the level of skill required. She says she'll cause some trouble if she doesn't get the job this week but none of us knows what she means by "trouble." The final kicker is that this is our only female manager at any level.

3. You probably aren't aware of this, but every year Al Tech has a company party for its employees and their spouses. I have been in charge of the arrangements for the last few years. It's next Saturday at the local Elks club. Some of the people around the office have wondered if it wouldn't be wise to postpone it because of Rusty's accident. My feeling is that it's a bit late to cancel. Besides, it'll be months before Rusty can get back on his feet again. The Carter family started the tradition fifteen years ago and Stuart hates to see it abandoned. Al White thinks it's an awful waste of money but Dick says it's a real morale booster for his workers. I need to know about this no later than Monday afternoon.

4. One final thing, and this is a real winner. Somewhere in Rusty's pile of stuff there should be a copy of a letter from our receptionist. I'll just let you read it for the pure joy of the moment. When you have gotten off the floor let me know and we'll talk about it. By the way, she officially works for me.

EXHIBIT 2

From: Aaron McClosky
To: George Hayes
Date: August 13, 1982

Welcome aboard.

The fellows in engineering have been busy working up some new designs to expand our product lines. Stu Carter, Dick Simcox, and I have been going around for months trying to decide what to do with the extra capacity of the new paint line. We're all in agreement that the window and door lines will go on first. I guess you've got the figures on this, too. There is a lot of demand for white and brown frames on both the RV and MH window lines and the margins are a good deal better than for the unpainted units. However, I believe we'd better develop some new products quickly if we want to get above the low capacity utilization our current products will provide. Dick thinks there's no real problem here because he feels we can land a lot of contract painting jobs. As far as I know Stu hasn't even tried to check out that possibility.

I'm having one of the designers collect some of our more promising designs. She should have them ready for you by Monday. We've been working on the designs for a line of picture frames, some designer curtain rods, and a dynamite set of shower doors. For the last several years there has been talk around the sales office of redesigning our lines for the retail market but we never seem to get anywhere on this. Just when the designers get excited about a new product design, it seems like Stu comes up with a variation on our windows that the mobile home guys just "have to have." By the time that's taken care of the new products get lost in the shuffle. I sure hope that doesn't happen with the paint line ideas.

We really ought to move on this business so my department can develop prototypes by year end. After that it'll take at least six months to work out the bugs, let the dies, and get into production.

EXHIBIT 3

From: Albert White
To: George Hayes
Date: 8/13/82

Mr. Hayes:

Having just recently corresponded with you at headquarters concerning the latest quarterly report, I am certain you are well aware of our current position. This week I have been reviewing the updated estimates for the fourth quarter. In doing so I have been reminded of a potential problem to which you should be alerted. The details are attached but I have summarized the situation below. [Attachment not shown.]

On July 28, Stuart Carter got an order for 10,000 window units with storms and screens and 1000 patio doors. [Attachment shows this order to be worth just under $300,000.] The customer, a new one for us, is a large condominium developer with units in five states. The order was to be delivered by November 5. Normally an order of this size would be greatly appreciated. However, these units are all non-standard product for us. Though assembly will not be a problem, the glass will be. For some reason we cannot find any way to cut the glass without a great deal of waste. The upshot of this is that in figuring the costs on this order, given the price Stuart quoted, we would be selling the whole order at about break-even.

Rusty and I talked about this situation and decided that one solution to this problem might be to try to resell the order using painted extrusions from the new line. We sent Stuart back to the customer and the developer said he would let us know this Wednesday if the order would be changed. By changing to painted windows we were able to quote a price that covered us for the painting and the excess waste and provide a profit. However, there is a catch. The customer is willing to wait a bit longer to give us a chance to operationalize the paint line, as he is in the design stage of the development. However, he wants a penalty clause in the order in case we are late in delivering under the revised order. If for any reason the equipment isn't ready to go on time we will either have to pay a penalty or have the extrusions painted outside. Either way, we would lose about $10,000 on the order if the revised quote is accepted and the paint room isn't ready by November.

EXHIBIT 4

From: Stu Carter
To: George Hayes
Date: August 13

Sorry I won't be in town when you arrive at Al Tech. I've had a big sales trip planned to meet with several of our major window customers in the South. Rusty wanted me to drum up some firm orders for the new painted metal lines since we're going to be going on line soon. He was apparently concerned our customers wouldn't order the more expensive, painted products, given the recession. I told him not to worry, though, as the expensive stuff usually sells OK anyway, especially in the South where the economy isn't as hard hit.

Barb was lucky to catch me before I left. I'll be swinging on back through Cincinnati for the Manufactured Housing Suppliers Show, then home for the big party!

Oh, before I forget, sooner or later you're bound to hear about it. In fact, the lawyer was going to meet with Rusty this week. While I was on the road recently the Groves kid broke into my office. I know he rifled my desk because the drawers were an awful mess. I don't care what he says he was after, he's had it in for me ever since I fired his dad from the sales force a year ago. How did I know his old man, Marv, would end up marrying my secretary! I have a good notion to fire her when I get back. Marv Groves went over my head to Mc-Closky, insisting he could sell more to the chain stores if we had more retail lines. I told Marv to keep his nose out of the design department and when he didn't I finally fired him. Those guys in design would spend all their time on the new stuff instead of helping me out on the window lines. The MH guys are always hot for slick-looking new window designs. Now McClosky is convinced that the new paint line was put in just so his department could have some fun.

Gotta run.

EXHIBIT 5

From: Charles Weber
To: George Hayes
Date: 8/13/82

Mr. Hayes:

Ms. Curtis suggested I prepare a memo to advise you of any problems I may be encountering in Purchasing. I foresee two areas of concern.

First, it will be necessary for me to locate long-term reliable sources of supply for the paint facility. We have temporary sources for the materials we need for the forecasted window and door production through December. Beyond that we need to be concerned about the demands of any new product lines and/or contract paint work. We also have not accounted for the condominium order, should it require painting.

Second, I have been hearing some rumors that two of our major aluminum suppliers may be cutting back production further. In the last major recession several of the "majors" shut off some potlines [smelting equipment] to artificially tighten supplies so they could raise prices even in a period of slack demand. This strategy worked well last time, so I suspect the rumors may be true. I may know more by the middle of next week. One of our suppliers will have their regional sales manager in the area on the pretext of training a new territory representative. You might wish to join us on the morning of the 18th, should you be available.

The last time billets were in short supply both of our contract suppliers instituted a very restrictive policy before supplying us with metal. For each pound of aluminum we wished to purchase we had to turn in a pound of scrap at the going price. Obviously, we could not keep up such a practice for very long without severe production cutbacks. Otherwise, we would be forced into the spot market to fill our remaining needs. To anticipate this possibility it might be wise to begin stockpiling our scrap. This will hurt our quarterly cash flow, but may help protect our supply of new metal. The next regular scrap pickup is scheduled for Friday the 20th.

Just a reminder, the engineers from the paint equipment company will be here Tuesday. It might be a good time for you to learn more about the new facility firsthand.

If I can be of any additional help, please don't hesitate to ask.

EXHIBIT 6

From: Dick Simcox
To: George Hayes
Date: August 14, 1982

Just before shutdown on Friday I got a phone call from one of our large customers. Apparently Stu had left on his sales trip already, and due to the urgency of the call, his secretary transferred the call to me. Here's the trouble. Our trucks just delivered a shipment of our new hexagonal windows to our biggest MH customer. These babies were right on spec, exceeded federal standards by a mile—the designers did a bang-up job. These are the most expensive windows we make because of the unusual shape. The tooling is incredible and glass-cutting is a real chore. I was real proud of assembly when I inspected these before loading. My supervisor, Judy Mills, did a great job on this. I sure wish she'd get off her horse about this paint job; I need her here. Anyway, the bums wouldn't accept delivery of the order. They told the driver the latch was on the wrong side. What's more like it is that their business is really off and they stopped producing the model that uses the hex windows. The driver's bringing them back this weekend.

What's got me worried is that this was just the first batch. The order was for three times what we shipped. We got a big set of tools and hired and trained a guy just for this product, hoping to get some more customers for it next year. If we could get in touch with Stu we could get him to see the customer at the show this week. The next batch was already started but I canceled them on Friday night until we find out what gives here. Not filling this order will do some damage to our sales targets for the quarter.

What worries me most is that this could be a trend. If all our customers are hurting now, how are we going to sell the painted stuff? We've been counting on the higher margins there to offset some volume declines in other products. Rusty's been worrying about this, too. He told me just last week. But Stu is convinced there's no problem. Seems to me we ought to be out looking for some contract painting. It'll be a bad Christmas for a lot of our people if we have to cut back in the last quarter.

I can free up an hour or two any time after 10 a.m. Monday if you need me.

EXHIBIT 7

From: Barbara Curtis
To: George Hayes
Date: August 13, 1982

Below is a summary of Rusty's agenda for the week of August 16.

1. Luncheon with Alan Holtman at noon on Monday.
    Mr. Holtman is the attorney retained by Al Tech. The subject of the meeting is the trespass, breaking and entering charge pending against Mitchell Groves, age 16, stepson of Stu Carter's secretary.

    On July 31, the boy was apprehended inside our office building after he set off the silent alarm. He claims to have been looking for proof that his stepmother was having an affair with Stu. They both deny this. When the police searched the boy, they found nothing in his possession belonging to Al Tech. The Groves think the situation can and should be worked out at home, though they want the boy to pay for damages. Stu seems to want to press for prosecution.

2. Tuesday, 11 a.m. to 3 p.m. meet with Janice Schulcraft and Dennis Sanchez. These are the engineers from the paint equipment manufacturer. The subject of their visit concerns the finalization of the delivery and installation plans. Rusty had planned a tour of the building addition, now almost completed, lunch, and then a briefing session to include Messrs. Weber, White, and Simcox.

3. Wednesday, 7:45 a.m.
    Rusty had reservations to leave O'Hare for Cincinnati for the MH Suppliers Show, returning Friday after dinner. He was to meet Stu upon his arrival.

4. Saturday, 6 p.m. to midnight, annual party, Elks Club. Rusty was to deliver a short speech after dinner.

EXHIBIT 8

Unopened letter dated August 12, 1982:

Dear Mr. Wainscott:

Our office has on file your plans for the construction of an addition to your facility on Eleventh Street, including the remodeling of the south-side entrance. You may be aware of the fact that last Monday, August 9, the City Council approved proposed building code modifications which go into effect immediately.

One section of the revised code may impact on your current construction. This notification is intended to provide you with some warning that, as filed, your new premises may not pass inspection. It is to your benefit to discuss this situation with your architect and your general contractor as soon as possible.

Enclosed is a copy of the changes in the code as approved by the council. [Enclosure not shown.] If my office can help you in interpreting these changes or in answering any other questions, please let me know.

Sincerely,
(Signed) Stanley Lerner, City Engineer

EXHIBIT 9

Manila envelope containing petition: August 2, 1982

We the undersigned request that the management of Al Tech repair the employees' parking lot. Many of us damaged our tires and suffered wheel alignment problems after last winter from the deep ruts, potholes, and frost heaving problems. We also request that in fall the apples from the trees by the lot be swept up regularly so the lot is not an obstacle course to walk through.

[253 signatures followed]

EXHIBIT 10

Unopened letter dated August 10, postmarked New York:

Dear Mr. Wainscott:

For the past two years you have supplied our chain of stores with your aluminum extension ladders. Let me express to you again how pleased we all are here with the high quality and timely delivery of this product. It continues to be a strong item for us.

In light of recent and expected changes in both demographics and the economic climate, we have redefined our corporate merchandising strategy. It is our intention to provide more variety in home improvement products and hardware. To implement this strategy we are seeking reliable suppliers in such product lines to provide our chain with private label merchandise. We would be interested in talking with you about the possibility of contracting for an exclusive line of windows, doors, and porch enclosures.

Since this may require some rethinking of your firm's priorities, I have decided to approach you directly rather than contacting your sales department. We are very anxious to proceed and I am hopeful we can expand our already cordial business relations further. I am planning to be in Chicago for a regional meeting on the 19th of this month. If you will be available it would be no trouble for me to drive out to your office on the 20th to discuss this in more detail. If you wish to get together at that time please call my office by the 18th.

Sincerely,
(Signed) John Colby
Vice President,
Merchandising

EXHIBIT 11

Letter postmarked August 9, addressed to "Al Teck." Letter was handwritten and is reproduced verbatim below:

To the man who runs things at Al Teck,

I was at your factory a few weeks back to get a job that was in the Want Ads. The boss woodn't hire me. Over the week end I seen my sister inlaw She says I can sue your place cause I am pertecked class. To be nice I give you one more chance befor I get a loyer.

Marie Grace

EXHIBIT 12

Letter dated July 23, 1982, opened by Wainscott:

Dear Mr. Wainscott:

County General Hospital is vitally concerned with the increasing number of job-related accidents occurring in our community. In an attempt to ameliorate this trend we have added a Safety Consultant to our hospital staff. His job is to suggest specific improvements which can be implemented with minimal expense in offices and factories in our community.

The services of our Safety Consultant will be made available to local businesses under one of two programs: a per-diem consultation to our charitable contribution plan. The per-diem rate is $500. The charitable contribution plan is based on the actual savings accruing to each firm through the reduction in expenses from reduced insurance costs and direct company-borne medical costs. If your company institutes any of the improvements suggested by our Safety Consultant, rather than pay the per-diem expense you may elect to contribute 10 per cent of the first year's actual dollar savings to our hospital.

We at County General sincerely believe this program will benefit both the community and the businesses that are so critical to its welfare. Please feel free to make an appointment with me at your earliest convenience so we can confer on this matter.

Respectfully,
(Signed) Michael Franz, Administrator
County General Hospital

EXHIBIT 13

Unsigned, handwritten note, no date, found on the floor near the office door on Sunday morning:

To the new Acting General Manager

Sir, the foremen here at Al Tech got together after quitting time on Friday and talked about the situation since Rusty's accident. We're sure you're a good guy and all or the company wouldn't have sent you. We just want you to know that we think Dick [Simcox] should have gotten the job. It didn't need to go to an outsider.

EXHIBIT 14

Letter dated August 4, 1982, opened by Wainscott, postmarked St. Louis:

Dear Rusty,

It's about that time again. We need to make plans for this year's holiday break. Some of the others want to spend the week after Christmas lolling on the beaches in either southern California or Florida. I'm partial to the Gulf side of Florida because my in-laws are in the area, and my kids could spend the week with them. Do you have any preferences?

This sure was one heck of a good idea. I don't remember exactly whose it was though it's been three years now. Doesn't really matter. Since all the divisions are shut down for the holidays anyway and the only thing going on is inventory, we general managers might as well enjoy ourselves. Besides, last year Frank said our gossip about HQ really helped him when it came time to put together the report on closing down his Kirksville plant. Knowing how the guys at HQ felt about things saved him a couple of months time.

Well, give me a call as soon as possible so we can finalize our plans and make reservations. Say hi to your good-looking wife for me.

(Signed) Jonas [Calder, General Manager, Metal Stampings]

EXHIBIT 15

Envelope, hand addressed to Mr. Hayes:

I have been a bookkeeper in the Accounting Department for eight years and heard about your temporary assignment to Al Tech on Friday morning. My parents are retired and vacation in Florida during the winter. Their two-bedroom home is located about a mile from our office at 2132 Elm St. It's near an elementary school. I called my folks over the lunch hour and they offered to rent the house to you for $250 a month. They are leaving after Labor Day and won't be back until Easter. It's really a good deal as two-bedroom apartments in town are scarce and rent for about $350 a month. Let me know early in the week if you are interested.

Dotty Simmons

EXHIBIT 16

Handwritten note from Ben Brown, clipped to the letter below, dated August 11:

Rusty:

This is a xerox of a letter I just got today from Joyce Riley, the new receptionist. I don't know what you want to do about this, but we should talk about it on Friday, the 13th (unless you want to meet at the Olympus Club Saturday).

Ben

Dear Mr. Brown:

Since you are both my boss and the Personnel Director, I felt it was right to mention a problem I'm having to you. I feel I am being harassed on my job.

When I interviewed for work here I asked if it was all right to moonlight and you said I could use my own time as I wished. The truth was that I had a job then, and still do, working Friday and Saturday nights at the Olympus Club on Sycamore Street. Sooner or later you're bound to hear it so I'll tell you now that I work there as an exotic dancer.

It seems some of the workers who know I work in the factory told a couple of the office people about my moonlighting and several of them came to see me at work. The club was really busy the last couple of weekends. Now rumors are all over the place about me. I know it's true because I overheard some of the workers in the lunchroom talking about drawing straws to see who gets to bring paperwork over to the office from the factory. Some of our office people must even have told customers who call here, because visitors to our office have said a few things to me. I'm not really complaining about what they say to me or how they look at me. I'm used to that. But what happened recently really bothers me.

A woman called here two days ago, wouldn't say who she was, and accused me of all sorts of things with her husband. I finally got over that and then yesterday another woman called and said I was a loose woman who shouldn't be allowed to work in an office where nice husbands worked. She said if I didn't quit my job she'd tell the other wives and get me fired. I enjoy my work but I don't play around with married men and I don't want to give up either job. Can you help me?

(Signed) Joyce Riley

EXHIBIT 17

Letter dated August 4, 1982, opened by Wainscott:

Dear Mr. Wainscott:

In preparation for the coming year the Board of Education has voted its continuing support for our Career Day program at Central High School. Your firm's participation last year was appreciated and we hope you will again donate your time and effort to help ensure the success of this year's program.

Career Day is scheduled for Friday, January 7, 1983, from 9 o'clock to 4 o'clock. This year the Board has decided to cancel all classes for the day so the participating firms will have more space for displays and meetings than we had last year.

We need your response by August 20 so we may make the necessary arrangements. Thank you for your cooperation in our efforts.

Sincerely,
(Signed) Robert Wood, Superintendent of Schools

EXHIBIT 18

Note written to himself by George Hayes when he arrived in the office:

Catch 8:30 p.m. United flight from O'Hare on Friday for our anniversary on Saturday—get present.

FIGURE 1
Organization
Chart—Al Tech
Division

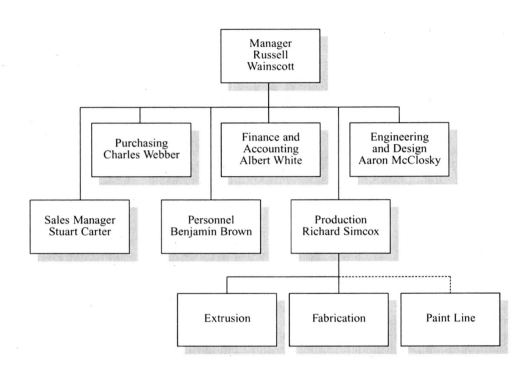

Edited by Paul F. Buller, Gonzaga University, and Randall S. Schuler, Rutgers University

BULLER | SCHULER

Managing Organizations and People

A Resource for Cases in Management, Organizational Behavior, and Human Resource Management

Abstract

Tyrone Hines, the recently promoted Vice President of the ZX Software Development Group, a unit of TaxPrep, Inc., must decide what actions to take to resolve simmering feuds and dissatisfaction within the Santa Cruz branch of his two-site organization. A corporate restructuring had led to the elimination of all but two of TaxPrep's software development sites and the splitting of the downsized development organization into two separate organizations: one devoted to the maintenance of the mainframe tax-preparation software programs, and the other dedicated to the development of the new ZX software programs designed for tax-return preparers use on personal computers. With the ZX development program months behind schedule, and faced with a corporate mandate to ensure that ZX software is generating profits by 1994, Hines is under pressure to resolve a perceived pay inequity that appears to be at the crux of the main conflict.

The case provides narrative data on TaxPrep's developmental history, as well as information on the firm's software development processes, organizational arrangements, external environment, evolving business strategy, and the compensation controversy within the Santa Cruz branch of the ZX development organization. Complicating the vice president's decision grid are several strategic, cost, and organizational climate imperatives that any acceptable solution must satisfy. The case concludes with the vice president's pondering what actions would be advised to eliminate the disgruntlement among interdependent members of the Santa Cruz team, as well as the suspicion and mistrust between the Santa Cruz site and the Tulsa base location for the ZX technology.

The ZX Software Development Group: Santa Cruz Site

In late 1992, Tyrone Hines, the recently promoted Vice President in charge of the ZX Development Group—one of two software development organizations within TaxPrep Inc.—was faced with a difficult problem. At the crux of the problem were perceptions by the Tax Specialists of a compensation inequity between themselves and the Tax Analysts at the Santa Cruz branch of the ZX Development Group. Although the intra-staff tensions and conflicts fed by these perceptions did not affect the ZX Group's Tulsa branch (which never had Tax Specialist positions), Hines nevertheless had reason to be concerned.

Software development teams at TaxPrep were highly interdependent, as were the individual task roles within the teams. Further, the ZX software development program was already months behind schedule. Without smooth working relationships within the teams, Hines knew that his prospects of meeting the fourth-quarter 1993 target date for the release of the new ZX software would be greatly diminished. He also knew that it was highly desirable to arrive at a resolution of the compensation issue that did not antagonize the Analysts or further inflame the Specialists.

Background on TaxPrep and Its Software Development Group

TaxPrep, Inc., one of several divisions of a large legal and business documents publishing firm, was founded in 1965. Its initial mission had been to "develop a product for processing computerized tax returns in a mainframe computer environment." During its first two decades of operation, the firm had grown steadily as it added depth and breadth to its product lines. By the early 1980s, TaxPrep could boast a complete line of individual and business tax-return services and products. Among the large service bureau tax-return processing firms, TaxPrep—which, by 1985, operated 23 tax-return processing centers nationwide—enjoyed a well-established market position that was the envy of many of its competitors.

TaxPrep's Initial Strategy: 1965–1991

By the end of its first quarter century of operation, TaxPrep, had captured a 25 percent market share in that part of the tax-return preparation business dominated by the national tax preparation services. This success was achieved despite TaxPrep's being the highest priced provider among the national tax preparation firms.

Terry Raphael, president, attributed TaxPrep's success to "[its] consistent attention to high-quality products, excellent customer service, and effective marketing." Particularly effective, he felt, had been TaxPrep's "pursuit of competitive advantage [via] excellent customer service." For example, given the importance that clients attached to fast turn-around of completed returns, TaxPrep moved to differentiate itself from its competitors by becoming, in 1974, the first firm to utilize courier services as an integral part of its operations. Competitive tactics such as these, Raphael explained, had earned TaxPrep strong customer loyalty, and propelled the firm's long record of rapid growth.

Initial Structure of the Software Development Staff

TaxPrep had centralized its mainframe software development staff at its corporate headquarters in Santa Cruz, CA. Until its 1991 downsizing, the Santa Cruz software staff, which was responsible for the development and maintenance of the mainframe tax-preparation software, consisted of 123 professionals. The staff was organized along product lines (e.g., individual versus business tax-return services), which were further divided along sub-product lines (see Exhibit 1).

Among the early development staff were fifteen Tax Specialists, many of whom had more than two decades of service with TaxPrep. These Specialists were experts in various facets of federal and state tax laws, which they regularly monitored for changes that would signal the need for periodic updates of the software programs. The remainder of the development group was evenly divided between Tax Analysts and Programmers, a few of whom had been with the firm for longer than ten years. Development staff members held college degrees in computer science, accounting, business/economics, or related disciplines. Many possessed graduate degrees in specialized fields. Nearly one-fifth of the Specialists and Analysts were certified public accountants and/or tax attorneys.

Changing Industry Dynamics: Consolidation and PC Technology

The impetus for the creation of the ZX Development Group could be traced to salient changes in competitive conditions during the early 1980s. Two trends in particular—increased industry consolidation and the popularization of personal computer-based, tax-return processing technology—had triggered a refocusing of TaxPrep's competitive strategy.

Changing Industry Dynamics—Industry Consolidation

As the computerized tax-return processing industry matured during the late 1970s, a wave of new entrants had begun penetrating the market. Their focus on regional niches soon led

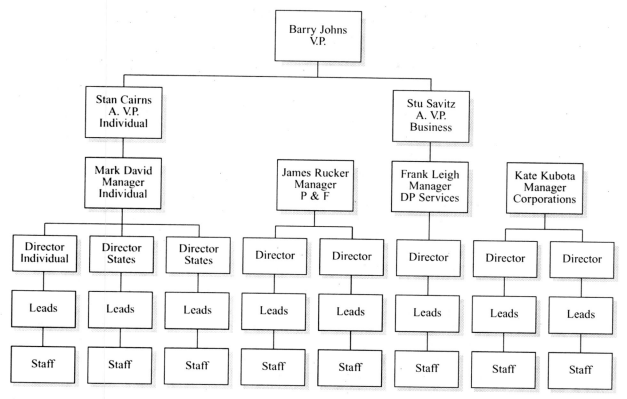

EXHIBIT 1
Mid-1985 Organization Chart for Mainframe Development Organization at TaxPrep's Headquarters

to the erosion of the dominance of industry giants such as TaxPrep and QwikTax (Tax-Prep's strongest national competitor) which vied for sophisticated larger customers, such as the "Big Five" certified public accounting (i.e., CPA) firms.[1] Many of the new entrants targeted local or regional CPA firms, aggressively using lower prices as a competitive weapon to pry market share from larger competitors.

In response to competitive inroads by these new entrants, major industry players—attracted by their small rivals' growing market shares—initiated vigorous acquisition campaigns. Industry consolidation proceeded at a brisk pace throughout the latter half of the 1980s.

TaxPrep's Response to Increased Competition. To protect its market share, TaxPrep's response to industry consolidation had been to implement its own acquisition strategy. During the period 1986-1989, the firm made six acquisitions, at a cost of $47.2 million, folding the acquired companies' tax preparation operations into TaxPrep's own mainframe computer processing services. TAXX (New Orleans) was acquired in early-1988; Accutax (Fremont, CA) was acquired in late-1988; and, ProfiTax (Rock Island, IL) was brought under TaxPrep's corporate umbrella in early-1989.

Two of the six acquisitions—Rock Island and Fremont—were designated as mainframe software development sites. These two additional development sites were assigned support roles in the work of the central mainframe software development organization at TaxPrep headquarters.

Changing Industry Dynamics—Emerging PC Technology
The popularization of the personal computer (PC) during the 1980s—which ultimately propelled a metamorphosis of the entire industry—had been the second impetus for the refocusing of TaxPrep's competitive strategy.

For the smaller tax preparer, and for those with less complex tax-return items, the advantages of the personal computer software were compelling. Such software made it possible for tax preparers to process an unlimited number of returns in their own offices on personal computers. In so doing, they could avoid paying the "per-return" fees charged by mainframe tax-return service bureaus. Aside from the per-return cost savings (after the "pay-back" period for the necessary computer hardware), PC tax return software offered a quicker turnaround via the merging of preparer and data processing roles.[2]

As the 1980s had drawn to a close, tax preparers were increasingly opting to invest in a PC-based tax-return processing system. And a host of new software startup firms, as well as a dozen major software companies, rapidly emerged to supply the requisite software. The increasing sophistication of PC-based tax-return processing software had begun to erode TaxPrep's market share, as even its sophisticated CPA-firm clientele became increasingly resistant to TaxPrep's high-end prices for mainframe tax-return processing.

TaxPrep's Response to the PC Software Threat. With its main competitive rivals scrambling to respond to the PC-based tax preparation technology, TaxPrep executives had soon concluded that the firm's long-term viability depended upon its ability to respond with TaxPrep's own PC-based tax-processing software. In late-1988, a task force of systems designers was commissioned to develop a PC software system. When, after more than a year of effort, they failed to produce a viable software package, TaxPrep began looking for a suitable acquisition candidate. SuperTax soon emerged as an attractive possibility.

Tulsa-based SuperTax had been in the mainframe tax-preparation business for six years when, in 1987, one of its software developers produced a new program which was intended as the basis for SuperTax's entry into the PC software market. The new software "ZX" because of the developer's fondness for the Nissan sports car of the same name— was written in "C," a fourth-generation computer language that obviated the traditional programmer role.

Limited financial resources, and an overly optimistic assessment of the time required to perfect the revolutionary new technology, had led SuperTax to prematurely abandon its mainframe products in order to focus on the ZX technology. This fateful decision led to a series of financially draining events, culminating in SuperTax's bankruptcy before ZX development was completed. In October 1989, TaxPrep executives, having read an internal assessment of the ZX product, bought SuperTax's ZX technology and customer lists. With this acquisition, TaxPrep began its transition from service-bureau provider of tax services to PC software provider.

The Formation of the ZX Development Group

Although TaxPrep executives knew that the mainframe product line would eventually be abandoned, they also recognized that additional development work was required to make the ZX product marketable. Hence, it was decided to continue to extract revenues from TaxPrep's 17,000 mainframe customers during the expected 24-month transition to the ZX program.

Initially, TaxPrep retained SuperTax's three development sites—Tulsa, where the individual-filer tax system was being developed; Roanoke, VA, where the business-filer tax system was under development; and Tampa, FL, where the "tool set" was being created—in order to be assured of the continued expertise of the SuperTax development staff. These three sites were added to TaxPrep's three existing mainframe software development sites and placed under the direction of the Vice President of Tax Systems Development. (See Exhibit 2.)

By late-1990, however, a precipitous decline in revenues—triggered by both the 1990-91 national recession and the continued hemorrhaging of market share as PC-based tax-preparation software firms siphoned off TaxPrep customers (see Exhibit 3)—led to a major downsizing and restructuring of the TaxPrep organization, including the development group. Within the Santa Cruz headquarters alone, the sales force was shrunk by 40 percent, while most other employee positions were reduced by half. All but a few of the Santa Cruz Programmers were released, as senior management looked toward the planned phase-out of the mainframe systems. By mid-1991, the erstwhile Santa Cruz development group of 150 Programmers, Analysts, and Specialists had become a 62-person group of comprised mostly of Analysts and Specialists.

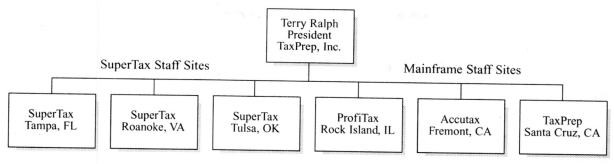

EXHIBIT 2
Pre-1991 Organization Chart for Mainframe & ZX Development Organizations at TaxPrep, Inc.

A few months later, it was decided to consolidate the ZX development effort into just two locations, Tulsa and Santa Cruz. Tyrone Hines, then head of the Tulsa ZX development team, was promoted to Vice President, in charge of all ZX development work, which was to be directed from the Tulsa site. Explaining the underlying rationale, Hines stated:

Corporate had wanted to avoid closing the four sites. Personnel at all six sites had been through a lot of disruption in a short period of time—with the layoffs that accompanied the acquisitions and with the insecurity within our mainframe group caused by the shift toward the PC software technology. After the corporate-wide layoffs [mandated] as a result of 1990s bleak financial results, we hadn't wanted to put them through more change.

But communication among the different sites responsible for various pieces of the software had become a nightmare. Then, too, the Rock Island and Fremont site staffs, with no experience in working with the ZX product, were too far up the learning curve to be of any real assistance. From a value-added perspective, corporate realized that the overhead cost of operating out of six development sites just couldn't be justified. The Santa Cruz/Tulsa pairing offered [us] the ability to develop a full product line at the least cost. . . . Santa Cruz offers some needed ZX development expertise, but Tulsa is the core of our ZX expertise.

EXHIBIT 3
Trends in Revenues and Profits: 1982–1992

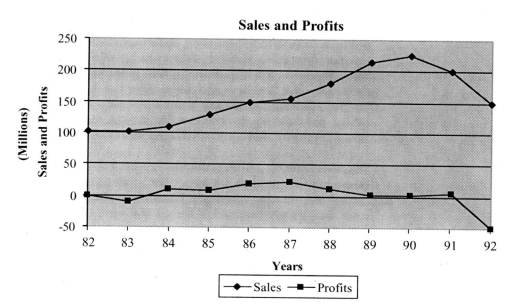

Along with the reduction in sites, the ZX development teams at both Santa Cruz and Tulsa were bolstered to handle the increased workload. Top-notch technical personnel from several locations (mainly, Roanoke and Tampa) were offered the opportunity to transfer to Tulsa or Santa Cruz. Those who had not wished to transfer were terminated.

The Development Process for Tax Preparation Software

In Tyrone Hines' view, dissatisfaction with the compensation system originated with changes in software development tasks that had resulted from TaxPrep's 1989 strategic decision, reinforced by its 1991 restructuring, to commit fully to the PC tax-preparation software market.

Mainframe Software Development Process: 1965–1993

TaxPrep's software development process was team-based. The development group was organized by product line (see Exhibit 1), with multiple teams involved in the development of a given product: three teams (for an individual-tax product), and five teams (for a business-tax product).

Team Organization and Staff Duties. Teams typically consisted of a director, a lead analyst, six to nine tax analysts, several tax specialists, six to nine Cobol programmers, and a lead programmer. The team director was responsible for the hiring, scheduling, and evaluation of staff members. During tax season, the director usually held daily status meetings to ensure that the team's products were being synchronized with those of the other development teams, with whom the team's products were interdependent. The lead analyst, the director's principal assistant, trained new team members, monitored team members' status reports, and performed various special project assignments.

The tax analysts and programmers were responsible for developing and maintaining their assigned tax products. The tax analyst's role entailed the following major duties: (i) analyzing applicable tax laws and tax forms to ensure compliance of the assigned tax-return product; (ii) upon changes in tax laws, developing specifications for programmers' use in changing the software program; (iii) maintaining a set of test files for each assigned tax product and, for quality control purposes, running that set of tests before a new program release was transmitted to preparers; and, (iv) responding to Program Error Reports received from the processing centers, and arranging for programmers to correct the problem before the next program release.

Programmers put the specifications from the tax analysts into the program and did the initial testing to ensure that the program performed as intended. They were also responsible for making the program as efficient as possible.

Finally, tax specialists performed the review function, evaluating all work done by the tax analysts. As such, they were essentially supervisors of the analysts' work.

The seasonal nature of the tax-preparation business made the jobs of tax analyst and programmer especially demanding. In the mainframe software era, the job of tax analyst was more demanding than that of the specialist, who mainly performed a review function. Yearly changes in federal and state tax laws necessitated long hours of overtime for the analysts, who were kept busy from the moment new laws were promulgated until they met TaxPrep's deadline (usually late-December or early-January) for integrating these modifications into the computer programs. The months immediately preceding the onset of the annual tax season were especially intense periods of overtime for the analysts.

Selection/Training and Performance Appraisal Systems. A minimum of two years' tax experience was required for the analyst position; programmers were required to have "some" programming experience. Vacant specialist positions were usually filled by top-notch analysts who had reached the top of the analyst job grade. Finally, because of the criticality of teamwork in the software development process, team directors sought to assess the likely degree to which each prospect would "fit" with other members of the team.

On-the-job training and periodic in-house classes on special topics were the most common forms of skills enhancement for new hires. Those who desired to obtain a Master's degree in a relevant field received tuition-reimbursement.

Team directors (who were typically promoted from the ranks of senior analysts) performed an annual review of each team member's performance, using a modification of an instrument developed by Hay Associates. Areas assessed included *Know How, Problem Solving,* and *Accountability.* These appraisals became the basis for merit increases and promotions.

Compensation Systems. Tax analysts received overtime pay to compensate them for the many extra hours of work required during the intense tax-preparation season. Although their overtime usually averaged more than 200 hours per person, maximum compensation was set at 10 percent of the total number of normal hours in a work year (i.e., 200 hours), or 10 percent of their salaries.

By contrast, tax specialists were not entitled to overtime compensation because in their supervisory capacity overtime work was rarely necessary under the mainframe system. Specialists were, however, eligible for a year-end bonus of $1,500, a long-established sum devised as means of compensating specialists for their ineligibility for overtime pay.

ZX Software Development Process: 1991–1993

With its purchase of the ZX product, TaxPrep's customary software development process underwent several changes.

Changes in Team Member Tasks. The fourth-generation computer language used in the ZX technology permitted the Analysts themselves to write the PC tax programs. The result was the 1991 layoff of nearly all the remaining programmers—a move that had accentuated feelings of insecurity within both development organizations. As Hines explained it:

The ZX Development Group was carved out of the development staffs at the various sites. Mainframe software development will continue for the next year or so, but everybody knows that the ZX product is the wave of the future. So, we have a serious morale problem and tension between the ZX Group, which is seen as a kind of "elite" staff, and the mainframe personnel, who sense that they're to be phased out along with the mainframe product.

Additionally, although tax analysts remained responsible for developing various tax preparation programs, their jobs also broadened somewhat to include duties that the programmers performed in the mainframe software development process. That is, using the user-friendly language at the core of the ZX technology, analysts also wrote the programs, integrating updated laws for the various tax forms and schedules.

With the built-in test protocols of the ZX technology largely obviating supervisory review of analysts' work, the role of specialist lost much of its distinctiveness. Specialist duties were now basically indistinguishable from those of the analysts. Further, both jobs now required overtime. However, with no overtime compensation forthcoming, specialists—already feeling demoted by their ZX work assignments—firmly resisted the idea of working overtime.

Magnitude of the Perceived Compensation Inequity. Depending on a tax analyst's experience and seniority, salaries ranged from $30,000 to $60,000, with the average analyst earning approximately $50,000 in 1993. The average overtime pay for analysts was about $5,000. By contrast, tax specialists' salaries ranged from $40,000 to $72,000, with the average specialist earning about $58,000 in 1993. A flat $1,500 per person bonus was available to tax specialists.

Santa Cruz site ZX team directors were increasingly concerned that the compensation controversy had begun to impede team effectiveness. It was because of their expressions of concern to Hines' two direct reports at the Santa Cruz site (see Exhibit 4) that Hines felt compelled to find a way to resolve the matter.

ZX Team Performance Problems at the Santa Cruz Site

The Santa Cruz ZX Development Group staff experienced difficulty from the very beginning of their work with the ZX program, which was completely new to them. The new program did not initially execute as well as had the old mainframe system, which had been around for so long that virtually all the bugs had been removed. In Hines' words, ZX development progress at the Santa Cruz site had been "painfully slow."

EXHIBIT 4
Organization Chart of the Post-1991 ZX Development Group of TaxPrep, Inc.

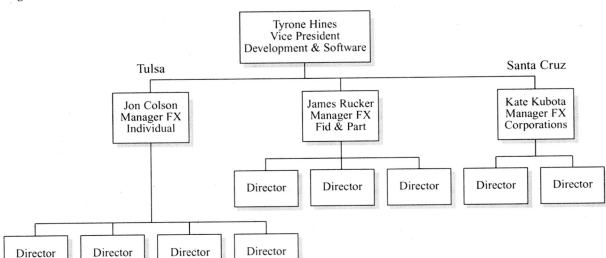

Further, the old mainframe system had a large number of periodic releases during the course of each year. This meant that any problems in the program would be discovered via customer feedback and could normally be corrected in the next weekly program release— of which there were normally fifteen during the program development season. Because of this, Hines perceived that the Santa Cruz analysts had become "somewhat complacent in their programming tasks."

By contrast, because ZX customers bought a finished software product that was supposed to work on their in-house computer system(s), *first-time* accuracy of programming was of prime importance. Further, there were only five releases on the ZX program during the TaxPrep software development season. And most "fixes" in a ZX program often necessitated time-consuming diagnostic calls between the customer and ZX analysts. "Walking" a customer through a programming problem over the telephone usually proved frustrating to both the customer and ZX software personnel.

Defining the success of the analysts' products in terms of "correctness of execution of complicated tax calculations" and "ease of use by the preparer," Hines was concerned that the Analysts be held accountable for their products both before and after they were released to the customer. "Unlike the situation in consumer-oriented software products," he noted, "telephone support [at TaxPrep] doesn't produce revenues. The level of telephone support is a pretty good indication of errors or substandard work that we've simply got to control."

Several mechanisms were used for process control. An Automatic Call Distribution, a telephone feature which indicated which analysts had been available for customer calls during a given time period, yielded a report indicating who took calls, how many calls were taken, when, and the minutes per call. A Query Report, generated by Customer Service, provided documentation on program errors. A third report, prepared by Marketing, tracked the number and type of enhancements added to each product. Finally, quality-control check systems involving "compare programs," were used to run a new product against the same set of test files used to identify bugs in the earlier version of a product.[3]

Other Inter-Development Staff Frictions

Aside from the Specialist/Analyst frictions at the Santa Cruz site, which were Hines' immediate concern, there were frictions elsewhere within the larger development organization. First, the insecurity and demoralization afflicting the downsized mainframe development staff was negatively impacting working relationships between mainframe and ZX staff members at Santa Cruz. The two staffs were not highly interdependent, but there were periodic needs for task interaction between members of the two groups. Hines' direct reports at the Santa Cruz ZX site had advised him that these interactions were increasingly frought with problems—e.g., resistance by the mainframe staff to informational exchanges with their ZX counterparts.

Moreover, given their on-going problems in mastering the ZX technology, Santa Cruz ZX staff personnel had become fearful of losing their work to the Tulsa site. This insecurity added an edginess to the required frequent communications between the two ZX staffs, and worked against the smooth and easy flow of information between the two sites.

The Criticality of Maintaining TaxPrep's Competitive Edge

As he pondered the situation, Hines—whose mandate it was to begin showing a profit on a full line of ZX software by 1994—was mindful of several issues that bore the resolution of the compensation issue. Foremost was the necessity of maintaining TaxPrep's reputation for high quality and excellent service, as the firm continued its metamorphosis into a provider of PC-based tax-return software. This could only be done if interdependent ZX development teams maintained easy communications and working relationships. A second consideration was senior management's current emphasis on cost containment. Hines knew that any modifications in ZX staff compensation would have to have a minimal cost impact.

Finally, Hines realized that his prospects for success in selling even a minimal cost solution would be enhanced to the extent that he could demonstrate to the president that the proposed change(s) would not add to the friction between the ZX and mainframe development teams. Given Terry Raphael's concern about the morale of the mainframe staff, Hines knew that any proposed ZX compensation changes would have to be seen as neutral in their impact on the personnel responsible for TaxPrep's still vital mainframe business.

Endnotes

1. Early tax software programs were designed to run on large mainframe computers, and to print out on impact printers in triplicate. The process required a tax-processing service bureau's customers ("preparers") to fill out input sheets, which were sent to a central (or regional) processing center where a powerful mainframe computer was located. The customer would receive the completed tax return within several days of completion of the input sheet.

2. Among the hurdles that mainframe-service customers faced in decoupling their operations from those of the service bureau mainframe tax-return processors were: (i) the substantial initial investment in computer hardware; (ii) the limited computing power of the earlier PC hardware and the relative lack of sophisticated coding in earlier PC software—constraints which greatly hampered their utility for complex tax-return processing (e.g., depletion, depreciation, and alternative minimum tax calculations); (iii) the necessity of the PC-based preparer's developing proficiency in a computer operating system and in software application; and finally, (iv) the more limited number of program "fixes" (i.e., new CD releases)—normally, just four or five program updates per tax-return season—available to the PC-based preparer who, in addition, would be faced with a four- or five-week delay in obtaining an updated program with which to devise a corrected tax return. On this final disad-

vantage: service bureau firms offered weekly program updates during tax season—thus reducing turnaround time for a corrected tax return to about a week, including the time required for the development group to remove the program "bug."

3. Among the documents TaxPrep employed to aid in the smooth and timely release of tax products were the following:

   - *Suggestion Record Document*: for proposing an enhancement to a program. These were reviewed by a committee which prioritized the approved proposals.
   - *Program Change Sheet*: for tracking changes in government tax forms so that every item would make it into the updated tax programs. Analysts were responsible for preparing these forms and for verifying the indicated program updates.
   - *Problem Error Report*: for documenting program bugs. Analysts were responsible for program corrections.
   - *Graphics Routing Slips*: for specifying procedures to follow in routing instruction guides, interview forms, and output forms to the TaxPrep Graphics Department.
   - *Instruction Guide Format*: for specifying how to standardize the format and language (e.g., wording, tense) of Instruction Guides written for the tax preparers.

BULLER | SCHULER

Managing Organizations and People
A Resource for Cases in Management, Organizational Behavior, and Human Resource Management

Abstract

At 2:53 A.M. on September 22, 1993, the *Sunset Limited*, Amtrak's only transcontinental passenger train, plunged into Big Bayou Canot, killing 47 passengers. Eight minutes earlier at 2:45 A.M., a towboat, pushing six barges and lost in a dense fog unknowingly bumped into the Big Bayou Canot Bridge knocking the track out of alignment. The train, traveling at a speed of 72 mph in the dense fog, derailed as a result, burying the engine and four cars deep in the mud and muck of Big Bayou Canot. Besides those who did not immediately perish, those still alive struggled to survive by any means possible. In the minutes and hours that followed, more lives were lost in this one moment than in the 23-year history of Amtrak.

This case, derived from secondary sources, illustrates the difficulty of assigning responsibility in situations that are managerially and technically complex, especially when they deal with highly emotional and sometimes disastrous events. It also addresses the difficulty of recognizing reasonable alternative solutions to major issues once they have been systematically identified. As such, the case examines the tradeoffs between the costs of corporate ethics and social responsibility, government regulation, fail-safe systems, and public welfare. And, it raises issues regarding the extent to which corporations should be expected to respond to government recommendations versus government mandates.

The Wreck of Amtrak's *Sunset Limited*

At 2:33 A.M. on September 22, 1993, the *Sunset Limited*, Amtrak's only transcontinental passenger train, eased out of the Mobile, Alabama, station to continue its streak eastward, 33 minutes behind schedule—scheduled departure was 2:00 A.M. (Figure 1). It had been delayed in New Orleans for repairs to an air conditioner and toilets on two cars. The train, as it left the Mobile station, consisted of three locomotives and eight cars and carried 202 passengers with a crew of 18. By the time the train was ten miles out of Mobile, it had reached a speed of 72 mph (authorized speed was 70 mph). The green signals indicated that the train was free to "proceed" at maximum track speed in spite of the dense fog, which reduced visibility to a few yards. At about 2:53 A.M. at Mile Post 656.7 on the Chesapeake and Ohio (CSX) main track, the *Sunset Limited* approached a wood-and-steel bridge spanning a navigable estuary called "Big Bayou Canot." Although the National

■ H. Richard Eisenbeis, University of Southern Colorado

1

FIGURE 1
Mobile, Alabama, and Vicinity Showing Location of Wreck of Amtrak's *Sunset Limited*

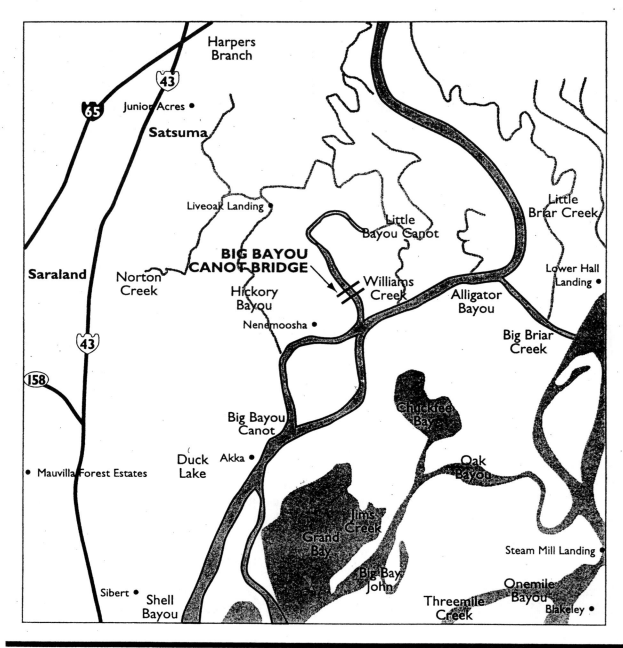

Transportation Safety Board (NTSB) had recommended that all railroad bridges over navigable bodies of water be equipped with sensors to detect bridge damage, the Big Bayou Canot bridge was not so equipped.

Bruce Barrett, a locomotive engineer, has described what might have been occurring in the cab of Amtrak engine Number 819 prior to the wreck.

This scenario is based upon my 17 years' experience as a locomotive engineer on a major western railroad and upon the compilation of bits and pieces of data from public records and accounts of the accident.

Engineer Michael Vincent was at the controls of the two-week-old General Electric "AMD-103" locomotive. Engineer Billy Rex Hall was in the cab with Vincent along with Ernest Lamar Russ who was qualifying as an Amtrak engineer on this portion of the run.

I can almost see the instrument lights as they cast a soft, orange glow across the cab of the locomotive, highlighted by the light from the train's headlight bouncing off the impenetrable fog. I can hear the three men calling out the colors of the railroad signals (sort of like traffic lights for automobiles) as they came into view and discussing the restrictions that would affect the train over the next few miles. The new locomotive, shaped like a bullet, would have been a topic of conversation. Engineers enjoy comparing the "old days" with the new technology as it responds to the movement of their hands on the controls as the train clipped along at 103.53 feet per second. While the headlight beam may have reached 1,000 feet in clear weather, given the dense fog, the visibility would more likely have been less than 100 feet. As the Bayou Canot Bridge appeared in the fog, they would have had no hint of what lay ahead. Even if the headlight had detected the slight shift of the tracks to the left, there would have been less than a second for Vincent to react. I can see his hand as he reached too late for the emergency brake as the 150-ton locomotive turned into an uncontrollable beast and lurched to the left, starting a dive that would bury the locomotive 46 feet—equivalent to five stories—into the muddy bank of the bayou.

I can sense the bridge collapsing under me and momentarily hear the locomotives and lead cars dropping into the water and debris below. I can feel the locomotive's windshield glass against my face and hands as it shatters inward. I can see myself recoiling in terror as water and mud extrude into the cab, helplessly entombing me and my two companions in our muddy coffin.

None of the engineers survived. The three locomotive units came to rest on the east side of the bayou. Part of Unit 819 was buried about 46 feet in the mud, and the part protruding above the embankment caught fire and burned. The verified records indicate that in addition to the engines, a baggage car, a baggage-dorm, and two coaches of the eight-car train dove into the 16 feet of water below the bridge. The last four cars remained on the bridge.

The passenger cars in the bayou immediately began to fill with water, and the diesel fuel from ruptured locomotive fuel tanks began to burn atop the water. While some passengers were able to fight their way to the surface, others were hopelessly trapped in the wreckage. Parents lifted children to safety and, in their continuing efforts to save others, became victims themselves. Others dove repeatedly into the black waters in attempts to save fellow passengers.

Darkness prevailed outside the cars after the derailment. Battery-powered emergency lighting, available inside coaches, provided some illumination; but only the train crew had penlights to use while walking down the tracks in the dark. Once the cars entered the water, the emergency lighting became inoperable, further complicating evacuation from the submerged cars. Without light from a few penlights and from the fire that ensued following the accident, no light would have been available. Because emergency lighting was unavailable in the submerged cars, passengers had difficulty locating and moving to exits.

Since most on board service crewmembers were asleep in the dorm coach and since the train attendants were in the cars on the bridge, passengers in the submerged cars had to make decisions on their own and evacuate without assistance. Fortunately, a few passengers took control of the situation, located exits, and told others what to do.

Both the conductor and the assistant conductor were in the diner car, the next to the last car on the train. The assistant conductor reported that the accident took place without warning—no setting up of the brakes, no horn blast, and no communication to the loco-motive crew. He was thrown onto a table in front of him and then into the middle of the car. The conductor was thrown over him. When the train stopped, the conductor attempted to contact the engineers in the lead locomotive using his portable radio but received no reply.

The badly shaken but otherwise uninjured assistant conductor instantly contacted Warren Carr (the CSX trainmaster) who was responsible for monitoring all traffic in this portion of the CSX system and requested immediate assistance. But, in the confusion and blackness he was able to give only a general location of the wreck.

The New York Times article entitled "Report Revises Times in Train Wreck" published October 8, 1993, includes transcripts of three calls to 911 placed by Amtrak employees immediately after the accident (Figure 2).

Neither Carr nor the Mobile Police Department's 911 operator were successful in their first attempts to contact the Coast Guard due to an incorrect listing of the number in the Mobile telephone directory. And, because there were no coordinated emergency re-sponse maps for the area, a confused 911 operator had a difficult time understanding the location of the wreck site being described by Mr. Carr. These two factors had the effect of slowing rescue efforts considerably.

Immediately after the wreck, Amtrak crewmen and passengers noted a "large marine vessel 150 yards or more to the south." It was later identified as the *Mauvilla*. Survivors thought it strange that the *Mauvilla* did not move in to assist in the rescue efforts until 15 to 25 minutes after the crash.

FIGURE 2
Transcripts
of 911 calls

Transcripts of three calls placed to 911 after the crash of the Amtrak *Sunset Limited* September 22 follow:

FIRST CALL: 3:01 A.M.
The first two calls came from officials of CSX Transportation Inc., owner of the tracks and bridge. Warren Carr, an assistant terminal trainmaster in Mobile, apparently made the first, to the Mobile police dispatcher.

Mr. Carr tells the operator a train has derailed at Bayou Sara drawbridge and that he understands people are in the water and the bridge is on fire. There are references to Prichard, a small town on the edge of Mobile and Chickasabogue, or Chickasaw Creek, five miles southwest of the accident site (Figure 3).

911:     Where is this? Where is that located?
CARR: It's off the Mobile River.
911:     Um-hm.
CARR: It's north of Chickasabogue draw. You can't . . .
911:     You can't . . .?
CARR: You can't get there, can't get there by vehicle.
911:     O.K., is that going to be, is that going to be in Prichard, north of Chickasabogue? Is that going to be it?
CARR: It's north of Chickasabogue.
911:     Um-hm.
CARR: It's a passenger train. I got people in the water. I got cars on fire.
911:     O.K., but . . .
CARR: It's a derailment.
911:     O.K., a derailment, but is it in Prichard, there by Chickasabogue Creek?
CARR: No, it's on the river.
911:     On the Mobile River?
CARR: You can't get to it over the road.

(continued)

FIGURE 2
Transcripts
of 911 calls—
continued

911:      O.K.

CARR: You're going to have to get some helicopters and boats and Coast Guard and all those people.

Later, Mr. Carr gets frustrated as he tries to give a location.

CARR: No, it's, it's south of Mobile River, north of Chickasabogue River.

911:      South of . . .

CARR: North of Chickasabogue, at the next major creek, north of Chickasabogue.

911:      And south of, what other river was that?

CARR: South of Mobile River. It's right along beside Mobile River, where Bayou Sara comes off the Mobile River.

911:      Bayou Seven?

CARR: Get me ahold of the Coast Guard.

SECOND CALL: 3:10 A.M.

The second call was from Ronnie Seymour, an assistant CSX supervisor for bridges and buildings in Mobile. During this call operators confirmed that the train was carrying passengers and began to grasp the scope of the disaster. (Figure 4 provides a sequence of events.)

911:          Can you tell me what the train was carrying?

SEYMOUR: The passengers.

911:          Passengers? (She then speaks to another operator.) It's going to be Saraland, but it's a passenger train that's derailed . . . crew in water, the train's on fire.

911:          So it is a passenger train?

SEYMOUR: Yes, ma'am.

911:          O.K., sir. It's going to be Saraland's but we have notified the proper authorities, O.K.?

SEYMOUR: Thank you very much.

THIRD CALL: 3:16 A.M.

The third call, 26 minutes after the accident is believed to have occurred, was from an unidentified Amtrak supervisor on the train.

AMTRAK: We're on, we're on the Mobile River.

911:          You're on the Mobile River?

AMTRAK: On the Mobile River. We've got cars burning. They're over, the bridge is out. There's people in the water. We're trying to help them, but we need all kind of help.

911:          So the bridge is out?

AMTRAK: Yes, ma'am, we need help. Send help, please.

Later, after telling the supervisor help is on the way, the operator asks about the location of the wreck.

911:          This is the bridge that's out?

AMTRAK: Yes, ma'am. The bridge is out. Yes, ma'am.

911:          O.K., which bridge is this that's . . . that's out?

AMTRAK: Ma'am, I don't know. We're on the Mobile River.

911:          You're on the Mobile River?

AMTRAK: That's all I know.

911:          But you don't know which bridge it is?

AMTRAK: No, ma'am. No, ma'am. I haven't been informed by the conductor. (The supervisor can be heard yelling: "John! John!" apparently to the conductor.)

The supervisor ends the call by telling the operator, "Ma'am, I have to go and assist these folks."

Source: The Associated Press

FIGURE 3
Mobile River Chart

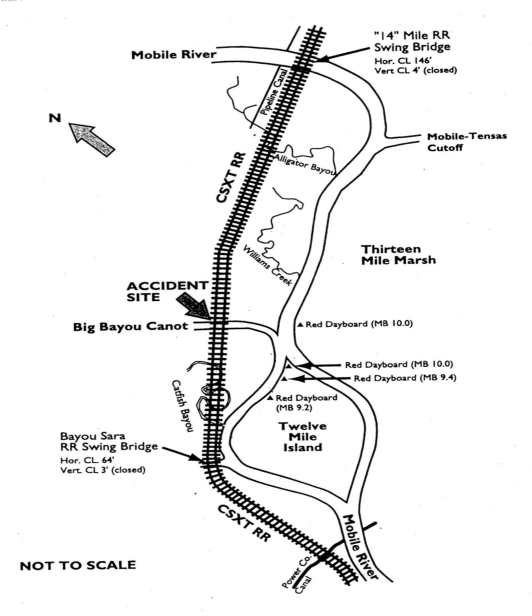

Note: The accident site at Big Bayou Canot Bridge is in close proximity to the Mobile River, which has a deep and wide channel heavily utilized by commercial traffic. Big Bayou Canot, a tributary of the Mobile River, has a natural channel like the Mobile River. There are few natural landmarks that allow mariners to visibly distinguish this waterway and the Mobile River. The geography of Bayou Sara and Big Bayou Canot, and the Mobile River in the vicinity of the CSX railroad bridge, is similar enough that in periods of reduced visibility or at night time, mariners could become disoriented without additional aids. There are no obstructions or other hindrances to navigation between the Mobile River channel and the bridge site, thereby allowing commercial vessels unrestricted access to the bridge site. Vessels transiting the Mobile River may enter the Big Bayou Canot in error, particularly at nighttime or during periods of limited visibility.

FIGURE 4
Times Relevant
to Accident

	Sequence of Events		
Sunset Limited		*Mauvilla*	
9/21/93			
9:30 P.M.	Crew on duty, New Orleans		
		11:30 P.M.	Pilot on watch
11:34 P.M.	Train 2 departed New Orleans		
9/22/93			
		12:55 A.M.	Departed National Marine fleet, mile 5, Mobile River
		2:15 A.M.	Radioed towboat Thomas B. McCabe
2:30 A.M.	Arrived Mobile		
2:33 A.M.	Departed Mobile		
		2:45 A.M.	hit bridge
2:53 A.M.	Derailment		
2:56 A.M.	Assistant conductor radioed "MAY DAY"		
2:57 A.M.	CSX dispatcher notified		
3:00 A.M.	CSX called 911		
		3:05 A.M.	Radioed "MAY DAY"—lost tow, need help
		3:07 A.M.	Reported fire via radio
		3:08 A.M.	Cost Guard advised captain of accident

**On Board the
*M/V Mauvill***

Meanwhile, a short distance away at about 2:45 A.M., towboat captain, Andrew Stabler, realized that the "bump" that had awakened him from a sound sleep a few minutes earlier was more serious than simply glancing off the river bank in the dense fog. His tow, the *M/V Mauvilla* (*Mauvilla*), owned by Warrior and Gulf Navigation Company (WGN) had been traveling up the Mobile River pushing a string of six barges of coal, cement, logs, and woodchip on its normal run to Birmingham and Tuscaloosa. Pilot Willie Odom, who was piloting the towboat while Captain Stabler napped, became lost in the fog and turned into Big Bayou Canot by mistake. Even though the towboat was equipped with radar, Pilot Odom had not been adequately trained in its use. National transportation regulations state that when boats become lost in foggy conditions, they must notify the Coast Guard immediately; however, this did not occur. River charts show the Big Bayou Canot Bridge as a trackline over the waterway but do not state its name, clearances, or the fact that it is a fixed bridge. The waterway was without channel markers and was restricted to barge traffic. Nevertheless, it was listed as a "navigable waterway" by the United States Coast Guard.

On September 10, 1994, the National Transportation Safety Board published the official account of activities aboard the *Mauvilla* immediately after it collided with the bridge (Figure 5).

**Who Was
Responsible?**

The United States District Court for the Southern District of Alabama trial records describing the accident read as follows:

The incident occurred in the early hours of September 22, 1993, in state territorial waters near the Port of Mobile, Alabama. At approximately 2:45 that morning, a commercial towing vessel named the M/V Mauvilla *("Mauvilla") was traveling north on the Mobile River pushing a tow of six loaded barges toward a destination some three hundred and fifty miles upriver. The vessel, owned and operated by Warrior and Gulf Navigation, Inc. (WGN), was carrying a crew under command of a captain and pilot.*

Early in the voyage, the Mauvilla *was enveloped by a heavy fog that had settled on the river. The pilot of the vessel, with his visibility of the waterway compromised, decided*

**FIGURE 5
NTSB Official
Account**

Pilot Odom stated as he maneuvered upstream, that he saw an object on his radar that appeared to be lying across the waterway. No river charts were on board the towboat or were they required to be. Odom said that he never considered the object might have been something other than another towboat and barges that had swung out from the bank. In fact the object was the single-track Big Bayou Canot railroad bridge, which has a vertical clearance of about 7 feet and is part of the CSX track system. The lead barge of the *Mauvilla* had a total height of 7 feet 10 inches.

At some point as he continued toward the bridge, Odom placed the throttles of the *Mauvilla* in reverse. He testified that he was "still trying to figure out what was in front of me. And, I never could." He said he felt a "bump" and thought he had run aground. The deckhand on duty testified that he also felt the "bump" while sitting in the galley and noted the time as 2:45 A.M. In fact, the lead port and starboard barges of the *Mauvilla* had struck the south and center piers of the bridge's through-girder span. The forward center barge, which protruded about 5 feet ahead of the port and starboard barges, struck the east girder between these two piers, displacing the south end of the girder span 38 inches to the west. This caused the east girder to obtrude into the space traversed by trains.

As a result of the collision, the port string of barges broke free from the tow. In the process of trying to retrieve the loose barges, the *Mauvilla* backed into the east bank of the Big Bayou Canot, where it remained pinned for about 8 minutes until about 2:53 A.M.

When the on-duty deckhand went on deck shortly after the collision with the bridge, he saw flames and said he heard "a hiss like a roar but not a boom or nothing like that." The deckhand estimated that the fire started 5 to 10 minutes after he felt the "bump." Odom then radioed the Mobile River bridge tender[*] and asked whether anyone had reported a fire: The tender replied, "No."

When Captain Stabler arrived in the wheelhouse shortly after he felt the "bump" and assumed control of the tow from the pilot, the starboard quarter of the towboat was up against the bank, limiting the vessel's movement. At about 3:05 A.M. Captain Stabler, concerned about his situation with the loose barges, broadcast a distress message on VHF/FM Channel 16:

"Mayday, Mayday, Mayday, the motor vessel Mauvilla [garbled], got a tow broke up right below anchorage end of pier and seems to have a cable or something wrapped in the wheel, barges adrift southbound. . . . If anybody down there can help rounding them up, I would appreciate it."

The U.S. Coast Guard Group Mobile (Group) received the radio transmission: the radio operator on watch responded and asked for a position.

Captain Stabler replied: "We're between the upper end of Twelve Mile Island and the old maritime cut, somewhere in that area and I'm not exactly sure on the mileboard, over."

Responding to the Group radio operator's questions about 3:06 A.M., Captain Stabler said that four people were on board, that the *Mauvilla* was unable to move, and that the vessel was in no danger of sinking.

About 3:07 A.M., the Group told the captain that a train had derailed.

Captain Stabler replied, "I believe we're right below the train. . . . They's a helluva fire in the middle of the river and there ain't supposed to be no fire up here and, like I say, I don't know exactly where we at. It's so foggy I can't tell . . . by looking at the radar, so there's something bad wrong up here."

The Group's operator asked Captain Stabler about 3:11 A.M. whether he was involved in the train derailment.

He replied, "I can't tell you for a hundred percent whether I'm involved or not. We are right below it, I'm not sure what's going on. I come up here it was so foggy I can't tell where I'm at. . . . I can't get away from the barges where I'm at. I'm gonna try to get out of here and see if I can't go up there and help somebody."

After extensive maneuvering of the *Mauvilla*'s engines and rudders, Captain Stabler was able to free the towboat from its position between the bank and the port string of barges. He then ordered the deckhands to release the towboat from the barges that remained together, maneuvered the *Mauvilla* to the port side of the tow, and pushed all six barges onto the bank. Leaving the barges pushed into the northeast bank, he moved the towboat toward the fire. About 3:19 A.M., Captain Stabler called and advised the Coast Guard that he had his barges under control and that he would try to render assistance to survivors.

---

[*]The Mobile River bridge tender is responsible for raising and lowering the 14-mile swing bridge (draw bridge) across the Mobile River for river traffic. Because clearance of the bridge above the water is 4' and because river traffic on the Mobile River is heavy, the bridge tender typically knows the location of all river boats in the vicinity of the bridge at all times.

to secure the Mauvilla *and wait for the fog to abate. However, while attempting to secure the* Mauvilla *to the riverbank, the pilot allowed the vessel to veer into the mouth of Big Bayou Canot, a tributary of the Mobile River.*

Unaware of what had transpired, and under the mistaken belief that he was still navigating on the Mobile River, the pilot continued to search for a place to secure the Mauvilla *and its tow. While this task was being undertaken, an object appeared on the* Mauvilla's *radar screen that the pilot believed to be another vessel to which he could secure his vessel. The object was in fact a railroad bridge, owned and maintained by CSX, that crossed Big Bayou Canot.*

As the pilot steered the Mauvilla *toward the object, the tow struck a bridge support causing a portion of the track to become laterally misaligned. Soon after, a passenger train, operated by Amtrak, derailed while attempting to traverse the damaged section of rail. Three locomotives, two passenger coaches, a crew dormitory car, and a baggage car tumbled into the bayou, resulting in the death of forty seven persons on the train, numerous personal injuries, and extensive property damage to the train and bridge.*

The crash precipitated the filing of over one hundred personal injury and wrongful death suits against WGN, the pilot and captain of the Mauvilla, *CSX, and Amtrak. The Judicial Panel on Multidistrict Litigation consolidated these actions in the United States District Court for the Southern District of Alabama for all pretrial proceedings.*

The media is often quick to assign blame for tragic accidents. Those cited in this particular tragedy for being totally or partially responsible were the National Transportation Safety Board (NTSB), Amtrak, CSX, WGN, the U.S. Coast Guard, the towboat captain, the pilot, and the Alabama Emergency Response Network. However, because of the technical complexities involved, determining responsibility is not a simple matter. The managers of the organizations involved, the public administrators, and the individuals involved tended to have different perceptions than the media had regarding blame and how to prevent similar accidents in the future. A shocked nation was left pondering why this tragedy occurred, who was responsible, and what measures should be taken to prevent the recurrence of such a tragedy in the future.

Appendix A

Passenger Transportation in the United States

People in America log more business and pleasure passenger miles than those in any other country in the world. In 1990, airlines, railroads, and bus lines in the United States accounted for 423.7 billion passenger miles and $30.76 billion in revenues.

Of the three modes of public transportation, railroads allow passengers a more leisurely mode of transportation at fares higher than bus fares but lower than airfares. Cross country and commuter train passenger miles averaged 12.26 billion per year between 1983 and 1989, reaching 13.24 billion passenger miles in 1990. Cross-country train travel in 1990 accounted for 6.04 billion passenger miles or 46 percent of this total versus 56 percent for commuter travel.

Cross-country passenger trains are operated by the North American Passenger Corporation, commonly known as "Amtrak." In stark contrast to crowded inter-city commuter trains, these trains offer passengers a nostalgic journey into the past by providing roomy accommodations with large floor-to-ceiling windows and vista domes. Amtrak also offers fine dining, a secure and relaxed environment, and first-class sleeping accommodations. Coach prices are reasonably affordable and the sleeping cars are still less costly than first-class airfare.

In the 1950s, air travel was rapidly gaining in popularity and the automobile continued to chip away at the railroads' customer base. In a bold plan designed to win back the public to rail travel, the railroads introduced air-conditioned, stainless steel streamliners with all the luxuries of a fine hotel. This proved to be "a final ill-fated attempt by the railroads to trim costs and to dull the attraction of a vastly improved interstate highway system." Passenger miles continued to plummet as travelers turned to the faster air travel and the ease of automobile travel on the nation's interstate highways. The actual cost of providing basic passenger service, much less providing luxury service, dropped revenues below the break-even point.

By the late 1960s, rail passenger service costs exceeded revenues. A study by the Interstate Commerce Commission (1968) of eight major carriers recorded average passenger train expenses of $1.83 for every $1.00 of passenger train revenue. In addition, passenger trains slowed the departure and arrival of highly profitable freight trains because passenger trains were accorded scheduling priorities. Ultimately, declining patronage and mounting losses forced many railroads to discontinue passenger service. By 1970, virtually all passenger trains had disappeared from the nation's railroads.

Amtrak. The few passenger trains that remained in service were "nationalized" on May 1, 1971, when the government-formed, semi-public National Railroad Passenger Corporation (NRPC) was given a charter to run the nation's railroad passenger service. This organization evolved into the North American Passenger Association (Amtrak). As with the aviation and highway systems, Amtrak has been subsidized by the federal government throughout its 23-year existence, just as aviation and highways are subsidized.

With the help of these hefty government subsidies and passenger revenues, Amtrak succeeded in forging a profitable national railroad passenger transportation network from a hodge-podge of run-down equipment and facilities inherited from an obsolete transportation system. New cars and locomotives were purchased to replace outdated cars and equipment. Run-down facilities with high operating costs were rebuilt or were replaced with new construction.

By 1996, Amtrak had received almost $15 billion in federal subsidies and the NRPC still continues to be a burden to taxpayers:

Federal subsidies to Amtrak (1993 to 1996)

$ 731 million
909 million
1,000 million
700 million

Amtrak itself owns and maintains only 730 route miles of track located mainly in the Northeast to compete with the airline commuter traffic between Boston, New York, Philadelphia, Baltimore, and Washington, D.C. The remainder of the 23,270 miles of track on which Amtrak operates is privately owned and maintained by other railroads. Since its inception in 1971, Amtrak has carried passengers over 119 billion passenger miles. In its 27-year history, Amtrak has had 88 passenger fatalities due to train accidents, or .073 fatalities per 100 million passenger miles. This compares to a passenger fatality rate for planes of .025; buses .028; and automobiles, 1.03.

Chesapeake System Railroads (CSX). CSX Corporation is a Fortune 500 transportation company providing rail, intermodal, container shipping, barging, and contract logistics services worldwide. Holdings include CSX Transportation Inc., Sea-Land Service Inc., CSX Intermodal, Inc., American Commercial Lines, Inc., and Customized Transportation, Inc. In 1997, CSX generated more than $10.6 billion of operating revenue. CSX owns and maintains the track on which the Big Bayou Canot disaster occurred.

Financial Highlights (In Millions)

Summary of operations	1997	1996	1995	1994
Operating revenue	$10,621	$10,563	$10,304	$9,409
Operating expense	$ 9,038	$ 9,014	$ 8,921	$8,227
Restructuring charge	—	—	257	—
Total operating expense	$ 9,038	$ 9,014	$ 9,178	$8,227
Operating income	$ 1,583	$ 1,522	$ 1,126	$1,182
Net earnings	$ 799	$ 855	$ 618	$ 652

Warrior and Gulf Navigation (WGN). Organized in 1940, WGN had about 225 employees. Of that number, 45 were towboat captains or pilots, and 54 were deckhands. The remaining employees were managers, support personnel, and terminal operators. The company and the American Waterways Operators, Inc., consider WGN a medium-size operation; at the time of the accident it had about 250 barges and 24 towboats.

The company typically moves six barges in a tow and occasionally eight. In the fast current of high-water conditions, tow size is usually held to four barges. One operator and one deckhand stand watch on a towboat on a 6-hour-on, 6-hour-off rotation, which is typical for the type of towing operation the company is engaged in. Between 1981 and 1994, the company experienced 45 reportable marine accidents, including the Big Bayou Canot accident. The 3.75 accidents-per-year average equates to 0.2 accidents per towboat-tow per year. A local Coast Guard official stated that he thought that WGN's accident record was better than average for inland towing companies.

Appendix B

Safety Issues, Regulations, Recommendations, and Procedures

Amtrak. Prior to the accident, Amtrak used signs and placards, as well as briefings, to inform passengers about the safety features on its trains. Both on board service personnel and conductors had responsibility for safety on Amtrak trains and Amtrak's manuals stated that such briefings be routinely given at all stations. Signs in Amtrak cars indicated the location of first-aid kits, fire extinguishers, and emergency windows; signs on the ceilings adjacent to emergency windows were phosphorescent. Each emergency window had signs explaining how to remove it from both the inside and the outside. Signs posted in the car vestibules and elsewhere throughout the cars also gave instructions about window removal.

Although the collision of the *Mauvilla* with the Big Bayou Canot Bridge displaced the south end of the structure about 38 inches horizontally, the rails remained intact. Had the rail broken as a result of the collision and subsequent displacement of the bridge and track, the signal at Bayou Sara, about 1.7 miles from the accident sight, would have displayed a red or "stop" aspect. Because the rails remained intact, the signal circuitry was not interrupted. The signal displayed for the *Sunset Limited* was clear or "proceed," as the assistant conductor confirmed when he heard the locomotive crew call the signal over the radio.

Towboat Regulations. Title 46 of the Code of Federal Regulations Parts 24 through 28 set forth equipment requirements for uninspected vessels (under 1,600 tons). The regulations cover life preservers and other life saving equipment; fire extinguishing equipment; emergency position indicating radio beacons for vessels on the high seas; and cooking, heating, and lighting systems as well as other equipment. They do not cover navigation equipment. Thus, the *Mauvilla*, an uninspected towboat of less than 1,600 tons, was not required to be fitted with a radio, charts, or a compass.

Bridge Regulations. No single entity is responsible for the safety of the nation's bridges. Federal, state, and local governments, as well as private industry, share the responsibility. This fragmentation of authority often leads to a piecemeal, uneven approach to bridge safety. Additionally, bridge safety involves several transportation modes including marine, railroad, and highway; and several federal agencies including the Coast Guard.

NTSB first addressed the issue of bridge alignment protection after a Union Pacific freight train, traveling westbound at 50 mph, struck a displaced bridge at Devil's Slide, Utah, on November 17, 1979, derailing 5 locomotive units and 56 cars. Damage estimates exceeded $5 million. As a result of its investigation of that accident, the Safety Board issued Safety Recommendation R-80-36, asking the Federal Railroad Association (FRA) to study "the feasibility of installing on bridges a mechanism to indicate when bridges are displaced."

On May 6, 1981, the FRA responded, noting that the 98,000 route miles of track in the continental United States contain some 85,000 bridges. The cost of installing a detection device on each of these bridges would be about $850 million; maintenance costs would total an additional $85 million per year. CSX alone has 11,000 railroad bridges in service. The FRA also noted that of the 41,627 railroad accidents that occurred between 1976 and 1979, only 20 were caused by displaced bridges or bridges that failed under load.

Module 4

Organizational Control, Power, and Conflict

Cases Outline

BULLER | SCHULER

Managing Organizations and People

A Resource for Cases in Management, Organizational Behavior, and Human Resource Management

Abstract

This descriptive case chronicles a dispute that erupted in 1994 between Pearl Jam, arguably the most popular alternative rock band in the United States, and Ticketmaster, the nation's premier ticket distribution company. The dispute was ongoing as of 1996, when the case ends. For its 1994 summer tour, Pearl Jam decided to try to limit the price of tickets to its concerts to no more than $20, to accommodate the limited resources of its teenaged fans. To this end, the band priced tickets at $18 and proposed to Ticketmaster that service charges be limited to no more than 10 percent of the value of the ticket. Ticketmaster refused, saying it would lose money. After the first round of negotiations failed, both organizations escalated the conflict. The dispute, which continued into 1996, harmed both parties. Pearl Jam was unable to proceed with its concert schedule without the cooperation of Ticketmaster, and canceled its entire 1994 summer tour. In 1995 and 1996, the band attempted to tour without the company, using small venues and alternative ticketing systems. Both tours were plagued with numerous problems, many related to ticket sales. In 1996, Ticketmaster failed in its bid for the lucrative contract to sell tickets to the Summer Olympic Games, citing distractions caused by its dispute with Pearl Jam.

Pearl Jam's Dispute with Ticketmaster

The two witnesses raising their right hands to be sworn on June 30, 1994, seemed strikingly out of place in the wood-paneled chambers of the House of Representatives Government Operations Committee. Stone Gossard, guitarist for the popular Seattle-based alternative rock bank Pearl Jam, was wearing velvet shorts, a loose pink shirt, and rope shoes. Jeff Ament, the band's bassist, was sporting pencil-thin trousers, a black leather jacket, and a backwards-facing Supersonics cap. "I am not used to doing this sort of thing," Gossard commented awkwardly as he began his testimony, "so bear with me if it's a little rough."

■ By Anne T. Lawrence, San Jose State University. An earlier version of this case was presented to the annual meeting of the Western Casewriters Association in March 1997. This case was prepared from publicly available sources and from materials provided by Pearl Jam and its attorneys, Ticketmaster Corporation, and the U.S. Department of Justice, solely for the purpose of stimulating student discussion. All events and individuals are real. Copyright 1998 by Anne T. Lawrence. All rights reserved.

1

The grunge rock superstars had come to Washington to testify in support of the band's charges that Ticketmaster Corporation, the nation's premier ticket distribution company, was guilty of antitrust violations. In a formal complaint filed earlier with the Department of Justice, Pearl Jam had argued that Ticketmaster's exclusive contracts with many of the nation's biggest concert venues and promoters had given the company a virtual monopoly over ticket sales for many kinds of events. Ticketmaster had used their market power unfairly, the band charged, to drive up service charges, increasing the cost to concert-goers—including Pearl Jam's cash-strapped teenaged fans.

Waiting to testify later in the hearing was Frederic D. Rosen, Ticketmaster's feisty and blunt-spoken chief executive. Calling the band's charges "a work of fiction," Rosen maintained that Ticketmaster did not set the price of the tickets. "The acts determine their own price," he asserted. "We have nothing to do with that." His organization's convenience charges, he maintained, were fully justified by the service provided to customers.

The congressional hearing was just the latest salvo in what *Billboard* magazine called the "unusually public and freewheeling business dispute" between Pearl Jam and Ticketmaster. In June 1994, the dispute seemed rapidly to be spiraling out of both sides' control, threatening their reputations and ability to pursue their very different artistic and business objectives.

Ticketmaster, Inc.

Ticketmaster Corporation, the object of Pearl Jam's complaint, was the most successful ticket service company in the United States. Its corporate mission, in its CEO's words, was to provide "automated ticketing services to organizations that sponsor events in order to allow their customers the ability to purchase tickets to those events from outlets or over the telephone." In 1994, the company had 4200 employees and outlets in 40 states, and processed over 38 million phone calls a year.

In 1994, Ticketmaster dominated the market for ticket sales to big name events at big venues. The company held exclusive contracts with about two-thirds of the nation's major stadiums, arenas, and amphitheaters—including such entertainment powerhouses as Madison Square Garden, the Meadowlands (New Jersey), the Great Western Forum (Los Angeles), the Boston Garden, and the Astrodome (Houston). It sold tickets on a nonexclusive basis for many other major venues. In 1993, Ticketmaster sold 55 million tickets, generating $191 million in revenue and a net profit of $7 million.

Ticketmaster had not always been the market leader. In 1982, when Rosen took over leadership of the company, Ticketmaster had been a nearly moribund regional ticketing service owned by the Pritzker family of Chicago. At that time, the ticketing service industry was dominated by Ticketron. A subsidiary of Control Data Corporation, a mainframe computer manufacturer, Ticketron had built a successful business in the 1970s by selling box office computer equipment to arenas and stadiums and by providing off-site ticket sales, mainly at department stores.

Rosen's strategy for the upstart rival Ticketmaster was to provide superior, inexpensive ticketing services to venue owners based on a new generation of minicomputers. Rather than make money from selling computer hardware, he would make money from "convenience" charges to the customer. Rosen purchased inexpensive minicomputers and hired programmers to write software enabling them simultaneously to serve numerous telephone operators and sales outlets, such as record stores. "We were able to make a P.T. boat act like an aircraft carrier," Rosen's programming chief later commented.

Throughout the early and mid-1980s, Rosen aggressively wooed venue owners across the country, signing them to exclusive three to five year contracts to provide ticketing services. The advantages of Rosen's pitch to the venue owner were obvious. The venue owners did not need to purchase expensive computer hardware or worry about it breaking down. Someone else would handle ticket sales. Rosen also offered to rebate a share of service charges to venue owners—often up front at the time the contract was signed. And the cost of the system was largely born by the customer, in the form of service charges added to the ticket price.

Throughout the 1980s, as it expanded its network of contracts with venues and promoters, Ticketmaster also acquired or entered into joint ventures with many of its regional rivals, such as TicketPro, Ticket World, and BASS. By the late 1980s, Ticketron was on the ropes, losing $2 million in 1989 and $7.5 million in 1990. In 1991, after efforts to find another buyer failed, the Justice Department approved the sale of Ticketron contracts (although not its computers) to Ticketmaster. Rosen's conquest of the industry was virtually complete.

In 1993, Seattle billionaire Paul G. Allen, co-founder of Microsoft Corporation, purchased an 80 percent share of Ticketmaster from the Pritzker family for $300 million. The Pritzkers retained 12 percent; the balance was owned by several individuals, including Rosen.

Pearl Jam

While Rosen was busy locking up contracts with major entertainment venues and promoters, the musicians who were to form his company's future nemesis, Pearl Jam, were beginning to make names for themselves in Seattle's fertile alternative rock scene of the late 1980s.

The Seattle music scene was in many ways unique. The city's geographical isolation from the rock industry capitals of New York and Los Angeles made it possible for a distinctive musical genre to emerge there. The city had its own network of clubs featuring alternative music, a progressive college radio station at Evergreen State College that favored independently-produced cuts, and a shoe-string alternative record label called Sub Pop. These factors helped support an unusually large number of innovative bands, including Nirvana, the first one to achieve significant commercial success.

Pearl Jam formed in 1990. In addition to Ament and Gossard, both veterans of the Seattle music underground, the band included lead vocalist and songwriter Eddie Vedder, percussionist Dave Abbruzzese, and guitarist Mike McCready. From the outset, the key figure in the band was the charismatic Eddie Vedder. The group's lead singer had an intense relationship with his youthful fans, with whom he strongly identified. Unlike many rock stars, he often wrote his fans personal letters, becoming—as he put it—"a part of their lives." Vedder was also more political than many of his grunge rock peers. He sported a tattoo of the insignia of Earth First!, a radical environmental organization, and over the years organized benefit concerts supporting abortion rights, international human rights, and youth voter registration, among other causes.

In spring 1991, Pearl Jam began playing club dates around Seattle, and almost immediately began attracting interest from major record companies. They eventually signed with Epic Records, a division of Sony. They released their first album, *Ten*, in August, and began touring in the U.S. in spring 1992.

The band's musical style combined elements of punk, classic rock, and blues. *Newsday* called Pearl Jam's music "a chaotic mix of muscular rhythms, piecing guitar hooks, and gut-wrenching lyrics." Part of the band's secret was its ability to cross over various formats. Cuts were played not only on "alternative rock" stations, but were also picked up by "heritage" or "classic rock" stations. In 1991, testifying to its crossover strength, the band won honors both for Favorite New Artist (Pop/Rock) and Favorite New Artist (Hard Rock) at the American Music Awards.

By the mid-1990s, Pearl Jam was being called the "hottest rock act" of the decade. Without a doubt, the band was a runaway commercial success. Although the band did not report its earnings, by 1996 it had sold over 17 million albums in the United States alone, and by one estimate as many as 30 million internationally. At the standard music industry rate of between $2.00 and $3.00 per "piece" for artist and songwriter royalties, the band might have made as much as $75 million on record sales alone—excluding revenue from tours, merchandising, and endorsements (several band members endorsed guitars and other products). Rosen was not off the mark when he pointedly remarked at one point, as his dispute with Pearl Jam was being characterized as a David versus Goliath struggle, "They make more money than we do."

Although the band was extraordinarily successful, its members were apparently unmotivated by a desire for commercial success and appeared, in some instances, almost ignorant of the business aspects of their enterprise. At the congressional hearing in 1994, for example, the subcommittee chair asked band members their reaction to losing an estimated $2 million by canceling their summer 1994 tour. Ament replied, "I am not really sure how much money we forfeited. In a lot of cases the money at this point really isn't that important to us . . . [Making money] has never been our major goal."

The Dispute Heats Up

Almost as soon as Pearl Jam began to tour in 1992, it began to tangle with Ticketmaster. As a band that had burst on the scene to almost immediate mass popularity, Pearl Jam quickly learned that venues big enough to accommodate its legions of fans in many—or even most—cases had exclusive deals with Ticketmaster.

Troubles between the two organizations started with a few relatively minor skirmishes.

- In 1992, the band staged a free concert for its fans in a park in Seattle. For security reasons, attendance had to be limited to 30,000, requiring the distribution of tickets. Ticketmaster agreed to provide ticketing for $1.50 per ticket, angering the band—who did not want fans to have to pay at all. Ultimately, the city government handled the ticketing.
- In December 1993, the band scheduled a benefit concert at the Seattle Center Arena, with the proceeds to go to charity. Ticketmaster, which handled ticketing for the Arena, initially agreed to the band's request that it donate a portion of its service charge receipts to charity, but reneged just as the tickets were about to go on sale. After what the band's attorney called "a tense impasse," Ticketmaster finally agreed to make a contribution—although not at the level it had initially promised.
- In March 1994, the band asked Ticketmaster to disclose the service charge separately on the face of the ticket for a concert in Chicago. When the ticketer refused, Pearl Jam threatened to perform at another venue. Ticketmaster backed down, but said it would not necessarily agree to separate disclosure elsewhere.

After this incident, Pearl Jam began to experiment with alternative ticketing arrangements. In Detroit, the band attempted to distribute tickets through its fan club. Ticketmaster threatened the promoter, with whom it had an exclusive contract, with a lawsuit. In New York, the band tried to sell tickets over the radio; in this instance, Ticketmaster threatened a lawsuit against the venue owner. Pearl Jam later reported that during this period, Ticketmaster told the band's manager through third parties that they should "watch their backs" and threatened to sue the band if it interfered with the company's exclusive contracts.

Ticketmaster made it clear to venue owners and promoters that it would not tolerate any breach of its exclusivity contracts. In March 1994, the North American Concert Promoters Association, a trade group, sent a memo to its members—addressing them as "brother raccoons"—stating in part:

Ticketmaster has indicated . . . that they will aggressively enforce their contracts with promoters and facilities. Ticketmaster's stance is that they have been loyal to their partners in this business and they hope & expect that their partners will reciprocate.

A subsequent update noted that the ticket service company "views the Pearl Jam issue as an all or nothing proposition, meaning that they will not agree to handle half of the available inventory on a show in any situation where a contract exists."

The Convenience Charge Issue

Against the background of these skirmishes, Pearl Jam began to organize their summer 1994 tour. The band decided to try to limit the price of tickets to its concerts to no more than $20, to accommodate the limited resources of their teenaged fans. To this end, the band priced their concert tickets at $18 and, through promoters, approached Ticketmaster with a proposal to limit their convenience charges to no more than 10 percent, or $1.80, per ticket. Gossard later explained that the band had "made a conscious decision that we do not want to put the price of our concerts out of the reach of our fans." The band also insisted that the service charge be listed separately on their tickets and that no paid advertisements appear on the reverse side.

Ticketmaster rejected the band's proposal, arguing that it would have lost money with a $1.80 service charge. The ticketer did make an indirect offer to the band, through intermediaries, to compromise on the issue. Rosen later explained:

Various promoters spoke to the group—we had no direct contact with them—and told them we would compromise on this matter. We agreed to lower our service charges to $2.25 to $2.50, depending on the area.

The company refused to go lower, arguing that it "should not have to do something that essentially costs [the company] money just to resolve a conflict with a rock band." Pearl Jam refused this offer.

In mid-April, the band canceled its entire 1994 summer tour, citing the difficulties of touring without Ticketmaster. The band stated, "Ticketmaster has in essence dug its own grave on this issue. It is unwilling to be in step with the times and to cooperate with a band whose business ideals are commendable, given the state of the world today."

The Anti-Trust Complaint

On May 6, Pearl Jam's attorneys in the Los Angeles office of Sullivan & Cromwell filed a formal complaint against Ticketmaster with the Antitrust Division of the U.S. Department of Justice, at the band's request.

At the heart of Pearl Jam's antitrust complaint was the charge that Ticketmaster had "a virtually absolute monopoly on the distribution of tickets to concerts." The band and its attorneys charged that Ticketmaster had used "kickbacks" to promoters and venue owners to obtain exclusive contracts. The ticketer had then used its market domination illegally to push up service charges to "exorbitant" levels. The band's attorneys also charged that Ticketmaster's efforts to enforce its contracts with promoters and venues constituted a "group boycott," illegal under the Sherman Antitrust Act, that had the effect of preventing the band from using alternative methods of ticketing.

Ticketmaster defended itself vigorously against each of these allegations. With respect to the monopoly issue, the company pointed out that although it dominated the market for ticket sales for events at major stadiums, when all entertainment events were included, it controlled just 2 percent of the national ticket market. It faced competition from other ticketers in many regional markets; and the rise of new technologies (such as on-line ticketing) also posed a competitive threat to the company.

Its exclusive contracts with venue owners and promoters, Ticketmaster pointed out, were openly negotiated and subject to renewal every five years or so. Such arrangements were common in the industry; for example, arenas and stadiums typically signed exclusive deals with service providers for everything from parking to hot dog concessions. Up front fees paid by the service provider to obtain these deals were widely used and in no way illegal.

Service charges were not excessive, Ticketmaster argued. Data provided by the company showed that in 1994, the average convenience fee per ticket was $3.15, representing 12.5 percent of the ticket price. The company claimed that its profit per ticket averaged less than ten cents. Over the period 1990–1994, the service charge had increased on average 5.9 percent a year. Over the same period, ticket prices had increased at an average annual rate of 4.7 percent.

The company also stated that its charges were justified by the convenience provided. Customers were able to order tickets by phone, using a credit card, or at convenient outlets. They could obtain the "best available" seat, since inventory was centralized. Box office camp outs were virtually eliminated. Ticketmaster also provided information about events over the phone. In fact, the company reported that 4 of every 5 calls received in 1994 did not result in a sale at all; the customer had simply called for information, which was given for free.

Pearl Jam's attorneys responded that these assertions were "highly dubious, if not intentionally misleading." They stated:

It is true that Ticketmaster operates in a narrow segment of the broad business of selling tickets to entertainment events in this country. Within that segment, however, Ticketmaster wields enormous clout by virtue of its exclusive dealing arrangements with venues and promoters.

The band's attorneys also called Ticketmaster's accounting figures, showing a profit of less than ten cents a ticket, "ludicrous." Sullivan & Cromwell argued that this amount represented profit *after* deduction of large executive salaries, depreciation and amortization expenses that did not represent real cash outlays, and payments to venues and promoters to secure contracts. Sullivan & Cromwell also challenged the $3.15 average service charge, saying that Ticketmaster had distorted the figure by including charges on cheaper movie tickets.

Both sides in the antitrust dispute had their supporters. Representatives of several other bands, including R.E.M., Aerosmith, and the Nitty Gritty Dirt Band, testified before Congress in support of Pearl Jam's position. Several private parties, mostly Ticketmaster's competitors, filed their own antitrust lawsuits. Several consumer organizations—including Consumers Against Unfair Ticketing, U.S. Public Interest Research Group, and the Consumer Federation of America—also sided with the band. In several states, legislators introduced bills to limit service charges. Promoters and venue owners, however, generally backed Ticketmaster, citing satisfaction with the company's service.

Life Without Ticketmaster

As the Justice Department investigation dragged on, and several private lawsuits against Ticketmaster winded their way through the federal courts, Pearl Jam decided to go ahead and mount their 1995 summer tour without Ticketmaster, using alternative ticketing and venues not under contract with them.

In February 1995, while this tour was still in the planning stage, a music industry executive tried to arrange a meeting between Fred Rosen and Pearl Jam manager Kelly Curtis. According to Ticketmaster's publicist, the band "crushed the mediation attempt." The band itself had no comment on this incident.

The band's effort to mount an independent tour was beset with difficulties from start to finish. "We'll do it," said band manager Curtis. "We've made our bed; now we'll sleep in it," she said. "But it's a pain in the ass." Life without Ticketmaster required the band to play in non-traditional venues, work with non-established promoters, and use novice ticket distributors. The band's managers checked out parks, car race tracks, horse tracks, and soccer fields. But inadequate parking, poor sight lines, and security worries rendered most of them unsuitable.

The 1995 tour got off to a very rocky start. Several early concerts were canceled because of poor weather and security problems. On June 24, Vedder abruptly walked off stage mid-set in a concert in San Francisco's Golden Gate Park before 50,000 fans, saying he was ill with the stomach flu. The following day—little more than a week after its start—the band abruptly canceled the remaining dates on its scheduled eleven-city tour. Its publicist offered the following explanation:

The cancellation was brought on by the business problems and controversies surrounding the band's attempt to schedule an alternative tour . . . [Pearl Jam] wanted to focus on its music, but instead has been faced with continued controversies associated with attempting to schedule and perform at alternative venues.

Tickets already sold for remaining shows were refunded.

Few other artists joined Pearl Jam's crusade. Although a number of other artists had supported the band's position in the Congressional hearings, none were willing to put the success of their tours on the line. Some observers concluded that Ticketmaster's apparent victory, in fact, had scared off other acts from trying to bypass the dominant ticketer. "[The dispute] showed how hard it is to tour outside the system. To mount a tour in the 'outback' is tough," said an executive of a regional ticketing company.

On July 5, 1995, the Justice Department issued a one-sentence press release, closing without comment its antitrust investigation of Ticketmaster, saying only that it did not have sufficient basis to bring charges. The department said it would continue to monitor competitive developments in the ticketing industry. Pearl Jam called the decision a "cave in." Ticketmaster issued a brief statement, saying that the action confirmed their belief that the antitrust charges "had no merit."

Ticketmaster had little further to say in public after the Justice Department announcement. The whole affair, however, may have softened Ticketmaster's unwillingness to negotiate service charges with top acts. For example, the company agreed to lower its service charge on Garth Brooks tickets, at his manager's request. But the dispute with Pearl Jam had clearly distracted the ticketer. In July 1995, Ticketmaster lost the huge contract to handle ticketing for the 1996 Summer Olympics to a joint venture between IBM and ProTix, a regional ticketer. Rosen said that Ticketmaster had been so "preoccupied" dealing with the antitrust investigation that it had not had time to address the Olympic Committee's concerns.

In the summer of 1996—shortly after a federal court in St. Louis dismissed the consolidated class-action lawsuit against Ticketmaster—Pearl Jam attempted once again to mount a tour without the ticketer. "We made a stand, and we're going to stick with it," Ament told the press. "Everything Ticketmaster stands for is what we're fighting against."

With a year's experience, things went a little more smoothly. But alternative ticketers used by the band were not always reliable, and many big markets—such as Boston—were bypassed entirely because of a lack of suitable venues. And ironically, even with the use of alternative ticketers, service charges were not much different from what Ticketmaster had offered in March 1994. Commented the editor of the concert trade magazine *Pollstar* of Pearl Jam's continuing crusade, "They're sacrificing millions by doing a tour this way. I don't see it having any impact on Ticketmaster, or anybody else but Pearl Jam."

References

1. All Things Considered [transcript of Public Radio broadcast], "Pearl Jam's Controversy with Ticketmaster Discussed," June 18, 1995.
2. Arnold, Gina, *Route 666: On the Road to Nirvana*, New York: St. Martin's Press, 1993.
3. *Business Week*, "Will Ticketmaster Get Scalped?" June 26, 1995.
4. *Billboard*, "New Set Pits Pearl Jam vs. Fame," October 16, 1993.
5. *Billboard*, "R.E.M. OKs Ticketmaster for Tour; Meanwhile, Pearl Jam Sticks to Guns," January 14, 1995.
6. *Billboard*, "How David Became the Industry's Goliath," July 9, 1994.
7. *Billboard*, "Play-by-Play Account of Pearl Jam Saga," July 8, 1995.
8. *Billboard*, "U.S. Drops Probe of Ticketing Business; Justice Department Finds No Fault; Ticketmaster Prevails," July 15, 1995.
9. *Billboard*, "Fans Sidelined by Flip Flops in Pearl Jam's Tour," July 8, 1995.
10. *Charleston Gazette*, "Creating a Stink Over Ticket Prices," July 28, 1994.
11. *Consumer Reports*, "Your Entertainment Dollars: Concert Tickets: Better Days Ahead?" August 1995.
12. *Contra Costa Times*, "Pearl Jam's Ticketing Fiasco Deserves No Encore," October 8, 1995.
13. *Daily Record*, "Court Dismisses Antitrust Suit Against Ticketmaster," June 5, 1996.
14. Morrell, Brad, *Pearl Jam: The Illustrated Biography*, New York: Omnibus Press, 1993.
15. *Newsday*, "Sun Around the Bend," August 25, 1996.
16. *Oakland Tribune*, "Problems Force Pearl Jam to Cancel Its Tour," June 27, 1995.
17. Romanowski, Patricia, ed., *The New Rolling Stone Encyclopedia of Rock and Roll*, New York: Fireside Press, 1995.
18. *St. Petersburg Times*, "Getting a Charge Out of Tickets," [profile of Frederic Rosen], September 20, 1992.
19. *St. Petersburg Times*, "Pearl Jam Tickets On Sale by Phone Today," August 24, 1996.
20. Sullivan & Cromwell, "Memorandum of Pearl Jam to the Antitrust Division of the United States Department of Justice Concerning Anticompetitive Actions Engaged in by Ticketmaster Holdings Group Ltd.," May 6, 1994.
21. Sullivan & Cromwell, "Supplemental Memorandum of Pearl Jam to the Antitrust Division of the United States Department of Justice Responding to Various Assertions Made by Ticketmaster Corporation," July 20, 1994.
22. Ticketmaster, Inc., "Facts About Ticketmaster and the Ticket Service Industry," n.d., approximately June 1995.
23. *USA Today*, "Ticketmaster's Cyberfuture is On-Line," March 10, 1995.
24. U.S. Department of Justice, "Antitrust Division Statement Regarding Ticketmaster Inquiry," [press release], July 5, 1995.
25. U.S. House of Representatives, Committee on Government Operations, Subcommittee on Information, Justice, Transportation, and Agriculture, "Pearl Jam's Antitrust Complaint: Questions About Concert, Sports, and Theater Handling Charges and Other Practices," June 30, 1994.
26. *U.S. News and World Report*, "Recording Sound Sales," September 25, 1995.
27. *The Wall Street Journal*, "Ticketmaster's Mr. Tough Guy," November 6, 1994.
28. *Washington Times*, "Consumer Groups Go After Ticketmaster," March 22, 1995.

BULLER | SCHULER

Managing Organizations and People

A Resource for Cases in Management, Organizational Behavior, and Human Resource Management

Abstract

Due to rapid growth in sales, Mr. Tanaka the production manager of Suntory is under pressure to increase production. Along with this pressure, there is some concern that the (aesthetic) quality of the product is being compromised. While there are no complaints either from the marketing department or buyers, Mr. Tanaka is concerned about the quality problems. He has correctly identified the labor-intensive ribbon-tying process on the bottles as the bottleneck in the production line. He is acutely aware that improved worker productivity in this part of the line is needed to increase production. He must now decide upon a plan of action to deal with the production and quality concerns.

Suntory

Mr. Tanaka, the production manager in charge of Royal 60 whiskey, sat reflecting on the forecasted demand provided to him by the marketing department. He wondered about the impact of this increase on the production line, and what this meant in terms of gearing up for increased production. Demand of Suntory's upscale Royal 60 whiskey was expected to increase rapidly. Over the next two years it was expected to grow over 40 percent. Forecasts predicted even more dramatic growth for the two years following that. The questions that preoccupied Mr. Tanaka were: (1) whether the current production capacity was sufficient, and (2) whether major changes would be required to meet this growing demand.

Marketing and Product Image

Royal 60 was one of a line of whiskeys marketed by Suntory in Japan. Its specific target market was the urban, upper-middle class Japanese manager. Over the years Suntory had built a cultural ambiance around Royal 60 that conveyed a feeling of understated European class: a drink for men who were quietly self-assured, who were neither rich nor by any means poor, who were somewhat cosmopolitan, but not overly so, and who appreciated the good things in life.

Part of Royal 60's distinctive product image was its packaging, which included a ribbon fastening cap to bottle. It was a distinctive feature not found on most domestic or

■ This case was written by Allan Bird and Suresh Kotha, both from the Stern School of Business, New York University. This case was prepared as basis for class discussion rather than to illustrate either effective or ineffective handling of administrative situations. Reprinted with permission.

imported brands of whiskey. The ribbon was perceived to make the whiskey more European by implying an association with European brandies and cognac which came similarly packaged. It also suggested Old World craftsmanship and elegance: the type of detail not found in a product that the average consumer would buy.

Production, Bottling, and Packaging

At Suntory, whiskey was produced using processes that were fairly standardized in the industry. Except for some automation, the method currently in use was similar to the one that had been in practice for centuries. The process essentially involved three stages. During stage one, whiskey mash was fermented and then distilled. This stage was automated at Suntory. In the second stage, distilled spirit was placed in wooden casks and then stored in large warehouses for anywhere from five to thirty-five years. From time to time, testers sampled the distilled spirit to check for proper color and taste. When the distilled spirit reached an appropriate level of maturity, processing moved into the third stage. During this stage, spirits of various ages were blended together to achieve the right color and taste. Royal 60, representing one such blended product line, was one of Suntory's higher quality brands.

After blending, the bottling of Royal 60 proceeded through a series of semi-automated and automated steps. The bottling process began with the sterilization of bottles in a hot water bath. Once sterilized, bottles were then filled with blended whiskey, capped and passed on to the labeling area where gold colored labels were applied automatically. The bottles then proceeded to the most labor-intensive step in the process—the tying of the distinctive ribbon to the Royal 60 bottle. The fastened caps were secured to the bottle by means of a hand-tied ribbon which was attached to the bottle by means of a machine-sealed wax stamp. Finally, the bottles were put into boxes and prepared for shipping to distributors.

Problems and Concerns

A quick review of the Royal 60 bottling line by Tanaka revealed that the ribbon-tying phase of the line represented the slowest-moving part of the process. With rapidly increasing demand it was apparent that productivity improvements in the ribbon-tying phase were essential if Suntory was to increase production levels without raising production costs. With this understanding, Tanaka began to examine the ribbon-tying process in more detail. He noticed that ribbons were tied manually on an assembly line of twenty workers (all women) during the stage prior to shipment. The manual process took eight steps, as shown in Exhibit 1. A ribbon was folded in half and then tucked back through the fold to

**EXHIBIT 1
Steps in Tying
Ribbons on
Royal 60**

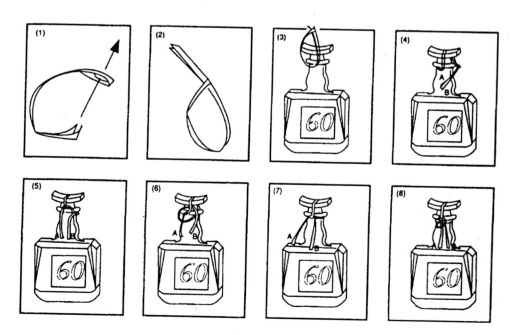

form a loop. The loop was next hooked over the left side of the bottle and the top of the cap. It was then wrapped around the bottle, from back to front. At the front, one end was passed through the initial loop from the inside, while the other end was passed through the loop from the outside. The two ends were then drawn tight, and the second end was tied around the first in a half-clove hitch. Employing this procedure, a line worker tied an average of three and a half bottles per minute. This translated into an average line speed of seventy bottles per minute.

From his detailed examination, it was clear to Tanaka that the ribbon-tying line was experiencing no major problems. He was aware that his workers were consistently meeting schedules and there was no known delay in product shipment in the past. However, he noticed differences in the knot sizes, resulting from the way they were tied. At that moment he was not sure whether these differences mattered. But he suspected that they did detract from the bottle's overall appearance. Further, two other things concerned him: (1) there were no standards or established specifications for the knot tying process, and (2) no final quality inspection of the product was undertaken before it was shipped.

Later during a conversation with Sato of the production research department, Tanaka learned that the placement of the knot varied as a result of worker inexperience, fatigue, or occasional worker inattention. Since it was the last operation before boxing, it was hard to catch mistakes. Even when an off-center knot could be identified and corrected, the adjustment took time, thus further slowing down the line. Also according to Sato, one of the most difficult aspects of the work for new employees was learning how to properly set the loop so that it would stay anchored and centered. If drawn too tightly, the loop tended to pull the knot to the left of center. If not drawn tightly enough, the loop would loosen, thus shifting the knot to the right of center. It currently took nearly sixty days for a new line worker to reach the average level of proficiency at this task. In addition, Sato noted that the resulting off-center knot did detract from the bottle's overall appearance. However, he did point out that he was not aware of any complaints from the marketing department.

According to Sato a complete automation of the ribbon-tying process was impossible. Automation of the process up to step 7 (see Exhibit 1) was certainly feasible, though it would require a sizable capital investment. However, Sato warned that it would still be necessary to retain workers to perform steps 7 and 8. Nonetheless, with automation the total number of workers on the line could be reduced. The production department estimated that each machine could on the average process six bottles a minute. Tanaka was aware that, given the current budgetary pressures, senior management was not inclined to provide major funds for this product line.

Tanaka's investigations led him to focus increasingly on the current production facility capacity to keep up with rising demand. The main bottleneck was the ribbon-tying operation—the slowest phase of the bottling line operation. In addition, there was no space on the current line to expand the number of workers; nor was it clear that automation would be economically justifiable given the fact that it would still be necessary to retain workers to complete the final stages of the tying process. Given Tanaka's conservative nature and the fact that the optimistic forecasts provided by the marketing department might never materialize, it seemed to him more prudent to wait before making major changes.

Enter the Violets

In the meantime, Tanaka decided to approach the Quality Control (QC) circle named as Violets[1] on the ribbon-tying line to see what they could come up with. A previous QC circle had recommended the use of pre-glued ribbon (see Exhibit 2b). The standard, pre-glued loop had cost 78.2 per unit as opposed to 14.7 per unit for the pre-folded variety (see Exhibit 2a) and resulted in a 16 percent productivity increase, thus more than offsetting the added cost. Perhaps, Tanaka hoped, the Violets could find ways to increase productivity that would serve, at the very least, as a short-term response to demand pressures.

After meeting with Mr. Tanaka, the circle began to discuss ways to increase productivity. They felt strongly that occasional defects and problems related to the centering of ribbon knots were symptomatic of inefficiencies in the ribbon-tying process and that steps to remove these inefficiencies could both improve quality and, more importantly, raise productivity.

EXHIBIT 2
Types of Ribbons
Used on the
Ribbon Tying
Line for Royal 60

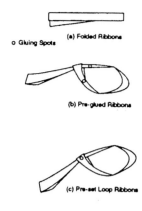

During one of their meetings it was suggested they experiment with a preset loop (see Exhibit 2c) rather than use a pre-glued ribbon. After some experimentation on the production line, the group proposed that pre-folded ribbons be glued in two places, thus facilitating the early part of the tying process (i.e., forming the ribbon into a loop). Also the use of a pre-set loop would make centering automatic, thereby reducing the amount of time it took new workers to get up to speed. They began exploring this possibility by surveying workers on the line as to what the ideal loop size should be (see Exhibit 3 for results of the survey). Based on these findings the circle decided on a loop size of 160 mm.

While the cost of pre-set loop ribbons would remain unchanged, the members predicted a slight increase in line speed resulting from this change. While making the knot tying process easier, the pre-set loop would also reduce some of the problems associated with sizing and centering of the knots. Thus, as part of a three-month test run, an order was placed for 50,000 such pre-set loop ribbons. The loop size was specified as 160 mm with a tolerance of plus or minus 2 mm.

In using these ribbons it was found that the line speed did increase to 74 bottles per minute, with individual workers tying an average of 3.7 bottles per minute. This represented a 5.7 percent increase in a line productivity. But it was not without its problems.

New Concerns

While the new pre-glued ribbons were being tested on the line, members of the quality circle sampled ribbons received to check if they met specifications. They randomly selected 480 ribbons from a consignment of 9,300 ribbons for measurement (see Exhibit 4 for results of this survey).

EXHIBIT 3
Histogram of Survey
Results for Preferred
Loop Size

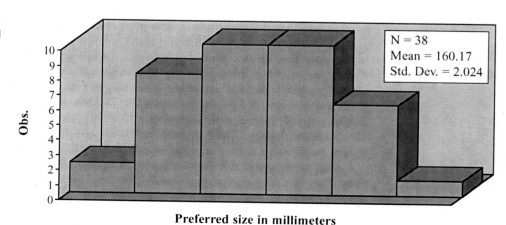

N = 38
Mean = 160.17
Std. Dev. = 2.024

Preferred size in millimeters

**EXHIBIT 4
Histogram of
Loop Size from
Random Sampling**

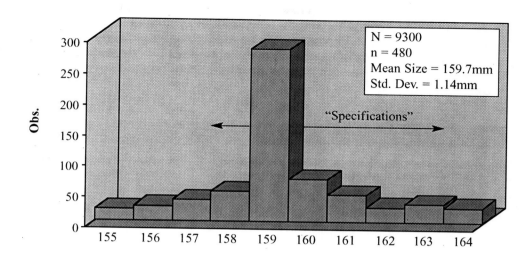

A survey of line workers indicated that there were also problems with ribbon quality. On some ribbons there was too much glue which caused the ribbons to stick together occasionally. It was also painful to the fingers when the glue hardened. Workers also complained about the look of the ribbons, some of which seemed to have been crushed during transportation.

The identification of variations in loop size extending outside the specifications encouraged the circle to examine how ribbons were produced by the supplier. They learned that their supplier wove fibers into ribbon, winding the ribbon onto large spools. The spools were then taken to a cutting room where they were measured, cut to a uniform length and tied into bundles. The bundles were then delivered by the supplier to fifty housewives. These women formed the pre-set loop ribbons by folding the pre-cut ribbon in half, measuring 160 mm from the fold on a ruler, forming a loop, and then gluing the loop at the appropriate spot. Ribbons were then tied in bundles of 100 and picked up by the supplier for delivery to Suntory. In an effort to understand the process better, a member of the QC circle sampled twenty pre-set ribbons from each housewife working for the manufacturer. The results from 6 representative housewives are shown in Exhibit 5.

The members discussed these new concerns at the next Violets Circle meeting with Tanaka. Had they created more problems than they had solved? True, they had achieved a productivity increase, but their actions created a whole range of additional concerns that needed to be dealt with immediately.

**EXHIBIT 5
Breakdown
by Housewife
of Random
Sampling Results**

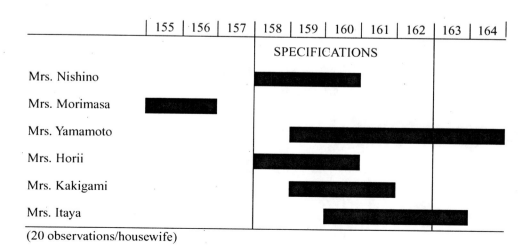

(20 observations/housewife)

Tanaka, returning to his office from this latest meeting with the QC members, focused his thoughts once again on the ribbon-tying process. He was not sure what to do next. He wondered if there had been any value in involving the Violets. While he was contemplating more changes, he wondered how the marketing people would react if he recommended doing away with the ribbon tying process completely.

Endnote

1. The Violets consisted of eight workers on the ribbon-tying line ranging in age from 19 to 56 years, with an average age of about 37 years. This recently formed group met once a week to discuss ways to increase productivity and improve the quality of the final product.

BULLER | SCHULER

Managing Organizations and People

A Resource for Cases in Management, Organizational Behavior, and Human Resource Management

Abstract

This case illustrates the challenges expatriates have working in countries that operate with different, yet acceptable, business practices. The protagonist in the case is confronted with what he considers a bribe during the course of negotiations. "Baksheesh" is not bribery in East Africa, it is considered an acceptable practice, a token offering in return for favors. The expatriate in the case is confronted with situations requiring him to decide what to do. Thus far he has resisted taking baksheesh. He has seen some results of this decision. He may be about to see more when he visits a local government official about his construction plans.

Baksheesh

It was the middle of the night. My legs and neck ached as I stood up in the aircraft, but, as a young man about to start his first expatriate assignment, I was thrilled to be in East Africa. Outside, the air was hot and against the night sky the terminal building was flood-lit. A small crowd of people moved out towards the aircraft, eager to meet relatives who had been to Europe on business, expats back for another tour of duty and, most important of all, to receive supplies of fresh food, newspapers, and other goods from Europe.

The General Manager of the local company, Mr. Lagarde, stood there on the tarmac to welcome me. He was French, in his early fifties, and had spent the last fifteen years as an expatriate in Africa, moving from country to country every three or four years. He seemed friendly enough and spoke to me in fatherly tones. I was far younger than he and had only worked for the company a year. I thought that he might resent my university background and early promotion to line responsibility overseas, but I also realized that he desperately needed a willing subordinate to manage an investment program to repair and rebuild the company's facilities, which had fallen into disrepair.

The local company marketed oil products in the country and used its storage facilities in the port for trans-shipment to neighboring countries as well. The oil storage tanks which sat between the small two-story office block and the Red Sea were built in 1936, but since the closure of the Suez Canal, they had been little used. The company had run down its operations and was only just profitable. It was wholly owned by one of the oil majors but was fully autonomous in day-to-day operations. With about one hundred local staff and three expatriates, it was too small to receive much attention from the parent company other than an annual review of the business plan. In 1983, an unexpected upturn in business had put new demands on the facilities which no longer met the appropriate safety standards. I was sent out for eighteen months or so with a mission to patch up the damage and update the facilities where necessary.

To meet my objectives, storage tanks, pumps, and pipework would need to be replaced section by section in order to keep the depot operational. The work would have to be done by local contractors as the company only employed a small maintenance crew of semi-skilled workers, and I would depend on these contractors to do their work properly and finish on time. I was pleased when, in the first couple of weeks, a number of them came to see me in my office. As they had no offices and ran their business from their cars, they would turn up at any time and would sit outside waiting for me to arrive. They would come in, usually alone, introduce themselves, and sit down. I explained to them that each section of the work would need to be bid for and that I would contact them soon.

Sapid Guedi must have been the fifth such contractor to come and see me. He told me that his firm had worked for my company for many years and hoped that we would have a long and fruitful relationship. He reached into his pocket and pulled out a gold chain which he held out to me as a "gift for my lady."

I was shocked. I had imagined this scene many times but felt unable to respond. This was "baksheesh," not a bribe relating to a particular job or contract, but a token offering which, he hoped, would win him my favor. Eventually, I thanked him but explained that I could not accept his gift which, in any case, was not necessary. He replied, "but your predecessor took my gifts."

Suddenly I felt quite alone. I had assumed that my colleagues would turn away baksheesh but now I wasn't sure. I said no again, led him out of my office, then sat back and thought about my position. I was flattered that my position justified such treatment but was upset that he thought I might accept his gift. I realized that I would have to establish a position of principle in order to avoid this problem in the future.

Within the company I felt that I could trust no one. Guedi had made me realize that my expatriate colleagues could possibly be taking bribes. A couple of days later, the General Manager came into my office and asked me to consider a particular contractor for a forthcoming job, explaining that he had been "recommended by a Minister." He was probably quite honest and his story was probably true, but I had a lingering doubt in my mind. I never told him what had happened with Guedi and, more generally, we never discussed the subject of bribery.

Two months or so later, I had settled down in both the country and the company. I had moved into a small apartment in town away from my colleagues but close to a number of other expatriates. I had a small jeep to get me around and had built up an active social life. I did have some problems when the Port Police began to stop and search the jeep on my way into work every day, but I had learned to be patient and they gave up after a week. I later found that Guedi arranged this "stop and search" to put me in my place. Other contractors had, apparently, heard that I was "clean" and I got no more offers of baksheesh.

At work, things were going well, and I had established a good rapport with the clerical staff and the manual labor out in the depot. Some of them, in fact, seemed more able and enthusiastic than the local managers. In the morning the office was simply chaotic with suppliers running around chasing lost invoices and the local managers running around chasing their staff. In the afternoons, however, the managers would get their jobs done with some help from the expatriates. These able young men were being managed by four local managers who could barely read and write. Amongst the four was a man called Ismail Farah. He was the ringleader and had ambitions of being promoted to the post of Operations Manager, a job which had always been done by an expatriate. Previous General Managers had considered him for the post but none had recommended him, despite the company's declared policy of promotion for nationals wherever possible. I wondered why.

Before leaving for Africa I was told that two of the last three General Managers had had nervous breakdowns which had caused them to be repatriated but I was also told that these were caused by "age" in one case and "marital problems" in the other. The standard of living of the expats in the country was not high, but there was no particular hardship to explain why two previously successful managers should crack up in this way. I was told that one of them would come to the office at night and work through the company's accounts. On one occasion, he was found sitting on the floor in tears by his secretary when she arrived in the morning. If life outside the company were not responsible, what within it could cause this level of anxiety?

I stood on the quay in the Port late one night, watching our men couple up hoses to a tanker which had to discharge oil into the storage tanks. As I looked down the quay I could see someone walking up towards me. It was Ismail. He came up, and we chatted for a few minutes before he started to tell me about his career and how he had been overlooked for promotion. I pointed out that I had not discussed his position with the General Manager but that the company would promote nationals whenever possible. It was a weak reply, but it was honest.

Ismail was the most talented of the four local managers, but I didn't know him well enough to form any other opinion. He seemed pleased that I would discuss the matter with him and hoped that we would "be good friends." He started to talk about the past, about how the country had broken away from colonial rule, and about the company's development through this time. Eventually, he started to talk about the first of the General Managers who had had a nervous breakdown. He smiled and appeared to mock the man's misfortune. "That man was trouble to me. He was a racist and he was weak. He treated us like children so we behaved like children. We would make mistakes in our work that he could never find and it drove him crazy."

I was stunned. I must have looked quite shocked too, because he went on to say, "Don't worry, you'll be all right, you are my friend." This time I went to see the General Manager. We talked about Ismail and his past which, it transpired, had been well documented in appraisal reports. He had the support of a minister within the government which prevented us from firing him. There was nothing we could do.

Eventually, I had come to terms with both internal and external threats and had learned to be cautious in my dealings. I had good working relationships with a number of contractors and no problems dealing with the local authorities. When the Chief of Port Police came to see me in my office, I assumed that his visit was a courtesy call.

He sat down and, after a few minutes' discussion, started to explain that his mother was ill and needed health care he could not pay until he received his pay at the end of the month. "Could you, as a personal favor, lend me the money until the end of the month?" I had had similar requests before and knew that the story was almost certainly a fabrication. "I'm sorry, I would help you if I could, but I have no money in this country." He leaned across the desk and beckoned me forward so that he could whisper into my ear, "But I know that you have money in your account file in the bank." I felt quite sick. I had lied, and he knew it. Although his request was clearly extortion, I felt guilty. I stood up, told him that he must have made a mistake, and led him out of my office. Later that day I went to see the bank manager. As upset about the leak in confidential information as I had been, he gave me an overdraft so that, from that day on, I never did have any money in the bank.

As work in the Port depot progressed, we decided to invest in a small office block out at the airport to house the aviation manager and the fifteen staff responsible for fueling European airlines as they stopped over en route to and from the Indian Ocean. It would be a small, single-story Arab-style building, and it had been designed by a young French architect, resident in the country, who reckoned that it would cost about $200,000 to build. Five contractors had bid for the construction work, and I had awarded the contract to the lowest bidder, subject to planning approval being granted. To get the approval, the architect had completed the necessary forms and had submitted them in the company's name to the Ministry of Public Works six weeks beforehand. We hadn't received any reply in writing when Abdi Issa, officer in charge of planning at the Ministry, called me by phone. "I have a few queries about the drawings you submitted with the planning application forms for your new airport office; nothing serious, the sort of thing we should discuss around the table. Could you come in and see me tomorrow morning in my office?" I wondered, now what?

BULLER | SCHULER

Managing Organizations and People

A Resource for Cases in Management, Organizational Behavior, and Human Resource Management

Abstract

This case describes the conflict between two groups that appears to be anchored in the personality of a manager of one of the groups. The manager over both groups, John, is faced with the questions of what are the real causes of the conflict and what to do about the conflict. As with groups in conflict, each makes strong statements about the other that makes it difficult to determined the source of the conflict. A primary challenge of this case is to develop the means and sources of data collection to determine the causes.

Conflict Management

Area Manager John H. was surprised and astounded by the conversation he had just heard if you could call it a conversation! He could hardly believe that two of his key managers could be involved in such a bitter feud. One accused the other of trying to undermine his department by stealing his best people and the other accused in rebuttal that the other manager was simply finding excuses for his bad management. There had been accusation and counter-accusation followed by hot denials and bitter recrimination. He finally decided there was nothing to be gained by further outbursts and sent both men back to their departments. This, he hoped, would give them a cooling off period and himself a chance to try and sort it all out.

It wasn't unusual for Technical Development and Product Engineering to have these differences, but they rarely took on such a heated aspect. John's thoughts turned to Ralph, Manager of Technical Development. He had come highly recommended by the president of another division. He had been very successful in development work and seemed well suited to this assignment. In his six months on the job he had reorganized several sections and initiated new projects. It wasn't spectacular but it appeared competent from all John could see. There had been a few gripes that he was too aloof and reserved, but that was natural in view of the man he had replaced. It always took a little time for these management transitions to settle down. It appeared Ralph was aware of his problem since he had inserted a new manager under him (Frank) who was effective in personal relationships. It was too early to tell how that was working out but it seemed a wise move.

John knew there were problems, however. He had talked with Personnel after the recent Opinion Survey and learned the morale in Ralph's group was down from its usual mark. There seemed to be more employee apathy, more lateness and absences, and more transfer requests. This latter issue was the most surprising since there were few such requests usually. It was odd to find morale at such a low ebb since the group was well knit and had strong group identity. Personnel had talked informally with a few of the people and their view was (1) the work load was too low and they didn't feel meaningfully utilized and (2) they felt their present management was too distant and reserved.

It was difficult to put these in perspective. From Ralph's viewpoint the low work load was directly traceable to the "game" George was playing. He contended one of George's people would request a "sizing" for a particular job. His people would carefully give cost, technology, and schedule estimates, but then nothing happened. One of his people would call over to find out where the work requisition was and would be told the job had been canceled by George. His manager would be offered a much smaller job—provided they transferred the people key to the former job request—"to help keep your people busy." When this finally came to Ralph's attention he "hit the roof" and this is what led to the recent confrontation. George's views varied greatly, hence the hot argument.

George had been in the department longer than Ralph. He was known as an effective, "hard-nosed" manager who got the job done. He was ambitious and had grown rather rapidly over the last two years. He was adaptable as shown by the fact that he had made the transition from Chemistry to Product Engineering. The Product Engineering Department had a poor reputation prior to George's moving over and he had been instrumental in changing its image to a very positive one. As a result the department had grown considerably under George. All in all it was a good record.

George contended Ralph was an inefficient manager, with too much fat in his organization, who was unwilling to cut back to a reasonable level. As a result Ralph was pricing himself out of the business. He had to cancel jobs because the costs were prohibitive. George laid some of the blame on the previous manager, Henry, claiming it was Henry's doing that caused the lab to reach the present ridiculous size. George felt Ralph should reevaluate his situation and curtail the department size and become competitive again. If the cost problem had merit as an argument it could go back to Henry. There was nothing to indicate Ralph's costs were out of line with past history.

George freely admitted to wanting several of Ralph's people. He felt they would be better placed and better utilized in his area, but he hotly denied he had "played any games" to get them. The pressure of the new releases had caused a backlog in his department and he could use expert help.

John wondered why George steadfastly refused to use the Technology group. He was slipping schedules and the overtime costs would eventually overtake the claimed excessive costs of Ralph's group. He wasn't in any serious trouble as yet and might be gambling he could pull his chestnuts out by the transfer of a few key people. If this was his gamble he might be trying to force Ralph's hand.

John decided he had better talk to Henry in order to clarify this matter further. After that was concluded he sorted out the following impressions. Henry had no love for Ralph. He felt it was still his "shop" and Ralph was doing a poor job of taking over. On the other hand Henry supported Ralph's contentions about George. He indicated he had similar problems in the past and had called him on it a number of times. He flatly denied that the group was too large and indicated it would function well if George didn't feel he had to save the managership of all operations necessary to his function. The conversation left John more puzzled than edified.

Well, there it was. All made good points. If George is correct an overhaul is in order and Ralph should get his costs in line. If Ralph is right George must be stopped from disrupting the department and risking full project success for the sake of his own gain. In all probability both have valid points and the problem will be how to respond appropriately to both managers.

<table>
<tr><td>

Ralph's Viewpoint

</td><td>

Ralph was transferred into this division after several successful projects in Engineering Development. He came highly recommended by the president of another division, under whom he had worked, and was deemed a candidate for higher management in the near future.

There was little doubt about his technical competence. He was informed and innovative. He preferred small groups to large, complex ones, and this was a partial reason for giving him this assignment. Higher growth would depend on his ability to handle larger groups. For this reason the job had been enlarged to encompass additional functions. This meant Ralph had a substantially larger group to manage than his predecessor.

Although Ralph never commented on his reaction to this change in operations for him, he appeared a little overwhelmed by it. He spent considerable time in his office planning and integrating the various functions. He only rarely met with the Lab people and had staff meetings on an irregular basis. It must be emphasized he had been in the job only about six months and still was getting his feet on the ground.

He had never been much of a delegator. Some of this was by temperament and some from the nature of the reward structure. He had been heard to comment: "I do my business in the halls. When I run into the Division President and he asks about my project I can get away with maybe one 'I don't know' and after that I'm known as an 'I don't know guy.'" The result was a tendency to know details that usually are reserved for subordinates. The new job stretched him to the point that he had greater difficulty doing this, but it may account for the inordinate amount of time he spent in his office.

In his approach to others he was direct and confronting. People knew where they stood, and in general their comments indicated they liked this style of managing. He was aware he interacted somewhat stiffly with others and this had occasioned the insertion of Frank at the Lab level. In addition he was planning to change some of the procedures Henry had instituted, and he felt Henry would be an obstacle to these plans. Frank would be a major factor in assuring that the new procedures went as smoothly as possible.

His relationship to Henry was cordial but distant. He had no particular dislike for Henry, but felt the group could be more effectively organized. He was in the process of developing these plans when the problem broke.

His relationship with John, the Director, was essentially OK as far as one could tell. On the whole his "clout" with John was undeveloped, as was his impact on his peers. He seemed to be regarded as an unknown quantity—perhaps something of a threat in view of his reputation.

He was disappointed with the way the meeting turned out. He didn't like shouting matches but he wasn't going to stand by and have George put him or his Lab group down. He was sure they were effective and as soon as he completed some of the new project planning he knew their work load would be more than adequate. He was familiar with people trying the kind of thing George was doing and the only way to avert it was through direct confrontation. He only wished he could better predict John's reaction.

</td></tr>
<tr><td>

Henry's Viewpoint

</td><td>

Henry was an "old timer" and had been the Lab's Manager for many years. He was affable and outgoing, walking the shop regularly and on a first-name basis with virtually everyone in the Lab. It had been his assignment to create and staff the Lab, and over the several years he managed it he exercised care in the selection and placement of the staff. It had been generally conceded the Lab was staffed with topnotch people.

The Lab group had strong ties with one another. There were a few who had turned down promotions in order to remain with the group. That it was not all one big happy family was indicated by a few dissidents who felt they had been passed over for promotion. On the whole, however, they worked well together and enjoyed a favorable reputation by all concerned.

As Henry had indicated, George had tried to lure some of his better talent away during the recent past. Henry learned of these rather quickly because of his close relationship

</td></tr>
</table>

to the group and he effectively aborted each of these. George had finally given up on this and had gone to outside recruiting for the talent he wanted. This meant a slower indoctrination process for him and slowed down his growth potential. It was Henry who first became aware that George was up to his "old tricks."

He probably should have gone to Ralph with the information about George but he felt at odds with Ralph's methods. He resented the staff role into which he had been put, even though medical advice was the basis for the move. He sensed that Ralph was planning changes and he had not been consulted. When Frank was brought in he felt even more resentful. He regarded his assignment as a "make work" one and did not feel meaningfully utilized. He still felt a strong proprietary interest in the Lab group and would take whatever measures he could to prevent its disruption.

Given a choice of choosing between Ralph or George he would choose Ralph, and eventually this choice had to be made. In his meetings with John he had been fully candid regarding George's tactics and hoped this once John would put a stop to them. He did it more to ensure the Lab remaining intact than because of Ralph. He certainly didn't want to see the Lab destroyed after all the years he'd spent building it to its present state.

George's Viewpoint

George was dynamic, energetic, and technically proficient. He had taken over the Product Engineering group when it was regarded with disfavor and had steadily built into its present respectable state. He had ambition and sought to enlarge his sphere of influence whenever possible. He viewed the situation in this way. "I like this environment. It is highly fluid and I have a lot of freedom to do things the way I believe they should be done. I get reprimanded when I make a mistake—and that's only fair as far as I'm concerned. My attitude is to take over and operate any group I can. If I'm successful it will soon come under my jurisdiction. I keep pushing until I'm told to stop by someone who can make it stick."

This had been George's method of operation as long as he had been a manager. It had paid off handsomely for him, and from the Company's standpoint they had benefited too. His group was well-managed, competently staffed, and morale was at least as good as one could find in the Division. His people were loyal to him and respected his ability. He had considerable "clout" because of his past success and had more than the usual influence with the Director.

He had no personal antipathy for Ralph. He was anxious to secure some of the key Lab people and honestly believed they would be more effective in his organization. He felt this would be better for the Company and would provide the people with greater opportunities for growth. There was some accuracy to the latter, but the former was a matter of opinion.

As he regarded the Lab group he felt they were overstaffed and underutilized. He didn't think Ralph was effective in moving to reorganize the department and felt the people were fair game for his managerial approach.

(It was interesting to this observer that direct methods were never utilized. The ground rules permitted making offers to people in other departments, through promotions, raises, etc. Why George never did was unclear.)

George felt he was an effective manager, better than his peers (possibly including the Director). He felt Ralph was running a country club and that it needed effective management. If possible he wanted to absorb the Lab into his operation, but that would require a restructuring of the organization. Since the Lab served many groups in addition to his, his functions would have to be broadened, an unlikely move at this time.

He was taking a calculated risk in not using the Lab for some of his immediate jobs because he might well get into a last minute "crunch" and, failing to meet schedule, lose some of the ground he had gained. On the other hand if he could secure some key people, he could come in on schedule and be in a position to take over other Lab functions that would arise later. In the meantime it would appear as if the Lab was not as necessary because of the low work load. He, at this time, was the major user of the Lab—although this was not always the case. This depended on the development cycle, which was at a low ebb for other groups, but would probably pick up fairly soon.

All in all George was satisfied with his progress and felt he had a good chance at the Director's job when John was promoted. He wasn't happy about this current situation with Ralph, but felt he could weather it and perhaps make Ralph appear foolish or somewhat less competent. It would be a good time for a put-down, his being new and all. The last meeting with John left him uncertain as to where each stood. He was sure he had not heard the last of the situation.

BULLER | SCHULER

Managing Organizations and People
A Resource for Cases in Management, Organizational Behavior,
and Human Resource Management

Abstract

This is a disguised company case that describes a traditional male-dominated manufacturing environment and its impact on female employees. One of the female employees files a formal complaint with the EEOC alleging sexual harassment at Flagstone. The case describes the nature of the work environment at the plant and the company management's unsuccessful attempts to change the work climate. The case illustrates the challenges of changing company culture and the role of management in leading effective change.

Iroquois Container Corporation: Flagstone Operations (A)

Paul Barker pulled out of the plant gate and turned onto the country road that took him home. It was a crisp, clear November 1993 day and a beautiful time of year for northern New Mexico. But Paul wasn't thinking about the beauty of the season or the scenery. Yesterday one of his technicians, Sherry Thompson, notified him that she would be off work for an unspecified time from "stress-related illness due to a hostile work environment." However, that he was losing a good employee for possibly a month or more was the least of his worries. Instead, this was all too similar to an event that had occurred five years earlier. In 1988, a Flagstone Operations employee in another department, Brenda Riley, had filed a sexual harassment and disparate treatment lawsuit stemming from a "hostile work environment" and in 1991 was awarded a $500,000 settlement. The actions and behaviors of Sherry were closely paralleling those of Brenda prior to her lawsuit. Paul thought, "I have the feeling that the company is headed for more 'disparate treatment and sexual harassment' litigation."

Iroquois Container: Flagstone Operations

The Iroquois Container Corporation is a relatively profitable diversified manufacturer with facilities located throughout the Western United States. The company has never been in serious financial straits and in 1993 its assets approached one-half billion dollars. The Flagstone Operation of the Iroquois Container Corporation is located in a small northern New Mexico town. For many years the town had had only one major source of employment, a molybdenum mine. In the late 1960s, the mine shut down leaving a large pool of skilled labor available at relatively low wages. Iroquois decided to locate its Flagstone plant there in 1970. Flagstone employed a total of 93 people, including 14 women, in its four units: Plant Maintenance, Operations, Warehousing, and Technical Services (Exhibit 1). The Technical Services Department was the only unit not unionized. The management team at the plant was entirely male and was primarily made up of mechanical, chemical, and electrical engineers with college degrees. Some non-degree holding individuals, however, had risen through the union ranks and moved into management.

Most of the large Hispanic population in the area (approximately 50%) lived at or slightly above the poverty level, and families did not encourage education beyond high school. The local cultural norms were such that even exceptional Hispanics were discouraged from pursuing a college education, and those that did go away to college and graduated seldom returned to the area. As a result, 13 of the 15 managers at Flagstone were white middle-class males (all with engineering degrees), recruited from other Iroquois facilities. All but three of the employees in the Technical Department were Anglos.

Women Employees at Flagstone

Historically, the dominant culture of the town valued the tradition of single breadwinner families. Men worked outside the home while women stayed home to take care of domestic chores. However, closure of the mine and the loss of those high-paying jobs, plus

EXHIBIT 1
Iroquois Container Corporation: Flagstone Operations

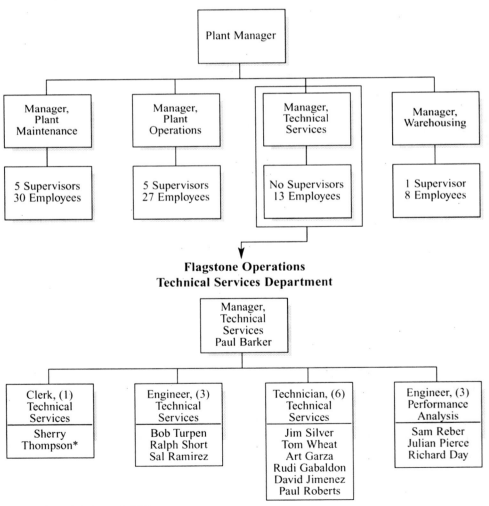

*Promoted to technical status in 1987

inflation and the desire to maintain a relatively high standard of living, forced many women to seek employment outside the home. In spite of these added responsibilities, traditional domestic values did not change and women continued to be responsible for most of the household chores.

There were, however, many employment barriers for women in the area and at Flagstone. The town's culture discouraged women from holding jobs that had traditionally been held by men. The union had not particularly encouraged females to join its ranks; and because the unemployment rate in the area was high and the pay at Flagstone was considered very good, turnover at the facility was low. In addition, the physically demanding work, the dirty and noisy environment, and the "good ole' boy" network made it difficult for women to be accepted as equals. To be fully accepted by her male co-workers, a woman had to become "one of the boys" and behave in a manner compatible with the overall norms of the prevailing organizational culture. Bantering and jokes, practical and otherwise, including behaviors that might be considered harassment, were the traditional means of communicating acceptance. Thus, few women had ever applied and a still smaller number had been hired to work at the plant.

Iroquois Container and Sexual Harassment

Following the filing of a formal complaint in 1984 with EEOC by Brenda Riley, who had been employed at Iroquois for four years, Iroquois management recognized that sexually explicit behavior could no longer be tolerated in its facilities. In 1985, management directed that all pornographic and sexual material be removed from the workplace in all of its plants and issued the following statement: "All lewd jokes and sexually intimidating and derogatory speech will cease immediately. Behavior is to be professional and non-threatening at all times." A formal policy statement forbidding all forms of sexual harassment was also inserted in all employee manuals and posted at each workplace. Unfortunately, this directive did little to change the work environment or employee attitudes and behaviors.

The company voluntarily began EEO training classes for management personnel in 1986, and in November 1987, Iroquois required all Flagstone employees to attend a "pluralism" class that, in part, addressed issues of sexual harassment. However, Iroquois had not made efforts to assess whether sexually hostile work environments existed at any of its plants. It took no company-wide proactive measures other than posting policy statements and holding management and worker education classes at its various facilities voluntary for the employees. Although Iroquois reacted to specific complaints, none of the men against whom the charges were made were ever disciplined.

Before Riley filed her second sexual harassment complaint in December 1987 and her lawsuit in June 1988, the work environment plant-wide contained calendars of nude women, pornographic magazines, sexual and racial jokes, and sexually oriented language. According to one plant supervisor, "In general, women throughout the facility were looked upon primarily as sex objects created to satisfy primal sex drives." Several men in the unit seemingly took pride in their ability to intimidate and offend females who came into their work area.

Between 1980 and 1991, the plant's 14 female employees were subjected to various forms of physical and sexual harassment. Recurring examples of sexual harassment and hostility toward female employees over the years included: Women being hit on their helmets with crescent wrenches with such force that the helmets were dented; car windows and windshields being broken; work gloves being filled with caustic materials; male employees entering women's restrooms when women were inside; women having their breasts and genitals fondled while being held by male co-workers; women being slapped on their buttocks and openly propositioned; and pornographic materials being openly displayed and accompanied by sexually explicit graffiti directed at specific female employees. For example, a sign posted in the control room in the summer of 1987 read: "SEXUAL HARASSMENT IN THIS AREA WILL NOT BE REPORTED; HOWEVER, IT WILL BE GRADED." One of Iroquois' posted official policy statements on equal employment opportunity, dated October 2, 1987, was altered to read that sexual advances were "welcome."

When female employees asked for advice or assistance, they were often insulted and made to feel stupid. Although unit managers were aware that such events were illegal under the EEOC Guidelines, they did little to stop these behaviors. When the women did muster the courage to approach their supervisors to tell them of the harassment, more often than not they were blamed by their supervisors for not attempting to "fit in better."

Because the prevailing mores of the Flagstone culture had become so deeply ingrained, the new sexual harassment policy mandated by management in 1985 was very unpopular and largely ignored. One reason was that the vast majority of the employees, whether male or female, didn't view these behaviors as offensive. The typical employee response to the mandate was, "This new policy is just the latest fad dreamed up by top management to make our jobs a little less enjoyable." In response to management's pressure to enforce its sexual harassment policies, many employees continued to violate company policies and retaliated with even more sexually explicit, aggressive behavior.

Rather than risk decreased production or retaliation for enforcing the company's stated sexual harassment policies, supervisors did little more than require the removal of the pornographic materials from open view. In reality, these policies served only to drive the harassing behaviors underground. Nevertheless, a few well-founded complaints surfaced. Flagstone's plant manager responded by issuing a memo on November 24, 1987, reaffirming Iroquois' EEO policy and identifying more specifically what constitutes sexual harassment. But, he later admitted that even after the company's efforts to eliminate sexually explicit graffiti and obscene materials, the problem persisted. It was not until after Brenda Riley filed her lawsuit in June 1988 that management began to become fully aware of the depth, breadth, and severity of the problem.

Technical Services Department

In July 1990, the Technical Services Department consisted of 14 people, 13 men and one woman, Sherry Thompson. Three of the men had engineering degrees. The others had received technical training in the military that qualified them for their jobs with Iroquois. Although engineering functions were important throughout the plant, those engineering tasks performed in the Technical Services Department were the most critical to the daily operations of the facility. This department housed the engineers and technicians who had the responsibility for overseeing and controlling the highly complex continuous process technology that was at the heart of Flagstone's profitability. Even with an engineering degree or military training, because of the complexity and skill levels required for employees to achieve competency, a long training period was needed before employees could gain a working knowledge of the intricacies of the process. Skill requirements were such that if key employees were suddenly to leave the organization, the plant would potentially have to curtail production sharply or shut down completely resulting in the loss of millions of dollars in revenues before replacements could be found. In addition, demand within the industry for individuals with these skills was such that they were highly mobile, even in times of economic downturn. Therefore, employees in the Technical Services Department were the most pampered in the plant. Because Technical Services personnel were considered professional employees and advancement within the unit was unencumbered by union seniority clauses, they were usually the first to be considered for and promoted into management positions. Nor, was the department bound by rigid union job descriptions. This gave the unit the flexibility to rotate assignments and to train new employees efficiently and effectively. As a result the work tended to be less routine and boring, and employees had the flexibility to adjust their hours to fit personal needs. Technical Services personnel also benefited from an attractive variable compensation plan.

Sherry Thompson

Sherry Thompson had been raised in a small Midwest community where she graduated from high school near the top of her class. After moving to New Mexico in 1984, she was hired by the Technical Services Department and met the challenges of her new job with zeal and enthusiasm. Within a relatively short time, she had mastered the job for which she was hired, department clerk, and was promoted to technical status. Her efforts and accomplishments were rewarded with high performance ratings and regular salary increases.

Even though Sherry was a very competent and productive employee, she had had her share of troubles at home, including a recent difficult divorce from an alcoholic husband. As a result, she found herself as a single parent of three teenaged boys, all of whom were said to have behavior problems.

One of Sherry's sons, along with another teenager, was involved in the theft of a handgun. While the other teenager was holding the gun, it discharged and the bullet hit her son in the leg. Sherry denied that her son was involved in the theft of the weapon and filed a wrongful injury lawsuit against the parents of the other teenager. After the trial, in which she received a substantial settlement, it was rumored that Sherry had confided to her friends that she knew that her son was equally as guilty as the other teenager.

Sherry also had problems at work. Although a very competent technician, men found her physical stature (6'4", 200 lbs.), rough talk, and abrasive personality to be intimidating. She had few friends, male or female, at Flagstone, the closest one being Brenda Riley. Sherry had complained to Brenda and others that she found the sexually explicit behaviors offensive and intimidating, but was afraid to voice her discomfort and complain to management for fear of not being accepted and for fear of reprisal. However, after Riley's lawsuit against Iroquois Container, in which Brenda reportedly received a $500,000 settlement, Sherry decided that she no longer had to tolerate the sexually offensive conduct in the unit. She began to insist that management enforce the company's new policies against such behaviors. Subsequently, Sherry complained almost daily to her supervisor about the men's behavior.

As the men learned of her complaints, they began to perceive her as being the sole source of management's continued pressure to do away with their old ways. Newspaper clippings about battered and victimized females and anti-feminist literature were "mysteriously" posted on the bulletin boards near Sherry's work station. Once, someone broke into her office during the night and placed a button reading "The Perfect Bitch" on her desk. On one occasion a male employee asked, "Why is your ass so big?" And, on another, when she complained that the men never said anything nice about women, one of the men mocked her by saying, "My don't your breasts look pretty today." In addition, Sherry experienced all the same hostile and sexual harassing behaviors that women at Flagstone had been subjected to in years past.

Sherry's supervisor seemed unwilling to take charge of the problem. Although he promised her he would discipline the men for violating company sexual harassment policies, he failed to take appropriate action when infractions occurred. Typically, her supervisor would handle her complaints by saying, "You're overreacting, Sherry," and on one occasion, he even disciplined her after she complained to another manager about her supervisor's failure to deal with the problem. Without her supervisor's support, Sherry knew her complaints would only serve to encourage the men to continue their behavior. Nevertheless, she persisted. In April 1990, Sherry's complaints finally caught the attention of middle management. This, plus the pending lawsuit in the Brenda Riley harassment case, was in no small part the reason for the demotion and transfer of Sherry's supervisor to another Iroquois plant in September 1990. In October of that year, Paul Barker was brought in from another Iroquois facility as head of the Technical Services Department.

Shortly after Paul Barker's arrival at Flagstone, Sherry, perceiving that the situation was still not improving quickly enough under Paul's leadership, filed a formal complaint with the State Equal Employment Opportunity Commission alleging "sexual discrimination due to a sexually hostile work environment." She also went on record as stating that the other women at the plant intentionally tried to make her look bad by complaining about her performance and by spreading malicious rumors about her. In Sherry's opinion,

"They didn't want the work environment to improve because they liked and participated in the rough language and lewd behaviors, and they viewed me as a troublemaker. Typically, when I went into the front office, the clerk greeted everyone by name except me. Julie, the warehouse clerk, would not help me unless she absolutely had to. She frequently bypassed me to wait on anyone who came to the counter after I did. When she finished, she would walk away and leave me standing at the counter so that I had to call someone else to wait on me."

Sherry also said that while she was at work, her car had frequently been spat upon and the paint scratched. On two other occasions her car windows were broken and on one other occasion oil was poured down the side of her car.

Paul Barker

For ten years Paul had worked at other Iroquois facilities. Three years before his transfer to Flagstone he had been promoted to Technical Services Manager at one of the company's smaller plants in Salt Lake City. At the Salt Lake plant he gained a reputation of being able to deal successfully with thorny personnel problems including sexual harassment.

In 1991, Paul had received a call from corporate headquarters telling him that he was being reassigned to the Flagstone Operations. This was done at the request of the Flagstone Plant Manager who believed that because of his record at Salt Lake, Paul could handle the difficult task of enforcing the company's sexual harassment policy and resolving the interpersonal conflict and other behavior problems within the Technical Services Department. Paul had accepted the transfer knowing that career-wise it would be his toughest assignment yet. Upon arriving at Flagstone, the Plant Manager told him that sexual harassment complaints had escalated to their highest point ever.

On Paul's first day at Flagstone, he met with his work unit to introduce himself and to explain why he was there. When he asked if there were any questions, as might be expected, the first question concerned the demotion and transfer of his predecessor. But, before Paul could answer, Sherry interrupted and asked him about his stance on sexual harassment. He immediately seized this opportunity to address the company's harassment policies. He concluded by saying,

"Behaviors perceived to be harassment will not be tolerated. I expect that employees will coordinate work assignments and collaborate with one another without hostility at all times. Furthermore, violations of the company's sexual harassment policy will result in severe disciplinary action including termination."

Connie Williams

One of Paul's first initiatives at Flagstone was to solicit the advice and support of Connie Williams, an associate assigned to Iroquois' Organizational Development Department. Connie was a specialist in evaluating workplace environments, developing transition plans for new managers, and assisting managers and work units in implementing those plans. Paul and Connie had collaborated on several occasions to resolve behavioral issues at the Salt Lake plant.

Paul especially admired her ability to deal with personnel issues including sexual harassment. Even though the men in Paul's unit had little respect for females, Connie soon proved to be an exception. She had a commanding presence, demonstrated a high level of expertise in her field, and spoke with authority. When she heard derogatory or sexist remarks, Connie's language skills enabled her to rephrase these remarks in such a way as to embarrass the perpetrators.

By March 1991, Connie and Paul had developed a series of questions and conducted individual interviews to assess employee attitudes and perceptions concerning the work unit, management, and the overall work environment. To assure confidentiality and encourage more reliable feedback, Connie conducted the interviews individually away from the plant site. As a result of the interviews, Connie perceived a certain level of mistrust among the employees toward Paul and herself and doubt about the purpose of the survey. However, she believed most of the employees had answered the questions honestly.

Their responses described a work environment ranging from supportive to sexually hostile. The interviews further revealed that most of the male employees believed Sherry Thompson was solely responsible for the prevailing behavioral problems and the "uncalled-for-pressures" from management stemming from enforcement of the company's sexual harassment policies.

During a second round of off-site meetings with individual employees in April 1991 to inform employees of the results of the interviews and to discuss their significance, it became even clearer that Sherry was the target of a substantial amount of hostility, distrust, blame and anger for insisting sexual harassment was a major problem at Flagstone.

Upon reviewing the results of these meetings, Paul reaffirmed his resolve "to do everything within my power to end the hostilities and sources of sexual harassment within the plant."

The Hostile Environment Resurfaces

For a few months following the meeting, the work environment seemed to improve; but over the next year, offensive language, pornography, and dirty jokes again became problematic. On August 23, 1992, Sherry informed Paul that she had been "raspberried" several times recently while attempting to page someone on the public address system. And, shortly after the August 23 incident, Sherry told Paul that one of her few friends, a fellow employee, had been physically threatened by other employees for associating with her. Upon investigating and finding the allegations to be true, Paul disciplined the guilty employees by giving them stern warnings and by placing letters of reprimand in their personnel files.

It was also at this time that Paul began to recognize that management initiatives to eliminate Flagstone's sexually hostile work environment were having little impact upon the behavior of certain employees. He believed that the only way to permanently resolve the problem was to transfer or terminate several key personnel. When he approached his superiors at Flagstone with this recommendation, they ignored his suggestion.

No additional complaints were heard from Sherry until November 1993, when she notified Paul that she had been diagnosed as being clinically depressed, as a result of incessant exposure to a hostile work environment. She also told him, "An awful lot of hostility continues to exist in the plant with much of it directed toward me and my friends." When asked to name specific people and events, Sherry said, "Sam Reber instigates much of the hostility and then backs out to let his co-workers pick up where he leaves off. If I object at all, they gang up on me. Instead of one person teasing or harassing me, there will be four or five."

Upon hearing this, Paul asked Sherry what she expected him to do. Sherry said, "It is the responsibility of management to provide me with a workplace free of harassment and intimidation. I *don't* want to leave; so I expect management to do what is necessary to stop these awful behaviors." Once more Paul approached his superiors and once more management chose to ignore the situation.

Paul's Personal Assessment

After dinner at home that cool November evening, Paul continued to reflect upon his attempts to eliminate sexual harassment and remove hostility in the department and what he must do to resolve the problem with Sherry.

"In my three years as manager, I believe I've worked diligently to do away with sexual harassment and resolve interpersonal conflict within the department. I've disciplined several people who violated sexual harassment policies by placing strong letters of reprimand in their personnel files and have brought these behaviors to the attention of my superiors. It's been a tough job to get the men to change their behavior, but I believe I've eliminated a large part of the problem. For the most part, the employees seem to be enjoying their work and getting along.

"I'm well aware, though, that I still may have a problem with four of the men in my department who treat Sherry very poorly and who, from the very beginning, have been the worst offenders of the harassment policies. I've had the feeling that these men are still harassing Sherry but I have no proof. No one, not even Sherry or her friends, has said anything. Because it has been more than a year since Sherry lodged her formal complaint, I'm really surprised that she's given notice of a prolonged leave of absence citing continued sexual harassment and a hostile work environment.

"After three years of attempting to deal with this mess in a civilized way and making recommendations to my superiors on how to solve the problem and continuously being ignored, I'm fed up. It's about time I take more drastic measures. While I can't change what has happened in the past, I can perhaps do some things to improve the future. I believe that Sherry's absence from work for a month or more will only make the situation worse. The workers in the department will think they have finally succeeded in driving Sherry

away, and I can't let that happen. Up until now, my philosophy and my efforts to get these men to change their behaviors and attitudes toward women have failed. I'm now convinced that this is the time to insist on major changes in the department. Things are already in a state of chaos. I guess it's about time I really shake things up! But how?"

Iroquois Container Corporation: Flagstone Operations (B)

Late the next afternoon, Paul's immediate supervisor received the following memorandum.

MEMORANDUM

TO: George White, Manager, Flagstone Operations

FROM: Paul Barker, Manager, Technical Services Department

DATE: November 12, 1993

SUBJECT: Assessment of Department Behaviors

You are aware of Sherry Thompson's absence and her claim. Although I'm in agreement with the Company's position to contest her claim, it is important that we deal with any hostility towards her which may be present.

The problem is not Sherry Thompson, and the solutions are not simple. Any major corrective action will likely result in a temporary negative impact on our production. The hostility is obvious, yet in most cases I am unable to identify the perpetrators. When management intervenes, the hostility gets worse and less work gets done. Obviously, we must gain control of this situation. I believe the problem lies within a core group of four TSD employees who are perpetuating the hostility.

All are top technical performers in key positions. Their hostility is directed in a subversive and subtle, but effective, manner. At this point I'm quite sure they will not commit an obvious policy violation that will result in disciplinary action. But, I don't believe the problem will disappear if they continue to work here. In order for my department to provide the service the plant requires to operate, I will need help from executive management in replacing these people should we remove them from the plant. I do not believe that terminating these individuals from the Company is necessary. Simply removing them from this plant and separating them through relocation to other plants may be sufficient to eliminate the behaviors and still allow us to retain their technical skills.

The hostility towards Sherry Thompson is plant-wide and is generated primarily by people with a high level of seniority or technical knowledge. They seem to be unable or unwilling to accept the fact that the environment which they built and perpetuated is unacceptable. They do not see themselves as being wrong and do not see their jobs as being in danger. The newer people (those with less than 4 years at Flagstone) realize what a tremendous job opportunity they have. Most of the newer people want no part of the hostility and avoid it when possible.

All of the senior TSD people involved in the conflict have the knowledge and capability to shut the plant down for an extended period. Theoretically, they could create a condition with the plant control systems that would shut down the plant for weeks. Because they see the Company as totally dependent on their knowledge and ability, which it is, they do not see their jobs as being in danger. As a result, they see little need to change their behavior or comply with the company policy.

As I see it, the solution to our problem is to transfer three people: Sam Reber, Paul Roberts, and Sherry Thompson. Paul Roberts is usually around when problems arise between Sam and Sherry. If this does not send the message to the people who are on the "fringe" of this problem, it is possible that Bob Turpen and Richard Day will need to be removed as well. Removing all four of these men will eliminate the group who at times refer to themselves as "the bad boys." Sherry is an excellent employee and a true asset to Iroquois. I believe that Sherry should be offered an attractive opportunity to work elsewhere in the Company. This will get her into a place where she can start again.

This will require that we delay the overhaul and startup of production unit #3. If we wait until spring to transfer these people, we will so severely erode the effectiveness of the fabrication unit that the overhaul will be extended indefinitely. *If we are going to initiate the transfers, we must do it now.* Also, if we wait until after the overhaul to remove these people, we've lost the opportunity of giving our junior level employees valuable overhaul and startup experience with these systems. In addition, I feel that a strong emotional shock is necessary to send the message to our people that we are serious about our expectations of their behavior, and this is it! Nobody in this plant should perceive themselves to be irreplaceable.

Two of my new and very capable junior-level technicians have not been a part of this problem and would welcome the opportunity to step into one of the vacated positions. The other positions would be filled with personnel from other operations within the company.

There is also an issue regarding other managers in the plant. There are other managerial personnel that are unwilling to act or see themselves as unable to do anything about the situation. I have been challenged personally by other managers in my attempts to correct the situation. I believe that if we are to really resolve this issue, it may be necessary to remove some management personnel as well. Those who are "on the fringe" will likely respond when they see their peers terminated because of their inaction on this issue.

The changes I am recommending should definitely improve behaviors in the Technical Services Department. We need to recognize that although the workers and some managers complain that Sherry is the problem, the real problem is that their attitudes, perceptions and behaviors are not compatible with what is expected in today's equal opportunity workplace. If anything, we should thank Sherry for her willingness to expose the magnitude of the problem. Unfortunately, the hostility generated against Sherry is so pervasive and subversive in this plant that a significant number of personnel changes may be required to change the prevailing attitudes concerning Sherry within the plant. Whatever we do will most likely have a negative impact on production. In my opinion, however, the anticipated short-term production problems will be much easier to deal with than another major discrimination lawsuit.

As George read Paul's memo, his frustration and anger began to rise, "Damn it! I thought we were beginning to get this sexual harassment B.S. under control. That's what we hired Paul for! There has to be some way to resolve this issue without transferring the three employees most responsible for the successful operation of my plant."

BULLER | SCHULER

Managing Organizations and People

A Resource for Cases in Management, Organizational Behavior, and Human Resource Management

Abstract

AstroTech, one of the world's foremost and progressive organizations, is a strong proponent of modern management and organizational behavior techniques and processes. This case illustrates the interpersonal, political, and socioeconomic relationships that surface in complex organizations when priorities and time/goal perspectives conflict. It addresses problems that arise from contrasting leadership styles and management philosophies, differences in time/goal perspectives among units, intra-individual role and interpersonal conflict, line/staff conflicts, and the political and power struggles that commonly occur in organizations. The case also calls attention to the dilemmas faced by individuals when their professional, ethical, and moral values differ from others in positions of power within the organization.

Astrotech Fuel Systems (A)

Shortly after responsibility for completion of AstroTech's Autoflow project had been removed from under Jim McGee's direction, the staff at the Fuel Systems Division was informed that Roger Banter, the absentee General Manager of the Fuel Systems Division, would make one of his rare visits to the Texas facility. Jim anticipated that Banter's visit was to propose that the heavy focus currently placed on Engineering should now be shifted to Marketing. But, during his visit and much to Jim's surprise, Banter made it a point to visit privately with him. As usual, Banter wasted no time on trivialities:

Jim, I've discussed your situation with Corporate Headquarters and suggest you call your previous boss about the possibility of a transfer back to your old job in Utah. You've not yet gotten a black eye in the company, but I'm concerned that if you stay here any longer, you will. Otherwise, any potential you might have for a promising career in this organization could very well be nothing more than wishful thinking.

As Banter stood and prepared to leave, Jim said:

Wait a minute! I feel I've made significant improvements to the engineering and quality systems here. I've developed a number of new products, increased the department's capability level and brought many of our poorly designed products up to specifications. I'd like to know what it is that I've done wrong. I've invested a lot of energy here. Although I admit I've not gotten along well with the staff even though I've tried, I like it here and would like to stay.

■ H. Richard Eisenbeis, University of Southern Colorado.

Banter hesitated for a second, turned, and said:

After all this is settled, you and I will sit down and talk, even if I have to come to Utah to do it.

Banter quickly exited, and Jim was left alone in his office in a state of confusion and astonishment. Jim believed that he had always been good about recognizing his own mistakes and weaknesses and being able to accept the truth. But, he found it extremely difficult to accept blame for things he didn't believe he was guilty of. Many thoughts raced through his mind as he considered his next move.

AstroTech and the Fuel Systems Division

AstroTech, one of the United States foremost and largest corporations, was involved in virtually all facets of manufacturing auxiliary equipment for the aerospace and airline industries. During the decade of the 1990s, annual revenues for the corporation exceeded $4 billion. Although in a "cutting edge" industry, the organization had tended to conform most closely to the divisionalized bureaucratic structure (Exhibit 1); however, it seemed to be transitioning toward a more organic structure.

The Fuel Systems product line had been acquired by AstroTech three years previously from a small, independent manufacturer of fuel systems serving the aeronautical industry. AstroTech's stated objective for this new division, consisting of 60 employees, was that it was a first step toward becoming the major supplier of aircraft fuel systems for the aerospace and aircraft industry. Although most of the original rank and file employees were retained, Fuel Systems' management was replaced by AstroTech personnel immediately upon acquisition. New and old employees alike believed that because of the facility's location and the generous salary and benefit packages that "this is the closest we'll ever get to living in paradise." They were all committed to seeing that the undertaking become a profitable and permanent facility within AstroTech.

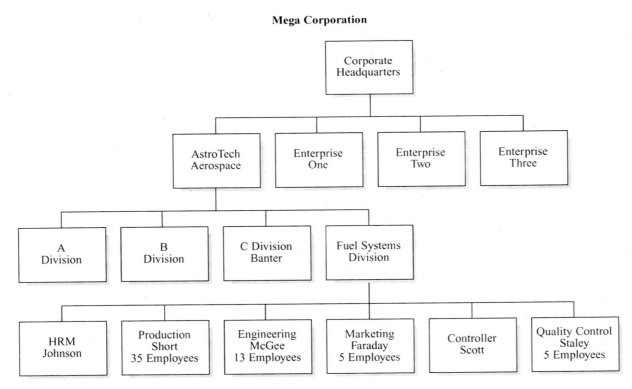

EXHIBIT 1
Organizational Chart before Phalen's Departure from the Fuel Systems Division

During its three years as a division of AstroTech, Fuel Systems had generated between $6 to $8 million in revenues annually. When compared to other units within the corporation—the smallest of which generated over $200 million in revenues annually—some thought it a stretch of the imagination to assign Fuel Systems "division" status. Instead, they thought it should have been designated as a product line attached to one of the other divisions. Whereas top-of-the-line products manufactured by Fuel Systems sold in the range of $6,000/unit, more sophisticated, state-of-the-art units manufactured by competitors ranged from $10,000 to $60,000/unit. But, because Fuel Systems' product line was unique to AstroTech and because it was perceived as having substantial long-range growth and profit potential, the unit was separated from the rest of the corporation and accorded divisional status. A downside to this was that, because it represented a relatively small investment compared to other divisions, Fuel Systems received only minimal oversight from corporate headquarters.

Jim McGee and AstroTech

Jim had begun his career with AstroTech Corporation at AstroTech's Composite Systems Division in Utah. Years of dedication and hard work earned him the challenging and satisfying position of Manager of Engineering and Quality. Although he was viewed by most as being a task master, he was respected for soliciting input from colleagues and subordinates before making decisions that would affect their welfare. Given his success in the Composite Systems Division, it came as no surprise to others when Jim was selected by the Corporation's Human Resource Department in conjunction with the corporate Vice-President of Technology to head the Engineering Department of the Fuel Systems Division. Jim welcomed his promotion and new responsibilities and was assured that he would play a key role in the success of the operation. Although he had been with AstroTech for ten years and had advanced rapidly in the corporation, unbeknownst to Jim, he was not in the least prepared for the challenges he would face and the compromises that would have to be made if he were to survive in his new position and in the corporate arena.

Prior to this most recent promotion, Jim's career with AstroTech had been marked by a continuous stream of accomplishments and promotions in Utah and at a previous assignment in Virginia. Although most of his experience was in mechanical and materials engineering, he had acquired a solid foundation in aerospace-related engineering and quality systems applicable to electronics-dominated fuel systems. Jim prided himself on his tenacity, his ability to motivate, and his ability to resolve complex problems. He was optimistic that the successful completion of this assignment would further enhance his career with the corporation.

The Concern for Quality Control

Jim had been on the job only a few days when he became painfully aware that interpersonal relationships within the unit were far from what had been conveyed to him during his interview with George Phalen, the division's president. Jim knew that the division was struggling and that he was part of a team charged with turning it around, but he was astonished at the extent of quality control improvements that would have to be made immediately if the unit was to meet corporate goals. Not only did he find that many of Fuel Systems' product lines were on the verge of becoming obsolete, but he also found that none of them met FAA specifications. Records indicated that the previous owner had almost certainly altered data to pass FAA inspections.

Jim also discovered that Phalen was far more interested in increasing unit output and sales than identifying and solving the major quality problems that had come with the acquisition. He was convinced that if major system design changes were not initiated immediately, the division's works-in-progress would continue to be substandard and that Corporate management's reputation for high-quality aerospace systems and engineering would be compromised.

Jim was concerned that Phalen minimized the importance of the need for upgrading these systems. It appeared to Jim that many at AstroTech ignored the fact that the division could be fined and/or shut down if its internal quality control systems did not comply with FAA regulations and that individuals could even be imprisoned for severe infractions. Mindful of the magnitude of the issues involved, Jim knew he could help the fledgling business meet quality expectations if he could somehow get through to Phalen that the current quality control systems were substandard. Jim also realized that he needed to do this without creating negative publicity for the corporation or without ruffling Phalen's feathers.

During the first few weeks on the job, Jim assessed the strengths and weaknesses of the division's quality control systems until he was sure of what needed to be done to meet quality standards. Shortly thereafter, at a bimonthly staff meeting, Jim attempted to offer suggestions on how to improve the division's control systems but was quickly cut off by Phalen's comment:

Don't waste your time on that; what we need here are new products. That's why we brought you in, and that's what you need to focus on.

Phalen then went on to describe how he and the Director of Operations, Ben Short, had "whipped the Engineering Department into shape" during the three months the department operated without a manager prior to Jim's arrival. Both Phalen and Short stated that before they became personally involved, the Engineering Department personnel "were poorly managed and sluffed-off."

George Phalen

George Phalen had been employed by AstroTech about five years prior to the Fuel Systems acquisition. He had been hired at the corporate level and was reputed to have had close ties with one of the corporate Vice-Presidents. Phalen had risen very quickly within the firm and left no doubts of his desire to someday manage at the corporate level. Upon being chosen to manage the Fuel Systems Division immediately after it was acquired, he saw this as a major opportunity to favorably impress managers at the top level of the organization. Because Fuel Systems was out of the mainstream of the organization and received little or no oversight from corporate headquarters, Phalen was able to manage with minimal accountability. From the onset, he appeared to have become obsessed with power. He ran a tight ship and insisted that tasks be completed immediately and be done his way regardless of subordinate suggestions or company policy. The fact that Phalen consistently overestimated sales projections contributed substantially to an ongoing pressure situation for the unit. In addition, Phalen had had no experience in dealing with the FAA. However, away from the plant, he was described as being very likeable and sociable, and a good family man and neighbor.

Ben Short

Short was a long-time employee with the organization and was considered by upper management to be an excellent production manager. He was transferred from another division to Fuel Systems to head up production immediately after Fuel Systems had been acquired by the parent organization. Short was looked upon as a "pure operations person"; that is, highly production oriented and "one who got things done." He was extremely loyal and dedicated toward achieving the new division's goals and objectives. Short was described by others in the plant as "being so firmly anchored as to be able to withstand a tornado."

Short made it clear to Jim that he believed engineers needed to be ridden hard to get results, and if they couldn't or wouldn't perform, they should be fired. He said:

After all, the success of this business depends upon quick sales. We don't have time to baby people. There are lots more engineers out there where these guys came from. You design the products and I'll build them; it's that simple. We straightened everything out for you before you got here, so stay on top of those guys or you'll lose the momentum. You have to show them who's boss, or they'll walk all over you.

Jim was taken aback by Phalen's and Short's comments concerning his department's priorities and how to motivate Engineering personnel. In addition, he noticed that on occasion Short was extremely gruff and aggressive with production workers. This was not a good sign in light of the fact that personnel from Engineering would be required to work closely with Production. The production departments with which Jim had been associated elsewhere in AstroTech were very professional and collegial, as well as productive. He was certain that his engineers would resign should they be subjected to Short's harsh leadership, and he knew that he couldn't afford to lose the few engineers he had.

Fuel Systems Engineering Department

In analyzing the situation, Jim asked Engineering personnel about how the unit functioned prior to his arrival. He learned that he was the fourth Engineering Manager since AstroTech purchased the business three years earlier. Although it concerned Jim that two of the previous engineering managers had had successful careers with AstroTech until joining the division, he remained optimistic that he would be successful. He thought:

After all, since I've been able to overcome some major obstacles in two larger divisions, I should be able to do the same in this, the smallest division.

Jim was particularly concerned about the lack of depth of his technical staff. While they were very dedicated, only 3 of the 13 members possessed engineering degrees. In addition, the group was currently in the process of developing or modifying over 20 products, a ratio deemed "aggressive" in any business. Also, given the limited resources at his disposal, Jim was convinced that Phalen's and Short's emphasis on high volume production would result in the division's demise. His most pressing concern, the lack of the highest level of quality control systems, intensified his resolve to improve them.

As he became more familiar with the existing systems, Jim realized the magnitude of the task before him. The previous owner had run the business as a "garage shop" with very few formal control systems and had done little to train his people in FAA or aerospace regulations. In further discussions with Phalen and Short, it became evident to Jim that only he understood the full impact of noncompliance with these regulations. He found it ironic that although Phalen and Short had created an overwhelming myriad of development programs during their brief, but "successful," stint in Engineering, they had little knowledge of the level of work required to develop and qualify highly technical products that would meet stringent FAA regulations and customer expectations.

As weeks grew into months, Jim attempted to simultaneously keep up with new product development and the improvement of system quality processes. In addition, he devoted considerable time to addressing problems associated with existing product lines. Several of these designs failed to meet specifications and mandated immediate redesigns. As a result, department personnel were asked to put in extensive overtime. Jim, himself, exceeded 75 hours per week on a regular basis. He believed that leading by example was the catalyst that motivated his personnel to work these overtime hours without complaining. Although the department had jelled as a team, Jim observed the workload was wearing on individuals who began taking shortcuts that he feared would create future problems.

It was evident to Jim that he could not design the necessary quality control systems required, develop new products, and service existing product lines with the limited personnel and resources at his disposal. This being the case, Jim approached Phalen and insisted: (1) that he be permitted to change priorities from developing new products to servicing existing product lines and (2) that he be given more technical personnel to enable him to focus more on meeting quality standards. Irritated by Jim's demands, Phalen accused him of not being able to manage his people. He said:

Jim, you need to sit on these people and kick them into gear to get work out of them. It's about time you quit letting them manage you. I need these products, and you're overdue. My advice to you is to get your department under control.

Jim was becoming more concerned by Phalen's refusal to realize the seriousness of the situation. Jim thought:

He simply doesn't want to hear about it. To hell with product development, I'll just have to do what I know is right.

In a subsequent staff meeting, it was announced that annual sales for the division were substantially below projections and that the division was continuing to "bleed red ink." Controller Willard Scott emphasized that the division had not once met sales projections or turned a profit in the three years since becoming part of AstroTech and that "it's high time we find out why." When individual staff members were asked for their opinions, a consensus emerged that the main reason for the division not reaching Phalen's goals was that they were unrealistic. It was obvious to Jim that Engineering was not the only unit having serious problems. Phalen countered their concerns with:

That's pure nonsense! If Engineering would develop the products they are assigned to and if Marketing would generate the sales that they've committed to, achieving these goals would be a piece of cake. You people just need to work smarter. If you don't have the right people, then get rid of the ones you have and find the right people.

As was typical of Phalen's staff meetings, he then began pitting staff members against one another by blaming the failure of one unit to meets its goals on one or more of the other units. Phalen would simply make a series of accusations and then sit back and watch the fireworks. At times, just when it appeared as if problems were near being resolved, Phalen would make new accusations to rekindle the flames. These staff meetings were notorious for lasting 3 to 4 hours, and the badgering and yelling that occurred usually precluded any constructive thought. The end result was exhaustion and frustration especially considering the workload that awaited staff in their respective departments. Phalen would also meet one-on-one with staff members and initiate rumors purposely designed to create conflict. He had once boasted to Jim, "I believe in managing with chaos. You must keep people on their toes and guessing in order to keep the upper hand."

Staff Concerns

In the ensuing months, the staff secretly met on several occasions to discuss the plight of the division and how to best deal with Phalen's unorthodox management tactics. Because Phalen had a history of creating untenable situations for people and then firing them, claiming to his superiors that the person was dishonest or incapable, extreme caution was necessary. With the division performing as poorly as it was, the staff was concerned that, once again, Phalen would attempt to buy himself time by blaming various personnel for the division's woes and terminating them. At the end of one long, frustrating day, Jim's top mechanical engineer approached him and said:

Jim, I've had enough. This place is just too crazy, and nobody outside of Engineering has a clue about what it takes to develop these products. I've decided to accept a position with another company.

Jim was devastated. The engineer's resignation had been preceded by two top draftsmen for essentially the same reasons.

It was at this time that Jim found an unexpected ally in Short who also began to distance himself from Phalen. Both Jim and Short agreed to use their contacts elsewhere in the corporation to discreetly let people know that all was not well at the Texas facility.

The resignation of key people and the fact that the Engineering unit continued to fall behind did have one positive effect. Jim was finally able to persuade Phalen to give him permission to hire additional personnel as well as to replace those who had left. Jim was fortunate to be able to hire three, very capable, new engineers. He was now confident that the unit would be able to meet performance expectations and would become a force to be reckoned with in the marketplace. But, he also knew that they must focus on the most critical projects if this was to become a reality. Jim was a strong believer in the old adage, "You can do many things poorly, or you can do a few things well."

The Morale Survey

But, focusing on the most critical products was not to be the case. Phalen insisted that his original performance expectations for the division and the Engineering unit remain unchanged. By the end of Jim's first year, frustration at all levels of the division was clearly evident. People were tired of the excessive workload and the perceived lack of Phalen's desire, or possibly his ability, to fix things. This frustration was further aggravated by the fact that Phalen was the only person who ever went home on time and rarely put in more than a 40-hour week. Morale was at an all-time low. But, spirits were lifted when it was rumored that the division was slated for an employee morale survey. Upon receiving confirmation that the survey was to be administered, the staff agreed among themselves to be honest in their responses and make Corporate Headquarters aware of Phalen's exploitive leadership style and the negative impact it continued to have on productivity and employee morale. Even though the engineering staff members were aware that their answers would be collected separately from the rest of the plant and, therefore, identifiable, they resolved that the Phalen "issue" had to be addressed and agreed to give identical responses to questions in spite of potential consequences.

One month later when the results of the survey were returned, Phalen had not fared well. Although negative comments occurred randomly, one set of particularly negative comments were sequentially numbered. It didn't take Phalen long to determine that these had originated in the Engineering Department and to identify the most negative comments as Jim's. With few exceptions, the other staff groups had failed to live up to their part of the agreement. Phalen called Jim into his office and laid out the entire list of his responses, including Jim's request for a new General Manager, and asked him point-blank:

Are these your comments and would you explain to me why you wrote them?

Noting that Phalen was uncharacteristically calm, Jim responded:

George, I was pretty upset over the way you were handling things when we filled out the surveys. As you are aware, we have a big difference in opinion over what the priorities should be in Engineering, as well as what we should ship and not ship and when.

The discussion did not last long.

Shortly after the survey and perhaps as a result, Phalen fired the Director of Marketing, confidently claiming that, "I made more sales on my last public relations trip than he did during the entire year." The subsequent search for a replacement led to the addition of Dick Faraday as the Director of Marketing. Like most of the management staff, Faraday came from another AstroTech division. He had a very confident air about him and was quickly able to prove his expertise. Rumors quickly emerged that Phalen had handpicked Faraday to become his heir apparent, and the two bonded quickly. Within a few weeks of his arrival, it was apparent that Faraday sided with Phalen in virtually all matters concerning personnel, product development and service, and quality control.

As the weeks passed, Phalen increased his demands on the Engineering Department and intensified his personal attacks on Jim. For the first time since coming to AstroTech, Jim had serious concerns about job security and his future with the company. He addressed these concerns by working feverishly to stay ahead of Phalen's demands, but contrary to Phalen's wishes, insisted on keeping the FAA and quality issues as his top priority because of the potential legal and ethical ramifications of shipping substandard products. Should loss of life occur as a result of inadequate quality control systems, Jim believed that he would ultimately be held responsible. Once in the past the Corporation had gained notoriety for not adhering to quality specifications in the aircraft industry with near disastrous results. Jim knew that the potential for a similar tragedy existed if quality control was not maintained at the highest level. Because of his emphasis on quality, it was inevitable that development projects would slip—and they did.

Jim often received the support of staff members from other departments and occasionally Short. Arron Staley, the Quality Manager, initially backed Jim but quickly came under fire by Phalen for it. Although Staley continued to back Jim privately, he became much less supportive of him in public. Jim frequently reminded himself that the others, including Short, had not been fully honest when they failed to make their concerns known on the survey.

Product X

A major conflict arose when Engineering detected a design flaw in Product X that was under long-term contract. Having experienced no problems with the product, the customer was unaware of the flaw. Jim announced the existence of the flaw in a staff meeting and recommended that shipments be delayed until the customer could be informed. Phalen immediately rejected Jim's proposal and demanded that the division keep shipping the product until the "real problem" was identified. However, with the exception of Phalen and Faraday, the staff members agreed that AstroTech should fix the problem and immediately inform the customer of the product's limitations. In support of Phalen, Faraday emphatically disagreed and stated that he would continue to ship the product until Engineering could come up with an acceptable solution. A heated discussion over the product continued for the entire afternoon, but nothing was accomplished—neither side was willing to make concessions. Much to Jim's dismay, Staley remained quiet during the discussion. However, two weeks later, having had enough of Phalen and Faraday's attempts to compromise product quality, Staley resigned.

Because of Jim's previous experience with quality systems and control, Phalen decided that Staley's position would not be filled and assigned responsibility for product quality to Jim's department. Unfortunately for Jim, the Quality Department was even more understaffed than the Engineering Department. Jim had argued emphatically that a replacement for Staley was critical, but Phalen and Faraday denied Jim's request on the grounds that they could not afford to replace him at that time.

After several weeks of debate, the issue of the faulty design of Product X reached a point where Jim felt that he had no alternative but to apprise the customer. Furthermore, as the Manager of Engineering and Quality, Jim believed that informing the customer was well within his area of responsibility. Jim met privately with Phalen to make one final attempt to get his permission to do so. Surprisingly, Phalen agreed and gave Jim discretion on how best to approach the customer. Fearing that Phalen would change his mind, Jim acted immediately without attempting to inform Faraday. He knew, given the stand that Faraday had taken in previous discussions, that he would do all he could to change Phalen's mind.

When Jim informed the customer about the deficiencies of Product X, its management expressed concern but were appreciative. Company representatives assured Jim that they would continue to order the product once the design flaws were corrected. Faraday's response was as expected. Upon learning of Jim's actions, he immediately demanded a staff meeting. Jim was shocked when Phalen claimed that he had not given permission. This was the final straw for Jim. After two hours of heated accusations and counter-accusations, Jim once more re-stated the actual chain of events and rebuked Phalen for his failure to admit that he had given Jim his authorization. Phalen finally admitted, "Jim you're right. I did give you my consent." Jim looked at Phalen in disbelief and disgust and, exhibiting behavior that was entirely out of character, stormed out of the meeting.

In the weeks following the Product X meeting, Phalen and Faraday increased their personal attacks on Jim and exerted even more pressure on Engineering to develop additional products. Faraday even began adding products to the list for which there were no customer orders, in an attempt to show that Marketing was doing its job "of creating the vision needed for the unit to achieve its stated sales goals." Unfortunately, these new demands took resources away from critical projects already underway, which caused Engineering to fall further behind. Jim pressured Phalen and Faraday to prioritize projects so that a "critical few" could be completed, but they insisted that efforts continue on all projects.

Shortly thereafter, word was received from Corporate Headquarters that the division had six months to prepare for a major FAA quality audit—the first of its kind for the new division. Jim argued that it was imperative that the division pass this audit if it was to continue manufacturing and shipping aerospace products. The staff finally agreed that it would be necessary to completely overhaul the existing quality control systems. The task of developing new and revamping old systems was placed solely on Jim. Although he realized the importance of completing this task, he also knew that the amount of time involved would conflict even more with Phalen's push to bring new products to market.

As weeks grew into months, the strong support Jim received from his technicians and engineers gave him confidence that he was acting in the best interests of the Corporation. However, his anxiety concerning job security and career advancement continued to increase.

An Unexpected Visitor

The debates and personal attacks during staff meetings had risen to an unprecedented level, and Jim had given up all hope that Corporate Headquarters would act on the survey results. Willard Scott, the Controller who had frequently complained in staff meetings of being forced to "work the books," accepted a transfer to another unit within AstroTech. Only Jim, Short, and Jill Johnson, the Human Resource Manager, remained of the staff who had completed the morale survey. Jim was convinced that he could not withstand the combined attacks of Phalen and Faraday and that his days with the Corporation were numbered.

Staff members were stunned, but pleasantly surprised, when one day without warning, a Senior Vice-President from New York showed up and terminated Phalen because of his "continued inability to meet division objectives." The out-and-out relief felt by Jim and Short was offset by Faraday's visible disappointment. His displeasure intensified when the Senior Vice-President announced that Phalen's position would not be filled because of the small size of the Fuel Systems Division. Instead, all five of the staff department heads would report directly to Roger Banter, the General Manager of a much larger division based in Indiana (Exhibit 2).

EXHIBIT 2   Organizational Chart after Phalen's departure from the Fuel Systems Division

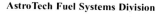

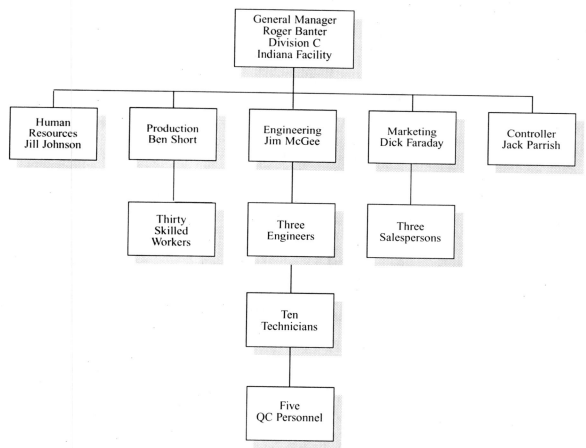

Faraday and Short knew Banter from previous assignments and were familiar with his reputation in the corporation as a strong, fair leader. The staff was generally pleased with his selection as the person to head the division. However, when Banter informed them that his contact with them would be through weekly teleconferences, they were disappointed that he was to be an absentee manager. Upon being informed of Banter's expectations for the division, the staff met to discuss how to avoid further conflict and resolved to make a fresh start. They agreed that they would forego one-on-one discussions with Banter unless they were initiated by Banter himself and that they would interact with him only during staff meetings. But, it soon became apparent to all that Faraday communicated more frequently with Banter than anyone else did and that these exchanges were not always initiated by Banter. Although Faraday had been the driving force behind the "group communication agreement," he ignored the agreement more than anyone.

FAA Inspection Anxieties

Even though the FAA audit was only two months away, Faraday again began to openly criticize Jim for spending too much time designing and revamping the quality control systems and not spending enough time developing new products. Because the Engineering Department was failing to develop new products that would sell, there was a growing concern among the staff about the division's future. They began to agree with Faraday. Nevertheless, Jim persisted in his attempts to convince the others of the importance of the audit, but because they were not knowledgeable of the time commitments and tradeoffs between new product development and implementation of the quality control systems, he met with minimal success. Jim was especially disturbed by lack of support from Short. Jim believed it ironic that Short had been responsible for AstroTech's Quality Control prior to Staley's arrival.

Staff members who had previously blamed Phalen's leadership style as being responsible for low productivity and failure to develop new products had now shifted the blame to Jim and his engineering group. This shift of blame was instigated by Faraday. Pressures on Jim to change his priorities increased and individuals from other departments began to distance themselves from him and his group. In spite of this increasingly hostile environment, the Engineering and Quality Control personnel continued to show Jim strong support. He also received encouragement from production operators who preferred his leadership style to the autocratic styles of Short and Faraday.

A new Controller, Jack Parrish, was finally hired to replace Willard Scott who had quit the division several months before. Parrish was a young CPA who openly discussed his desire to make a positive impact on the division in order to prove his mettle with Corporate Headquarters. Soon after joining the Fuel Systems Division, Parrish claimed that the Engineering Department was "out-of-control" because of its overcommitment to quality. Faraday, capitalizing on Parrish's allegations, called a staff meeting to discuss them. He began by saying, "Jim, I no longer have confidence in your ability to manage your department." He then gave the group a detailed explanation why he believed Engineering's priorities were the major cause of the division's inability to meet its goals. When Jim attempted to defend his priorities, it was evident that those few from other departments who had previously supported him no longer did. After Jim had had his say, Faraday quickly ended the meeting.

Even without the support of the other staff members, Jim was still convinced he was right. He was upset that his priorities and his management abilities were being questioned. Recognizing that he was in a tough spot, he decided it was time to consult one-on-one with Banter and get his opinion. He knew that to successfully plead his case with Banter he had to be completely open and honest and to avoid implying that other staff members were guilty of any wrongdoing. In his conversation with Banter, Jim said:

My main reason for calling is to ensure that you're aware of the staff's concern relative to my performance. They've stated that they've lost confidence in my ability to set priorities and to manage the Engineering Department. Perhaps you can offer me some guidance. I'd like to discuss this with you in detail at your earliest convenience.

Other than this, little of substance was said. However, Jim expected to hear from Banter before too much time had passed.

At the next staff meeting, Jim told the group that he had shared their concerns with Banter. The entire staff was angered by his disclosure. Faraday quickly accused Jim of breaking the trust of the group members by going to Banter without their permission. In defense Jim said:

First off, Banter is my direct boss, and I should be able to talk to him about issues concerning my personal performance. Secondly, you're the ones who said I was performing poorly. All I did was inform Banter of your opinions. How can you find fault in this?

As usual, Faraday was the first to censure:

He may be your boss, but you should have discussed these issues with us before you called him. Here again, you've shown that you can't be trusted.

Jim looked at everyone in disbelief, noticing that most staff members refused to make eye contact. He then said:

This whole thing is ridiculous. I've got work to do.

With this, Jim left the meeting.

Frustrated, Jim shared the gist of the meeting with a senior engineer who said:

Jim, this is absurd! Everyone knows the hours we're working and that you're the first one in at 5:00 A.M. and you're lucky to leave by 7:00 P.M. We're in here 7 days a week. Why aren't they here during those hours to work with us as a team? What do they expect from us anyhow?

Actually, Short did spend considerable time in the facility, but Faraday, Parrish, Johnson, and their departmental personnel didn't come close to the time Engineering invested in these projects.

The AutoFlow

During the ensuing weeks, Faraday continued to denigrate Jim to the staff for calling Banter as well as for informing the customer months before about the flaws in Product X. Faraday further aggravated the situation by calling a meeting initiating the development of another new product, the AutoFlow, which would be one of the largest projects ever undertaken by the division. Because of its size and complexity, Engineering estimated a major design effort of 15 to 18 months to develop and qualify. Nevertheless, Marketing demanded that the product be operational and fully qualified by the FAA within 6 months. Given their concerns about the future of the division and the perceived sales potential of the AutoFlow, the staff sided with Faraday. Once more, Jim believed he was being set up to fail. His initial reaction was that he saw no possible way to meet this schedule but added that Engineering would do its best to complete the project "as soon as possible." He also reminded them that the division had never developed and qualified a new product in less than 12 months.

Jim's working relationships with other staff members had become strained to the breaking point, and he was now clearly the odd man out. He found it hard to believe that his status had fallen from being "one-of-the-group" to "most-wanted-out-of-the-group" in such a short period of time. Faraday's calls to Banter increased and it was evident that he had gained Banter's confidence. Furthermore, no matter what information Jim volunteered in staff meetings, Faraday was quick to discredit or discount it, and there was little support from the rest of the staff, most notably, Short. In fact, the relationship between Short and Jim had deteriorated to the point where on one occasion they became entangled in a very public and violent debate on the production floor. Accusations were exchanged and the debate escalated with Short losing control and physically attacking Jim. The two were immediately separated by nearby workers and an "emergency" staff meeting was called.

Jim and Short explained to the rest of the staff that they were under a lot of pressure at the time of the incident. The altercation arose over who was to pick up a corporate executive at the local airport. Jim had initially been designated to meet this person and bring him to the plant. When time approached for the executive's arrival and Jim was not to be found, Short made arrangements to meet the visiting dignitary. About the time Short was to leave for the airport, Jim appeared on the scene. Each insisted that he was responsible for bringing the corporate officer to the facility. The argument that ensued resulted in Short connecting with a strong right hand that ended up with Jim having to pick himself up off the floor. By the end of the meeting, the staff agreed that the incident would be kept under wraps and not leaked to colleagues in other divisions or to Corporate Headquarters. Jim knew that he could have Short fired, or even arrested. However, because of his past friendship with Short and understanding the pressures they were all under, Jim decided to "sweep it under the carpet." But, it was clear that irreparable damage had been done.

Thanks for Nothing

The FAA audit took place two weeks later and lasted for four days. Fortunately, all of Jim's hard work paid off and the division passed with flying colors. The Engineering and Quality Department personnel were ecstatic. Although Short threw a plant-wide party for Jim to celebrate the effort and its success, after the party Faraday immediately called a meeting that included Jim, Parrish, Short, and himself. Its purpose was not to apologize for being unduly critical of Jim or to congratulate him further but quite the opposite. He got right to the point:

Jim, we'd like you to know that we believe you obviously put too much effort into the audit preparation. Even though you got an "A" we needed only a "C." The wasted effort could have been better applied to new product development.

Jim then reminded the group that the FAA inspector had given them the high grade because of the extensive effort for compliance on the part of "the facility." Although the auditor was well aware of the quality problems inherited from the past owner, he agreed to limit his audit to the present and to base it on the processes designed by Jim's group; ensured processes that quality standards would continue to be met in the years to come. Jim's argument—that the audit would have failed had the facility not been able to show strong potential for continuous process improvement—fell on deaf ears.

Almost Accomplishing the Near Impossible

The 6-month deadline for completion of the AutoFlow project arrived all too soon. Engineering had put in a Herculean effort and had completed the design, but the project was still in the qualification phase. What made the feat even more remarkable was that Engineering had accomplished the task with very little assistance from Marketing. Although Marketing was responsible for submitting to Engineering a preliminary product specification based on the customer's needs, no such specification was ever provided. Because Jim and his group knew that any delay in the project would eventually be blamed on them, they created a specification and copied it to Marketing. When they received no feedback, they interpreted it as tacit approval to proceed. Six months later, irritated when Jim informed him that an additional 2 to 4 weeks would be required to complete the project, Faraday scheduled a staff teleconference with Banter. During the conference he made it a point to say:

I would be selling the AutoFlow units now if I had had a completed design from Engineering, but as usual they're behind schedule.

After Jim had answered a few technical questions from Banter about the status of the project, the conference ended.

While the Cat's Away

Having not taken any time off during the 18 months he had been with the division, Jim scheduled a 3-day vacation for his family. He looked forward to getting away from the stress, but because of the pressure to complete the AutoFlow project, he informed the staff at its next meeting that he was canceling his vacation in order to speed up completion of the project. Jim was surprised when Short said, "Don't be crazy. You need some quality time with your family. Go! You've earned it." Knowing how much his family was looking forward to time away, Jim was pleased that the staff appreciated his hard work and encouraged him to go.

When he returned, Jim was furious when he learned that during his absence the staff had called Banter and reiterated their lack of confidence in Jim's ability to manage and to complete the AutoFlow project. Faraday had also reaffirmed his belief that he could sell hundreds of the units as soon as they were qualified. He had told Banter that he had three customers with approved budgets waiting for this product and three more that were very interested and that he could easily have sold over a million dollars of the AutoFlow unit within the next six months if Jim had finished the design on time. Faraday had also convinced Banter to have the AutoFlow project reassigned to Short's unit.

During the next scheduled teleconference after Jim's return, Jim tried to change Banter's mind by pointing out that the AutoFlow was one of the most ambitious projects ever undertaken by the division and that its completion was only two weeks away. However, Banter's decision—to remove the project from Jim's control—stood. Jim attempted to discuss the issue privately with Banter but was unable to contact him by phone or to arrange a meeting. Jim experienced deep feelings of anxiety, rejection, frustration, anger, and . . . betrayal.

True to Jim's prediction, Short's unit was able to complete the project within two weeks and prototypes were submitted to FAA for approval. Initial units were fabricated for Marketing and sent to pre-selected airlines for performance verification and to generate sales for the new product line. Although still smoldering from losing the AutoFlow project, Jim was extremely proud of his Engineering team. They had labored against all odds, working seven days a week for six and a half months, to develop this new product in record time. Field tests had proven that the units exceeded even the Engineering team's expectations. Furthermore, the AutoFlow surpassed performance standards of their competitor's product and also sold for less. In spite of all this, Marketing had yet to secure a single contract for this new, superior product. With the year rapidly coming to a close, sales goals for the division appeared more and more out of reach.

Abandoned and Alone or Where Do I Go from Here?

Jim's thoughts returned to Banter. In the few hours since Banter's departure, many questions continued to weigh heavily on Jim:

Why is it that no one is willing to give me credit for my accomplishments here at Fuel Systems? The FAA would have shut us down had it not been for my efforts and persistence. Besides, I was able to accomplish these things with few resources and under adverse circumstances. Where did I fail? What could I have done differently? Was I wrong for not compromising my concerns for quality? Should I leave the division and return to Utah and my old job, or should I stay here and fight it out? What does the future hold should I choose to stay? While staying would carry risk, would not my leaving be viewed as an admission of my incompetence and reduce my chances for advancement within the corporation?

This last point was the toughest one for Jim to swallow.

Edited by Paul F. Buller, Gonzaga University, and Randall S. Schuler, Rutgers University

BULLER | SCHULER

Managing Organizations and People
A Resource for Cases in Management, Organizational Behavior, and Human Resource Management

Abstract

Seeking to make the topic of whistleblowing personally relevant and meaningful to undergraduates, we have developed a brief case exercise, based on the fictionalized and embellished experience of a former student of the first author. The decision of the prospective whistleblower, a part-time business student working as a first-line supervisor at a restaurant, (1) involves an organizational scenario in which students can readily picture themselves and (2) does matter, to a number of stakeholders, including the supervisor's friend (knowing the victim of wrongdoing may increase the likelihood of whistleblowing). The protagonist merely suspects her manager of stealing, until she hears concrete evidence of it from her assistant manager, who does *not* want to take action. This case therefore asks students to think about the extent to which it is ethically appropriate for a prospective whistleblower to force another member of his or her organization to become an unwilling collaborator in the reporting of misconduct. Also, the supervisor perceives that their company has an old boys' network, and her assistant manager presumes that their miscreant male manager has allies in high places. The case thus also addresses political aspects of whistleblowing decisions and outcomes.

Unsavory Problems at Tasty's: A Case Exercise About Whistleblowing

Emily Brown, a part-time business administration student, has been supporting herself and paying tuition at Teaberry University for the past five years by working at Tasty's, a family-style restaurant. During the last three years, she has been a supervisor there. Tasty's, which runs 37 franchises in the northeastern U.S., has experienced some financial difficulties in the last year. About six months ago, as a result of declining revenues, Tasty's closed several stores in the district where Emily works. Many employees lost their jobs; their more fortunate co-workers were offered jobs at stores that remained open. Emily's store survived the recent spate of closings, but her general manager, Connie O'Hare, was transferred to a store outside the district. Before her transfer, Connie had been general manager at Emily's store for eight years. Her subordinates had enjoyed their jobs and worked hard. They were proud that their Tasty's was one of the strongest performers in the district, and attributed their store's continuing viability in large part to Connie's managerial talent.

■ Debra Comer, Hofstra University, and Gina Vega, Merrimack College.

Replacing Connie as their general manager was John Tadmore. John had been the general manager at another Tasty's for barely two years at the time of his transfer to Emily's store. John, whose own store had closed, was delighted by the transfer, which cut his commute in half. Emily, for her part, was infuriated that John was actually benefiting from the closing of his store, whereas Connie was being shuffled around without any regard for what she—or her subordinates—wanted. She chalked up Connie's transfer to the old boys' network at Tasty's, which has no female division managers and only a handful of women at the level of district manager (see Figure 1). The scarcity of women in top leadership positions had been the only feature of the company that bothered Emily, who, until recently, had otherwise considered Tasty's an ideal employer.

Within the first month of John's arrival, the store was showing signs of neglect. Orders weren't placed on time, the employee schedule was always finished late and frequently contained gaps and/or overlaps, and the level of grime and grunge had hit an all-time high. Perhaps most troubling, money seemed to be disappearing. Registers were short on a regular basis by twenty dollars or more, the change fund (kept in the safe) was often missing money, and bank bags were coming up short. In her five years at Tasty's, Emily had never witnessed a situation like this one. Despite her lack of any solid evidence, she suspected John of stealing from the store. Meanwhile, John was accusing others. He blamed a light bank bag on a new employee, and a $40 register shortage on Martin Pine,

FIGURE 1
Organization
Chart of Tasty's

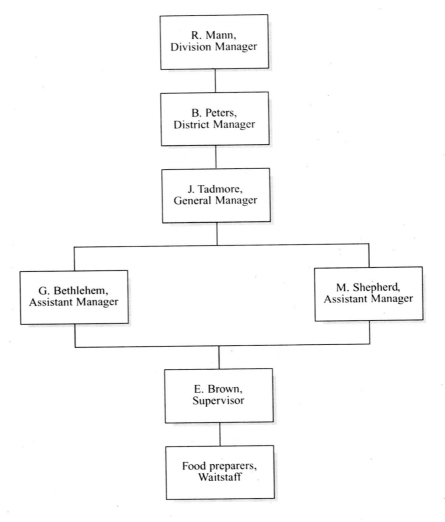

Note: Emily Brown is one of eight supervisors at her store.

one of Emily's closest colleagues. Perturbed and feeling helpless, Emily turned to Ginger Bethlehem, one of her assistant managers.

E: *Ginger, I need to talk to someone about what's been going on in the store.*

G: *O.K. Have a seat. I'm listening.*

E: *Since Connie left, everything's been going down hill. Scheduling is a mess, the store is not as clean as it should be, and, of course, there's the mysterious disappearing money. John has been blaming other people of stealing, but I think he is the real thief!*

G: *Emily, I've never seen you so upset!*

E: *Well, John has been unfairly accusing innocent people. Martin is a good friend of mine. I've known him for more than three years and I know he would never steal period, let alone from the store. He loves his job as much as I do, or, as much as I did, anyway. Did you know Marty was thinking about leaving?*

G: *No, I didn't know that. That's too bad. He's a solid performer.*

E: *I can't prove anything, Ginger, but I'd bet that John is the culprit. I mean, the way he's so quick to blame others. You're an assistant manager; can you talk to him about this?*

G: *What could I say that would make a difference? Listen to me, Emily. Last week, at the end of the night, John and I were getting ready to close up. I was exhausted, so I headed toward the ladies' room to splash some water on my face to perk up for my drive home. But I noticed my right earring was missing, so I started crawling around, looking for it. When I finally found it, I heard some sounds at the register. I stayed crouched down, so John couldn't see me. But I could see him. He took three bills from the stack of twenties and stuffed them in his back pocket.*

E: *John thought he could get away with it because he thought you were in the bathroom.*

G: *Exactly.*

E: *What did John say when you told him?*

G: *Told him?!?! What, are you kidding me? John is doing my performance review next month, and I'm not going to say or do anything to ruin my chances of getting the raise I deserve.*

E: *Have you spoken with Blake Peters?*

G: *The district manager! Why do you want me to stir up trouble? Besides, Emily, Blake and John went to college together. I could be wrong, but I'm guessing that that's how John got to be our general manager after his store was closed.*

E: *But you don't know for sure. Don't you think Blake should know? John's getting away with stealing, and he's ruining our store and driving away capable employees. It's not fair!*

G: *Who told you life is fair? Well, I have to get back to my paperwork now. Please, Emily, do us both a favor and forget I told you anything.*

Emily left Ginger's office, more upset and confused than she'd been before entering. She recognized that maybe Ginger was right that it wouldn't accomplish anything to speak with Blake. But knowing that John was hurting the store and people in it was eating away at her. She couldn't respect Ginger's decision to keep quiet. She wondered whether she should try talking to Blake, or whether it made more sense to go over Blake's head and speak with Richard Mann, her division manager. For years, Emily had loved working at Tasty's. Now, she dreaded going to work. She knew one thing for sure: She had to do something, even if it meant resigning. She didn't think she could stay at Tasty's if the current situation continued.

Module 5

Human Resource Management

Cases Outline

BULLER | SCHULER

Managing Organizations and People

A Resource for Cases in Management, Organizational Behavior, and Human Resource Management

Abstract

Precision Measurement of Japan (PM-J) is a joint venture formed between Takezawa Electric Company (TEC) and Precision Measurement, Inc. (PMI). PMI is a Minneosota-based manufacturer of high-quality measurement and instrumentation equipment that formed the joint venture to penetrate the Japanese market. PM-J operates in a highly competitive domestic market in Japan. In order to maintain a competitive posture in Japan, PM-J must resolve two preliminary issues and then move on to the hard task of recommending a labor market strategy for the company. The preliminary issues include: (1) is a joint venture partner dumping worn-out human capital into PM-J? and (2) is PM-J's salary scale appropriate? Information needed to handle these issues is provided in the case. The more serious issue is appraising the various labor market strategies for recruiting engineers against various possible "states of the world" as they affect the labor market for engineers. Primary among the important variables will be Japanese action on import penetration and its effects on the labor market for engineers.

Precision Measurement of Japan

Precision Measurement of Japan (PM-J) is a joint venture company between Takezawa* Electric Company (TEC), a Japanese electrical equipment manufacturing company, and Precision Management, Inc. (PMI), a Minnesota-based manufacturer of measurement devices. Major markets for these devices are chemical processes, pipelines, aircraft and aerospace, and power generation. As a multinational corporation, PMI is faced with the problem of penetrating the Japanese market before one of its Japanese competitors perfects the various gauges and shuts the U.S. company out of the Japanese market. In order to penetrate the Japanese market, PMI has entered into a business relationship with TEC, thus forming a quasi-Japanese company, PM-J. This step was intended to increase PMI's credibility with the Japanese, and to forestall a Japanese competitor from using its

■ Carlson School of Management, Case Development Center, University of Minnesota (Industrial Relations, James G. Scoville).

* I am also indebted to referees who commented on the case. One of their suggestions was a brief guide to pronunciation of the Japanese names in this case. In general, each vowel merits a syllable; thus, "Tah.Keh.zah,wah." The only exception is when "i" serves as a "y," as in the name of Keio ("Kayo") University. All "sh" combinations in this case are pronounced as in "shoe."

1

protected domestic market to work out bugs, employ economies of scale, undercut PMI's pricing scheme, and generally take over the world instrument market. This would seriously, perhaps fatally, affect PMI's visibility.

The Problem

The problem faced by his company, according to Joe Smith, president of PM-J, is that the Japanese instrument companies are becoming more visible and are developing broader product lines, which may directly affect PM-J's market share. Corporate PM-J headquarters is genuinely concerned that the Japanese long-term plan is to capture and dominate the world instrument markets just as they have taken over camera, automobile, video recorder, and other high-tech markets. The instrument market could be the next Japanese strategic industry.

Currently, the Japanese tend to dominate only their domestic instrument markets, says Smith. This could change by working their familiar strategy. This is accomplished by closing the Japanese markets to foreign competition, acquiring volume and experience in domestic markets, and basing foreign marketing on that experience.

The usual Japanese strategy is to either (1) obtain licenses for advanced technology from other companies (usually from the United States) and then improve the technology and market it alone or (2) use some company's proven distribution to establish a market base and then go it alone. Both of these approaches save considerable time and expense to the Japanese company, thus freeing resources and capital for quick and effective marketing of the new and/or improved technology. Smith reports that two competitors gained real substance in this manner.

After penetrating the foreign markets with this strategy, excellent service and responsiveness from the Japanese companies are generally reported. The Japanese will, no doubt, continue their patient, persistent way of presenting high-technology, high-performance products which are backed by quality service. Even though they gain market position slowly, says Smith, once the Japanese establish accounts, their outstanding customer relations and excellent service record often mean they keep the accounts; the non-Japanese are then in a position of lost accounts and a declining market share.

Objective

PMI wishes to establish a permanent position in the Japanese domestic market. Additionally, it would be preferable that any Japanese competition be retarded by PMI's establishment of a strong sales and manufacturing posture in Japan. To acquire and maintain a market share in the instrument industry, PMI must establish credibility as a viable company; this it sought to do by combining with TEC. By establishing PM-J, PMI is demonstrating a long-term commitment and significant investment in Japan. In its efforts to capture the Japanese market, PM-J is faced with two overriding questions:

1. Is it possible to hire a sufficient number of qualified sales engineers (preferably newly graduated) to increase sales, establish quality accounts, and achieve a reasonable profit growth?
2. In what manner might PM-J increase its market position and distribution in the Japanese market?

The answers to these questions are complicated by a variety of socioeconomic factors unique to Japan.

The Country

Japan has a small amount of inhabitable land located on a number of mountainous islands, with few natural resources, but abundant human resources. Pressured by the need to import almost all raw materials, including 100% of all oil, the Japanese economy grew at phenomenal rates during the 1960s and 1970s. During this period, Japanese industrial products moved from a reputation as cheap and flimsy to a position known for quality and reliability. This achievement was attained in part through protective import practices and a coordinated industrial strategy featuring cooperation between major manufacturing groups and the government, especially through activities of the Ministry of International Trade and Industry (MITI).

The Company

Precision Measurement, Inc. was founded in the mid-1960s to produce a wide range of measurement and instrumentation equipment. Over the years, the company has remained at the forefront of this industry and continues to this day to pursue cutting edge research. In recent years, the company's financial strength has been sustained by a classic "cash cow"—a gauge for measurement of flow and pressure. The success of this gauge relies on two factors—(1) very fine and precise machining of high-quality material to strict quality standards and (2) an ingenious application of elementary principles of physics. Neither of these constitutes a substantial barrier to Japanese competition: machining materials to high standard is straightforward; even the casewriter's late 1950s high school physics allows him to understand the way the gauge works!

Staffing Implications

To penetrate the Japanese domestic market, an optimal staffing pattern must be generated which would yield the desired sales capability. (Manufacturing takes place in the United States, with the gauge being modified to the customer's needs in Japan by production engineers and technicians.) PM-J's president supplied a table (Exhibit 1) of desired staffing patterns from the beginning of 1999 through 2001, which focuses on their probable staffing needs. Although PM-J found it very difficult to hire the eight engineers who presently represent the company, it is now faced with the need to engage seven more in just two and one-half years.

Engineering Labor Markets in Japan

The nature of Japanese labor markets, particularly for professionals and managers, directly affects attainability of the staffing patterns outlined by the company. Modern, large Japanese organizations generally hire people as they finish school for "lifetime employment." The employee then receives a traditional training, which consists of considerable job rotation and general training which develops broad skills; the employee, therefore, expects a pay system based primarily on length of service with the company rather than job-specific performance. Thus, PM-J's competitors would typically hire engineers on completion of university training and employ them until their early to mid-50s. Then, as is the practice with many managers, the senior employees are transferred to subsidiaries, client organizations, smaller plants, or less demanding jobs.

A small company like PM-J cannot easily compete in the labor market because it cannot guarantee its own survival for the career lifetime of the employees. Small organizations are more likely to go out of business and are, even if they survive, less likely to obtain a major share of the product market. This fact does little to instill confidence in the new graduate who expects lifetime employment as a condition of employment. The same weakness generally applies to foreign companies in Japan. They often do not share a commitment to lifetime employment, traditional pay systems, or a long business presence in Japan. This image, formed by some foreign companies that came to Japan and then laid off many people or totally withdrew, is widespread among Japanese professionals.

PM-J has generally been unable to recruit the immediate postgraduate because it is both small and foreign. This has necessitated acquiring its engineering force in various ad hoc ways, predominantly relying on recommendations from its joint venture partner, TEC. While not optimal, it has at least allowed the company to develop a skeleton staff.

EXHIBIT 1
Projected Staffing Patterns, 1999-2001

	April 99	Dec 99	Dec 00	Dec 01
Administration	5	5	5	5
Secretarial/Clerical	5	5	5	5
Engineering	8	11	13	15
Sales & Marketing (3)				
Engineering Services Group (3)				
Production (2)				
Production Technicians	2	3	3	3
	20	24	26	28

EXHIBIT 2
Sales and Support Force, Spring 1995

Name	Source	Annual (million yen) including bonuses	Average pay at large companies* (million yen)	Performance evaluation
Sato	small company experience, recommended by the general manager of PM-J	9.5	9.7	55% effort rating; lower segment on performance
Suzuki	formerly a representative for PM-J	7.3	5.8	80%
Takahashi	TEC (age: late 40s)	7.3	7.2	75-85%
Watanabe	Nihon Medical (age: early 50s), recommended by a classmate who is now a professor	9.5	9.5	very high
Tanaka	junior high school education plus 20 years in the instrumentation sales business; answered an ad in a trade journal			N/A
Ito	TEC (age: 32)	5.8	5.8	90%
Kobayashi	new university graduate	2.9	3.0	N/A
Saito	TEC (age: about 40)	6.3	6.3	very high
Yamamoto	TEC (age: mid 40s)	8.4	7.8	very high

* Equal to 18 months salary in the average large company, no housing or other allowances figured in. The extra six months' pay reflects the average level of bonuses in Japan. At present, large Japanese companies pay roughly 2 months' salary as a bonus three times a year (late spring, late summer, and at the Christmas—New Year's season).

Source: Japan Institute of Labor Statistical Reports, and Japanese Ministry of Labour (www.mol.go.jp/info/toukei.english/b_0l.htm).

The first two columns of Exhibit 2 show the name and recruiting source of engineers currently employed by PM-J. The third and fourth columns show the salaries of these people (millions of yen per year) as compared with the average pay of employees of the same age and education in large companies in Japan. The final column shows each employee's job performance evaluation as reported by company president Smith. Exhibit 2 clearly demonstrates that PM-J's hiring pattern has strongly deviated from the stereotypical post-university hire/lifetime employment pattern of the Japanese industry in general.

Alternatives to the Current Situation

Given the staffing and recruiting patterns of Japanese industries and the staffing dilemmas faced by PM-J, what alternative plans of action are available to a small, foreign company that will promote its slated objectives of expanded sales and increased market share? If PM-J is to predominate in the Japanese market, what alternatives to its current pattern of hiring mid-career engineers could move the company toward hiring newly graduated, qualified engineers? Are there changes occurring in the Japanese labor culture which might benefit PM-J if the company recognizes and adapts the changes to fit its needs?

Attracting Younger Engineers

How might PM-J increase its hiring ratio of younger engineers directly out of school? Will it be as difficult to hire new graduates in the future as previous experience suggests? The latter situation seems to be loosening a bit as professors' influence in directing students has declined. Indeed, some students are more willing to consider employers other than just the very largest and more traditional Japanese companies. Furthermore, the typical lifetime employment pattern seems to be eroding as some younger professionals with relatively recent dates of hire move to new companies after only three or four years of employment. Organizations like The Recruit Center (a major recruiting and placement organization providing extensive published information on companies as prospective employers) and "headhunters" are supporting these changes in employment patterns by publicizing employment opportunities and company characteristics. Young professionals in engineering and other technical fields are beginning to rely on such data in making career decisions.

The advantages of this alternative, i.e., to employ personnel agencies, are straightforward. First, PM-J could more readily advertise the benefits and opportunities it is able to provide to career-minded professionals via the agencies and headhunters; as third parties, can confer as they present the company as a stable organization that demonstrates Japanese characteristics. Third, recruitment agents are financially motivated to match employers and employees; PM-J can capitalize on this by requesting younger, well-educated, technically qualified engineers who have a potentially longer career life with the company.

The principal disadvantages of personnel agencies are their high cost to the small organization in terms of money and CEO time. Further caveats must be noted: graduates of the best Japanese universities and engineering programs (University of Tokyo and Keio University) would probably not be interested in employment agencies, because they would most likely be recruited by the large domestic companies via contacts with university professors. Likewise, headhunters would be less able to lure young new hires from large companies to work for a smaller foreign-based firm. Additionally, if PM-J accepted a large proportion of graduates from second and third tier universities, it would be unable to generate a level of credibility which a workforce of "better" educated employees from top-rated universities would confer.

Attracting Female Engineers

One intriguing labor market strategy might be to get women into PM-J's labor force as sales engineers. A growing number of women are enrolled in engineering programs of Japanese universities. Their employability, at least in principle, should be enhanced by equal opportunity legislation recently passed by the Diet (Japan's Parliament). More distant observers, including some at the corporate offices of PMI, have occasionally brainstormed about job redesign and the use of women engineers; U.S.-based students may almost think this a natural option.

Practical reaction at PM-J, however, stresses that the acceptability of women in many Japanese work roles is not immediately forthcoming. Moreover, it will be even longer in coming within the industrial setting where men are almost exclusively employed and where evening entertainment of customers is an expected job component.

Engineers vs. Salespeople

A variant on the idea of increasing the number of engineers at PM-J is to reduce the company's reliance on engineers by employing non-technically trained salespeople; the sales component of the engineers' positions would be eliminated or substantially decreased. After all, engineers don't do all the selling in the United States; rather, they provide technical backup and design work after the salesperson has made the pitch.

Perhaps it is feasible to explore hiring graduates of technical high schools and vocational schools for sales, following the example set when Tanaka was hired (Exhibit 2). This could be accomplished by multiple testing (less restricted in Japan than in the United States) and increased training to identify and qualify strong sales candidates. In fact, PMI in the United States and other organizations in Japan succeeded in using a combination of both occupations in marketing products.

By using non-engineering salespeople, PM-J could easily expand its labor force with younger employees. Unfortunately, the company is small and foreign; in reducing the perceived qualifications of its salesforce it will suffer a further loss of credibility conferred on employees holding an engineering degree from a respected university.

Maintaining Status Quo

Staying with the status quo is another strategy. PM-J could continue using mid-career people. Most of these employees have been recruited from the joint venture partner, TEC. This method is relatively inexpensive, because the initial recruitment, selection, and training costs are absorbed by TEC since the engineers began employment there. An advantage of this method is that the engineers with 25 to 30 years' experience have far more business contacts than do fresh graduates. The principle disadvantage is that one cannot be certain that the TEC engineers are quality employees. After all, why should TEC give up its best people to PM-J and retain the marginal employees for its own use? It's quite conceivable that the joint venture could be receiving some of the less productive TEC personnel. This also perpetuates the current dilemma of a salesforce in its early to mid-50s, which does not assist the company's image, credibility, or ability to capture the difficult Japanese market.

A further complication in PM-J's reliance on TEC's transferred employees is that many mid-career professionals may be loyal to their previous employer; this will not result in a highly motivated salesforce that will be prepared to endeavor diligently to promote a new employer in the market.

Supplementing the Status Quo

Another strategic option is to supplement the status quo (hiring mid-career professional engineers) with headhunters and/or employment agencies such as The Recruit Center. Headhunters are more prevalent in the Japanese labor market recently, and many Japanese companies report some successes in employing their services. Even though such agencies and headhunters are quite expensive and time-consuming, they do represent one means in filling gaps created by internal rotations of employees or vacancies resulting from terminated employees. Perhaps the most likely recruit from headhunting would be in the 28- to 30-year-old range who is making a career move. Although not fresh from school, these engineers would still be relatively recent university graduates with respectively longer career lives ahead of them. This would tend to stabilize PM-J's engineering and salesforce turnover while simultaneously conferring the credibility to be gained from the honored university degree.

Toward an Appraisal of These Options

The likely success of these various strategies clearly depends on the prospective state of the Japanese engineer labor market. PM-J's hiring success will be directly enhanced by any developments that reduce the number of engineers absorbed by the rest of Japanese industry and by its ability to gain credibility as a stable "Japanese" company. Indirect effects are also possible.

For example, it's likely that any developments that loosen the supply of male engineers will make it even more difficult for female engineers to be accepted, especially in sales. Thus, a reliable forecast of engineering labor market conditions in Japan is central to any strategy recommendation to PM-J.

Future Labor Market Developments

Effects of an Aging Workforce
The Japanese labor force and population has aged in recent years, pressuring the social insurance and retirement systems, similar to the U.S. situation. This has led the government to explore postponing pension age from about 60 to 65. The Japanese employment system for engineers (among other professions) initially moves employees in the 50 to 55 age range to secondary employment (within the firm) or to other employers.[1] Since the government has made early pension less likely, it seems that in coming years more men will seek longer second careers. As noted, this would dampen women's employability. It would also increase the availability of engineering resources to a company like PM-J.

The Decline of New Workers
The declining number of young people entering the labor market and the declining pool of new engineering graduates implies that small companies like PM-J are more likely to be squeezed out of the market. Based on present hiring patterns, 80% of the graduates of the top 10 Japanese engineering schools would be recruited and absorbed by a select group of employers consisting of the largest domestic and foreign organizations. This tightening of the youth market decreases the viability of a strategy aimed at hiring fresh graduates into small, foreign companies.

Foreign Product Competition and the Japanese Labor Market

One must consider the labor market effects of opening Japanese product markets to foreign competition. If Japan concedes to growing pressure from its allies to reduce import tariffs and trade barriers, who will be hit hardest? Which Japanese industries will be hurt by a policy of greater import penetration into Japan? First of all, it is not probable that agriculture will be hit heavily. Even though Japanese food prices are three to six times the world level, it's unlikely that the government would chance eroding its support base among small farmers. This is due to the fact that import restriction policies have supported the relatively large agricultural population who have in turn faithfully supported the incumbent government party, the Liberal Democrats, since the late 1940s.

Are import penetration liberalizations for non-agricultural products apt to affect big companies like Matsushita, Hitachi, or Asahi? These firms run the Japanese "economic miracle" and are closely tied to government policy through the coordinating activities of the Ministry of International Trade and Industry. Such an alliance between government and big business is likely to forestall serious import impacts on the key companies. Thus, won't any opening of Japanese markets to U.S. imports probably be designed to have the most impact on items produced by smaller businesses? As these smaller businesses cut back on employment, won't they have the effect of loosening the labor market exactly where PM-J is located (in terms of company size)?

Political considerations aside, it is also true that small-scale industry in Japan has much higher labor costs (relative to larger enterprises) than in the United States or Germany (another major trading country). Increased foreign product-market competition and a resulting loosening of the smaller-company labor market would increase a surviving small foreign company's ability to recruit and retain qualified employees.

To the extent that Japanese trade policy is liberalized, PM-J should be more successful on all fronts in trying to hire engineers in competition with Japanese firms. On the other hand, the staffing demands of other foreign firms, which either expand or enter Japan as a result of this trade policy liberalization, will have to be taken into account.

Product Market Issues

Having considered some major human resource dynamics affecting PM-J's penetration into the Japanese market, it is necessary to review what product market considerations are relevant to the company's success of PM-J in the Japanese market.

Standards are most frequently mentioned as problems or barriers by would-be American importers of technical equipment. Japanese standards are simply not the same as the United States and are very difficult to understand or change. With respect to the "cash cow gauge," PM-J spent six or seven years on the standards acceptance process.

The biggest issue regarding the product market is the prospect for increased penetration of imports into the Japanese market. Japanese government policy on this is evolving. Whether this will help sell PM-J's product, only time will tell. But if it becomes easier for foreign firms to bid on government jobs (pursuant to GATT agreements), PM-J might see a direct sales payoff in major government projects.

Issues from this Case

There are at least two preliminary issues to address in this case.

First, is TEC doing its job? Are they providing qualified people to the joint venture, PM-J, or are they "dumping" marginal employees who are past their peak performance and on the downslide?

The second preliminary issue that the student should address is whether PM-J's pay scale is appropriate. Data in Exhibit 2 provide comparisons with big companies' pay levels.

The Longer-Run Labor Market Strategy Options

One can identify the risks, benefits, and costs of various alternatives (including staffing options) against the backdrop of various "states of the world." Those states of the world will be dominated by the degree to which government policy changes so that PM-J (or more radically, a lot of foreign competition) is able to penetrate domestic markets in Japan. Some engineering labor market strategies will be higher risk and lower risk, with higher and lower costs and payoffs, depending what one thinks will happen to the engineering labor market and PM-J's ability to penetrate the product market. Although Japanese government policies on foreign access to markets may dominate the scene, other things that will impinge upon the labor market should be considered:

- the aging population
- shortages of youth entering the labor force
- increased numbers of people (early to mid-50s) seeking longer second careers
- increased number of women seeking positions
- changing Japanese culture and labor markets
- changing values
- economic and banking conditions[2]

Considering the case as a whole, the basic issue can be starkly posed: How should PM-J attempt to recruit enough people to permit an effective penetration of the Japanese product market on which the survival not only of PM-J, but of its parent PMI, may depend?

Endnotes

1. The age-related pay system (nenko), plus the common decline of productivity after a certain age, older workers tend to become more and more expensive rapidly.

2. The website japanjin.com provides useful information.

BULLER | SCHULER

Managing Organizations and People

A Resource for Cases in Management, Organizational Behavior, and Human Resource Management

Abstract

This case is effective in getting students to think of the human resources department in business terms. Mike Mitchell has recently been selected to become the vice president of human resources at the North American branch of Swiss Bank Corporation (SBC). Driven by his entrepreneurial talents, Mike has taken on the challenge of making the human resource (HR) department of SBC, North America more strategic in its orientation and activities. The case identifies the major elements of his plan to reposition and "customerize" the HR department.

Bringing HR into the Business

Mike Mitchell left the Bank of Montreal to become vice president of human resources at the North American branch of the Swiss Bank Corporation (SBC) in the autumn of 1993. It was a move up for him in terms of status, responsibility, monetary compensation, and challenge. Of these, it was the challenge that was most intriguing to Mitchell. In his mid-30s, he saw this as the perfect time to take a risk in his career. He realized that if he succeeded he would establish a prototype that could be marketed to other firms. In addition, success could lead to further career opportunities (and challenges). While he had a general idea of what he wanted to do and had gotten verbal support from his superiors, the senior vice president of human resources and the president of SBC, North America, the details of exactly what he was going to do and how he was going to do it, remained to unfold.

In 1992 the parent company of SBC (a $110 billion universal bank) headquartered in Basel, Switzerland decided it needed a clearer statement of its intentions to focus its energies and resources in light of the growing international competition. Accordingly, it crafted a vision statement to the effect that the bank was going to better serve its customers with high-quality products that served their needs rather than just those of the institution. While the North American operation was relatively autonomous, it was still expected to embrace this vision. The details of its implementation, however, were in local hands. For the human resources side, the hands became those of Mitchell.

While Mitchell had spent some time in human resources at the Bank of Montreal in New York, the bulk of his work experience was as an entrepreneur in Montreal, Canada. It

■ This case was prepared by Randall S. Schuler, Rutgers University, who expresses his appreciation for the cooperation of Michael Mitchell.

was this experience that impacted his thinking the most. Thus, when he came to the SBC, his self-image was a business person who happened to be working in human resources. It was in part because of this image that his stay at the Bank of Montreal was brief: human resources was still a bit too conservative for his style. Too many of his ideas "just couldn't be done." In interviewing with the top managers at SBC, however, they warned him of the same general environment. He thus knew he would have to go slow to change almost 1,000 employees including his own department of 10 employees, but he really didn't know what this meant. He knew, however, that he wanted to reposition and "customerize" the HR department at SBC. He knew that this was necessary to connect the HR department to the business.

He identified the four major aspects for his program to reposition and customerize the HR department so that it could become current with the state-of-the-art and practice and so that it could be connected to the business (and develop a customer-focus attitude). The four aspects included: gathering information, developing action agendas, implementing those agendas, and then evaluating and revising those agendas.

Gathering Information. Finding out how things are done involves asking the customers, diagnosing the environment, and asking the HR department itself. From the customers Mitchell learns the nature of the business strategy and how HR generally can fit with or help that strategy. He also learns what they now get from the HR department, what would be the ideal, and how the ideal could best be delivered. This analysis is done for each activity in HR as well as the entire department and the staff. From the environment Mitchell learns what other companies are doing with their HR departments and their HR practices. He looks at competitors and those in other industries in order to see the possibilities for the entire department and for each HR activity. From the HR department he learns how they see themselves in relation to servicing their customers; their knowledge of strategy; how they think the customers perceive the department; and their desire to improve, to be the best or whatever they want.

Developing Agendas. Making agendas based upon this information is the second aspect of Mitchell's plan. This involves feeding the information back to the HR department and letting them draw up plans (agendas) for resolving any discrepancies between what they are doing and what their customers want. But in order for the department to do this they really need to determine a vision of themselves what they want to be vis-a-vis themselves and the rest of the organization. They also need to determine if their current ways of operating and the current structure are sufficient to move ahead. If not, then the HR department needs to get themselves reorganized. This can be occurring while they are developing the agendas. The HR department may need to get new skills if they are to be successful in implementing their new vision (especially if they decide to be current and customer-oriented). Once the vision starts taking shape and the agendas are drawn up, the HR department can establish a game plan for how they will get their agendas implemented. They then need to get line approval for moving ahead with the implementation. Top management and line managers immediately impacted should give approval.

Implementing the Agendas. This third aspect involves the HR department going out and meeting with the customers to discuss the agendas. While this aspect will involve responding to specific needs of the line managers, it may also involve selling the line managers on other activities. Now that the HR department is being more strategic and customer-oriented, they will begin to develop programs that go beyond the regular administrative activities and services that it generally provides the line managers. These will be based upon the ideas of the HR department. They will get these ideas upon their knowledge of the strategy, the competitors, what other successful firms are doing, and their knowledge of HR practices. Because these services are new, they will need to be sold to their customers, at least at first. Once successful they will develop a demand of their own. So in addition to implementing the specifically agreed-upon agendas and contracts, this aspect will include developing and implementing (and selling) new programs.

Evaluating and Revising. Part and parcel of the agenda setting is the development of contracts. These specify what will be delivered to the customer. The customer then has the right to appraise the work delivered. Based on these appraisals by the line managers, the agendas become evaluated. Revisions and adjustments can then be made for improvements the next time around. The contracts, however, may not be the only way to appraise the work of the HR department. Other criteria may be used (although they could be put into the contract) based on the desire of the HR department. Such criteria could include the reduction in turnover from better selection procedures or an increase in the number of new ideas or innovations from a change in the HR practices to facilitate the innovative strategy of the business.

Implications for the HR Department

There are several implications for the HR department (Mitchell and his staff) in their efforts to reposition and customerize.

1. A major one is the need for the HR department to be reoriented. Its mind-set has to be strategic and customer-oriented.
2. The HR department needs to become a constant gatherer of information: from the internal environment and the external environment. They need to know the opportunities and the possibilities for HR practices and how to implement these ideas with and for the line managers. Consequently, they need to know the competition, the business strategy, and how the competition can be beat in relation to the current assets of the company and those that they could or need to develop.
3. The HR department needs to identify what level of excellence they want to attain. In doing so they will identify the speed and quality at which they will be a strategic player and fulfill their managerial and operational roles.
4. HR managers and staff will need to work closely with the line managers in designing systems to get them the needed services and information. They will need to work with the line managers to develop contracts by which the HR department will be evaluated by the line managers.
5. The HR department will be changed so that there is more of a generalist rather than a specialist orientation. There will be a greater team orientation also.
6. Things will never be the same. This goes for the HR department and the entire competitive marketplace. This means that the HR professionals in the department will be always on the go, gathering, servicing, evaluating, revising and, most of all, listening. And because the business will be changing all the time, the HR department will need to always be changing what it delivers. Nonetheless the opportunities for making things better and the company and its people more competitive and successful are endless and challenging!

Implications for the Line Managers

There are also several implications in the repositioning and customerization program for line managers.

1. The line managers need to work closely with Mitchell and his staff to gather information on what is now happening and what is desired. Line managers will also have to share their views on the strategy of their business with Mitchell. Together, they become partners in the business. The line managers need to be willing to accept a new role being played by Mitchell and his HR staff.
2. The line managers need to work closely with the HR staff in developing the agendas for action. They need to be willing to spend time with the staff to look at each of the HR activities now being provided by the HR department.
3. The line managers need to work with the HR staff in appraising the success of the HR efforts. They do this through the development and use of the contracts established with the staff.
4. The line managers need to be ready to talk with and listen to Mitchell and his staff as they propose new programs to improve the chances for gaining competitive advantage through the use of human resources.

The Benefits from the Partnership

The results of this partnership may be well worth the costs involved in the changes necessary to ensure repositioning and customerization. As far as Mitchell is concerned, there are several products from a repositioning and customerization program. They include:

- enhancing the quality and responsiveness of the HR department
- developing the HR department in terms of new jobs (skillwise), providing new excitement and building commitment to the company's mission, goals, and strategies
- HR becoming linked with the business
- HR becoming integrated with the corporate strategy
- HR becoming market- or customer-oriented and gaining a flexibility to respond to and anticipate changes
- criteria being developed by which to evaluate and revise the behaviors of the HR department
- HR gaining an ability to develop and use HR practices to gain competitive advantage
- HR gaining an awareness of the potential ways different HR practices can be done by constantly monitoring what other successful companies are doing
- HR becoming more keenly aware of the internal and external environment
- standard products of the HR department being provided more efficiently
- new products and services being developed
- software being developed as a way to deliver the new products
- new services and products being sold outside the company
- the HR department changing dramatically and consequently becoming an example for the rest of the company regarding change
- the HR department becoming a place where everyone wants to work
- HR's services and products becoming sought after

Discussion Questions

1. Who are the customers of Mitchell and his HR staff?
2. What must Mitchell do in order for his staff to be able to do the things necessary to reposition and customerize?
3. Do you think that the line managers will cooperate with Mitchell and his staff? What will it take to see that they do? What would be their reasons for resisting a partnership with the HR department?
4. Develop a matrix with projects, dates, milestones, and people involved (i.e., HR, line managers, and employees) for Mitchell and his staff.

BULLER | SCHULER

Managing Organizations and People

A Resource for Cases in Management, Organizational Behavior,
and Human Resource Management

Abstract

This case is an integrative case designed to provide an overview of the human resources
management process. Focused on the startup of a new organization, The Tall Pines Hotel
and Conference Center, it sets into bold relief many of the issues involved in linking
human resource management with strategy. The case centers on the dilemma faced by Gordon McGregor, hotel manager, in attracting qualified personnel to open a new facility. At
stake here is both the urgency of the present situation and the long-term necessity to develop a human resources staffing system to meet future needs.

The Tall Pines Hotel and Conference Center

Gordon McGregor sorted through his morning mail to find the report from Natalie Sharp
about the open house sponsored by the hotel for job applicants. With the sounds of ham-
mering and the smell of fresh paint all around, he was eager to get a picture of his new staff
as he neared the opening of the hotel in about two months. He pushed aside samples of
carpeting left by a subcontractor this morning to read the five-page report from Natalie.

As hotel manager, Gordon was faced with the last of the major hurdles in getting Tall
Pines open—the filling of about 315 positions ranging from bellhops and butchers to
clerks and chambermaids. The grand opening scheduled for May first made it imperative
to bring his full staff on board and get them trained and operational quickly. He had
brought in most of his managerial and supervisory staff over the past six months. Many
had come from other hotels in the nationwide chain. Some he had worked with in other
parts of the chain in his 15 years in the system, so there was a sense of excitement about
being together as a team to create something brand new. Today marked the beginning of
the final phase of his plan to manage his own hotel successfully.

The Tall Pines Hotel

Gordon had been involved in the planning of the hotel for about two years. Corporate management had selected the site four years ago on the basis of a careful study by its market
research staff of the southeastern part of the United States. They were interested in launching a new concept in hotels and had chosen the city of Riverton (pop. 95,000), located in
the suburbs of Roosevelt City, a major city in the Southeast. The entire metropolitan area
had grown dramatically since the early 1960s to a total population of about 1.9 million,
with further growth forecast for the next 15 years before a leveling off would occur.

■ Reprinted by permission of D. Jeffrey Lenn, George Washington University, 1986.

Riverton comprised about half the area and two-thirds the population of one of the counties that surrounded Roosevelt City. Growth in population, wealth, and industry had been concentrated in the suburban counties, although there was new interest in the revitalization of the old downtown area. Riverton had been especially aggressive in its plan to attract new industry with the creation of an economic development committee, which had been successful in enticing a number of high-technology firms to open offices or build small facilities within the city limits. Many offices had moved from Roosevelt into the suburbs to take advantage of lower taxes, new buildings, and a pool of skilled workers. Shopping centers, restaurants, and housing developments mushroomed to meet the demands of the population shift.

Corporate management saw the opportunity to fill a niche in the suburbs because of the lack of hotel and conference space. They purchased an 18-acre tract on a major highway that entered Roosevelt City from the south on the west side of Riverton. It was to be developed as a campuslike setting with the preservation of 2 major pine groves and the expansion of a natural lake. The hotel had been constructed in line with these plans to include 350 rooms, 2 swimming pools, 3 restaurants, small shops, and a small exercise and weight room. An outdoor jogging trail was being completed as well. The conference center was built to cater to corporate meetings with secretarial services, teleconferencing facilities, and even access to personal computers. The entire facility was oriented toward comfortable stays of extended periods as well as overnight lodging.

An architect of national reputation had designed the building to become a focal point for the surrounding area. Twin towers jutted through the pines to provide the foundation for a five-story atrium. The glass enclosure provided light and freshness to the restaurants and public space below. The building was striking as viewed from the interstate in both directions, standing boldly against the horizon and rising from the pine groves. Tall Pines was a particularly appropriate name for the entire center, which could act as a comfortable retreat from both city activity and corporate life.

The building had also been controversial. The Riverton Board of Architectural Review was besieged by complaints about the design. But support from the city council and the mayor dissolved the opposition quickly. Projections of a $3.8 million payroll and annual tax bills of $350,000 for the city and $420,000 for the state made the entire project highly appealing. The board voted unanimously to accept the architectural plans.

Natalie Sharp, Director of Personnel

Last November, Gordon had hired Natalie Sharp to become his director of personnel. She had worked for two other hotel chains after college and then been hired three years ago to help with the opening of a new 100-room hotel in the southwest. She had done an outstanding job of staffing this hotel set in the center of an older city undergoing major renovation. Corporate management was enthusiastic about her potential and had urged Gordon to consider her for the job. Two days of interviews at Tall Pines confirmed this potential as well as the experience he needed in opening a new hotel.

Natalie was given the responsibility for the entire staffing process, although Gordon had made it clear that his department managers had the final authority for those working in their departments. Supervisory personnel were hired with Natalie confirming managerial decisions and working out job descriptions, salaries, and other specifics for each position.

Her major task was the recruitment and hiring program for the bulk of the staff to ready the hotel for opening on May 1. She and Gordon had met in the middle of January to review her plan. She had worked closely with the state Department of Employment Services as well as Riverton's Employment Options Office to arrange for a Job Fair on February 15. Held at a local school on a Saturday, the fair was designed to attract candidates and provide a screening session and even some first-round interviews. Tall Pines would provide a good package of benefits on top of a competitive wage:

- Blue Cross/Blue Shield
- Paid vacation (after one year)
- Pension plan (vested after seven years)

- On-site job training
- Educational benefits

Natalie had convinced Gordon that although minimum wage would be the controlling factor for many entry-level positions, the promise of raises in six months was needed as an inducement for retention of good employees.

Natalie believed that the primary pool of candidates would be found in Roosevelt City and Riverton. The figures provided by a local government agency supported her belief that a number of people would apply for the various positions to be filled.

Local Unemployment Rates*	
Metropolitan area	3.7%
Roosevelt City	8.1
Riverton	5.0
All suburbs	3.7

*December figures.

An advertising campaign directed toward the larger metropolitan area, coupled with state and city support, should yield at least double the number of candidates needed for each position. Natalie had shown Gordon a series of articles in the Metro Star, the major daily, about a large hotel opening last year in the center of Roosevelt City. Over 11,000 applications were made for 350 positions; the articles included pictures of long lines of people trying to get through the door for interviews. Tall Pines would find an eager group ready to work at its hotel.

The Disappointing Report

The note of optimism of last month was missing from the short report on yesterday's Job Fair. Just over 200 people had applied for the 315 positions. Of these, only 75 had been screened and interviewed. Most had little experience in the hotel business but seemed capable of on-the-job training. The applicants were mostly from the surrounding towns in the county and Riverton, with a few from Roosevelt City.

Natalie had done an informal survey of her small cadre of interviewers late in the afternoon. Applicants had concerns about wage scales and transportation. Unskilled workers with some experience found it difficult to believe that they would start at minimum wage, saying that they could get more at many fast-food chains. Three employees from Big Tex, a regional hamburger chain, had come to the fair together and reported that the chain had just upped starting salaries for counter help to 75 cents above minimum wage. Natalie's follow-up call to Big Tex, as well as her conversation with a representative of the county chamber of commerce, had confirmed that many employers were offering hourly wages in excess of minimum wage simply to fill empty positions.

The concerns about transportation were more difficult to bring into focus. Natalie pieced together a picture of Tall Pines being out of the way for most people using public transportation. A few asked about whether the hotel planned to provide bus transportation into Roosevelt City. It had taken them nearly an hour from home with a transfer from a subway stop onto a bus, which dropped them off about 3 blocks away. Riverton residents indicated that it took 30 minutes to get over from the east side of the city, which meant crossing the interstate because the bus route ended there. Location clearly was a factor in keeping applicants away.

The Stream of Telephone Calls

Gordon's optimism about his gala opening was suddenly deflated by this report. Natalie's conclusion was concisely stated in one sentence:

I have arranged another Job Fair in 10 days with the hope that our results will be better this time.

He wondered whether there would be enough candidates for the remaining positions and whether there would be enough time to train them after all of the necessary personnel paperwork had been completed.

His thoughts were interrupted by a call from his secretary indicating that a reporter was on the line from the *Riverton Telegram*, asking questions about the Job Fair. He directed the call to Natalie's office. A call from the *Metro Star* was also redirected. But he did take a call from the Riverton mayor's office to assure them that the hotel had the hiring situation under control with the opening still set for May 1. Later in the afternoon, the director of one of the associations scheduled to hold a conference at the hotel during the first week called to ask about the opening. Bad news travels fast! thought Gordon as he hung up with another set of assurances to the anxious director.

Natalie sailed into the office to report on the two phone calls from the press. Both had received information about the disappointing turnout at the Job Fair and were interested in both the reasons and the impact on the opening. She thought that it would be difficult to assess the impact of the publicity until the morning editions were out. Gordon suggested a breakfast meeting with the hotel's top staff to discuss the problem and work toward a solution.

The Breakfast Staff Meeting

Both papers covered the story with short articles hidden away in the second sections. The *Telegram* headline read:

NEW HOTEL NEEDS 240 WORKERS

It briefly described the low turnout at the Job Fair with a listing of the positions still available. A quote from Natalie indicated that another fair would be held in the near future. The story was done in a generally favorable light with emphasis on new business within Riverton, which the hotel should attract.

The *Star* headline was more critical:

NEW SUBURBAN HOTEL SURPRISED TO FIND FEW APPLY FOR 315 JOBS

The new twin towers were pictured along with a sheet from the fair that listed the jobs available at the hotel. Natalie was quoted about the continuing search to be carried out as well as the types of benefits offered by Tall Pines. A representative of the Roosevelt City Office of Job Services was quoted: "It's not so much that people here won't look in the suburbs; it's that once you cross over that city line, there is a mental barrier about being away from home. Employers have to offer good jobs, good transportation, and a lot of encouragement to get people to apply." A union office spokesman wondered whether people were discouraged because Tall Pines is a nonunion hotel. A man who had been offered a second interview at the fair indicated that he would rather work close to his home in Roosevelt City, but had been out of work for four months and needed the job.

Gordon and Natalie agreed that neither article gave a negative perspective on hotel management, but questions could be raised about postponement of the opening. Clearly, it was important to follow up with the Riverton mayor's office as well as meeting planners who had scheduled the hotel opening for May and June to assure them that the situation would be under control. Contact with the Roosevelt City Office of Job Services was mandatory now.

At the meeting, Gordon asked Natalie to review her report as well as the press clippings for the assembled department heads. They both answered a number of questions about the Job Fair and the type of applicants at the fair. Gordon suggested that they delay the discussion about the future until later in the meeting so that all of the facts surrounding the problem could be sorted through carefully. It became clear that many departments could operate for the first two weeks in May on a reduced staffing pattern using supervisory personnel to fill in. But a full staff was essential to accommodate the anticipated increase in business.

The meeting then turned to a brainstorming session to help Natalie develop a strategy for attracting people who would be good candidates to fill the remaining positions. The group agreed that four areas merited further consideration:

- *Advertising campaign*
  Directed particularly toward Roosevelt City and Riverton with focus on benefits of working at Tall Pines.
- *Upgrade of wage scale*
  Additions to minimum wage for entry-level jobs in order to be competitive.
  Necessity for incentive pay to retain good employees.
- *Transportation system*
  Necessity for assistance to workers coming from both Riverton and Roosevelt City in particular because of their reliance on public transportation.
- *Cooperation with public agencies*
  Cultivation of relationships with a number of agencies to identify other applicant pools.

Gordon asked Natalie to make use of these ideas in the development of a plan to fill the 240 remaining positions. He assured the managers that he would call them the next day with a finalized plan to meet the objective of full staffing by May 1. In the meantime, he would handle the public relations aspect of the issue through his office. The meeting adjourned with an agreement that any hotel was only as good as its personnel.

Reflections Over Lunch

As manager of Tall Pines, Gordon enjoyed a number of perquisites unavailable in other jobs. Today, he was delighted to initiate one of those—access to the best meals from the hotel kitchens. Jack Sanders, the sales and convention manager, wheeled in a cart of delectable dishes prepared by one of the French chefs interviewing for the position as head chef. Expecting to join Gordon for lunch, he set a small table for two and uncorked a bottle of wine. As he settled into one of the chairs and pulled out his napkin, Gordon interrupted: "Sorry, Jack. This is a working lunch for me with all of this hiring mess on my mind. You're welcome to take a plate back to your office, but I need to be alone to get a handle on this situation." Jack excused himself, a full plate and wineglass in hand, while Gordon settled into his chair.

The meal was excellent, with the wine chosen for its appropriate balance with the food. Gordon thought about his fortunate managerial situation—no fast-food lunches, no traveling throughout the week, and no narrow job responsibilities. All of these were left behind for any hotel manager. There was a sense of excitement about what lay in store for him both here at Tall Pines and within the larger national organization as it expanded.

But the past day had drowned out much of that excitement. What seemed so close to completion was now filled with a number of questions. Could Tall Pines attract a good staff? Could they be trained and on the job by May 1? How costly was it going to be to pay a competitive wage? Could he instill within the staff a sense of pride about Tall Pines? Could the hotel open on May 1?

The smell of paint, the carpet samples, and even the faint sound of hammers now came into fuller focus as he asked the last question. Where had he gone wrong in the development of his plan to open the hotel? Why didn't he foresee a potential problem about staffing earlier? Getting the right people seemed like the easiest of his plans to implement. Now it looked like an impossible task. With a cup of coffee in hand, he moved back to his desk to begin the process of solving the problem he faced.

BULLER | SCHULER

Managing Organizations and People

A Resource for Cases in Management, Organizational Behavior, and Human Resource Management

Abstract

Don English, corporate vice president of human resources at Bancroft, is planning to move human resources in a strategic direction. Even though Bancroft has made tremendous strides in quality in recent years, partly through the contributions of the human resource department, Don believes that more can be done. As part of his plan, Don is considering ways that his HR department can involve Bancroft's suppliers in the company's strategy to improve quality.

A Broader View Seizes More Opportunities

Don English, corporate vice president in charge of human resources, is now finally able to take a pause from the continuous stream of fire fighting activity he has been engaged in since he came to Bancroft 10 years ago! Like many of his colleagues in other firms, Don's knowledge of human resource management came as much from doing it as anything else.

His constant fire fighting activity tended to keep him pretty narrowly focused. Because of his workload, he rarely read personnel journals or attended professional conferences. Recently, however, things have been easing up. He has been able to recruit and train almost all the division managers in charge of human resources. Now they can do most of the fire fighting—at least that's what Don is planning on. And he has been doing more reading than ever before. Of course, Don has not been totally out of touch with the rest of the world on the growing importance of human resource management planning. When he started filling the slots for division personnel managers, he made sure that it was a learning experience for him. Don always required job candidates to prepare a one-hour talk on the state of research and practice in different areas of personnel, e.g., selection, appraisal, compensation, and training. He would even invite MBA candidates who had no course work in personnel and ask them to relate their field of interest to human resource management.

Don is planning to become the chief executive officer of Bancroft or some other firm of similar or larger size within the next five to seven years. He thinks he can achieve this

---

■ This case was prepared by Randall S. Schuler, Rutgers University.

if he remains in human resources and does an outstanding job. He will have to be outstanding by all standards, both internal and external to the firm. From his interviews during the past three years, Don knows that it is imperative to move human resources in a strategic direction while at the same time doing the best possible job with the "nuts and bolts" activities.

During a moment of reflection, Don begins to scratch some notes on his large white desk pad. In the middle is Bancroft. To its left are its suppliers and to its right are its customers. In his head are all the human resource practices he is so familiar with. He has a hunch that there must be a way to use the firm's expertise in performance appraisal and training to help Bancroft be more effective. Bancroft has been learning tremendously from its five-year drive to improve quality, but during the past year, quality gains have slowed. Bancroft must continue to improve its quality, but large internal quality gains are becoming more and more difficult as Bancroft climbs the learning curve. Don wonders: How can he help Bancroft experience the excitement of seeing large gains in quality improvement again? Don circles the list of suppliers and begins to formulate a plan that will improve his chances of becoming CEO. He now seeks your advice in exactly what to do and how to go about doing it.

Discussion Questions

1. Let's assume that Don has gotten the approval from his boss to help Bancroft's suppliers. Should he work with them all or decide to just start with one or two and see how it goes?
2. If Don can do anything to help his suppliers with their human resource management activities, what should he focus on the most?
3. Should Don actually go into the suppliers and do their HR work or should he train the suppliers' HR professionals at Bancroft?

BULLER | SCHULER

Managing Organizations and People

A Resource for Cases in Management, Organizational Behavior, and Human Resource Management

Abstract

Katia Gore, an emergency room nurse, has been physically assaulted while on her shift by an "impatient" patient. The hospital's Executive Administrator, Hamilton Bronson, and the Head Nurse of the emergency room, Edith Warner, are meeting to discuss the facts of the incident. Decisions must be made regarding how to preempt—and protect against—violent attacks.

Moon Over ER

Six o'clock on a Sunday morning was an unusual time to find the executive administrator of Metropolitan Hospital, Inc. holding a problem-solving session with a head nurse. Nevertheless, Hamilton Bronson, Executive Administrator, and Edith Warner, Head Nurse in the emergency room (ER) during the previous shift, were finally sitting down to discuss the tragic event that had occurred several hours earlier. Katia Gore, an ER nurse, had been physically assaulted during her shift by a patient.

Because of the incident and the resulting turmoil, on top of the lean staffing and high demand in the ER, Nurse Warner had been in a frenzy, keeping the ER running as smoothly as could be expected. Now that Warner's shift was over, Bronson wanted to get the facts first hand from her.

The Setting

Metropolitan Hospital, Inc. is a 500 bed, for-profit facility located in an urban sector of a major U.S. city. Metropolitan is recognized as one of a few dominant hospitals in a highly competitive market. The hospital and the market, though, had experienced profound changes in recent years.

During the early 1990s, the health care industry began a process of restructuring itself into a "managed-care" system. Previously, health care services had been paid for on a "fee-for-service" basis; insurance companies—or individuals receiving medical attention—would pay the going rate for health care services. Under the new managed-care system, health care providers entered into contractual agreements with health management organizations (HMOs) to provide medical services for the HMOs' members. The health care

■ This case was prepared by Steven J. Maranville and J. Andrew Morris, Cameron School of Business, University of St. Thomas. Reprinted by permission.

providers were compensated through a method known as "capitation," by which health care providers received a specified annual amount for the care delivered to each HMO member—regardless of the number of visits or procedures performed. Consequently, health care providers were compelled to contain their costs to ensure the contractual relationship would be profitable.

Hospitalization had always been a major health care expense. Consequently, to lower their costs, health care providers avoided hospitalization for their patients, and when hospitalization was absolutely necessary, the length of hospital stays and the procedures performed were kept to a minimum.

This reduction in the demand for hospital services had a second-order affect on the operations of hospitals. Hospitals also had to contain costs to remain solvent. A leading source of cost containment had come through "reorganizing" and the "downsizing" or "rightsizing" of personnel. The health care industry was highly labor intensive and accounted for a vast amount of health care expense. Labor, though, was seen as being more variable than capital expenses in hospitals. Consequently, staff sizes in hospitals were reduced to achieve "optimal" productivity.

Sometimes, however, the lean operations of hospitals would come into conflict with patients' desires for responsiveness. ERs were quite vulnerable to these staffing issues. For example, as an urban hospital, Metropolitan's ER was frequently in high demand by those who were in need of critical, emergency care as well as by those who were without medical insurance or a primary care physician.

The Incident

Nurse Warner looked pensive as she described the night's events to the hospital's executive administrator. "I remember Katia laughed when I told her last night's shift was going to be a nightmare. All the factors were right for an extremely busy shift. It was the second night of a three-day holiday weekend. The weather has been hot and steamy. And, as silly as it may seem, the moon was full. Unfortunately, my prediction was all too true. The waiting room was crowded from 10:00 p.m. on with patients and families. Most were having to wait over an hour to see a doctor since, of course, the most critical cases got first attention. The problem was there were so many critical cases and not nearly enough doctors or staff. Lately, with the move to managed-care, staffing has been getting worse.

"Looking back, I should have done something sooner. Nobody wants to wait in the ER. Just after 2:00 a.m., a patient who had been waiting for over an hour started to become restless and rowdy. He demanded attention on several occasions, but his problem just wasn't that serious. I told him myself that he'd have to wait. As I was walking away, Katia came through the waiting area behind me. The patient leaped to his feet and demanded that Katia get him into the emergency room. Katia told the patient that more serious cases needed her attention. At that moment, the patient lost it. He was a large man about 40 years old. He grabbed Katia by the arm, threw her against the wall, and began swinging wildly at her, hitting her in the face and shoulders. People started screaming and running. The lounge was in a terrible commotion. Finally, the man was forced away by several other nurses and patients.

"The man was apprehended, but Katia was in pretty bad shape. So, we examined her and ran some tests. There don't appear to be any serious injuries. She's resting now in a recovery room on the fourth floor."

The Decision

Bronson wanted to act quickly before emotions at the hospital and in the community could get out of control. A violent encounter such as this one could have devastating implications for morale— not to mention the enormous expenses associated with the hospitals potential liability. Further, news of the incident could severely effect Metropolitan's image and market share.

Bronson commented, "We're used to the occasional squabbles between staff. We work in a high-pressure setting. But, physical attacks—especially from patients—are quite different. Even though hospitals attend to patients who have sometimes been the victims of violence, hospitals shouldn't be the scenes of violence. Nurses can't be afraid to perform their work."

Bronson and Warner knew that, while this episode of violence caught them by surprise, the possibility of this type of violence occurring more frequently was growing. The hospital needed to take actions that would preempt—or at least protect—its employees from violent behavior.

BULLER | SCHULER

Managing Organizations and People

A Resource for Cases in Management, Organizational Behavior, and Human Resource Management

Abstract

Heartland State Bank is a large independent bank in the $500 million to $1 billion dollar range located in a moderate-sized mid-western market with several major regional/national competitors. The bank's market enjoyed a strong economy in early 1998 and a tight labor market. The local economy was dominated by service industries, such as government, education, real estate, medical services, and insurance. In a planning meeting held in January 1998, HSB's Senior VP of Human Resources reported to the other members of senior management that the bank was suffering from a problem of employee turnover that was costing the bank more than $400,000. Based on this report, the senior officers determined that Marilyn Harrison, the SVP/HR, should prepare a plan to solve this problem, enabling the bank to achieve its objective of being the "employer of choice" in its market, enhancing "employee delight," and achieving an overall reduction in employee turnover from roughly 23 percent of the workforce annually to 18 percent. The problem was complicated by a planned conversion of the bank's information systems that was expected to create a great deal of stress for all staff.

Heartland State Bank (A): The Employee Turnover Problem

The senior management team at Heartland State Bank met for their annual off-site strategic planning retreat in a small resort town in January 1998. The first part of the meeting consisted of status reports from each of the bank's five senior managers. While the bank had enjoyed a record year of profits and growth, the report from the Senior VP of Human Resources, Marilyn Harrison, was quite troubling. She reported that while the level of turnover for bank employees in 1997 had declined from the loss of more than a third of the workforce in 1995 to only about a quarter, she felt the rate was still unacceptably high. Further, she also reported that the turnover in 1997 cost the bank more than $410,000. At that point Ms. Harrison presented her full report including various tables which included a thorough analysis of the problem. The obvious question that faced both the HR manager and the managers of the bank as a whole for 1998 and beyond was what should the bank do about this problem, especially since one of its primary strategic priorities was to provide superior personal customer service.

Background

Heartland State Bank (HSB) was the largest *independent* bank in its moderate-sized mid-western home market city and the state in which it was located. HSB had assets in the $500 million to $1 billion range. While the bank had several branches in its home market, it was confined to that market by the state banking laws in force at that time. The city's economic base was dominated by service industries such as government, education, medicine, insurance, real estate, and finance. In addition, with one notable exception, HSB's numerous competitors were all branches of large regional or national bank holding companies. While their competitors had formidable resources far in excess of HSB's, their policies were largely determined by managers in headquarters located in other states, giving HSB the opportunity to project itself as the largest "hometown" bank in its market. There was one other independent bank in HSB's market. Although this bank was considerably smaller than HSB, it had a far higher return on investment than any bank in the market.

Like much of the country in 1997, HSB's home market had enjoyed several years of solid economic growth at or above the national average and an unemployment rate far below state and national averages. A number of the city's major employers, including a major insurance company, had enjoyed several years of very strong growth. While such growth would normally be considered good fortune in any community, the high concentration of growth in knowledge-based service industries greatly strained the supply of qualified workers. Consequently, the potential labor market had shrunk to a very low level, putting modest upward pressure on wage rates and costs for employers seeking to hire such workers. Furthermore, as the supply of qualified workers declined, employers increasingly turned to less qualified individuals, forcing training costs to rise. The longer the growth continued, the more expensive employee turnover became and the more opportunities a firm's best employees had to better themselves by changing jobs.

Bank Strategy

Heartland State Bank had several key goals and strategies:

1. *Maintain asset quality superior to all competitors*—Although the bank was one of the fastest growing and most aggressive lenders in its market, it had the lowest level of problem loans as a percent of total assets of all the major banks in the state and this rate was among the lowest in the country.
2. *Acquire and maintain a strong customer base through the development of desirable products and high-quality personalized customer service*—For HSB to achieve this trademark goal it would have to depend greatly on the quality and training of the bank's personnel and the presence of a stable staff. Customers liked to see a familiar customer service representative (CSR—sometimes referred to as a teller) or consumer banker when they came to the bank to do business.
3. *Enhance the level and quality of the bank's core earnings (operating earnings excluding adjustments to loan reserves)*—Although the bank had achieved several consecutive years of record earnings, the rising costs of personnel promised to put an increased strain on their record.
4. *Achieve superior growth in assets and earnings*—Although this goal had become increasingly important, achieving consistent growth in the bank would eventually require corresponding growth in capacity through a combination of productivity gains and an increase in the size of the bank's workforce. This would, in turn, create increased costs for both training and employee acquisition.

The ability of HSB to achieve these goals also depended on its sources of competitive advantage. Overall, HSB had a reputation as a high service bank and its customer list included many of the most prominent organizations and individuals in its market, which was the largest market in the state. HSB excelled in two key product market areas, commercial lending and trust-related services, such as commercial trusts and commercial cash management. Commercial cash management accounts were especially important because of the large amounts of funds they supplied to the bank to support its growth. Furthermore, these commercial accounts were companies that had a number of employees who might be enticed to become customers of the bank.

Dominance in HSB's particular product markets required a good deal of personal service by high-quality personnel to acquire and keep such customers happy, both at the counter and in the "back office." As with any business, the largest and most profitable customers were regularly sought by all the market's competitors. HSB felt that its ability to keep and satisfy prominent customers was largely a function of its people. To gain access to the quality staff it felt it must employ, a key priority for HSB was to become the employer of choice for its employees. Management felt that one key to becoming the employer of choice was to offer very competitive compensation and benefits. Although this practice enabled the bank to build a quality workforce, its personnel costs were relatively high compared to the bank's peers and turnover, while recently lower than the levels experienced by its competitors, was still higher and more costly than was desirable. Based on these priorities and related personnel issues, including turnover, a major strategic priority for 1998 was to enhance staff recruitment, development, and retention. The bank set a goal to reduce overall staff turnover from 23.2 percent of the total workforce in 1997 to 18 percent in 1998, or a decline of just over 22 percent in the annual turnover rate.

Staff Turnover

Problem Scope

In her initial presentation, Ms. Harrison noted that in 1995, terminations of all types—voluntary and involuntary—equaled 34.4 percent of HSB's staff. This proportion declined to 24.4 percent in 1996 and 23.2 percent in 1997. In general, the employees who left the bank were predominately non-officer personnel (87 percent), female (76 percent), from the consumer/retail division of the bank (54 percent), and voluntarily separated (83 percent). The average age of employees leaving the bank was 33 years, compared to an average age of 43 for all employees. The average tenure of those who left was 3 years, 6 months. Table 1 summarizes the departmental breakdown of the turnover expressed in employee equivalents along with the average organizational tenure in years and months for each position.

Reasons for Leaving

As a matter of policy Ms. Harrison or members of her staff interviewed each employee who left the bank. Table 2 presents the results of those exit interviews for 1997 and shows that the employees who left HSB in 1997 did so for a variety of reasons, with the most prominent being to take advantage of new opportunities. Ms. Harrison deemed this particular reason *avoidable* because she felt that if suitable opportunities had existed at the bank, these employees would not have left. Based on the reasons employees gave for leaving, Ms. Harrison determined 46.3 percent of the bank's turnover could be classified as avoidable. Ms. Harrison also felt that 9.3 percent of the employee separations could be classified as *possibly avoidable* because they involved situations that might have been remedied if management had addressed the problems of specific employee performance soon enough (see Table 2 for reasons). She also noted that low pay was not a specific reason given by anyone leaving in 1997.

Cost of Turnover

The final part of Ms. Harrison's report was an estimate of the cost of the turnover at HSB in 1997. Table 3 presents a breakdown of the total cost of employee turnover at HSB in 1997. The turnover costs shown in the table were estimated for each employee by his/her manager, with the help of the Human Resources staff. As shown in the table, the bank identified the following four types of turnover costs.

**TABLE 1
Turnover by
Department,
1997 Heartland
State Bank**

Department/ Position	Proportion of Terminations	Average Years	Tenure Months
CONSUMER/RETAIL			
CSR (Teller)	40.8%	1	2
Consumer Banker	7.4	9	8
Consumer Services Manager	3.8	15	10
Customer Support Representative	1.8	1	1
Subtotal	53.8	3	4
HUMAN RESOURCES			
Administrative Assistant	1.0	8	8
Subtotal	1.0	8	8
TRUST			
Benefits Administrator	3.8	2	5
File Clerk	1.8		2
Investment Representative	1.8	2	2
Senior Trust Administrator	1.8		7
Trust Assistant	1.8	7	8
Trust Operations Clerk	1.8	11	0
Subtotal	12.8	3	9
LENDING			
Mortgage Loan Processor	5.6		11
Administrative Assistant	3.8	8	8
Collections Representative	3.8	6	9
CRA Officer	1.8	2	10
CRA Compliance Assistant	1.8		6
Credit Analyst	1.8	1	6
Subtotal	18.6	3	10
FINANCE/OPERATIONS			
Funds Transfer Specialist	3.8	3	11
Accounting Analyst	1.8	1	10
Accounts Payable Clerk	1.8		4
Cost Accounting Analyst	1.8	3	4
Operations Clerk	1.8		7
Wire Transfer Specialist	1.8	1	5
Administrative Assistant	1.0	8	8
Subtotal	13.8	2	8
TOTAL/AVERAGE	100.0%	3	6

Source: HSB organizational study.

1. *Separation costs*—include the cost of an exit interview plus administrative and record keeping activities associated with separation.
2. *Replacement costs*—include advertising, pre-employment administrative functions and record keeping, selection interviews, pre-employment tests, and selection meetings.
3. *Training costs*—include books, manuals, reports, education (workshops and employee's compensation while attending), one-to-one coaching (compensation of both the employee and the coach), and compensation of new employee until s/he gets up to "par."
4. *Lost productivity*—includes overtime, temporary employees, lost fees, supervisory time, etc. while the position is vacant.

TABLE 2
Reason for HSB
Employees Leaving
the Bank—1997

Reason for Leaving HSB	Proportion of Total
AVOIDABLE*	
New opportunities	35.2% †
Working conditions	11.1 ‡
Subtotal	46.3
POSSIBLY AVOIDABLE*	
Performance	5.6
Attendance record	3.7
Subtotal	9.3
GENERALLY UNAVOIDABLE*	
Relocated	9.2
Return to school	7.3
Misconduct	5.6
Personal reasons	5.6
Health reasons	5.6
Retired	3.7
Self employment	3.7
Other	3.7
Subtotal	44.4
Total	100.0%

Reasons taken from comprehensive exit interviews.

† This reason might include pay issues, but no one specifically stated this.

‡ This would include all conditions, including employee perceptions of management, although no one specifically complained about his/her manager.

* The classification of reasons for leaving as avoidable, possibly avoidable, and unavoidable was created by the HR department. *Avoidable* turnover was that which the bank felt it could reduce by some type of positive action. *Possibly avoidable* turnover related to people who left because of factors that might have been remedied by management before they became problems. *Unavoidable* factors were reasons the bank felt it could do little to change.

Source: HSB organizational study.

TABLE 3
Cost of Turnover
at HSB—1997

Department	Term. %	Separation Costs	Replacement Costs	Training Costs	Lost Productivity	Total Cost
Consumer	53.8%	$1,568	$16,993	$166,204	$45,100	$229,865
Human Resources	1.0	23	440	1,750	980	3,193
Trust	12.8	384	4,311	41,269	9,030	54,994
Lending	18.6	516	7,422	45,041	14,605	67,584
Finance/Operations	13.8	402	4,800	38,243	11,010	54,455
Totals		$2,893	$33,966	$292,507	$80,725	$410,091
% of Total		0.7%	8.3%	71.3%	19.7%	

Source: HSB organizational study. Data estimated by department managers based on definitions of costs provided by the organization's HR Division.

The Teller Problem

At HSB, as in most banks, the primary retail customer contact person was the teller or customer service representative (CSR). As shown in Table 1, this position was the biggest problem area, accounting for more than 40 percent of total turnover, and Ms. Harrison thought it would be the most difficult part of the problem to solve. Though HSB paid its employees more than its other bank competitors, this entry level position didn't pay qualified individuals as much in absolute terms as they could earn at other employers in the area. For some people, money wasn't the only concern. They wanted certain types of schedules to accommodate the needs of their children, for example. Tellers didn't have much opportunity for advancement, so individuals seeking career growth would be unlikely to remain in the position for very long.

MIS Conversion

In addition to its more general needs, the bank also faced a major short-run issue in 1998, converting its MIS services to two new vendors. This process would involve virtually the entire year and promised to be complex, time-consuming, and stressful for nearly all employees in the bank. All employees would have to be trained in the new system, a process that would tax the already overworked Human Resources Division. Furthermore, many key employees would have to take time off from their already busy schedules to engage in numerous team meetings and planning sessions to set up the bank for the conversion that was scheduled to take place in early December. The senior management team was quite concerned that this process could result in the loss of some key employees or at the very least, productivity would be significantly reduced as these people tried to balance their lives. As the group discussed these issues, it was suggested that some system of random rewards or "perks" be devised to reduce the stress and enhance the quality of work life for the staff. While the exact nature of such a system was left up to Ms. Harrison to devise in consultation with the rest of her Senior Management colleagues, it was suggested that management offer employees symphony tickets, seats in its VIP box at the local baseball park, tickets for families of employees to the local amusement park, and so forth.

Future Goals and Strategies

After presenting her report, Ms. Harrison began a general discussion of possible options the bank could evaluate to solve its turnover problem. After discussing the topic for more than an hour, a number of goals and actions were identified and placed in HSB's strategic plan for 1998. In addition, it was decided that Ms. Harrison would follow up her initial report with a more detailed plan showing how the firm could achieve its long-run goal of becoming the "employer of choice" for its employees.

Objectives

1. Reduce turnover among all employees to 18 percent of the workforce in 1998.
2. Increase the tenure of lower level customer service personnel and reduce teller turnover to 30 percent of the total (from just over 40 percent as shown in Table 1).
3. In the long run, increase the average age, maturity, and tenure of bank personnel, especially in lower level positions. (Ms. Harrison is keenly aware that as the bank tried to achieve this goal, she would have to exercise great care to conform to all statutes and regulations associated with fair hiring practices.)
4. Increase the level of employee delight. (Note: the term "employee delight" was developed by the firm's CEO after he and several senior managers attended a presentation given by several key managers of the Walt Disney Co. At that presentation the Disney officials talked of that firm's emphasis on "delighting" its customers. HSB's CEO asked his team to transfer this concept to the treatment of its staff and consider how the bank might delight its *employees*. While the general notion of delight seemed clear to most of the senior managers, perhaps as a measure of satisfaction, no specific definition or list of factors that might actually comprise employee delight was developed by early 1998.)

Actions

1. The Human Resources Division will prepare a plan for achieving its turnover objectives for 1998 and beyond. The plan is to be prepared in the first quarter, implemented in the second quarter, and reviewed and revised during the year, as necessary. This plan should be comprehensive and include, but not be limited to, consideration of the following:
   - Enhance the CSR (teller) position by various means, such as bonuses, scheduling considerations, multiple grades within the position, deferred incentives (paid only after a certain job tenure is achieved), etc.
   - Provide extra pay for working at peak times.
   - Implement special recognition programs.
   - Conduct employee attitude surveys.
   - Assign mentors to new employees.
   - Utilize referrals from current employees and customers to find mature individuals who might be recruited for CSR positions.
2. The HR division will also prepare a related plan addressing the goal of enhancing "employee delight." This plan should not only allow the bank to enhance the level of employee satisfaction, but should also contribute to a reduction in turnover.
3. HR will work with other managers to take whatever actions are necessary to make certain that the loss of any key personnel does not reduce the quality of customer service or damage any customer relationships.

The Challenge

HSB utilized several methods for assessing its employees and their attitudes. It conducted anonymous surveys of employee satisfaction through 1995. It also surveyed each employee's perception of the "internal service" of each functional area of the bank every six months. In this latter survey each employee was asked to rate the service provided by each of roughly 60 functional areas of the bank from which they might require services in a given six-month period. Loan officers, for example, would be asked to rate the service provided by the bank's credit analysts and/or account managers. Scores on this latter survey had risen continuously for more than four years. In addition, the bank also prided itself on its internal communication. It conducted regular all-employee meetings to provide feedback on major bank events and published a regular newsletter to provide focused communication on various issues, including employee recognition.

Based on this information, the bank felt that it was informed about the attitudes and concerns of its staff. Still, Ms. Harrison felt that somehow the bank was insufficiently informed about employee needs and attitudes or it should be able to keep its employees for more than the current 3½ year average (Table 1). She wondered what she needed to know to develop the new plans. Since departing employees never mentioned compensation as a problem and so many other reasons were given, it was hard to focus on a specific set of actions that might solve the retention problem. How could the bank lower its turnover and achieve employee delight? This problem was even more critical in this coming year because of the bank's scheduled MIS conversion. Ms. Harrison wondered if the bank might use the conversion process to test some of the suggested techniques for enhancing employee delight by giving random rewards to employees under stress or for working above and beyond what was required. She also worried that perhaps the bank's goal to reduce turnover to 18 percent was too optimistic, after all, much of the turnover was unavoidable, but the goal was in her MBO plan for the coming year and her 1998 bonus would depend, in part, on achieving her assigned goals.

BULLER | SCHULER

Managing Organizations and People

A Resource for Cases in Management, Organizational Behavior,
and Human Resource Management

Abstract

Heartland State Bank was a large independent bank in the $500 million to $1 billion dollar range located in a moderate-sized mid-western market with several major regional/national competitors. The bank's market enjoyed a strong economy in early 1998 and a tight labor market. The local economy was dominated by service industries such as government, education, real estate, medical services, and insurance. In a planning meeting held in January 1998, Marilyn Harrison, the Senior VP of Human Resources reported to the other members of senior management that the bank was suffering from a problem of employee turnover that was costing the bank more than $400,000. Upon hearing this report, the senior management team asked Ms. Harrison to propose a plan to solve this problem and present it at the bank's April planning meeting. She prepared a draft plan, which is presented in the case. In spite of this promising first step a number of issues remained to be resolved before the bank could achieve its HR goals.

Heartland State Bank (B): Planning for Employee Delight

In January 1998, the senior management team at Heartland State Bank (HSB) had met for their annual off-site strategic planning retreat. One of the issues introduced in that meeting was the need to reduce turnover among the bank's staff. As a result of that meeting Marilyn Harrison, Senior Vice President of Human Resources, had been charged with the responsibility to accomplish the goal of reducing staff turnover from roughly 23 percent of the workforce in 1997 to 18 percent in 1998. In support of this goal Ms. Harrison was asked to develop a plan for reducing turnover, which included a plan for enhancing "Employee Delight" and ultimately making HSB the "Employer of Choice" in its market.

Ms. Harrison's task was complicated by the fact that in addition to the bank's normal activity in 1998, it would also be implementing a major conversion of all of its item processing and information systems to a new vendor. This activity was expected to create considerable stress on all the bank's staff, although key staff were expected to shoulder the largest part of the burden. In this atmosphere the bank would be trying to achieve significant growth, maintain a high level of customer service, maintain asset quality, and significantly reduce the staff turnover. At the beginning of this task Ms. Harrison had considerable doubt about achieving her assigned goal and was concerned because her annual bonus would depend in part on this outcome.

In April 1998, the bank's senior management team assembled once again to review their current strategic plan. At that meeting, Ms. Harrison was to present her preliminary plans for reducing turnover, making HSB the "Employer of Choice" in its market, and achieving "employee delight." While Ms. Harrison and her human resources team had done considerable research in preparing for the April meeting, she was still faced with a number of unanswered questions. How much would the plan cost? Would it work? Even if the plan was adopted immediately, only eight months remained in 1998 and she still had to achieve her goal of reducing turnover to 18 percent of the workforce.

Background

Heartland State Bank (HSB) was the largest *independent* bank in its moderate-sized midwestern home market city and the state in which it was located. HSB had assets in the $500 million to $1 billion range. While the bank had several branches in its home market, it was confined to that market by the state banking laws in force at that time. The city's economic base was dominated by service industries such as government, education, medicine, insurance, real estate, and finance. In addition, with one notable exception, HSB's competitors were all branches of large regional or national bank holding companies. While their competitors had formidable resources far in excess of HSB's, their policies were largely determined by managers in headquarters located in other states, giving HSB the opportunity to project itself as the largest "hometown" bank in its market. There was one other independent bank in HSB's market. Although this bank was considerably smaller than HSB, it had a far higher return on investment than any bank in the market.

Like much of the country in 1997, HSB's home market had enjoyed several years of solid economic growth at or above the national average and an unemployment rate far below state and national averages. A number of the city's major employers, including a major insurance company, had enjoyed several years of very strong growth. While such growth would normally be considered good fortune in any community, the high concentration of growth in knowledge-based service industries greatly strained the supply of qualified workers. Consequently, the potential labor market had shrunk to a very low level, putting modest upward pressure on wage rates and costs for employers seeking to hire such workers. Furthermore, as the supply of qualified workers declined, employers increasingly turned to less qualified individuals, forcing training costs to rise. The longer the growth continued, the more expensive employee turnover became and the more opportunities a firm's best employees had to better themselves by changing jobs.

Bank Strategies and Objectives

Heartland State Bank had several key goals and strategies:

1. Maintain asset quality superior to all competitors by maintaining the lowest level of problem loans to total assets in their market.
2. Acquire and maintain a strong customer base through the development of desirable products and high-quality personalized customer service.
3. Enhance the level and quality of the bank's core earnings (earnings excluding adjustments to loan reserves).
4. Achieve superior growth in assets and earnings.

The ability of HSB to achieve these goals also depended on its sources of competitive advantage. Overall, HSB had a reputation as a high service bank and its customer list included many of the most prominent organizations and individuals in its market, which was the largest in the state. HSB excelled in two key product market areas: commercial lending and trust-related services such as commercial trusts and commercial cash management. Commercial cash management accounts were especially important because of the large amounts of funds they supplied to the bank to support its growth. Furthermore, these commercial accounts were companies that had a number of employees who might be enticed to become customers of the bank.

Human Resources

Dominance in HSB's particular product markets required a good deal of personal service by high-quality personnel to acquire and keep such customers happy, both at the counter and in the "back office." As with any business, the largest and most profitable customers were regularly sought by all the market's competitors. HSB felt that its ability to keep and satisfy prominent customers was largely a function of its people. To gain access to quality staff, a key priority for HSB was to become the employer of choice for its employees. Management felt that one key to becoming the employer of choice was to offer very competitive compensation and benefits. Although this practice enabled the bank to build a quality workforce, its personnel costs were relatively high compared to the bank's peers and turnover, while recently lower than the levels experienced by its competitors, was still higher and more costly than desirable. Accordingly, the bank set several personnel-related objectives for 1998.

1. Reduce turnover among all employees to 18 percent in 1998.
2. Increase tenure of lower level customer service personnel and reduce teller turnover from 40 percent to 30 percent of total turnover.
3. Begin to increase the average age, maturity, and organizational tenure of bank personnel, especially in lower level positions.
4. Increase the level of employee delight. (Note: the term "employee delight" was developed by the firm's CEO after he and several senior managers attended a presentation given by several key managers of the Walt Disney Co. At that presentation the Disney officials talked of that firm's emphasis on "delighting" its customers. HSB's CEO asked his team to transfer this concept to the treatment of its staff and consider how the bank might delight its *employees*. While the general notion of delight seemed clear to most of the senior managers, how this variable might be measured or more precisely defined had not been determined at the time of the April 1998 meeting. It was apparent at that meeting that the term was meant to define a high level of employee satisfaction.)

To achieve these specific staffing objectives the human resources division was asked to prepare two plans that might be combined into a comprehensive HR employee retention strategy. The first plan was to be comprehensive and include, but not be limited to, consideration of the following strategies or actions:

1. Enhance the customer service representative (CSR, also known as a teller) position by various means such as: bonuses, scheduling considerations, multiple grades within the position, and/or deferred incentives payable only after the employee achieved some set level of job tenure.
2. Provide extra pay for working at peak times.
3. Implement special recognition programs.
4. Conduct an employee satisfaction survey (to determine the level of satisfaction and identify work related factors that would enhance that satisfaction and/or delight the bank's employees).
5. Assign mentors to new employees.
6. Utilize referrals from current employees and customers to find qualified individuals who might be recruited for CSR positions.

In addition, HR was asked to prepare a second plan to specifically address the goal of enhancing employee delight. This plan was to suggest the means by which the bank could raise the level of employee satisfaction and/or delight, as well as contribute to a reduction in turnover and an increase in employee experience and maturity.

Proposed Plan   At the April planning meeting Ms. Harrison presented her proposed plan to the senior
management team. That plan was based on information from two sources: the bank's own
survey and exit interview data and external research conducted by HR staff on factors believed to affect employee tenure and satisfaction.

Bank Employee Trends

In her initial presentation, Ms. Harrison noted that in 1995, terminations of all types—
voluntary and involuntary—equaled 34.4 percent of HSB's staff. This proportion declined
to 24.4 percent in 1996 and 23.2 percent in 1997. In general, the employees who left the
bank were predominately non-officer personnel (87 percent), female (76 percent), from
the consumer/retail division of the bank (54 percent), and voluntarily separated (83 percent). The average age of employees leaving the bank was 33 years, compared to an average age of 43 for all employees. The average tenure of those who left was 3 years, 6
months. Table 1 summarizes the departmental breakdown of the turnover expressed in
employee equivalents along with the average organizational tenure in years and months for
each position.

As a matter of policy Ms. Harrison or members of her staff interviewed each employee who left the bank. Table 2 presents the results of those exit interviews for 1997 and
shows that the employees who left HSB in 1997 did so for a variety of reasons, with the
most prominent being to take advantage of new opportunities. Ms. Harrison deemed this
particular reason *avoidable* because she felt that if suitable opportunities had existed at the
bank, these employees would not have left. Based on the reasons employees gave for leaving, Ms. Harrison determined 46.3 percent of the bank's turnover could be classified as
avoidable. Ms. Harrison also felt that 9.3 percent of the employee separations could be
classified as *possibly avoidable* because they involved situations that might have been
remedied if management had addressed the problems of specific employee performance
soon enough (see Table 2 for reasons). She also noted that low pay was not a specific reason given by anyone leaving in 1997.

Research Findings

Ms. Harrison and her staff also looked at a variety of sources (books and trade journals)
to see what various experts had to say about what creates employee delight (satisfaction).
The research provided much information and Ms. Harrison identified several common
conclusions concerning employee preferences and needs such as:

1. Compensation, while not necessarily the most important factor in retaining employ-
    ees, is still important.
2. With today's family complexities and workloads, work arrangements such as flexible
    schedules, short work weeks, and comp time are important. (Comp time—or paid
    time off—is given to non-exempt employees instead of overtime pay for extra hours
    worked. Comp time must be given at a rate of 1.5 hours for every overtime hour
    worked and must be given under specific conditions and restrictions.)
3. A preferred organization provides opportunities for advancement, especially for
    women.
4. The employer should respect the employees' need for balance between work life and
    family life.
5. The company should help workers with family demands such as child care and de-
    pendent care, for example.
6. The organization should provide a pleasant and comfortable personalized working en-
    vironment and show respect for its employees and their opinions and contributions.
    In addition, casual dress is increasingly popular, especially among "back office" per-
    sonnel.
7. Employees also like to work for an organization they respect and whose goals and
    strategies they understand. They want to be part of a successful organization.

Table 3 summarizes a list of factors employees at various levels find important to their
commitment to their organizations.[1] One of the interesting findings of this particular study

TABLE 1
Turnover by
Department,
1997 Heartland
State Bank

Department/ Position	Proportion of Terminations	Average Years	Tenure Months
CONSUMER/RETAIL			
CSR (Teller)	40.8%	1	2
Consumer Banker	7.4	9	8
Consumer Services Manager	3.8	15	10
Customer Support Representative	1.8	1	1
Subtotal	53.8	3	4
HUMAN RESOURCES			
Administrative Assistant	1.0	8	8
Subtotal	1.0	8	8
TRUST			
Benefits Administrator	3.8	2	5
File Clerk	1.8		2
Investment Representative	1.8	2	2
Senior Trust Administrator	1.8		7
Trust Assistant	1.8	7	8
Trust Operations Clerk	1.8	11	0
Subtotal	12.8	3	9
LENDING			
Mortgage Loan Processor	5.6		11
Administrative Assistant	3.8	8	8
Collections Representative	3.8	6	9
CRA Officer	1.8	2	10
CRA Compliance Assistant	1.8		6
Credit Analyst	1.8	1	6
Subtotal	18.6	3	10
FINANCE/OPERATIONS			
Funds Transfer Specialist	3.8	3	11
Accounting Analyst	1.8	1	10
Accounts Payable Clerk	1.8		4
Cost Accounting Analyst	1.8	3	4
Operations Clerk	1.8		7
Wire Transfer Specialist	1.8	1	5
Administrative Assistant	1.0	8	8
Subtotal	13.8	2	8
TOTAL/AVERAGE	100.0%	3	6

Source: HSB organizational study.

is the difference in the ranking of retention factors at each level of the organization. Three of the top four factors for top level employees were monetary in nature, whereas front line employees weighted their choices far more in the direction of quality of work life issues. This may be a result of their age and the likely age of their families or it may be a function of their cultural attitudes. However, what this information shows is the importance of the quality of work life for lower level employees and that no plan will satisfy all employees in the same way.

Other research supports these results and shows that employees are especially sensitive to the way they are treated by the firms that employ them. Such factors as training and orientation programs, mentoring programs, being part of an effective work group, and frequent productive and/or supportive feedback from supervisors all rate as important

TABLE 2
Reasons for HSB Employees Leaving the Bank—1997

Reason for Leaving HSB	Proportion of Total
AVOIDABLE*	
New opportunities	35.2%†
Working conditions	11.1‡
Subtotal	46.3
POSSIBLY AVOIDABLE*	
Performance	5.6
Attendance record	3.7
Subtotal	9.3
GENERALLY UNAVOIDABLE*	
Relocated	9.2
Return to school	7.3
Misconduct	5.6
Personal reasons	5.6
Health reasons	5.6
Retired	3.7
Self employment	3.7
Other	3.7
Subtotal	44.4
Total	100.0%

Reasons taken from comprehensive exit interviews.

† This reason might include pay issues, but no one specifically stated this.

‡ This would include all conditions, including employee perceptions of management, although no one specifically complained about his/her manager.

* The classification of reasons for leaving as avoidable, possibly avoidable, and unavoidable was created by the HR department. *Avoidable* turnover was that which the bank felt it could reduce by some type of positive action. *Possibly avoidable* turnover related to people who left because of factors that might have been remedied by management before they became problems. *Unavoidable* factors were reasons the bank felt it could do little to change.

Source: HSB organizational study.

TABLE 3
Most Important Factors for Retaining Employees

SENIOR EXECUTIVES	%	MIDDLE MANAGERS	%	FRONT LINE	%
Compensation & benefits	67%	Compensation and benefits	61%	More careful hiring	57%
Stock options	52%	More careful hiring	54%	Compensation and benefits	50%
More careful hiring †	47%	Tuition reimbursement	41%	Tuition reimbursement	47%
Profit sharing	27%	Stock options	32%	Training programs	45%
Retention bonuses	26%	Casual dress code	31%	Orientation programs	39%
Tuition reimbursement	23%	Exit interviews	28%	Casual dress code	38%
Casual dress code	22%	Flexible hours	25%	Flexible hours	33%
Exit interviews	19%	Profit sharing	23%	Health insurance	29%
Flexible hours	18%	Orientation programs	22%	Exit interviews	28%
Orientation programs	5%	Retention bonuses	20%	Profit sharing	17%

† "More careful hiring" may be interpreted to mean that senior executives would like firms they work for to be selective in their hiring of new executives who will become their colleagues.

Source: F. Hansen. "Currents in Compensation and Benefits." *Compensation and Benefits Review*, September/October 1998, pp. 6–15. (See endnote.)

to employee retention. In her report to the senior management team, Ms. Harrison included a list of factors she hypothesized as potentially able to positively influence employee satisfaction/delight (Table 4).

Planning Process

On the basis of the HR department's research, Ms. Harrison developed a preliminary four-step process for devising a comprehensive plan for improving employee retention and enhancing employee delight.

1. Assess Employee Opinion
   - Administer a modified version of an employee opinion survey previously administered in 1995. Modifications will include specific questions concerning employee preferences for various "delight" factors.
   - Conduct focus groups for employees at various levels of the organization based on information gleaned from research and the survey. These focus groups may be managed by an outside facilitator.
2. Analyze Survey Information
   With the help of an outside consultant the bank will compile and analyze the survey data to create a prioritized list of employee delight factors.
3. Benchmark Other Organizations
   Gather information on employee retention techniques from other organizations, both in banking and in other industries, to determine best practices. May be done through

TABLE 4
Employee Delight Factors Identified by HR Heartland State Bank

Employee Delight Factor	Family	Individual	Monetary
Saving bond for new child			X
Summer jobs for employee child	X		
Casual dress		X	
Leased fitness center	X	X	
Four day work week	X	X	
Flexible work schedule	X	X	
Free meals		X	
Profit sharing			X
Matching charitable gifts		X	
Employee PC purchase program	X	X	
Birthday off		X	
Days off for service tenure		X	
Discounts for employees at local businesses	X	X	
Designated free parking		X	
College scholarship program	X		
Free family dinner nights	X		
Thanksgiving turkey	X		
Freedom to personalize office		X	
Presidential recognition for special events	X	X	
Discounted movie passes	X	X	
Corporate concierge	X	X	
Surprise treats (food, etc.)		X	
Payout of unused leave time			X
Discounted trips	X	X	
Increased internal promotions		X	
Tickets to major attractions		X	
Babysitting subsidy when working overtime	X	X	X
Work at home program	X	X	

site visits and through tele-conferencing. HR will collect benchmark data on recruiting strategies, employee turnover, employee satisfaction, recognition programs, and benefit packages.

4.   Develop and Implement the Employee Delight Plan

Once the HR department determines the relevant delight factors, it will analyze the cost of each factor, determine metrics for evaluating plan performance, and devise the final plan and a schedule for phasing in its implementation.

- Costs—proposed employee delight factors will be evaluated to determine their short- and long-term costs.
- Performance measurement—before implementing any plan for improving retention/delight, the bank must decide what measures of performance it will use to determine the plan's success.

Factors under consideration included:

- Turnover—has turnover improved?
- Tenure—is the average tenure at the bank increasing?
- Recruiting—is the time required to recruit new employees decreasing? This could indicate an improved reputation as the area's employer of choice.
- Referrals—have the number of successful referrals from employees increased?
- Satisfaction—will a follow-up survey in two years show increased satisfaction with the bank's HR practices?

A major element of the proposed plan was the gathering of information concerning employee attitudes. HSB already utilized several methods for assessing its employees and their attitudes. It conducted anonymous surveys of employee satisfaction in 1995. It also surveyed each employee's perception of the "internal service" of each functional area of the bank every six months. In this latter survey each employee was asked to rate the service provided by each of roughly 60 functional areas of the bank from which they might require services in a given six-month period. Loan officers, for example, would be asked to rate the service provided by the bank's credit analysts and/or account managers. Scores on this latter survey had risen continuously for more than four years. In addition, the bank also prided itself on its internal communication. It conducted regular all-employee meetings to provide feedback on major bank events and published a regular newsletter to provide focused communication on various issues, including employee recognition.

Planning Questions

When Ms. Harrison presented her report to the senior management team, there was a good deal of discussion about various issues related to the plan. For example, some senior managers wanted to know who would select the factors to be included. Would individual managers have any discretion as to how they treated and/or rewarded their particular employees or would this have to be coordinated across various departments? What would HR's role be in making such choices and in the problem of enterprise-wide coordination? How would this plan be coordinated with the MIS conversion planning process?

The managers were also concerned about the power these factors would have to achieve the desired result. Once a specific delight factor was implemented would it become permanent and be given to everyone automatically? Would everyone get the "Thanksgiving turkey," or just a selected few? Would people become jealous if they didn't get a reward their friend got? One of the key elements of the plan suggested in the January meeting was the notion of using spontaneous rewards to reinforce particular acts of "organizational heroism." Would that be part of the plan, or would all rewards eventually become expected and eventually lose their power to motivate? Other managers wondered if HR considered the table of potential delight factors provided in the report (Table 4) to be exhaustive. Should mentoring play a key role in the overall plan?

Ms. Harrison and her colleagues also wondered what role recruiting should play in achieving the goal of reducing turnover. The bank typically used standard approaches to recruiting such as advertisements, employee referrals, and occasionally staff recruitment agencies. They also maintained contacts with other bankers and on occasion hired personnel from their competitors. Should they fine-tune this process to hire particular types of individuals for the teller position? To do this effectively they would have to know more about what could motivate individuals to stay in these positions. They would also have to do this in a way that conformed to applicable laws controlling hiring practices. Was it possible to retain a teller for more than a year or two?

Ms. Harrison left the April meeting with several questions and concerns. With all her other responsibilities it had taken some time to create this initial plan and many questions would have to be faced before finalizing it. She also knew she only had two-thirds of the year left for her department to achieve its personnel turnover goals. Almost half of the bank's turnover was unavoidable so all of the reduction would have to come from the other half. Finally, the plan's success would undoubtedly be affected by the ongoing systems conversion and the impact of this factor would be hard to predict. She also knew she had a lot to do and not much time in which to get the job done. Finally, she wondered if the bank was on the right track in tackling this problem. Since the bank's turnover level was roughly similar to other firms, was this really a problem worth this much time and expense? Only time would tell.

Endnote

1. Data in Table 3 come from a study of employee preferences reported in: F. Hansen. "Currents in Compensation and Benefits." *Compensation and Benefits Review*, September/October 1998, pp. 6-15. While this article was not available to Ms. Harrison at the time of the case, it does summarize much of the research she uncovered from other sources.

Part 6

Managing Diversity

Cases Outline

BULLER | SCHULER

Managing Organizations and People

A Resource for Cases in Management, Organizational Behavior, and Human Resource Management

Abstract

As workforces become more diverse, they begin to face many new human resource issues. The Barden Corporation case illustrates four people-related business concerns: the influx of immigrants, the need for skilled workers, the increasing number of older workers, and the growing number of employees who are out of shape that results in safety and health concerns. The case setting is the Precision Bearing Division of the Barden Corporation in Danbury, Connecticut.

Managing Workforce Diversity: People Related Issues at the Barden Corporation

Introduction

The largest segment of the business at the Barden Corporation is the Precision Bearings Division. It manufactures high-precision ball bearings in a range of sizes for machine tools, aircraft instruments and accessories, aircraft engines, computer peripherals, textile spindles, and medical and dental equipment. Presently, the division employs about 1,000 people, which includes a marketing department and a small corporate staff. It was founded during World War II to manufacture the special bearings needed for the Norden bomb-sight. It has been non-union since that time (which gives you a hint about the culture). The following description is told by Mr. Donald Brush, Vice President and General Manager of the Precision Bearings Division.

Background

Reporting directly to me is a small staff comprising a manufacturing manager, a quality manager, an engineering manager, a director of manufacturing planning, and a director of industrial relations (see Exhibit 1). We meet together several times a week to discuss current problems, as well as short- and long-range opportunities and needs. On alternate weeks we augment this group by including the supervisory personnel who report to the senior managers listed above. I might interject here that all supervisors meet with hourly employees on either a weekly or bi-weekly basis to review specific departmental successes and failures, and otherwise to keep employees informed about the business and to encourage ownership of their own jobs. The managers themselves meet on call as the

■ This case was prepared by Randall S. Schuler, Rutgers University, who expresses his appreciation for the cooperation of Donald Brush.

EXHIBIT 1
Precision Bearings Division

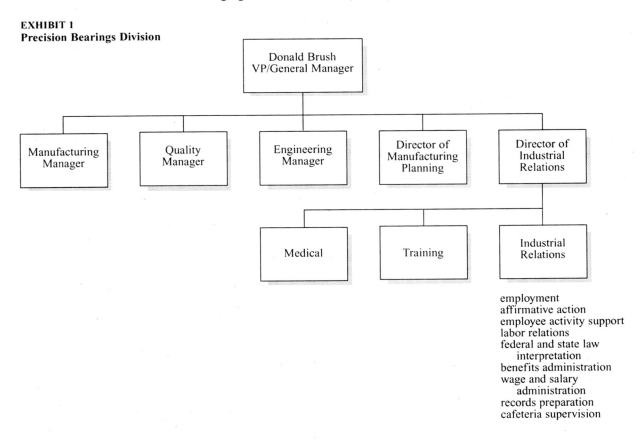

Employee Relations Committee to discuss and recommend approval on a wide range of issues that include the evaluation and audit of hourly and salaried positions, as well as the creation or modification of all divisional personnel policies.

A few words about our Personnel (or Industrial Relations) Department. (You will notice that the term "Human Resources" does not yet roll off our tongues easily, but we understand what it means.) There are six employees who together provide the basic services of employment, affirmative action, employee activity support, labor relations, interpretation of the plethora of federal and state laws, benefits administration, wage and salary administration, records preparation and maintenance, cafeteria supervision, and so on. There are, in addition, two people who coordinate our rather extensive training activities.

As presently organized, the Medical Department comes under the supervision of the director of industrial relations. Its authorized staff includes a medical director, the manager of employee health and safety (who is an occupational health nurse), a staff nurse, a safety specialist, and a secretary/clerk.

The development and execution of plans and programs, including those of a strategic nature, almost invariably involve the active participation of Personnel. And that's how we want it to be. On the other hand, the Personnel Department doesn't run the business. By this I mean they don't hire or fire, promote, or demote. They don't write job descriptions or determine salaries or wages, etc., etc. All these things are done by the line managers with the Personnel Department providing a framework to ensure consistency and that all actions are appropriate to company goals. You might say that Personnel is our "Jiminy Cricket"—they are there for advice, consent and, importantly, as a conscience.

During the past several months we have been running into many issues that are affecting the very essence of our business: growth, profits, survival, and competitiveness. Because the issues involve our human resources, we call them people-related business issues. Would you please give us your experience, expertise, and suggestions as to how we can solve them? Thanks! The following briefly describes the nature of each of the four issues.

Issue: Recruiting and Training New Hourly Employees

The need to recruit and train approximately 125 new hourly workers to respond to a surge in business in a high cost of living area at a time when the unemployment rate is no more than 2.5% is very challenging. By mid-1989 it had become evident that we had an opportunity to significantly increase our business. In order to achieve otherwise attainable goals, we have to increase our hourly workforce by a net of about 125 employees (that is, in addition to normal turnover, retirements, etc.) in one year. I have asked Personnel to test the waters, recognizing the unemployment in the Danbury labor market has reached an unprecedented low of about 2.5%.

Issue: Safety and Occupational Health Issues

The need to create a heightened awareness by the workforce for safety and occupational health considerations is very important. This is an evolving mission born of a dissatisfaction on our part about "safety as usual." Over the years, Barden employees have assumed that, because we are a metal working shop, people were just going to get hurt. But we cannot afford to have people get hurt and miss work anymore. Yet, as our workforce ages, the employees seem to get out of shape and become more injury and illness prone.

Issue: Spiraling Health Costs of an Aging Population

The spiraling health costs of an aging and sometimes out-of-shape workforce are very costly. All employers face this. Barden's problem is a little unique in that hourly employees tend to stay with the company and retire from the company. For example, we still have several employees whose careers began with us 45 years ago shortly after the company was founded. Our average age approaches 45 for employees and their dependent spouses. Generally, our jobs do not require much physical effort, and it's easy to become out of shape and overfed. As a consequence, they get sick, use hospitals, and have accidents.

Issue: New Machines and the Development of Qualified Workers

The technological evolution of increasingly complex machinery and related manufacturing equipment and the development of trained workers to operate and maintain these machines and equipment, are important facts of life. This process is unceasing and requires a good deal of planning for both the short and the long run. For example, where will we be next year or five years out in order to remain competitive in terms of cost, quality, and service? Buying and rebuilding machines is part of the story. Running them efficiently is quite another. As you know, modern equipment of this sort requires operational people who are not only knowledgeable about the turning or grinding of metals, but also conversant with computerized numerical controls. The employee who sets up and operates a $500,000 machine must be well-trained. Yet having trained people is getting more difficult.

Summary

Mr. Brush knows that these four people-related business issues all reflect the increasing diversity of the workforce. Because of this, he knows that these issues will be around for a long time. Therefore, he requests that you provide him with action plans that can offer long lasting solutions (if at all possible!). He would also appreciate having any more facts related to the four issues identified.

BULLER | SCHULER

Managing Organizations and People

A Resource for Cases in Management, Organizational Behavior,
and Human Resource Management

Abstract

The Propmore Corporation presents an intricate case of sexual harassment that requires a good deal of ethical decision making on the part of a relatively new purchasing manager, Don Bradford. The overriding ethical issue illustrated by the case is that of fairness. In the three parts of the case, Bradford must consider decisions that test his ethical principles and his sense of "fair play." He must balance his responsibilities to all stakeholders.

Propmore Corporation

Situation I

Overview

Don Bradford was on the fast track at the Propmore Corporation. But he wished he could slow things down a bit, given several hard choices he had to make.

Propmore Corporation was a good place to work. It had sales of about $500 million per year, a net profit margin of 5 percent, and a return on equity of 15 percent. Propmore made several key components used by the aerospace industry and consumer goods market. It was a leader in its field. The company was organized by product divisions, each reporting to the Executive Vice President. Its operations were decentralized, with broad decision-making capability at the divisional level. However, at the corporate level functional departments (Purchasing, R&D, Personnel, and Marketing) set company policy and coordinated divisional activities in these areas. Propmore was financially successful, and it treated its people well, as Don Bradford's experience showed.

After earning his MBA four years ago from a respected state university, Don quickly rose through the ranks in Purchasing. At age 31, he holds the prestigious position of manager. (See the organizational chart in Exhibit 1.) Before joining Propmore, Don earned a B.S. in engineering and worked for three years in the aerospace industry as a design engineer. During his first three years at Propmore, Don was a buyer and received "excellent" ratings in all his performance appraisals.

**EXHIBIT 1
Propmore
Organizational
Chart**

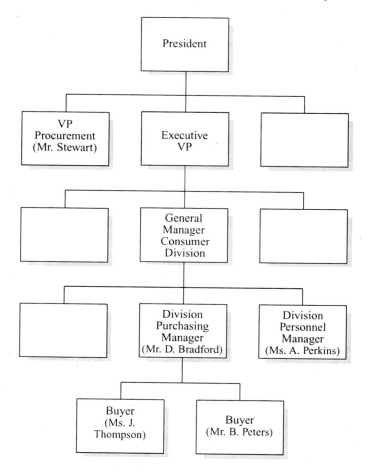

As Purchasing Manager, Don enjoyed good working relationships with superiors and subordinates. He was accountable directly to the consumer Division General Manager and, functionally, to the Corporate Vice President of Procurement, Mr. Stewart. His dealings with these people were always amiable and he came to count upon them for technical guidance, as he learned the role of Divisional Purchasing Manager. Don had several staff assistants who knew the business of buying and were loyal employees. He had done a good job of handling the resentment of those passed over by his promotion to manager, and he had developed a good deal of trust with the buying staff. At least he thought he had—until Jane Thompson presented him with the first in a series of dilemmas.

Jane Thompson, age 34, had been with Propmore for 10 years. She had a B.A. in English Literature and 2 years experience as a material expediter before coming to Propmore. Initially hired as a purchasing assistant, Jane became a buyer after 2 years. She enjoyed her job and the people she worked with at Propmore. In 4 years of working with Don, Jane had come to admire and respect his approach to management. She appreciated his sensitive yet strong leadership and saw him as an honest person who could be trusted to look after the interests of his subordinates.

But the dilemma with which Jane now presented Don made him wonder whether he had the skill to be a manager in a major division.

A Luncheon Harassment

After a two-hour purchasing meeting in the morning, Bill Smith, an Airgoods Corporation Sales Representative, had invited Jane Thompson to lunch. They left at noon. An hour and a half later, Jane stormed into Don Bradford's office, obviously upset. When Don asked what was wrong, Jane told him in very strong terms that Bill Smith had sexually harassed her during and after the luncheon.

According to Jane, Bill made some sexual comments and suggestions toward the end of the meal. She considered this to be offensive and unwelcome. Jane, however, told Bill to take her back to the office. He attempted to make light of the situation and said he was only joking, but on the way back he made some further comments and several casual physical contacts to which she objected. When they arrived at the company, Bill was embarrassed and tried to apologize. But Jane entered the office before he could finish.

Jane demanded that the Airgoods Corporation be taken off the bidder list for the raw material contract and that Airgoods' President be informed of the unseemly and illegal behavior of one of his salespeople. She would also consider taking legal action against Bill Smith through the Equal Employment Opportunity Commission for sexual harassment. Also, Jane stated she would investigate suing the Propmore Corporation for failure to protect her from this form of discrimination while she was performing her duties as an employee of the company. At the end of this outburst, Jane abruptly left Don's office.

Don was significantly troubled. Jane played a critical role in getting bids for the raw material contract. He needed her. Yet he knew that if he kept Airgoods on the bidder list, it might be difficult for her to view this vendor objectively.

Don was somewhat concerned about Jane's threat to sue Propmore but doubted that she had a very good case. Still, such an action would be costly in legal fees, management time, and damage to the company's image.

Don wasn't sure what to do about the bidder list. Airgoods had an excellent record as a reliable vendor for similar contracts. Propmore might be at a disadvantage if Airgoods was eliminated. On the other hand, Don firmly believed in standing behind his subordinates.

At this point, he needed more information on what constitutes sexual harassment and what policy guidelines his company had established. He examined two documents: the EEOC Definition of Sexual Harassment (Appendix 1) and the Propmore Corporation's Policy HR-13, on Sexual Harassment (Appendix 2).

Appendix 1: Situation I

Equal Employment Opportunity Commission
Definition of Sexual Harassment

"Unwelcome sexual advances, requests for sexual favors and other verbal or physical contact of a sexual nature constitute sexual harassment when (1) submission to such conduct is made either explicitly or implicitly a term or condition of an individual's employment, (2) submission to or rejection of such conduct by an individual is used as the basis for employment decisions affecting such individual, or (3) such conduct has the purpose or effect of unreasonably interfering with an individual's work performance or creating an intimidating, hostile or offensive working environment."

"Applying general Title VII principles, an employer, employment agency, joint apprenticeship committee or labor organization (hereinafter collectively referred to as 'employer') is responsible for its acts and those of its agents and supervisory employees with respect to sexual harassment regardless of whether the employer knew or should have known of their occurrence."

—EEOC guideline based on the Civil Rights Act of 1964, Title VII

Appendix 2: Situation I

The Propmore Corporation Policy HR-13
Policy Area: Sexual Harassment

Purpose: The purpose of Policy HR-13 is to inform employees of the company that the Propmore Corporation forbids practices of sexual harassment on the job and that disciplinary action may be taken against those who violate this policy.

Policy Statement: In keeping with its long-standing tradition of abiding by pertinent laws and regulations, the Propmore Corporation forbids practices of sexual harassment on the job which violate Title VII of the Civil Rights Act of 1964. Sexual harassment on the job, regardless of its intent, is against the law. Employees who nevertheless engage in sexual harassment practices face possible disciplinary action, which includes dismissal from the company.

Policy Implementation: Those who wish to report violations of Policy HR-13 shall file a written grievance with their immediate supervisors within two weeks of the alleged violation. In conjunction with the Legal Department, the supervisor will investigate the alleged violation and issue his or her decision based upon the findings of this investigation within 30 days of receiving the written grievance.

Situation II

Gathering More Information

Don Bradford had met Bill Smith, the Airgoods Corporation salesperson, on several occasions but did not feel he really knew him. To learn more about Bill, Don talked with his other key buyer, Bob Peters. Bob had dealt with Bill on many contracts in the past. After Don finished recounting the incident concerning Jane, Bob smiled. In his opinion, it was just a "boys will be boys" situation that got blown out of proportion. It may have been more than a joke, but Bob did not think Bill would do something "too far out." He pointed out that Bill had been selling for 10 years and knew how to treat a customer.

Don's next step was a visit to the division personnel office. In addition to going through Jane's file, he wanted to discuss the matter with Ann Perkins, the division's Human Resource Manager. Fortunately, Ann was in her office and had time to see him immediately.

Don went over the whole situation with Ann. When he had finished his account, Ann was silent for a minute. Then she pointed out that this was a strange sexual harassment situation: it did not happen at the company, and the alleged harasser was not a member of the Propmore organization. The extent of the company's responsibility was not clear.

She had heard of cases where employees held their companies responsible for protecting them from sexual harassment by employees of other organizations. But the harassment had taken place on company premises, where some degree of direct supervision and protection could have been expected.

Ann filled out a slip authorizing Don to see Jane's personnel file. He took the file to an empty office and went through its contents.

There were the expected hiring and annual evaluation forms, which revealed nothing unusual and only confirmed his own high opinion of Jane.

Then Don came to an informal note at the back of the file. It summarized a telephone reference check with the personnel manager of Jane's former employer. The note indicated that Jane had complained of being sexually harassed by her supervisor. The personnel manager had "checked it out" with the supervisor, who claimed "there was nothing to it." The note also indicated that Jane was terminated two months after this incident for "unsatisfactory work."

Don returned to his office and called his functional superior, Mr. Stewart, to inform him of the situation. Mr. Stewart was the Corporate Vice President of Procurement. He had known Bill Smith personally for a number of years. He told Don that Bill's wife had abandoned him and their three children several years ago. Although Bill had a reputation for occasional odd behavior, he was known in the industry as a hard-working salesperson who provided excellent service and follow-through on his accounts.

Situation III

A Telephone Call

Don felt he needed even more information to make a thorough investigation. He contemplated calling Bill Smith. In fairness to Bill, he should hear his version of what happened during the luncheon. But he knew he was not responsible for the actions of a non-employee. Furthermore, he wondered if talking to Bill would upset Jane even more if she found out. And would it be a proper part of an investigation mandated by company policy?

As Don considered his options, the phone rang. It was Bill Smith's boss, Joe Maxwell. He and Bill had talked about the luncheon he said, and wanted to know if Jane had reported anything.

"Don, I don't know what you know about that meeting," said Joe, "but Bill has told me all the facts, and I thought we could put our heads together and nip this thing in the bud."

Don wasn't sure if this call was going to help or hinder him in his decision making. At first, he felt Joe was trying to unduly influence him. Also, he wasn't sure if the call was a violation of Jane's right to confidentiality. "Joe, I'm not sure we should be discussing this matter at all," said Don. "We might be jumping the gun. And what if Jane—"

"Wait, wait," Joe interrupted. "This thing can be put to rest if you just hear what really happened. We've been a good supplier for some time now. Give us the benefit of the doubt. We can talk 'off the record' if you want. But don't close the door on us."

"Okay," said Don, "let's talk off the record. I'll hear Bill's version, but I won't reach a conclusion over the phone. Our policy requires an investigation, and when that's complete, I'll let you know our position."

"Gee, Don," said Joe, "I don't think you even need an investigation. Bill says the only thing that went on at lunch was some innocent flirtation. Jane was giving him the old 'come on,' you know. She was more than friendly to him, smiling a lot and laughing at his jokes. Bill saw all the signals and just responded like a full-blooded male."

"You mean Jane was the cause of his harassing her?" Don asked.

"No, he didn't harass her," Joe said with urgency in his voice. "He only flirted with her because he thought she was flirting with him. It was all very innocent. These things happen every day. He didn't mean any harm. Just the opposite. He thought there was a chance for a nice relationship. He likes her very much and thought the feeling was mutual. No need to make a federal case out of it. These things happen—that's all. Remember when you asked out one of my salespeople, Don? She said 'no,' but she didn't suggest sexual harassment. Isn't this the same thing?"

"I don't know. Jane was really upset when she came to me. She didn't see it as just flirting that went on," said Don.

"Come on, Don," insisted Joe. "Give her some time to calm down. You know how women can be sometimes. Maybe she has PMS. Why don't you let things just settle down before you do anything rash and start that unnecessary investigation? I bet in a couple of days, you can talk to Jane and convince her it was just a misunderstanding. I'll put someone else on this contract, and we'll forget the whole thing ever happened. We've got to think about business first, right?"

Joe Maxwell's phone call put things in a new light for Don. If it was only innocent flirtation, why should good relations between Propmore and Airgoods be damaged? Yet he knew he had an obligation to Jane. He just wasn't sure how far that obligation went.

BULLER | SCHULER

Managing Organizations and People

A Resource for Cases in Management, Organizational Behavior, and Human Resource Management

Abstract

In many organizations, the procedures used to select candidates for promotion to higher levels in the organization are poorly designed and/or poorly implemented. This state of affairs creates problems for both the organization, which suffers because it fails to promote the best people for the job, and the employees, who view promotions as a reward for a job well done and as opportunities to advance their careers. This case illustrates 2 primary principles that should drive the decisions about how to select people for promotion: (1) finding the best candidates for the job, and (2) ensuring that the procedures are perceived as fair and equitable by everyone who participates. Realistically, a third consideration that will usually become important at some point is cost.

Promotion to Police Sergeant

Until recently, selection of candidates for promotion to police sergeants at State University was done unsystematically. Job analysis was not the foundation for selection decisions but rather intuition and subjective judgments. The presence of a legal imperative and a desire to make better and more objective selection decisions resulted in a program to develop new promotion procedures.

State University is a large university with eight campuses spread throughout the state. Each campus has its own police department. Although the eight campuses are fairly autonomous and independent, there is a central administration group which coordinates certain functions, including personnel. Legally the police departments are responsible for their selection and promotion decisions; they are not governed by the personnel group in central administration nor by the campus-based personnel departments. But the chiefs recognize that their expertise is limited and so they regularly seek advice and guidance from the campus and central administration personnel departments.

The eight campuses differ from each other in many ways, including size (from 4,000 students at the smallest campus to 30,000 students at the largest campus), location (both urban and rural), and age or time in existence (from as young as 10 years to as old as more than 100 years). Corresponding to these differences among the campuses are differences in the composition, philosophies, and histories of the police department, each run by its own police chief. Of particular importance in 1983 was an ongoing rivalry between two large departments, one in the northern part of the state and the other in the southern part of the state; each was vying for recognition as the "best."

Despite competition among the departments, all eight police chiefs recognized the value of pooling their resources to maintain a single promotion procedure (or test) for selecting sergeants. By having a single procedure, a rank-ordered list of all university police officers qualified for promotion could be developed and made available to all campuses. Each list had a two-year life. During these two years, whenever a vacancy for sergeant came up on any of the eight campuses, the people at the top of the list had first priority for promotion. Approximately 20 vacancies occurred during a list's two-year life, and usually about 150 of the 250 police officers met the minimum requirements for promotion (i.e., two years of college credits, two years of police experience, and completion of a state-sponsored management training course).

Because of the attractive small selection ratio, the police chiefs wanted to improve their selection procedures so that the 20 vacancies were filled with the very best of the 150 eligible police officers. Accordingly, the university agreed to pay for a consultant to work with the police and personnel groups to design a high-quality promotion procedure for sergeants. They hired Gerri Smith from a prestigious consulting firm specializing in selection.

Getting Started

As with previous consulting assignments of this type, Ms. Smith knew that the development of a new promotion procedure would take time and involve several components. These components, beginning with job analysis, are outlined in the sequence through which Ms. Smith proceeded. This outline is shown in Exhibit 1.

Job Analysis

In 1979, six of the eight police departments had hired a firm to conduct job analyses of all jobs within their departments. The method the firm had used appeared to be the critical incident technique (CIT), but it was difficult to tell for sure because the documentation of the job analysis procedures had been retained by the consulting firm. The police chiefs contacted the firm after Ms. Smith pointed out to them that this documentation would be critical should they ever need to defend in court decisions they made using the results of the job analysis. Unfortunately, the particular consultant they had worked with four years ago was no longer with the firm and the documentation was nowhere to be found.

Neither Ms. Smith nor the police chiefs had anticipated this problem. They had hoped to have their promotion list ready in four months. If they did a job analysis, they knew they might have to wait six or seven months before seeing that list. After discussing the matter at length, the chiefs decided that in the long run it was in their best interest to collect systematic, up-to-date job analysis information, so they asked Ms. Smith to get started.

**EXHIBIT 1
Components of
the Promotion
Test Developed
by Ms. Smith**

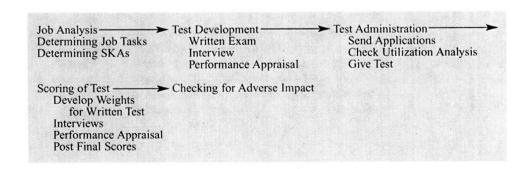

Job Analysis ──────▶ Test Development ──────▶ Test Administration ──────▶
Determining Job Tasks   Written Exam   Send Applications
Determining SKAs   Interview   Check Utilization Analysis
                               Performance Appraisal   Give Test

Scoring of Test ──────▶ Checking for Adverse Impact
     Develop Weights
        for Written Test
     Interviews
     Performance Appraisal
     Post Final Scores

Phase I: Determining Job Tasks

Usually Ms. Smith likes to use an extended CIT method of job analysis but in this case it was not practical. To do so, she would have had to travel to eight locations that were hundreds of miles apart from each other. Both time and budget constraints ruled this out. Therefore, Ms. Smith decided to combine features of the CIT and GOJA methods. This creative solution was possible because the Uniform Guidelines recognize that there is no one best method of job analysis. As long as the method used provided information about the importance, frequency, difficulty, and trainability of one's job tasks, it would probably hold up to the scrutiny of the courts.

Ms. Smith conducted the job analysis for sergeants as follows: First, she asked each police department to send copies of the job descriptions for all of their sergeants. These gave her a general working knowledge of what the job of sergeant involved. Next, she developed a form that she would send to each sergeant to fill out. This form asked the sergeant to list all of his or her job duties and then, for each duty or task, to rate how frequently it was performed relative to other duties, how important it was to the job overall, how difficult it was to perform, and the amount of training that would be needed to teach someone to perform the duty. This form was sent to each sergeant, who filled it out and then reviewed it with his or her commanding lieutenant. If the lieutenant felt any qualifications or changes were needed, these were noted in a designated space. Both the sergeant and lieutenant then signed the form to indicate they had reviewed it together. Finally, the chief reviewed the form, added any comments he felt were appropriate, and signed it. The original copy of the form was kept by the campus police department and a photocopy was sent to Ms. Smith.

Using the information from the completed forms, Ms. Smith generated a list of eight job domains, which she believed, based on the data she had collected, represented the tasks relevant to the job of a sergeant. Then, for each domain, she listed all of the specific tasks that she felt belonged to the domain. For each task, she recorded the corresponding ratings of frequency, difficulty, importance, and trainability (FDIT ratings). This list of domains and tasks was then sent back to 12 randomly chosen sergeants and 3 lieutenants who reviewed it. Ms. Smith asked these reviewers to study the list she had generated and evaluate whether the domains made logical sense to them and whether the tasks within each domain belonged there. They returned their suggestions for revision to Ms. Smith in writing. She then finalized the list, which is shown in Exhibit 2.

Phase II: Determining Skills, Knowledge, and Abilities (SKAs)

Now that the major job tasks had been identified, Ms. Smith needed to determine the SKAs required to perform those tasks. Then methods of assessing applicants' relevant SKAs could be designed for use as a selection test.

To find out which SKAs were important for performing a sergeant's job, Ms. Smith went back to the experts—the sergeants and lieutenants. In order to record their judgments in a systematic way, Ms. Smith designed a simple matrix for the job experts to complete. The headings on the 8 columns of the matrix were the names of the domains generated in Phase I of the job analysis. The labels for the 17 rows of the matrix were names of abilities, knowledges, and skills that she believed someone might need to perform well as a sergeant.

This domain's X abilities matrix was sent to all sergeants and lieutenants along with a list of the tasks that belonged in each domain and definitions of each ability. The job experts completed the matrix by indicating the importance of each ability for performing the tasks in each domain. Using these ratings, Ms. Smith determined the nine SKAs that were most important to assess in order to predict performance as a sergeant (see Exhibit 3).

Test Development

The police refer to the process through which sergeants are selected as the Sergeants' Promotional Exam (SPE). Traditionally, SPE has three components: a written exam, an interview, and an evaluation of past performance. These three components have always been used by the university police departments and they are typically used by city and state police departments as well. The police chiefs wanted Ms. Smith to maintain the three

EXHIBIT 2
Job Domains for the
Position of Police
Sergeant

		Average Ratings			
		F	D	I	T[a]
Domain:	Law enforcement activities including patrolling, investigating, apprehending.	6.2	5.8	6.3	5.1[b]
Sample tasks:	1. responding to call for crime in progress 2. cultivating sources of street information				
Domain:	Adaptability to the job, including completing work in a timely manner, attention to detail, willingness to assume accountability for one's work.	6.4	3.3	5.7	4.0
Sample tasks:	1. accepting orders or assignments 2. keeping up-to-date files				
Domain:	Dealing with the public.	6.7	4.9	5.2	4.1
Sample tasks:	1. referring citizens to other agencies 2. interviewing witnesses				
Domain:	Personal appearance and demeanor.	6.7	2.7	5.3	2.9
Sample tasks:	1. physical fitness activities 2. maintenance of uniform and equipment				
Domain:	Supervision and leadership.	4.7	6.4	4.8	6.7
Sample tasks:	1. working with a rookie or new transfer 2. supervising an investigation				
Domain:	Report writing.	5.9	4.6	5.5	5.1
Sample tasks:	1. writing up findings for an ongoing investigation 2. writing descriptions of events that occurred during on-site call				
Domain:	Teamwork, including working with other professionals both inside and outside of the department.	5.4	5.1	5.7	4.3
Sample tasks:	1. requesting assistance from other officers 2. teaching knowledge and skills to other officers				

[a] F = Frequency of task performance; D = Difficulty; I = Importance; T = Trainability.
[b] Ratings were made using a scale of 1 to 7. Values shown are means obtained by averaging across all items in the domain.

EXHIBIT 3
SKAs Assessed by
the Sergeant's
Promotional Exam

		Exam Component in which SKA Was Assessed[a]		
Skills, Knowledges, & Abilities	I[b]	Written	Interview	Performance
1. Knowledge of State and Federal Law	6.7	x	x	x
2. Knowledge of Local Procedures and Regulations	6.6	x		x
3. Writing Ability	5.2	x		x
4. Communication Skills	5.8		x	x
5. Reasoning Ability	5.0		x	x
6. Skill in Interpersonal Relations	6.1		x	x
7. Knowledge of General Management Principles	5.4	x		
8. Reading Ability	4.9	x		
9. Leadership Skills	4.8		x	x

[a] An "x" indicates the ability was assessed by that component of the exam.
[b] I = Importance rating of the ability. The value shown is a mean obtained by averaging the importance ratings of the ability for all job domains.

components of SPE, but they were eager to have the content of each component revised and updated. So the major questions were: (1) Which SKAs should be assessed by each component? and (2) How exactly should each SKA be measured?

In deciding how to design the SPE, Ms. Smith kept several things in mind: First, she knew that written tests were more likely than interviews and performance ratings to have impact against minorities, especially blacks and Hispanics. Second, she was wary of interviews because she knew they are difficult to standardize and make reliable. Third, she preferred to assess as many SKAs as possible using the most job-related method possible, which in this case was the performance appraisal. Finally, she knew that each of the three methods at her disposal (written test, interview, performance ratings) had both strengths and weaknesses, so the best strategy would be to measure all SKAs using more than one method, if possible.

The three components of the SPE Ms. Smith designed are described in detail below. Throughout these next sections, reference is made to a Task Force. This Task Force was organized to assist Ms. Smith with her task of developing the tests. It consisted of three chiefs and two lieutenants.

The Written Exam

During Phase II of the job analysis, 17 SKAs had been rated for their importance to a sergeant's job performance. Of these, 9 were judged to be relatively high in importance. Five of the 9 were judged to be appropriately assessed in a written exam: reading skills, writing skills, knowledge of basic management principles, knowledge of state and federal laws, and knowledge of university regulations and procedures as described by the local General Orders manual. The 2 skill areas had been rated as relatively less important than the 3 knowledge areas, so the proportion of test items devoted to each skill or knowledge area was adjusted to reflect the importance ratings.

Usually, the most difficult part of developing a written test is writing the test items. Fortunately, the Task Force had the advantage of being able to obtain potential items from a state agency that maintained a bank of thousands of test items for law enforcement exams. Upon request, this agency randomly selected a total of 400 items relevant to the SKAs to be assessed on the exam. Each member of the Task Force then reviewed all 400 questions and noted any objections they had. At a group meeting, the Task Force discussed their evaluations of the 400 items. Their goal was to select a total of 100 of the best items. The decision rule they used to eliminate items from the pool of 400 was to eliminate any item to which any member of the Task Force had objections. This reduced the pool to fewer than 200. Finally, redundant items were eliminated and the final 100 items were chosen to fit the goal of distributing items across the 5 knowledge and skill areas according to the relative importance of the areas.

As already noted, one disadvantage of written tests was that minorities tend to score lower than whites, resulting in adverse impact for selection decisions based on written tests. Test experts now realize that a major source of unfairness in written tests is that often the reading skill needed to take the test is higher than the skill needed to do the job in question. To decrease the potential for unfair discrimination, any written tests used for selection should be checked to ensure that the readability level of the test is equal to or below the readability level of written materials typically encountered in the job. Therefore, as the last step in developing the written test for the SPE, Ms. Smith conducted readability analyses of the test and of samples of department memos, regulation manuals, legal documents, and correspondence taken directly out of the record files of current sergeants. This analysis showed the reading skill needed to take the test was somewhat less than the skill needed to read materials from the sergeant's actual files.

The Interview

In the past, the police department interviewed only candidates who passed the written test. This practice meant that the chiefs had to decide on a cut-off point to define what a passing score would be for the written exam. They had always found this to be an extremely difficult judgment to make and wanted to avoid making that judgment this year. Their solution to the problem was to allow everyone to go through the interview process and not use the written test as a hurdle. This solution fit the chiefs' philosophy that someone who does well in the interview should be able to have that compensate for a low score on the written test, but it creates a practical problem: How could they interview approximately 100 candidates spread throughout a large state in a manner that everyone perceived to be standardized and fair, without incurring prohibitive expenses?

Ideally, it seemed that fairness and standardization could be best attained by having only one interview board (or panel), rather than having one panel at each of the eight campuses. But this would mean unbearably high travel costs—either the board members would have to travel around the state, or applicants would have to travel to the board. The Task Force decided the only practical solution was to set up two interview boards, one in the northern half of the state, and one in the southern half. This solution presented a real challenge to Ms. Smith who had to develop an interviewing procedure so sound it could not be attacked as possibly giving an unfair advantage to candidates in either half of the state. Ms. Smith realized that this challenge could be met only with a structured interview conducted by trained interviewers.

The first order of business was to solicit volunteers to serve as interviewers. The chiefs believed the interviewers should represent the following: the Affirmative Action officers from central administration, the general university community, the local communities by which the campuses were surrounded, the state law enforcement agencies, and their own departments. The group included the people to whom the chiefs felt most directly accountable, the people to whom the chiefs wished to demonstrate the credibility of their departments, and the people for whom the chiefs felt their departments should serve as role models. The Task Force was given the responsibility of creating two interview boards. Each board was to have one member to represent each of the five groups listed above.

After the interview boards were set up, Ms. Smith arranged a one-day training session for the interviewers. Her objectives for this training session were as follows:

- Develop a set of four or five questions that would be used for all interviews.
- Develop standards to use in evaluating candidates' responses to each question.
- Generate consensus among the interviewers about what they were to accomplish with the interview process.
- Give the interviewers an opportunity to role play an interview session.
- Develop an appreciation among the interviewers of the seriousness of their task and the problems inherent in accomplishing it (e.g., rater errors and biases, primacy and recency effects, and possible boredom and fatigue).

In order to accomplish these objectives, Ms. Smith did several things. First, prior to the training session she identified five SKAs (based on her job analysis) that could potentially be assessed in an interview. For each of these SKAs, she asked a few lieutenants to suggest interview questions that would tap the SKAs. Using these suggestions, she generated a list of about 20 potential interview questions. She sent this list, along with a short manual on interviewing and a job description for sergeants, to all members of the interview boards. The interviewers were asked to review this material prior to the training session.

At the training session, Ms. Smith reviewed several principles of interviewing and explained her objectives to the board members. She explained her belief that the only way to accomplish the objectives was for the interviewers to spend the day communicating and problem solving together. She turned over to them the task of selecting four or five questions that they all agreed were appropriate, and for which they were able to specify standards to be used in evaluating the candidates' responses. The interviewers struggled for several hours with this task, which they were surprised to find so difficult. By the end of the day, they had developed four questions they could all live with and a conviction that the interview process would be standardized and fair. At the end of the day, one of the interviewers—a 20-year veteran of a large city's police department—admitted to Ms. Smith that he came to the training session believing the day would be a waste of time because there was nothing he didn't already know about interviewing. To his surprise he came away feeling that every interview board should go through a similar process before they began evaluating candidates, especially since their evaluations can strongly influence the careers of young officers.

Performance Appraisals

The third component of the SPE was a performance appraisal of each candidate. Ms. Smith was happy to learn that the department already had a good performance appraisal procedure that was used for promotion decisions. The system worked as follows: For each candidate, all of the department officers who knew the candidate (this was typically three or four people) filled out a detailed appraisal form. The appraisal form accessed seven domains of job performance. For each performance domain, 8 to 12 specific tasks were listed. The officers evaluated the candidate's performance of each task using a 10-point rating scale. These ratings were averaged and multiplied by 10 to yield one overall performance score.

Administering the SPE

At the same time the three test components were being developed, Ms. Smith and the Task Force were planning for the administration of the tests. Only internal applicants were allowed to take the SPE, so the recruiting process was simple. All university police officers were sent a letter that described the testing procedures in detail. An application form was sent with this letter instructing all interested persons to apply by a particular date.

Although it was routine practice for the department to use only internal recruiting for the SPE, the chiefs always felt obliged to justify this practice. The major argument against the practice of internal recruiting was that it would perpetuate any existing underrepresentation of minority groups. To counter this argument, the chiefs sent a utilization analysis to the university's AAP officer, who compared this information to their routinely collected availability data. Because the police department had an aggressive recruiting program for entry-level positions, this comparison usually revealed that minority groups were not underrepresented in the pool of potential internal applicants.

The written exam was scheduled for a Saturday morning, and the police chiefs were all instructed to take this into account when assigning duties during that period. All interviewing was conducted the week after the written test. The officers completed their performance appraisals during that week also. Candidates were told the final list of total scores would be posted three weeks after the date of the written test.

Scoring the SPE

Final SPE scores were created by adding together the weighted scores from each component. The written test was weighted 50 percent, and the interview and performance appraisal were each weighted 25 percent. The final list of promotion candidates consisted of a rank ordering of everyone who had completed all three phases of the SPE based on the overall scores. This list was posted in each of the eight campus police departments along with a notice encouraging all applicants to speak with their chief to obtain detailed feedback.

The chiefs chose to weight the written test more heavily than the interview and performance appraisal primarily because they and their patrol officers all believed the written test was the most objective component of the SPE, and thus was the least subject to the criticism that favoritism determined the scores. Initially, the chiefs had suggested to Ms. Smith that the performance appraisal be weighted only 10 percent because it was the component believed to be the most subjective. However, Ms. Smith countered that the performance appraisal was the most job-related component and therefore was probably the most valid predictor. The 50-25-25 weighting system was eventually agreed upon to take into account these and other similar types of concerns.

Checking for Adverse Impact

As noted previously, this university's police departments viewed themselves as leaders in the field of law enforcement practice. Consequently, they were particularly concerned about maintaining a force that was balanced with respect to the races and sexes. Recall that it was primarily this concern that led the departments to use a compensatory selection model rather than use the written test as a hurdle and therefore have to impose an arbitrary cut-off score for that component.

Ms. Smith believed that when management is sincerely concerned about the potential discriminatory effects of their selection procedures, the best guarantee for preventing unfair discrimination is information. Therefore, her last task for the police department was to conduct numerous analyses that illustrated the effects certain types of policies could have on their selection process. For example, one analysis involved computing adverse impact figures (using the 80 percent rule and a computer) under the assumption that the top 10, 20, or 30 candidates, respectively, would eventually be promoted from their list. This analysis revealed that strong adverse impact against blacks would occur if only the top 10 candidates were promoted, that using the top 20 candidates would cause less adverse impact, and that no adverse impact would occur if the top 30 candidates were promoted (see Exhibit 4). Similarly, Ms. Smith demonstrated the adverse impact of each of the three components of the SPE and the effects that changing the weighting system would have with respect to adverse impact. Because adverse impact was associated only with the written test, the adverse impact of the total SPE was directly affected by the weight given the written test—the higher the weight of the written test, the more adverse impact of the SPE overall. To reduce the potential adverse impact of the SPE, the weight of the written test should be reduced.

Ms. Smith concluded her consulting assignment with the police chiefs. It is now up to them to fairly utilize, evaluate, and update the promotion procedures Ms. Smith helped them design. What problems, challenges, and issues face the police chiefs in carrying out the procedures developed by Ms. Smith?

EXHIBIT 4
Analysis to
Check for Potential
Adverse Impact

	Asian	Black	Hispanic	Am. Indian	White	Males	Females
Test Component	(n=23)[a]	(n=37)	(n= 11)	(n=3)	(n=71)	(n=118)	(n=27)
	% of Subgroup Who Are Among the Top 20 Candidates						
Written	(5)[b]22%	(2) 5%[c]	(1)9%[c]	(1)33%	(11)15%	(14)12%	(6)22%
Interview	(6) 26%	(3) 8%[c]	(1)9%[c]	(0) 0%[c]	(10)14%	(16)14%	(4)15%
Performance Appraisal	(5) 22%	(5)14%	(0)0%[c]	(1)33%	(9) 13%	(15)13%	(5)19%
	% of Subgroup Who Are Among the Top 30 Candidates						
Written	(7)30%	(7)19%	(2)18%	(1)33%	(13)18%	(22)19%	(8)30%
Interview	(7)30%	(6)16%	(2)18%	(1)33%	(14)20%	(24)20%	(6)22%
Performance Appraisal	(5)22%	(6)16%	(2)18%	(2)67%	(15)21%	(25)21%	(5)19%

[a] n = indicates the total number of job applicants in the subgroup.
[b] Values in parentheses represent numbers of applicants.
[c] Indicates that adverse impact defined by the 80 percent rule exists for the subgroup in comparison to the majority group (whites or males).

BULLER | SCHULER

Managing Organizations and People

A Resource for Cases in Management, Organizational Behavior, and Human Resource Management

Abstract

Propco, a subsidiary of a large, diversified manufacturer of advanced technology products, is a leading U.S. producer of a variety of marine systems products. Due to a dramatic decline in defense spending beginning in the later 1980s, Propco has been seeking ways to reduce its costs. One of the primary strategies has been to cut spending through employee layoffs. In 1991, Propco had a work force of about 14,000 people, 3.2 percent of which were minorities. By January 1, 1993, the firm's employees totaled about 10,000 with just under 1.1 percent comprised of minorities. This case provides an "inside" look at the human impact of downsizing strategies and corporate diversity programs. In particular, it highlights the challenges of attracting and maintaining a diverse work force in a declining business.

Propco, Inc.

Allied Technologies Corporation (ATC)

Founded in 1918, Allied Technologies is a diversified designer and manufacturer of advanced technology products and is one of the largest private employers in the state of Rhode Island. Headed by Joseph R. Wagner, the company is comprised of 10 operating units. These units conduct their businesses within four principal industry segments or lines of business—Marine Systems, Construction, Power, and Motor Parts. During 1991, the major business units within these four segments held, in most instances, rankings of either number one, two, or three in their major lines of business.

Revenues for 1991 totaled $16,427 million, with an operating income of $892 million. Non-U.S. operations accounted for 41 percent of sales in 1991, while U.S. Government business comprised 23 percent of sales.

Historically, at least half of ATC's revenues were derived from the military sector. Cuts in defense budgets for marine products (e.g., submarine engines, screw propellers, and environmental control systems), both in the U.S. and in other developed countries,

■ This case was written by Richard D. Freedman, Stern School of Business, New York University. Reprinted with permission. This case is based upon a real situation, certain facts have been changed, and the names of the corporations and the names and titles of individuals have been disguised.

have reduced requirements for military submarines and ships and related equipment from U.S. suppliers. Total U.S. defense spending peaked in 1985, and current budget requests indicate a further 4 percent decline in spending by 1993.

Wagner stated:

Beyond the problems in the military business, the plant closings and layoffs are intended to make the company more efficient. We have begun a transformation more profound and more potent than any single event in the corporation's recent history . . . sadly, though, 13,900 jobs must be eliminated in order to attain this efficiency.

Consequently, according to many experts, diversification of their operations into non-military marine areas is one of the most promising strategies for survival. In fact, ATC is following a diversification strategy. ATC has grown from a narrowly focused marine company in the 1970s with revenues of less than $2 billion, to what is today a $16 billion enterprise. Based on 1991 sales, the firm is one of the largest U.S. industrial companies, and one of the tenth largest U.S. exporters.

According to Wagner,

We have built the Company in order to be profitable in the face of declining Pentagon expenditures; the firm is reducing its reliance on defense contracts. We are now selling more products overseas. The Company is very strong and viable.

But some of ATC's operating units—such as Propco—whose primary task was to develop and construct military equipment, have suffered extensive financial losses because of the reductions in the military budget in the post-cold-war era.

Overall, the Corporation's earnings for the first nine months of 1991 were down 65 percent from the equivalent period of 1990. In 1991 ATC suffered its first annual operating loss in three decades.

Propco

Propco was the creation of a 1929 consolidation of HLL Vessels and the Excelsior Screw Propeller Company. At that time, Propco was the largest manufacturer of marine propellers in the world. Its specialty was the development and construction of screw propellers for submarines. A major risk to submarines is their location by enemies using instruments that detect the sounds and signals they make. Propellor screws are a major source of such "noise." Consequently the design and manufacture of better screw propellers is a significant issue in submarine development. Propco is renowned for its leadership in screw propellor development.

Although the advent of the jet age did not eliminate ocean-travel, it did reduce their commercial business and require that the company acquire other types of businesses. In the 1950s, with the development of an electronics group and a new engineering group, the division diversified into other marine and space systems especially in the defense industry.

At present, under the leadership of Malden K. Ruhn, Propco is a leading domestic producer of a number of Marine Systems products. Its major production programs include engine controls, environmental controls, marine-engine controls, and propellers for commercial and military boats.

The Marine Systems business is affected by many different factors: rapid changes in technology; lengthy and costly development cycles; heavy dependence on a small number of products and programs; changes in legislation and in government procurement and other regulations and procurement practices; licensing or other arrangements; substantial competition from a large number of companies; and changes in economic, industrial and international conditions. In addition, the principal methods of competition in the Marine Systems business are price, delivery schedules, product performance, service, and other terms and conditions of sale. Consequently, in times of recession and reduced government spending, firms heavily involved in the production of these systems must seek to reduce production and cut costs in order to remain profitable.

One primary way in which the company sought to cut spending is through employee layoffs. In 1991, Propco had a workforce of approximately 14,000 people, 3.2 percent of which were minorities. As of January 1, 1993, the firm's employees totaled 10,000 with just under 1.1 percent comprised of minorities.

Corporate Restructuring

In 1991 there was a sharp decline in ocean traffic, construction, and engine production. This marked the first time that ATC's core commercial markets simultaneously hit the bottom of their industry cycles. In addition, government reassessments of the military threat from the former Soviet Union—and efforts to reduce the U.S. deficit—resulted in fewer defense procurement contracts being awarded.

Consequently, in early 1992, ATC management announced that it would eliminate 15,297 jobs, including 8,143 in Rhode Island, by the end of 1994. At the time of this announcement, the Company had over 50,000 employees based in Rhode Island. The proposed cuts represent over 7.5 percent of the over 100,000 workers employed worldwide by the sprawling company—virtually all parts of the company will be affected. The largest job losses will be in the divisions that produce defense products.

According to CEO Wagner,

The Corporation is embarking on a sea of change that will produce a leaner, tougher-minded company capable of enduring the current recession, and seizing opportunities as they arise in the future. The harsh reality is that a shrinking military budget means fewer orders for the company's military marine equipment and sophisticated electronics.

The goal of the restructuring plan is to reduce costs by $1.2 billion a year by 1994 in order to improve the Company's financial performance. The Company has said that the layoffs would save $500 million a year; closing plants will add another $400 million by early 1993; and improvements in design, engineering and manufacturing will add an additional $500 million in projected savings.

Repercussions for Propco Employees

As part of the reorganization announcement by ATC, Propco was instructed to lay off 925 employees. According to corporate spokespeople, most of the reductions are being accomplished through severance and enhanced early retirement programs. The official statement released by Propco's public relations department is:

We understand the difficulties that our employees are under during this time of restructuring; however, it is in Propco's long-term interests to become a much leaner and more flexible organization. In order for our Company to compete effectively and efficiently, we must cut costs where possible. It is our understanding that the reorganization will be completed soon.

But while ATC executives emphasize the necessity for the layoffs and paint a positive picture of the Corporation's recent balance sheet performance, Propco employees appear to be much more pessimistic about this latest round of employee firings. Below are the comments of some of Propco's former and current employees who have witnessed, and experienced, the effects of the restructuring program.

Vincent S.

(Vincent is a White, 33-year-old Operations Center Manager at Propco. He received his MBA in Operations by attending school at night while working for the company. Vincent is married and is the father of newborn twins. He has been with the company for six years.)

Propco has been laying off people for close to two years now. Each new quarter we receive fewer Marine Systems orders. Unfortunately, this leads to another round of layoffs. It's not that our people don't know how to project orders. Look, the entire industry is suffering and our customers have had to cut back, most times at the last minute. They have to look out for their bottom line, just like we do.

It's frustrating. It's frustrating as hell. My men look to me for answers as to when this is all going to end, but I know little more than they do about future economic performance. Of course morale is very low. "Was the last layoff the last?" is the most unanswered question among the guys. Every time a new wave of layoffs comes around you can feel the tension. People barely speak to each other, and no one wants to speak to me. You can see the fear in people's eyes.

I'm scared too. I'm not really afraid of losing my job. I'm afraid that someone is going to take their anger out on me. Every time my boss calls a meeting I'm scared that I have to lay off more men. In December I had to lay off 50 people right after Christmas. I was told that would be the last of the reduction from my unit. But two weeks ago I was told to reduce my numbers by another 20 men. You have no idea how hard it is to tell a man who is old enough to be your father, that he's fired. It really is hard. Men have cried and begged for their jobs. Let me tell you, I don't sleep well at night when I have to do this. I don't park my car in the employee parking lot when I lay people off. Some of the manager's cars have been scratched or dented after they lay off people. Telling people who have worked for a company for 20 or 30 years that they are no longer needed is one of the hardest things I have had to do in my life. I hope this all ends soon.

These constant layoffs have been really hard on everyone here. At first the unions took a hard-line stance—an "us vs. them" mentality. But after the fourth round of layoffs they decided to cooperate in order to make the firm more competitive. They know that in the long run this is what's best. Because union leadership decided to cooperate, we were able to adopt many Japanese-style manufacturing models. This has not prevented layoffs, but it has resulted in a more accurate determination of the number of employees that should be dismissed.

The bottom line is that everyone wants Propco to remain competitive so that when things get better, corporate headquarters will keep Propco in Rhode Island.

The layoffs have caused the level of distrust between the hourly employees and senior management to increase a great deal. Hourlys think management is incapable of saving the company, is not making any sacrifices (for example they recently received bonuses), and sees them as process components instead of human beings. Senior management thinks that hourlys are incapable of understanding the market situation, are not helping to regain competitiveness, and are spoiled union babies. I'm sort of in the middle of all this since I'm not a part of senior management, and I'm not an hourly employee. I'm the guy that gets the job of actually laying off my workers.

Richard C.

(Richard is a White, 48-year-old Manager of Central Purchasing. He received his undergraduate degree in Finance from an Ivy League university. He is married and a father of three teenagers. Richard has been with the company for 27 years.)

I was laid off right before Christmas. I can honestly say that I had no idea whatsoever that I would be let go. I mean, I have been with Propco for 27 years. It's home to me, and the people there are my family. Or so I thought. I guess I got too complacent. You figure, "I'm part of management. I make $85,000 a year. I'm secure." Do you know that my boss wouldn't even look me in the eye when he told me? I really thought we were friends. We used to be a team in the company golf tournaments. I'm sure it was hard on him, but at least he still has his job.

At first they offered me an early retirement package last November. The package included a payment of $15,000 and, get this, three months of medical before my benefits would run out. At first I turned the package down, but my boss told me that if I didn't take it I would be fired anyway. Some choice.

I understand that the economy is in a recession, but you figure that if you put in as much time as I did with a company, nothing will ever happen. You'll retire and receive a good pension. Now I'm mailing out resumes and cover letters, something I never thought I would have to do again. Propco is a great company to work for; I loved it there. But apparently the feeling was not mutual. Do you know that the company did not give me any career counseling? At least the hourly workers get that.

What went wrong? Who knows? I guess the company screwed up. It's not my concern now. The only thing on my mind now is how to take care of my family. My wife works, but we need to have a second income. I made some connections with other firms in the industry while I was at Propco. Hopefully something comes through soon.

Carl G.

(Carl is a 35-year-old, African-American former screw propeller grinder. He was employed at Propco for 12 years. Carl has taken courses toward an undergraduate degree in Sociology from a local university. He is divorced.)

Yeah, I was a grinder at Propco for 12 years before the layoff. I made $15.22 an hour to grind metal off of a military screw forging. Sounds really hard, but it was just manual labor; a lot of lifting and hard work, but it was easy once you got used to it. I have to say, though, that most of the unit's grinders were Black. I used to hear some of the White union guys joking and calling our area "the plantation," saying what we did was "slave labor." They weren't lying. I was there for 12 years and I never could seem to get promoted out of that area. Most of the time, new Black guys were put in our area. Not to say that Propco has a lot of Black workers—they don't. That's a different story, though, but it seems strange to me that a company that is 15 minutes from Hartford and 50 minutes from New Haven has so few minorities in their plant.

Out of the 10 Blacks in my section, 4 have been laid off. You see, union people know when they will be laid off because its done by seniority. Those people with the most years don't have to worry. But since most of the Black guys are what they call "recent hires," they are the first to be fired. You know the old saying. That's the name of the game.

What was it like to be Black at Propco? Well, you never quite feel comfortable there. You feel like what you are, an outsider. The foreman watches you all the time. He's never as easy with you as he is with the White guys. He checks your time card. He calls you at home to make sure that's where you are, when you call in sick. When the rest of the guys go play golf, you're never invited. They just assume you don't know how to play. Or else they just don't want you around. When there's some kind of party, either you're not invited, or they invite you at the last minute. The White guys talk to you when they want to know how to do something. Otherwise, for the most part, they act like you're not there. There are some White guys who are cool; they try to get to know you. But for the most part, you are looked down at, even though they are doing the same kind of work.

The Black guys in my area were lucky, though, because we had each other. We laughed and talked and told stories. We did our own thing. We covered for each other, and helped out when someone fell behind. We had our own parties. We went out together. We helped each other.

Propco has diversity meetings all the time. They say they're trying to find ways to hire more minorities and women. I haven't seen any real progress. It seems more like talk to me. Sometimes I think that they only had the Blacks that they did there because of the government contracts. You see, whenever you do work for the government, you have to have a certain number of minorities. It could be that Propco only hired the minorities that it did because of that.

Don't get me wrong, Propco is a pretty good company to work for. You get health, dental, a savings plan, and free education. Even after the layoff my benefits will last for one year. Also, the union gave us job counseling and assistance. I received one week's pay for every year of employment as severance pay. But, there is no doubt that a lot of people in management are prejudiced. I used to hear jokes all the time about minorities. You know, sexual jokes, stupid jokes, that type of thing. Usually you try to ignore it. It's hard. I guess I'm lucky. I just found another job. Most everyone I know is still looking. Maybe things are getting better.

Samuel L.   *(Samuel is a White, 36-year-old foam machinist. He recently received a B.A. in Psychology from a local college by attending night school. He is married and has two children. Samuel was employed at Propco for 14 years.)*

I knew it was coming, but I prayed that the economy would get better before it was my time to get the pink slip. In a way it's a relief that it finally happened. Every time layoffs were announced, I couldn't sleep. I couldn't eat. I yelled at my family. I was very difficult to live with. The waiting got to be too much. Even being at work was hard. The guys walked around like someone had just died. It was real uneasy there. Guys who used to be friends, barely spoke to each other. I guess it was the tension. Everyone looked at each other like they were enemies. Like the next guy would take their jobs from them. It was really rough.

I was a foam machinist at Propco; I put a regional blade spar into a die machine and injected high pressure foam that forms an X-10 screw shape. Big deal. I doubt that I can find another job doing the same thing. Not that I would want to, but what else can I do? I have a degree, but what do you do with it? Psychology. What a useless degree unless you go back to school. I can't do that now. I guess I'm lucky since my wife makes a pretty good salary, and she can support the family until I can find another job.

I made good money at Propco—$15.35 an hour. But management sure as heck makes a lot more. And you don't see too many of them getting laid off. It's always the same. Management gets paid a lot of money to "manage," but the people who actually do the work get $15.00 an hour. Then when management messes up the company, they fire the people who work and keep the people who think. Does this make any sense to you? They could fire a couple of "thinkers" and save more money than if they fired 20 of us. But, hey, what do I know? I'm just an hourly.

Race relations at Propco? What about it? There were a few Black guys there not a whole lot though. I never had any problem with them. They were just like any of the other guys to me. I mean they worked hard. Everyone at Propco did. I heard a few guys telling race jokes. But they told other kinds of jokes too. You know, like jokes about Polish people, Italian people, women, sex. The people who told those jokes were jerks. I don't have a problem working with Black people. As long as the guy does his work, he's all right with me.

The Black guys sure did stick together. They ate lunch together. Clocked in and out together. I guess I understand. There just weren't that many of them. I'm sure I would be like that too. But you know, the Italian guys were sort of like that too. Strength in numbers I guess.

I feel sorry for all of us now. I know that the economy has been bad, but Allied Technologies is a rich company. It's huge. Something else could be done. They could work with the governor; maybe negotiate tax breaks. They could try lots of things. You're damn right I'm angry. I worked at that place for 14 years. And what do they do for me? They fire me to save themselves.

Steven H.

(Steven is a 38-year-old, African-American Division Manager at one of Allied Technologies Corporation's other operating units. Prior to his present position, he was assigned to corporate headquarters where he had frequent interaction with Propco managers. He has an engineering degree from an Ivy League university and advanced studies in business and Human Resources. He has been with the company for eight years. Steven is married.)

Out of over 3,000 people at Propco, there are only 81 Black salaried workers. When I say salaried, that includes clerks, buyers, and secretaries, as well as unit managers. Out of that 81, only 7 are actually managers of people. And after the next round of layoffs, I expect that number to drop. Black managers are an endangered species here at Propco, and in fact throughout ATC.

It's just a fact that Black salaried workers have a higher propensity of getting laid off. Propco's culture—like other ATC operating units—is one of institutional racism. For example, in one of their units there are 400 employees. Only 15 of those people are Black. That was last October. Now I understand that there is only one Black salaried employee. And he's there because somebody high up likes him.

The bottom line is that Black employees at Propco don't have a support network. There is a lot of nepotism there, so that when it comes time to lay off salaried workers, those who don't have real friends often find themselves on the unemployment line. Face it, people don't lay off their friends and family. This situation generally applies to salaried workers, since hourly workers are laid off based upon seniority.

To further exacerbate matters, it is difficult for Black employees to take additional training and education classes that would assist in making them more competitive. I am not saying that these individuals are not already highly qualified. Management does not tend to hire minorities unless they are superior achievers. It is just that it is essential for a manager's career to always look like he is trying to improve his leadership skills.

But then again even education is no safety net. Here is a classic example. There was a Black employee at Propco who had started as an hourly and had worked his way up to a position as a $40,000 a year manufacturing engineer. When his mentor left, he was demoted back to an hourly worker as a dispatcher. And this guy had an engineering degree. It goes without saying that he left Propco.

Is Propco consciously racist? I tend to think so. I can't tell you how many diversity meetings friends of mine have attended where someone from upper management would say, "we can't find qualified minority candidates to fill our positions." That whole argument is ridiculous. Propco participates in a program where minority college students are given summer internships at the company. They are also assigned a mentor from the management ranks. These kids are not dumb. Their grade point averages are in the 3.3 range. How many are with the company now? None. This is despite the fact that over 90 percent of the interns get superior ratings on their summer performance. I think this speaks for itself.

I believe that something has to be done to address the racist mentality around the entire corporation. I hate being the one who has to defend my race all of the time, but there are very few others that care. I'm doing what I can, but I can't fix the problem alone.

Do I see a future for myself here? ATC is doing great things. I think that if I hang in here long enough, I can make a difference. I want to help qualified minorities—not just Blacks—get into these large firms. ATC has a lot to offer employees. But if it gets too tough for me, I don't think I'll have a problem finding another position somewhere else.

Propco's Human Resource Policies

The ATC Human Resources Department has issued policy statements over time regarding layoffs, diversity, and minorities that the company indicates are the basis for its layoff decisions. All divisions have to rigorously adhere to these policies. All of them have been developed with the direct involvement and approval of the CEO, Joseph R. Wagner. Wagner has given numerous speeches stressing the importance of diversity in corporate life in general and ATC in particular. ATC donates considerable money to civil rights organizations and Wagner himself has received several humanitarian awards.

It is the position of Allied Technologies Corporation to hire qualified candidates regardless of race, creed, color, sex, or ethnic origin. We have an ongoing diversity program in place in which we hope to devise ways to introduce more minorities and women into our businesses. For the past two years the Company has participated in an internship program in which minority college students are given the opportunity to work in some of our business units during the summer. It is our hope that the students will learn from, and enjoy, their intern experience and consider working for ATC upon graduation.[1]

As far as industry standards are concerned, the Company is on an even keel with other firms of its size when it comes to the number of minority employees that it employs.

There is a concerted effort on the part of the executives at ATC to hire the best people for the job, and that is what we do.

In laying off union workers, we adhere to the union contract and lay them off in order of seniority.

Endnote

1. As of now, Propco does not have any of the former interns in its employ, although some have graduated from college.

BULLER | SCHULER

Managing Organizations and People

A Resource for Cases in Management, Organizational Behavior,
and Human Resource Management

Abstract

Acoma Pueblo may be the oldest continuously inhabited site in the continental U.S. Early visitors came in the 1930s and, in the 1980s, mainly due to the efforts of one visionary manager, the Acoma tribe slowly and conscientiously developed its visitor program to attract and educate people from throughout the world. What began as a modest and small business that could shut down its operation for tribal ceremonials is now a profitable and highly visible entity that must respond to customer demand. Existing in a fragile environment of place, people, and culture, the newly created Tribal Business Board and seasoned tourism program manager are learning to respond to the marketplace that is largely non-tribal and, at the same time, to preserve their heritage and traditional Pueblo tribal traditions, values, and practices. Acoma Pueblo's economy was relatively small and undeveloped until the mid-1980s. The fundamental management question for the tribe is how it can effectively enhance the tribal economy by developing its tourism program and some other businesses without compromising its cultural heritage and traditions. By utilizing modern management techniques, the tribe has an opportunity to enhance its economic viability and generate revenue that will help other business development activities.

The Business of Culture at Acoma Pueblo

Overview

The manager of the Acoma Pueblo Tourism Center is dedicated to educating non-native people about the Southwestern American Indians, especially the Acoma Pueblo Tribe. As the years pass, more and more visitors are attracted to Old Acoma, also known as "Sky City." The tour and center have become a successful business that is outgrowing the capacity of its facilities. The manager needs to address these issues with the traditional Tribal

■ This case was prepared by Regina Gilbert and Helen J. Muller, Anderson Schools of Management, University of New Mexico. The authors acknowledge the University of New Mexico departments for their support of this study. We appreciate the generous contributions of people associated with the Acoma Tourism Program towards this case study, especially Ms. Mary Tenorio. We extend our thanks to Evalena Boone, BBA, Chris Day, B.S. Candidate, and Anita Sanchez, MBA Candidate for their work on earlier phases of this case study. We are grateful to Asbjorn Osland for his constructive comments and suggestions.

1

Council members, who oversee the visitor's center for approval to expand the present center so it can accommodate the increase in tourism. Business development can benefit the Acoma Pueblo Tribe but not at the expense of its cultural traditions and values.

Acoma Pueblo

Acoma Pueblo is a federally recognized American Indian tribe in Cibola County, New Mexico. It is one of 19 Pueblo Indian nations in the state who continue to live within their own enriched traditional values known to them since the beginning of time. As an American Indian community, the Acoma people are proud of their history, heritage, and cultural values that have kept them unique in the face of Spanish and American colonists. The Acoma Pueblo people are a distinct tribe that has its own religion, culture, and language; they are divided into clans. Each of the tribal clans, 14 in all, has its particular spiritual significance. The Acoma people are known by their clan which is traced through the mother's side; the mother passes her clan designation to her children. This constitutes the matriarchal descent pattern that most Pueblo tribes follow.

Within the matriarchal tradition, women are responsible for the family and the home and do not enter sacred kivas where religious ceremonies are practiced. A woman is considered head of the household, has possession of the house, and hands down the ownership of the house to her youngest daughter. The youngest daughter is responsible for taking care of family members. If an Acoma man marries outside of the tribe, it is expected that he will move to his wife's location.

The language of the Acoma people is part of the Keresan tribal language and is shared with the people of Laguna Pueblo and some of the Rio Grande Pueblos. The Pueblo of Acoma is adjacent to the Pueblo of Laguna. Granted a tribe may live in close proximity to another tribe and some similar characteristics may exist, but there are no two American Indian tribes entirely alike.

Acoma Pueblo is only one federally recognized American Indian tribe out of 511 distinct tribes within the United States (see Tiller, 1996). There are an additional 200 or so unrecognized tribes that occupy various areas in the United States. Tribal people live in a variety of environments, either on or off the reservations that may occupy rural areas or cities. The Pueblo of Acoma has an interstate highway (I-40) cutting through its reservation. Fifteen miles to the west of Acoma is the town of Grants while to the east is the city of Albuquerque 56 miles away.

The Acoma Tribe has reservation land where a majority of the tribally enrolled members occupy their homes. Based on a 1995 census, approximately 6,091 people live on the reservation including both tribal and non-tribal individuals. Many of the people who live on the reservation commute to the surrounding urban areas for employment. Reservation land is also known as trust land, land held in trust by the federal government that is intended for tribal use. The reservation of Acoma Pueblo expands over 378,114 acres: the Tribe owns 377,794 acres and 320 acres are owned by individual tribal members.

Old Acoma is one of three villages on the Acoma reservation; the other two villages are Acomita and McCartys. Old Acoma is referred to as "Sky City" because of its significant location. Sky City is the center of attraction for tourists who come from miles around to view the spectacular site.

History of Old Acoma— "Sky City"

Old Acoma or Sky City is unique in its history. Archaeologists trace its occupation back to at least 1150 A.D. Sky City is still occupied by tribal elders who continue to live as they did many years ago. Currently, there are about 30 people in Sky City, only a handful of people. The Acoma Tribe preserves Sky City by not contaminating it with today's modern utilities, such as running water, sewer service, natural gas, and electricity. The people who live on the mesa top store their drinking water and replenish it daily, use lanterns at night, cook their food in wood stoves and their bread in ovens that are built outside the home, and have out-houses for facilities. Just being within the village, a visitor is set back into time and can experience a sense of peace and tranquillity.

Sky City acquired its name due to the site it occupies. The village of Old Acoma stands on a mesa top 365 feet above the surrounding valley of sparse, dry farmland with a mixture of pinon and juniper trees. Once on top of the mesa, you are able to see for miles in all directions. There is a beautiful view of Mount Taylor at over 11,000 feet in the distance and if you look down from the mesa you are able to see the fields of the villagers who grow watermelon, corn, and other native foods.

The village consists of 250 dwellings. Even though only a handful of people live at Sky City year round, other tribal members come back to the village during ceremonial events throughout the year. Many of the homes at Sky City are used during the ceremonies to feed family members, as a resting place for the young and old, and as a place where everyone can reunite as a family. American Indian cultures are very family oriented. For the people of Acoma, it is important to family members that they all return periodically to the Pueblo for their traditional ceremonies. During this time, all family members share the closeness and security which brings about happiness and joy to everyone.

The people of Acoma chose the location of Sky City for one reason. Acoma oral history tells the story about the beginning of time or "how we came to be at Acoma." In the Keresan language, Acoma is known as "*Hak'u*" which means a "place of readiness." Also in the Acoma native language, *Hak-u* means "to prepare." As the Acoma tradition tells it, the location of Acoma was actually prepared for the people. Orlando Antonio, a senior tour guide at Sky City, describes the story which Acoma oral history refers to as the creation story:

Before we evolved from our hole in the ground as whole, there was a religious leader who evolved first. What was he looking for? He was looking for the place that had been prepared for the Acoma people. Again Hak'u means prepared. So when he migrated south, every little hill side he came to he would yell out the word Hak'u . . . no response. Every butte he came to, Hak'u, nothing. Then he came to Enchanted Mesa, he yells out the word again, Hak'u. Guess what he probably heard? His echo. So the leader says to himself, okay, I have found the place that has been prepared for the Acoma people. Then I must return and let the Acoma people know. He returns and the evolution of the Acoma people begins.

For centuries, Enchanted Mesa (nearby to the Sky City mesa) served a band of Acoma ancestors as a dwelling, storehouse, and fortress.

The "new home" for the Acoma people at Enchanted Mesa stood 400 feet above the valley floor. A series of single-file handholds and steps cut into the towering rock provided access. Then, one day during a violent storm, part of the descent-pathway crumbled leaving a young girl with her grandmother trapped on the mesa top. Rather than starve, they leapt to their deaths. Upon hearing of this event, the tribal elders realized that they must move to a different mesa, one known as "Sky City," to reestablish their homes and continue to live their lives as Acoma people.

Many people considered Sky City an ideal site for protection from marauding enemies. Before settlers occupied the surrounding valley, nomadic American Indian tribes would raid the area for their livelihood, stealing food and supplies. During this time the Acoma Pueblo people farmed and raised many fruits and vegetables below Sky City. But times have changed. During the past 37 years, some people moved to nearby Acomita and McCartys to continue farming with irrigation readily available from the Rio San Jose river. However, there are still some Acoma people who continue the ancient tradition of dry land farming at Old Acoma.

History of Tourism at Sky City

The idea of being in the tourism business is new to the Pueblo of Acoma because it began with the people of Sky City in the beginning of the 1900s even though it wasn't realized as such. The enterprise that started out as touring an historical Pueblo village and seeing "real live" American Indians has become one of New Mexico's top five tourist spots attracting more than 115,000 visitors a year.

The tourism business at Sky City has a unique history and is connected to the San Esteban del Rey Mission which occupies the mesa top among the houses. The mission was begun in 1629 under the direction of Friar Juan Ramirez of Spain and was completed in 1640. Friar Juan Ramirez chose the people of Acoma for conversion to Christianity (Catholicism) because he had heard that they held the distinction of being the most rebellious of all the southwestern tribes. He was determined to save these rebels because he believed it was his work as a man of the church. Friar Juan Ramirez set out on the journey to Acoma alone. When he arrived there, warriors greeted him with arrows. The villagers feared any visitor with white skin because such previous encounters had resulted in war, bloodshed, and the loss of many people.

According to Acoma legend, Friar Juan Ramirez gained entry to Old Acoma because he saved an infant falling off the high edge as he approached the mesa to deliver his message of the church. The people of Old Acoma and the tribal leader considered the delivery of the child to its mother to be a miracle. Knowing how high their mesa was and seeing a man in a robe must have made the people of Acoma believe that the Friar, a white man, had special powers.

This event bestowed a special significance to Friar Juan Ramirez and allowed him to stay with the people of Acoma. Friar Juan Ramirez did not reveal until years later that the infant girl had fallen onto a ledge, was stunned, and he had simply picked her up. This "miracle" inspired the devotion of the Acoma people to Friar Ramirez and it helped to build San Esteban del Rey Mission. The establishment of the mission resulted from peace yet the Spaniards indentured the Acoma people to build it.

As time passed into the current century, the church caretakers needed financial assistance to maintain the mission and to preserve its significance. The manager says that there are records dating back to the 1930s showing the number of visitors at Sky City who made monetary donations to the mission to help with renovations. In those days, the mission caretakers' families served as tour guides and they told the history of the mission and of the Pueblo.

Hollywood motion pictures in those days (and even today) depicted Natives as savages. These images instilled the visitors' conceptions of American Indians' appearance and livelihood. The visitors who arrived during those times came from other missions and included curiosity seekers and historians. A rudimentary road that was built for a motion picture in the 1920s served as the only access route to the top of the high mesa. Most of the visitors had to park below the mesa and walk up the road to the top. Before that time, toeholds carved into the cliff functioned as the access route to the top. That depicts the beginning of a tourism activity at Sky City: visitors came to see the historic San Esteban del Rey Mission and made monetary donations for the restoration and preservation of the mission. The mission, moreover, is registered as a National Historic Landmark.

Another significant event helped boost the tourism program: This was the building of a paved road to the top of Sky City that was made possible by the Tribal government.

A Pueblo Government

The Acoma Tribal Council chose to retain its traditional tribal form of government (Tiller, 1996). In 1934, the United States government established the tribal government system under the Indian Reorganization Act (IRA), and tribes could choose a traditional or constitutional type government. Yet, Indian people did not have the right to vote in New Mexico state elections until 1948.

The U.S. federal government considers the tribes on the reservations to be quasi-sovereign, domestic, and dependent nations. Such sovereign rights include the power to determine their own form of government, to define conditions for membership in the nation, to administer justice and enforce laws, to tax, to regulate domestic relations of its members, and to regulate property use. Each tribal entity has its own governmental organization that usually opts for a constitution and council that oversees tribal businesses, finances, programs, and policies. Because the tribes are inherently sovereign, individual states may not exercise authority over them unless authorized by Congress.

Because sovereignty means the power or authority to govern, and because tribes are sovereign, they must be allowed to choose the manner and form by which they will govern. Many Native Nations chose to adopt constitutional government models similar to that of the United States. Others, like Acoma Pueblo, chose to retain their traditional form of governance. Under traditional forms, religious leaders (also known as *caciques*) or tribal chiefs maintain the authority to make decisions on behalf of their tribe. The United States recognized this type of government in treaty agreements with the various tribes. The

Supreme Court decreed that American tribes are not required to function under a "normal" constitutional government if they so chose. Therefore, the Pueblo of Acoma could select their traditional form of government with one particular clan having responsibility for appointing the 12 Tribal Council members and officers of the Pueblo (Tiller, 1996).

Economic Growth in Tourism

The Acoma Tribal Council members began to see an opportunity for tribal economic development by focusing on the tourism trade that the mission caretakers had managed. They knew the mission still received donations from visitors. During the 1960s to the mid-1980s, the Tribal Council formalized the tourism business. The Council, as a traditional government, looked to the tribal elders for wisdom, took traditions and customs as decision-making tools, and progressed by abiding to traditional Pueblo religion and values.

Within a few years, the Tribal Council constructed a dwelling at the Sky City entrance for use as a "guide office." Visitors would pay a small fee here to be guided within the village. After years of operation, however, the office could not handle the influx of visitors because Sky City had limited parking facilities.

After deliberating the situation, the Council agreed to use some land at the base of Old Acoma to build a new visitor's center that would be a mandatory stop and a starting point for the Sky City tour. The inclusion of modern utilities added to the relatively large construction costs of the center. Since Sky City had no electricity, it had to be brought in from the village of Acomita, 11 miles away. With construction plans in hand, they began to install water and sewer at the new visitor's center. Utilities near the tourist center went underground to preserve the beauty of the land as it has been seen for centuries. Now, as you travel to Sky City you do not see electrical poles.

After installation of the utilities' infrastructure, construction began on the visitor's center building and parking facilities. The new center could not have been built without financial support from the federally sponsored Economic Development Administration (EDA) that assisted economic development on American Indian reservations. The Tribal government's proposal to EDA for the tourism facility was a success. In 1978, the Pueblo of Acoma Tourist Visitor's Program officially opened its doors at the new center.

The new tourism center had a snack bar and gift shop at the same counter. The snack bar sold a few items of food including candy and drinks. The gift shop sold postcards, Acoma pottery, T-shirts, and other small items. Even though a restroom existed, both the visitors and the employees had to share it. A six-passenger van transported the visitors up to Sky City from the beginning when the center first opened its doors.

Initially, the visitor's center had a handful of employees, and visitors paid a reasonable fee for the tour. At this time, no formal structure to the tour existed. Visitors were shuttled to the mesa top and guided through the village. They asked many questions as they went from site to site: how the people at Sky City cook their food, where they get their drinking water, and why the people chose to live a life style without any utilities. More specific questions focused on the Acoma people: how is it possible to construct the earthen dwellings, what is a *kiva* and what is its significance, and what religion do the people practice? The tour guides gave out information based on their own personal knowledge from stories that had been passed on to them as young children. They answered questions as best they could about the Acoma people and their long history.

Acoma people are well known for their unique pottery and their hard work to create the beautiful designs of parrots and detailed art work with different designs that represent the rain, the sun, and the other elements of the Earth. The residents of Sky City saw an opportunity to make some money from the visitors who came on the tour. The women set up a stand in front of their houses and displayed their pottery. Visitors are fascinated by the beauty of the intricate pottery designs, and their purchases have helped these "works of art" to become famous. The hard work put into the visitor's center by the Tribal Council spoke for itself. The revenue from the tourists, who stood in awe of the wondrous ancient site, enabled the Tribe and the center to break ground into something big.

Economic development through tourism is a management strategy to foster economic independence. Developing an ancestral site as a tourism attraction must be balanced with business concepts involving fiscal accountability, on the one hand, and with preserving the delicate cultural traditions and harmony of the Pueblo people on the other hand. While Native people throughout the world share many of the same challenges, and certain Native traditions and values may appear to be similar, they do not share the same culture. The preservation of the Sky City historical site, its location and spirituality, and its peacefulness are features that attract the visitors from all over the world to the "place of readiness" (see Appendix A).

The Manager's Role

It was not until 1986 that Mary Tenorio became involved with the Acoma Tourism Center. A social worker by profession, Ms. Tenorio came to work for the tourism center as a retreat from her previous job. She had intended to stay with the center for a year to recover from job burn-out. The Acoma Tribal Council granted her job request and she became the ninth permanent staff member. During her first year, Ms. Tenorio worked as a cashier and assisted the manager to develop forms for a better accountability system.

From then on, Ms. Tenorio developed other forms to account for inventory, for record-keeping of tour fees, where visitors traveled from, and for inventory of merchandise. Because the forms contained detailed information, she believed that any person should be able to look at a particular sheet at the end of the day and review the information about how many people took the tour. Ms. Tenorio played a major role in transforming the tourism center into a business entity.

As the years went by, Ms. Tenorio continued to work at the tourism center. She enjoyed her job and continued developing the tourism center to make work more efficient. She did not entertain any thoughts about returning to her old profession because she enjoyed the challenges in the tourism industry. Having a little business background from classes she took at a local community college, she continued to learn the basic concepts of business in her day-to-day experience.

A few of her successes in the early years of her work at Acoma included the approval by the Acoma Tribal Council of a cultural and historical "script" for use by all tour guides. She redesigned brochures and promoted the Sky City tours through advertising. With much motivation and devotion to her job, she traveled to different areas around the state and requested that the colorful brochures be inserted into conference packets. She also distributed brochures to local business outlets that promoted tourism information. In sum, she put much hard work and effort into developing the Acoma tourism program.

As Ms. Tenorio continued to work on promoting the tourism center in the early 1990s, she realized that the existing building could not handle the increasing inflow of tourists. She decided to request funds from the Tribal Council to expand the facility. As part of this expansion request, she included a plan to expand the restroom as there was only one facility for everyone.

She realized that dealing with the members of the Tribal Council would require hard work. The traditional form of Pueblo government is associated, for the most part, with cultures characterized by reliance on a council of elders, highly valued communal and kinship bonds, and decision making through consensus building. These different frameworks of tribal cultural norms and contemporary business organizations introduced an important organizational dynamic for tourism development (see Appendix B for comparisons between Anglo business-oriented and traditional Pueblo cultural patterns).

She learned how to formally address the Council and, at the same time, to talk professionally in her native tongue, and to show her respect to the Councilmen. Along these lines, she made a considerable effort to advocate for the effective protection of the community's interests as it embarked upon increasing its business participation in the business framework of the tourism industry.

Because the Tribal Council members recognized Ms. Tenorio's potential and her capabilities, they grew to respect her as a professional business woman. Soon, she was promoted to the position of director of the visitor's center. In this new position, Ms. Tenorio's responsibility expanded. Due to the respect bestowed by the Tribal Council, she developed more confidence in her working relationships.

Ms. Tenorio wanted to be more professional in her approach to management and, at the same time, she felt it important to honor traditional Pueblo customs. Thus, she needed to redefine her method of working with the Council when she had to request changes for the visitor's center. She eventually developed a strategy that reflected a "win-win" situation for both the Pueblo and the program. People were inspired by the decision to make improvements to the visitor's center.

Although Mary Tenorio's story may now seem like a success, she did go through a challenging learning period to gain the Council members' respect and in learning to effectively process her suggestions. As a result she says: "I have developed 'thick skin,' which allows me to handle any situation that may come my way in the future."

Development of the Business Board

A Business Board was established in 1997 and reports to the Tribal Council. The purpose of the Board is to place all of the Tribe's economic development under the direction of the Business Board instead of the Tribal Council. This allows the Tribal Council to concentrate on other policy and administrative matters while still maintaining oversight of business development on the reservation. Other tribes follow this practice.

Several years ago, the Tribal Council conducted a formal assessment of all the business activities of the tribe. The committee with this charge realized the need to create a group of business professionals who understood the concepts of managing economic development. It recognized, furthermore, that a substantive difference between business affairs and traditional tribal governmental affairs exists. With a casino now under the Tribe's operation, an additional reason for the new Board became apparent. The State Indian Gaming Regulatory Commission had advised on the separation for business on one side and governmental affairs on the other.

Before the Business Board existed, a tribal official oversaw the tourism center and found this to be a difficult task because there were so many different matters to attend to that made it hard to have a person available during working hours. Now, the visitor's center administrative staff has a formal chain of command to follow with ready access to an office and person to whom they can report. Indirectly, the tourism program is still under the Tribal Council because it represents the people.

One of the many advantages for the five new members of the Business Board is that business activities are now separated from tribal politics. Work on economic development issues have a quicker turnaround time. Another advantage is that appointments are staggered in three-year terms. Consistency can be maintained by the Board with regard to the business functions that must operate in a professional manner.

The Council appoints the Business Board members. Three Acoma tribal members and two non-tribal members, one of whom is non-Indian currently serve on the Board. Of the two non-tribal board members, one is an attorney from Albuquerque and the other is married to an Acoma family member. The Board has a charter with by-laws; it makes recommendations to the Governor concerning business opportunities from "outside" corporations as well as local tribal entrepreneurs. Currently, the Business Board has eight business operations under its direction. There is a need for additional staff. The President of the Board is a full-time employee of the Council. The other Board members serve on a voluntary basis. Support staff is provided by the Acoma Tribal Administration.

The Tourism Program Today

Acoma Pueblo draws thousands of visitors every month of the year. The tourism center now houses the admissions office, a small restaurant, a gift shop, and a museum. The admissions office handles the ticket sales for the tours and the permits for still-cameras only. The restaurant's menu offers both Anglo-American and traditional Pueblo dishes as well as snack-bar type items. The gift shop sells merchandise such as Acoma Pueblo pottery, jewelry, T-shirts, posters, and postcards. The hand-crafted items are bought directly from local Natives who guarantee the authenticity of their work. Commercial items are usually purchased from "outside" businesses. The center's museum, with its "1,000 Years of Clay" exhibit, depicts the history and customs of the early inhabitants of Acoma. A comfortable bus takes visitors up to the mesa top.

The guided tour of Sky City lasts approximately one hour and involves a one-mile walk. As people become more aware of the history of the Americas, their curiosity deepens about American Indian people. This is apparent at Acoma: visitors continue to be fascinated by its rich culture and historical significance. For example, they learn that Acoma is one of the oldest continuously inhabited villages in North America, and that, in 1599, a famous battle over religious freedom was fought between Conquistadors and the Acoma people. Having an opportunity to experience and learn about another culture is the very origin of why people visit Sky City.

The essence of the tourism program is to teach the world about the Acoma Pueblo people. There are individuals who still believe that Natives wear buck skins, beads, and feathers. They believe, furthermore, that American Indian people live in desolated areas; have tipis for homes; have no formal education; and that Native men are either warriors, alcoholics, or are uncivilized. These common misconceptions of Native people are corrected by the patient Acoma Pueblo tour guides during the educational tour at Sky City.

According to the records kept by the center, the top 10 states of annual visitor origin are: California, Colorado, Florida, Illinois, Massachusetts, New York, Ohio, Pennsylvania, Tennessee, and Texas. Visitors come from every state in the U.S. and from around the world: Australia, Canada, England, Germany, Holland, Italy, Sweden, and Switzerland to name a few. With this in mind, the visitor's center is planning to market their program to people in other countries. The Acoma Tourism Center is developing a web site as a marketing tool in the future. With the overwhelming influx of tourists, once again, the center has outgrown its existing facilities.

The number of visitors fluctuates during the year. The busiest time is from May through October. Tour companies, both large and small and both local and national, bring buses filled with customers; public schools bring children on field trips. And the various events in surrounding cities, such as the Albuquerque International Balloon Fiesta and the Gallup Inter-tribal Indian Ceremonial, draw visitors to Acoma. The slowest time of the year is November through April when the cold winter months causes the drop in visitors. Although Sky City is open year round, the Tribe closes the facilities a few times a year in observance of its religious ceremonies. This is a point of discussion by managers and Business Board members because visitors travel for miles to visit Sky City.

The tourism center has 6 management positions with 27 permanent employees. During the summer months, there are 50 to 55 employees all of whom are members of the Acoma Pueblo tribe. The center is organized into departments: security, facility maintenance, gifts, admissions, kitchen, and administration. Non-management personnel include: tour guides, vendor-guides, bus drivers, security guards, custodians, sales clerks, cashiers, and cooks.

Permanent and part-time staff in the areas of hospitality and customer service as well as some other areas participate in training programs. Some of the training contractors include: 1) Fred Pryor Seminars, 2) Marriott, 3) U.S. Forestry Department, and 4) New Mexico Department of Tourism. Ms. Tenorio stresses the importance of incorporating ethical values and practicing professional manners along with relying on traditional values as a framework in staff training activities. The articulation of traditional Pueblo values are critical for motivating employees and these are conveyed by stressing the importance of Acoma history and the significance of the staff's role in portraying Acoma's history to visitors.

Staff meetings are positively oriented to correct any misunderstandings or problems staff may encounter while in the presence of non-tribal visitors who may convey negative feelings or stereotypes towards the Acoma people and its particular cultural traditions. All staff members receive training to become experts on the history of Acoma. No one is to say the three deadly words: "I don't know." The culturally-based attractions and the hospitality of the destination tour-hosts serve to empower the Acoma people. The manner in which the Acoma Pueblo hosts interact with visitors is a critical determinant of the travel experiences and resulting satisfaction of guests. Visitors upon returning home can influence others to visit the Pueblo.

A substantial amount of revenue is brought into the Acoma tourism business. It is estimated that over $1 million is generated on a yearly basis. This revenue is used for operating costs and the remaining profits go into the "general tribal account." At Acoma Pueblo, the strategies and projects that are most likely to lead to tribal financial success must be based on community control rather than on individual enterprise. Funds generated by tribal enterprises go directly into the community to help with water lines, road maintenance, and community centers used by the elderly and youth. The tourism center, furthermore, is establishing scholarships and internships for employees who are seeking higher education. Acoma Pueblo tradition means that the Tribe must first be able to take care of its own people before it can contribute to others.

The spread of tourism is driven, in part, by a perpetual search for new destinations and, in part, by an increasing interest in and marketing of things natural or unspoiled. Acoma Pueblo offers a natural beauty that is unspoiled. The Acoma Tourism program gives a clear picture of how Acoma Pueblo was many years ago and shows how, over the centuries, it resisted outside Euro-American influences that sought to change its culture and traditions.

Appendix A

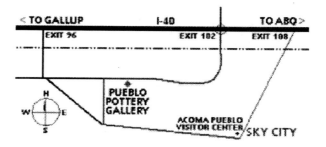

Source: Map courtesy of Wingspread Guides of New Mexico. Picture provided by http://gopher.nara.gov/exhall/originals/ acoma.html. "National Archives, Still Picture Branch, Records of the National Park Service." Photograph courtesy of National Archives, Ansel Adams (Photo Number 79-AAA-1).

Appendix B   **Traditional Acoma Pueblo Tribal and Anglo-American Cultural Patterns**

Category	Acoma Pueblo	Anglo
Interaction	Communication is face-to-face and verbal; consensus-oriented and status conscious.	Communication is written and spoken. Differences of opinion are encouraged as is competition.
Association	Family organization based on *clan*; matriarchal in origin; land is held by youngest daughter.	Family organization based on nuclear family. Land is individually owned.
Authority	Ascribed authority—spiritual leaders have significant power; today tribal government is based on traditional appointed system.	Secular authority, achieved status, U.S. federal system of government with elected representation.
Work	Originally agrarian based; "work" is part of life activity and may be subordinated to other activities such as traditional religious ceremonies.	Industrialized economy; technical orientation; work holds high priority in life; people value money and material goods.
Temporality	Present-oriented. Time measured by the season or task to be accomplished (cyclic-oriented).	Time measured by minutes and hours and is extremely important; time is lineally-oriented.
Learning	Teaching is verbal; learning is by mimic and rote; instructors are respected elders.	Teaching is multifaceted— emphasis is on practical & applied. Teachers have college degrees.
Spirituality	Religion is an integral part of life in general and in everyday life; religion pervades all activities.	Religion and work are separate entities and is so stated in the Constitution.
Natural Resources	Adapts and respects the environment. People and nature are integrated and inseparable.	Seeks to control and exploit the environment. People are separate from nature.

Sources: Acoma Pueblo material is adapted from Muller (1998), Winfield (1995), Stewart & Bennett (1991), and the members of the American Indian Business Association, NM; Anglo material is adapted from Harris & Moran (1991) and Stewart & Bennett (1991).

BULLER | SCHULER

Managing Organizations and People

A Resource for Cases in Management, Organizational Behavior,
and Human Resource Management

Abstract

Allan Hill is an American HR consultant hired by a Latin American company (*Staffing, Inc.*) specializing in personnel recruitment and selection. Allan was hired to help *Staffing* improve the processes and procedures they implement when making recommendations regarding personnel searches ranging from entry-level employees to high-level executives. The key objective of this case is to illustrate fundamental cross-cultural differences in making personnel selection decisions. While the American consultant was concerned about identifying job-related KSAs, *Euro-Latin Bank's* VP for HR suggested attributes related to the candidates physical appearance, sex, and age. Although equal employment opportunity (EEO) laws exist in most Latin American countries, these laws are rarely enforced.

Personnel Selection Procedures in Latin America

The following case is based on a true story. Names have been changed to protect the identity of those involved.

Allan Hill is an American Human Resources consultant hired by a Latin American company (*Staffing, Inc.*) specializing in personnel recruitment and selection. Allan was hired to help *Staffing* improve the processes and procedures they implement when making recommendations regarding personnel searches ranging from entry-level employees to high-level executives.

At the time when Allan was hired, selection decision-making processes conducted at *Staffing* were mostly subjective. For instance, no standardized tests were in use and interviews were unstructured and conducted by a single interviewer. In addition, there were no procedures in place to assess the effectiveness of *Staffing's* hiring recommendations. In other words, for those hired, there were no follow-ups to assess how their performance compared to those hired based on other recruitment firms' recommendations.

Allan's suggestions included the use of tests to assess knowledge, skills, and abilities (KSAs) needed for specific jobs, and the use of structured interviews. Allan also

■ Herman Aguinis, University of Colorado at Denver

recommended telephone interviews with *Staffing's* clients to collect information regarding performance levels of employees hired based on *Staffing's* recommendations.

Allan was successful at making the selection process more objective, standardized, based on KSAs required by the various positions, and fair. *Staffing* was doing very well and its clients were very happy with the changes in selection procedures and follow-up evaluation methods.

One of *Staffing's* largest clients, a European bank's subsidiary in this Latin American country (*Euro-Latin Bank*), made a request for "10 people to occupy teller positions." Based on this request, ads were published in several local newspapers and over 400 applications were received. *Staffing* screened out about 50 percent of these applicants based on various reasons (e.g., no experience, no minimum educational qualifications). Those remaining in the pool of applicants were administered a basic math and verbal skills test as well as a structured interview. Based on test and interview results, *Staffing* referred 30 finalists to be interviewed by *Euro-Latin Bank's* HR department.

A few days later, *Staffing* received a call from *Euro-Latin Bank's* Vice President for HR. He was very upset and disappointed with *Staffing's* recommendations. He said, "Teller positions are critical for our business and we cannot afford to have the kind of people you recommended doing the job." When asked what was the problem with the candidates recommended, he said, "I want you to send me well-qualified candidates, and by this I mean blond women who are at least 1 meter 65 centimeters tall and between the ages of 22 and 29 years."

The following questions can be used to generate group discussion:

1. Assume you are *Staffing, Inc.'s* CEO. What do you do? What are the factors you consider in making your decision regarding how to respond to the request?
2. Assume you are Allan Hill. What do you do? What are the factors you consider in making your decision regarding how to respond to the request?

Module 7

Motivation and Performance

Cases Outline

Managing Organizations and People

A Resource for Cases in Management, Organizational Behavior, and Human Resource Management

Abstract

Fred Maiorino had been one of Schering-Plough's top sales representatives, but he was now 63 years old and had refused his company's "early out" package. Early in his career, he settled in his sales territory of Southern New Jersey, which included its capital of Trenton, while making a good living and winning many performance prizes. More recently, however, under the guidance of the sales district's new sales manager, Jim Reed, a new personnel evaluation system has determined that Fred's performance has slipped badly. Jim tries to help Fred but to little effect. The breaking point between the two comes when Jim discovers that Fred has been submitting false activity reports over time spent making his rounds of doctors' offices and pharmacies.

Reed puts him on a six-month probation while stating specific sales goals that must be met. At the end of the probationary period, Fred had failed to attain the marketshare gains set for him. Fred was given another six-month probation to give him the benefit of the doubt, given his long service with Schering-Plough, but he failed again. Later, he was publicly fired in a restaurant he frequented with Reed and his company car and sales materials were confiscated.

Suffering hurt feelings, and feeling that he had been fired because of his age, Fred filed an age discrimination suit against his former employer. During the trial, it was found that the marketshare increase system for evaluating sales representatives favored the company's new, young sales reps while discriminating against its more senior ones. After eight days of testimony, the jury made a judgment of $8.44 million against Schering-Plough—the largest award in New Jersey's history.

How to Motivate Fred Maiorino?

After working for 35 years as one of Schering-Plough's top salespeople, Fred Maiorino stood in his suburban home's driveway on July 15, 1991 without a job, his car, or his pride. Just minutes before, he had been fired by his boss Jim Reed over coffee in Mastori's Diner and Restaurant in Bordentown, New Jersey. Reed had simply handed Fred a dismissal letter stating he was being fired for not meeting company sales goals, excessive tardiness, failing to call on key physicians, and ignoring suggestions for improving his performance. After the firing, Fred was followed to his home eight miles away where Jim stripped Fred of his company car and sales literature. The following month, Maiorino's place was filled by Eric Adeson, a new 24-year-old hire.

Maiorino had once been a top salesperson for Schering. Why did Fred's career turn out this way? Management says it tried hard to help Fred realize the company's sales goals. Despite Schering-Plough's motivational efforts, however, Fred was now without income and a job although he said he had "told Reed I planned to work till I was seventy."

Fred experienced great personal loss and pain because of the firing and how it had been handled. He said his "Life had been ruined." Furthermore, Fred believed his age was the true reason for the firing and he thought Schering had created an evaluation and motivation system that was prejudiced against its senior sales representatives.

Feeling he had grounds for a lawsuit and wanting back his job, Maiorino contacted the law firm of Barry & McMoran of Newark, New Jersey, in late July 1991. Fred's lawyers filed a thirteen-count complaint in April 1992, asserting, among other things, that Schering violated New Jersey law against age discrimination. See Appendix A for a summary of Fred Maiorino's claims.

After an unsuccessful attempt to settle out of court for $750,000, Fred's lawyers prepared for trial. They gathered evidence for two and one-half years and met Schering-Plough in court in mid-October 1994. After eight days of testimony and arguments, the trial's jury found in favor of Fred Maiorino, resulting in New Jersey's largest age discrimination award—a judgment of $8.44 million.

Fred's Sales Career at Schering-Plough

Fred Maiorino joined Schering-Plough on March 26, 1956 as a 28-year-old college graduate. He began working his way up the sales force ladder through a series of successful assignments, primarily in the areas of eastern Pennsylvania and western New Jersey. On January 1, 1984, Fred was assigned to the newly-created South Jersey Sales district which specialized in promoting Schering's asthmatics products.

He then made his home in the Trenton, New Jersey, suburb of Hamilton Square and, over a thirty-year period, raised a family of five while becoming an institution as a drug salesman. Gerald Novik, a Bordentown, New Jersey, physician told how Fred "knew all the secretaries, all the nurses and he could get in, do his business and get out in minutes, while other sales reps would be sitting in the waiting room for hours." Dr. Loren Southern, a Princeton, New Jersey, allergist also attested to Fred's skills and stature in the medical community. "Fred was very effective [and] both knew what he was talking about and was a pleasure to deal with. If you needed anything, drug samples or information on side-effects, Fred would get it for you like that." Maiorino produced results for Schering-Plough as well as garnering a good living and company recognition and performance awards. By 1986, he was earning almost $40,000 a year plus about $10,000 annually in commissions, and he had been a member of Schering's Diamond 110 Club six times, an award given to those selling at least 110% of their annual sales quota. In early 1987, he was the top-ranked representative of the nine working in his district. This ranking earned him a weekend with his wife Cathy at a local resort along with pocket money of $250 and ultimately recognition as the company's representative of the year.

Fred's honors and glad tidings did not occur in a static organizational climate given the drug industry's competitive nature. Numerous personnel shifts and sales incentive changes were implemented in Schering-Plough's sales divisions from time to time, and in September 1987, Fred got James A. Reed as his new boss. Despite being top-ranked in his district in mid-1988, Reed gave Fred his lowest ever half-year performance evaluation of "Good." This evaluation was lower than any given to the district's other reps, all of whom were at least twenty years younger. Based on superior evaluations of "Very Good" and "Outstanding," their salaries increased about 12.7% while Fred's increased only 5%.

Schering-Plough

The Schering-Plough Corporation of Madison, New Jersey, came about through the 1971 merging of the Schering Company, a German firm created in 1928, and Plough of Memphis, Tennessee. During World War II, Schering's American assets had been seized and placed under a government-appointed director. When the war ended, the company's research efforts developed a number of drugs including Chlor-Trimeton, one of the first antihistamines, and the cold medicine Coricidin.

After its merger with Plough, Schering extended its product line to such cosmetics and items as Coppertone and Di-GeL. The antifungal Lotrimin AF was introduced in 1975, Drixoral began over-the-counter (OTC) cold remedy sales in 1982, and the anti-asthmatics Vanceril and Proventil began their respective sales in 1976 and 1981. Consumer products acquisitions were also made in the late 1970s and 1980s. These included Scholl foot-care products in 1979 and Cooper Companies in the eye-care field in 1988. In 1990, Schering-Plough sold its Maybelline cosmetics operation to Playtex, while obtaining in the same year FDA approval to sell Gyne-Lotrimin as a nonprescription treatment for yeast infections.

The company usually employs about 500 sales representatives who are assigned territories in which they manage all sales activities. Sales managers report to a district manager who supervises from 9 to 12 territories. These districts, in turn, are managed by regional sales managers. Over the course of Fred's career, Schering increased its American regions from eight to nine. The number of territories assigned to a district has frequently increased and decreased, and whole regions have either been disbanded or reformulated due to shifts in the population. Information on Schering-Plough's company performance during Fred Maiorino's last employment years is in Table 1. Figure 1 is a partial organization chart covering Schering's sales when Fred was fired.

Fred Maiorino specialized in detailing Schering's asthma products. Asthma, the industrialized world's most common chronic disease, is incurable and causes more than 5,000 deaths a year in the United States. About 4–6% of America's adult population and 20% of its children suffer from asthma. This group of about 12 million spends $6 billion annually for medicines that address the illness's symptoms. Asthmatics experience coughing, chest tightness, wheezing, and shortness of breath when they are suffering an attack. When under an acute attack, victims gasp for air and feel like they are drowning.

As the world's most commonly prescribed drug class, bronchodialators are prescribed which act to relax the bronchial passages' constricted muscles. These bronchodialators are self-administered and take many forms including suppositories, injections, and pills. The most popular usage is as an inhalant in the configuration of a puffer with the most effective bronchodialators being beta-2 agonists. These drugs are marketed by various companies under the brand names Brethaire, Maxair, Proventil, and Ventolin. As a group, bronchodialator sales rose 30% from 1983 to 1990.

In the early 1990s, Schering narrowly led this market's segment. Its sales on Proventil surged 36% to $79 million from 1985–1986 and another 56% from 1988 to 1989. Proventil sales in 1989 were over $135 million. Schering has also developed an improved inhalation device for the basic product and introduced sustained-release Proventil Repetabs in August 1986, to support Proventil's growth after it lost its patent protection in December 1989. Of the four brands available, over 95% of all sales have been equally divided between Proventil and Glaxo's Ventolin.

Schering-Plough and Glaxo also dominate the moderate asthma-sufferer market anti-inflammatory medication, in the form of inhaled corticosteroids and is most often prescribed and sold under such brand names as Aerobid, Azmacort, Beclovent, and Vanceril. Schering's Vanceril and Glaxo's Beclovent hold almost equal market shares. The sales of inhaled corticosteroids rose about 3% from 1983 to 1990.

TABLE 1
Selected Company Information

Company Information	1987	1988	1989	1990	1991
Sales ($000,000)	2,699.0	2,969.0	3,158.0	3,323.0	3,616.0
Net Income ($000,000)	316.0	390.0	471.0	565.0	646.0
Income Percent of Sales	11.7%	13.1%	14.9%	17.0%	17.9%
Earnings per Share	$1.37	$1.74	$2.09	$2.50	$3.01
Dividends per Share	$0.51	$0.70	$0.89	$1.07	$1.27
Employees	21,700	22,400	21,300	19,700	20,200

Source: "Schering-Plough Corporation," *Hoover's Company Profile Database*. 1995. Austin, TX. The Reference Press.

**FIGURE 1
Partial 1992
Schering-Plough
Sales Organization**

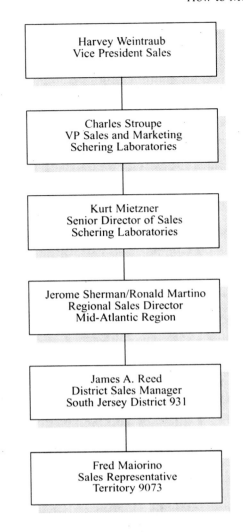

**Jim Reed
Tries to Turn
Fred Around**

In February 1987, Jim Reed, a veteran Schering manager in his sixties, was named general sales manager in charge of Fred Maiorino's South Jersey sales district—a district whose territories would vary from 9 to 12 over the next few years. As shown in Figure 2, the district's major city is the state capitol of Trenton, and Fred's sales territory contained this city and its surrounding Mercer County. Table 2 presents data on factors related to health care product sales applied to Fred's territory as well as in New Jersey and the United States.

When Reed first came to the district, he turned to Fred for help and leadership in increasing Schering's sales. Maiorino recalls being told, "You're one of the senior men here. I'll need your help." At this time, Reed also implemented a new system for measuring sales representative performance that had been created by Schering in mid-1987. Instead of the firm's usual sales quota system, salesmen were now rated by two basically different measures—one which was quantitatively objective and the other which employed critical incidents of effective and ineffective sales rep actions as behavioral benchmarks.

The quantitative component was based on ranked by-product market share gains. These were reported in the company's semi-annual Therapeutic Class Report (TCR). The critical incident component was a compilation of behaviors witnessed by the district sales manager when making joint calls with his sales reps. Tables 3 and 4 present Fred's first Pharmaceutical Sales Representative (PSR) evaluation under the new system. A "V" stands for "Very Good" where "Results clearly exceed most position requirements. Performance is of a high quality and is achieved on a consistent basis." A "G" stands for

FIGURE 2
New Jersey and the South Jersey Sales District

Trenton

TABLE 2
Health Care Market Attractiveness Factors (Averages for 1988–1990)

Attractiveness Factor	Trenton Metro	New Jersey	United States
Median age	34.4	34.8	33.7
Population per square mile	1,432.0	992.1	70.5
Household growth	-0.8%	-0.9/0	0.2%
Household buying income	$39,766.00	$36,404.00	$22,944.00
Annual household buying power Growth	8.2%	5.8%	8.1%
Annual retail sales growth	2.0%	3.6%	5.2%
Drugstore sales/Retail sales	3.1%	2.9%	3.6%
Annual drugstore sales growth	-1.2%	4.6%	4.9%
Drugstore sales per household	$694.10	$632.12	$676.81

Source: Annual surveys of buying power, *Sales & Marketing Management*, August issues 1988–1990.

"Good" where the sales rep has demonstrated "Competent and dependable level of performance. Meets all performance standards of the job." Figure 3 cites the company's rationale and use of its behaviorally anchored rating scales (BARS).

In mid-1989, Reed was reviewing Schering's national sales figures and noted Fred's sales on Proventil ranked him 469th in a national sales force of about 500 representatives. While his sales were much better on other drugs, Jim focused on Proventil and Fred's poor performance against Cibaei's Breathine. Reed wrote a July memo to Fred saying in part that his performance was "well below what you are capable of" and encouraged him to do better. He concluded, "Fred, the first four months of 1989 were not good ones—but they are now history."

In addition to offering written encouragement, Reed started coaching Fred and provided him with medical journals so he could improve his sales pitches. Reed also increased the number of sales calls he made with him and suggested that he set realistic goals for himself on a quarterly, product-by-product basis. In response to this latter suggestion, Fred scrawled an early May 1989, memo to Reed stating "I have opted not to do this at this time, but would like to make the following statement instead: I have always, during my long career with Schering, strived to do the best that I can do, be the best that I can be, and that is all anyone can expect of me. Of course, this is nothing new as I will, as in the past, continue to do the same."

On October 10, 1989, Reed's confidence in Fred broke down completely. At about 10:30 a.m. Jim drove through Fred's neighborhood, after conducting an interview with a job candidate in the area, and saw his White Dodge in his driveway although company

TABLE 3
Fred Maiorino's
Objective Evaluation
Under Schering's
New System

| | **PSR Performance Evaluation**
Second Half 1987
Region: 08—District: 931—Territory: 9073 | | | | | |
| **TCR Performance and Ranking** | | | | | | |
Product	**1986** **Market** **Share**	**1987** **Market** **Share**	**Point** **Change** **1986-87**	**Percent** **Change** **1986-87**	**1987** **District** **Standing**	**1987** **Regional** **Standing**
Proventil Inhaler	51.95	49.69	−2.26	−4.35	2	21
Proventil Repetabs	.00	3.09	3.09	.00	7	53
Proventil Solution	.00	5.03	5.03	.00	7	55
Proventil Tablets	3.52	57.22	23.70	70.70	1	1
Proventil Family	42.36	49.42	7.06	16.67	1	2
Theo-Dur Spray	4.21	2.93	−1.28	−30.40	7	40
Theo-Dur Tablets	53.85	66.51	12.66	23.51	1	13
Trinalin	10.62	10.69	.07	.66	9	80
Vancenase	17.03	16.67	−.36	−2.11	8	76
Composite	35.09	43.91	8.82	25.14	1	8
Quota Attainment						
Percent Attainment:	124.74					
District Standing: 1						
Regional Standing: 12						

Source: Plaintiff's Exhibit P–8.

policy says representatives are supposed to be on the road by 8:30 a.m. The checking of sales representatives' driveways was consistent with Schering policy which suggests occasional "quality checks" on its call activity requirements. One method proposed by Schering's personnel department for performing these quality checks was:

You may station yourself in the general vicinity of a representative's residence to make sure that the representative leaves home within normal working hours and then follow the representative on territory to make sure that the representative actually calls on physicians and accounts.

Upon discovering Fred's car, Reed said he "was pretty darned upset. I had really knocked myself out to help him get higher numbers . . . and I said, 'My God, all the work I'm doing and he's, he's home.'" Jim then telephoned his regional sales manager, Ronald Martino, who said, "Don't say anything about this to Fred" and told him to spotcheck his driveway for additional transgressions. From early November to early January 1990, Reed drove 70 miles from his Landenberg, Pennsylvania home to check Fred on five different days at 20-minute intervals from 8:00 a.m.–10:00 a.m. Each time his car was in his driveway, although Fred had marked his activity report as having worked full days.

With this evidence, Schering's managers met and Ron Martino drafted a memo warning Maiorino about his tardiness. Martino was overruled by head quarters, however, which ordered a two-day suspension to be served without pay on February 13–14, 1990 for activity report falsification. Reed told Fred about his suspension at their usual Bordentown diner whereupon Fred became "defensive, almost paranoia-like [and] asked me why I had been checking on him . . . after 33 years of loyal and dedicated service, I should not question his integrity. . . . There were several short, unbridled bursts of emotion on his part which included statements such as, 'I am not going to take this spying.'"

Despite the ill-will growing between them, Reed continued his efforts at improving Fred's sales. On one occasion, while visiting one of the territory's pharmacies, the two went through its computer files and located the physicians who were "whales" or large-volume drug prescribers but were not included amongst his Focus Cards. From this experience, Reed concluded Fred was not targeting the correct doctors and that "he was flying by the seat of his pants" in working his territory.

TABLE 4
Fred Maiorino's
BARS Evaluation
Under Schering's
New System

	Competency	Rating	Performance vs. Responsibilities
I.	Ability to use non-selling time in doctor's office effectively and establish productive relations with office personnel	V	Mr. Maiorino uses the strong rapport that he has developed with office personnel to complete appointments with busy physicians. He gains information about the physician's likes and dislikes from the nurses and receptionists.
II.	Ability to make an effective sales presentation	V	Fred gives a very comprehensive detail with the advantages of his products as compared to his competition. He is trusted and (sic) respected in the offices of his physicians.
III.	Ability to answer objections and gain commitment from M.D.	V	The combination of product knowledge and sales skills enables Fred to overcome implied objections to the use of his products. He closes as well as anyone that I have worked with as a manager.
IV.	Ability to use sales aids, samples, and literature	V	Mr. Maiorino routinely checks the inventory of his sample products in the physicians' office. He has a thorough knowledge of our various selling aids, and routinely leaves file cards for future reference by the physician. His need in this area is to have a better knowledge and use of the clinical reprints.
V.	Ability to work with retailers	V	Fred has developed a strong and respected rapport with his pharmacists throughout the years. This rapport affords him information of the prescribing habits and physicians in the surrounding area.
VI.	Ability to work with wholesalers	N/A	
VII.	Ability to work with hospitals	V	Mr. Maiorino had the responsibilities of a hospital representative a few years back and this experience shows in his knowledge of the politics of hospitals. He understands formularies, how to get products approved, and then how to build volume.
VIII.	Maintain high level of Schering product knowledge, competitive products, and the marketplace	V	Fred can cite problems of competitive products and show advantages of the Schering product. He has a solid understanding of the pharmaceutical industry.
IX.	Ability to plan a sales call	G	Fred packs sales aids as needed (visuals, reprints, PI sheets, etc.) in his detail bag for ready reference.
X.	Ability to adhere to plan of action	G	Positive in accepting new ideas and suggestions at sales meetings. Uses selling aids and samples as outlined in Home Office action plans.
XI.	Ability to organize and manage territory to achieve maximum productivity	G	From the years of experience in his present territory, Fred knows the physicians, nurses, and receptionists. This rapport gains him access to many hard-to-see physicians.
XII.	Ability to handle administrative duties in accordance with sales management policies and direction	G	Mr. Maiorino is very prompt with his weekly and monthly routine mail. His need (sic) to use the many successful years of experience in compiling a more reflective Monthly report. He has been a very successful PSR and has the knowledge to evaluate selling material, medical trends, and selling techniques.

Source: Plaintiff's Exhibit P–8.

FIGURE 3
Schering-Plough's
Purpose and Use of
the BARS System

Policy and Procedure

The Behavior Anchored Rating Scale (BARS) for PSRs was developed to help give an accurate measure of a person's overall performance. The traditional method of judging solely by the bottom line (i.e., sales results) ignores other factors intrinsic to the individual's performance. It also does not yield information on how results were achieved or how to establish programs to improve performance. In short, a bottom-line approach by itself does meet the need to be objective in evaluation of performance. However, it does not provide feedback on an individual's strengths or weaknesses.

As an alternative to traditional methods, a behavioral focus to performance appraisal and training presents a more functional approach. There are many advantages to anchoring evaluation to job-related behavior, Of major importance is the fact that behavior can be observed, and people can learn behavior. Behavior can be taught.

When behaviors (observable acts) are properly collected and classified, they generate a Behaviorally Anchored Rating Scale (BARS). The basic idea is to look at an individual's behavior as compared with behavioral standards identified as above average, average, or below average in their performance. Emphasis is placed on the behavior that can be seen as directly leading to the desired competency. There are four basic steps to developing a BARS. (1) Descriptions of particularly effective or ineffective performance are gathered. These must be examples of actual observed behaviors. (2) The behaviors are sorted into categories that reflect a specific competency (for example, ability to use sales aids and literature). (3) Managers are then asked to write statements describing specific behavior that falls between the extremes for each competency. (4) The managers are asked to place each statement on a five-point scale, ranging from outstanding to unsatisfactory. Since the behaviors are specific to a particular position, and are developed by the people who are in a position to judge relevancy (district managers), the BARS offers a meaningful assessment for PSR performance. In practice, you should regularly observe and record examples of your representatives' behavior as outlined using the established BARS competencies. In fact, the PSR Sales Skills Profile, Goals Performance Review, and the Annual Evaluation all utilize the BARS.

Source: District Manager Policy and Procedure 40–82, Schering Corporation, March 16, 1987.

Based on this observation, Jim wrote a memo on June 22, 1990 to Maiorino regarding his territory's zip codes 8609, 8620, 8610, 8618, 8540, 8648, and 8619 stating "One wonders whether you have identified your 'whales' and, if so, are you calling on them with appropriate frequency, using selling aids effectively, and probing to find why the physicians in these . . . zips prefer the single action tablets Ventolin and Breathine" of our competitors? He then cited Fred for "unacceptable territorial management" and placed him on a probationary program that was to last for six months until December 31, 1990. While on probation, he had to match the district's average marketshare gains for Proventil inhalers, solution, and Repetabs, Vancenase AQ, Vanceril, Theo-Dur, and Eulexin. Reed stated this improvement could be obtained by "dedicated and diligent territorial management skills. Such skills would include the identification of territorial 'whales,' knowledge of their prescribing habits, and appropriate call intervals utilizing current selling aids in tandem with a well thought-out presentation" as well as "the sponsorship of influential speakers at county medical society meetings, HMOs, or gatherings of potential prescribers of our products, at least one per quarter." If these goals were not accomplished, "appropriate disciplinary action will be taken up to and including discharge."

By the probationary period's end, however, Fred had met the goals for only two of seven drugs. Of the district's nine sales representatives, he was ranked eighth in marketshare and ninth in marketshare gain. Accordingly Reed recommended on February 20, 1991 that Fred be fired. Sherman, Reed's new boss as of early January 1991, ordered a new probation, however, as he stated it "was not clear as to what goals had to be achieved for what period of time. . . . In addition to that, I felt that I wanted to focus a program on the most important products that we had and not as many as [previously listed], giving Mr. Maiorino the benefit of the doubt of a long-service employee and that we should make sure that there was no question in his mind as to what was expected of him." During this second probation, Maiorino had to meet the sales goals of Schering's two most important products, Proventil Repetabs and Vancenase AQ, while not letting the sales of the other five drugs slide. If he failed to perform in either category, he would be fired.

By the time this new probation ended on May 31, 1991, the district's marketshare gain for the Proventil Repetabs was 4.6% while Fred's was only 3%. He also fell short on the

Vancenase AQ with the district's marketshare growth amounting to 1.6% and Fred's amounting to only 0.4%. Accordingly, the dismissal letter Reed handed Fred in Mastori's Diner said he had "no alternative but to terminate your employment with Schering effective immediately."

Fred Defends Himself

Although it took almost three years for his career to unravel, Fred traced the start of his problems to May 1989. In that month, Schering announced its "Voluntary Enhanced Retirement Program to all employees aged 55 and older." This program was not part of a personnel reduction effort and, in fact, the company had hired 75 to 80 young sales reps in anticipation of many employees accepting the company's "early out" package. Of the 98 eligible representatives, however, only 29 accepted the offer, thereby leaving Schering with excessive sales reps.

Reed discussed the retirement plan with Fred in September but he turned it down, noting he had a boy in college and had to pay for weddings. During the ensuing discussion, Fred was told he was foolish for not taking the retirement plan and shortly thereafter, Reed began gathering evidence of Fred's poor territorial management practices of which activity report falsification and tardiness were his initial transgressions.

Regarding the evidence Reed had compiled, Fred had asked for specific dates so he could offer an explanation or present any extenuating circumstances. Reed refused the request although Fred explained he could have been late some days because his wife had been sick, one day his mother-in-law had had a medical emergency and had to be taken to the doctor, and on other days he could have been suffering dizziness from his early morning high blood pressure medication.

Regardless of when he started his workday, Fred said he put in a full day's work, and Schering acknowledged it did not know when his workdays ended. Moreover, in an April 5, 1989 memo, Reed had encouraged his sales reps to be flexible about their work habits, and Fred reasoned he was merely applying that flexibility to his own situation. Reed had written, "By now you know that we really mean to implement the territory management concept. You have complete freedom to plan your own physician/pharmacy/hospital call schedule. All we expect of you is that you put in a full day's work each day." When asked why he did not confront Maiorino the first time he saw his car in the driveway and issue him an oral warning as dictated by company policy, Reed replied, "[I] wanted to see, was he going to compound [the tardiness] by lying on his activity report." See Figure 4 for Schering's progressive discipline policy for absenteeism.

**FIGURE 4
Schering-Plough's
Progressive
Discipline
Absenteeism Policy**

Supervisors are responsible for monitoring absence occurrences and may hold a discussion with an employee at any time that there are questions or concerns about the frequency or number of occurrences. Also, employees may request information from their supervisors concerning their own occurrence record at any time. In all instances in which an employee reaches the level of four (4) occurrences or three (3) occurrences and ten (10) days during a calendar year, he may expect his supervisor to initiate a discussion to review the nature and causes of absences. The primary purpose of such discussions is to improve attendance and to insure appropriate corrective action. Following such action, if attendance does not improve, an employee is subject to further disciplinary action as follows:

Within a Calendar year

Occurrences		Occurrences/Days	Disciplinary Action
5	or	4/12	Verbal Warning*
6	or	5/17	Written Warning
7	or	6/22	1-Day Suspension
8	or	7/27	5-Day Suspension
9	or	8/32	Discharge

*Verbal warnings are voided at the end of the calendar year in which the warning was given, provided the employee has had no additional occurrences.

Source: *Schering-Plough Employee Handbook*, p. 13.

Fred also stated that he had implemented many of Reed's suggestions. Maiorino held a dinner and Pulmonary-Allergy Symposium in Trenton in mid-December 1988, with Dr. James Fish as its speaker. On June 22, 1989, another symposium was held in Trenton on prostate and bladder cancer. Both symposia were attended by most of Fred's Allergy, Urology, and Oncology doctors. Maiorino's "Plan of Action" memo of July 9, 1990 cited other activities such as increased "calls on my whales, [the] possible addition of more new whales by more prospecting of newer physicians who are using products similar to our lines of products, or using good amounts of Schering products and have a potential for increasing to a much broader use of our products."

Although Fred had written an earlier September 15, 1989 memo that "I have always tried to do the best that I can and after all is said and done, this is all anyone can do," the stress was starting to take its toll and he felt the probations had been administered unfairly. His first probation required him to meet the district's average marketshare gains for seven drugs, although the district's eight other sales representatives were never held to the same performance standard. Fred was not informed of his second six-month probation (which ran from January 1991 to May 1991) until March 1991. Nor was he made aware that the probation was retroactive to January 1991. Fred had only three months to improve his performance and, more importantly, he was not told what goals he had to fulfill until after being informed of the probation.

Under a system created by Reed, performance goals could not be ascertained before the fact as they were based on historical sales results. Reed would rank his reps based on moving 12-month totals compared to this-year/last-year quarterly totals. When asked if Schering authorized him to use this system, he answered, "Gee, that's hard to answer the way you ask it. I have the right, in my judgment, to motivate representatives, to coach, to teach, to counsel, and I find that competition is a very strong motivating force. There's nothing that says that I cannot do something like this. A ranking report is quite motivational."

As a result of what he felt were unfair management practices, Fred's behavior with customers started to change. Jim Vizzoni, the operator of two Trenton, New Jersey, pharmacies noted, "Fred was an outgoing, happy-go-lucky guy, but you could see he was getting upset. The problem, he said, was his boss."

The Battle Continues

Upon winning his lawsuit for illegal discharge based on age, Fred exclaimed, "Justice has been done, and this shows the system works for old people as well as young people. Hopefully, this will prevent Schering-Plough and other corporations from illegally terminating longtime employees." The company, however, did not walk away and give up the fight. Company spokesperson Linn Weiss said, "Schering-Plough believes that the verdict is not justified in fact or law."

As of early 1996, Fred had not collected his jury-dictated award and Schering's lawyers indicated the company would appeal the Elizabeth, New Jersey, Superior Court decision. Schering also challenged the legal fees paid to Fred's lawyers. Fred is still without a job, after having worked temporarily for another drug company for nine months. Schering has discontinued the incentive system it inaugurated in 1988. The question remains, however, did Schering-Plough treat Maiorino unfairly or was he just a recalcitrant, "over the hill" salesman who had to be removed for the sake of sales force productivity? If Fred needed to be motivated or taught new ways of being more effective, could Schering's management have handled the situation better?

Discussion Questions

1. What qualities do veteran sales representatives such as Fred Maiorino bring to their jobs? What qualities do young sales representatives bring to their assigned territories? In the drug industry, which of the two age groups do you feel are preferable?

2. Fred was fired for deficient performance. Can Schering-Plough objectively substantiate its assessment that Fred was a poor-performing sales representative?

3. What basic virtues does the BARS system possess as a performance evaluation device? What faults does it possess? Appraise the quality of Schering-Plough's use of its BARS.

4. In evaluating sales performance, Schering-Plough switched from a quota system to a ranked marketshare increase system. Viewed from both motivational and objective measurement perspectives, what are the advantages and disadvantages of each system?

5. In terminating Fred Maiorino, did Schering-Plough give him "due process"?

6. A number of approaches to ethical decision-making behavior exist, namely the utilitarian approach, the individual rights approach, and the justice approach. Looking at the overwhelming factors in Schering-Plough's situation, was its ultimate decision to fire Fred Maiorino correct given the concerns of each of these approaches?

7. There are a number of responsibilities firms must fulfill or actions they have to do if they are to remain viable. There are a number of other responsibilities or actions they should do and might do. Where on this spectrum of obligations do you believe Schering-Plough operates?

8. What did Schering-Plough do to help Fred Maiorino improve his performance? To what degree did Fred himself frustrate his employer's attempts to improve his performance?

Appendix A: Summary of Specific Claims

In filing his claim, Fred Maiorino made the following allegations against Schering, Ronald Martino, James A. Reed, and several unnamed defendants.

1. Unlawful discrimination because of age in violation of N.J.S.A. 10:51-2(d) New Jersey Law Against Discrimination in retaliation for refusing the early retirement offered in 1989. An additional claim of unlawful age discrimination was filed for refusing to accept a later early retirement offer made in 1990.

2. Wrongful termination.

3. Unlawful discrimination by imposing different terms and conditions of employment than those imposed on younger employees. These terms and conditions included subjecting him to monitoring while younger employees were not monitored in the same fashion, and failure to advise him of their monitoring him and presenting him with their findings at the time of each monitoring occasion.

4. Breach of good faith and fair dealing when they placed him on his probations.

5. For causing severe embarrassment, emotional distress, physical distress, and humiliation as a direct and proximate result of their acts and omissions.

BULLER | SCHULER

Managing Organizations and People
A Resource for Cases in Management, Organizational Behavior, and Human Resource Management

Abstract

A manager of a dining room is faced with the selection of the anticipated replacement for a key employee. The manager thinks aloud to a student intern and asks for her advice. The dining room is one of two food service operations in a large, urban medical center. The other food service outlet is a cafeteria in a new part of the medical center—and has drawn customers and profitability away from the dining room. Centralized purchasing, a history of adversarial union relations, and a small, experienced staff with idiosyncratic skills and relationships complicate the replacement dining room situation with which the manager works.

The Kriendler Executive Dining Room

It was mid-August and it had been a hot, humid New York City summer. Kathy, the summer intern and a third-year hospitality college student from upstate, was filling out requisition forms for the next day. She looked up as Artie, the manager of the R.W. Kriendler Executive Dining Room, entered the office from the kitchen, sat down, lit a cigarette, and loosened his tie. Exhaling, Artie turned to Kathy, and sighed, "I can see that this Ann situation is going to cause a lot of problems." Kathy laid down her pen, turned to face Artie, and asked "What's up?" She knew the signs—Artie was going to use her to think out loud, something that was happening with increasing frequency as the summer wore on. Artie smiled, and said. "Kath listen up, I'd really value your advice on this one." Kathy nodded and listened closely.

Foodservice at Mount Sinai

The Bob Kriendler Executive Dining Room is located in the Mount Sinai Medical Center, which overlooks New York City's Central Park and is on the edge of Spanish Harlem. The medical center, covering nearly four square blocks, includes a 1,122-bed hospital and a major medical school. The hospital has recently been expanded, and added a new pavilion where rooms were arranged around a glass atrium. The pavilion was designed by the world famous architect I.M. Pei and is an impressive sight that can be seen from the Triboro Bridge.

The medical center has two eating facilities, the Plaza Cafeteria, located in the new North Pavilion, and the Kriendler Dining Room, located in the Annenberg building, nearly two blocks away but accessible via indoor corridors. The Plaza Cafeteria is serviced by the main kitchen located one floor below it in the same building. The main kitchen includes a large storeroom, a kosher kitchen, and the Central Tray Service which prepares all patient meals. The main kitchen is run very strictly and sanitation is of the highest priority. About 100 employees and 20 managers are responsible for the hospital's foodservice. Most of the managers, however, are not hospital employees but rather work for a foodservice contract company. The majority of the foodservice workers are middle-aged, represent several minorities, have families, and commute from one of the five boroughs of New York City via bus and subway. Every hospital worker must join the Hospital and Healthcare Workers Union, Local 1199.

Through negotiations, the union determines the wages, hours, vacations, and protects the rights of all hourly hospital employees. The employees are often heard to complain about the union, for example about the dues that are automatically taken out of their weekly paycheck. When the union went on strike a few years ago, many of the employees scabbed and came in to work despite their affiliation. Getting their paychecks and feeding their families seems to be more important than union loyalty. Despite this lack of loyalty, however, if any members feel that their rights are being infringed upon they call on a union delegate without hesitation. Any arbitrary action taken by a manager can lead to a grievance and the history of many drawn out battles and the resulting paperwork has led to most managers' resentment of the union.

The Plaza Cafeteria serves breakfast, lunch, and dinner as well as snacks in between; it is open almost straight through from 6 a.m. to 10 p.m., seven days a week. It services hospital employees, some administrators, doctors and nurses, and most hospital visitors. The cafeteria offers a variety of moderate quality foods at reasonable prices. The seating area seats approximately 300 and has an attractive view of Central Park.

The other dining facility, Artie's unit, is the Kriendler Executive Dining Room. Its clientele is made up of hospital executives, doctors, medical school personnel and students, and some hospital visitors. Kriendler offers higher quality food and therefore is priced on a more upscale level. It is only open for lunch from 11 a.m.–2 p.m., Monday through Friday. It is located on the fifth floor of the Annenberg building on a floor with most of the medical school offices, including the dean's and registrar's office. It is not located near any of the hospital patient floors.

In the past year, the Kriendler Dining Room has experienced a drop in volume and profits. Several factors are responsible for this. First, with all of the renovation and reconstruction going on, many of the previous employee and visitor traffic patterns have been altered. The operating rooms used to be located in the Annenberg building's upper floors making it convenient for doctors and nurses to simply take the elevator down to the fifth floor for lunch. Now the operating rooms are located in the new hospital in the same building as the Plaza Cafeteria. The old cafeteria had been located in the building next to Annenberg, in the basement, and had no windows. It was not in a high-profile location, nor was its atmosphere very appealing. The new cafeteria is very attractive, very bright, and is in a high-traffic area, right off the glass atrium, close to the new main entrance of the medical center. As Artie has often been heard to say, "The first thing that hits you when you walk into the hospital is the smell of french fries!" Due to its location and the curiosity of patrons, the new cafeteria has taken over a large portion of Kriendler's business. What Artie counts on is the fact that Kriendler serves higher quality products, his patrons get better service, and can enjoy their meal in more pleasant surroundings. Artie hopes that when the "curiosity phase" passes, some of his old patrons will realize that the cafeteria is serving the same mediocre food it was before and return to his facility. Since Kriendler prides itself on its better quality and better service, each member of Kriendler's 12-person staff makes Kriendler what it is. Throughout foodservice at Mount Sinai, Kriendler's employees are known to be the best.

Kriendler's Personnel

Artie Thompson is the Dining Room manager. Artie awakens daily at 4:30 a.m. to commute to the hospital via the Long Island Railroad and the New York subway system. He arrives just before 6 a.m. and leaves about 3:30 p.m. This does not include either the nights he stays when the catering department has special functions in the dining room where he monitors their goings-on and makes sure they leave the kitchen spotless, or the weekends he comes in when the engineering department has to make repairs that cannot be done during the week. Not one item enters the kitchen or is prepared that Artie does not inspect. His major responsibilities include ordering all the food for the unit (done through the main foodservice purchasing department but he orders higher quality products than the main kitchen does), inspecting the items upon receipt, and overseeing production (at times directly assisting) and training staff. Artie remains in the serving area throughout the hours of service and makes repeated trips through the dining room to see that standards are maintained. As the manager, Artie is responsible for all aspects of the dining room's operation. His style is to ponder every decision very carefully.

Every Kriendler staff member has very specific duties that they have learned to perform, for the most part without flaw. Most know each other's positions, so substituting is not a problem when someone calls in sick. In the winter, when absenteeism increases, this occurs frequently.

The key position is that of the cook. This position has been filled for the last 15 years by a man characterized by his colleagues as a hot-tempered and rather gruff man named Lenny. Lenny says he does not like change of any kind and has been observed to get into screaming arguments (complete with expletives) with Artie over menu changes. Kriendler operates on a four-week menu cycle. Four hot entrees are offered daily, rotating among eight each week, which Lenny is responsible for preparing. There are items that he says he "hates" to prepare and "if it were up to him," Kriendler would serve the same four entrees every day every week. Four times a year Artie redesigns the menu. He keeps up on trends in the food industry and tries to implement them where he can at Kriendler. He gives Lenny advance notice, usually about one month, as to the changes and does ask his opinion. Lenny knows that the menu is changed periodically but he always explodes at Artie as if he were changing a 20-year-old tradition and just wants to complicate Lenny's life. Lenny also lets it be known if he does not care for a particular item, e.g., "I don't know how Artie expects to sell this @#$%!" Despite his complaining and personal dislike of certain entrees, he is a perfectionist and will pull something off the steamline if it looks less than appealing. Lenny is known to be extremely reliable and very fast. No matter what might occur, at 11:00 sharp, the steamline is full and ready to serve customers. If Lenny does call in sick, which is rare, Artie takes over as cook. Having to accomplish his managerial tasks, when he cooks, Artie ends up staying into the evening on these days.

The next three most important positions are held by the women that prepare the salads and desserts. The lead position is that which is held by Ann. Her shift begins at 6 a.m. and at that time she prepares one of the regular cold salad plates as well as her station in the serving area, which is made-to-order cold sandwiches. The atmosphere in the kitchen during this morning prep time varies, usually based on the mood of Lenny. If he and Artie have an argument in the morning, the staff always takes the side of Lenny, agreeing with him over Artie. Some days Lenny puts on some music and the staff chats lightheartedly with each other, especially on pay day. Other days the kitchen is silent, with everyone seemingly absorbed in their own thoughts. More popular than the steam table items, Ann's station receives the most customer demand. Greeting every customer with a smile and a kind word, she moves the line along quickly and efficiently. If she runs out of anything either she herself will go into the kitchen to get an item or she will ask someone else if she is busy. She works closely with the hot sandwich server, Ray, whose station is adjacent to hers. Being less busy than Ann, he often helps out if many people are waiting. Ann's job is stressful in that she is on her feet for almost three hours straight and some of her customers are less than patient and polite. She is as happy as everyone else when 2:00 arrives. On days that Ann calls in sick, one of the other women takes her spot and the slack is taken up by Artie and the other workers. Customers always ask for her when she is absent and say they notice a difference in service. Now as Ann approaches the age of 55 and her 31st year of service to the hospital's foodservice department, Artie will be faced with filling this key position in about two months.

The other two cold prep positions are held by Flora and Averil. Flora, who prepares the desserts and one of the cold salad plates, usually fills in for Ann in her absence. In fact, other workers overheard her say more than once, "I better get that spot when Ann leaves." According to her co-workers, she is a good worker; however, she often complains and calls in sick rather frequently. Flora performs, in Artie's view, at the minimum level required; she never exceeds her duties and even her own tasks are not always completed. She takes many breaks and likes to sample many of the food products. Averil, the third cold prep employee, was promoted from within the unit from the dishroom. She is extremely reliable and will pick up the slack of any of the other workers. If she notices a task that needs to be done, she does it; she does not have to be told or asked. She could fill in almost every position if necessary. As Artie has said, "Lenny, Averil, and I could run this place by ourselves if we had to!"

The fifth production position is the steamline server, who serves all of the hot items. The position is held by Peter, a Jehovah's Witness who never loses his temper or is impolite to customers. He must work closely with Lenny since he has to ask him to replenish the line and Lenny closely observes the way Peter serves his food. When Lenny sees something he does not like he tells Peter in no uncertain terms, without hesitation. Peter takes Lenny's often harsh remarks good naturedly and tries to stay on Lenny's good side. He too was promoted from within; his previous position was potwasher. Peter serves as an information source for Artie as well as running personal errands for him on occasion, such as picking up and depositing his paycheck. Since he is so trustworthy, Artie knows he can ask these things of Peter in complete faith of his word. Peter is well-liked by both the customers and the other staff members.

The remaining five positions are the three sanitation men and the two cashiers. While these positions affect the customers less than the others, they do affect the overall running of the unit. They are an integral part of the staff and contribute to the working atmosphere as well as enhancing or detracting from the efficiency of the unit.

Artie Thinks Out Loud

"I know Flora assumes the slot is hers but I don't want to put her there. She cannot stand that long; her legs can't take it. She calls in sick enough already. She's slow and just doesn't have that rapport with the customers. I can't fool around with that spot—it's our biggest profit maker and I won't jeopardize it by putting someone there who may frustrate our customers. I would like to put Averil there; she's our strongest worker. But that would cause conflict with Flora and then who am I going to replace Flora with? None of our sanitation people have the skills or even capability to be in a demanding production position. I don't think Averil even wants the job.

"What I would like to do is get someone from downstairs (one of the main kitchen workers). There is this one woman, Gloria, who is very good and friendly also. I asked Peter for her home phone number since he is friendly with her and I knew he wouldn't say anything to the rest of the crew. She is definitely interested and I told her to keep it in mind and I'd let her know. She has worked up here before for me on occasion and I'm sure she would pick up the routine just fine. But again, I can see resentment arising because of this alleged break in protocol. The union could be called in and, even though they would not really have a case, they could hold me up for a while. I can't afford that!

"My third possibility is just hiring someone new from the outside. This might avoid some conflict, but then I would have someone who is completely new to Mount Sinai, possibly even to foodservice although I wouldn't accept anyone from Human Resources who was. That adjustment period might really bog us down. He or she would also have to get used to and be accepted by the rest of the crew. If they don't work out, what am I going to do with them? I can't fire them because of the union!"

Artie looked at the ceiling, took a long drag on his cigarette, and continued, "Although things are picking up, sales haven't been great. I can't afford to make the wrong decision here—I'd be digging myself a bigger hole. Well, I'm glad I have some time to think about it but I really have to get moving. Kath, why don't you think about this a bit and let me know what you would do if you were me?"

BULLER | SCHULER

Managing Organizations and People

A Resource for Cases in Management, Organizational Behavior, and Human Resource Management

Abstract

Nordstrom has been one of the most successful retailers in recent years based on its tradition of outstanding customer service. This case describes the management practices that have shaped the customer-oriented culture of Nordstrom and contributed to its success. The human resource management activities that produce its highly motivated sales force are particularly emphasized. Yet, not all employees at Nordstrom have reacted positively to its management practices. A number of employees have viewed the company as being unfair and unethical in its dealings with them. Dissatisfied employees have even organized a unionization campaign. An interesting feature of the case is the positive and negative perceptions of current and former employees to "The Nordstrom Way."

Nordstrom

In 1880, John W. Nordstrom left Sweden and sailed to the United States. Twenty-one years later, with a $13,000 fortune struck in Klondike gold, he opened up a shoe store in Seattle. Today that small downtown store is a shoe and apparel empire with almost 100 outlets in more than 10 states.

Nordstrom is one of the most successful department stores with 1995 sales of $3.9 billion and net earnings of $203 million.[1] During the 1980s and 1990s, the company doubled its size from 29 to 89 stores, opening outlets across California and eastward, in Virginia, Washington, D.C. and, most recently, in Paramus, New Jersey. Sales and net earnings grew comparably. In 1995 profits were up 45% and same store sales were up 4.4%.[2] The number of Nordstrom employees has grown to 35,000.

Despite its recent expansion, Nordstrom has remained a family operation. Grandsons John, Bruce, and Jim are all co-chairmen and Jack McMillan, a Nordstrom by marriage, is the company's president. Nordstrom has no chief executive. The company prides itself on having cultivated a family orientation among its workers. All employees are made to feel like members of a family sharing in "the Nordstrom Way."[3]

The Nordstrom Way is perhaps what has set the department store apart from its competition. It is customer service like no one else offers, service above and beyond the call

■ This case was prepared by Richard D. Freedman and Jill Vohr, Sterns School of Business, New York University. Copyright © 1991 by Professor Richard D. Freedman. Reprinted and updated with permission.

1

of duty. At Nordstrom, service is an art form. The store hosts gala dinners and fashion shows, has valet parking, concierges for special requests stationed near every store's entrance, and soothing ballads played on Steinways at every store accompanying eager smiles from salespeople ready and willing to go to great lengths to please the Nordstrom customer. Such amenities have won Nordstrom customer loyalty and affection. In Seattle, it is common to see bumper stickers that proclaim: "I'd rather be shopping at Nordstrom's." Bruce Nordstrom says of the company's customer service tradition: "We were raised sitting on a shoe stool on our knees in front of a customer. And that is both a literal and figurative posture . . . a born servant, if you will. There's nothing wrong with that. We're proud of it . . . and I think our people know that that's what we do."[4] Nordstrom employees, 'Nordies,' all have similar characteristics. They are upbeat, ambitious but, at the same time, selfless. The Nordstrom store directory describes the Nordie service expectation:

Our staff is genuinely interested in seeing that all your needs are met. They are professionals—will help you with everything from gift suggestions to wardrobe planning. They will even accompany you from department to department until you find exactly what you're looking for.[5]

Nordies keep personal books listing each of their customers and record every activity and correspondence. Thank-you letters are sent to customers for purchases regardless of how small. One man was sent a thank-you note for buying only a pair of socks.[6] Nordies will personally deliver purchases as well, outside of work time and even on holidays, all to cultivate that special relationship and trust that has resulted in Nordstrom's faithful customer base and glowing sales record.

Thank-you letters and personal deliveries only barely suggest what the Nordstrom Way entails. One employee spent over three hours on Easter Sunday finding a customer's house so he could deliver a stuffed rabbit to the customer's wife in person.[7] Another employee searched every store in the company to find a blue shirt with a white cuff and white collar that a customer had seen in an ad. Although the employee never found the shirt in his size, she personally delivered one to him at work the next morning. She had sewn a blue and white shirt together.[8]

What motivates Nordstrom employees to go to such personal trouble for their customers? High salaries for one. Nordstrom employees earn some of the highest salaries in the retail business. Pat McCarthy, a longtime Nordie, is one of them. Twenty years at Nordstrom has enabled him to cultivate a strong, loyal customer base that has brought him commissions of $80,000 plus a year.[9] "It's really a people job, which I love," says McCarthy. "Every year my sales have gotten progressively better."[10] Base pay rates are also high—between $5 and $11 an hour, which is well above the industry standard of $6 to $7.[11] High salaries have given Nordstrom a reputation that attracts good salespeople. Company officials say as many as 2,000 employment applications are received when 100 new entry-level openings are announced.[12]

All salespeople start "on the floor," and the company has a strict policy of promoting only from within. Potential managers are required to have at least two years' experience selling, and are promoted after less time only under special circumstances. Promotions for all Nordies are based on three criteria: customer service, productivity, and teamwork. If a salesperson has good team spirit, a solid record of fine customer service, and high sales per hour (SPH), after an appropriate length of time with the company, that employee will likely be promoted to department manager. Similarly, a manager whose department goals have been successively reached or surpassed over his or her length of employment, has fine customer service skills, and good relations with employees will rise to buyer or store manager positions.

Employees receive little formal training when they are hired or promoted to a new position. Most of the training is informally provided through on-the-job communication. What formal training they do receive is of a practical nature, e.g., scheduling procedures, salary and commission determinations, and benefit opportunities. The three Nordstrom performance criteria (customer service, productivity, and teamwork) are emphasized, although trainees are not told how these criteria are evaluated. Trainees are encouraged to seek information from co-workers and superiors who are described as friendly and accessible. Personal books are provided for use in keeping records of customers, sales, thank-you letters, and letters from customers. New employees are also given their own set of business cards to emphasize entrepreneurial opportunities and to encourage them to develop a solid customer base.

Not long ago, Nordstrom replaced its 20-page rule book with a one-page sheet and a few words of wisdom: "Use your best judgment in all situations," and "Do whatever it takes to make the customer happy."[13] Nordstrom gives people the freedom to do whatever it takes to make the customer happy (as long as it's legal). The company has since continued to maintain a decentralized approach to management. Managers are given significant freedom to operate their departments in the Nordstrom way. Individual creativity is a by-product of freedom. They are responsible for hiring, scheduling, and evaluating their crew and receive little guidance in the form of written company policies. Nordstrom hires people that will create their own business, and strict policy might stifle ingenuity and creativity. Therefore, most of the information guiding salespeople is received from their managers and not dictated from above. As described by regional personnel director Molly Goe, each department manager runs his or her department like an individual boutique.[14]

Managers are solely responsible for evaluating their employees. According to personnel manager Mary Kim Stuart, no specific, company-wide evaluation forms are used for salespeople and managers.[15] Rather, each manager designs his or her own evaluation system. If the manager considers an aspect of an employee's performance worth noting it is communicated to the store manager. The store manager, in turn, decides whether to note it in the employee's file.

Like their salespeople, managers are "on the floor" selling and receive a commission. However, their base salaries are much higher. Consequently, although commissions provide managers with an incentive to sell, they are less critical for their income than for salespeople.

All Nordstrom salespeople are on a commission system called a draw. Hourly rates are determined based on the salesperson's abilities and length of employment with the company. Commission percentages for salespeople are strictly based on SPH. Employees receive either their commission percentage times their total sales for that pay period or their hourly rate times their total work hours depending on which is higher. For example, Joe Demarte, Nordstrom's vice president of personnel, explains that a salesperson with a 6.75% commission who works 40 hours for $10 an hour and sells $10,000 worth would earn $675 rather than $400. If he sold $1,000 worth, he would earn his hourly wage and no commission.[16] Consequently, only if an employee's sales are high relative to the hours they have worked, will they receive a commission. The higher the total dollar sales, the higher the commission. The incentive is to generate high pace and high-dollar sales.

Although most of the training is implicit, Nordstrom's expectations of its employees are explicit. "The life of a Nordstrom salesperson is defined by goals. Daily, monthly, quarterly, and annual goals; departmental, storewide and company goals; qualitative and quantitative."[17] These goals are formulated at the top by senior managers and trickle down through the hierarchy to departmental managers who are responsible for meeting designated sales quotas for their departments. Managers' salaries, commissions, and bonuses depend on whether or not they attain these goals. Successive failure to reach targets can lead to dismissal. The same is true for salespeople. Managers encourage salespeople to reach high SPH levels. Some even set specific targets for their employees to ensure the attainment of their departments' sales quotas. Managers are free to implement their own approach to productivity as long as it achieves set targets and is consistent with the Nordstrom Way.

SPHs must be kept above a specified minimum level or a salesperson will not receive commission. Low SPHs reflect poor performance and can therefore be grounds for dismissal. Charts are displayed on bulletin boards in back rooms that rank employees by SPH. Ranking reflects an employee's sales ability on the floor. A red line across the chart designates the minimum SPH level necessary to receive a commission. Employees use these charts to keep tabs on their performance and see themselves in relation to their co-workers.

Everyone is formally and informally aware of their sales performance. In addition to the SPH chart, employees can keep track of their performance on computer printouts available in back offices that list their sales by employee identification number. Salespeople often know each other's number and can see how they stand in relation to one another. To keep it that way, some store managers broadcast the prior day's top 20 salespeople over a loudspeaker each morning. Numerous sales contests operate as incentives. For example, free dinners are given to employees who make the most multiple-item sales to individual customers. Often, within a department, a $20 bill is passed around throughout the day to the salesperson who has rung up the highest single sale. At the end of the day, the winner gets to keep the $20 bill. Top salespeople are named "Pacesetters," which carries with it roughly the status of a varsity letter on a high school athlete's jacket. Motivational skits are used to generate sales enthusiasm. Managers dress up as Kermit the Frog to get employees whipped into a selling frenzy, or a department's staff performs the Michael Jackson song "Beat it" with the words, "Charge it."[18] Nordstrom also offers a course on self-motivation encouraging salespeople to ask themselves what they want to accomplish each day to spur them to take responsibility for their own future. Many do, especially the successful ones. Employees seem to know precisely what they want and need to achieve. One top salesperson stated, "The first year I consciously set quarterly goals to achieve the Pacesetter requirement. My second year my personal goal was $500,000, and I paced myself accordingly. My third year I wanted to achieve $1 million in total sales. To accomplish this I set monthly and quarterly quotas and closely monitored my progress."[19] Clearly, the best salespeople are entrepreneurial self-starters.

Managers are also encouraged to be self-motivated. "Every year the company's managers gather in meetings where they publicly state their store or departmental goals for the next 12 months. Then their bosses will reveal their own goals for the same manager, sometimes with a dramatic flourish."[20] Working at Nordstrom is not for everybody. The company has very high expectations. If you don't meet them, you're gone.

Good customer relations the Nordstrom Way are also important. Employees buzz with tales of extraordinary efforts made by salespeople. Peer competition and pressures to be a member of "the Nordstrom family" keep salespeople striving for a popularity that is based on their sales ability. Rewards for customer satisfaction are high. Bonuses up to $100 are awarded to salespeople with the best customer relations. Managers read letters received from pleased customers aloud at company meetings and over the loudspeaker. Whoops and cheers are heard from listeners. The salespeople who received the letters are honored as "Customer Service All Stars."[21] Their pictures are hung on the wall next to the customer service desk. They receive extra discounts on store merchandise and commendations on their personal records.

To check on the customer service provided by their employees, Nordstrom periodically dispatches "secret shoppers," people who pretend to be shoppers.[22] Salespeople are encouraged to be friendly and warm. Nordstrom does not tolerate rude behavior towards its customers. Smile contests are conducted to motivate courteous behavior. Pictures of smiling employees are taken and displayed in the lunchroom. Those that smile the most on the job receive the highest praise. "Recognition is the number one motivation," says Demarte with respect to Nordstrom contests. "We recognize our top performers constantly, as well as our customer service heroics."[23]

Most Nordstrom employees strongly uphold the Nordstrom philosophy of service. Some are almost religious about it, happily dedicating their lives to master "The Nordstrom Way." Yet, other employees feel the customers are catered to at the expense of their own working conditions, that systems meant to encourage employees actually oppress them, placing them in an environment of constant pressure, harassment, and competition. Some employees began to accuse Nordstrom of unfair labor practices. The United Food and Commercial Workers Union, of which only 2,000 of the 30,000 Nordstrom work force are members, became involved.[24] Accusations of "off-the-clock" work and overbearing work pressures dominated complaints.

All employees are expected to contribute to stocking, delivering, and picking up merchandise. Much of this work is done off the clock, past the end of a shift, on the weekends, or through breaks and lunches. Also employees are expected to maintain close relations with their customers, which implicitly entails thank-you notes and sometimes personal deliveries. The Nordstrom practice is not to include the hours spent at these activities in the total hours worked for each employee's pay period. Union leader, Joe Peterson, in his fight against Nordstrom and what he feels is grossly unfair treatment of employees, continues to search for and encourage employees to hop on the bandwagon. Over 500 complaints were filed with the workers' union and as more complaints poured in, the union set up an 800 hotline to handle them. An article in *The Wall Street Journal* included several stories told by Nordstrom employees themselves.

Taking Out the Trash

A divorced California homemaker who returned to the job market at 40, Patty Bemis joined Nordstrom in 1981, lured by the promise of a bigger income and the "status" of induction in the Nordie elite. She stayed for eight years. "They came to me," she recalls of the Nordstrom recruiters. "I was working at The Broadway as Estee Lauder's counter manager and they said they had heard I had wonderful sales figures." Ms. Bemis was thrilled. "We'd all heard Nordstrom was the place to work. They painted a great picture and I fell right into it." She found herself working progressively harder—for less money and amid more fear. "The managers were these little tin gods, always grilling you about your sales," she recalls. "You feel like your job was constantly in jeopardy. They'd write you up for anything, being sick, the way you dressed." Once, she had to get a doctor's note so she wouldn't get in trouble for wearing low-heel shoes to work. Sufficiently cowed, she reported to work even when she had strep throat. Worn down by pressure, "the girls around me were dropping like flies," she says. "Everyone was always in tears. You feel like an absolute nothing working for them."

Ms. Bemis was consistently one of her department's top sellers, but some years she only made $18,000, far below what she had expected she would earn. She won a company-wide sales contest, and received "a pair of PJs," she recalls. "Whoopiedoo!" And she logged many unpaid hours delivering cosmetics to customers and unpacking hundreds of boxes of makeup. "Working off the clock was standard," crucial to elevating sales per hour. "In the end, really serving the customer, being an All-Star, meant nothing; if you had low sales per hour, you were forced out."

During a big Clinique sale, Ms. Bemis says she worked 12- to 15-hour shifts for a number of days without overtime pay or a day off. On the drive home at 10:30 on the tenth night, she passed out at the wheel and slammed into the freeway's center divider, she says. While she was at home recovering from head injuries, she recalls, "The manager kept calling me and saying, 'Patty, we can't hold your job much longer.'" Her doctor told her she should stay out a few weeks but she didn't dare. "Now, I know I have all these rights. But at the time all I knew was I had to have that job."

She finally left last spring. "I just couldn't take it anymore—the constant demands, the grueling hours. I just said one day, life's too short." She took a sales post at Scandia Down Shops, where she says she makes $400 more a month than at Nordstrom. "And I can sleep at night."[25]

A Broken Clock

The first time Lori Lucas came to one of the many "mandatory" Saturday morning department meetings and saw the sign—"Do Not Punch the Clock." she assumed the managers were telling the truth when they said the clock was temporarily out of order. But as weeks went by, she discovered the clock was always "broken" or the timecards were just missing.

Finally she and several other employees just marked the hours down on their timecard manually. She and another employee recall that their manager whited-out the hours and accused the two of not being "team players."

The department meetings "were unbelievable," Ms. Lucas recalls. "There you'd be at seven in the morning and they had all these security guards dressed up like the California Raisins, with plastic garbage bags stuffed with M&Ms around their midriffs. And all you can hear is people chanting, 'We're number one!' and 'You want to do it for Nordstrom.' Finally I went up to the store manager and said, 'What is this all about?' and she said, 'You are here to learn the Nordstrom Way.'"

The Nordstrom Way involved an endless round of contests ("Who Looks More Nordstrom" was a popular one, intended to encourage employees to shop at the stores) and the daily recital of "affirmations" ("I only sell multiples," was one chanted by salespeople).

And the Nordstrom Way, Ms. Lucas discovered, meant working for free. "My manager would say, 'You go clock out and come down and we'll talk.' That was her little trick way of saying there's nonsell work to do."

Like most salesclerks at Nordstrom, Ms. Lucas also had daily quotas of thank-you letters to write, and monthly customer service "books" to generate photo albums that are supposed to be filled with letters from grateful customers. ("People would get so desperate they would have their friends and relatives write fake letters for them," Petra Rousu, a 10-year salesclerk veteran, recalls.) Such duties, Ms. Lucas says, were supposed to be tackled only after hours. "I'd be up till 3 a.m., doing my letters, and doing my manager's books," she says. "Before you know it, your whole life is Nordstrom. But you couldn't complain, because then your manager would schedule you for the bad hours, your sales per hour would fall, and next thing you know, you're out the door."

The pressure eventually gave Ms. Lucas an ulcer, she says. One day after working 22 days without a day off, she demanded a lunch break. On her hour off, she applied for and got a new job elsewhere and gave notice as soon as she returned. "I remember thinking, I'm making less than $20,000 a year. Why am I killing myself? Nordstrom was the most unfair place I ever worked."[26]

Staying on Top

For nearly two years, Cindy Nelson had stayed on top of the chart in one of the Bellevue, Washington, stores. She was on her way to making "Pacesetter" again. . . . A clique of salesclerks on the floor—led by numbers two and three on the charts held a pow-wow one day, decided that Ms. Nelson must be stealing their sales and vowed to have her "watched," according to court depositions that later became part of a suit filed by Ms. Nelson against Nordstrom in Bellevue, Washington.

On September 29, 1986, Cindy Nelson reported for work and was immediately whisked into the personnel office. The department manager had before her five notes of complaint from the salesclerks, all unsigned, which claimed Ms. Nelson had been stealing sales.

Ms. Nelson asked to inspect the sales receipts in question and confront her accusers, but the manager, Rhonda Eakes, refused. "I just didn't feel that it was any of her business," Ms. Eakes explained later in her deposition. Then she told Ms. Nelson that she was fired. (All of the managers and employees involved in Ms. Nelson's firing declined comment, referring queries to Mr. Nordstrom, who said, "That gal wasn't a good employee.")

"I was totally stunned," recalls Ms. Nelson, who had a stack of customer service citations in her file and had been told she was about to make manager. She was also, up until then, "your 100-percent gung-ho Nordie. This whole time I thought I was going to be this great Nordstrom person and now I was nothing, a nobody. I became an emotional wreck."[27]

Other criticisms were made of Nordstrom. Allegedly employees were required to purchase and wear Nordstrom clothing while on the job.[28] The company was also accused of having discriminatory practices.[29] Part of becoming a Nordie, employees say, involves acquiring a certain look. Lupe Sakagawa, a top salesperson, recalls that on her first day on the job, her manager strong-armed her into buying $1,400 of the "right" clothes—all from the department. But that wasn't enough: The store manager then called her in and told her, "Correct your accent." Ms. Sakagawa is Mexican. "It was very hard for me to prove myself," she says, "because of that image of the Nordstrom Girl—blond hair, young, and cute."[30] Nordstrom has since hired a black human resources officer and the company reports that 25.6% of all its employees are minorities.[31]

Other sentiments were brought to the attention of the media through Peterson, who felt employees are being exploited. Peterson specifically criticized the SPH incentive. He believed that in order to keep SPH up, employees were encouraged to keep their work hours down. Consequently, they could not record hours spent doing certain nonselling chores (stock taking, personal deliveries, thank-you notes) on their time sheets. Nordstrom's position was that the employees are compensated by commissions that actually pay them for doing extra tasks. Employees willingly donate their time. It is not explicitly required of them. Peterson argued that ". . . If one employee is donating a lot of time, it forces others to do the same or it creates an atmosphere where everyone is playing on an unequal playing field."[32] Because employees who log only sales times have higher SPH than co-workers who clock in all other business and support activities, employees are motivated to decrease their nonsales hours. They work off the clock to be awarded better shifts and more hours. In response, Demarte insisted that because SPH is the objective performance evaluation factor . . . that's what people focus on."[33] Evaluation is not based just on SPH. People who perform the best are also best in giving the customer service and working as a team. Yet, Demarte does admit there is pressure. "People who perform the most effectively are the ones we need to have on the floor. Therefore, there's this pressure to be better."[34] Middle management encourages workers to get jobs done within certain time frames and if they can't meet the deadlines, exert "implied pressures" on their salespeople to get the job done after work hours. President Jack McMillan insists that "the system is as level a playing field as you can find for people to rise up quickly on their own merit. Everybody starts on the selling floor and the ones that show initiative, creativity, and desire rise up in the system and become department managers. Those department managers that show the ability to make things happen rise up to be buyers or store managers or vice presidents. We think it's a great system, but it's obvious there are some glitches in it. One way to control selling costs—not the right way—is to encourage people to get the work done in a certain time frame. If they can't get it done, then there is implied pressure to work off the clock. We are responsible for the pressure from middle managers. There was no plan or scheme, but it happened. I guess you could say we were negligent for not knowing, but we are responsible for it."[35] Recently Nordstrom set aside $15 million to pay back employees who had performed off-the-clock services.[36]

Despite Nordstrom's promises of back pay the union still fought them, pointing a finger at Nordstrom's high turnover rates, even for the retail industry. Nordstrom replied that although salespeople who regularly had trouble meeting sales quotas or coping with pressure to improve their performance were dismissed, these employees usually leave of their own volition. Having been made to feel uncomfortable or inadequate in the Nordstrom culture that celebrates accomplishment, they recognize that they do not belong. They leave before the company has cause to dismiss them. Nordstrom compensates by attempting to hire people who are innate Nordies. The company's hiring philosophy supports their decentralized management style. Bruce Nordstrom is quoted as saying, "All we do is hire nice, motivated, hardworking people and then we leave them alone to do what they do best. The system is to have self-empowered people who have an entrepreneurial spirit, who feel that they're in this to better themselves and to feel good about themselves and to make more money and to be successful."[37] Jim Nordstrom adds, "There's expectations on our people. And when people apply for a job any place, they want to work hard and they want to do a good job. That's their intention. And our intention is to allow them the freedom to work as hard as they want to work."[38] However, miss your quota three months in a row, and you're out. "If you don't like to win, it's hard to be successful in this company," says Midwestern regional manager Bob Middlemas.[39]

Although there were several complaints, it seemed that most Nordstrom employees also did not support their union leader's accusations. In December 1990, more than half of the 1,850 employees left the union after membership became optional.[40] With continued pressure by Peterson, a former Nordstrom shoe salesperson, Nordstrom responded with an anti-union campaign. And in July of 1991, employees consisting of salespeople, office workers, clerks, and display workers at five stores in Seattle voted by more than a 2-to-1 ratio to end union representation altogether.[41] Indeed, several employees speak in favor of Nordstrom stating that they love working for the company and do not want anything changed.[42]

"It's a feeling, it's family," Ms. Sargent says enthusiastically. "Sure, during the busy seasons, you do work six to seven days a week, but being in the store with the Christmas tree here, you create your own memories." Ms. Sargent, who has worked for Nordstrom in Seattle for seven years, says she doesn't mind working for free. "When I go home and do follow-ups or write thank yous, I think it's inappropriate to be charging the company for that."

At the San Francisco store, another set of employees testify to the company's virtues. "Here at Nordstrom, I feel I can be the best that I can be," says Doris Quiros, a salesperson in the women's sportswear department. While other retailers "give you a big book of rules, when I came here, Nordstrom gave me one with only one rule: Use your best judgment. That's because they want me to be my own boss." In the women's shoe department, Tim Snow, a former waiter, says people are impressed now when they learn where he works. "You can be at the grocery store and you show them your ID card and they'll start right off on how much they love to shop there."[43]

If happy employees are not enough to justify the existing Nordstrom system, the company's success and their numerous satisfied customers are. "They treat you with the most reverence you can imagine," one customer said after a salesperson offered her the option of either wearing a Nordstrom dress that had a run in it and returning it at her convenience for a full refund or taking $100 off the price. "It's so darn easy to go in there."[44] Betsy Sanders, the head of the company's Southern California division, sometimes stands at the store exit at night as the store closes and says good night to departing customers. One evening, as she bade some shoppers farewell, she heard one say: "What kind of drugs are these people on? Even the doormen are nice."[45]

Looking for ways to attract more customers, Nordstrom introduced a mail-order catalog. In its first year, 1994, it attracted 300,000 shoppers. At the same time Nordstrom introduced a proprietary Visa credit card and went on-line with its Nordstrom Personal Touch America on market place MCI (http://www.internetmci.com/marketplace, 6870401@mcimail.com, or http://www.nordstrom-pta.com).

Endnotes

1. *Hoover's Company Profile Database*, 1996, The Reference Press, Inc., Austin, TX.
2. Ibid.
3. Robert Spector and Patrick D. McCarthy, *The Nordstrom Way* (New York: John Wiley & Sons, Inc., 1995); Charlene Marrner Solomon, "Nightmare At Nordstrom," *Personnel Journal* (September 1990): 77.
4. Marti Galovic Palmer, Producer, "The Nordstrom Boys," *60 Minutes*, Vol. XXII Num. 33 (May 6, 1990): 8.
5. "How Nordstrom Got There," *Stores* (January 1990): 68.
6. Mary Kim Stuart, Nordstrom Personnel Director (Paramus, New Jersey) telephone conversation with author, November 9, 1990.
7. "The Nordstrom Boys," *60 Minutes*: 8.
8. Ibid.
9. Susan C. Faludi, "At Nordstrom Stores, Service Comes First—But at a Big Price," *The Wall Street Journal* (February 20, 1990).
10. Ibid.
11. Seth Lubove, "Don't Listen to the Boss, Listen to the Customer," *Forbes* (December 4, 1995): 45–46; Dori Jones Yang, "Will 'The Nordstrom Way' Travel Well?" *Business Week* (September 3, 1990): 83.
12. Joyce Anne Oliver and Eric J. Johnson, "People Motive Redefines Customer Service," *HR Magazine*, Vol. 35 Iss. 6 (June 1990): 120.
13. Mary Kim Stuart interview, November 9, 1990.
14. Solomon, "Nightmare At Nordstrom," p. 77.
15. Mary Kim Stuart interview, November 9, 1990.
16. Solomon, "Nightmare At Nordstrom," p. 79.
17. Richard W. Stevenson, "Watch Out Macy's, Here Comes Nordstrom," *New York Times* (August 27, 1989): 39.
18. Ibid.
19. Ibid.
20. Ibid.
21. Solomon, "Nightmare At Nordstrom," p. 83.
22. Faludi, "At Nordstrom Stores, Service Comes First—But at a Big Price."
23. Solomon, "Nightmare At Nordstrom," p. 77.
24. Ibid., 78.
25. Faludi, "At Nordstrom Stores, Service Comes First—But at a Big Price"; Spector and McCarthy, *The Nordstrom Way*.
26. Ibid.
27. Ibid.
28. Solomon, "Nightmare At Nordstrom," p. 78.
29. Faludi, "At Nordstrom Stores, Service Comes First—But at a Big Price."
30. Ibid.
31. Solomon, "Nightmare At Nordstrom," p. 78.
32. Ibid., 80.
33. Ibid., 81.
34. Ibid.
35. Robert Spector, "Nordstrom Discusses Its Problems," *Women's Wear Daily* (March 27, 1990): 18.
36. Solomon, "Nightmare At Nordstrom," p. 80.
37. "The Nordstrom Boys," *60 Minutes*: 10.
38. Ibid.
39. Lubove, "Don't Listen to the Boss, Listen to the Customer," p. 46.
40. "Nordstrom Workers in Seattle Reject Union," *New York Times* (July 20, 1991).
41. Ibid.
42. Solomon, "Nightmare At Nordstrom," p. 77.
43. Faludi, "At Nordstrom Stores, Service Comes First—But at a Big Price."
44. Richard W. Stevenson, "Watch Out Macy's, Here Comes Nordstrom," *New York Times* (August 27, 1989): 38.
45. Ibid., 40.

BULLER | SCHULER

Managing Organizations and People

A Resource for Cases in Management, Organizational Behavior, and Human Resource Management

Abstract

This case describes the factors contributing to Southwest Airlines' phenomenal success. It provides an overview of the airline industry and the forces that comprise industry structure and attractiveness. The central factors underlying Southwest's success in this competitive industry include: the leadership of CEO Herb Kelleher, a competitive strategy based on cost leadership, a culture, and human resource management practices that encourage superior performance. The case highlights several challenges facing Southwest Airlines (SWA) as the company seeks to sustain its growth and profitability.

Southwest Airlines

The tale of two men, one airline, and a cocktail napkin . . . "Let's start our own airline," Rollin W. King said to his friend Herb Kelleher in a bar years ago. "Convince me," Herb replied. Rolling drew a triangle connecting Texas' major cities on a cocktail napkin. He said, "We could offer fares so low people would fly instead of drive." Herb paused, placed his drink on the napkin, then spoke "Rollin, you're crazy. Let's do it."[1]

Introduction

Southwest Airlines is currently facing a multitude of challenges to its historically successful business strategy that has created concerns about its ability to grow in the future.

■ S.E. Jackson and R.S. Schuler, *Managing Human Resources: A Strategic Partnership Perspective* (Mason, Ohio: South-Western 2003). An interactive multimedia version of this case is available at http://www.i-case.com.

Credits: Ari Ginsberg and Richard Freedman prepared the original version of this case with the research assistance of Bill Smith. It is used here with their permission. They thank Myron Uretsky, Eric Greenleaf, and Bethany Gertzog for their valuable comments and suggestions. They also appreciate the careful review, corrections, and helpful recommendations made by Susan Yancey of Southwest Airlines on an earlier version. The case is intended to serve as the basis for class discussion rather than to illustrate either effective or ineffective handling of an administrative situation. A glossary of their key terms appears in Appendix A.

The case was updated in 2001 by Randall S. Schuler, Susan E. Jackson, and Kristin Nordfors. Materials to update this case were taken from the web site of SWA and the case materials (including Appendicies B and C) of Megha Channa, Olympia Cicchino, Shirish Grover, Mohini Mukherjee, and Drew Von Tish, all students in the Rutgers University Master's of HRM program and is used with their permission. Additional materials and insights provided by the students at the GSBA-Zurich.

These challenges are both external and internal. External challenges include competition and price pressures, current conditions in the airline industry stemming from deregulation and continued access for competitors to short haul markets that have long provided the company with significant profitability and competitive advantage. Internally the company faces challenges such as finding continued access to talent that is selected very carefully, and at the same time are very competitively compensated resulting in relatively low labor cost for the company. The continued access to and availability of talent has direct impact on Southwest's operating strategy of being the cheapest and most efficient airline that in turn depends upon highly motivated employees who deliver outstanding customer service.

Southwest's former CEO and current Chairman Herb Kelleher has created a unique culture that has been sustained during the company's 30-year life. He is the figurehead that embodies the company's greatest strengths. The unique culture that has been created by Southwest and championed by its chairman has been able thus far, to sustain its recruitment and retention goals for the types of employees it targets. Employee ownership has been used extensively to tie the fortunes of the company with those responsible for it and to retain employees who might otherwise look to Southwest's competitors. Employee satisfaction and the recognition that Southwest is one of the best companies for attracting, developing and retaining talented people, makes it a well-oiled industry leader.

The question is can Southwest continue its profitability, outstanding level of customer service, and reputation for being low cost, on time, and safe in the context of a limited pool of market talent, which is at the heart of its competitive advantage. Can the company maintain its relatively low turnover rate even though the demand for skilled labor has put significant pressures on recruitment and retention of employees? Can the firm continue to spend so much time and money on recruitment and training and remain competitive and equally profitable with all of the external conditions applying pressure on its business at the same time? Will the fact that Herb Kelleher is no longer Southwest's CEO and James Parker has assumed the position hurt the company's reputation in the marketplace and cause it to lose its unique identity and cachet?

In addition to these questions, all of the external environmental issues such as more direct competition, weakened labor relations, and the change from a short-haul airline to a longer-haul airline, will have an impact on the future growth and success of the company. The strategies that have been so successful in the past will have to be modified to allow the company to grow into other markets, and these modifications will come with all their accompanying challenges. The key to these challenges may be the company's understanding and appreciation of its people.

Background

Few industries have experienced the turmoil faced by the U.S. domestic airline business during the past two decades. Once characterized by high wages, stable prices, and choreographed competition, the industry changed swiftly and dramatically when deregulation took effect in 1978. Several of the strongest and greatest airlines (e.g., Pan Am, Eastern) disappeared through mergers or bankruptcies. Strikes and disruptions interfered with companies' attempts to reduce costs. New competitors aggressively swooped into the marketplace; the majority failed.

The industry is again in a period of high demand and expanding profitability. Despite the volatile conditions and many organizational failures, one carrier grew and prospered throughout this entire period—Southwest Airlines.

Southwest was controversial from its inception. Although the Texas Aeronautics Commission approved Southwest's petition to fly on February 20, 1968, the nascent airline was locked in legal battles for three years because competing airlines—Braniff, Trans-Texas, and Continental—fought through political and legal means to keep it out of the market. Through the efforts of Herb Kelleher, a New York University law school graduate and the airline's former chief executive officer and current chairman of the board, Southwest finally secured the support of both the Texas Supreme Court and the United States Supreme Court.

Southwest emerged from these early legal battles with its now famous underdog fighting spirit. The company built its initial advertising campaigns around a prominent issue of the time as well as its airport location. Thus "Make Love, Not War" became the airline's theme, and the company became the "Love" airline. Fittingly, LUV was chosen as the company's stock ticker symbol. Southwest went on to see successful growth through three distinct periods. The "Proud Texan" period (1971–1978) saw the establishment of a large city-service network within its home state of Texas. Because it did not engage in interstate commerce, the fledgling carrier was not subject to many federal regulations, particularly those imposed by the Civil Aeronautics Board (CAB). The second phase, "Interstate Expansion" (1978–1986), was characterized by the opening of service to 14 other states. Interstate expansion was made possible by, and thus coincided with, the deregulation of the domestic airline industry. The most recent phase, "National Achievement" (1987–present) has been a time of considerable growth, distinguished recognition, and success.

Despite its past success, Southwest Airlines now faces new challenges that raise concerns about its continued ability to grow. Ironically, many of these concerns are a result of changes brought about by Southwest itself. Some of them are external, such as imitation by competitors who are becoming more efficient and the limited size of the shorter-haul flight markets in which Southwest developed a core competency. Others are internal, including the emergent problems of managing a larger, more complex organization, and a culture that might have been dependent on the charisma of a single individual, Herb Kelleher, or that may not play well to the new audiences needed for future growth. Will Southwest Airlines be able to continue its remarkable success or will emerging conditions seriously threaten Southwest's future prosperity?

The Airline Industry

The competitive environment in which Southwest operates can be subdivided into different value-added stages, customer and service segments, and competitor groups.

Airlines engage in several value-adding activities. These include aircraft procurement, aircraft maintenance, reservation systems, schedule and route planning, in-flight services, and after-flight services. Competitors may differ in their involvement in these activities. For example, Southwest performs some in-house maintenance but offers no post-flight services. By contrast, American Airlines owns and markets its own reservation system, and Allegis, as United Airlines was known briefly in 1987, at one time operated a car rental agency (Hertz) and two hotel chains (Hilton and Westin).

Airlines compete for three primary types of customers: travel agents, corporate travel managers, and individual travelers. The two major categories of passengers are leisure travelers, who tend to be quite price-sensitive, and business travelers, who are more concerned with convenience. To satisfy the different needs of some or all of these groups, airlines present a wide variety of services, depending on their strategy.

Passenger service can be categorized along a number of dimensions. For example, airlines differ by geographical coverage; some specialize in short-haul service while others provide a vast network of interconnected long-haul and short-haul flights on a global basis through a network of strategic alliances. They also differ in how their routes are structured within the territories they serve. The two extremes are point-to-point and hub-and-spoke. The former is characterized by direct service between two points. The latter is characterized by complex, coordinated routes and schedule structures that channel passengers from numerous far-flung airports (the spokes) through a central airport (the hub). The hub itself has many costly infrastructure requirements (baggage handling systems, large terminals, maintenance facilities, and parts inventories). To address the pricing complexity created by multiple traffic flows through a hub, hub-spoke carriers conduct complicated yield and inventory management calculations. The result of this complexity is that the hub-spoke pricing structure is systematically different from point-to-point pricing. These added complexities allow a carrier to offer flights between more "city-pairs" than it could under a point-to-point network. For a company that relies on a network, like an airline or telephone company, competitive advantage accrues from economies of scope, i.e., the geographic reach of that network. Economies of scope do not necessarily complement economies of scale, and in fact are often achieved at the expense of scale economies and vice versa. Thus, although the hub-and-spoke system is driven by economies of scope, each strategy, hub-and-spoke or point-to-point, has its own inherent cost and organizational implications.

Passenger service can also be characterized in terms of breadth. An airline may choose to provide a broad gamut of services including meals, advance seat assignments, and frequent flier programs (full service), or it can offer only Spartan services (no-frills). A further differentiation is the number of service classes offered. Most airlines have two classes of service, first and coach. Some offer three classes, first, business, and coach (United and American on select flights), others offer only coach (Southwest), and a few offer only first class (Midwest Express). In addition to the direct cost of providing differentiated service, amenities such as first class seating and in-flight meals indirectly affect the cost structure of an airline by limiting the number of seats its aircraft can hold. Because Southwest does not currently offer meals or first class service, its 737-300 holds 137 seats whereas a United Airlines 737-300 holds only 128 seats.

U.S. airlines can be categorized into three major competitor groups based on geographical coverage. First are the "major" national airlines. They include: America West Airlines, American Airlines, Continental Airlines, Delta Airlines, Northwest Airlines, United Airlines, and Southwest Airlines. Second are the regionals, which include Airtran (formerly ValuJet), Frontier Airlines, Alaska Airlines/Horizon Air, and many others. Third is the commuter or "feed" carriers, most of which operate as extensions of the majors. These carriers use mostly turboprop or regional jet equipment and fly routes that are generally less than 500 miles. Some of these carriers include Atlantic Coast Airlines, which operates as United Express; Atlantic Southeast Airlines, which operates as Delta's Business Express; Comair Holdings, another Delta commuter; Mesa Air Group, which operates its own flights as well as feeder flights for United; SkyWest, Inc.; and numerous others.

Competitive Environment

The *Airline Deregulation Act of 1978* redefined the industry by eliminating the ability of the CAB to set fares, allocate routes, and control entry and exit into markets. Unfortunately, most airlines were hamstrung by high cost structures, including exorbitant labor costs and highly inefficient planes and infrastructure facilities. In the aftermath of the complete removal of entry and price controls by 1980, competition intensified considerably as new entrants cherry-picked the large carriers' most profitable routes. This led to an extended period of severe industry shakeout and consolidation.

Structural Characteristics

The industry's structural characteristics make it a tough place to be very profitable. The overall industry is not highly concentrated, although it has become more concentrated since deregulation. Nevertheless, most discrete markets are served by a limited number of carriers. In the oligopolistic markets in which most airlines compete, the pricing actions of one company affect the profits of all competitors. Intense price wars have been a frequent event in the industry. Because competition varies from route to route, a carrier can dominate one market, be dominated in another, and face intense rivalry in a third. As a result of the hub-and-spoke system, airlines face head-to-head competition with more carriers in more markets.

Suppliers tend to have relatively high bargaining power. Certain unions are in a position to shut down airlines. Airplane manufacturers (Boeing, Airbus) have considerable power in altering the terms of purchase for planes. Furthermore, the business is capital intensive and requires very large expenditures for airplanes and other infrastructure.

Despite difficult economics, the industry is still attractive to new entrants. There are few substitutes for long-haul air travel. In addition, most of the incumbents have high cost structures that are exceedingly difficult to improve significantly. Carrier failures and downsizing have also created a large supply of relatively new "used" aircraft and the cost of acquiring aircraft is reduced further by the practice of aircraft leasing. Given high debt levels and low profitability in comparison to other industries, most airlines, including

Southwest, have begun to lease their planes rather than purchase them. In light of high debt and low profits, the depreciation tax shield is not as valuable to the airlines. By leasing, carriers can "sell" that tax shield to the leasing company, actually creating value for the carrier. As a result, entry barriers are not as high as one would expect in other capital-intensive industries.

Furthermore, new entrants generally gain significant cost advantage by securing lower labor costs because they are not burdened by the unfavorable union contracts that affect many older airlines. Many of the union contracts agreed to by the major airlines call for higher pay and contain work rule provisions that reduce labor productivity. In addition, new entrants are sometimes able to gain favorable terms by purchasing excess capacity of other airlines, such as training and maintenance.

Profitability

In order to survive and profit in this tough environment, airlines attempt to manipulate three main variables: cost, calculated as total operating expenses divided by available seat miles (ASM); yield, calculated as total operating revenues divided by the number of revenue passenger miles (RPM); and load factor, calculated as the ratio between RPMs and ASMs, which measures capacity utilization. Thus, profitability, defined as income divided by ASM, is computed as:

$$\text{Profitability} = [\text{yield} \times \text{load factor}] - \text{cost}$$

The major airlines have faced intensive competition from low-price airlines during the past 10 to 15 years. While these low-priced airlines expanded the market for air travel, they also placed great downward pressure on the prices of the majors, thereby reducing their yields. To compete, the majors engaged in great cost-cutting efforts.

Capacity

JP Morgan analysts believe that the most important factor influencing pricing in the long term will be the falling industry cost curve. They point out that low-cost airlines have already lowered and inverted the traditionally downward sloping industry cost curve. "With it they have pressured fares industry-wide, but particularly in short-haul markets where their impact on costs have been most dramatic . . . the airlines that are increasing capacity are those lowest on the industry's cost curve."[2] This shift has occurred because of the growth in low-cost, short-haul travel.

Outlook

Lehman Brothers analysts concluded that the U.S. airline industry was entering a mature and more stable phase, as the major restructuring it required was largely accomplished. In their view, this restructuring was driven by two key developments. First was the retrenchment of the majors into their core hubs. Second was technology diffusion, which occurred when the weaker airlines upgraded their systems technology regarding pricing and yield management and eliminated many disparities among major carriers.

Arenas of competition have also shifted. This trend was heightened by the events of September 11, 2001, and the public's concern about flying. Low-cost carriers, including Southwest Airlines and Shuttle by United, dominate short-haul capacity in the west. Expansion of the low-cost carriers now seems to be increasing, and competition appears to be increasing. Meanwhile the east coast is still dominated by high-cost carriers such as Delta and Continental, although they are facing significant profitability issues. Consequently, it is not surprising that the low-cost airlines have targeted the east as a major arena for expansion. Southwest's invasion of Florida and Providence, Rhode Island, is a noteworthy example. In the northeast, capacity reduction by high-cost competitors such as American and Continental has also enhanced the opportunities for low-cost airlines such at JetBlue, which now has a hub at JFK and wants to add a plane a week to its fleet from now until 2008! As carriers learn to adapt the low-cost formula to the geographic, climatic, and market intricacies of the northeast, low-cost operations will likely continue to expand.[3]

Southwest Airlines' Mission and Objectives

Southwest Airlines' mission focuses to an unusually large degree on customer service and employee commitment. According to its annual report, the mission of Southwest Airlines is "dedication to the highest quality of Customer Service delivered with a sense of warmth, friendliness, individual pride, and Company Spirit." Indeed, Southwest proudly proclaims, "We are a company of People, not planes. That is what distinguishes us from other airlines and other companies." In many respects, the vision that separates Southwest from many of its competitors is the degree to which it is defined by a unique partnership with, and pride in, its employees. As stated in its *Annual Report*:

At Southwest Airlines, People are our most important asset. Our People know that because that's the way we treat them. Our People, in turn, provide the best Customer Service in the airline industry. And that's what we are in business for—to provide Legendary Customer Service. We start by hiring only the best People, and we know how to find them. People want to work for a "winner," and because of our success and the genuine concern and respect we have for each of our Employees, we have earned an excellent reputation as a great place to work. As a result, we attract and hire the very best applicants. Once hired, we train, develop, nurture, and, most important of all, support our People! In other words, we empower our Employees to effectively make decisions and to perform their jobs in this very challenging industry.

The airline's goal is to deliver a basic service very efficiently and safely. This translates into a number of fundamental objectives. A central pillar of its approach is to provide safe, low-price transportation in conjunction with maximum customer convenience. The airline provides a high frequency of flights with consistent on-time departures and arrivals. Southwest's employees also aspire to make this commodity service a "fun" experience. Playing games is encouraged, such as "guess the weight of the gate agent." The fun spirit is tempered so that it is never in poor taste and does not alienate business travelers.

Southwest Airlines' Strategy

Southwest Airlines is categorized as a Low Fare/No Frills airline. However, its size and importance have led most analysts to consider it to be one of the major airlines despite its fit in the low-fare segment. In a fundamental sense, Southwest's business-level strategy is to be the cheapest and most efficient operator in specific domestic regional markets, while continuing to provide its customers with a high level of convenience and service leveraged off its highly motivated employees. Essentially, Southwest's advantage is that it is low-cost and has a good safety reputation.

Cost Leadership

Southwest operates the lowest cost major airline in the industry. The airline devised a number of clever stratagems to achieve this low-cost structure. For example, by serving smaller, less congested secondary airports in larger cities, which tend to have lower gate costs and landing fees, Southwest can maintain schedules cheaply and easily. Southwest's approach is also facilitated by its focus on the southwest and other locations with generally excellent weather conditions, which leads to far fewer delays. Moreover, by following a point-to-point strategy, Southwest need not coordinate flight schedules into connecting hubs and spokes, which dramatically reduces scheduling complexity and costs.

Route Structure

Historically, Southwest has specialized in relatively short-haul flights and has experienced considerable threat from providers of ground transportation (cars, trains, and buses) because the buyers of these short-haul services tend to be quite price sensitive. Southwest has widened the market for air travel by attracting large numbers of patrons who previously relied on ground transportation. For example, before it entered the Louisville to Chicago market, weekly traffic totaled 8,000 passengers. After Southwest entered the market, that number grew to over 26,000. This increase in traffic is now recognized as

"The Southwest Effect." Emphasis on short-haul flights has also allowed them to pare costly services such as food, which passengers demand on longer flights. Passengers are provided with only an "extended snack"—cheese, crackers, and a Nutri-Grain bar.

Turnaround Time

Its route structure has helped Southwest to experience the most rapid aircraft turnaround time in the industry (15–20 minutes versus an industry average of 55 minutes). Interestingly, Southwest's "20 Minute Turnaround" can be traced directly to the carrier's first days of operation in Texas when financial pressures forced the company to sell one of the four Boeing 737s it had purchased for its initial service. Having only three planes to fly three routes necessitated very rapid turnaround.

Rapid turnaround time is essential for short-haul flights because airplanes are airborne for a smaller percentage of time than on long-haul flights. Faster turnaround also allows Southwest to fly more daily segments with each plane, which in turn increases its assets' turnover. Their ability to maintain this practice is being challenged by the increased security requirements, but so far they seem to be doing well. Time will only tell what the exact impact of the *Airline Security Act* signed into law by President George W. Bush on November 19, 2001.

Fleet Composition

Southwest has the simplest fleet composition among the major airlines. The company only flies Boeing 737 planes and has committed to fly the 737 exclusively through 2004.

In choosing the fuel efficient 737, Southwest developed a close relationship with Boeing that enabled it to develop comparatively favorable purchase terms. Although Southwest flies a number of model variations of the 737, the cockpits of the entire fleet are standardized. Therefore, any pilot can fly any plane, and any plane can be deployed on any route. In addition to helping capture scale economies at a much smaller size than its larger competitors, the homogenous fleet composition reduces the complexities of training, maintenance, and service. It is difficult to calculate the large savings associated with this approach, but they exist in almost all operating areas including scheduling, training, aircraft deployment and use, wages and salaries, maintenance, and spare parts inventories.

Travel Agency Exposure

According to its Annual Report, Southwest sells over 70 percent of its seats directly rather than through travel agents (compared to the industry average of 20 to 25 percent), thereby saving the 10 percent commission paid to travel agents. This also alleviates the need to participate in many of the travel agent reservation systems.

While this reduces the company's breadth of distribution, it helps to reduce commission payments and Computer Reservation System (CRS) fees, which are approximately $2.50 per flight segment.

Gates

Access to gates is often a constraining factor in the ability of airlines to expand because major airports have limited numbers of gates and most are already taken by other airlines. An emphasis on less crowded secondary airports has alleviated this problem for Southwest. Southwest purchases or leases gates at airports, as opposed to renting the gates of other airlines, which enables the airline to use its own ground crews.

Connections

Southwest does not offer connections to other airlines, which simplifies its ground operations. However, this also limits access for many passengers, particularly from international flights.

Fare Structure

Southwest also controls costs through its simplified fare structure. While Southwest's major competitors have complex fare structures and use computers and artificial intelligence programs to maximize passenger revenues, Southwest offers no special business or first-class seating. Rather, they generally offer a regular coach fare and a limited number of discounted coach fares.

Labor

Labor is the largest cost component of airlines despite the heavy capital investment demanded in the industry. Southwest's labor costs are roughly 30 percent of revenues and 40 percent of all expenses. This represents about 8 cents per seat mile. About 82 percent of Southwest's employees are unionized. Given the ability of unions to bring carrier operations to a halt, it is not surprising that they wield considerable power. The International Association of Machinists and Aerospace Workers (IAM) represents customer service and reservation employees; the Transportation Workers Union of America (TWU) represents flight attendants; the Southwest Airline Pilots' Association (SWAPA) represents pilots; and the International Brotherhood of Teamsters (IBT) represents aircraft cleaners, mechanics, flight training instructors, and others. There are also some other smaller unions.

In an industry where unions and management have often been at war—and where unions have the power to resist essential changes—the quality of their relationship is a crucial issue. Perhaps one of the best examples of this is the 1994 agreement between Southwest Airlines and SWAPA. The pilots agreed to keep pay rates at existing levels for five years, with increases of 3 percent in three of the last five years of the ten-year deal (five-year base term, with an additional five years unless it is terminated by the union). Pilots can earn additional pay based on company profits. The pilots also obtained options to acquire up to 1.4 million shares of company stock in each of the ten years, in accord with market prices on the date of the deal. Pilots hired between 1996 and 2003 obtain lesser amounts of options at 5 percent over the then market value of the stock. Maximum pilot salary at Southwest is $148,000 yearly while at United it is $290,000 yearly. At JetBlue it is $115,000.

Customer Service

Southwest's approach to customer service is one of its core strategies. Its "Positively Outrageous Service" (POS) is different from the customer service associated with other major airlines. Service is provided with friendliness, caring, warmth, and company spirit—staff go out of their way to be helpful. This approach to service leverages Southwest's outstanding relationship with its employees. However, this stellar customer service does not include costly amenities like reserved seats or food service, and only offers very limited automatic baggage re-checking. By emphasizing flight frequency and on-time performance, Southwest has redefined the concept of quality air service. This unusual approach has allowed Southwest to differentiate its service while maintaining its cost leadership strategy.

Marketing

Marketing savvy also plays a key role in Southwest's strategy. Since Southwest's inception, the major elements of the product offering have been price, convenience, and service. As a Texas native serving mostly Texas markets, it has played the role of the hometown underdog, fighting against the majors. Now, when Southwest enters a new market, they use a sophisticated combination of advertising, public relations, and promotions in the belief that once people fly Southwest they will be hooked.

Growth

Despite its remarkable growth in what had been until recently a relatively moribund industry, Southwest has not emphasized growth as an objective. In fact, Herb Kelleher has expressed a "go-slow" philosophy. For example, Southwest will not enter markets unless it perceives favorable conditions, which range from the wishes of the local community to the availability of an appropriate labor supply. Given its record of success and its reputation, it is not surprising that there are many communities that want Southwest to serve their markets. After all, good air service is considered by most communities to be an essential aspect of economic development. However, Southwest's policy prohibits accepting monetary subsidies or other incentives that cities and airports offer to gain air service. Southwest has also demonstrated a remarkable ability to manage its growth, an essential commodity in an industry known for its complexity. The inability to manage rapid growth has been blamed for the failure of many carriers, including Braniff, PeopleExpress, and ValuJet.

Organization

Structure

Southwest, like most airlines, is a formal and centralized organization. Organizationally, Southwest is structured according to functions. The nature of operations in the airline business is quite mechanical. That is, airline operations naturally aim for efficiency and consistency. They are not spontaneous—they value clock-like behavior. Planes must be in certain places at certain times and must be operated safely and efficiently. Safety itself requires following very rigorous procedures to ensure proper maintenance and training. The reputation of an airline can be seriously damaged by only one or two serious accidents. Therefore, the organization of Southwest is characterized by a high degree of formalization and standardization.

Reporting to Vice Chairman of the Board and Chief Executive Officer (CEO) James Parker are Colleen Barrett, President and Chief Operating Officer; and Gary Kelly, Executive Vice President and Chief Financial Officer. Perhaps the most influential is Colleen C. Barrett who is in charge of such key functions as marketing, sales, advertising, human resources, customer relations, and governmental affairs. John G. Denison is Executive Vice President in charge of Corporate Services, which includes finance, legal, facilities, reservations, revenue management (pricing), and systems (including computer services and telecommunications). There is one other Vice President reporting to Parker, Al Davis, who is in charge of internal auditing and special projects. For operations controller functions he reports to Gary Barron.

How has Southwest Airlines maintained high levels of customer and employee satisfaction in the context of a functional organization? The company uses a number of mechanisms to allow employee participation. The fundamental concept is the notion of a "loose-tight" design. Within the context of tight rules and procedures, employees are encouraged to take a wide degree of leeway. The company maintains rather informal job descriptions and decentralizes decision making regarding customer service. So while there is very high standardization regarding operations, it is low with respect to customer service. Employees are empowered to do what is necessary to satisfy customers. Flight attendants are allowed to improvise cabin instructions and employees play practical jokes on each other and customers. Positively Outrageous Service in action! The company management operates with an informal open door policy that allows employees to circumvent the formal hierarchy. Employees are encouraged to try things, knowing they will not be punished.

Southwest's organization is considerably simpler than its major competitors. Most of its competitors must manage the spatial complexity of far flung international operations and contend with the added intricacies of hub-and-spoke systems. These large international carriers are also involved in complex alliances with other airlines in foreign markets to augment the scope of their services. They manage code sharing arrangements with small regional domestic carriers. In short, the large carriers are complex networks, with more complicated organizational management issues.

Size

Southwest operates in more than 57 cities in 29 states and employs over 30,000 people. As of 2001, this consists of approximately 6,228 flight personnel; 1,049 maintenance workers; 13,148 in ground customer service; and 2,519 in management, marketing, accounting, and clerical positions. Southwest has become such a popular employer that it received 216,000 resumes in the year 2000 and hired 5,134 new employees. Southwest is still a relatively small company compared to the other major airlines. It ranks eighth in revenues and fifth in passenger boardings. Southwest's Available Seat Miles (ASMs) total less than a quarter of American Airlines, and it operates a fleet of only 352 aircraft compared to about 700 aircraft for American. Nevertheless, Southwest is the largest carrier in a significant number of the markets in which it flies and the dominant airline in the short-haul niche of the airline business.

Adaptability

Southwest has been a very nimble organization, quick to take advantage of market opportunities. For example, when American Airlines and USAir scaled back their California operations, Southwest quickly took over the abandoned gates, acquired more planes, and now has 50 percent of the California market. Another example is Southwest's expansion into the Chicago Midway market following the collapse of Midway Airlines. Much of this flexibility stems from the company's remarkable labor relations. In addition, although Southwest is still purely a domestic carrier, it is developing a strategic alliance with Icelandair, a small North-European carrier.

Human Resource Management

At Southwest Airlines the human resource function is called the People Department. According to the department's mission statement: "recognizing that our people are the competitive advantage, we deliver the resources and services to prepare our people to be winners, to support the growth and profitability of the company, while preserving the values and special culture of Southwest Airlines." The crucial importance of human resources to the strategy of Southwest has made the People Department more organizationally central to the company than its counterparts are at its competitors. Given Southwest's reputation as a great place to work, it is no wonder that so many people apply for each job opening

Unique Approach Aligned with Culture

Southwest Airlines distinguish themselves from their competitors by doing many things differently. One of the most striking differences is how it goes through the selection process. It begins with Chairman Herb Kelleher who states, "We like mavericks—people who have a sense of humor. We look for attitude. We'll train you on whatever you need to do, but the one thing we can't do is change inherent attitudes."[4] Libby Sartain, Southwest's "Vice President of People," remarked that the company has had to become more and more creative in how it finds candidates.[5] In a typical year she noted that the company hires 4,000 to 5,000 people. In the past, about one out of four applicants would be interviewed and less than 3 percent would actually be hired. In theory, the odds of getting into Harvard are higher.[6]

Hire Based on Attitude

What does Southwest look for in the selection process? The approach places great emphasis on hiring based on attitude. During the interview process, there may not be a fixed set of skills or experiences that are examined.[7] The search is for something that Southwest considers to be much more elusive and important—a blend of energy, humor, team spirit, and self-confidence. These key predictors are used by Southwest to indicate how well applicants will perform and fit in with its own unique culture.

The hiring process at Southwest also emphasizes the importance of hiring people who are inclined toward teamwork. Ann Rhodes, former Vice President of People, stated that one of the important unwritten rules at Southwest was that "you can't be an elitist." Southwest actually uses a personality test to rate candidates (on a scale from one to five) on seven separate traits.[8] The seven areas evaluated include cheerfulness, optimism, decision-making skills, team spirit, communication, self-confidence, and self-starter skills. Anything less than a three is considered cause for rejection. With this methodology, the airline has chosen to use a multiple hurdles approach where an applicant must exceed fixed levels of proficiency on all of the predictors in order to be accepted. With this approach a higher rating in one area will not compensate for a lower score on one of the other predictors. Southwest believes in these seven predictors and that failing to make the grade in even one will guarantee that the person will be unsuccessful on the job.

Interview Based on Strategy

The process of selection based on the seven predictors applies to everyone from pilots to mechanics. In the words of Libby Sartain, "We would rather go short and work overtime than hire one bad apple." In addition to the evaluation of the seven predictors, Southwest uses other methods in the selection process. The process begins like most companies with an interview. The interviewer looks for team-oriented people with prior work experiences that match. A common theme in screening all candidates revolves around people skills. According to Gittell,[9] the easiest way to get in trouble at Southwest is to offend another employee. Even when pilots are interviewed, the airline went out of their way to find candidates that lacked an attitude of superiority and who seemed likely to treat coworkers with respect. Southwest's system for selecting its people is time intensive but based on a history of bringing in people that fit into the culture of the company.

The selection process at Southwest includes panel interviews, which can be an efficient, reliable, and cost-effective means of screening candidates. For example, a panel of representatives from the People Department and the In-flight Department may interview candidates for a flight attendant job. Panel interviews tend to produce more consistent results since interviewers hear the same response at the same time. A series of one-on-one interviews will come next with a variety of people. The system used by Southwest follows the basics of good interview design by including structured questions, systematic scoring, multiple interviewers, and interviewer training.

Southwest publicly explains almost every detail of the practices it uses to select employees. In theory, any company could attempt to copy the process and claim it as their own. It would probably fail for a number of reasons. First, Southwest expends much more energy and time than most companies do. In order to find the right people they spend the money up front in the selection process in the belief that it becomes worthwhile over time. So, not every company would be willing or able to make that type of investment. Second, Southwest's selection process matches the culture of the company. They value people and "walk the talk" when it comes to finding the right employees. Some additional quotes from Herb Kelleher back this up:

Other companies don't value attitude. They don't pay all that much attention to it. They don't make it a priority. I've been with companies where they have an opening, and you know what they consider the function of the personnel department? To plug a hole as quickly as they possibly can. That's quite different from what we do in many cases. Some years ago our VP of the people department told me they had interviewed 34 people for a ramp agent position in Amarillo, TX, and she was a little embarrassed about the amount of time it was taking and the implied cost of it, and my answer was: if you have to interview 134 people to get the right attitude on the ramp in Amarillo, TX, do it.

Developing the Process

The People Department, which is the HR function at Southwest Airlines, developed its interview process in collaboration with Development Dimensions International, a consulting firm that specializes in designing sound selection procedures. "The procedures at Southwest Airlines adhere to the basic principles of good interview design: structured questions, systematic scoring, multiple interviewers, and interviewer training."[10]

Benefits of Centralization and Role of the People Department

The overall selection and placement process at Southwest is centralized like the rest of the organizational structure of the airline. The centralization of this process helps make the best candidate available for the right job (that is, it makes the placement process successful and feasible). Having trained people involved in the selection and placement decision improves the efficiency of the process and also reduces the risk of bias or unfair judgements. It also helps the operating managers to concentrate on their job while also remaining involved in selection and placement decisions without personally formulating the process. This of course is a huge benefit in terms of keeping decisions and policies consistent throughout the organization.

The People Department at Southwest enjoys an extremely important role in its selection and placement process. This kind of a centralized process helps the organization as the applicants have to go to one place to apply for any position, and specialists trained in selection techniques can assist in the process of deciding which candidates should be hired and where they ought to be placed. Southwest keeps the line managers and other employees involved in the process, which serves to its benefit for a number of reasons. Employees who get the opportunity to contribute in the selection of their team members also become more committed to helping them succeed and it also provides them with a sense of urgency. The involvement of all levels of management and employees along with the HR department in the selection and placement process helps Southwest build a strong network of employees, who could then successfully forward the organization's mission of providing the right attitude and service to its customers.

The Decision-Making in Selection and Placement

The People Department has sound procedures that are in place for any level of selection, be it in the form of interviews or written assessments. The selection and placement decisions would however finally be made by a combined panel of line managers and specialized representatives from the People Department. Going by Chairman Herb Kelleher's deep involvement and his interpersonal demeanor in the management of Southwest, one could also assume that he would have the final say in any placement and selection decisions. In his own words, "My name is Herb/Big Daddy—O/You should all know me/I run this show."[11] Selection and placement decisions at Southwest seem to be made by line managers and senior management with full participation of present employees in the spirit of true partnership. The People Department is responsible for designing the process and is largely responsible for attracting, helping in the selection and placement of, and retaining a strong set of employees.

All of the various applications go through the People Department and prospective candidates are then interviewed and tested for *aptitude and attitude* by a panel of interviewers in keeping with a consistent process that is developed by the HR function. Once selection decisions are made, placement of the right individual in the right position is once again done with the involvement of all levels of employees from that department along with specialists.

For instance, at Southwest Airlines, a panel of representatives from the People Department and the In-flight Department first interviews candidates for flight attendant positions. Before the selection process is finished, they also have one-on-one interviews with a recruiter, a supervisor from the hiring department, and a peer. Sound procedures can be quite useful in these interviews. Poorly conducted interviews may yield very little useful information, and may even damage the image of the organization, which is very important to Southwest.

As mentioned earlier though, while employees and their feedback is valued at Southwest, it seems from the workings of the management headed by Herb Kelleher that final decision-making powers are largely vested with the management of the company. This process seems to have worked quite well for Southwest Airlines.

Libby Sartain, Vice President of People, and her team have spent years analyzing the staff at Southwest and have calibrated their questions to the specific needs and requirements of each job, as well as attributes like judgment and decision-making skills. The process can take up to six weeks before anybody is hired. About 20 percent of recruits fail to make it through the training period at The University of People in Dallas.

The time and money spent on the recruitment process has resulted in a turnover rate of 9 percent, the lowest in the industry. Traditionally, the HR department does not do much to endear itself to finance. However, Southwest's CFO, Gary Kelly believes investing in hiring is vital. "If you are not going to work hard to get people who are a good fit, it will hurt you. For example, we have never had a strike. What airline is even close to being able to say that?"

The predictor most stringently used for selection and placement of employees is personality and values. A panel of representatives from the People Department and the In-flight Department first interviews the candidates for flight attendant jobs. Before the selection process is finished, they will also have one-on-one interviews with a recruiter, or supervisor from the hiring department and a peer. The selection is highly systematic and a multiple hurdles approach combined with a good interview design—structured questions, systematic scoring, multiple interviews, and interviewer training—implies that only the best candidates get selected. The selection of candidates that fit the organizational culture of Southwest is undoubtedly critical to the success of Southwest.

This has enabled Southwest to maintain a strong, unified culture in the face of enormous growth and to groom management talent within it. This is reflected at the senior management level, where promotions within the ranks have led to all but five positions being occupied by insiders, some of them having started their careers in entry-level positions. Internal politics is not apparent from the sources available to us. We can, however make the assumption that involvement of politics in decision making is always a possibility.

As Southwest grows, sustaining this zeal is likely to get harder. Previously, the question that was frequently asked was: After Kelleher, Who? According to Bob Crandell, ex-CEO of American Airlines, "The kind of contribution Kelleher can make to Southwest is to select the next leader and help the next leader make a successful transition." Well, he did just that in 2001.

It was recently announced that James Parker, presently the vice president would take over as the CEO for Kelleher. It is to be seen whether Parker and his team can continue the growth and success Southwest has been enjoying for the past three decades. Now everyone will be watching to see if the success of SWA has been a function of the unique person or not.

Training

In an organization where attitudes, culture, and fit are so important it is natural that the company places such a great emphasis on socialization and training. McDonald's has its Hamburger University, Southwest has its University for People. Everyone at Southwest has a responsibility for self-improvement and training. Once a year, all Southwest employees, including all senior management, are required to participate in training programs designed to reinforce shared values. Except for flight training, which is regulated and certified, all training is done on the employee's own time. Nonetheless, the training department operates at full capacity, seven days a week. The fun spirit of Southwest emerges in graduates very early. For example, a class of new pilots stumbled into Kelleher's office wearing dark glasses and holding white canes.

Labor Relations

The importance of labor relations cannot be underestimated in a company that is about 82 percent unionized. Here again Kelleher's unusual abilities emerged. Somehow he was able to convince union members and officials to identify with the company. Time will tell if Parker can have the same success. So far, especially during the difficult time in 2001, success continues. This is further described in the following section entitled "Southwest Airlines Performance Indicators."

Compensation

It is also noteworthy that in an era when chief executive pay has escalated to huge amounts, Kelleher was named one of the lowest-paid chief executive officers in Dallas on a performance-adjusted basis. Furthermore, company officers do not get the perks often enjoyed by their counterparts in comparable organizations—no cars or club memberships—and they even stay in the same hotels as flight crews. Southwest has refused to compete for executive talent based on salary.

Culture

The most distinguishing feature of Southwest Airlines is its culture. When competitors and outside observers describe Southwest, they tend to focus on its cultural attributes. Herb

Kelleher made the development and maintenance of culture one of his primary duties. The culture permeates the entire organization and sends clear signals about the behavior expected at Southwest. To promote employee awareness of the effects of their efforts on the company's bottom line, *LUV Lines* (the company newsletter) reports break-even volumes per plane. The newsletter informs employees not only of Southwest's issues, but competitor news as well. The belief is that informed employees are better equipped to make decisions.

One of the shared values is the importance of having fun at work. Humor is a significant aspect of the work environment. Such attributes are believed by senior management to enhance a sense of community, trust, and spirit and to counterbalance the stress and pressures of the mechanistic demands of airline operations.

Another characteristic is the cooperative relationship among employee groups. This can be an advantage in functional structures, which are notorious for generating coordination problems. In other airlines, work procedures clearly demarcate job duties. However, at Southwest everyone pitches in regardless of the task. Stories abound of pilots helping with baggage and of employees going out of their way to help customers. In one particularly bizarre story, an agent baby-sat a passenger's dog for two weeks so that the customer could take a flight on which pets were not allowed. Employee cooperation impacts the bottom line. When pilots help flight attendants clean the aircraft and check in passengers at the gate, turnaround time, a cornerstone of the low-cost structure, is expedited.

Because of its team-oriented culture, Southwest is not stifled by the rigid work rules that characterize most competitors. As a result, Southwest has tempered the stringent demands of a functional structure with the liberating force of an egalitarian culture. One excerpt from Southwest's "The Book on Service: What Positively Outrageous Service Looks Like at Southwest Airlines" is rather instructive:

"Attitude breeds attitude . . ." If we want our customers to have fun, we must create a fun-loving environment. That means we have to be self-confident enough to reach out and share our sense of humor and fun—with both our internal and external customers. We must want to play and be willing to expend the extra energy it takes to create a fun experience with our customers.

Just as the words "it's not my job" can take away the source of life for a consumer-oriented business, the words "it's just a job" are equally as dangerous. Positively Outrageous Service cannot be learned from a book or manual; it cannot be artificially manufactured; and it is not required by law. It is born and bred in each individual according to his or her experiences, attitude, and genuine desire to succeed—both personally and professionally. Service does not start at the beginning of each work day, nor does it end when you go home. It is a very real part of you . . . it's your company; your success; your future.

This approach certainly contributes significantly to the lowest employee turnover rate in the industry (7 percent) and the highest level of consumer satisfaction.

Despite all of the freedom that the culture permits in some areas, the company also employs very stringent controls. Perhaps the best example is that Herb Kelleher himself had to approve all expenditures over $1,000!

Forged over 30 years, Southwest's culture has been a source of sustainable competitive advantage. A Bankers Trust analyst put it this way:

Southwest has an indefinably unique corporate culture and very special management/employee relationship that has taken years to cultivate. Employees have long had a significant stake in the company; employee ownership and employee contribution to wealth creation are not ideas that are alien to the workforce of Southwest Airlines since it is emphatically not "just a job." Then, too, the relationship is not merely spiritual—the employees have come to trust the only company that has a record of 23 consecutive years of earning stability combined with an impressive record of stock appreciation unmatched by virtually any company . . . within or beyond the airline industry. The pilots are well compensated relative to the industry average, and they understand that. The challenge was to find creative ways to tie together the fortunes of the company with those responsible for it without risk or destruction of shareholder value . . . and, unlike the employee groups at other major airlines, the Southwest pilots understand that.[12]

Management

Until Parker arrived as CEO, there was no doubt as to who is in charge at Southwest. In this respect Southwest is like most of the other airlines, centralized with a very strong, if not dominating CEO. What set Herb Kelleher apart was his charismatic nature. His friendly, participative, deeply involved, and caring approach was and is revered throughout the organization. A very large number of employees know the chairman, and he is reputed to know thousands of them by name. Nonetheless, it is also known that behind the scenes he can be extremely tough, implying that his public and private personae can be quite different.

Herb Kelleher, age 68, started Southwest with a former client, Rollin King, who is still a member of the Board of Directors. King supposedly presented his idea for a low-cost Texas-only airline based on the success of Pacific Southwest Airlines in California to Kelleher over dinner at the St. Antony Club in San Antonio. The original "Love Triangle," the foundation of Southwest's strategy, was drawn on a cocktail napkin.

Kelleher's management style, which had been described as a combination of Sam Walton's thriftiness and Robin Williams's wackiness,[13] seems to have been consistent right from the beginning. Direct, visible, and, some would say, even bizarre, he has attended company parties dressed in drag and appeared in a company ad as Elvis. Known for constantly showing the flag in the field and interacting with large numbers of employees and customers, Kelleher is reputed to have engaged people in conversations for hours, at all hours, about company and industry issues, often with a drink in his hand. He almost always seems ready for a party, and this fun-oriented atmosphere pervades the organization. The company newspaper, *LUV Lines*, has a column, "So, What Was Herb Doing All This Time?" recounting the CEO's activities. Following his example, Southwest employees are well known for going the extra mile. Among the stories of such behavior is that of a customer service representative who stayed overnight at a hotel with an elderly woman who was afraid to stay alone when her flight was grounded due to fog. The agent "knew" that was what Herb would have done.

Kelleher replaced formal strategic planning with "future scenario generation," arguing that "reality is chaotic, and planning is ordered and logical. The meticulous nit-picking that goes on in most strategic planning processes creates a mental straightjacket that becomes disabling in an industry where things change radically from one day to the next."[14] It seems likely that Parker will continue these practices, but his style may be quite different. Time will tell.

One of the most powerful departments is the Customer Department headed by Colleen Barrett, Executive Vice President, and Parker's right-hand. She is the senior female in the airline industry, and provided the organizational balance for Kelleher. She is known to be a stickler for details. She plays another unofficial role, acting as an ombudsman for customers and as an internal management expert.

In the early 1990s Barrett set up a company culture committee, comprised of people from all geographic areas and levels of the company. The committee, which meets four times a year, is charged with preserving and enhancing the company culture. One of the committee's successes is illustrated by the company organization. It is well known that functional structures such as Southwest's are designed to promote specialization and scale economies, but often at the expense of teamwork and coordination. As these organizations grow they become even more difficult to operate in an integrated manner. The committee developed a number of initiatives to improve cross-functional cooperation. One example is that all company officers and directors have to spend one day every quarter in the field—working a real "line job."

Technology

Like all airlines, Southwest is a very heavy user of computer-related technology. This technology supports all activities from scheduling to reservations to general operations support. The network is built on four superservers and a reservations subsystem that connects more than 5,000 PCs and terminals across the country. Remote locations communicate with the servers using TCP/IP across Novell LANs.

This network supports a reservation system that has enabled Southwest to be the first carrier to offer ticketless travel on all of its flights. Over 80 percent of Southwest's seats are now sold ticketless. The ticketless system offers significantly improved customer service by eliminating lines at ticket counters. The system also reduces costs; it is estimated that it costs an airline from $15 to $30 to produce and process a single paper ticket.

Customers using the Southwest ticketless system can purchase a seat on a Southwest flight by telephone or on the Internet. Customers receive a confirmation code, which is traded for a boarding pass at the airport. The concept of ticketless travel originated at Morris Air, a Salt Lake City airline acquired by Southwest in 1993. Although policy and operational differences prevented Southwest from adopting the Morris system, the company was able to accelerate the development of its own system with the assistance of Evan Airline Information Services, a consulting firm that helped to develop Morris Air's system. The first ticketless passenger boarded a Southwest plane only four months after development began.

All Internet activities are concentrated under Kevin Krone, Vice President—Interactive Marketing. Marketing activities explicitly build on the Internet as a primary marketing channel. Krone's activities are closely coordinated with the requirements and support facilities of Rapp's department. Southwest was the first carrier to host a web site, http://www.iflyswa.com, which was deemed "Best Airline Web Site" by Air Transport World. It recently launched a joint venture with Worldview Systems to enhance its Internet presence.

Southwest Airlines Performance Indicators

There are many different criteria that can be used to evaluate Southwest's success in achieving its basic objectives. Certainly Southwest's different constituencies look at its performance in different ways. Southwest takes particular pride in the following accomplishments:

- 30 years of safe, reliable operations;
- number one in fewest Customer complaints for the last nine consecutive years in the Department of Transportation's Air Travel Consumer Report;
- in the top five of Fortune's "100 Best Companies to Work for in America" for the past four years;
- five consecutive years of Triple Crown Customer Service;
- nine consecutive years of increased profits and 28 years of profitability;
- recognition as one of the top ten places to work in Robert Levering and Milton Moscowitz's book, The Best 100 Companies to Work for in America;
- top ranking in the Airline Quality Survey conducted by The National Institute for Aviation Research for two of the last three years;
- consistent financial success that provides thousands of jobs in the aerospace industry; and
- a route system that has grown to 58 airports in 29 states, carrying more than 60 million customers on 352 Boeing 737 aircraft.

Check the magazine stories and the web site regularly to update these performance figures.

No issue is more important than safety and security. One need only to study the checkered history of ValuJet or Air Florida to see what one catastrophic crash can do to an airline when the airline is perceived to have been at fault. Meanwhile, Southwest maintains a 30-year safety record and is generally acknowledged to be one of the world's safest airlines.

Of course, Southwest's customers remain one of the company's main constituencies. Despite its "no-frills" orientation, Southwest consistently receives the highest rankings for customer satisfaction. This is achieved through the successful management of customer expectations. By emphasizing low price and consistency, Southwest has successfully redefined the concept of quality airline service. For example, the "Triple Crown Award" goes to the airline, if any, which has the best on-time record, best baggage handling, and fewest customer complaints according to statistics published in the Department of Transportation (DOT) Air Travel Consumer Reports. First won by Southwest in 1988, the airline has won the award every year since 1992. No other airline has ranked on top in all three categories for even a single month, although Continental Airlines is catching up fast!

Given its mission, employee satisfaction is another important indicator of company success. Personnel are a crucial determinant of organizational performance throughout the industry. Labor costs are about 40 percent of operating costs in the industry, while at Southwest they are considerably lower. As noted, labor relations is an important determinant of company survival. Southwest has one of the lowest personnel turnover ratios in the industry. It began the first profit-sharing plan in the industry, and employees now own about 12 percent of the stock. *Fortune* has named Southwest as one of the best companies for attracting, developing, and keeping talented people. In 1997, *Fortune* ranked Southwest first on its list of the "100 Best Companies to Work for in America," and Southwest has been in the top five for the past four years.

Southwest has had generally peaceful and cooperative labor relations throughout most of its history. One salient result of management-labor harmony is that Southwest employees are the most productive in the industry. A single agent usually staffs gates, where competitors commonly use two or three. Ground crews are composed of six or fewer employees, about half the number used by other carriers. Despite the lean staffing, planes are turned around in half the time of many rivals. Southwest pays its pilots wages that are comparable to the major carriers, but pilot productivity (e.g., number of flights per day, number of hours worked) is considerably higher.

Despite its low-cost structure, Southwest is not able to control all costs. Perhaps the most important uncontrollable element is fuel, which has varied from 78.7 cents per gallon in 2000 to 55.2 cents per gallon in 1995. One advantage that larger, broader scope carriers have is a more limited exposure to fuel price volatility. Broader scope allows them to take advantage of geographic differences in fuel prices, and deeper pockets allow them to hedge against future price increases. However, Southwest does have the advantage of a younger and more fuel-efficient fleet than its larger competitors.

Market share is another indicator of an organization's performance. By this criterion, Southwest also ranks at the top of the industry. For example, it consistently ranks first in market share in 80 to 90 of its top 100 city-pair markets, and overall has 60 to 65 percent of total market share. Because of the "Southwest Effect," the carrier gains this share by growing the size of each of its markets—this is achieved by a fare structure that is on average $60 lower than the majors.

The Challenges Ahead

Southwest Airlines is no Johnny-come-lately. Its basic strategy of consistent low-cost, no-frills, high-frequency, on-time air transportation with friendly service is a recipe that has been refined throughout the company's 30-year life. It has worked for the company in periods of catastrophic losses for the industry as well as in times of abundance. Southwest has been able to compete successfully both with the major airlines and those that have been formed to copy its formula.

Opportunities for Growth
Southwest apparently recognizes the potential saturation of its historic markets and the limited number of attractive short-haul markets. Therefore, it has expanded into some longer-haul markets. Longer-haul not only provides avenues for future growth, but also provides potentially higher margins. On average, the company's cost per ASM is about 8 cents. However, on its longer routes costs are as low as 4 cents per ASM. Furthermore, as mentioned, the 10 percent ticket tax has been replaced with a combination ticket tax and takeoff fee. This increases the attractiveness of longer-haul flights.

Analysts see growth directions in the invasion of new markets, such as Florida, as well as in the addition of new city-pairs to Southwest's point-to-point network. In 2000, Southwest began service in Albany and Buffalo, and in 2001, entered West Palm Beach.

Limits to Growth

As critics have noted, there are many challenges on the horizon. Southwest will eventually saturate its historic niche. The company currently flies into 58 airports with more than 2,700 flights per day. Its old strategy of focusing on good climates and smaller, less congested airports has contributed to Southwest's low costs. Many believe that poor weather conditions can affect Southwest's ability to maintain on-time performance and can significantly impact down-line operations. This is magnified by a schedule based on a rapid turnaround, which leaves little leeway for flight delays. Southwest entered and then left the Denver market when bad weather forced an unacceptable number of delays and canceled flights.

This puts a limit on growth because there are only a finite number of markets that can satisfy these criteria. Thus, Southwest has begun to enter markets in poorer climates and to introduce longer-haul flights. Providence, Rhode Island, one of the newer locations, is not a good weather location. There are about 56 airports in good weather locations with populations of over 100,000. Southwest currently serves 36. It is unclear how much demand for point-to-point service exists in the remaining 20.

If Southwest decides to introduce food services as an amenity for longer-haul flights, it would require galleys and onboard services that would significantly boost the cost of operation of those airplanes. Longer flights also result in fewer flights per day and may serve to drive down yield. A mixture of galleyed and non-galleyed aircraft will also make fleet scheduling less flexible. Furthermore, there will be a greater need for functions in the organization responsible for new elements such as national marketing, the frequent flier program, interline agreements, new geographic operations, and possibly food services.

People and culture also are major concerns to further expansion. Southwest is highly selective; it consequently needs a large pool of applicants in order to find a few people good enough for the culture. With labor shortages across the country, it may be difficult to attract large pools of applicants. Without the selectivity, Southwest may not be able to get the human resources it needs in order to differentiate itself from others. The unique culture of Southwest helps make the company really fly. As companies expand, particularly in geographic location, they often find that it becomes increasingly more difficult to maintain the same culture. This is particularly true if the culture is built around the persona of one major leader such as Herb.

Competition

During the last several years, the gap between Southwest and the rest of the majors has narrowed as other carriers have attempted to emulate Southwest's formula. Larger airlines have developed lower cost short-haul divisions. Continental, United, and Delta have all introduced an "airline within an airline" to lower costs for short-haul flights. These separate divisions may hire their own pilots and ground support at much lower costs under separate contractual relations with unions. Under these arrangements pilots can often be employed for less than half the cost of the parent airline. This, not surprisingly, has led to some bitter disputes between management and unions. For example, at American Airlines the unions have seen this as a management tactic for shifting their members from high- to low-paying jobs with the same duties.

At the same time, Southwest has adopted many of the features that the majors use to support their large networks. As Southwest has grown in scope, it has introduced national advertising, including NFL sponsorship; a frequent flier program, including a branded credit card; and interline and marketing agreements with international carriers. Southwest's operations at Nashville are developing into a hub. The carrier's average stage length has also increased over the last several years. Southwest has now expanded into geographic markets and climates that are not as compatible with its original fair-weather, low-congestion strategy. Its flights now compete head-to-head with some of the major carriers.

Recent successes of Continental Airlines under the leadership of Gordon Bethune are most impressive. He has virtually turned the airline around 180 degrees. In the near term Continental seems likely to be one of SWA's strongest competitors, in addition to Jet-

Blue.[15] JetBlue, under the leadership of David Neeleman, the opposite in personality from Herb Kelleher, is fast becoming a no-frills airline for Southwest to take seriously. It has a similar philosophy as SWA, e.g., it has just one type of plane, the Airbus A320, and doesn't serve meals. It does, however, let passengers pick their seats, has leather upholstery, free satellite TV and a frequent flier program. Neeleman has big plans SWA cannot afford to ignore.[16]

While SWA and JetBlue are just thinking about going global, Ryanair and EasyJet based in Britain are expanding their networks out of Britain and setting up bases in Europe where low-fare airlines are few and far between. Crossair is now a player in this important market along with Virgin Express. These two carriers are now in a regulatory environment that SWA faced in 1978, i.e., one that is becoming much more deregulated thanks to the EU legislation that took full effect in 1997 that allows any qualified airline to fly anywhere within the EU without government approval. Although both these low-fare airlines are copying much of the SWA model, greater social costs and much more attractive high-speed rail alternatives make running a low-cost operation successfully in Europe a bit more challenging as Virgin Express and Debonair have learned. Nonetheless, low-fare air travel is growing 25 percent yearly in Europe![17]

Appendix A	**Glossary of Terms**	
	ARC	Airline Reporting Corporation. An organization owned by the airlines that serves as a clearing house for processing airline tickets.
	ASM	Available Seat Mile. One ASM is one sellable seat, flown for one mile. For example, a 138 seat Boeing 737 traveling 749 miles from LGA to ORD (LaGuardia to O'Hare) represents 103,362 ASMs.
	Class of Service	The fare level at which a ticket is sold. This does not refer to the cabin in which the passenger flies. For example, a United Airlines' availability display shows the following classes of service for coach: Y B M H Q V. By subdividing coach into classes, airlines can control inventory and manage yield.
	Code Share	An interline agreement by which two carriers are able to apply their flight numbers to the same plane. This often includes an interline connection. For example, American Airlines and South African Airlines code share on SAA's flight to JHB (Johannesburg). The flight has an AA flight number and an SAA flight number. AA can sell it as an American Airlines flight.
	CRS	Computer Reservation System. Allows airlines and travel agents to reserve and sell seats on airline flights. CRS companies include Apollo, Sabre, System One, and Worldspan.
	Direct Flight	Any flight designated by a single flight number. Direct flights can include multiple stops and even changes of aircraft. For example, Pan Am Flight 1 at one time made 11 stops as it flew "round the world" direct from LAX to JFK.
	Full Fare	Designated as "Full Y." The undiscounted first, business, or coach fare. For domestic fares, this is used to calculate the level of discounted fares. Full Y is rarely paid for domestic flights, but is common on international flights when inventory is scarce.
	Interline Agreement	Refers to various agreements between carriers. Common interline agreements concern the transfer of baggage, the endorsement and acceptance of tickets, and joint airfares (for example, a passenger flies USAir from Albany to JFK and then SAS to Copenhagen).
	Inventory	The number of seats available for each class of service for a given flight. For example, a USAir flight may have no K inventory

available (seats to sell at K class fare levels) although higher priced H seats may be available. Both seats are in coach.

Load Factor   The percentage of ASMs that are filled by paying passengers. Can be calculated by dividing RPMs by ASMs.

O&D   Origin and Destination. Refers to the originating and terminating airports of an itinerary segment. Connection points are not counted in O&Ds. This is different from city-pair, which refers to the origination and termination of a flight segment. For example, for a passenger traveling on NW from HPN (White Plains) to SMF (Sacramento), the O&D market is HPN-SMF. The city-pairs flown will be HPN-DTW and DTW-SMF (White Plains-Detroit, Detroit-Sacramento)

Restricted Fare   Any fare that has restrictive rules attached to it. Common restrictions include Saturday Night Stayover, Advance Purchase, Day/Time of Travel, Non-Refundability, and Class of Service. Generally, lower fares have greater restrictions.

RPM   Revenue Passenger Mile. One passenger paying to fly one mile. For example, a passenger who pays to fly from LGA to ORD represents 749 RPMs. The class of service and fare paid are not considered in calculating RPMs.

Stage Length   The length of a flight segment. The stage length between LGA and ORD is 749 miles.

Unrestricted Fare   A fare with no restrictions. Often, this is not the full fare. For example, American's Y26 fare is an unrestricted fare, but still lower than the full Y fare.

Yield   Measured as revenue per RPM.

Appendix B   Interview of Joanna DePinto, employee in marketing division of Southwest Airlines, conducted by the team on telephone on March 23, 2001.

1. When you got hired, what was the process?
    I was an intern in Austin, when I applied. I got interviewed by a bunch of people many times. Group interviews are a big deal at Southwest. They see your ability to communicate well and get along with other people. You meet the group you will be working with and they see how you get on with them.
2. Do you know of any other companies, that have the same selection process?
    No! Well, not exactly the same selection process. Some companies like Compac and Cisco are trying to emulate us. They are hiring people not just for technical skills but also for their people skills.
3. Who do you think makes the final decision about selection?
    The applicants work with a recruiter through all rounds of interviews, but I think the final decision is made by the manager of the department and the director.
4. What impacts the decision-making process most at Southwest?
    Everyone works towards the good of the company. It all comes down to what is best for the company. Cost saving is very important. As far as hiring is concerned, it is definitely about the kind of person you are. They hire for personality and train for skill.
5. So attitude and personality are the key drivers at Southwest?
    Oh! Absolutely!
6. What about internal politics in hiring and selection?
    There is no infighting or disagreement. People really try and do what is best for the company. I don't think there is any internal politics that affects decision making. People enjoy coming to work everyday; there is no cut throat competition or anything.

7. What is Herb like?

    Oh! He is awesome! He is a wonderful man, very reachable. The first day I went to work, he got into the same elevator as me and kissed me! I got like quite excited, 'Herb Kelleher kissed me.' When I reached my office I told my colleagues about it and they said, 'Oh! But he kisses everyone!'

Appendix C

Question 1A: Describe the Hiring Process at Southwest

Southwest Airlines tries to fill all vacancies from within the Company if at all possible. The reason for this is because we are making the assumption that someone who is already employed by us has the "spirit" and attitude and work ethics we want, whereas we would be taking a chance by hiring from outside. The theory is that we will hire for attitude and train for skill. Obviously, there are times when we must hire from outside. First, of course, we do as close a match as possible for the job requirements—although if an internal doesn't meet all the requirements but does meet most of them and has a great attitude/spirit, we will give them a chance at interviewing for the position.

Our interview process can be quite strenuous. We do group interviews for some front line positions such as Flight Attendant or Reservation Sales Agent. This would consist of a team of interviewers and each asks questions that the applicants respond to. Then each interviewer gets to cast a vote for or against bringing each applicant back for a second interview. From this point on, the process is similar for all job applicants. The second interview (for those who participated in group interviews) and the first interview for other applicants usually consists of a smaller interview team. The questions are asked by all of the interviewers but they are basically "behavior based" questions. This means that applicants will be asked to describe a time in their past work life when they were faced with a certain situation. The response should include what the situation was, what the applicant did or how they handled it, and finally what was the result. For example, if the job required good conflict management skills, an interviewer might ask the applicant to describe a time when they were in a heated disagreement with a coworker—what was the situation, how did you handle it, and what was the result? The response from the applicant is a predictor of the behavior this potential employee would use in the future on this job if hired.

When the interview is over, all interview team members must come to a consensus as to whether to hire this individual or, as is frequently necessary, to bring the applicant back for a third interview. If there is a third interview, the next higher level of leadership will be involved. Sometimes, depending on the position being interviewed for, interviews can continue all the way through the Vice President. An example of that is that anyone taking a position within our People Department (human resources) or even just moving from one position to another within the People Department will interview first with a recruiter and interview team consisting of peers and first level leadership for that position, and continue all the way through our Vice President of People.

This is time consuming; however, we are more confident of getting the right person in the right position. Also, you should be aware that we frequently start with a pool of applicants but end up reposting the job. The reason this happens is that we do not take the best person in the pool; instead we are looking for the best person for the job and if we don't find him or her in the pool, then we start over. An empty desk for a period of time is sometimes a price we pay in order to find the best fit.

Question 1B: Can Any Company Duplicate What Southwest Does? Have Any Tried or Benchmarked and Then Launched Their Own?

Many companies have benchmarked Southwest for numerous reasons. In fact, SWA at one time hosted a "Culture Day" for outside companies because we had so many requests. We have stopped doing this because it got so big, it was taking us away from what we should be doing. I'm sure that some of those organizations have listened to what they were told and did try to implement some of what we do. However, I do not know who did not do it, nor do I have information on how successful they were. Obviously, there is a down side to the way we approach hiring. Lots of organizations probably decided not to put the extra burden on other employees by having a position vacant for very long and using resources in the hiring process for such a long interview process.

Question 2: Who Makes the Selection and Placement Decisions at Southwest?

I believe I answered this question in 1A above. To recap, the decision is a joint decision of the interview team if it is a front line position. If not front line, then not only does the interview team have to be in agreement, but all the leaders involved in the interview process. If any one of them kicks back on an application, it can take that applicant out of the running.

Question 3: What Impacts the Decision-Making Process the Most at Southwest? Do Politics Impact the Process?

The hire/no hire decision is based on how well of a match the applicant is to the requirements of the job PLUS their attitude/spirit—it takes both! As far as politics are concerned, even Herb stays out of the hiring process. It is the least political, buddy-buddy system that it can be.

Question 4: How Important Is the Selection and Placement Process to Southwest's Success?

Southwest Airlines has a unique culture and our financial success as an airline is founded on that culture; it is what makes us "different." We like to have fun, we love a challenge, we are made up of people who take accountability for their actions and for the success of our airline—we, therefore, believe in hard work/hard play. We like people who are willing to work outside the lines and are willing to step up to the plate and make a decision. We don't like people who take themselves too seriously, are complainers or not willing to "do whatever it takes." Not everyone is fit for this environment. If we do not continue to employ "the right stuff," our culture, overall, could fail. How important is the selection and placement process to Southwest's success? I don't know a word descriptive enough! Let's just say it is crucial!

—Pat Janson, Facilitator
University of People, Career Development Services
People Department, Southwest Airlines
March 27 and April 4, 2001

Endnotes

1. Brooker, K., "The Chairman of the Board Looks Back," *Fortune* (May 28, 2001): 63–76.
2. JP Morgan, Short-haul Competitive Update (April 16, 1996): 3; _____,"Snip, snip, snip," *The Economist* (October 13, 2001): 59–60.
3. Brown, E., "A Smokeless Herb," *Fortune* (May 28, 2001): 78–79; Zuckerman, L., "Airline Based at Kennedy Expands West," *The New York Times* (May 23, 2001): C1,6.
4. CEO Profile of Herb Kelleher, *Chief Executive Magazine* (March 2000).
5. Wong, N. "Let Spirit Guide Leadership" *Workforce* (February 2000): 33–36; Donnelly, G., "Recruiting, Retention & Returns," *CFO* (March 1, 2000).
6. Gittell, J.H. "Paradox of Coordination and Control," *California Management Review* (Spring 2000): 101–117.
7. Carbonara, P. "Hire for Attitude, Train for Skill," *Fast Company* (August 1996): 73–78.
8. Brooker, K. "Can Anyone Replace Herb?" *Fortune* (April 17, 2000): 186–192.
9. Gittell, J.H. *op cit.*
10. Jackson, S.E., and Schuler, R.S. *Managing Human Resources through Strategic Partnership* (Mason, Ohio: South-Western 2003).
11. Jones, K. "Herb's Flight Plan," *Texas Monthly* (March 1999); Zellner,W. "Southwest: After Kelleher, More Blue Skies," *Business Week* (April 2, 2001): 45.
12. Lee, V. "Impacts of Deregulation and Recent Trends on Aviation Industry Management," *Bankers Trust Research* (August 30, 1996): 16; Tully, S. "From Bad to Worse," *Fortune* (October 15, 2001): 119–28; Conlin, M. "Where Layoffs Are a Last Resort," *Business Week* (October 8, 2001): 42; Ewing, J., D. Fairlamb, and K. Capell, "The Fallout in Europe," *Business Week* (October 8, 2001): 52–53.
13. Myerson, A.R. "Air Herb," *The New York Times Magazine* (November 9, 1997): 36.
14. Freiberg, J. and K. Freiberg, *NUTS! Southwest Airlines' Crazy Recipe for Business and Personal Success* (Austin, TX: Bard Books, 1996); Oppel, R. "Southwest Manages to Keep Its Balance," *The New York Times* (September 25, 2001): C6.
15. "Outlaw Flyboy CEOs," *Fortune* (November 13, 2000): 237–250.
16. Brown, E. *op cit*; Zuckerman, L. "JetBlue, Exception Among Airlines, Is Likely to Post a Profit," *The New York Times* (November 7, 2001): C3.
17. "The Squeeze on Europe's Air Fares," *The Economist* (May 26, 2001): 57-58; Done, K. "Ryanair Continues to Escape Turbulence," *Financial Times* (November 6, 2001): 23.

BULLER | SCHULER

Managing Organizations and People
A Resource for Cases in Management, Organizational Behavior, and Human Resource Management

Abstract

Lincoln Electric, the world's largest maker of arc-welding products, employs 2,400 workers in two U.S. factories near Cleveland and an equal number in eleven factories located in other countries. The company has a sales force of more than 200 persons. This case provides an in-depth look at the company's strategy and human resource management practices that have helped it to achieve and sustain a competitive advantage in the industry. Among the human resource management practices illustrated are the company's renowned incentive management and bonus systems, employee involvement programs, high performance work culture, and informal structure. Several interviews with employees provide insight into the impact of these practices.

The Lincoln Electric Company

People are our most valuable asset. They must feel secure, important, challenged, in control of their destiny, confident in their leadership, be responsive to common goals, believe they are being treated fairly, have easy access to authority and open lines of communication in all possible directions. Perhaps the most important task Lincoln employees face today is that of establishing an example for others in the Lincoln organization in other parts of the world. We need to maximize the benefits of cooperation and teamwork, fusing high technology with human talent, so that we here in the USA and all our subsidiary and joint venture operations will be in a position to realize our full potential.
—George Willis, former CEO, The Lincoln Electric Company

Today, The Lincoln Electric Company under the leadership of Donald Hastings, is the world's largest manufacturer of arc-welding products and a leading producer of industrial electric motors. The firm employs almost 4,000 workers in three U.S. factories near Cleveland and almost an equal number in factories located in other countries. This does not include the field sales force of more than 200. The company's U.S. market share (for arc-welding products) is estimated at more than 40 percent.[1]

■ This case was written by Arthur Sharplin. It is adapted here by R.S. Schuler and used with the permission of Arthur D. Sharplin.

The Lincoln incentive management plan has been well known for many years. Many college management texts make reference to the Lincoln plan as a model for achieving higher worker productivity. Certainly, the firm has been successful according to the usual measures.

James F. Lincoln died in 1965 and there was some concern, even among employees, that the management system would fall into disarray, that profits would decline, and that year-end bonuses might be discounted. Quite the contrary—since Lincoln's death, the company appears as strong as ever. Each year, except the recession years 1982 and 1983, has seen high profits and bonuses. In 1995, Lincoln Electric's centennial, sales for the first time surpassed $1 billion. While there was some employee discontent about relatively flat bonuses in 1995, employee morale and productivity remain very good.[2] Employee turnover is almost nonexistent except for retirements. Lincoln's market share is stable. The historically high stock dividends continue.

A Historical Sketch

In 1895, after being "frozen out" of the depression-ravaged Elliot-Lincoln Company, a maker of Lincoln-designed electric motors, John C. Lincoln took out his second patent and began to manufacture his improved motor. He opened his new business, unincorporated, with $200 he had earned redesigning a motor for young Herbert Henry Dow, who later founded the Dow Chemical Company.

Started during an economic depression and cursed by a major fire after only one year in business, the company grew, but hardly prospered, through its first quarter century. In 1906, John C. Lincoln incorporated the business and moved from his one-room, fourth-floor factory to a new three-story building he erected in east Cleveland. He expanded his workforce to 30 and sales grew to over $50,000 a year. John preferred being an engineer and inventor rather than a manager, though, and it was to be left to another Lincoln to manage the company through its years of success. In 1907, after a bout of typhoid fever forced him from Ohio State University in his senior year, James F. Lincoln, John's brother, joined the fledgling company. In 1914 he became the active head of the firm, with the titles of General Manager and Vice President. John remained president of the company for some years but became more involved in other business ventures and in his work as an inventor.

One of James Lincoln's early actions was to ask the employees to elect representatives to a committee which would advise him on company operations. This "Advisory Board" has met with the chief executive officer every two weeks since that time. This was only the first of a series of innovative personnel policies which have, over the years, distinguished Lincoln Electric from its contemporaries.

The first year the Advisory Board was in existence, working hours were reduced from 55 per week, then standard, to 50 hours a week. In 1915, the company gave each employee a paid-up life insurance policy. A welding school, which continues today, was begun in 1917. In 1918, an employee bonus plan was attempted. It was not continued, but the idea was to resurface later.

The Lincoln Electric Employees Association was formed in 1919 to provide health benefits and social activities. This organization continues today and has assumed several additional functions over the years. In 1923, a piecework pay system was in effect: employees got two weeks paid vacation each year, and wages were adjusted for changes in the Consumer Price Index. Approximately 30 per cent of the common stock was set aside for key employees in 1914. A stock purchase plan for all employees was begun in 1925.

The Board of Directors voted to start a suggestion system in 1929. The program is still in effect, but cash awards, a part of the early program, were discontinued several years ago. Now, suggestions are rewarded by "additional points" which affect year-end bonuses.

The legendary Lincoln bonus plan was proposed by the Advisory Board and accepted on a trial basis in 1934. The first annual bonus amounted to about 25 percent of wages. There has been a bonus every year since then. The bonus plan has been a cornerstone of the Lincoln management system and recent bonuses have approximated annual wages.

By 1944, Lincoln employees enjoyed a pension plan, a policy of promotion from within, and continuous employment. Base pay rates were determined by formal job evaluation and a merit rating system was in effect.

In the prologue of James F. Lincoln's last book, Charles G. Herbruck writes regarding the foregoing personnel innovations:

They were not to buy good behavior. They were not efforts to increase profits. They were not antidotes to labor difficulties. They did not constitute a "do-gooder" program. They were expression of mutual respect for each per son's importance to the job to be done. All of them reflect the leadership of James Lincoln, under whom they were nurtured and propagated.

During World War II, Lincoln prospered as never before. By the start of the war, the company was the world's largest manufacturer of arc-welding products. Sales of about $4,000,000 in 1934 grew to $24,000,000 by 1941. Productivity per employee more than doubled during the same period. The Navy's Price Review Board challenged the high profits. And the Internal Revenue Service questioned the tax deductibility of employee bonuses, arguing they were not "ordinary and necessary" costs of doing business. But the forceful and articulate James Lincoln was able to overcome the objections.

Certainly since 1935 and probably for several years before that, Lincoln's productivity has been well above the average for similar companies. The company claims levels of productivity more than twice those for other manufacturers from 1945 onward. Information available from outside sources tends to support these claims.

Company Philosophy

James F. Lincoln was the son of a Congregational minister, and Christian principles were at the center of his business philosophy. The confidence that he had in the efficacy of Christ's teachings is illustrated by the following remark taken from one of his books:

The Christian ethic should control our acts. If it did control our acts, the savings in cost of distribution would be tremendous. Advertising would be a contact of the expert consultant with the customer, in order to give the customer the best product available when all of the customer's needs are considered. Competition then would be in improving the quality of products and increasing efficiency in producing and distributing them; not in deception, as is now too customary. Pricing would reflect efficiency of production; it would not be a selling dodge that the customer may be sorry he accepted. It would be proper for all concerned and rewarding for the ability used in producing the product.

There is no indication that Lincoln attempted to evangelize his employees or customers—or the general public for that matter. Neither the former chairman of the board and chief executive, George Willis, nor the current one, Donald F. Hastings, mention the Christian gospel in their recent speeches and interviews. The company motto, "The actual is limited, the possible is immense," is prominently displayed, but there is no display of religious slogans, and there is no company chapel.

Attitude Toward the Customer

James Lincoln saw the customer's needs as the raison d'etre for every company. "When any company has achieved success so that it is attractive as an investment," he wrote, "all money usually needed for expansion is supplied by the customer in retained earnings. It is obvious that the customer's interests, not the stockholder's, should come first." In 1947 he said, "Care should be taken . . . not to rivet attention on profit. Between 'How much do I get?' and 'How do I make this better, cheaper, more useful?' the difference is fundamental and decisive." Willis, too, ranks the customer as management's most important constituency. This is reflected in Lincoln's policy to "at all times price on the basis of cost and at all times keep pressure on our cost. . . ." Lincoln's goal, often stated, is "to build a better and better product at a lower and lower price." James Lincoln said, "It is obvious that the customer's interests should be the first goal of industry."

This priority, and the priority given to other groups, is reflected in the Mission and Values Statement and the set of Goals shown in Appendix A.

Attitude Toward Stockholders

Stockholders are given last priority at Lincoln. This is a continuation of James Lincoln's philosophy: "The last group to be considered is the stockholders who own stock because they think it will be more profitable than investing money in any other way." Concerning division of the largess produced by incentive management, he wrote, "The absentee stockholder also will get his share, even if undeserved, out of the greatly increased profit that the efficiency produces."

Attitude Toward Unionism

There has never been a serious effort to organize Lincoln employees. While James Lincoln criticized the labor movement for "selfishly attempting to better its position at the expense of the people it must serve," he still had kind words for union members. He excused abuses of union power as "the natural reactions of human beings to the abuses to which management has subjected them." Lincoln's idea of the correct relationship between workers and managers is shown by this comment: "Labor and management are properly not warring camps; they are parts of one organization in which they must, and should, cooperate fully and happily."

Beliefs and Assumptions About Employees

If fulfilling customer needs is the desired goal of business, then employee performance and productivity are the means by which this goal can best be achieved. It is the Lincoln attitude toward employees, reflected in the following comments by James Lincoln, which is credited by many with creating the success the company has experienced:

He is just as eager as any manager is to be part of a team that is properly organized and working for the advancement of our economy. . . . He has no desire to make profits for those who do not hold up their end in production, as is true of absentee stockholders and inactive people in the company.

If money is to be used as an incentive, the program must provide that what is paid to the worker is what he has earned. The earnings of each must be in accordance with accomplishment.

Status is of great importance in all human relationships. The greatest incentive that money has, usually, is that it is a symbol of success. The resulting status is the real incentive. . . . Money alone can be an incentive to the miser only.

There must be complete honesty and understanding between the hourly worker and management if high efficiency is to be obtained.

These beliefs and assumptions have helped shaped Lincoln's human resource objectives. These are shown in Appendix B.

Lincoln's Business

Arc-welding has been the standard joining method in shipbuilding for decades. It is the predominant way of connecting steel in the construction industry. Most industrial plants have their own welding shops for maintenance and construction. Manufacturers of tractors and all kinds of heavy equipment use arc-welding extensively in the manufacturing process. Many hobbyists have their own welding machines and use them for making metal items such as patio furniture and barbecue pits. The popularity of welded sculpture as an art form is growing.

While advances in welding technology have been frequent, arc-welding products, in the main, have hardly changed. Lincoln's Innershield process is a notable exception. This process, described later, lowers welding cost and improves quality and speed in many applications. The most widely used Lincoln electrode, the Fleetweld 5P, has been virtually the same since the 1930s. The most popular engine-driven welder in the world, the Lincoln SA-200, has been a gray-colored assembly including a four-cylinder continental Red Seal engine and a 200 ampere direct-current generator with two current-control knobs for at least four decades. A 1989 model SA-200 even weighs almost the same as the 1950 model, and it certainly is little changed in appearance.

The company's share of the U.S. arc-welding products market appears to have been about 40 percent for many years. The welding products market has grown somewhat faster than the level of industry in general. The market is highly price-competitive, with variations in prices of standard items normally amounting to only a percent or two. Lincoln's products are sold directly by its engineering-oriented sales force and indirectly through its distributor organization. Advertising expenditures amount to less than three-fourths of a percent of sales. Research and development expenditures typically range from $10 million to $12 million, considerably more than competitors.

The other major welding process, flame-welding, has not been competitive with arc-welding since the 1930s. However, plasma-arc-welding, a relatively new process which uses a conducting stream of super heated gas (plasma) to confine the welding current to a small area, has made some inroads, especially in metal tubing manufacturing, in recent years. Major advances in technology which will produce an alternative superior to arc-welding within the next decade or so appear unlikely. Also, it seems likely that changes in the machines and techniques used in arc-welding will be evolutionary rather than revolutionary.

It is also reasonable to observe that Lincoln Electric's business objectives, shown in Appendix C, are likely to change in an evolutionary rather than a revolutionary way.

Products

The company is primarily engaged in the manufacture and sale of arc-welding products—electric welding machines and metal electrodes. Lincoln also produces electric motors ranging from one-half horsepower to 200 horsepower. Motors constitute about eight to ten percent of total sales. Several million dollars have recently been invested in automated equipment that will double Lincoln's manufacturing capacity for one-half to 20 horsepower electric motors. The electric welding machines, some consisting of a transformer or motor and generator arrangement powered by commercial electricity and others consisting of an internal combustion engine and generator, are designed to produce 30 to 1,500 amperes of electrical power. This electrical current is used to melt a consumable metal electrode with the molten metal being transferred in super hot spray to the metal joint being welded. Very high temperatures and hot sparks are produced, and operators usually must wear special eye and face protection and leather gloves, often along with leather aprons and sleeves. Lincoln and its competitors now market a wide range of general purpose and specialty electrodes for welding mild steel, aluminum, cast iron, and stainless and special steels. Most of these electrodes are designed to meet the standards of the American Welding Society, a trade association. They are thus essentially the same as to size and composition from one manufacturer to another. Every electrode manufacturer has a limited number of unique products, but these typically constitute only a small percentage of total sales.

Welding electrodes are of two basic types: coated "stick" electrodes and coiled wire. Coated "stick" electrodes, usually 14 inches long and smaller than a pencil in diameter, which are held in a special insulated holder by the operator, who must manipulate the electrode in order to maintain a proper arc-width and pattern of deposition of the metal being transferred. Stick electrodes are packaged in 6- to 50-pound boxes.

Coiled wire, ranging in diameter from 0.035' to 0.219', is designed to be fed continuously to the welding arc through a "gun" held by the operator or positioned by automatic positioning equipment. The wire is packaged in coils, reels, and drums weighing from 14 to 1,000 pounds and may be solid or flux-cored. For more information on products visit the Web site **http://www.Lincolnelectric.com**.

Manufacturing Process

The main plant is in Euclid, Ohio, a suburb on Cleveland's east side. The layout of this plant is shown in Exhibit 1. There are no warehouses. Materials flow from the half-mile long dock on the north side of the plant through the production lines to a very limited storage and loading area on the south side.

Materials used on each work station are stored as close as possible to the work station. The administrative offices, near the center of the factory, are entirely functional. A corridor below the main level provides access to the factory floor from the main entrance near the center of the plan. *Fortune* recently declared the Euclid facility one of America's 10 best-managed factories, and compared it with a General Electric plant also on the list:

Stepping into G.E.'s spanking new dishwasher plant, an awed supplier said, is like stepping "into the Hyatt Regency." By comparison, stepping into Lincoln Electric's 33-year-old, cavernous, dimly lit factory is like stumbling into a dingy big-city YMCA. It's only when one starts looking at how these factories do things that similarities become apparent. They have found ways to merge design with manufacturing, build in quality, make wise choices about automation, get close to customers, and handle their workforces.

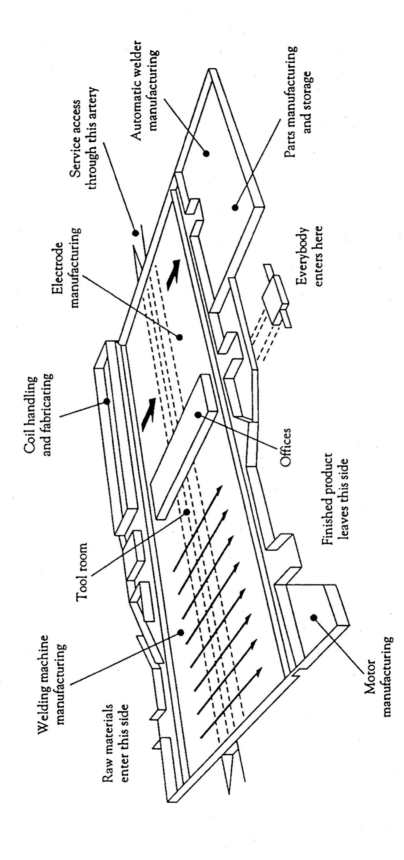

EXHIBIT 1
Main Factory Layout

Another Lincoln plant, in Mentor, Ohio, houses some of the electrode production operations, which were moved from the main plant. Electrode manufacturing is highly capital intensive. Metal rods purchased from steel producers are drawn down to smaller diameters, cut to length, and coated with pressed-powder "flux" for stick electrodes or plated with copper (for conductivity) and put into coils or spools for wire. Lincoln's Innershield wire is hollow and filled with a material similar to that used to coat stick electrodes. As mentioned earlier, this represented a major innovation in welding technology when it was introduced. The company is highly secretive about its electrode production processes, and outsiders are not given access to the details of those processes.

Lincoln welding machines and electric motors are made on a series of assembly lines. Gasoline and diesel engines are purchased partially assembled but practically all other components are made from basic industrial products, e.g., steel bars and sheets and bare copper conductor wire.

Individual components, such as gasoline tanks for engine-driven welders and steel shafts for motors and generators, are made by numerous small "factories within a factory." The shaft for a certain generator, for example, is made from raw steel bar by one operator who uses five large machines, all running continuously. A saw cuts the bar to length, a digital lathe machines different sections to varying diameters, a special mining machine cuts a slot for the keyway, and so forth, until a finished shaft is produced. The operator moves the shafts from machine to machine and makes necessary adjustments. Another operator punches, shapes, and paints sheetmetal cowling parts. One assembles steel laminations onto a rotor shaft, then winds, insulates, and tests the rotors. Finished components are moved by crane operators to the nearby assembly lines.

Worker Performance and Attitude

Exceptional worker performance at Lincoln is a matter of record. The typical Lincoln employee earns about twice as much as other factory workers in the Cleveland area. Yet the company's labor cost per sales dollar is well below industry averages. Worker turnover is practically nonexistent except for retirements and departures by new employees. Turnover is less than 4 percent for employees who have been on the jobs for at least 18 months.[3]

Sales per Lincoln factory employee currently exceed $150,000. An observer at the factory quickly sees why this figure is so high. Each worker is proceeding busily and thoughtfully about the task at hand. There is no idle chatter. Most workers take no coffee breaks. Many operate several machines and make a substantial component unaided. The supervisors are busy with planning and recordkeeping duties and hardly glance at the people they "supervise." The manufacturing procedures appear efficient—no unnecessary steps, no wasted motions, no wasted materials. Finished components move smoothly to subsequent work stations. Appendix D includes summaries of interviews with employees.

Organizational Structure

Lincoln has never allowed development of a formal organization chart. The objective of this policy is to ensure maximum flexibility. An open door policy is practiced throughout the company, and personnel are encouraged to take problems to the persons most capable of resolving them. Once, Harvard Business School researchers prepared an organization chart reflecting the implied relationships at Lincoln. The chart became available within the company, and present management feels that had a disruptive effect. Therefore, no organizational chart appears in this report.

Perhaps because of the quality and enthusiasm of the Lincoln workforce, routine supervision is almost nonexistent. A typical production foreman, for example, supervises as many as 100 workers, a span-of-control which does not allow more than infrequent worker-supervisor interaction.

Position titles and traditional flows of authority do imply something of an organizational structure, however. For example, the Vice President, Sales, and the Vice President, Electrode Division, report to the President, as do various staff assistants such as the Personnel Director and the Director of Purchasing.

Using such implied relationships, it has been determined that production workers have two or, at most, three levels of supervision between themselves and the President.

Human Resource Policies

As mentioned earlier, it is Lincoln's remarkable human resource practices that are credited by many with the company's success.

Recruitment and Selection

Every job opening is advertised internally on company bulletin boards and any employee can apply for any job so advertised. External hiring is permitted only for entry-level positions. Selection for these jobs is done on the basis of personal interviews—there is no aptitude or psychological testing. A committee consisting of Vice Presidents and supervisors interviews candidates initially cleared by the personnel department. Final selection is made by the supervisor who has a job opening. Nonetheless, it is increasingly desirable that factory workers have some advanced math skills and understand the use of computers. Out of over 20,000 applications received by the personnel department during a recent period, relatively few were hired in 1994–1995. Consequently Lincoln's expansion is becoming increasingly dependent upon getting employees qualified to work in the Lincoln environment, within the famous incentive system.[4]

Job Security

In 1958 Lincoln formalized its guaranteed continuous employment policy, which had already been in effect for many years. There have been no layoffs since World War II. Since 1958, every worker with over two year's longevity has been guaranteed at least 30 hours per week, 49 weeks per year.

The Policy has never been so severely tested as during the 1981 to 1983 recession. As a manufacturer of capital goods, Lincoln's business is highly cyclical. In previous recessions the company was able to avoid major sales declines. However, sales plummeted 32 percent in 1982 and another 16 percent the next year. Few companies could withstand such a revenue collapse and remain profitable. Yet Lincoln not only earned profits, but no employee was laid off and year-end incentive bonuses continued. To weather the storm, management cut most of the non-salaried workers back to 30 hours a week for varying periods of time. Many employees were reassigned and the total workforce was slightly reduced through normal attrition and restricted hiring. Many employees grumbled at their unexpected misfortune, probably to the surprise and dismay of some Lincoln managers. However, sales and profits—and employee bonuses—soon rebounded and all was well again.

Performance Evaluations

Each supervisor formally evaluates subordinates twice a year using the cards shown in Exhibit 2. The employee performance criteria, "quality," "dependability," "ideas and cooperation," and "output" are considered to be independent of each other. Marks on the cards are converted to numerical scores which are forced to average 100 for each evaluating supervisor. Individual merit rating scores normally range from 80 to 110. Any score over 110 requires a special letter to top management. These scores (over 110) are not considered in computing the required 100-point average for each evaluating supervisor.

Suggestions for improvements often result in recommendations for exceptionally high performance scores. Supervisors discuss individual performance marks with the employees concerned. Each warranty claim is traced to the individual employee whose work caused the defect. The employee's performance score may be reduced, or the worker may be required to repay the cost of servicing the warranty claim by working without pay.

Compensation

Basic wage levels for jobs at Lincoln are determined by a wage survey of similar jobs in the Cleveland area.[5] These rates are adjusted quarterly in accordance with changes in the Cleveland area wage index. Insofar as possible, base wage rates are translated into piece rates. Today the average Lincoln factory worker earns $16.54 an hour vs. the average $14.25 manufacturing wage in the Cleveland area. Practically all production workers and many others—for example, some forklift operators—are paid by piece rate. Once established, piece rates are never changed unless a substantive change in the way a job is done results from a source other than the worker doing the job.

EXHIBIT 2   Merit Rating Cards

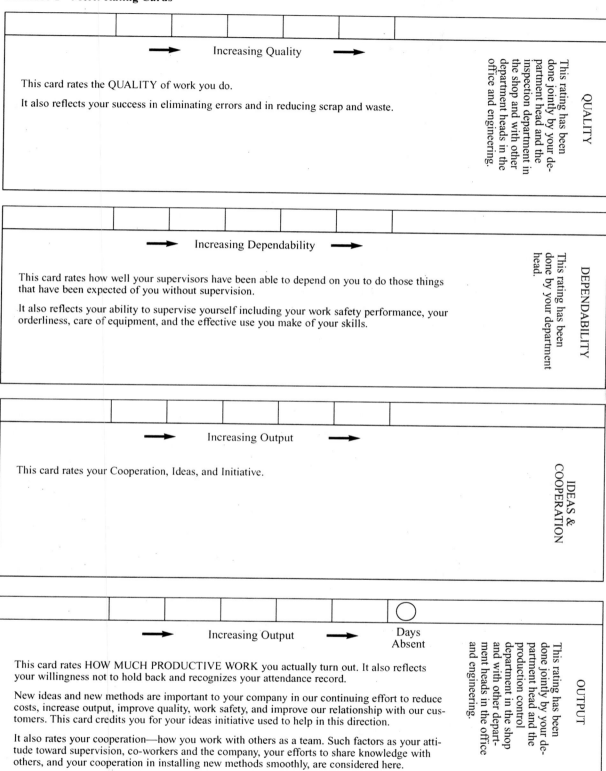

QUALITY

Increasing Quality

This card rates the QUALITY of work you do.

It also reflects your success in eliminating errors and in reducing scrap and waste.

This rating has been done jointly by your department head and the inspection department in the shop and with other department heads in the office and engineering.

DEPENDABILITY

Increasing Dependability

This card rates how well your supervisors have been able to depend on you to do those things that have been expected of you without supervision.

It also reflects your ability to supervise yourself including your work safety performance, your orderliness, care of equipment, and the effective use you make of your skills.

This rating has been done by your department head.

IDEAS & COOPERATION

Increasing Output

This card rates your Cooperation, Ideas, and Initiative.

OUTPUT

Increasing Output   Days Absent

This card rates HOW MUCH PRODUCTIVE WORK you actually turn out. It also reflects your willingness not to hold back and recognizes your attendance record.

New ideas and new methods are important to your company in our continuing effort to reduce costs, increase output, improve quality, work safety, and improve our relationship with our customers. This card credits you for your ideas initiative used to help in this direction.

It also rates your cooperation—how you work with others as a team. Such factors as your attitude toward supervision, co-workers and the company, your efforts to share knowledge with others, and your cooperation in installing new methods smoothly, are considered here.

This rating has been done jointly by your department head and the production control department in the shop and with other department heads in the office and engineering.

In December of each year, a portion of annual profits is distributed to employees as bonuses. Incentive bonuses since 1934 have averaged about 90 percent of annual wages. The average bonus for 1995 was $18,887. Even for the recession years 1982 and 1983, bonuses had averaged $13,998 and $8,557, respectively. Individual bonuses are proportional to merit-rating scores. For example, assume the amount set aside for bonuses is 80 percent of total wages paid to eligible employees. A person whose performance score is 95 will receive a bonus of 76 percent (0.80 × 0.95) of annual wages. While these percentages have often resulted in high total compensation, some employees believe that their bonuses are not rising fast enough, despite rising profits. This reflects the firm's decision to use the money to expand the operations rather than put them into higher bonuses. It also reflects the fact that there are more workers today sharing in a bonus pool that is only a little higher than in many years in the 1980s.[6]

Vacations
The company is shut down for two weeks in August and two weeks during the Christmas season. Vacations are taken during these periods. For employees with over 25 years of service, a fifth week of vacation may be taken at a time acceptable to superiors.

Work Assignment
Management has authority to transfer workers and to switch between overtime and short time as required. Supervisors have undisputed authority to assign specific parts to individual workers, who may have their own preferences due to variations in piece rates. During the 1982–1983 recession, 50 factory workers volunteered to join sales teams and fanned out across the country to sell a new welder designed for automobile body shops and small machine shops. The result: $10 million in sales and a hot new product.

Employee Participation in Decision Making
Thinking of participative management usually evokes a vision of a relaxed, non authoritarian atmosphere. This is not the case at Lincoln. Formal authority is quite strong. "We're very authoritarian around here," says Willis. James F. Lincoln placed a good deal of stress on protecting management's authority. "Management in all successful departments of industry must have complete power," he said. "Management is the coach who must be obeyed. The men, however, are the players who alone can win the game." Despite this attitude, there are several ways in which employees participate in management at Lincoln.

Richard Sabo, Assistant to the Chief Executive Officer, relates job enlargement/enrichment to participation. He said, "The most important participative technique that we use is giving more responsibility to employees. We give a high school graduate more responsibility than other companies give their foremen." Management puts limits on the degree of participation that is allowed, however. In Sabo's words:

When you use 'participation,' put quotes around it. Because we believe that each person should participate only in those decisions he is most knowledgeable about. I don't think production employees should control the decisions of the chairman. They don't know as much as he does about the decisions he is involved in.

The Advisory Board, elected by the workers, meets with the chairman and the president every two weeks to discuss ways of improving operations. As noted earlier, this board has been in existence since 1914 and has contributed to many innovations. The incentive bonuses, for example, were first recommended by this committee. Every employee has access to Advisory Board members, and answers to all Advisory Board suggestions are promised by the following meeting. Both Willis and Hastings are quick to point out, though, that the Advisory Board only recommends actions. "They do not have direct authority," Willis says, "And when they bring up something that management thinks is not to the benefit of the company, it will be rejected."

Under the early suggestion program, employees were awarded one-half of the first year's savings attributable to their suggestions. Now, however, the value of suggestions is reflected in performance evaluation scores, which determine individual incentive bonus amounts.

Training and Education

Production workers are given a short period of on-the-job training and then placed on a piecework pay system. Lincoln does not pay for off-site education, unless very specific company needs are identified. The idea behind this latter policy, according to Sabo, is that everyone cannot take advantage of such a program, and it is unfair to expend company funds for an advantage to which there is unequal access. Recruits for sales jobs, already college graduates, are given on-the-job training in the plant followed by a period of work and training at one of the regional sales offices.

Fringe Benefits and Executive Perquisites

A medical plan and a company-paid retirement program have been in effect for many years. A plant cafeteria, operated on a break-even basis, serves meals at about 60 percent of usual costs. The Employee Association, to which the company does not contribute, provides disability insurance and social and athletic activities. The employee stock ownership program has resulted in employee ownership of about 50 percent of the common stock. Under this program, each employee with more than two years of service may purchase stock in the corporation. The price of these shares is established at book value. Stock purchased through this plan may be held by employees only. Dividends and voting rights are the same as for stock that is owned outside the plan. Approximately 75 percent of the employees own Lincoln stock.

As to executive perquisites, there are none—crowded, austere offices, no executive washrooms or lunchrooms, and no reserved parking spaces. Even the top executives pay for their own meals and eat in the employee cafeteria. On one recent day, Willis arrived at work late due to a breakfast speaking engagement and had to park far away from the factory entrance.

Financial Policies

James F. Lincoln felt strongly that financing for company growth should come from within the company—through initial cash investment by the founders, through retention of earnings, and through stock purchases by those who work in the business. He saw the following advantages of this approach:

1. Ownership of stock by employees strengthens team spirit. "If they are mutually anxious to make it succeed, the future of the company is bright."
2. Ownership of stock provides individual incentive because employees feel that they will benefit from company profitability.
3. "Ownership is educational." Owner-employees "will know how profits are made and lost; how success is won and lost. . . . There are few socialists in the list of stockholders of the nation's industries."
4. "Capital available from within controls expansion." Unwarranted expansion would not occur, Lincoln believed, under his financing plan.
5. "The greatest advantage would be the development of the individual worker. Under the incentive of ownership, he would become a greater man."
6. "Stock ownership is one of the steps that can be taken that will make the worker feel that there is less of a gulf between him and the boss. . . . Stock ownership will help the worker to recognize his responsibility in the game and the importance of victory."

Until 1980, Lincoln Electric borrowed no money. Even now, the company's liabilities consist mainly of accounts payable and short-term accruals. The unusual pricing policy at Lincoln is succinctly stated by Willis: "At all times price on the basis of cost and at all times keep pressure on our cost." This policy resulted in the price for the most popular welding electrode then in use going from 16 cents a pound in 1929 to 4.7 cents in 1938. More recently, the SA-200 welder, Lincoln's largest selling portable machine, decreased in price from 1958 through 1965. According to Dr. C. Jackson Grayson of the American

Productivity Center in Houston, Texas, Lincoln's prices increased only one-fifth as fast as the Consumer Price Index from 1934 to about 1970. This resulted in a welding-products market in which Lincoln became the undisputed price leader for the products it manufactures. Not even the major Japanese manufacturers, such as Nippon Steel for welding electrodes and Saka Transformer for welding machines, were able to penetrate this market.

Substantial cash balances accumulated each year preparatory to paying the year-end bonuses. Modest success with international expansion put some pressure on what was basically a conservative financial philosophy. However, the company borrowed money in 1992 to pay for employee bonuses in the United States. In 1995 Lincoln issued $119 million of new stock. This sale created greater public ownership. As a consequence, Don Hastings remarked that the company must now consider not only the employees but its shareholders, customers, and suppliers.[7] For more current financial information visit Lincoln's Web site.

How Well Does Lincoln Serve Its Stakeholders?

Lincoln Electric differs from most other companies in the importance it assigns to each of the groups it serves. Hastings identifies these groups, in the order of priority ascribed to them, as: 1) customers, 2) employees, and 3) stockholders. As suggested, the 1995 stock issue increased the salience of the stockholders.

Certainly the firm's customers have fared well over the years. Lincoln prices for welding machines and welding electrodes are acknowledged to be the lowest in the marketplace. Quality has consistently been high. The cost of field failures for Lincoln products was recently determined to be a remarkable 0.04 percent of revenues. The "Fleetweld" electrodes and SA-200 welders have been the standard in the pipeline and refinery construction industry, where price is hardly a criterion, for decades. A Lincoln distributor in Monroe, Louisiana, says that he has sold several hundred of the popular AC-225 welders, which are warranted for one year, but has never handled a warranty claim.

Perhaps best served of all management constituencies have been the employees. Not the least of their benefits, of course, are the year-end bonuses, which effectively double an already average compensation level. The foregoing description of the personnel program and the comments in Appendix D further illustrate the desirability of a Lincoln job.

While stockholders were relegated to an inferior status by James F. Lincoln, they have done very well indeed. Recent dividends exceeded $11 a share and earnings per share have approached $30. In January 1980, the price of restricted stock, committed to employees, was $117 a share. By 1989, the stated value, at which the company will repurchase the stock if tendered, was $201. A check with the New York office of Merrill Lynch, Pierce, Fenner and Smith at that time revealed an estimated price on Lincoln stock of $270 a share, with none being offered for sale. Technically, this price applies only to the unrestricted stock owned by the Lincoln family, a few other major holders, and employees who have purchased it on the open market. Risk associated with Lincoln stock, a major determinant of stock value, is minimal because of the small amount of debt in the capital structure, because of an extremely stable earnings record, and because of Lincoln's practice of purchasing the restricted stock whenever employees offer it for sale. The 1995 stock sale has changed this situation dramatically. The stock now trades freely on the NASDAQ stock exchange.

A Concluding Comment

It is easy to believe that the reason for Lincoln's success is the excellent attitude of the employees and their willingness to work harder, faster, and more intelligently than other industrial workers. However, Sabo suggests that appropriate credit be given to Lincoln executives, whom he credits with carrying out the following policies:

1. Management has limited research, development, and manufacturing to a standard product line designed to meet the major needs of the welding industry.
2. New products must be reviewed by manufacturing and all producing costs verified before being approved by management.
3. Purchasing is challenged to not only procure materials at the lowest cost, but also to work closely with engineering and manufacturing to assure that the latest innovations are implemented.

4. Manufacturing supervision and all personnel are held accountable for reduction of scrap, energy conservation, and maintenance of product quality.

5. Production control, material handling, and methods engineering are closely supervised by top management.

6. Management has made cost reduction a way of life at Lincoln, and definite programs are established in many areas, including traffic and shipping, where tremendous savings can result.

7. Management has established a sales department that is technically trained to reduce customer welding costs. This sales approach and other real customer services have eliminated nonessential frills and resulted in long-term benefits to all concerned.

8. Management has encouraged education, technical publishing, and long-range programs that have resulted in industry growth, thereby assuring market potential for The Lincoln Electric Company.

Sabo writes, "It is in a very real sense a personal and group experience in faith—a belief that together we can achieve results which alone would not be possible. It is not a perfect system and it is not easy. It requires tremendous dedication and hard work. However, it does work and the results are worth the effort."

Appendix A   **Mission and Values Statement**
The mission of The Lincoln Electric Company is to earn and retain global leadership as a total quality supplier of superior products and services.

Our Core Values

As a responsible and successful company in partnership with our customers, distributors, employees, shareholders, suppliers and our host communities, we pledge ourselves to conduct our business in accordance with these core values:

- Respond to our customers' needs and expectations with quality, integrity and value
- Recognize people as our most valuable asset
- Maintain and expand the Lincoln Incentive Management philosophy
- Practice prudent and responsible financial management
- Strive continually to be environmentally responsible
- Support communities where we operate and industries in which we participate

To Realize Our Mission and Support Our Core Values, We Have Established the Following Goals:

Respond to Our Customers' Needs and Expectations with Quality, Integrity and Value

- Assure value through innovative, functional and reliable products and services in all the markets we serve around the world.
- Exceed global standards for products and service quality.
- Provide our customers with personalized technical support that helps them achieve improvements in cost reduction, productivity and quality.
- Lead the industry in aggressive application of advanced technology to meet customer requirements.
- Invest constantly in creative research and development dedicated to maintaining our position of market leadership.
- Achieve and maintain the leading market share position in our major markets around the world.

Recognize People as Our Most Valuable Asset

- Maintain a safe, clean and healthy environment for our employees.
- Promote employee training, education and development, and broaden skills through multi-departmental and international assignments.
- Maintain an affirmative action program and provide all employees with opportunities for advancement commensurate with their abilities and performance regardless of race, religion, national origin, sex, age or disability.

- Maintain an environment that fosters ethical behavior, mutual trust, equal opportunity, open communication, personal growth and creativity.
- Demand integrity, discipline and professional conduct from our employees in every aspect of our business and conduct our operations ethically and in accordance with the law.
- Reward employees through recognition, "pay for performance," and by sharing our profits with incentive bonus compensation based on extraordinary achievement.

Maintain and Expand the Lincoln Incentive Management Philosophy
Promote dynamic teamwork and incentive as the most profitable and cost-effective way of achieving:

- A committed work ethic and positive employee attitudes throughout the Company.
- High-quality, low-cost manufacturing.
- Efficient and innovative engineering.
- Customer-oriented operation and administration.
- A dedicated and knowledgeable sales and service force.
- A total organization responsive to the needs of our worldwide customers.

Practice Prudent and Responsible Financial Management
- Establish attainable goals, strategic planning, and accountability for results that enhance shareholder value.
- Promote the process of employee involvement in cost reductions and quality improvements.
- Recognize profit as the resource that enables our Company to serve our customers.

Strive Continually to Be Environmentally Responsible
- Continue to pursue the most environmentally sound operating practices, processes and products to protect the global environment.
- Maintain a clean and healthy environment in our host communities.

Support Communities Where We Operate and Industries in Which We Participate
- Invest prudently in social, cultural, educational and charitable activities.
- Contribute to the industries we serve and society as a whole by continuing our leadership role in professional organizations and education.
- Encourage and support appropriate employee involvement in community activities.

Appendix B   **What Are the HR Objectives of Lincoln Electric?**
- To "maintain and expand the Lincoln Incentive Management Philosophy"
- To "recognize people as [their] most valuable asset"
- To promote training, education and development that broaden employee skills
- To "maintain an affirmative action program and provide all employees with opportunities for advancement commensurate with their abilities and performance regardless of race, religion, national origin, sex, age or disability"

Appendix C   **Business Objectives of Lincoln Electric:**
- To be a global leader in price and quality and serve the customers first
- To "earn and retain global leadership as a total quality supplier of superior products and services"
- To "respond to [their] customers, integrity and value"
- To "practice prudent and responsible financial management"
- To "strive continually to be environmentally responsible"
- To "support communities where [they] operate and industries in which [they] participate"
- To "maintain an environment that fosters ethical behavior, mutual trust, equal opportunity, open communication, personal growth and creativity"
- To promote feedback

The Lincoln Electric Company 15

- To "demand integrity, discipline and professional conduct from [their] employees in every aspect of [their] business and conduct [their] operations ethically and in accordance with the law"
- To "reward employees through recognition, 'pay for performance,' and by sharing [their] profits with incentive bonus compensation based on extraordinary achievement" as a means of motivation
- To "promote dynamic teamwork and incentive"

Appendix D   Employee Interviews

Typical questions and answers from employee interviews are presented below. In order to maintain each employee's personal privacy, fictitious names are given to the interviewees.

Interview 1

Betty Stewart, a 52-year-old high school graduate who had been with Lincoln 13 years was working as a cost accounting clerk at the time of the interview.

Q: What jobs have you held here besides the one you have now?
A: I worked in payroll for awhile, and then this job came open and I took it.
Q: How much money did you make last year, including your bonus?
A: I would say roughly around $25,000, but I was off for back surgery for a while.
Q: You weren't paid while you were off for back surgery?
A: No.
Q: Did the Employees Association help out?
A: Yes. The company doesn't furnish that, though. We pay $8 a month into the Employee Association. I think my check from them was $130.00 a week.
Q: How was your performance rating last year?
A: It was around 100 points, but I lost some points for attendance for my back problem.
Q: How did you get your job at Lincoln?
A: I was bored silly where I was working, and I had heard that Lincoln kept their people busy. So I applied and got the job the next day.
Q: Do you think you make more money than similar workers in Cleveland?
A: I know I do.
Q: What have you done with your money?
A: We have purchased a better home. Also, my son is going to the University of Chicago, which costs $13,000 a year. I buy the Lincoln stock that is offered each year, and I have a little bit of gold.
Q: Have you ever visited with any of the senior executives, like Mr. Willis or Mr. Hastings?
A: I have known Mr. Willis for a long time.
Q: Does he call you by name?
A: Yes. In fact he was very instrumental in my going to the doctor that I am going to with my back. He knows the director of the clinic.
Q: Do you know Mr. Hastings?
A: I know him to speak to him, and he always speaks, always. But I have known Mr. Willis for a good many years. When I did Plant Two accounting I did not understand how the plant operated. Of course you are not allowed in Plant Two, because that's the Electrode Division. I told my boss about the problem one day and the next thing I knew Mr. Willis came by and said, "Come on, Betty, we're going to Plant Two." He spent an hour and a half showing me the plant.
Q: Do you think Lincoln employees produce more than those in other companies?
A: I think with the incentive program the way that it is, if you want to work and achieve, then you will do it. If you don't want to work and achieve, you will not do it no matter where you are. Just because you are merit rated and have a bonus, if you really don't want to work hard, then you're not going to. You will accept your 90 points or 92 or 85, because even with that you make more money than people on the outside.
Q: Do you think Lincoln employees will ever join a union?
A: I don't know why they would.

Q: So you say that money is a very major advantage?

A: Money is a major advantage, but it's not just the money. It's the fact that having the incentive, you do wish to work a little harder. I'm sure that there are a lot of men here who, if they worked some other place, would not work as hard as they do here. Not that they are overworked—I don't mean that—but I'm sure they wouldn't push.

Q: Is there anything that you would like to add?

A: I do like working here. I am better off being pushed mentally. In another company if you pushed too hard you would feel a little bit of pressure, and someone might say, "Hey, slow down, don't try so hard." But here you are encouraged, not discouraged.

Interview 2

Ed Sanderson, a 23-year-old high school graduate who had been with Lincoln four years, was a machine operator in the Electrode Division at the time of the interview.

Q: How did you happen to get this job?

A: My wife was pregnant, and I was making three bucks an hour and one day I came here and applied. That was it. I kept calling to let them know I was still interested.

Q: Roughly what were your earnings last year including your bonus?

A: $45,000.

Q: What have you done with your money since you have been here?

A: Well, we've lived pretty well and we bought a condominium.

Q: Have you paid for the condominium?

A: No, but I could.

Q: Have you bought your Lincoln stock this year?

A: No, I haven't bought any Lincoln stock yet.

Q: Do you get the feeling that the executives here are pretty well thought of?

A: I think they are. To get where they are today, they had to really work.

Q: Wouldn't that be true anywhere?

A: I think more so here because seniority really doesn't mean anything. If you work with a guy who has 20 years here, and you have two months and you're doing a better job, you will get advanced before he will.

Q: Are you paid on a piece rate basis?

A: My gang does. There are nine of us who make the bare electrode, and the whole group gets paid based on how much electrode we make.

Q: Do you think you work harder than workers in other factories in the Cleveland area?

A: Yes, I would say I probably work harder.

Q: Do you think it hurts anybody?

A: No, a little hard work never hurts anybody.

Q: If you could choose, do you think you would be as happy earning a little less money and being able to slow down a little?

A: No, it doesn't bother me. If it bothered me, I wouldn't do it.

Q: Why do you think Lincoln employees produce more than workers in other plants?

A: That's the way the company is set up. The more you put out, the more you're going to make.

Q: Do you think it's the piece rate and bonus together?

A: I don't think people would work here if they didn't know that they would be rewarded at the end of the year.

Q: Do you think Lincoln employees will ever join a union?

A: No.

Q: What are the major advantages of working for Lincoln?

A: Money.

Q: Are there any other advantages?

A: Yes, we don't have a union shop. I don't think I could work in a union shop.

Q: Do you think you are a career man with Lincoln at this time?

A: Yes.

Interview 3

Roger Lewis, a 23-year-old Purdue graduate in mechanical engineering who had been in the Lincoln sales program for 15 months, was working in the Cleveland sales office at the time of the interview.

Q. How did you get your job at Lincoln?
A: I saw that Lincoln was interviewing on campus at Purdue, and I went by. I later came to Cleveland for a plant tour and was offered a job.
Q: Do you know any of the senior executives? Would they know you by name?
A: Yes, I know all of them—Mr. Hastings, Mr. Willis, Mr. Sabo.
Q: Do you think Lincoln sales representatives work harder than those in other companies?
A: Yes. I don't think there are many sales reps for other companies who are putting in 50- to 60-hour weeks. Everybody here works harder. You can go out in the plant, or you can go upstairs, and there's nobody sitting around.
Q: Do you see any real disadvantage of working at Lincoln?
A: I don't know if it's a disadvantage, but Lincoln is a spartan company, a very thrifty company. I like that. The sales offices are functional, not fancy.
Q: Why do you think Lincoln employees have such high productivity?
A: Piecework has a lot to do with it. Lincoln is smaller than many plants, too; you can stand in one place and see the materials come in one side and the product go out the other. You feel a part of the company. The chance to get ahead is important, too. They have a strict policy of promoting from within, so you know you have a chance. I think in a lot of other places you may not get as fair a shake as you do here. The sales offices are on a smaller scale, too. I like that. I tell someone that we have two people in the Baltimore office, and they say "You've got to be kidding." It's smaller and more personal. Pay is the most important thing. I have heard that this is the highest paying factory in the world.

Interview 4

Jimmy Roberts, a 47-year-old high school graduate who had been with Lincoln 17 years, was working as a multiple-drill press operator at the time of the interview.

Q: What jobs have you had at Lincoln?
A: I started out cleaning the men's locker room in 1967. After about a year I got a job in the flux department, where we make the coating for welding rods. I worked there for seven or eight years and then got my present job.
Q: Do you make one particular part?
A: No, there are a variety of parts I make—at least 25.
Q: Each one has a different piece rate attached to it?
A: Yes.
Q: Are some piece rates better than others?
A: Yes.
Q: How do you determine which ones you are going to do?
A: You don't. Your supervisor assigns them.
Q: How much money did you make last year?
A: $53,000.
Q: Have you ever received any kind of award or citation?
A: No.
Q: Was your rating ever over 110?
A: Yes. For the past five years, probably, I made over 110 points.
Q: Is there any attempt to let the others know . . . ?
A: The kind of points I get? No.
Q: Do you know what they are making?
A: No. There are some who might not be too happy with their points and they might make it known. The majority, though, do not make it a point of telling other employees.

Q: Would you be just as happy earning a little less money and working a little slower?

A: I don't think I would, not at this point. I have done piecework all these years, and the fast pace doesn't really bother me.

Q: Why do you think Lincoln productivity is so high?

A: The incentive thing—the bonus distribution. I think that would be the main reason. The paycheck you get every two weeks is important too.

Q: Do you think Lincoln employees would ever join a union?

A: I don't think so. I have never heard anyone mention it.

Q: What is the most important advantage of working here?

A: Amount of money you make. I don't think I could make this type of money anywhere else, especially with only a high school education.

Q: As a black person, do you feel that Lincoln discriminates in any way against blacks?

A: No. I do not think any more so than any other job. Naturally, there is a certain amount of discrimination, regardless of where you are.

Interview 5

Joe Trahan, a 58-year-old high school graduate who had been with Lincoln 39 years, was employed as a working supervisor in the tool room at the time of the interview.

Q: Roughly what was your pay last year?

A: Over $56,000, salary, bonus, stock dividends.

Q: How much was your bonus?

A: About $26,000.

Q: Have you ever gotten a special award of any kind?

A: Not really.

Q: What have you done with your money?

A: My house is paid for, and my two cars. I also have some bonds and the Lincoln stock.

Q: What do you think of the executives at Lincoln?

A: They're really top notch.

Q: What is the major disadvantage of working at Lincoln Electric?

A: I don't know of any disadvantage at all.

Q: Do you think you produce more than most people in similar jobs with other companies?

A: I do believe that.

Q: Why is that? Why do you believe that?

A: We are on the incentive system. Everything we do, we try to improve to make a better product with a minimum of outlay. We try to improve the bonus.

Q: Would you be just as happy making a little less money and not working quite so hard?

A: I don't think so.

Q: Do you think Lincoln employees would ever join a union?

A: I don't think they would ever consider it.

Q: What is the most important advantage of working at Lincoln?

A: Compensation.

Q: Tell me something about Mr. James Lincoln, who died in 1965.

A: You are talking about Jimmy Sr. He always strolled through the shop in his shirt sleeves. Big fellow. Always looked distinguished. Gray hair. Friendly sort of guy. I was a member of the Advisory Board one year. He was there each time.

Q: Did he strike you as really caring?

A: I think he always cared for people.

Q: Did you get any sensation of a religious nature from him?

A: No, not really.

Q: And religion is not part of the program now?

A: No.

Q: Do you think Mr. Lincoln was a very intelligent man, or was he just a nice guy?

A: I would say he was pretty well educated. A great talker—always right off the top of his head. He knew what he was talking about all the time.

Q: When were bonuses for beneficial suggestions done away with?

A: About 18 years ago.

Q: Did that hurt very much?

A: I do not think so, because suggestions are still rewarded through the merit rating system.

Q: Is there anything you would like to add?

A: It's a good place to work. The union kind of ties other places down. At other places, electricians only do electrical work, carpenters only do carpentry work. At Lincoln Electric we all pitch in and do whatever needs to be done.

Q: So a major advantage is not having a union?

A: That's right.

Letter from the CEO to Our Shareholders

Each of you is aware that your company faced enormous challenges in 1993. Those challenges required a focused, creative and positive leadership approach on the part of your management team. As I write this, first quarter 1994 results indicate that the domestic economy is continuing its upward surge. Because of the many tough decisions we had to make in 1993, we are now poised to take advantage of an improved economic climate. Even though much of my personal time has been devoted to overseeing the situation in Europe, excellent results are being achieved in the U.S.A. and Canada.

During 1993, a thorough strategic assessment of our foreign operations led to the conclusion that Lincoln Electric lacked the necessary financial resources to continue to support twenty-one manufacturing sites. We did not have the luxury of time to keep those plants operating while working to increase our sales and profitability. As a result, with the endorsement of our financial community, the Board of Directors approved management's recommendation to restructure operations in Europe, Latin America, and Japan.

The restructuring included closing the Messer Lincoln operations in Germany; reducing employment throughout Lincoln Norweld, which operates plants in England, France, the Netherlands, Spain, and Norway; and closing manufacturing plants in Venezuela, Brazil, and Japan. The result was a workforce reduction totaling some 770 employees worldwide. We are not abandoning these markets by any means. Rather, the restructuring will allow us to retain and increase sales while relieving us of the high costs associated with excess manufacturing capacity. Now that the restructuring has been accomplished, we operate fifteen plants in ten countries. This capacity will be adequate to supply the inventory needed to support our customers and an increasingly aggressive marketing strategy. We are internationally recognized for outstanding products and service, and we have been certified to the international quality standard ISO-9002.

It was not easy for Lincoln Electric to eliminate manufacturing capacity and jobs. However, I must point out that the overseas companies were given repeated opportunities to turn their performance around. In all fairness, no one anticipated the depth of the recession that continues to devastate Europe, and particularly Germany. But we could not in good conscience, risk both the continuous erosion of shareholder value and the jobs of our dedicated U.S. employees by remaining unprofitable in these manufacturing operations.

For the second year in the history of this company, it was necessary to take restructuring charges that resulted in a consolidated loss. The restructuring charge totaled $70,100,000 ($40,900,000 after tax), and contributed to a consolidated net loss for 1993 of $38,100,000, compared to a $45,800,000 consolidated loss in 1992.

In 1993 our U.S. and Canadian operations achieved outstanding results with increased levels of sales and profitability and a significant gain in market share. We made a huge step forward by concentrating on the "Top Line" to meet one of our major goals— manufacturing and selling $2.1 million worth of product from our Ohio company each day from June 1 through the end of the year. Our Canadian company also made significant contributions with a 38 percent increase in sales. The bottom line automatically moved into greater profitability.

These impressive gains were not made without sacrifice. Lincoln manufacturing people voluntarily deferred 614 weeks of vacation, worked holidays, and many employees worked a seven day-a-week schedule to fill the steady stream of orders brought in by the sales department as we capitalized on an emerging domestic economy that we felt was being largely ignored by our major competitors. This remarkable achievement would never have been possible without the expert management of your President and Chief Operating Officer Frederick W. Makenbach. His leadership consistently inspired our employees and management team alike. The U.S. company's extraordinary performance encouraged the Board of Directors to approve a gross bonus of $55 million, and to continue the regular quarterly dividend payment throughout the year. As you know, the usual course of action for a company reporting a consolidated loss is to cut or defer bonuses and dividends. That these were paid is a tribute to our Board and their steadfast belief in the long range, proven benefits of the Incentive Management System. Thinking of the long term is critical to our process in a world that too often seems to demand instant solutions to complex problems. Your Chairman, your Board, and your management team are determined to resist that impulse. Currently, Lincoln people around the world are working diligently to formulate a Strategic Plan that will carry this company into the next century. An important element of this business plan will be our new state-of-the-art motor manufacturing facility, which is on schedule. Furthermore, we have strengthened our international leadership with the addition of executives experienced in global management to our Board and to key management posts.

While your company is indeed emerging from a very challenging period in its history, we project excellent results for 1994, with strong sales, increased profits, and the benefits of those developments accruing to shareholders, customers and employees. As the year proceeds, we will be looking forward to our Centennial in 1995. I am confident that you and I will enjoy celebrating that event together.

Sincerely,

Donald F. Hastings

Chairman and Chief Executive Officer (Retired May 1997)

Postscript: In Lincoln Electric's centennial year, 1995, sales topped $1 billion for the first time. It was also the year that Hastings eliminated the two-tier wage plan that was instituted in 1993. Under this plan, new hires started at 75% of the normal pay rate. This plan increased the turnover rate among the new hires and was regarded as unfair by senior workers. According to one of them, "If an individual shows he can handle the workload, he should be rewarded." As of 1997, Lincoln Electric appears to be back on track, committed as ever to its philosophy and values.[8] Although Donald F. Hastings has been replaced by Anthony A. Massaro, he continues to be an inspiration for the direction and spirit of Lincoln Electric.

Endnotes

1. T.W. Gerdel, "Lincoln Electric Experiences Season of Worker Discontent," *Plain Dealer* [Cleveland] (December 10, 1995).
2. Ibid.
3. Z. Schiller, "A Model Incentive Plan Gets Caught in a Vise," *Business Week* (January 22, 1996): 89, 92.
4. R. Narisetti, "Job Paradox Manufacturers Decry a Shortage of Workers While Rejecting Many," *The Wall Street Journal* (September 8, 1995): A4.
5. Schiller, "A Model Incentive Plan Gets Caught in a Vise," *Business Week* (January 22, 1996): 89, 92.
6. Gerdel, "Lincoln Electric Experiences Season of Worker Discontent," *Plain Dealer* [Cleveland] (December 10, 1995).
7. Ibid.
8. R.M. Hodgetts, "A Conversation with Donald F. Hastings of the Lincoln Electric Company," *Organizational Dynamics* (Winter 1997): 68–74; M. Gleisser, "Lincoln CEO's Formula: Mutual Trust and Loyalty," *Plain Dealer* (June 22, 1996): 2–C.

BULLER | SCHULER

Managing Organizations and People

A Resource for Cases in Management, Organizational Behavior, and Human Resource Management

Abstract

This case is an odyssey of the author's personal discovery working as an American expatriate in Paris in the late 1980s. The case illustrates some of the differences between the French and American cultures and how they manifest themselves into management styles. The case also provides some examples of right and wrong things to do as a leader in France. Ultimately this expatriate was successful, but only after a lengthy and frustrating conditioning process. The objective of this case is to familiarize American (or other) expatriates with the cultural expectations while managing in France. It's the first step in discovering "How To" be a successful expatriate manager in France.

An American in Paris

"April in Paris . . . chestnuts in blossom . . . holiday tables under the sun" . . . or so the song goes. But on this cold, rainy April day, it was just plain miserable. This would also accurately describe the mood of John Edwards, an American expatriate who had been living in Paris for just over six months. He was still struggling with the language, still struggling with the unfathomable bureaucracy, still astounded by the high prices of everything, and totally befuddled by his lack of ability to make anything positive happen at his work.

Just a short while ago it all seemed so perfect . . . an opportunity to manage his company's French subsidiary in one of the most beautiful cities in the world. After all, he had just come off a series of successful international ventures where he had started up the company's first foreign manufacturing operations, negotiated several successful licensing agreements, and managed technology transfers to several different European countries. He always chose Paris as his gateway city to Europe, using it as a base to move throughout the various European locations, and he spoke pretty good French (or so he thought). What a great city . . . the art, the music, the history, the architecture, the grand boulevards, the cafes, the restaurants, all combined to make this his dream location. This assignment as the new Directeur General was sure be an exciting and rewarding experience in a city that he loved!

■ Tom Morris, University of San Diego.

1

John's problems started immediately when attempting to converse with the engineers and technicians at his new Paris office. John had spent months in intensive training, refreshing his admittedly rusty skills in the French language. When his training was complete, his instructors assured him that he would have no trouble making himself understood anywhere in France. Well, technically they were correct. Everyone understood John just fine, and in fact thought he was quite articulate. The problem was, he couldn't understand them! They seemed to be speaking some sort of French dialect that he could not grasp. When he traveled outside of Paris in any direction, he understood people perfectly. But the Parisians seemed to speak very rapidly, use a lot of slang, and cut the endings off of all the words. It seemed like a different language. He was very disappointed, and ultimately had to hire a local language instructor to help him learn to understand "Parisian."

His office schedule was another mystery to John. Everyone started at 8 A.M., took an hour for lunch, but by 4 P.M. the office was empty. When he inquired about the missing hour, he was informed of the French national "35 hour rule." In order to help reduce unemployment, the French government had mandated that no workers could work more than 35 hours per week. And, they actually sent around inspectors to check on it! Of course, the companies must still pay the workers the same amount they had earned in 40 hours of work. It seemed that the government thought that companies could somehow pay the existing workers full wages for 40 hours, but hire additional workers to make up the difference in lost hours. The fact that this may make the company unprofitable somehow escaped their logic. John was still shaking his head over this bureaucratic craziness when Patrice, the accounting manager, handed him his "lunch tickets."

"What's this?" asked John.

"Your lunch tickets," replied Patrice.

"What are they for?"

Patrice looked quizzically at John and replied, "They are for lunch."

"What do you mean they are for lunch?" asked John. "What do I do with them?"

"You take them to a restaurant and pay for your lunch with them," Patrice explained patiently. "Every company provides lunch tickets for their employees, it's the law in France. The government wants to be sure all workers have a good, hearty lunch."

"You mean the company buys lunch for every employee, every day?" asked John.

"Of course," replied Patrice. "It's budgeted under miscellaneous expenses."

"Let me see if I understand this correctly," said John. "The government requires that I pay workers for 40 hours when they work only 35, and the government then requires that I buy lunch for all the employees every day?"

"That's right," said Patrice. "And, they also require that you pay an extra month's salary as a bonus each year. It's called the 13th month salary."

John stared blankly into space, not really believing what he had just heard, but somehow knowing that it was really true. "Is there anything else I should know?" he asked.

"Just that we always close the office down during the month of August and half of July when everyone goes on holiday," replied Patrice.

It was clear that John had a lot to learn about the French bureaucracy and the liberal employee subsidies that they forced upon their employers. No wonder everything was so expensive!

To make matters even worse, he did not really understand the huge cultural differences that existed between the American and French managerial culture. After negotiating with top level managers in a number of different countries, he thought that he understood national culture reasonably well, but he had never directly managed foreign nationals. He understood the correlation between national culture and managerial culture only in abstract, intellectual terms. A national culture is difficult enough to understand and articulate, but transferring that cultural concept into day-to-day managerial practice had proven to be even more difficult.

As an example, John had a recent cultural misunderstanding involving his secretary, Monique, whose title was Secretary to the Directeur General. It seemed that the order processing and order confirmation letters within the subsidiary were falling behind. Francois, his general sales manager, was beseeching John to hire another clerk to assist with the order processing and confirmation letters.

"John!" exclaimed Francois. "The customers are complaining that it is taking too long to receive their orders. We have a backlog of orders to be shipped longer than one week, and the salesmen's confirmation letters are just stacking up. We need to hire another clerk to help process orders and type the salesman's confirmation letters as quickly as possible."

"Well you're right about the order processing rate, and the salesmen's letters, we need to speed that up," answered John. "But I don't think that we need to hire another clerk, we just need to use our existing resources."

John had noticed that his secretary Monique seemed to have lots of spare time between telephone calls and devoted hours to manicuring her nails each day.

"I'll just ask Monique to lend a hand and type some of the salesmen's letters," said John.

"Oh, I don't think so, replied Francois. "She is the Secretary of the Directeur General and she doesn't type the salesmen's letters."

"Well, I'm the Directeur General," said John. "So I guess I'll just ask her to help out. This doesn't seem like such a big deal to me."

John called Monique into his small, but comfortable office overlooking the Seine and the Bois de Boulogne beyond.

"Monique, it seems that we are getting behind in sending out the salesmen's confirmation letters, and I wonder if you would mind helping out until we get caught up?"

"Do you mean typing the salesmen's letters?" asked Monique incredulously.

"Right," replied John.

"I am the Secretary of the Directeur General, and I don't type salesmen's letters," she exclaimed firmly.

"Well, I'm the Directeur General and I'd like you to help out with the salesmen's letters," directed John.

Monique's wide-eyed expression collapsed immediately into tears as she picked up her purse, purposefully walked out the office, and slammed the door. It was the last time that John saw Monique.

Several days later however, John was visited by a representative from the Ministry of Labor. It seemed that Monique had applied for unemployment compensation because she had been forced to quit her job due to "an unreasonable request for demeaning work outside her profession." After a brief discussion, the representative from the Ministry concurred with Monique and stated very clearly that the Ministry would award her 90 percent of her regular salary for the next year, or as long as it took for her to find another professional position of her liking. Naturally, John's company would be responsible for the payments.

John was dumbfounded. He was aware of the hierarchical nature of French society. He understood that the very top positions in industry, government, and society went to the graduates of the "Grandes Ecoles" (the great schools) of France, and that the other industry positions were ordered by the various levels of education received from other educational programs. The hierarchy went generally as follows:

Position	School
Enterprise management & high government posts	Grandes Ecoles
Professionals: engineers, attorneys, etc.	5 year university degree
Functionaries: bookkeepers, planners, etc.	2 year university degree
Operators: technicians, machinists, secretaries, etc.	Baccalaureate degree
Common workers: clerks, drivers, etc.	No Baccalaureate degree

Moreover, promotion from one level to another is very unusual. Once qualifications are obtained, there is little opportunity to improve later in one's career. There is however, a strong sense of honor associated with each rank, and individuals at each level are bound by this shared code of honor. After all "Honor is due to each according to their rank" (French proverb). Within each organizational level, a distinct "pecking order" exists based on the "intellectual nobility" of each position. Those positions that require some conceptual or independent thinking are considered nobler than those that do not. The job of management is to somehow maintain a clear chain of command while using the sense of honor as a tool to channel energies and increase efficiency in each hierarchical level. But one always maintains the hierarchy and its order.

Clearly, John had violated the nobility and honor of the Secretary of the Directeur General by asking her to perform the task of a lowly clerk. Francois understood this perfectly, but John did not heed his warning. The only thing he could do was to chalk it up to a learning experience via trial and error.

Following this incident, John reflected on his prior success as a manager in the United States. He always maintained a casual management style, allowed a lot of freedom with his subordinates, and it had served him well. He reasoned that since the French value independent thinking, they would respond well to a participative management system and would value a new sense of empowerment.

John gathered his staff together to gain some understanding of the problems within the organization and perhaps generate some potential resolutions. He had great hopes that he would stimulate an intellectual challenge for his staff. John gently prodded his staff with questions about the operation.

"What kind of problems are you experiencing?"

"How do you think can we improve our operation?"

He felt a growing uneasiness as his staff members shifted in their chairs and glanced apprehensively at each other. All seemed reluctant to participate.

"What's the matter?" pleaded John. *"Doesn't anyone have any ideas?"*

Finally Patrice, John's accounting manager, hesitatingly spoke.

"Why are you asking us this?" he questioned quietly.

"Because I want to improve our performance," replied John. *"You know these operations better than anyone else, surely you must have some ideas on how to make things work better."*

"But I thought you were supposed to do that," Patrice exclaimed. *"The Directeur General is supposed to know what to do to make everything work correctly."*

John was stunned, he had some ideas for improvement, but he wanted the ideas to come from them so they would have some ownership and some sense of empowerment to move things ahead. Obviously, this was not going to happen. John continued to try over the next couple of months to get his staff to assume some responsibility, but to no avail. They were polite, cooperative, and tried hard to accomplish everything he suggested. But, they felt no sense of ownership or personal challenge in anything they did. Empowerment and responsibility was the last thing in the world that they wanted.

It had been six months of trial and error learning for John. He was learning, but often lamented "It's too bad that so much of my experience has to come from making errors." It was now time for the corporation's regular meeting in Brussels. All the European managers would be there. John enjoyed these meetings because it allowed him to discuss common problems with his European counterparts. It had been a good year for the corporation in Europe with everyone, including John somehow meeting or exceeding their objectives. But John continued to struggle with his management style and shared his concerns with Michel, the Directeur General of the Belgian subsidiary.

Michel was a native Belgian, spoke fluent French, and understood the French culture very well. After all, it was one of the two official languages of Belgium that uniquely shared the French and Dutch cultures. Michel was also familiar with the American managerial culture as he had spent two years at corporate headquarters in the United States. As they spoke, Michel outlined his view of the American and French managerial culture on the back of his dinner napkin. He described the French managerial characteristics and how they were different from the American style of management.

"Management systems must reflect the cultural expectations of all the members of the organization," he said. *"In the U.S. you manage in a way that fits the American managerial culture, and in France you must meet the expectations of the French managerial culture. The respective management systems aren't right or wrong, they're just different."*

His cultural differences were expressed as follows:

	American	French
Organizational Style	Informal, mostly egalitarian, where everyone contributes equally. Organizational charts are to divide activities.	Formal and hierarchical. The organization chart defines positions of power.
Communication	Low context, direct and to the point.	High context, indirect and subtle.
Thinking	Straight forward, fact orientation, avoids complexity.	Circular, principal orientation, facts are a burden.
Protocol	Not significant.	Extremely important, individuals treated according to rank and honor.
Business Orientation	Practical and results oriented. Find a way to get it done any way you can.	Intellectual while maintaining a sense of logic. Form counts more than results.
Government & Business	Free market mentality. Government entrusted only to maintain competition.	Bureaucratic, designed to help employees and control business. Extremely liberal.
Management Style	Participative with shared decision making.	Authoritarian and autocratic, centralized decision making.
Meetings	Strict agenda, time budgeted to cover the agenda.	Floating agenda, concurrent mini-meetings. No closure.
Deadlines	Serious goals, not to be compromised.	Flexible, not taken very seriously.
Character of People	Extremely individualistic, everyone accepts their own responsibility.	Leaders are individualistic, subordinates collective. Only leaders are responsible.
Historical	Here and now, maybe short-term future perspective.	Extremely historical, all perspectives in terms of the past.
Task Orientation	Monochronic, serial . . . one thing at a time. Resolve one and move on to next. Eliminate alternatives.	Polychronic, multifunctional. Explore many alternatives simultaneously. Create alternatives.
Risk	Risk takers . . . they seek success.	Risk avoiders . . . they seek security.
Law	If it's the law...you follow it. If the light is red, you stop.	Everyone has the right to determine if a law is reasonable. If no one is coming, why would you stop for a red light?
Order	First come, first served. Everyone takes their place in an orderly way. Patience is a virtue.	What order? Go immediately to the head of any line. It's your right. Patience is for foreigners.

As John looked over the comparative factors, he began to formulate a different sort of managerial culture for his French office. He was slowly beginning to understand the reasons behind the behaviors. He suddenly understood the seemingly non-understandable difference between the French "erreur" and "faute." It is okay to be guilty of an "erreur" because no one is perfect, but one must never be guilty of a "faute" because that connotates guilt and responsibility for the "erreur." For example, if you back into someone's car and dent the fender, then this is an "erreur." But the "faute" belongs to the person who parked the car in the improper place where you could hit it. Of course no one would admit to this, because it would mean accepting responsibility. In the mind of the person who parked the car, this was an "erreur" to park it there, the one who backed into the car was guilty of the "faute." A true French person would never admit that they were responsible or at fault for anything.

As John began to reflect upon his insights to the culture, he began to think about his ability to become a competent French manager. When he arrived back in Paris, he was once again confronted by Francois.

"Since you have been gone, our customer problems have gotten even worse. Our orders are further behind than ever."

John thought to himself, "What actions can I take to resolve this problem? I don't even have a secretary to help out any more. How can you manage in a society where no one takes any responsibility for anything? How do I respond in a way that is consistent with the cultural expectation, and also get things done? What should I do now?"

Module 8

Communication and Group Dynamics

Cases Outline

BULLER | SCHULER

Managing Organizations and People

A Resource for Cases in Management, Organizational Behavior, and Human Resource Management

Abstract

Bob Marvin, president of Motor Parts Corporation (MPC), feels a great deal of conflict and frustration about how to deal with the behavior of one of his vice presidents, Al Shepherd. Al's wife, Ruth, has recently had a recurrence of a malignant brain tumor, and Al is spending more and more time away from work to be with her. Bob believes that Al's increasing absence from work and his preoccupation with his wife's problem is causing Al's performance to suffer. In addition, Bob thinks Al's behavior is beginning to affect the morale and performance of others who work with Al. Bob is even beginning to question Al's commitment to the organization.

Bob has chosen not to confront Al directly because he does not want to seem insensitive. Instead, he has asked Mike Jones, a management professor and planning consultant to MPC, as well as a good friend to both Al and Bob, to speak with Al. Al was quite open about his feelings with Bob. Al believed that he was performing his job duties adequately and expressed his loyalty to the company.

When Mike Jones reports the results of his conversation with Al, Bob becomes more puzzled about what to do. Later, when Bob finds out that Al is in Detroit at his mother's house (who is ill), he becomes really frustrated. (What Bob does not know is that Al is in Detroit closing the deal on a major account for MPC.) Mike asks Bob to talk to Al in a more straightforward way.

Motor Parts Corporation

Bob Marvin, president of Motor Parts Corp. (MPC), felt a great deal of conflict and frustration as he chaired the strategic planning meeting of his senior management team. Al Shepherd, his executive vice president, had just arose from the conference table and excused himself, saying:

I'm sorry but we have had a change in our chemotherapy appointment and I have to meet Ruth.

Ruth, Al's wife, had just recently learned that she had a recurrence of a malignant brain tumor. The prior bout, over only two years ago, had been difficult. Al was completely involved with his wife's fight against her illness. He had become about as expert as a layman could become on the disease, the many methods of fighting it, and the best institutions and physicians. He had accompanied her to virtually all medical appointments and procedures. When asked about her condition he would report to colleagues at great length and in technical detail. He was consumed by her situation. It had been a year since she had been given a clean bill of health when they were devastated to learn about her relapse. Now, the odds were against her. The doctors suggested a variety of alternative treatments, but at best her chances of surviving two years were less than one in three.

Bob, with great self-restraint, did not want to react at the meeting, and as hard as it was he tried to work around some of the issues that most directly affected Al.

Bob couldn't help but notice increasing, and less subtle references by others in the meeting to problems they had working around Al. After all, the organization had to go on. They all had their jobs to do, and while none had problems as severe as Al, many of them had their own serious problems. Jay Unger, VP Marketing had a son who had recently been expelled from college and was in rehabilitation with a drug dependency problem. Pete Arnell, was in the middle of a divorce. Bob himself, had his own problems, real problems.

At the end of the meeting he asked Mike Jones, who had happened to be at the meeting to return with him to his office. Mike is a management professor at the university and a consultant to MPC on planning issues.

What am I going to do about Al? As you know, after me, he has the most important job in this company. In fact, on a day-to-day basis he probably has the most critical job since all functions except for Finance, Legal, and Public Relations report directly to him. For the past few months he has been out of the office as much as he has been in it. Even worse, numerous meetings have been set to coincide with his schedule only to be aborted at the last second because he had to leave to take his wife to a medical appointment.

Now I just heard that our national sales meeting that has to be set up months in advance can't be scheduled because he is not certain about a procedure she has scheduled for about that time period.

His job requires considerable travel to regional offices and he just has not been doing enough of it. We have a number of new regional managers who are not getting enough guidance. We have some regional managers who are not doing a good job. They require closer supervision, if not replacement. Instead of dealing with these issues directly he is delegating supervisory chores to the two senior staff people in his department. For example, I know Joe Roderick is a great planner and earlier in his career he was a regional manager at Major Parts, but he is not their boss. I don't want lines of authority confused. I told that to Al when we created those staff positions.

You know that I try to keep in contact with our major customers. I have picked up hints that some of our regional people are just not performing adequately. He is not on top of things. Just look at how poor some of our regions are performing—Detroit and San Francisco are good examples. Our business is as dependent on service as price and quality. We can't afford not to be on top of things.

Just think about today. Here we are under all of this pressure from our Board to develop a new five-year plan. Even though our performance has been, on a relative basis, the best in the industry, they keep warning me that a company of our size has to do even better if it is going to avoid a takeover.

And you know we haven't been cheap. Salaries have risen around here faster than any place in the industry. I think that is only fair given performance. No one has done better than Al in the eight years that he has been here. He started at a rather low pay level and now is the highest paid executive in a comparable position in the industry.

Even though I have always had problems with his attention to detail and some of the people he has hired, I have no complaint about overall results. But we have to continue to improve.

By the way, you know that this is only part of the problem with Al. He's got to be one of the softest guys I've ever met. He stays home when he's got a bad cold, when there's a few inches of snow in his driveway. He was out a week last year with an ear infection. He is out about as much as any senior manager I've ever known.

You really have to wonder sometimes about his commitment. Some Board members have picked this up. To be honest, if something happened to me I don't think he would be a serious candidate for my job, even though they think he is very talented.

Mike couldn't help but think while Bob was talking. "If someone didn't know Bob they would think him quite callous if they overheard what he just said, but Bob is really a good person in his own way." He had known Bob for over 20 years. Their careers ran in parallels. Mike had been a consultant for three organizations that employed Bob, each watched the other move up their respective professions.

Bob was a rather shy person who frequently had to work in public. So he masked his shyness in formality. Although he encouraged subordinates to demonstrate initiative, he tended to carefully scrutinize their work, even the work of those in whom he had developed considerable confidence. He wanted things done the "right" way. He was often characterized as a perfectionist. He was as meticulous in his dress as his work. Despite his success, he was quite insecure. He worried most of the time.

Bob held himself to the same standard as others. It was an unusual evening or weekend that he would not spend much of his time working on the thick pile of papers he would take home and dictating one of the dozen or so memos that he would send to subordinates every day. He tried to overcome his natural reticence in public by carefully developed presentations. There were times that he could spend half a day preparing a 10-minute presentation to his Board. One problem with the approach was that he came across to some as stiff and cold. People who did not know him well thought of him as a rather dry and formal person, even bureaucratic. Bob had few friends. Those few who managed to get close to him over the years know him as a caring and brilliant executive.

Bob said little to Al because he wanted to be supportive, and he certainly did not want to be perceived by Al as not caring or putting his job ahead of his family. After all, no one spent more time thinking about family issues than Bob. So what he did was constantly send Al reminders about unresolved issues, press him for dates, and urge him to make trips in the field.

Well what have you said to him?" asked Mike.

I have stressed to him how important some of the meetings are and I have tried to alert him to some of the critical issues he has to handle."

He has indicated that he has been working on many of the problems at home and over the phone. He says he is in constant contact with his people over the telephone and that there are very few problems that he is not able to deal with. But that is simply not true.

You've known him for a long time. Why don't you talk to him and give me your assessment?"

The next week Mike asked Al out to lunch after they worked on the planning issues. Before lunch Mike couldn't help but review his impressions of Al. Al was like many people he had known who came up through sales. He was one of the most enjoyable people you could want to be around. He had an endless supply of the latest jokes—although he could be somewhat indiscreet as to who he told what joke. He was warm and friendly and showed great interest in the problems of the people he worked with—including his subordinates. He genuinely enjoyed helping his subordinates, although he was so busy that the lack of contact with him was a constant source of complaint. While this was a significant problem before the recurrence of Ruth's malignancy, now it was serious. Being liked was important to Al. His feelings would be hurt when he would hear about or sense the disapproval of a colleague. An ongoing source of conflict between Bob and Al was the fact that while Bob thought rules and regulations were meant to be followed, Al was inclined to overlook the rules, both for himself and others if the job was being done. Al was basically an optimistic person; he tended not to worry about the future, unless he had a specific problem he was forced to confront. He felt no need to control his subordinates if they were producing. After all, he had said to Mike many times what is the difference if he took time off if the job was being done?

After chatting for a while about issues that they were working on together Mike turned the conversation to Ruth's health. Al was quite hopeful about a new treatment available at the Morris Clinic. In fact, he had pulled strings with influential people and had a famous expert examine her. He advised an operation that would give her a one chance in three probability for surviving three years. Without the operation she had about a 15 percent probability. The operation would be in two months and she would have to remain at the hospital for a month. Of course, he would stay with her.

Mike asked about other relatives who could share the load. Their two children were away at college and he did not think it would be right to ask them. They were under enough stress at school and with their mother's illness. She had one sister who had two young teenagers so she could not help. Of course, he would not even consider leaving her alone.

Mike then asked: "Given all of the important issues you are working on and the people who look to you for supervision, how will you deal with your work responsibilities?"

Al said. "No problem, I've thought it through. First, I will set up in the regional office. I will try to be available for three hours a day, when I can leave Ruth. When there are significant problems with regional managers I'll fly them in to see me. After all, what's the difference if I fly out to see them or they come in to see me? As you know we hired Joe Roderick to handle major staff responsibilities like planning and executive development. He's had many years of supervisory experience, so he can handle any other issues that come up. So you can see that we ought to be able to handle the problems.

"I guess I ought to tell you that this illness has been very troubling, very difficult for me to handle. I haven't been sleeping well for weeks. The same thing happened the last time. So I've been getting up at 3 or 4:00 a.m. every day. I have been using that time very productively. It is incredible how much work you can get done through the computer tie in to the office when everything is so quiet."

Mike had the feeling that there was a lot more to the story than he was getting from Al, so he responded that, "It is clear that you've given this a lot of thought. But don't tell me what your plans are, tell me how you feel about things. The fact that you are having trouble sleeping is understandable, but it's also suggestive of deeper issues."

Al replied that, "It is very difficult for me now. I know that I am not 100 percent into my job. But let me remind you about what happened about a year-and-a-half ago. The presidency of Delta Corp., our major competitor, opened when Arnie Wyman had the sudden heart attack. Their Board hired that executive search firm to find candidates, and the partner managing the account knew me and wanted me to go on their short list. You'll surely remember that I came to you as a friend and discussed the situation with you. Everyone said I would be the prime candidate for the job.

"After thinking it over I decided not to interview with them. There were a lot of factors involved, of course. But in the end the determining factor was how MPC, and Bob in particular, treated me when we were having all those health problems. I felt, and I feel, part of a family. Families take care of their own in times of trouble. Mike, money can't buy that."

Mike later spoke to Bob about his lunch with Al. He tried to be descriptive and non-evaluative, urging Bob to speak to Al directly. Yet, after the discussion Bob seemed fixated on one point. He wondered whether Al's reference to being recruited away was a cryptic warning or a genuine statement of emotion. Or was it some combination?

Two weeks later Mike was in the office working with managers on some rather complex planning issues when he was called out of a meeting to take a long distance call from Al. Al was calling from Detroit where MPC had one of its most important regional offices and which happened to be his home town. While going over some of the planning issues Al interrupted the conversation, saying "Mike, I have to interrupt, I'm so excited, you'll never guess what happened last night. You know how long and hard we've been working on the Delta Corp. account. Tim Reynolds, our Detroit regional manager, finally set things up and we met with Delta's senior management team. We got the account! It will be at least $15,000,000 this year—almost 2% of our sales goal! Don't tell Bob, I want to break the news to him. This account was a real high priority for him."

A few hours later, toward the end of the day, Mike was just completing a meeting with Bob, when Bob said to him:

"You'll never guess the latest with Al. He is in Detroit. I tried to get him in the office yesterday morning on a very important issue, but Tim Reynolds said that he hadn't been in. He said that Al was at his mother's house. You remember that his dad died last year and his mother is alone and is in the early stages of Alzheimer's. He didn't get back to me until the late afternoon. Then he told me that he had to cancel some important meetings back here because he had to spend Friday in Detroit. It's obvious that he is taking advantage again. On top of everything else. I'm really frustrated."

"Well," Mike said, "Why don't you think about discussing it with him in a more straightforward way?"

Bob replied, "What's the use? You heard what he said. He has us over a barrel. He is staying with us because we treat him like family."

"Bob, are you being sarcastic?"

BULLER | SCHULER

Managing Organizations and People

A Resource for Cases in Management, Organizational Behavior, and Human Resource Management

Abstract

This case presents a number of difficult situations encountered by a contract negotiating team in a West African country. The cultural differences between doing business in West Africa and Peter Janes' expectations are explored. In addition, the situation leads Mr. Janes to question his basic values and presuppositions about his identity and integrity, through a rather bizarre incident. Finally, the question of the effectiveness of company policy is raised, particularly in relation to the structure of the negotiating teams and the relationship between headquarters and the team.

Contract Negotiations in Western Africa: A Case of Mistaken Identity

Peter Janes, a young member of Eurojet's Contracts Department, was on his way to Saheli in French-speaking West Africa to work on the complicated negotiations involved in selling a jet airliner to the Saheli government. He was not altogether thrilled with the assignment, and hoped it would be a quick deal, since financing seemed to be available for it. He had experience in contract negotiation in India, the Philippines, and Saudi Arabia, and most recently, Australia. At 27, he was one of the younger members of the department, but was seen as trustworthy with a high degree of motivation. If he succeeded, it would be the first deal he brought to closure on his own. But he had serious doubts about the project's feasibility or desirability. In addition, he had left behind what seemed to be the beginning of a great relationship in Australia, and he wanted to get back to his girlfriend. Furthermore, Janes had no desire to become a Francophone Africa expert within the company.

The Company Eurojet was one of the larger diversified aircraft manufacturers. It had developed a particular jet for Third World operations, able to operate from hot and high airfields, including unprepared strips. Orders, however, were hard to come by because of the difficulties of Third World financing and the poor financial condition of regional airlines. The company was therefore delighted to learn that its regional sales executive in Saheli, Mr. Ali Osaju, had found a potential sale in the country's desire for a presidential aircraft, along with its need for reliable regional air transport.

The sale looked even more possible when it was discovered that the government Export Import Bank had a substantial budget available for Saheli, making financing of the multimillion dollar aircraft feasible. It would be necessary to arrange an international commercial bank loan for Saheli as well. The potential of the airliner to earn revenue through regional transport was considered important in securing the loan.

The Negotiating Team

In December 1987, the Saheli government announced that they were ready to begin detailed negotiations. According to company policy, negotiations were conducted by the Contracts Department in close cooperation with sales and internal specialist functions. Mr. Janes, having just spent a hard-working three months—he had had four days off in the last six months based in Australia and working across southeast Asia on specialist leasing packages—was assigned to the team because of his Third World experience, and his ability to speak French. He had been with the company for about two years. He had no experience in Africa.

Mr. Osaju was a highly placed African of middle eastern origin, educated in Europe, with a background in aviation. He had joined the company at about the same time as Mr. Janes. He had no previous experience in selling high-tech capital goods, but had many good connections, and was seen as invaluable to the company because of his African cultural background, combined with his European education. He had been developing local contacts in Saheli by spending a week there every two or three months over the past two years.

The Negotiating Policy

The company's negotiating policy inevitably led to what was referred to as the "two-headed monster approach." The sales representative was responsible for initial discussions and for overall relations with the customer. The contracts representative was responsible for negotiating concrete offers and signing contracts and finance agreements on behalf of the company. This double approach led to varying degrees of tension between the members of particular teams as well as between the departments in general. Sales were particularly aggrieved that contracts operated on a worldwide rather than a regional basis.

Working in a team where both have important roles to play required considerable sensitivity. In his two years of working at Eurojet, Peter Janes was looked on by the sales people as a considerate and skilled negotiating partner. He was not likely to lose a contract that they had spent years developing because of cultural clumsiness. Nevertheless, he walked a very narrow line, as it was his role to say no to all the wishes of the customer which were not feasible from the company's perspective. As this was to be his first solo contract negotiation, and Ali Osaju's first sale with the company, they shared a certain personal enthusiasm for closing the deal.

The Negotiation: The Early Days

Eurojet was not the only company trying to sell a jetliner to Saheli. The Russians, who had had considerable influence over the country since its independence 20 years earlier, were very present, trying to sell their aircraft and to sabotage the deal with Eurojet. Mr. Janes and Mr. Osaju frequently received strange phone calls in their hotel rooms and were aware that all their telephone calls were bugged. Once, Mr. Janes returned to his room to find that his briefcase had been tampered with. In addition, another European company with a number of contracts in surrounding countries was trying to arrange a deal.

The main negotiating point of the team to begin with was to have the Sahelis accept one airplane that could be converted from a regional airliner to a VIP presidential jet. The Sahelis originally wanted a specially designed VIP jet, which would have cost an extra 10 million dollars and would never have been used other than for the president. The negotiations moved extremely slowly. Mr. Janes and Mr. Osaju spent hours waiting to see officials, chasing papers from one office to another. They became aware that no one official wanted to be responsible for making the decision, in case he would be blamed for it should things go wrong.

They spent many hours debating strategy in the bar of the hotel. Mr. Janes objected to Mr. Osaju telling him what to do. Mr. Osaju objected to Mr. Janes making issues too complicated for the client. The relationship was a very tense one. They both felt they were getting little support from the head office and that the circumstances they were working in were very difficult.

Mr. Janes began to feel he was in a no-win situation. He realized that the negotiating process could go on for months, and he knew that his colleague had already begun to take over his activities with multi-order prospects in Australia. Conditions at the hotel were not that comfortable, and both he and Mr. Osaju were paid on a salary only basis. There were no overseas allowances.

The lack of support from headquarters was a problem for both the negotiators. Communications were difficult, as they felt they could not talk freely over the telephone because of being bugged. Furthermore, they did not feel their contacts at headquarters would begin to understand the finer points of the negotiation difficulties. They did learn from headquarters that they were considered to be moving too slowly in making the deal.

There were constant discussions on finance, spares, configuration, certification, and training. All the legal and technical documents had to be translated from English to French, causing many minor but significant misunderstandings. In one case, the standard contract at home called for the Saheli government to waive its "sovereign immunity" and "contract in its private rather than its public capacity." Saheli had adopted the Napoleonic Code from France, and had no equivalent legal concepts. The courts in the home country have a very limited right to hear actions against the Crown, and they assume this element of the law holds true for all countries. The Saheli negotiators listened with polite disbelief to these explanations and sent a telegram to the president saying, "Sahelian sovereignty is being threatened."

Mr. Janes and Mr. Osaju decided on a very basic strategy of patience and a friendly, open manner. Establishing trust and preserving individual and corporate credibility were recognized as being vital. They placed great emphasis on simplifying the bureaucratic process. Two months of negotiating passed with no commitment in sight.

Eurojet management was beginning to show their lack of confidence in the deal. Peter Janes had committed them to one million dollars of expenditure on completing an airline to the Sahelis' expectations, so that it could be delivered on time, yet they saw no formalization of the contract, nor had they received any of the loan money. On the Saheli side, there was considerable nervousness about the commercial sovereign loans from the international banks.

Mr. Janes continued to make his daily round of visits to offices and homes, establishing himself as open and trustworthy and using his skill in expressing complex legal and technical terms in a simple way. He began to be aware of a warming of perceptions toward him. Up until then he had felt that the Sahelian officials were always guarded, on the defense in the presence of Eurojet's legal commercial representative. He thought that this was because it was his role to say "no" in the negotiations. In the third month of the negotiations, he received an extremely encouraging sign. A source close to the president had recently been quoted as saying, "He (Janes) doesn't say 'yes' very often, but when he says 'yes,' he means 'yes.'" This was the sign that they had been waiting for, that his credibility had been established and they could now begin to deal with some of the more sensitive issues in the negotiation.

Mr. Janes had adapted himself to local culture as much as he could. Although his natural inclination would have been to get things done quickly, deal with business first, and make friends later, he was aware that this was not how business deals were made in Saheli. So he spent many hours making friends, going to people's houses, walking around their businesses and factories. On one such occasion, he was walking around a factory with one of his friends, holding his hand as was the custom for Sahelian male friends. To his horror, a group of foreign diplomats came toward them on their tour of the factory. Mr. Janes was aware of an almost super-human effort on his part not to let go of his friend's hand and keep it relaxed, even as he felt the rest of his body stiffen with tension.

On another occasion, one of Mr. Janes' acquaintances attributes to him the status of being a great football (soccer) player. Peter thinks this person is just kidding at first, so he just "plays along with it." Later, when Peter's friends begin introducing him around as an international soccer player, it begins to worry him. He was unwilling to embarrass people by saying they were wrong, but was equally uncomfortable not striking down the myth. Perhaps it served some purpose. His status as an international soccer player was apparently much greater than that of a young lawyer; perhaps he needed a little extra to justify his power in negotiating and signing the contract. It was relatively easy to give indirect answers to questions, thus saving his conscience and protecting his strangely acquired status. Nonetheless, alluding to his legal training, Mr. Janes had said to Mr. Osaju at this time, "I can put my hand on my heart and say, 'I have not told a lie,' but I don't feel comfortable. We have worked so hard for credibility, I would hate a silly issue like this to backfire on us." At the time, they agreed to laugh off the issue, because so far the people involved were not main players in the negotiations.

Mr. Janes continued to make noncommittal replies and managed to avoid any further serious problems. Although greatly disturbing to him personally, it was a nonissue in terms of the negotiations. Fortunately for Peter Janes, he could discuss his feelings about the situation with Ali Osaju, and so relieve some of his own tension by laughing about the absurdity of it.

After 10 months of intense negotiations, the deal was almost called off by the negotiating team at the last minute. They had spent days retranslating the French contract back into English, and then sitting by a Sahelian typist who did not speak English saying each word to her phonetically so that she could type it. They both had had very little sleep in order to get the contract finished on time. When they finally went with the attorney general to the president's office to sign the contract, they were as usual kept waiting for a few hours. During that time, the attorney general reread the French contract and discovered numerous spelling mistakes in it. He then declared that he could not give it to the president in its present condition, and that the signing would have to be delayed for another week.

Ali and Peter both hit the walls—literally. It was the last straw. While Ali threw books and papers at the walls, Peter strode around the room shouting that unless they signed immediately, he was withdrawing Eurojet's approval of the contract. The attorney general stood his ground, and Ali and Peter stormed off to the hotel. They could scarcely believe what they had done after almost a year's worth of friendly and meticulous negotiating. Peter went to sleep, exhausted after the last 10 days of work and the loss of the contract.

He was woken four hours later to be informed that the attorney general was waiting to see him. He was escorted to an office across the road, where he found the attorney general in his shirtsleeves, sitting at a typewriter, carefully changing all the spelling mistakes himself. He wanted Peter to initial all the changes so that he would feel confident that no substantial changes were being made in the contract. The contract was signed the next day.

Epilogue

Despite Eurojet's advice, the aircraft was not handled by the national airlines but kept under the president's control, and so, rarely used. Debt servicing soon became a problem, and one year later, the aircraft was quietly and informally repossessed. Eurojet has offered to resell the aircraft, but the Saheli government balked at authorizing the sale.

Mr. Osaju spent one more year in Africa, and then was promoted to the Far East where he was made regional sales director. Mr. Janes was promoted to another program in early 1983, where he continued to work for the next four years.

BULLER | SCHULER

Managing Organizations and People

A Resource for Cases in Management, Organizational Behavior, and Human Resource Management

Abstract

George Stein, a college student employed for the summer by Eastern Dairy, must decide if he is going to remove the filters from the plant's piping and, thus, allow the current production run of milkshake mix to be contaminated with maggots. This course of action will save the company money, at least in the short run, and allow George's shift to go home on time. George is disturbed, however, by the thought of children drinking those milkshakes. The workforce is unionized and George is feeling pressure from some of his co-workers to cut corners. The night shift is staffed by a self-managed team and no members of management are on duty.

Does This Milkshake Taste Funny?

George Stein, a college student working for Eastern Dairy during the summer, was suddenly faced with an ethical dilemma. George had very little time to think about his choices, less than a minute. On the one hand, he could do what Paul told him to do, and his shift could go home on time. However, he found it tough to shake the gross mental image of all those innocent kids drinking milkshakes contaminated with pulverized maggots. If he chose instead to go against Paul, what would the guys say? He could almost hear their derisive comments already: "wimp . . ., wus . . ., college kid . . ."

Background   George Stein had lived his entire life in various suburbs of a major city on the east coast. His father's salary as a manager provided the family with a solid middle-class lifestyle. His mother was a homemaker. George's major interests in life were the local teenage gathering place—a drive-in restaurant—hot rod cars, and his girlfriend, Cathy. He had not really wanted to attend college, but relentless pressure by his parents convinced him to try it for

■ This case was prepared by Roland B. Cousins, LaGrange College, and Linda E. Benitz, InterCel, Inc., as a basis for class discussion and not to illustrate either effective or ineffective handling of an administrative situation. The names of the firm, individuals, and the location involved have been disguised to preserve anonymity. The situation reported is factual. The authors thank Anne T. Lawarence for her assistance in the development of this case.

a year. He chose mechanical engineering as his major, hoping there might be some similarity between being a mechanical engineer and being a mechanic. After one year at engineering school, however, he had not seen any similarity yet. Once again this summer, his parents had to prod and cajole him to agree to return to school in the fall. They only succeeded by promising to give their blessing to his marriage to Cathy following his sophomore year.

George worked at menial jobs each of the last four summers to satisfy his immediate need for dating and car money. He did manage to put away a bit to be used for spending money during the school year. He had saved very little for the day that he and Cathy would start their life together, but they planned for Cathy to support them with her earnings as a secretary until George either finished or quit school.

The day after George returned home this summer, he heard that Eastern Dairy might hire summer help. He applied at the local plant the next day. Eastern Dairy was unionized, and the wages paid were over twice the minimum wage George had been paid on previous jobs, so he was quite interested in a position.

Eastern Dairy manufactured milkshake and ice cream mix for a number of customers in the metropolitan area. It sold the ice cream mix in 5- and 10-gallon containers to other firms, which then added flavoring ingredients (e.g., strawberries or blueberries), packaged and froze the mix, and sold the ice cream under their own brand names. Eastern Dairy sold the milkshake mix in 5-gallon cardboard cartons, which contained a plastic liner. These packages were delivered to many restaurants in the area. The packaging was designed to fit into automatic milkshake machines used in many types of restaurants, including most fast-food restaurants and drive-ins.

George was elated when he received the call asking him to come to the plant on June 8. After a brief visit with the human resources director, at which time George filled out the necessary employment forms, he was instructed to report for work at 11:00 p.m. that night. He was assigned to the night shift, working from 11:00 p.m. until 7:00 a.m., six nights per week—Sunday through Friday. With the regular wages paid at Eastern Dairy, supplemented by time and one-half for eight hours of guaranteed overtime each week, George thought he could save a tidy sum before he had to return to school at the end of the first week of September.

When George reported to work, he discovered that there were no managers assigned to the night shift. The entire plant was operated by a six-person crew of operators. One member of this crew, a young man named Paul Burnham, received each night's production orders from the day shift superintendent as the superintendent left for the day. Although Paul's status was no different from that of his five colleagues, the other crew members looked to him for direction. Paul passed the production orders to the mixer (who was the first stage of the production process) and kept the production records for the shift.

The production process was really quite simple. Mixes moved between various pieces of equipment (including mixing vats, pasteurizers, coolers, homogenizers, and filling machines) through stainless steel pipes suspended from the ceiling. All of the pipes had to be disassembled, thoroughly cleaned, and reinstalled by the conclusion of the night shift. This process took approximately one hour, so all the mix had to be run by 6:00 a.m. in order to complete the cleanup by the 7:00 a.m. quitting time. Paul and one other worker, Fred (the mixer), cleaned the giant mixing vats while the other four on the shift, including George, cleaned and reinstalled the pipes and filters.

George soon learned that Paul felt a sense of responsibility for completing all of the assigned work before the end of the shift. However, as long as that objective was achieved, he did not seem to care about what else went on during the shift. A great deal of storytelling and horseplay was the norm, but the work was always completed by quitting time. George was soon enjoying the easy camaraderie of the work group, the outrageous pranks they pulled on one another, and even the work itself.

George's position required that he station himself beside a conveyor in a large freezer room. He removed containers of mix as they came down the line and stacked them in the appropriate places. Periodically, Paul would decide that they had all worked hard enough and would shut down the line for a while so that they all could engage in some non-work activity like joke telling, hiding each other's lunch boxes, or "balloon" fights. The balloons were actually the five-gallon, flexible liners for the cardboard boxes in which the mix was sold.

While George did not relish being hit by an exploding bag containing five gallons of heavy mix, he found it great fun to lob one at one of his co-workers. The loss of 10 to 40 gallons of mix on a shift did not seem to concern anyone, and these fights were never curtailed.

George quickly learned that management had only two expectations of the night shift. First, the shift was expected to complete the production orders each night. Second, management expected the equipment, including the pipes, to be spotlessly cleaned at the conclusion of the shift. Paul told George that inspectors from the county health department would occasionally drop by unannounced at the end of the shift to inspect the vats and pipes after they had been disassembled and scrubbed. Paul also told George that management would be very upset if the inspectors registered any complaints about cleanliness.

George did join the union but saw very little evidence of their involvement in the day-to-day operations of the plant. Labor relations seemed quite amicable, and George only thought of the union when he looked at a pay stub and noticed that union dues had been deducted from his gross pay. The difference George noticed in working for Eastern Dairy compared to his previous employers was not the presence of the union but the absence of management.

The Current Situation

Things seemed to be going quite well for George on the job—until a few minutes ago. The problem first surfaced when the milkshake mix that was being run started spewing out of one of the joints in the overhead pipe network. The pumps were shut down while George disassembled the joint to see what the problem was. George removed the filter screen from the pipe at the leaking joint and saw that it was completely packed with solid matter. Closer inspection revealed that maggots were the culprits. George hurriedly took the filter to Paul to show him the blockage. Paul did not seem too concerned and told George to clean the filter and reassemble the joint. When George asked how this could have happened, Paul said maggots occasionally got into the bags of certain ingredients that were stored in a warehouse at the back of the lot. "But you do not have to worry," said Paul. "The filters will catch any solid matter."

Feeling somewhat reassured, George cleaned the filter and reassembled the pipe. But still, the image of maggots floating in a milkshake was hard to shake. And, unfortunately for George, this was not the end of it.

Shortly after the pumps were re-started, the mix began to flow out of another joint. Once again, a filter plugged with maggots was found to be the cause.

For the second time, George cleaned the filter and reassembled the connection. This time Paul had seemed a bit more concerned as he noted that they barely had enough time to run the last 500 gallons remaining in the vats before they needed to clean up in preparation for the end of the shift.

Moments after the equipment was again re-started, another joint started to spew. When maggots were found to be clogging this filter too, Paul called George over and told him to remove all five filters from the line so the last 500 gallons could be run without any filters. Paul laughed when he saw the shocked look on George's face.

"George," he said, "don't forget that all of this stuff goes through the homogenizer, so any solid matter will be completely pulverized. And when it's heated in the pasteurization process, any bacteria will be killed. No one will ever know about this, the company can save a lot of mix—that's money—and, most important, we can run this through and go home on time."

George knew that they would never get this lot packaged if they had to shut down every minute to clean filters, and there was no reason to believe it would not be this way for the rest of the run. The product had been thoroughly mixed in the mixing vats at the beginning of the process, which meant that contaminants would be distributed uniformly throughout the 500 gallons. George also knew that 500 gallons of milkshake was very expensive. He did not think management would just want it dumped down the drain. Finally,

Paul was definitely right about one thing, removing all of the filters, a 10-minute job at most, would assure that they could get everything cleaned up and be out on time.

As George walked to the first filter joint, he felt a knot forming in his stomach as he thought of kids drinking all of the milkshakes they were about to produce. He had already decided he would not have another milkshake for at least a month, in order to be absolutely sure that this batch was no longer being served at restaurants. After all, he did not know exactly which restaurants would receive this mix. As he picked up his wrench and approached the first pipe joint that contained a filter, he still could not help wondering if he should not do or say something more.

BULLER | SCHULER

Managing Organizations and People

A Resource for Cases in Management, Organizational Behavior, and Human Resource Management

Abstract

Ellen, the program director of Omega House, a hospice, was wondering how to deal with the new development officer, George. He reported to her and was also part of a cross-program task force on fund raising within the Social Action Consortium (SAC), the umbrella organization for a variety of service agencies located in the Midwest. Ellen was accustomed to working in a team and found George's non-communicative approach disconcerting. She was puzzled as to how to deal with the situation. Was the problem with George structural rather than individual? George's structural place within SAC seemed unclear, with him seemingly reporting both to her and the SAC development office chief, who headed the task force. Thus, she asked herself, "Is the problem George's irresponsible and non-communicative behavior or is it confusion over who is to direct his efforts or both?"

Insubordination or Unclear Loyalties?

Background

Omega House was established for those terminally ill patients who need to find inner peace and dignity as well as the best in hospice care in their remaining days. It had been started by a group that had been unable to sustain it financially and had gone bankrupt and been closed for several years. Then, in the early 1990s, SAC agreed to assume responsibility for it. It is now one of many services provided by SAC. SAC brings together 17 different groups, including small social service agencies and donor organizations that wish to be involved in more direct service than contributing to a funding agency. For nearly 80 years it has provided service to the less fortunate and disenfranchised. It provides a wide range of services, in addition to Omega House, including the following: assorted special projects in the field of education, services to at-risk youth, shelters and apartments for those with special needs, services for people with HIV, addictions counseling, an inner-city health program and emergency food assistance, consumer credit seminars, and political advocacy for issues that effect the poor and disenfranchised. Its expenditures and revenues in 1995 were roughly $8 million.

Program Director

Ellen didn't get much sleep. Before, when she had been a full-time nurse, she used to fall asleep immediately after an exhausting but satisfying shift; she could leave the problems at work. However, now that she had become a manager, she found that things tended to

■ This case was written by Asbjorn Osland, George Fox University, and Shannon Shoul, University of Portland.

1

nag at her and keep her awake. Like today, George seemed to be insubordinate. She would never have spoken to her superior in that tone. Why did he think he could get away with it with her? Did she appear unsure of herself? Was George confused over where his loyalties should lie?

Ellen began working at the hospice as a registered nurse in patient care five years ago. Then, just over two years ago, she became the temporary program director, after her predecessor had been dismissed, and assumed the managerial responsibilities for Omega House, in addition to clinical oversight of patient care. Given her lack of managerial experience at the time of her temporary assignment, she had been promised managerial training but after two years was still waiting. Ellen felt very comfortable dealing with clinical care and was fortunate to have a strong clinical staff, an excellent and devoted kitchen crew, and a dedicated volunteer coordinator who organized the extensive services provided by the volunteers. However, she was less comfortable with her managerial duties in relation to SAC. Also, the troubled financial history of the Omega House concerned her. To further complicate matters, the SAC administration had proven both arbitrary and autocratic, in her experience. Though she lived through the bankruptcy, she missed the lean administrative structure Omega House had enjoyed before the bankruptcy and subsequent SAC ownership. Her clinical staff had also worked at Omega House before SAC assumed control and were often skeptical of SAC-mandated changes.

Additionally, she was not quite certain what George, Omega's new development officer, was doing. SAC's executive director had hired George immediately before she left to take another job with a prominent ecumenical relief organization. This left the organization without an executive director, as the board had decided to take some time to fill the leadership position. George seemed to spend most of his time with the other development people at SAC, working on the cross-program task force on fundraising. He was the only one with professional fundraising experience and many within SAC viewed him as an expert. Ellen understood that should George obtain a large grant for SAC, it could also help Omega House. However, it had been her experience that she had to fight hard for resources. Thus, when George had been assigned to her, she thought he would focus most of his attention on Omega House. Ellen understood that Omega House was one of SAC's only programs with active volunteers who could raise funds. Thus she understood that George could also be useful to other parts of SAC but still felt that since George had been hired with money from a grant given to Omega House, he should spend the bulk of his time serving their needs. Funds from this grant had also been used to purchase office equipment used by George and others.

Ellen had also come to suspect, based on gossip, that George's past job history involved a personal indiscretion that had led to his termination with another employer. This made it difficult for her to completely trust him.

What's George Up to?

Ellen entered the kitchen early Monday morning and said, "Hi Dan. What's for breakfast today?"

Dan, with his back to her, was gyrating to the rhythm of a CD blaring in the boom box. Dan's wide-ranging preferences for music ran from the church hymns he played on Sunday evenings to punk. Ellen was not quite certain where this particular CD fit on the continuum but took the liberty of turning it down. Dan turned and noted her presence, "Oh, hi you old bitty—don't you like my music? I suppose you'd prefer MUSAK," he responded in a playfully scornful tone. He then approached her and hugged her, stating, "It's nice to see you. What's up?" Their relationship represented the friendliness existing throughout the Omega staff: approachable, playful, and comfortable.

While attempting to wrap her arms around Dan's ample upper body, Ellen looked over his shoulder and noted a tray of long-stemmed glasses sitting on the counter in the dish washing area and asked, "Who passed on?" The long-stemmed glasses were used by the staff to honor one of the patients who had died. The average stay was only three weeks. To avoid developing the lack of feeling that one can find in service settings where people routinely suffered tragedy, the staff engaged in this ceremony each time someone died; they left a light on outside the person's room and shared a toast of a non-alcoholic sparkling beverage.

"Theo. He had been active all weekend. Fortunately, his immediate family was with him last night," Dan responded soberly. "Active" meant Theo had been showing the physical motions that were symptomatic of impending death.

They both paused a moment before continuing. The customary, "That's too bad," did not seem to fit as it was a hospice designated for people with terminal cancer or AIDS who were near death upon admission.

Ellen continued, "Say, what time did George come in on Friday? I was at the SAC office for a meeting. He usually comes through the kitchen. Did you happen to notice?"

Dan looked out the window and thought, "Let's see. I had finished breakfast and was outside having a cigarette. It must have been after nine. He seems to come at about that time except for a couple of times a week when he comes in while I'm doing the breakfast dishes, which would make it after 10:30."

Ellen thanked Dan and went to the portion of the old estate house where the patients were located. Her office was immediately behind the nursing station. She liked to be close to the action and sometimes wondered if she was cut out for chasing after administrative staff, like George, who weren't communicating regularly with her.

That morning she dealt with the customary managerial concerns for the first half hour and spent the balance of the morning reviewing the financial statements in preparation for the budget meeting the next day. She noted that while SAC's development efforts had seemed to improve funding for Omega, Omega's own fundraising efforts had resulted in little change from the previous year when they didn't even have their own development officer. Now that they had George, she had expected Omega's contributions to have risen. She also noticed that George's salary was charged to a grant destined in its entirety to Omega's budget. She thought to herself, "If George is working for Omega, these numbers ought to be changing. Since he's charged to Omega, I really should be more aware of what he's up to." She resolved to speak with George that afternoon.

Confrontation

Ellen walked up the stairs of the main portion of the house to the office, directly above the kitchen and Dan's blaring boom box and deep voice, where George worked. She found him at the photocopy machine. When he saw her he looked somewhat sheepish. Ellen noted that the yellow copies looked like fliers; she caught a glimpse of the image of a canoe and the words "Boundary Waters Adventure" before he hastily scooped the copies up and put them in the opened briefcase positioned unsteadily on top of the photocopy machine. "Just taking a few minutes to make some personal copies—I brought in my own ream of yellow paper. I hope you don't mind," said George, avoiding her gaze. He then cleared his throat and proceeded, "What can I do for you?"

"I don't want you making hundreds of copies on our machine. The paper is a minor expense but the copies are not. It's leased and we pay several cents per copy," said Ellen as forcefully as she could without shouting. She had not wanted their meeting to begin this way.

"Understood," responded George quickly. He continued, "I'd be happy to reimburse SAC for the copies. I've done 300."

"That would be nice," responded Ellen before continuing. She paused briefly while he closed his briefcase and went to his office. She followed him in and took a seat after he gestured to her to sit in the chair customarily occupied by the university intern, Lisa, who was off at a retreat for her university. Trying to change the mood from a disciplinary one, which she felt she had been forced into, to the collaborative tone she had intended, Ellen continued, "Say, I wanted to compliment you again on the 'casino night' last week. It went well and I've received several calls from people who attended." She was referring to a fundraising event they had held the previous week; it was an evening on the lawn where the sponsors, volunteers, and staff played various casino-like games. She wanted to begin with something positive, even though she had discovered that Lisa had a larger role in the arrangements than she would have expected from an intern.

George responded, "Well, that's what I'm here for."

Fundraising was a big issue with Omega and the SAC. Some of the low-profile SAC programs had been cut recently. Ellen had been told by SAC that her program would not be cut, but was concerned nonetheless since she wanted to upgrade some of their equipment as well as complete the remodeling of the facility. To do so, she needed more money and George had been recruited for that purpose. However, he seemed to spend a lot of time at the SAC office working with the cross-program task force on fundraising for the benefit of the overall organization rather than focusing on Omega.

Additionally, some of Ellen's uncertainty stemmed from the autocratic style the former SAC director had used to manage the various programs. Sometimes the director had seemed capricious in how she would arbitrarily fire program directors. Ellen also regarded her as insensitive; the director would come in, unannounced, leading a delegation of visitors through the facility. Since Omega was a hospice, Ellen felt that such visits should have been handled with greater sensitivity. Also, the director had tried to micro-manage many of the programs. She would make decisions about minutiae, sometimes change programs without consulting the program director, and involve staff from the various programs in SAC issues, such as the cross-program task force on fundraising. Ellen understood that this was a large concern for SAC and she knew that George, who was assigned to Omega, needed to participate in this fundraising task force at SAC. However, Ellen was concerned that Omega's internal fundraising efforts were not getting the attention they deserved from George. It was apparent to Ellen that Lisa, the student intern, had assumed a leadership role, filling the vacuum left by George. However, Lisa was temporary and should not supplant George.

With this in mind, Ellen then asked, "Say, I was wondering how it was going with the Omega committee you're leading for fundraising?" Ellen had formed an internal committee, comprised of both staff and volunteers (some of whom were donors), to generate ideas for fundraising. She had heard from committee members that George was difficult to communicate with and frequently did not attend the meetings. Still, Ellen was aware of how both the staff and volunteers comprised a group that had been together for years and that it would be difficult for George to be accepted immediately.

George responded assertively, "Look, I can't get the job done if I'm to work in committees all the time here and at SAC."

Ellen responded, quickly and decisively, "I asked you to be on that committee and I expected you to participate. These people have been a part of Omega for years and can contribute a great deal both in service and ideas. Those who are donors also provide a lot of financial support. They are the ones who keep us going. You can't ignore them. Furthermore, they need your fundraising expertise. I know it's difficult to enter an established group but you won't have a chance if they don't perceive you as more cooperative."

George responded, more carefully this time after noting Ellen's displeasure, "I had no intention of leaving anyone out of the loop or avoiding the committee. It's just that I'm part of SAC's cross-program task force. I had a few conflicts where I had to decide where to focus my energies. I felt I had to do what SAC wanted."

Ellen was now walking around the room. She listened, thought for a moment, and then responded, "I understand that you need to coordinate your Omega efforts with the SAC team's overall development plans and may be asked to do things with them. However, when I tell you specifically what to do, I expect you to do it."

George responded delicately, "Maybe you should speak with the SAC development officer so that we can all understand our jobs better."

Ellen felt she was not getting through to George. She stated, "You're assigned here. Your salary comes out of my budget. I don't see the confusion. Yes, I'll speak with the SAC development officer to clarify what it is I told you to do and why I want you to do it. But that won't change that you're working here for me. So please do what I say."

Ellen felt that she couldn't have been more explicit. However, later, on her way home, she wondered if the problem wasn't structural rather than individual. George reported to her and SAC's development chief. She recalled how SAC's development chief sat in on George's interview with her and lobbied for George because of his skills, which he said would round out SAC's development team. Thus, she wondered, "Is the problem George and what appears to be irresponsible and non-communicative behavior or is it confusion over who is to direct his efforts or both?"

BULLER | SCHULER

Managing Organizations and People
A Resource for Cases in Management, Organizational Behavior,
and Human Resource Management

Abstract

This is a classic case demonstrating group cohesion and competition in a dynamic organizational environment. The luggers haul meat that is regarded as a tough and dirty job. The butchers have the cleaner job of cutting the meat brought in by the luggers; the butchers have more status. Suddenly, there are some technological changes. The luggers' job becomes easier, a union is formed that provides the luggers more security and the luggers devise a method by which they can make more money. Because of the group size of the luggers they break into two sub-groups.

The Luggers Versus the Butchers

Food Merchandising Corporation had one of its warehouses in a small city in northern New Jersey. The main operation of the warehouse was to stock certain goods, and then ship them on order to various stores. The meat department handled packaged meats, and wholesale cuts of lamb, veal, and beef. Beef, by far the biggest and most expensive commodity, was generally bought from Midwestern packers and shipped either by railroad or truck. On arrival at the warehouse, the beef was in the form of two hindquarters and two forequarters, each weighing close to two hundred pounds. The problem was to get these heavy pieces of meat off the trucks (or freight cars) and onto the intricate system of rails within the warehouse. Freight was paid by the shipper.

Company and union rules proscribed warehousemen from unloading trucks. It became the function of the general warehouseman (designated "lugger") to assist in the unloading of the trucks, but with no lifting. If, however, the beef was shipped by rail, it became his function to unload the freight cars. After the meat was placed on company rails, it was pushed through the doors into the 35' warehouse where it was placed in stock until it was butchered. The butchery process involved several men. First, the meat went to

■ Robert E. C. Wegner and Leonard Sayles, Cases in Organizational and Administrative Behavior, 1972, pp. 42–48.
Reprinted by permission of Prentice-Hall, Inc., Englewood Cliffs, New Jersey.

the sawman. While someone steadied the meat on the rail, the rib, plate, brisket, and shoulder bones were severed. Then it was passed on to the cutters, who butchered it into several smaller wholesale cuts. After that the meat was again placed in stock to be shipped out by the night crews.

The "Luggers" Versus the "Butchers"

The operation of the warehouse involved two distinct functions: to unload and stock the beef, and then to butcher it. The unloading process was wholly different from butchering. It required physical strength and coordination to lift 200 pounds of beef all day. Furthermore, when the workload slowed down, the luggers were given different tasks. There was a degree of variety in their work. But the butchering function was very different. The men were geographically confined to the cutting line and performed the same basic operations day after day.

When the warehouse was unionized eight years ago, the men who had most seniority were given first option as to the jobs they preferred. Since many of these men were on the older side, they gravitated away from the more laborious general warehouse work toward the higher-wage butcher jobs. Consequently, two different types of individuals became associated with the two different types of jobs.

The eight butchers were engaged in the skilled practice of butchering meat. Most of them had been with the company for many years. For the most part, they were family men with many off-the-job responsibilities, were by no means in union affairs, and probably had more loyalty to the company than to the union local. They had a high number of social activities off the job, such as group picnics, bowling, golf, et cetera. The tedious boredom of their job was somewhat mitigated by these mutual activities and an atmosphere of good humor usually prevailed in their corner of the warehouse.

There were nine luggers, but two of these had been butchers until very recently. More will be said later about these men. A third man usually worked in another section. Thus the term "lugger" referred to a specific group of six general warehousemen. These men were younger and generally had less company time than the butchers, but this is not to say that they were young or new. Most of them were married, but treated their home responsibilities differently. For instance, the typical butcher would spend his night at home, and most of the luggers would spend their night working a part-time job.

Hank, Josh, and Mr. Abrams

Hank was the foreman. When he became foreman about 10 years ago, the men considered him a walking terror but a good foreman. Now he was considered neither. There were several reasons for this change. First, the coming of the union had made Hank more careful in the way he handled the men. Second, Hank had lost control of the luggers. After several fiery confrontations, he more or less left them alone. When it was necessary to give them an order, great explanations and apologies often accompanied it. His relationship with butchers, however, remained fairly intact. In effect, Hank was afraid of the luggers but not of the butchers. Third, when Mr. Abrams became manager two years ago it was his policy to use close personal supervision of the men to ensure efficiency. Mr. Abrams, therefore, usurped considerable portions of Hank's responsibility.

Josh was the union representative. He had built up a great friendship with Carl, the shop steward, and the other luggers. His relationship with the butchers, however, was strictly on a business basis. Usually this meant that the butchers complained about the luggers, but nothing really important was done about it.

Mr. Abrams' assistant was Lyle, nicknamed "the Puppy." Lyle used to follow Mr. Abrams everywhere he went, to the great enjoyment of the men. Thus came the nickname "Puppy."

The butchers took the brunt of Mr. Abrams' close supervision, mainly because they were confined to one spot, and were easy to observe. Also, this was where the real pressure had to be applied, for if the meat was not butchered, it could not be sent out and stores would run short. Mr. Abrams had the responsibility to ensure that stores were not short. He evidently felt that standing over the men (with the Puppy at his side) would cut down on the little games the men developed to break up their boring routine (talking, bathroom breaks, et cetera). The net effect was that the men, being old timers, took their breaks anyway but grumbled about being watched over. The luggers were harder to watch, being more spread out, and they also managed to gain some control over Mr. Abrams. He knew that an ill-timed remark or too much supervision would only result in later slowdowns by these men.

A Slow Change in Status

Six years ago the butcher's job was considered much more desirable than that of the luggers. At that time most of the meat was shipped by railroad. This necessitated a great deal of heavy work. Most of the men would have preferred the cold monotony of cutting meat to lugging 200 pounds of beef from a railroad car to a loading dock. It was at this point that two luggers, Brent and Terry, began to think of developing a system of portable rails that would be adaptable to the large variety of freight cars which came to the warehouse. The rails were successfully designed and developed by the two men. With the passage of time skill in their use was achieved, and the job of unloading freight cars became quite simple.

The ingenuity of two luggers was widely heralded about the warehouse and in the company, and recognition was given in due proportion. More importantly, a job that was undesirable before became quite attractive because the chief reason for its undesirability had ceased to exist. The main attractions of the butcher's job were reduced to the companionship of the group, the waning prestige of being a skilled workman, and the higher-wage-more-over time benefits. This was quite sufficient to keep them satisfied, if not as happy as before.

Hank's foremanship also suffered. At this date, his position had already been dealt a few blows by the union and the men. Now an innovation was introduced that had no place in his way of doing things. He preferred to completely ignore the rails and allow the luggers to use them as they saw fit. From the company's point of view, the use of rails in freight cars meant very little. Four men were still required in each car. Efficiency remained about the same because it took time to assemble and disassemble the rail system.

If the use of the rails had resulted solely in physical advantages, it is probable that the situation would have gone along unchanged. But the luggers were quick to discover an economic value in their use. The trucks coming in on the front docks had to be unloaded. Since freight was paid by the shipper, the company and union had worked out an agreement in which the trucker was responsible for delivering the meat to the dock. The warehouse workers were only to assist peripherally and were not permitted inside the trucks unless it was absolutely necessary.

The drivers were not happy with their lot of unloading up to 35,000 pounds of beef. Consequently, they often hired warehouse vagrants—men who sat around the warehouse waiting for such opportunities. The going rate was one dollar per 1,000 pounds: between $30.00 and $35.00 a truck. It generally took two hours to unload one truck. The enterprising luggers redesigned the rails for use on the trucks, and made it known that a tip of two dollars was in order for anyone who cared to use them. Since the railroad was making more and more use of piggyback services, the number of trucks as well as the amount of the tips began to increase.

A Dispute Develops

Last year, two butchers were given the option of working as luggers. They exercised the option, partly hoping to recuperate some of their wage losses by sharing in the tip money. It was not long before serious arguments developed between the old and new luggers. Beforehand, the luggers had worked out a one-for-you and one-for-me system with the trucks. Such an informal understanding was possible because this tightly cohesive group knew that petty bickering would soon take the problem out of their own hands. The two ex-butchers, however, had no desire to work with the old group. They were in no way amenable to tacit understandings that cut them out. Consequently, when the big trailers turned into the driveway, there began a jockeying for position.

Arguments developed, and other work suffered. When the two ex-butchers turned to the union, they found their upward paths of communication thoroughly blocked. Carl, the shop steward, was a lugger. It was to his disadvantage to press hard on behalf of the two ex-butchers. Josh, the union representative, was much too friendly with the luggers and no progress could be made here. Hank, the foreman, was worthless in this matter, and Mr. Abrams was too new at this stage to take action. For these reasons, and because of a normal reluctance to push grievances, little pressure was placed on the union.

Early last spring, following a series of flare-ups over equipment usage and truck tips, two "clubs" were formed: Club "Six" and Club "Three." Brent, one of the two rail designers, originated the idea of formalizing the two groups. Each club was given a separate locker for equipment. No exchanges were to take place. Members of Club Three (the two ex-butchers and a third who worked in a different part of the warehouse) were permitted to work a share of trucks proportional to club membership. Members of Club Six (the six original luggers) began a practice of pooling tips and dividing them equally.

At first the formalization of the two groups appeared to be a good solution. There were fewer arguments, and Club Three was reasonably satisfied. However, an unfortunate side effect developed. Previously, the distinctions between luggers and butchers were implicit and the warehouse as a whole was a friendly place. People knew who got along with whom, and friendships often crossed group lines. With the formalization, however, people began to class themselves as "in" or "out." Club Six members began to be more and more isolated among the twenty-five men who worked in this section of the warehouse. Butchers and luggers constantly complained about each other. Members of Club Six refused to work with members of Club Three, and much ill feeling was generated. But even so, had there been nothing else, these difficulties would probably not have caused any lasting problems. There was, however, something else—the piggyback development.

The railroads were making more and more use of piggyback trucking. This is a system whereby trailers are hauled part of the way by rail, and part of the way by road. As the number of freight cars decreased and the warehouse volume increased, more trucks began coming. These trucks had to be unloaded, and unloading was an expensive and time-consuming proposition. The use of rails on the trucks had cut down the time it took to unload. A good crew could "knock one off" in less than an hour, though the average time was about two hours. The luggers began to move into this very lucrative area. It became quite a steady thing for them to bring home an extra $30.00 or $40.00 per week. Occasionally, if things were slow enough, the luggers would work a truck on company time. Or they would begin setting it up about 3:30, so there would be no delay in getting it started at 4:00.

From a company viewpoint, there was no problem. Trucks were being emptied faster than ever before, even on the rare occasion when a truck came in purposely late. The more usual situation was either that there were too many trucks to unload in the normal day or that the truck was legitimately delayed. At any rate, the rails enabled the ordinary trucks to be unloaded much more rapidly and the experienced luggers often finished their after-hour trucks in half the normal time. Warehouse efficiency did not suffer.

The butchers, however, were not a happy group. They continued to work the same boring routine in the same 35°. Their income did not change. They watched the luggers develop into a very cohesive group and usurp their status position. They resented the different treatments meted out to the two groups. The luggers were given too much freedom, and the butchers were too closely supervised. The luggers quite often "couldn't" stay overtime, yet they could almost always work a truck. Nothing was ever said when luggers made excuses; but if the butchers did not want to stay, they were given a great deal of grief.

Pressure was applied, and it was not a rare thing to find butchers working three hours overtime for half the money the luggers made in an hour by working a truck. The obvious inequity was deeply resented. The luggers used company time to work trucks, or to set them up, and this violated the union contract. Yet nothing concrete was ever done to stop them. The butchers felt totally frustrated and disenchanted with what they had once considered as high-status jobs. Despite their innate conservatism and procompany attitude, they seriously considered a massive walkout to get their grievances heard.

BULLER | SCHULER

Managing Organizations and People

A Resource for Cases in Management, Organizational Behavior, and Human Resource Management

Abstract

This case illustrates the effect of poor management and inadequate job design on the motivation of a Guatemalan office of translators. A vacuum of leadership and supervision allowed an informal group with poor work norms to take over, creating a climate that resulted in low productivity and morale. The protagonist, a consultant, must determine what recommendations to make about who should run the department and how the work should be structured.

The Donor Services Department

Joanna Reed was walking home through fallen tree blossoms in Guatemala City. Today, however, her mind was more on her work than the natural beauty surrounding her. She unlocked the gate to her colonial home and sat down on the porch, surrounded by riotous toddlers, pets, and plants, to ponder the recommendations she would make to Sam Wilson. The key decisions she needed to make about his Donor Services Department concerned who should run the department and how the work should be structured.

Joanna had worked for a sponsorship agency engaged in international development work with poor people for six years. She and her husband moved from country to country setting up new agencies. In each country, they had to design how the work should be done, given the local labor market and work conditions.

After a year in Guatemala, Joanna, happily pregnant with her third child, had finished setting up the Donor Services Department for the agency and was working only part-time on a research project. A friend who ran a "competing" development agency approached her to do a consulting project for him. Sam Wilson, an American, was the national representative of a U.S.-based agency that had offices all over the world. Sam wanted Joanna to analyze his Donor Services Department, because he'd received complaints from headquarters about its efficiency. Since he'd been told that his office needed to double in size in the coming year, he wanted to get all the bugs worked out beforehand. Joanna agreed to spend a month gathering information and compiling a report on this department.

■ Joyce S. Osland, San Jose State University.

What Is a Donor Services Department in a Sponsorship Agency Anyway?

Sponsorship agencies, with multimillion-dollar budgets, are funded by individuals and groups in developed countries who contribute to development programs in less-developed countries (LDCs). Donors contribute approximately $20.00 per month plus optional special gifts. The agencies use this money to fund education, health, community development, and income-producing projects for poor people affiliated with their agency in various communities. In the eyes of most donors, the specific benefit provided by sponsorship agencies is the personal relationship between a donor and a child and his or her family in the LDC. The donors and children write back and forth, and the agency sends photos of the child and family to the donors. Some donors never write the family they sponsor; others write weekly and visit the family on their vacations. The efficiency of a Donor Services Department and the quality of their translations are key ingredients to keeping donors and attracting new ones. Good departments also never lose sight of the fact that sponsorship agencies serve a dual constituency—the local people they are trying to help develop and the sponsors who make that help possible through their donations.

The work of a Donor Services Department consists of more than translating letters, preparing annual progress reports on the families, and answering donor questions directed to the agency. It also handles the extensive, seemingly endless paperwork associated with enrolling new families and assigning them to donors, reassignments when either the donor or the family stops participating, and the special gifts of money sent (and thank you notes for them). Having accurate enrollment figures is crucial because the money the agency receives from headquarters is based upon these figures and affects planning.

The Cast of Characters in the Department

The Department Head

Joanna tackled the challenge of analyzing the department by speaking first with the department head (see the organizational chart in Figure 1). José Barriga, a charismatic, dynamic man in his forties, was head of both Donor Services and Community Services. In reality, he spent virtually no time in the Donor Services Department and was not bilingual. "My biggest pleasure is working with the community leaders and coming up with programs that will be successful. I much prefer being in the field, driving from village to village talking with people, to supervising paperwork. I'm not sure exactly what goes on in Donor Services, but Elena, the supervisor, is very responsible. I make it a point to walk through the department once a week and say hello to everyone, and I check their daily production figures."

Like José, Sam was also more interested in working with the communities on projects than in immersing himself in the details of the more administrative departments. In part, Sam had contracted Joanna because he rightfully worried that Donor Services did not receive the attention it deserved from José, who was very articulate and personable but seldom had time to look at anything beyond case histories. José never involved himself in the internal affairs of the department. Even though he was not considered much of a resource to them, he was well liked and respected by the staff of Donor Services, and they never complained about him.

The Supervisor

This was not the case with the supervisor José had promoted from within. Elena had the title of departmental supervisor, but she exercised very little authority. A slight, single woman in her thirties, Elena had worked for the organization since its establishment ten years earlier. She was organized, meticulous, dependable, and hard working. But she was a quiet, non-assertive, nervous woman who was anything but proactive. When asked what changes she would make if she were the head of the department, she sidestepped the question by responding, "It is difficult to have an opinion on this subject. I think that the boss can see the necessary changes with greater clarity."

Elena did not enjoy her role as supervisor, which was partly due to the opposition she encountered from a small clique of long-time translators. In the opinion of this subgroup, Elena had three strikes against her. One, unlike her subordinates, she was not bilingual. "How can she be the supervisor when she doesn't even know English well? One of us would make a better supervisor." Bilingual secretaries in status-conscious Guatemala see

**FIGURE 1
Organizational
Chart—Donor
Services Department**

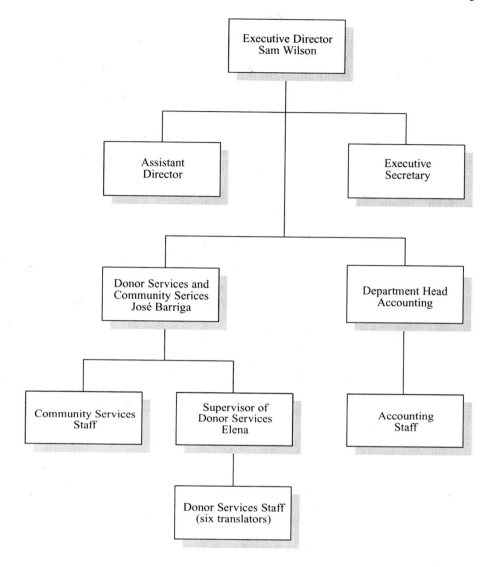

themselves as a cut above ordinary secretaries. This group looked down on Elena as being less skilled and educated than they were, even though she was an excellent employee. Second, Elena belonged to a different religion than the organization itself and almost all the other employees. This made no difference to Sam and José but seemed important to the clique who could be heard making occasional derogatory comments about Elena's religion.

The third strike against Elena was her lack of authority. No one had ever clarified how much authority she really possessed, and she herself made no effort to assume control of the department. "My instructions are to inform Don José Barriga of infractions in my daily production memo. I'm not supposed to confront people directly when infractions occur, although it might be easier to correct things if I did." ("Don" is a Latin American honorific used before the first name to denote respect.)

This subgroup showed their disdain and lack of respect for Elena by treating her with varying degrees of rudeness and ignoring her requests. They saw her as a watchdog, an attitude furthered by José who sometimes announced, "We (senior management) are not going to be here tomorrow, so be good because Elena will be watching you." When Sam and José left the office, the clique often stopped working to socialize. They'd watch Elena smolder out of the corner of their eyes, knowing she would not reprimand them. "I liked my job better before I became supervisor," said Elena. "Ever since, some of the girls have resented me, and I'm not comfortable trying to keep them in line. Why don't they just do their work without needing me to be the policeman? The only thing that keeps me from quitting is the loyalty I feel for the agency and Don José."

The Workers

In addition to the clique already mentioned, there were three other female translators in the department. All the translators but one had the same profile: in their twenties, of working-class backgrounds, and graduates of bilingual secretary schools, possessing average English skills. (As stated earlier, in Latin America, being a bilingual secretary is a fairly prestigious occupation for a woman.) The exception in this group was the best translator, Magdalena, a college-educated recent hire in her late thirties who came from an upper-class family. She worked, not because she needed the money, but because she believed in the mission of the agency. "This job lets me live out my religious beliefs and help people who have less advantages than I do." Magdalena was more professional and mature than the other translators. Although all the employees were proud of the agency and its religious mission, the clique members spent too much time socializing and skirmishing with other employees within and without the department.

The three translators who were not working at full capacity were very close friends. The leader of this group, Juana, was a spunky, bright woman with good oral English skills and a hearty sense of humor. A long-time friend of Barriga's, Juana translated for English-speaking visitors who came to visit the program sites throughout the country. The other translators, tied to their desks, saw this as a huge perk. Juana was the ringleader in the occasional mutinies against Elena and in feuds with people from other departments. Elena was reluctant to complain about Juana to Barriga, given their friendship. Perhaps she feared Juana would make her life even more miserable.

Juana's two buddies (*compañeras*) in the department also had many years with the agency. They'd gotten into the habit of helping each other on the infrequent occasions when they had excessive amounts of work. When they were idle or simply wanted to relieve the boredom of their jobs, they socialized and gossiped. Juana in particular was noted for lethal sarcasm and pointed jokes about people she didn't like. This clique was not very welcoming to the newer members of the department. Magdalena simply smiled at them but kept her distance, and the two younger translators kept a low profile to avoid incurring their disfavor. As one of them remarked, "It doesn't pay to get on Juana's bad side."

The Organization of the Department

Like many small offices in Latin America, the agency was located in a spacious former private home. The Donor Services Department was housed in the 40 × 30-foot living room area. The women's desks were set up in two rows, with Elena's desk in the back corner. Since the offices of both Wilson and Barriga were in former back bedrooms, everyone who visited them walked through the department, greeting and stopping to chat with the long-time employees (Elena, Juana, and her two friends). Elena's numerous visitors also spent a good deal of time working their way through the department to reach her desk, further contributing to the amount of socializing going on in the department.

Elena was the only department member who had "official" visitors since she was the liaison person who dealt with program representatives and kept track of enrollments. The translators each were assigned one work process. For example, Marisol prepared case histories on new children and their families for prospective donors while Juana processed gifts. One of the newer translators prepared files for newly enrolled children and did all the filing for the entire department (a daunting task). Most of the jobs were primarily clerical and required little or no English. The letter translations were outsourced to external translators on a piece-work basis and supervised by Magdalena. Hers was the only job that involved extensive translation; for the most part, however, she translated simple messages (such as greeting cards) that were far below her level of language proficiency. The trickier translations, such as queries from donors in other countries, were still handled by Wilson's executive secretary.

Several translators complained that, "We don't have enough opportunity to use our English skills on the job. Not only are we not getting any better in English, we are probably losing fluency because most of our jobs are just clerical work. We do the same simple, boring tasks over and over, day in and day out. Why did they hire bilingual secretaries for these jobs anyway?"

Another obvious problem was the uneven distribution of work in the office. The desks of Magdalena and the new translators were literally overflowing with several months' backlog of work while Juana and her two friends had time to kill. Nobody, including Elena, made any efforts to even out the work assignments or help out those who were buried. The subject had never been broached.

The agency was growing at a rapid pace, and there were piles of paperwork sitting around waiting to be processed. Joanna spent three weeks having each department member explain her job (in mind-numbing detail), drawing up flow charts of how each type of paperwork was handled, and poking around in their files. She found many unnecessary steps that resulted in slow turnaround times for various processes. There were daily output reports submitted to Barriga, but no statistics kept on the length of time it took to respond to requests for information or process paperwork. No data was shared with the translators, so they had no idea how the department was faring and little sense of urgency about their work. The only goal was to meet the monthly quota of case histories, which only affected Marisol. Trying to keep up with what came across their desks summed up the entire focus of the employees.

Joanna found many instances of errors and poor quality, not so much from carelessness as lack of training and supervision. Both Barriga and Wilson revised the case histories, but Joanna was amazed to discover that no one ever looked at any other work done by the department. Joanna found that the employees were very accommodating when asked to explain their jobs and very conscientious about their work (if not the hours devoted to it). She also found, however, the employees were seldom able to explain why things were done in a certain way, because they had received little training for their jobs and only understood their small part of the department. Morale was obviously low, and all the employees seemed frustrated with the situation in the department. With the exception of Magdalena who had experience in other offices, they had few ideas for Reed about how the department could be improved.

Module 9

Organizational Change and Transformation

Cases Outline

Edited by Paul F. Buller, Gonzaga University, and Randall S. Schuler, Rutgers University

BULLER | SCHULER

Managing Organizations and People

A Resource for Cases in Management, Organizational Behavior,
and Human Resource Management

Abstract

Harley-Davidson, not unlike a number of firms such as Steinway & Sons and Bose Corporation, seems to be occupying a prosperous niche by differentiating its products and services. More importantly, the firm has been able to successfully defend its niche. The case provides an opportunity to identify contingencies which support opportunities to earn above average profits in a niche market using a focused strategy.

Harley-Davidson company makes an attractive classroom learning vehicle for many issues including: (1) issues of international competition; (2) issues of ownership and control; (3) issues of technological innovation and path dependencies; (4) issues pertaining to integration across various functions of a business; (5) advantages of the value chain factors and quality of the company's management. Moreover, the transformation of the firm over the years raises a more general managerial and economic issue that is: *how may firms survive under what are often increasing demanding conditions of international business where competitors are resourceful and trade barriers are falling.*

Transformation at Harley-Davidson

There are very few products that are so exciting that people will tattoo your logo on their body.

—Richard Teerlink, Harley-Davidson CEO

Richard Teerlink, Harley-Davidson's CEO, was visiting the firm's factory at York, Pennsylvania, and was enjoying a private tour of the new additions to the Gott Motorcycle Museum. Seeing the firm's motorcycles from previous years reminded him of the history inherent in every Harley emblem. The firm's history was in his thoughts much more these days, as Harley-Davidson was about to celebrate its 92nd birthday. Over the last two decades, the firm had successfully shed its product and marketing doldrums, and was once again the market leader in the U.S. heavyweight motorcycle segment.

Teerlink was at the firm's York factory to review progress on the retooling of its production lines. Over time, the production processes at this factory had evolved to increase overall quality, efficiency, and worker involvement in manufacturing. Currently, Harley-Davidson had over 70 percent of the heavyweight motorcycle segment in the U.S. and had over a year of production backlogs. Despite a dramatic comeback from the brink of bankruptcy in the 1970s, Teerlink felt it was too early to rest on past laurels. He was concerned about the firm's growing production backlogs and renewed attempts by leading Japanese motorcycle manufacturers to gain market share in the heavyweight segment of the motorcycle industry. He was also faced with the need to examine Harley-Davidson's exports to Europe since Europe was emerging as the new battleground for heavyweight motorcycles.

Company Background

Harley-Davidson was founded in 1903 by Arthur and Walter Davidson and William Harley. Its first motorcycle was created on a part-time basis in a garage. Due to a stroke of luck, namely creating an engine that worked right the first time, the firm's motorcycles experienced phenomenal growth. In 1907, having sold 50 motorcycles the firm filed for incorporation with one full-time employee.

During these early years, the reputation of the firm was linked to Davidson's riding a Harley motorcycle to victory in a 1908 race and by the innovations pioneered by the firm. Innovations such as the V-twin engine, clutch, internal expanding rear brake, and three-speed transmission helped the growth of the firm.[1] By 1918 Harley-Davidson became the world's largest motorcycle company by producing 28,000 motorcycles (see Appendix A).

Despite a dedicated group of customers, the firm's fortunes were not insulated from economic pressures. The first downturn in the firm's fortunes occurred in the early 1920s when production dropped to 10,000. However, U.S. production rebounded to over 20,000 by the late 1920s only to plummet once again during the Depression years. Despite the decline, Harley-Davidson invested in R&D and experimented with its now famous V-twin design and a new four-cylinder engine. Minor improvements from these experiments increased the reliability of the machines throughout the 1930s. With the addition of the firm-developed electric starter, balloon tires, front brakes, and standardized parts, product quality also improved. Such improvements led consumers to choose Harley motorcycles, two-to-one, over the firm's arch rival, the Indian, the only other U.S. motorcycle manufacturer.

With the advent of the second World War and the military use of Harley motorcycles as dispatch and scout bikes, production soared to 29,000 units in 1943. In 1948, the firm opened a plant (Capitol Drive) in Wauwatosa, Wisconsin. It was a 269,000 square-foot facility that was purchased for $1.5 million in anticipation of postwar demand. However, in 1949 the firm's sales shrank to 23,740 units, considerably less than the firm's projected total of 43,250 units.

During the post-war period, Harley-Davidson experienced pressure from foreign imports, mostly from Europe. For the first time, American GIs stationed in the United Kingdom had developed a taste for British motorcycles such as the Norton and the Triumph. These motorcycles were smaller and more power efficient, and also handled better than U.S. built motorcycles. The firm's rival, the Indian, produced a British copycat in an attempt to lure customers away from Harley-Davidson. However, plagued by quality problems with this new entry, the Indian Motorcycle Company went bankrupt in 1953.[2]

By 1952, weak demand for motorcycles and Harley-Davidson's continued market share losses to European imports placed a heavy burden on the firm's financial resources. Part of the blame for this poor financial performance was internal; instead of reinvesting profits, the firm chose to award dividends to shareholders, which were often as high as 10 percent of earnings. The firm, however, managed to remain profitable by introducing larger, more powerful motorcycles. In the mid-1950s, motorcycle registrations in the U.S. amounted to 550,000 units for both new and used motorcycles. Harley-Davidson remained the undisputed leader of the market with over 60 percent market share and $20 million in sales.

The Harley-Davidson Mystique

From its original V-twin engine through its development of heavyweight bikes in the late 1940s and early 1950s, Harley-Davidson established an image of "raw power" which became its major selling point. Many aspects of the Harley motorcycle, such as the heavy use of chrome, its low-profile appearance, the styled tail fenders, and the chop of the front fork (i.e., the extension of the fork beyond plumb), highlighted the firm's unique image. The Harley motorcycle not only looked different, it sounded different. The growl of the Harley engine was, and still is, described as "a voice: a bassoprofundo thump that makes other motorcycles sound like sewing machines."[3]

Prior to the 1930s, Harley-Davidson's advertisements marketed the motorcycles as utilitarian vehicles. With the addition of new colors, decals, and stylized designs in the late 1930s the firm, however, adopted an "image and lifestyle" approach to marketing. Motorcycles were advertised in "biker" magazines and promoted mainly by word-of-mouth. Harley motorcycles were used by the U.S. military, highway patrol officers, the Hell's Angels, and Hollywood rebels including actors James Dean and Marlon Brando. Toward the end of the 1950s, this roster expanded to include young "Elvis-types" attracting dates with their Harley motorcycle. Given this customer base, the firm's advertisements often depicted leather-clad riders, military dispatch riders, or police officers on motorcycles. These advertisements cultivated an image of Harley motorcycles as "tough." Moreover, Harley-Davidson's motorcycles were often associated with people who were willing to break the "traditional" mold or willing to "live on the edge." In other words, the image reflected "rugged" individuality and "frontier" spirit. Over time, the Harley motorcycle became a part of American iconography and is now associated with the U.S. flag and the bald eagle, the national symbol of the United States. This association resulted in incredible brand loyalty, especially among U.S. customers that continues to this day. A "typical" Harley motorcycle owner cites the firm's American manufacture and "character" as its most attractive and distinguishable feature.

The Japanese Enter the U.S. Market

The post-second World War U.S. motorcycle market attracted the attention of Japanese manufacturers beginning with Honda. Upon entering the U.S. market in 1959, Honda "accidentally" uncovered a large untapped customer base of older males and younger women—a segment not well suited to the "tough" Harley motorcycles.

To target this group, Honda moved away from the traditions that Harley-Davidson had established to a more benign, family-oriented approach in advertising motorcycles. Their ad campaign "you meet the nicest people on a Honda" was communal, sweet, and family-oriented. Honda focused on smaller, faster, quieter, and less-expensive motorcycles. Its strategy was to enter one geographic region at a time with lightweight motorcycles (50 cc), then introduce more powerful 250 cc motorcycles, before targeting another geographical region. By 1965, Honda had made substantial inroads into the U.S. motorcycle industry; one out of every two motorcycles sold during that year in the U.S. was a Honda.

Other Japanese firms such as Yamaha, Suzuki, and Kawasaki soon followed. Similar to Honda's earlier entry, they marketed smaller, quieter, and more fuel-efficient motorcycles. Additionally, their motorcycles required little or no maintenance and were easier to handle compared to larger Harley bikes (Harley motorcycles weighed between 450 and 800 lbs). Such characteristics attracted younger riders, women, and older riders; riders who could not afford the more expensive Harley motorcycles; or bikers who did not want to tinker with the motorcycles, or those who could not muscle them around steep curves.

With the Japanese manufacturers' entry, the size and demographics of the U.S. motorcycle industry changed significantly. During the late 1960s and early 1970s, the demand for motorcycles grew rapidly. For example, 80 percent of motorcycle sales in the early 1960s were to first-time buyers. And between 1963 and 1973, motorcycle sales increased at an annual rate of 33 percent. Soon Japanese manufacturers accounted for more than 85 percent of U.S. motorcycle sales.[4]

Lead by Honda, the Japanese manufacturers were not only distinguished by their ability to create small engines but were skilled at mass-producing motorcycles efficiently. Japanese competitors offered quieter, better-handling motorcycles with more power at a lower price. They constantly improved and redesigned their products to counter potential market threats. Moreover, they were also able to reduce the time it took to introduce new models. Their ability to rely on internally generated funding, sourced primarily from *Keiretsu* banks, created a long-term profit orientation. Prices were set to increase market share without regard to short-term profits. Advertising expenditures were many multiples of competitor companies.[5] As evidenced by the rapid market share growth of Japanese manufacturers, consumers preferred the technical advances being offered by the Japanese motorcycle manufacturers.

Harley-Davidson executives did little to counter the advance of the Japanese competitors. Some Harley executives even believed that Japanese motorcycles would bring new riders to Harley-Davidson when they were ready to "step up" to larger and more powerful motorcycles. During this time, few if any technological improvements were made to Harley motorcycles. Unlike automobiles, motorcycle manufacturers did not have distinct model years.

The rapid expansion of the industry, combined with the practice of the Japanese manufacturers introducing multiple, high-quality models in quick succession, put Harley-Davidson at a distinct disadvantage. Despite increasing sales, the firm's overall market share declined and it was transformed into a "niche" player focusing on heavyweight motorcycles. Relative to the Japanese competition, the firm lacked resources to finance new product designs and expand production. In 1965, in an effort to raise capital, the firm went public after 60 years of private ownership. But unable to attract enough capital, the firm continued to face severe pressures from the Japanese manufacturers. Shortly after going public, Harley-Davidson was acquired in a friendly takeover by AMF, a heavy-industrial conglomerate looking to diversify into leisure products.

The AMF Years

Upon acquiring Harley-Davidson, AMF's CEO, Rodney Gott, noted: "There was a motorcycle craze. You could sell anything you could produce. We wanted to meet [this] demand."[6] To increase Harley-Davidson's production capacity, he committed AMF's capital expenditures to the firm's manufacturing plants.[7]

Production and Quality Problems

The influx of new capital, management, and marketing skills allowed Harley-Davidson to expand production from 15,475 units in 1969 to 70,000 units in 1973. Less-skilled workers were added to the production lines. In AMF's zeal to increase production, many quality issues were overlooked. Product quality decreased to an all-time low. The four-fold increase in production resulted in motorcycles that leaked oil on the showroom floor. Richard Teerlink, the firm's CFO commented on this process of decline:

In the early '80s, Harley's reputation for reliability and quality had fallen as steeply as its market share, which had dropped from 100% of the domestic market to a low of 23%. Brand-new Harleys sitting on the dealership floor had to have cardboard put down beneath them to sop up the leaking oil.

The Harley product that AMF had acquired was essentially a hand-crafted machine. Production drawings used to build motorcycles were not exact. Tolerances for the various components and processes were not well specified. However, a skilled workforce under the direction of family management was able to produce a small volume of quality products using craft methods of production. This mode of operating was less dependent on exact specifications than would be required employing a mass-production approach. Rather than reevaluate their approach to manufacturing and product quality, AMF managers added new features in an effort to attract customers from new market segments. According to a Harley executive:

The bottom line was that quality went to hell because AMF expanded Harley production at the same time that Harleys were getting out of date and the Japanese were coming into town with new designs and reliable products at a low price.

To challenge Japanese manufacturers in the smaller and faster-growing market segment, AMF entered into a joint venture with Ameracchi, an Italian company with production facilities in Italy. Ameracchi produced smaller, lower-priced Harley motorcycles that were sold in the U.S. Although these motorcycles expanded the firm's ridership, they did little to stop the Japanese. To earn larger margins, Harley dealers steered consumers to the larger, higher-margin motorcycles, thus further hindering the firm's effort to penetrate the small motorcycle segment. In assessing the AMF years, especially their expansionist strategy, William Davidson, the last "family" president of Harley-Davidson, noted:

They [AMF management] thought Harley-Davidson could become another Honda. That's ridiculous . . . Honda produced 3,518,000 units in 1982. No one can imagine Harley-Davidson ever producing one-tenth that many machines. We were never meant to be a high-production company.[8]

With little interest in the smaller Harley bikes, the firm terminated its Italian joint-venture in 1978.

On the marketing side, AMF hired Benton & Bowles to create advertising for all of AMF's leisure products including Harley motorcycles. Benton & Bowles were interested in expanding Harley-Davidson's share of the non-traditional market dominated by the Japanese. To help change its image, AMF's top management forced Harley-Davidson managers to remove their advertisements from certain previously successful, but less "high-tone" advertising outlets such as the Easy Rider. This change in advertising tactics and the lack of understanding of the Harley mystique it reflected, lead to an alienation of Harley's traditional customers—riders who were most likely to work on their own motorcycles, a necessity during this time as Harley's quality declined.

As the U.S.-motorcycle industry continued to grow, Harley-Davidson's overall share began to shrink rather rapidly. The Japanese manufacturers tightened their stranglehold on the segments not contested by Harley-Davidson.

The Japanese Target Harley-Davidson

In 1975, in an effort to target Harley-Davidson's market segment, Honda introduced the Goldwing, a 1000 cc motorcycle. Industry reports during that time described this motorcycle as the "most technologically sophisticated and complex heavyweight motorcycle available in the market." Soon Kawasaki followed suit with the introduction of its own heavyweight motorcycle. To Harley-Davidson's horror, its share of the "heavyweight" segment began to decline. Harley-Davidson was now faced with a situation where it was ceding ridership to the Japanese in the "traditional" biker segments, and not attracting customers in "non-traditional" segments.[9]

Honda, the largest of the Japanese producers, was the value-added leader during the mid-1970s. In the late 1970s, Yamaha made a conscious decision to displace Honda as the world's leading motorcycle firm by increasing production and introducing new models at lower prices. This move triggered a vicious price war between Honda and Yamaha that lasted for three years. With increased inventories and heightened competition resulting from this war, steep price reductions were undertaken by both Honda and Yamaha. The falling prices coincided with an economic downturn and declining overall market in the U.S. This combination of factors severely hurt Yamaha, forcing them to cede leadership to Honda. Unable to remain profitable at these deflated prices, Harley-Davidson was crippled.

By the late 1970s, the motorcycle boom was a faded memory with all manufacturers competing for market share in a stagnant market (see Exhibit 1). Japanese manufacturers continued to pressure Harley-Davidson by introducing newer and larger motorcycles. Between 1970 and 1980, Harley-Davidson's share declined by over 80 percent.

The Dramatic Turnaround

Toward the end of Gott's tenure as CEO of AMF, he hired Vaughn Beals to guide Harley-Davidson. As soon as Beals took over, he designed a 10-year product strategy with the help of long-time Harley managers. The plan included the development of a new family of performance engines, code named NOVA, which was supported by R&D funding from AMF. With Gott's departure, however, AMF's commitment to turning around Harley-Davidson waned. With its long-term profitability in question, tensions erupted between Harley-Davidson's managers and AMF's top management over operating costs and R&D funding of the NOVA project. By 1980, with Harley's profitability down, AMF began looking for a buyer.

The Buy Back

With continued losses facing Harley, Beals orchestrated a highly leveraged buyout with the help of a small group of Harley-Davidson managers. Able to raise only a small

EXHIBIT 1
U.S. Market
Shares of Leading
Motorcycle
Manufacturers

	Harley-Davidson	Honda	Suzuki	Kawasaki	Yamaha	Other
1980	30.8%	25.6%	12.0%	16.3%	13.3%	2.0%
1981	29.6%	33.9%	9.9%	15.1%	9.6%	1.9%
1982	28.8%	35.9%	10.5%	12.5%	10.1%	2.2%
1983	23.0%	44.3%	8.1%	9.4%	13.1%	2.1%
1984	26.9%	38.1%	7.1%	11.7%	13.8%	2.4%
1985	27.8%	38.8%	5.6%	10.7%	13.8%	3.3%
1986	33.3%	31.1%	6.9%	12.7%	12.6%	3.4%
1987	40.0%	29.4%	10.5%	11.2%	7.1%	1.8%
1988	46.5%	24.1%	6.6%	11.5%	8.9%	2.4%
1989	59.1%	14.9%	6.9%	7.6%	9.1%	2.4%

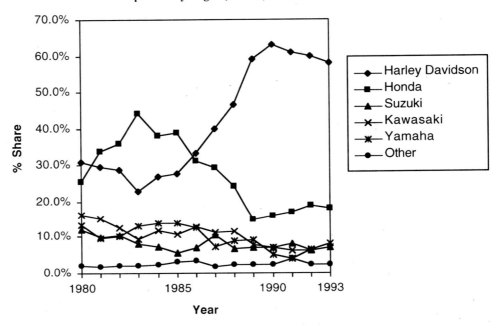

Super Heavyweight (850cc+) Market Shares Data

fraction of the $81.5 million buyback price, Harley-Davidson's top management took the rest on as debt.[10] This large debt not only severely constrained the strategic and long-term options available, but forced Harley's new owners to pare down costs and cut back motorcycle production. Because lenders financed only 13 cents out of every sales dollar, top management managed for cash flows rather than income.[11] Beals and his top management team reduced costs, trimmed the workforce, and renegotiated longer payouts with component suppliers. According to Teerlink, the firm's CFO at that time, the firm created a vision that was simple: survival.[12]

Learning from the Japanese

Once Harley-Davidson went private, Beals began to benchmark the firm against Japanese competitors. A group of senior managers visited Honda's plant in the U.S. After touring Honda's Marysville plant in Ohio, Tom Gelb, the Senior-VP for Operations recalled:

The [Honda] assembly line was neat and uncluttered—unlike our operation, where the line was always littered with parts and material. There was minimum paperwork and things flowed very smoothly.

In the Honda plant, inventory was controlled through a Just-in-Time (JIT) system that used no computers or automation. Moreover, motorcycles were built to order rather than for inventory. This shocked Harley-Davidson executives, whose multimillion-dollar inventory system at their York assembly plant required far greater amounts of buffer inventory for both work-in-process (WIP) and finished motorcycles. John Bleustein, the Senior-VP for Parts and Accessories acknowledged that:

[The Japanese] . . . were just better managers . . . and they understood how to do manufacturing a hell of a lot better, with less inventory and much higher quality.[13]

Beals concurred with his colleagues:

Harley-Davidson's production system was basically flawed. In this system, we gave the worker responsibility for quantity, not quality. Then we set up a whole police force for quality and a battalion of accountants to measure errors made in production.[14]

The differences between Harley-Davidson and Honda were striking. For example, only 5 percent of Honda's motorcycles failed to pass final quality inspection; over 50 percent of Harley's failed during the same test. According to Harley-Davidson's internal estimates, overall Japanese productivity was over 30 percent greater than Harley-Davidson. According to a report by the *Boston Consulting Group*, Honda's value added per employee was even better, on the order of two to three times that of its Japanese competitors, Suzuki and Yamaha.[15]

The Productivity Triad

Reflecting on the Honda visit, Beals and his management team recognized that the only way to compete was by improving the quality and production of Harley-Davidson's existing and new products. They realized that manufacturing motorcycles to sub-par quality standards, and then inspecting and reworking them, was an inefficient and costly way of operating. Because their end product was incapable of standing up to the Japanese entry in the heavyweight segment, Harley's entire manufacturing system needed to be modified, and fast.

Using Japanese production methods as a blueprint, top management teams formulated and implemented what they termed the *productivity triad*. This new approach involved (a) employee involvement, (b) use of JIT inventory practices, and (c) statistical operator control (SOC).

First, Harley-Davidson's senior executives reasoned that full participation (and ultimately support) of employees at all levels was the key to successful improvement of both the product quality and the production process. Line workers were encouraged to contribute to the decision-making process because they knew better than management what worked and what did not. All manufacturing workers were required to participate in the newly formed quality circles that were made directly responsible for improving motorcycle quality.

Second, a Materials-as-Needed (MAN) program was introduced. This was Harley-Davidson's version of Honda's JIT inventory control practices. It was implemented to free up much-needed cash by reducing work-in-process inventory. More importantly, it was hoped that lower inventory levels would make quality problems more apparent and force employees to take action.

Third, based on their observations at Honda, top management reasoned that training and empowering employees to measure quality and recommend change was essential for improvement. Under SOC, employees were now taught to see how quality problems developed and how they could be traced and corrected during the production process. Harley's top management hoped that process improvements utilizing tools that track conformance to specifications, coupled with employee incentive programs, would result in greatly improved product quality.

Finally, in 1983, in an attempt to gain time and protect itself from the Japanese inroads in the heavyweight segment, Harley-Davidson sought tariff protection from the U.S.

government. They requested, and were granted, a 5-year, self-liquidating tariff by President Reagan.

The production changes carried out under the *productivity triad* program and the renewed R&D expenditures instituted after the leverage buyout soon impacted the competitive capability of Harley-Davidson. For example, prior to the introduction of MAN, Harley-Davidson turned their inventory twice a year. Under the new system, inventory turn increased to 17. More importantly, lower inventory levels made quality problems more apparent and forced employees to take action.

Additionally, the success of the turnaround efforts showed in other improved statistics: productivity improvement went up by over 50 percent; work-in-process inventory was reduced by 75 percent; scrap and rework, a measure of quality improvement, was down by 68 percent; the firm's U.S. revenues increased by over 80 percent; international revenues by 1.7 times; operating profits increased by $59 million; and market share in the heavyweight segment, that was dropping precipitously earlier, now increased by 97 percent (see Exhibit 2). In light of this dramatic progress, the firm petitioned the U.S. government to lift the import tariff protection in 1987, one year ahead of schedule.

In 1989, the firm went public through a well received IPO. Richard Teerlink, the firm's CFO for six years, was promoted to CEO. Management and motorcycle enthusiasts attended the listing of Harley-Davidson on the exchange with great ceremony, replete with a motorcycle parade down Wall Street. Teerlink was now responsible for completing Harley's dramatic turnaround and for revitalizing the legendary Harley Mystique.

Harley-Davidson in the 1990s

The U.S. heavyweight segment of the motorcycle industry is extremely competitive but remains the most profitable segment of the motorcycle market. In 1994, this segment represented approximately 35 percent of the total U.S. motorcycle market (in terms of new units registered). Harley-Davidson, Honda, Suzuki, Kawasaki, and Yamaha are the major players. Competition is based upon price, quality, reliability, styling, product features, and warranties. The Japanese manufacturers have superior financial and marketing resources and are also more diversified with sales volumes greater than Harley-Davidson (see Exhibit 2 for Harley's financial performance).

Building a Learning Organization

In 1993, Harley-Davidson was attempting to transform itself from a very informal to a formal organization. Also, the firm began emphasizing organizational and individual learning at all levels through a program it termed the *Leadership Institute* (see Exhibit 3). Many changes were underway as noted by Teerlink:

The senior staff consists of me, my secretary, the CFO and our vice president of continuous improvement. The company eliminated the positions of senior vice president in marketing and in operations. We eliminated those jobs because they didn't add value our products. The people were auditors. They were checkers. Now we have teams—a create-demand team, a team that is in charge of producing our products, and a product-support team. Before Harley established these teams, people would go up to one boss and that boss would go over to another boss and he would go to still another boss. And we wondered why the Japanese beat us on the issue of time.[16]

To complement the structural changes, new rewards and incentive systems were introduced. Exhibit 4, Harley-Davidson's mission statement sets forth the firm's overall goals and direction. As explained by Teerlink:

We are changing our pay system to pay for performance. We needed our people to understand empowerment. An employee must make the decision that he or she wants more training—no one will tap you on the shoulder—but once you are there, we will help you. The executive committee was the first group to go through the [Leadership] Institute. We didn't want anyone to get the attitude that the executive committee doesn't have anything to learn. I'm a big believer in learning.[17]

	1994	1993	1992	1991	1990
	(In thousands, except per share amounts)				
Income statement data:					
Net sales	$1,541,796	$1,217,428	$1,105,284	$939,863	$864,600
Cost of goods sold	1,120,332	880,269	808,871	706,140	635,551
Gross profit	421,464	337,159	296,413	233,723	229,049
Selling, administrative, and engineering	261,157	267,353*	199,216	165,078	145,674
Income from operations	160,307	69,806	97,197	68,645	83,375
Interest income (expense), net	44	(831)	(4,912)	(7,312)	(9,701)
Other income (expense), net	1,718	(2,460)	(3,476)	(3,239)	(11,057)
Income before provision for income taxes, extraordinary items, and accounting changes	162,069	66,515	88,809	58,094	62,617
Provision for income taxes	57,797	48,072	34,636	21,122	24,309
Income before extraordinary items and accounting changes	104,272	18,443	54,173	36,972	38,308
Extraordinary items, net of tax	—	—	(388)	—	(478)
Income before accounting changes	104,272	18,443	53,785	36,972	37,830
Cumulative effect of accounting changes, net of tax**	—	(30,328)	—	—	—
Net income (loss)	$ 104,272	$ (11,885)	$ 53,785	$ 36,972	$ 37,830
Weighted average common shares assuming no dilution	76,198	75,900	71,778	71,160	71,152
Per common share:					
Income before extraordinary items and accounting changes	$ 1.37	$ .24	$ .76	$ .52	$ .54
Extraordinary items, net of tax	—	—	(.01)	—	(.01)
Accounting changes, net of tax	—	(.40)	—	—	—
Net income (loss)	$ 1.37	$ (.16)	$ .75	$ .52	$ .53
Dividends paid	$ .14	$ .14	$ .06	$ —	$ —
Balance sheet data:					
Working capital	$ 189,358	$ 142,996	$ 96,232	$ 64,212	$ 50,152
Total assets	739,215	583,285	522,164	474,233	407,467
Short-term debt, including current maturities of long-term debt	18,303	21,369	16,965	41,089	23,859
Long term debt, less current maturities	9,410	3,429	2,360	46,906	48,339
Total debt	27,713	24,798	19,325	87,995	72,198
Shareholders' equity	433,232	324,912	335,380	238,000	198,775

*Includes a $57 million charge related primarily to the write-off of goodwill at the Transportation Vehicles segment (Holiday Rambler).
**During 1993, the Company adopted accounting standards related to postretirement health care benefits and income taxes.

**EXHIBIT 2
Harley-Davidson
Selected Financial
Data**

The Leadership Institute was designed to introduce new workers to Harley-Davidson goals and culture while providing current workers with a better understanding of the corporate structure and the effects of external factors upon corporate performance. The firm also prepared nontechnical explanations of how cash flows and flexible production affect financial success. Line workers were exposed to the interrelation between products, sales, and profitability. Substantial changes in worker job descriptions, responsibilities, and production processes were undertaken in an effort to increase job-enrichment and worker-empowerment. These efforts were implemented through worker cross-training, expansion of job responsibility, and expansion of worker understanding of the overall production processes. In 1994, a new labor agreement was reached that allowed a general wage increase of 3 percent per year as well as an incremental annual payment and work rule change critical to the creation of a "learning" orientation. Recently, Peter Senge, an expert

EXHIBIT 3
Harley-Davidson:
Building a Learning
Organization

Three Job Areas for Learning

- THE WORK ITSELF: developing, producing, and selling products and services
  — Master all the skills necessary to do a quality job every time
  — Learn more of the theory behind and latest technology of your job
  — Branch out and learn related fields

- THE SUPPORTING SYSTEMS: all the systems and processes helping to complete the work
  — Improve the information you need
  — Improve equipment, tools, and supplies
  — Improve goal-setting and measurement (feedback)
  — Improve product/service flow and consistency

- HOW WE WORK: the collective way people think, act, and interact
  — Learn how your "product" is used; improve customer relations
  — Improve team problem-solving
  — Take responsibility and ownership
  — Always look (and be open) for ways to improve
  — Experiment with your and others' ideas
  — Improve supplier problem-solving

Learning Organizations

- . . . organizations that continually expand their ability to shape their future
- Break with tradition: the top thinks and everyone else acts . . . must merge thinking and acting in all jobs
- Learning is moving from thought to action

on learning in organizations, has been retained by top management to help improve Harley's performance as a "learning organization."

Marketing

As Exhibit 5 indicates, Harley-Davidson has led the U.S. motorcycle industry sales of heavyweight motorcycles. According to Harley's top management:

The management buyback of Harley-Davidson and the ensuing changes allowed Harley to regain its leadership position. There is a return to more customer focused advertisement and traditional advertising venues including the biker magazines shunned during the AMF years. More latitude was given to dealers in promoting the product, with greater focus on local and regional advertising. While previous quality problems prevented Harley-David-son from being seriously considered by first-time buyers, the firm's emphasis on quality has allowed the new advertising initiatives to work; today people are not only willing to consider Harley motorcycles, they are willing to wait for delivery.

Many industry observers believed that delivery delays served to enhance the Harley-Davidson image by making it public knowledge that demand vastly exceeded supply.

Harley-Davidson's marketing efforts are divided among dealer promotions, customer events, magazine and direct-mail advertising, public relations, and cooperative programs with Harley-Davidson dealers. The firm's expenditures on domestic marketing and advertising were approximately $65.6 million, $53.8 million, and $45.2 million during 1994, 1993, and 1992, respectively. Domestic motorcycle sales generated 50.3 percent, 51.4 per-

EXHIBIT 4
Harley-Davidson's
Mission Statement
and Operations
Philosophy

Harley's Mission Statement

Harley-Davidson's Worldwide mission is to:

- Preserve and perpetuate the Harley-Davidson institution through continuous improvement in the quality of our products and services and achievement of our financial goals.
- Provide motorcycles, accessories, and services to motorcyclists in selected niches.
- Provide the general public brand identified, products/services to enhance Harley-Davidson's image and attract new customers.
- Engage in manufacturing or service ventures that can add value (not only profit) to the motorcycle business.

Harley's Operations Philosophy

The company philosophy that will guide us to achieving success is to:

- Live by the corporate vision, values and issues.
- Perpetuate the heritage, tradition, and mystique of Harley-Davidson and seek to enhance it with new motorcycle products and services.
- Value our trademarks, patents, and copyright; vigorously defend them, and actively license our trademarks.
- Maintain an outward versus inward focus on products, service, and benchmarks of performance.
- Provide high customer satisfaction by supplying products and services that meet purchaser's expectations and offer value commensurate with the purchasing price.
- Rely primarily on a network of distributors and dealers for customer sales and services.
- Maintain a "close to the customer" philosophy with distributors, dealers, and current and potential customers.

Source: The Harley-Davidson Company.

cent, and 52.8 percent of revenues in the motorcycles segment during 1994, 1993, and 1992, respectively.

The balance of the revenues generated were a result of international sales (29 percent), accessories (16–18 percent), and licensing (1–2 percent). Domestic motorcycle parts and accessories sales comprised 17.8 percent, 17.4 percent, and 15.3 percent of net sales in the motorcycles segment in 1994, 1993, and 1992, respectively. Net sales from domestic motorcycle parts and accessories have grown 97.3 percent since 1991. Royalty revenues from licensing accounted for approximately 2 percent of the net sales from the motorcycles segment during 1994 (1 percent during 1993 and 1992). Although royalty revenues from licensing activities were small, the profitability of this business was high.

Harley motorcycles emphasized traditional styling, design simplicity, durability, ease of service, and evolutionary change. The firm's marketing approach emphasized four heavyweight segments: *standard*, which emphasized simplicity and cost; *performance*, which emphasized handling and speed; *touring*, which emphasized comfort and amenities

EXHIBIT 5
Shares of U.S.
Heavyweight
Motorcycle Market
(above 750cc Engine
Displacement)

	1994	1993	1992	1991	1990
New U.S. Registrations (1000s units):					
Total new registrations	116.2	101.4	86.4	74.3	78.5
Harley-Davidson new registrations	65.2	59.3	52.2	45.1	46.9
Percentage Market Share:					
Harley-Davidson	58.1%	58.4%	60.4%	60.7%	59.7%
Honda	19.1	17.7	16.4	17.3	18.7
Suzuki	8.7	9.4	9.4	7.6	5.7
Kawasaki	7.1	6.2	5.6	6.4	6.5
Yamaha	3.9	4.4	4.1	4.7	6.9
Other	5.1	3.9	4.1	3.3	2.5
Total	100.0	100.0	100.0	100.0	100.0

Source: Harley-Davidson, *Annual Report* 1994.

for long-distance travel; and *custom*, which emphasized styling and individual owner customization. The last two product segments—touring and custom—were the primary classes of heavyweight motorcycles offered by Harley-Davidson. The custom product line represented the firm's highest unit volumes and commanded a premium price because of its features, styling, and high resale value. In 1994, the firm manufactured and sold 20 models of touring and custom heavyweight motorcycles with suggested retail prices ranging from approximately $5,000 to $17,500. Together these two segments accounted for 76 percent, 75 percent, and 73 percent of total heavyweight retail unit sales in the U.S. during 1994, 1993, and 1992, respectively (see Exhibit 6).

While some accessory differences between Harley's top-of-the-line touring motorcycles and its competitors' exist, the suggested retail prices are comparable. The top of the firm's custom product line was typically priced at almost twice that of its competitors' custom motorcycles (see Exhibit 7). More importantly, according to the firm's surveys of retail purchasers:

[H]istorically, over three-quarters of the purchasers of its Sportster model [smallest displacement custom motorcycle] have come from competitive-brand motorcycles or people new to the sport of motorcycling. Since 1988, the Company's research has consistently shown a repurchase intent in excess of 92% on the part of purchasers of its motorcycles, and the Company expects to see sales of its 883 cc Sportster model partially translated into sales of its higher priced products in the normal two- to three-year ownership cycle.

**EXHIBIT 6
Harley-Davidson:
Segment Sales in
the U.S.–1992**

Segment	Market size (units)	HD Share (units)	HD share %
Custom	60,000	46,100	77%
Touring	17,000	6,084	36%
Standard	6,793	—	—
Performance	20,340	—	—

Source: Morgan Stanley & Co. Inc, Nov. 15, 1993.

**EXHIBIT 7
Harley-Davidson
Motorcycles—
Suggested Retail
Prices**

Model Type	Model Name	Suggested Price Ranges*
Custom Models		
FLHTCI	Ultra Classic Electra Glide—Fuel Inj.	$17,500
FLHTCU	Ultra Classic Electra Glide	$16,500 – 16,050
FLTCU	Electra Guide Classic	$14,300 – 13,850
FLSTC	Heritage Softail Classic	$14,100 – 13,875
Performance Models		
FLHT	Electra Glide Standard	$11,995
FLHR	Road King	$13,700 – 13,475
FLSTN	Heritage Softail Special	$13,650
FLSTF	Fat Boy	$13,650 – 13,425
Touring Models		
FXSTSB	Bad Boy	$13,850 – 13,700
FXDWG	Dyna Wide Glide	$13,650 – 13,500
FXSTS	Springe Softail	$13,600 – 13,375
FXSTC	Softail Custom	$13,350 – 13,125
FXDS-CONV	Dyna Convertible	$12,950 – 12,800
FXDL	Dyna Low Rider	$12,700 – 12,800
FXD	Dyna Super Glide	$11,995
Sportster Models		
XLH1200	Sportster 1200	$7,395 – 7,200
XLH883	Sportster 883 Deluxe	$6,195 – 6,120
XLH883	Sportster 883 Hugger	$5,775 – 5,700
XLH883	Sportster	$5,070 – 4,995

*Prices vary depending upon color and extras.

Source: *Motorcycle Milestones* by Cycle Trade, 1995.

Harley-Davidson distributed its motorcycles and related products in the U.S. through approximately 600 independently owned, full-service dealerships to whom the firm sold direct. With respect to sales of new motorcycles, approximately 75 percent of the dealerships sell Harley-Davidson motorcycles exclusively.[18] Harley-Davidson provided a variety of services to its dealers and retail customers including service training schools, delivery of its motorcycles, motorcycling vacations, memberships in an owners club, and customized software packages for dealers. The firm encouraged its motorcycle dealers to purchase and maintain adequate inventories of parts and accessories during the winter months in anticipation of the Christmas and spring selling season by offering its dealers special discounts and delayed billing terms.

When asked to differentiate Harley motorcycles from Japanese motorcycles, Teerlink responded:

Our sale is based on the hardware, but it's much more than that. Harley-Davidson doesn't sell transportation, we sell transformation. We sell excitement, a way of life. We had to give people a way to transform themselves. But a motorcycle—inherently an irrational device—need not be flawless. Indeed, one of the reasons people buy bikes is to get away from the increasingly over-sanitized way of life, to take some risks, to hone skills in a world that more and more doesn't want us to do such things.

Further, the firm differentiated itself from its Japanese manufacturers by offering support to various enthusiast and social groups. The Harley-Davidson Owners Group (HOG), formed in 1983 to encourage Harley-Davidson owners to become more actively involved in the sport of motorcycling, had approximately 270,000 members worldwide. It was the industry's largest company-sponsored motorcycle enthusiast organization. Interest among women riders is cultivated through "The Ladies of Harley," a group that aims to increase ridership and interest among young women motorcyclists. According to Harley-Davidson's internal marketing surveys:

The typical U.S. Harley-Davidson motorcycle owner is a male in his early forties, with a household income of approximately $65,200, who purchases a motorcycle for recreational purposes rather than to provide transportation, and who is an experienced motorcycle rider. Over two-thirds of the Company's sales are to buyers with at least one year of higher education beyond high school.

The firm encouraged motorcycle and accessory sales as well as customer allegiance by issuing the Harley-Davidson credit card to customers. Over 60,000 members use this form of credit for the purchase of a motorcycle, service, and accessories. Harley-Davidson accessories tend to be substantially more expensive than third-party vended accessories. In recent years, Harley-Davidson has licensed the production and sale of a broad range of consumer items, including T-shirts and other clothing, jewelry, small-leather goods, and numerous other products. It is expanding its licensing activity in the toy category. Although the majority of licensing activity occurred in the U.S., the firm has expanded this activity into international markets.

In 1993, the company acquired a 49 percent interest in the Buell Motorcycle Company, a manufacturer of performance motorcycles. This investment in Buell offers the possibility of gradually gaining entry into select niches within the performance motorcycle market. The firm was considering the distribution of a limited number of Buell motorcycles to select Harley-Davidson dealers. New products to be included are a line of racing bikes prototyped on the Buell Thunderbolt series, the VR-1000. The VR-1000 motorcycles have successfully competed on the international racing circuit over the previous 18 months.[19] Several top executives viewed Harley-Davidson's reentry into this performance segment as a return to its heritage of product innovation and development through lessons learned on the racetrack.

Manufacturing

In 1994, approximately 4,300 employees were employed in Harley-Davidson's motorcycle division. Production workers at the motorcycle manufacturing facilities in Wauwatosa and

Tomahawk, Wisconsin, are represented principally by the United Paperworkers International Union (UPIU) of the AFL-CIO, as well as the International Association of Machinist and Aerospace Workers (IAM). Workers in York, Pennsylvania, were represented principally by the IAM.

During 1993, the company unveiled a manufacturing strategy designed to achieve a goal of a 100,000 units per year production rate in 1996 (see Exhibit 8). According to Harley-Davidson:

The strategy calls for the enhancement of the motorcycles segment's ability to increase capacity, adjust to changes in the market place, and further improve quality while reducing costs. The strategy calls for the achievement of the increased capacity within the existing facilities (with minor additions) without a significant change in personnel. The Company began implementing the strategy in 1993 and estimates that it will reach the production goal of 100,000 units in 1995, more than one year ahead of schedule. In addition, the Company plans to increase annual production capacity to 115,000 units by 1997.

Under the plan, the Capital Drive plant in Wisconsin, was to be the proving ground for cellular manufacturing concepts. The factory was to be divided into three manufacturing groups: 1340 cc powertrain group, 883 cc and 1200 cc powertrains, and the transmission group. Within each of these groups, work-cells were to be structured around components in an effort to minimize work-in-process inventories and increase employee empowerment. Line workers, rather than managers, could order parts and tooling, decide scheduling, and inspect for quality. Because these cells supply the final assembly line as well as dealers, they were to be operated three shifts a day for five days a week.

At the final assembly plant at York, Pennsylvania, a traditional assembly-line approach was employed to manufacture Harley motorcycles. The line employed 81 workers which corresponded to one worker per station. The average daily production of this line was 200 motorcycles. Two new lines were being contemplated—one for the *Sportster* models and the other for *Touring* models.

The *Sportster* models were to be assembled on an innovative "hybrid" line that attempted to combine assembly-line and cellular manufacturing practices. The proposed line consisted of 15 stations on which three-person-worker teams would follow a motorcycle through all 15 stations. Thus, each three-member team was responsible for assembling the entire motorcycle. This line was to employ 45 people and was expected to produce 75 motorcycles a day. A second "hybrid" assembly line, similar to the *Sportster* line, was also being contemplated for *Touring* models. This line was to employ 25 stations and would have a rated production capacity of 110 motorcycles per day.

The move to two additional assembly lines—*Sportster* line and *Touring* line—were to be phased in over time. These changes were to be accomplished during normal operations and while meeting production targets. The firm had allocated over $200 million for capacity expansion and process improvement in manufacturing facilities.

EXHIBIT 8
Harley-Davidson:
Production
Capacity Data

	1987	1988	1989	1990	1991	1992	1993
Motorcycle shipments (units)	45,365	52,623	58,938	62,458	68,626	76,495	81,696
Motorcycle revenue/unit	$5,648	$6,269	$6,959	$7,769	$7,988	$8,661	$8,926
Production days	245	245	245	245	245	245	245
Shipments/day	185	215	241	255	280	312	333
Unit growth	15.0%	16.0%	12.0%	18.0%	3.6%	11.5%	6.8%

Source: Dean Witter Reynolds Company Report, July 21, 1994 and Morgan Stanley & Co. Inc., Company Report, Nov. 15, 1993.

Harley-Davidson has endeavored to establish long-term informal "partnership" relationships with its suppliers. It directly assists suppliers in the implementation of the manufacturing techniques employed by Harley-Davidson through training sessions and plant evaluations. To promote the "partnership" philosophy, the firm reduced the number of its manufacturing suppliers in recent years. Additionally, it conducts more business with suppliers that have implemented the same manufacturing techniques as its manufacturing operations. The firm purchased all of its raw materials, principally steel and aluminum castings, forging, sheet, and bars, and certain motorcycle components, including carburetors, batteries, tires, seats, electrical components, and instruments. Although certain components were secured from a limited number of suppliers, top management anticipated no significant difficulties in obtaining raw materials or components.

In general, Harley-Davidson does not experience seasonal fluctuations in production. This is primarily because of the strong demand for Harley-Davidson motorcycles and related products as well as the availability of floor-plan financing arrangements for its independent dealers. The financing provided allows dealers to build inventory levels in anticipation of the spring and summer selling seasons.

Questions Facing Top Management

Expand Production Capacity

In 1994, its share of the heavyweight market was 56.1 percent, down slightly from 58.4 percent in the previous year. This was primarily a result of constrained production capacity in a growing market. Domestic heavyweight registrations increased 15 percent and 17 percent during 1994 and 1993. Although Harley-Davidson managers did not expect the market to grow at these rates in the future, they felt that in order to maintain the firm's current level of U.S. sales increased production capacity was necessary. In 1994, Harley-Davidson had a backlog of motorcycle orders nearly a year long.

While the reduced employee turnover (1–2 percent) in recent years suggested a faith in new management, internal surveys showed that Harley-Davidson employees were wary of volume increases. Employees feared that volume will be increased at the expense of quality and hurt the Harley-Davidson name.

Overseas Production Capability

Questions involving production capacity also included whether Harley-Davidson should "export" production abroad. The concept of overseas manufacturing facilities was hotly debated by Harley-Davidson management. Some considered foreign production as inconsistent with "buying a piece of the American Dream." But others argued that foreign production was inevitable with growing overseas demand. Still others argued for an increase of domestic production for export.

Harley-Davidson's international sales were $263 million and $240 million, accounting for approximately 28 percent and 29 percent of net sales of the motorcycles segment, during 1993 and 1992, respectively (see Exhibit 9). According to Harley-Davidson executives:

[T]he international heavyweight market is growing and is significantly larger than the U.S. heavyweight market . . . [and Harley-Davidson] holds an average market share of approximately 15% in the heavyweight export markets in which it competes.

The firm had wholly owned subsidiaries in Germany, Japan, and the United Kingdom. The German subsidiary serves Austria, France, Denmark, Czech Republic, Hungary, and Poland. Foreign subsidiaries supply a network of 135 dealers. About 45 percent of these dealers sold Harley-Davidson motorcycles exclusively. In 1994, the firm was represented throughout the rest of the world by an independent network of distributors and direct sales dealers that included 15 distributors serving 16 country markets with approxi- mately 243 dealers. The remainder of the network included 14 direct sales dealers serving 14 country markets. Germany, Japan, Canada, and Australia, in that order, represent the firm's largest export markets. They account for approximately 60 percent of export sales.

Teerlink felt that to enhance international growth, the firm needed to reexamine its European strategy. Specifically, Harley-Davidson was considering ways to improve the

EXHIBIT 9
Worldwide Heavyweight Motorcycle Registration Data (above 750 cc Engine Displacement, 000s)

	1994	1993	1992	1991
North America (1):				
Total registrations	129.9	109.5	92.3	80.7
Harley-Davidson registrations	69.5	63.4	56.0	48.3
Harley-Davidson market share percentage	55.7%	57.9%	60.6%	59.9%
Europe (2):				
Total registrations	128.7	129.4	128.0	104.9
Harley-Davidson registrations	14.2	13.0	12.5	10.7
Harley-Davidson market share percentage	11.0%	10.1%	9.7%	10.2%
Japan/Australia (3):				
Total registrations	34.0	31.8	28.2	24.6
Harley-Davidson registrations	7.8	6.6	5.2	5.2
Harley-Davidson market share percentage	22.3%	20.9%	18.4%	21.1%

Notes
(1) Includes the United States and Canada
(2) Includes Austria, Belgium, France, Germany, Italy, Netherlands, Spain, Switzerland, and United Kingdom.
(3) Data for Queensland, Northern Territory and South Australia not available prior to 1993.

quality of the firm's distribution systems, dealer network, and customer support activities in Europe. According to industry reports, Europe was the world's largest heavyweight motorcycle market and was expected to become the next battleground for heavyweight motorcycles.

[T]he U.S. motorcycle market has become less and less important to the Japanese bike-makers . . . It's interesting that Honda's CB 1000 and Kawasaki's ZR (nee Zephyr) line of retro-standards came as a surprise to the U.S. arms of the two companies. They were designed for Japan, where that style of bike is riding a huge wave of popularity. Over here, they're just overpriced caricatures of performance machines we stopped building in our backyards 15 years ago. Likewise, the design of new sport bikes is largely driven by how well they will be accepted in Europe. Honda's CBR900RR was intended as a 750 until the Germans demanded more autobahn speed.[20]

According to industry observers, the belief that Japanese manufacturers no longer wish to contend for the American market may be unfounded. These observers pointed to Kawasaki's recent introductions that faithfully imitate the Harley motorcycle. (The radiator was hidden, more chrome was employed, and the Kawasaki four-cylinder engine had been configured to look like a Harley V-twin engine.) Also Kawasaki had launched a national advertising campaign which dropped the familiar themes in favor of leather-clad models.

Endnotes

1. Of these, the most distinctive innovation was the V-twin engine introduced in 1909. The V-twin engine derived its name from its cylinders, which were set opposite each other at a 45-degree angle. It gave Harley motorcycles an aggressive appearance and the ability to deliver broad but low-torque power. The V-twin engine's simple design allowed owners to tinker with their engines—a necessity at that time since motorcycle mechanics were virtually non-existent.
2. European motorcycles, lead by British firms, continued to gain popularity in the U.S. Responding to this growing foreign competition, Harley lobbied the U.S. government for a 50 percent tariff protection in 1950 because imports accounted for nearly 40 percent of new motorcycle registrations in the U.S. during that year. The Commission turned down Harley-Davidson's request. Additionally, it determined that Harley-Davidson was employing unfair trade practices because it had prohibited its dealers from carrying other brands, a violation of Federal Trade Commission rules developed for automobile dealers.
3. Reid, P. *Well Made in America*, New York: McGraw-Hill, 1990, page 5.
4. *Note on the Motorcycle Industry*—1975, Harvard Business School (578-210).
5. *Harley Davidson*—1987, Harvard Business School (292-082), page 4.
6. Reid, page 6.
7. At the time, motorcycle production was divided between the Juneau Avenue facility in Milwaukee and Wisconsin's Capital Drive plant. In 1972, AMF decided to shift all motorcycle production to Wisconsin while simultaneously refurbishing an idle bowling equipment plant in York, Pennsylvania, for motorcycle production. Upon installing state-of-art equipment, frame production and final assembly operations were moved to York in 1973. This refurbishment included the installation of a state-of-the-art inventory management system. The computer controlled inventory system cost $2 million and moved inventory from storage to production via conveyors which snaked over two miles within the plant. The Capital Drive plant was now dedicated to engine and transmission production and no improvements were undertaken during this time at this plant. The technological disparity between the two facilities, coupled with the 700-mile distance between them, created severe logistical problems in scheduling and coordinating the supply of engines (from Wisconsin) for the final assembly of motorcycles (at York). To add to the confusion, the oil crisis, resulting from the Arab oil embargo,

dramatically increased the cost of transporting components between fa-cilities and was extremely damaging to Harley-Davidson.

8. Wright, D.K., *The Harley Davidson Motor Company: An Official 90-Year History*, page 254.
9. Traditional bikers are those who tend to maintain and customize their own bikes. Non-traditional bikers included those recent converts to mo-torcycling who rode smaller bikes, mostly Japanese, and were less inter-ested in tinkering with their motorcycles.
10. Reid, page 4.
11. Reid, page 202.
12. Born to Be Real, *Industry Week*, August 2, 1993.
13. Ibid., page 15.
14. Reid, page 18.
15. See *Honda (A)*, Harvard Business School case (9-384-049), page 10 and the *Note on the Motorcycle Industry—1975*.
16. *Industry Week*, August 2, 1993.
17. Peak, M.H., Harley-Davidson: Going Whole Hog to Provide Stakeholder Satisfaction, *Management Review*, 82 (6): 53, 1993.
18. Among the factors affecting the volume of motorcycle sales are the availability and cost of credit to both retail purchasers and the number of Harley-Davidson dealers. In 1993, Harley-Davidson invested $10 million for a 49 percent interest in Eaglemark Financial Services, Inc., formerly Eagle Credit Corporation. This credit corporation provided motorcycle floor planning and parts and accessories financing arrange-ments to the firm's U.S. dealers. It also offered retail financing opportu-nities to domestic motorcycle customers.
19. Buell was a former Harley employee who left the firm to create a line of racing bikes powered by Harley engines mounted on modified Harley frames. Harley was a 49 percent owner of Buell.
20. *Management Review*, 1993.

Appendix A

Harley-Davidson History

1903   William Harley, and Arthur and Walter Davidson build a motorcycle in the shed in the Davidson's backyard

1907   Harley-Davidson Motor Company incorporated on September 17

1909   William Harley designs the first V-twin engine

1912   Harley introduces the first clutch on production vehicles

1915   Harley offers the first three-speed transmission

1918   Harley-Davidson is the largest motorcycle company in the world

1922   300,000 square-foot plant is built on Juneau Avenue in Milwaukee

1933   Great Depression—Harley production declines 80% to 3,700 motorcycles

1949   British competition enters the U.S. market

1953   Indian Motorcycle goes out of business leaving Harley as the last U.S. motorcycle manufacturer

1957   Harley introduces Sportster

1960   Japanese enter the lightweight (up to 250 cc) motorcycle market; Harley acquires Aermacchi, an Italian producer of lightweight motorcycles, for import into the U.S.

1960s   Japanese producers spark consumer interest in the light- and middleweight (250-500 cc) market signaling the start of the motorcycle boom

1965   Harley goes public

1969   AMF, Inc. takes over Harley with plans to capitalize on the bike boom

1973   Production divided between Capitol Drive (engine and transmission) and the New York, Pennsylvania, frame and final assembly plant

1975   Vaughn L. Beals appointed Chief Executive of Harley-Davidson

1978   U.S. government declines Harley's first request for foreign trade protection

1979   Sales reach 50,000 units; AMF declines Beals' request for R&D spending

1981   Harley management, led by Beals, purchases Harley-Davidson from AMF

1982   Harley implements the Productivity Triad

1987   Harley requests the lifting of the import tariff

1990   Harley establishes an Employee Stock Program

1992   Harley creates a new production strategy; anticipates production to reach 100,000 units by 1996

1995   100,000 production target achieved; market share exceeds 60% in the super-heavyweight segment

BULLER | SCHULER

Managing Organizations and People

A Resource for Cases in Management, Organizational Behavior, and Human Resource Management

Edited by Paul F. Buller, Gonzaga University, and Randall S. Schuler, Rutgers University

Abstract

This case describes the process by which Aid Association for Lutherans (AAL) and, more specifically, one of its departments, Insurance Product Services (IPS) were transformed from traditionally structured to team-based organizations. The case provides considerable detail regarding the planning and implementation of this transformation. The transformation required an integration of strategy, organizational structure, human resource management practices, and other systems within AAL and IPS.

Organizational Change: Planning and Implementing Teams at AAL and IPS

All across the United States, millions of Americans buy a variety of insurance products each year. They buy them from insurers like Met Life and Prudential, the so-called commercial insurers, and from Aid Association for Lutherans (AAL) and Knights of Columbus, the so-called fraternal benefit societies. Unlike commercial insurers, the approximately 200 fraternal benefit societies that are exempt from certain taxes serve up a mix of financial products, good works, member services, and sometimes social activities. Generally founded at the turn of the century by immigrants to provide for each other in tough times, the groups were among the first to offer insurance to working-class people. Although the societies account for less than 2 percent of the new life insurance policies written each year, about 10 million Americans buy life insurance and annuities—and sometimes health insurance, disability insurance, and mutual funds—from them.

A key concern for anyone when buying life insurance is a company's financial soundness. In this regard, fraternal societies appear to be ahead of the pack. There have been no losses to policyholders in recent memory, said a spokesman for A.M. Best, an independent agency that reviews and rates the insurance industry on the basis of overall performance and financial strength. But a few societies have merged because of declining membership. Of the 42 fraternals rated by the agency, 30 fall in the top six of its 15 rating categories, and the 6 largest fraternals, after which size drops off considerably, are in that upper tier. The largest of these is Aid Association for Lutherans.[1]

■ This case was prepared by Jerome Laubenstein and his team members at IPS department of AAL. It is used here by permission. Reprinted from Randall S. Schuler, *Managing Human Resources*, 6th Edition. West Publishing Company, 1996.

Aid Association for Lutherans (AAL)

AAL is a fraternal benefit society that provides fraternal benefits and financial security for Lutherans and their families. Individuals who purchase financial products from AAL also become members of AAL and join one of over 8,600 local volunteer service chapters called branches. Through the volunteer efforts of 1.6 million members, branches are provided opportunities to help themselves, their churches, and communities. Members also receive free educational materials on family and health topics. AAL also offers scholarship opportunities for members as well as grants to help Lutheran congregations and institutions. In total, nearly $62 million was spent on AAL's fraternal outreach last year.

AAL's financial products include individual life, disability income and long-term care insurance, and annuity products. Our subsidiary company, AAL Capital Management Corporation, offers mutual funds to our members. The AAL Member Credit Union is an affiliate that offers members federally insured savings accounts, a credit card, and various types of loans and home mortgages.

AAL assets under management are over $12 billion. Total annual premium income is over $1.5 billion. AAL is among the top 2 percent of all U.S. life insurers and is the nation's largest fraternal benefit society in terms of assets and ordinary life insurance in force. AAL also maintains an A+ rating, the highest possible, from A.M. Best and also maintains a Duff & Phelps AAA rating and a Standard & Poors AAA rating, both the highest possible.

AAL markets its products and services in all 50 states and the District of Columbia through a sales staff of over 2,400 employees. Corporate headquarters are located in Appleton, Wisconsin, where over 1,400 are employed. (Note: Staffing numbers throughout this paper are in terms of "full-time equivalents" or FTEs. Since a sizable number of regular part-time employees are utilized, the actual number of people employed is greater than stated.)

Organizational Change at AAL

AAL's organizational change, which was dubbed "Renewal" and "Transformation," officially began in December 1985 with the engagement of Roy Walters and Associates as consultants for a diagnostic process. But we can trace the beginnings of this change effort back years before that time.[2]

Some seeds were planted during the period of some very successful product introductions in 1982. The focus and energy level of the organization during that time was exciting, even though we were up to our ears trying to keep up with business due to the phenomenal success of our universal life product. We can remember saying that we should have one of these situations every two years or so, for the energizing effects it had on us and the organization.

With the introduction of these new products, we also ushered in a new awareness of the shrinking margins in financial services and our needs to rein in expenses in order to stay competitive. In addition, our president and CEO had announced his upcoming retirement, and our new president, Dick Gunderson, came in September 1985 from another life insurance organization. Studies of the insurance industry convinced Gunderson that the association had to cut costs by over $50 million over the next five years to stay competitive. In so many ways, the question on the minds of some senior managers was: What choices could be made now to position AAL for the future? Organizational change or transformation became the answer.

Positive Dissatisfaction

One of the hardest parts about the change effort was the fact that AAL was not in crisis. The good news is that this gave us the luxury of time to change and adjust; the bad news is that it's difficult to motivate oneself to go through the effort of change when things are going so well. Many of the concerns mentioned were like clouds out at the distant horizon; sales, financial, and fraternal results were continuing to grow and seemingly there was nothing in the status quo that would point to the need for fundamental change. As our consultant Bob Janson pointed out, what we did need to discover and tap was the sense of what he termed "positive dissatisfaction" within the organization—the feeling that even if AAL was doing well, we have an even higher potential to reach.

Where Are We?

The first task of the change effort was an organizational diagnosis to seek out this positive dissatisfaction. A team of 12 managers was trained in a structured interview process, then went out and conducted over 200 interviews in a diagonal slice of the home office and field. The team asked people what AAL's strengths and weaknesses were in 10 categories: Control, Culture, Management Style, Marketing, Mission, Historic Strengths, Productivity, Quality, Structure, and Technology.

Those team interviews were a great experience; people in our organization did share their hopes and dreams for what AAL could become and their frustration that we weren't working as effectively as we could to reach those dreams. People identified many strengths on which to build: our members and market, financial strength, fraternal focus and reputation, dedicated employees—both home office and field. But as the team reported out to a larger management group in May 1986, there were areas that needed attention. Our consultant has often told us since this time that he had never seen an organization so "ripe" for change.

AAL's Vision

In a process working in parallel with the diagnosis, 100 of AAL's managers also worked on the development of a vision statement[3] for the organization. The result was viewed as a reaffirmation of what AAL had become and what we stood for. It reads as follows:

AAL, the leader in fraternalism, brings Lutheran people together to pursue quality living through financial security, volunteer action, and help for others.

So, six months from the start of the transformation process, AAL had both a vision statement and a current snapshot of the organization; when the two were compared, the gaps that needed to be addressed came into clearer focus. We were set to launch our efforts to close these gaps in order to position ourselves even more strongly for the future. The working theme at that time was "Touch Tomorrow Today."

Closing Gaps

The first gaps to be addressed were in the areas of 1) organizational structure, 2) management style, and 3) marketing strategy. Efforts to study and recommend ways to close the gaps between our current situation and our vision in these three areas were launched anew still employing participative methods. For example, for the structure study, a team of six managers was charged to develop alternative proposals for restructuring the organization through the two management levels below the president. The recommendations were developed by the team with input from a larger circle of managers, then finally delivered to the president. He chose to reorganize AAL using many of the concepts recommended and the new organization was put into place late in November 1986. The reorganization was significant; 25 of the top 26 positions in the organization had changes in responsibility, including significant changes in senior management.

The efforts in other areas continue to this day. A new marketing strategy was completed in the fall of 1988. Work progressed this past year at defining a more precise vision of desired management style and assessing ourselves as managers (and having employees assess us) against that vision. We have also produced a technology strategy in response to a gap-closing need and are now wrestling with ways to address the productivity and quality variables in a more direct way.

Organizational Change Results

Our corporate restructuring, just by its nature, has been the most visible result. Frankly, after restructuring at the top of the organization was over, it was hard to convince employees that the change process was not complete.

In response to our expense challenges, the organization also achieved its downsizing goal of 250 positions by 1990. This was primarily accomplished through an early retirement window offered in 1986, as well as through attrition.

Structure and personnel changes can always be disrupting, but were especially so in our organization. Not only were we a part of a very stable industry, we were one of the largest employers in a relatively small community, with very low turnover. One of the key elements of our change process, I feel, is the guarantee of continued employment that was built into our change effort. As Robert Waterman of *In Search of Excellence* fame terms it, there is a need to maintain "stability in motion" throughout renewal. We strive to give our managers and employees the freedom and courage to reorganize and try new ways of work by placing a safety net underneath them. Employees whose positions are eliminated during the change process, or who turn out to have a mismatch of skills for new ways of work become members of a program. The program helps assess skills, finds temporary work assignments, offers support, and works to find them internal placements, field transfer, or voluntary outplacement.

Now for the sharper focus on the planning and implementing of teams within a key service area of AAL. We'll tell you about the transition of a large service department set against the backdrop of this larger change effort.

Organizational Change of the Insurance Product Services Department: Planning and Implementing Teams

The Insurance Product Services Department (IPS) provides all services related to the individual life, long-term care, and disability income insurance product lines, from the initial underwriting of contracts to the ultimate handling of claims. IPS currently consists of 426 employees, about 30 percent of the home office employees.

Phase I—"Identifying the Need"

The desire for a new organizational design for IPS had its roots in the corporate change study and subsequent corporate reorganization described above. As a result, the change efforts of IPS management were fully supported by Gunderson and top management in the spirit of corporate renewal. IPS management had the freedom to proceed with the restructuring of the department without the need for periodic presentations and approvals.

The major concerns that came out of the corporate change study regarding the "old" insurance product services environment were:

1. It was not considered to be truly customer-oriented because of its functional rather than wholistic approach to service.
2. Most decisions were made very high in a hierarchical organization with as many as six levels of supervision. As a result, decisions were made some distance from the problems that negatively impacted timeliness. They were also made by people other than those who knew most about the "problems." That had a negative impact on the quality of the decisions.
3. Skills and abilities of people were underutilized and many jobs tended to be boring because of their narrow scope.
4. Productivity was viewed from a functional perspective rather than from an integrated perspective.
5. Recent marketing successes had caused significant growth in staff and related expenses. Top management felt it was excessive growth.

Related to this last point, the change of IPS was addressed in an environment that called for the downsizing of the corporate staff by 250 over a five-year period. Corporate staff numbered 1,556 on Jan. 1, 1987.

As part of the corporate change action, a new IPS department head was put in place in December 1986. Jerome (Jerry) Laubenstein, a former marketing executive, was noted for his participative style. He was given the charge to "regionalize" the service function in an effort to get closer to the customer and to address the corporate downsizing goal as it related to the significant growth experienced by IPS in recent years.

Jerry then brought in a new senior level departmental management team in January 1987. This new senior management team consisted of five individuals to manage five geographic service regions. These people were selected for their action-oriented management style, creativity, and their demonstrated willingness to take calculated risks—a contrast to the risk-averse former culture. They were also selected because of their management strengths and highly participative management style. Technical insurance knowledge, though desirable, was not felt to be essential.

Phase II—"Setting Broad Parameters"

The second week after selection, the new IPS management team (Jerry Laubenstein, the department head, and his five regional managers) came together in an off-site retreat to address the approach to be used for redesigning the department. The first step was to develop a vision for the new IPS organization. The result was a simple statement that read "regionalization plus 'one team' processing" and included the following list of "desired outcomes":

1. A "customer driven" organization. (Customers were identified as field staff and members.)
   Being customer driven was perceived to include:
   - Listening to customer for wants/needs.
   - Being responsive and pro-active to customer wants/needs.
   - Acknowledging that the customer's problem is the provider's problem.
   - Seeing the provider as problem solver rather than order taker.
   - Informing/educating the customer.
   - Using customer-informed measures on how we're meeting their needs.
2. A strong "team" relationship with the field staff and internal support units. The need for "networking" was heavily stressed.
3. A "flat" organization with fewer levels of supervision and fewer staff.
4. "One stop" processing as fully as possible to avoid the delays and lack of ownership associated with an assembly-line approach.
5. A quality management team that would model participative management, more involvement of employees in deciding how work was to be accomplished, and more decision-making authority for employees in carrying out their day-to-day assignments.

A very simple mission statement was also established for the new organization:

IPS Mission

"To enable the agent, the primary customer, to do an even better job of serving the policyholder, the ultimate customer."

Phase III—"Design and Development"

The design process did not begin with the self-managing team concept as a goal. However, the design process did begin with a strong desire to obtain "buy in" by employees to the need for restructuring. Therefore, one of the first major tasks of the new departmental management team was to communicate the reasons for pursuing a change in work design to every employee in the department. The reasons for change really were restatements of what individuals had related to the corporate change interview teams.

Communications. Because AAL had no facility to bring the entire IPS staff together at one time (484 people at that time), the first attempt at communication to all employees was through the existing functional management structure in IPS. They were asked to conduct unit meetings, explaining the reasons for and parameters around which a new organization would be developed. Information and support materials were provided to facilitate communication. This approach met with limited success.

More Communication. A second effort was structured around large group meetings with approximately 100 employees per group. AAL CEO Richard Gunderson and Jerry Laubenstein, IPS department head, also participated. This attempt met with more success. Periodic unit meetings, led by the new regional managers, were continued. A departmental newsletter was also established. The newsletter was distributed to all IPS employees to provide continuing communications as the process progressed through the planning and implementation stages of the redesign. As we look back we'd reaffirm the fact that good solid communication cannot be over-emphasized in a restructuring process such as AAL experienced.

Design Teams. Because the "new" management team was committed to a highly participative team-oriented management style, it involved a significant cross section of employees in the departmental "redesign." Ten teams (approximately 125 employees) were appointed from lists of employees nominated by managers, supervisors, and employees. Team members consisted of employees from all levels within the organization. The teams and team charges were as follows:

- STRUCTURE TEAMS—Three of the 10 teams were charged to independently propose a new departmental structure, taking into account several "givens" such as regional organization and a maximum of three levels of supervision.
- PHYSICAL RESOURCES—Was charged to address the physical resource issues that need to be dealt with in any organization.
- MANAGEMENT STYLE TEAM—Was charged to address management style and to propose a "culture" in which employees could grow and perform in the spirit of service excellence.
- MANAGEMENT INFORMATION TEAM—Was charged to evaluate the types of management information needed to manage the operation.
- FIELD INPUT TEAM—Was charged to gain agent (customer) input on our EDP support services.
- EDP RESOURCE TEAM—Was charged to look at the impact on our EDP support services. IPS is a highly mechanized operation and, as a result, the impact on EDP operations was quite significant.
- OPERATIONS TEAM—Was charged to look after ongoing operations during the renewal effort.
- CELEBRATION TEAM—Finally, a team was appointed to plan and administer appropriate and timely celebration events to highlight specific milestones and successes along the way.

The results produced by these teams in a very short, three-week period were phenomenal. It should be noted that these results were achieved while employees continued to handle normal work activities.

Role Clarification. It was important during this time to clearly articulate the role of teams within a participative management decision-making process, especially when proposals required modification or rejection. It was IPS management's experience that employees tended to confuse the various teams' roles of providing input with management's accountability for making decisions. Managers, on the other hand, had to remember the need to explain why team decisions were modified or rejected. Looking back, it probably would have been better to label the approach as "high involvement" rather than "participative management." Doing so may have avoided some misunderstandings.

Decision Making and Implementation

Two of the three structure teams submitted organizational proposals that closely parallel our current design. These proposals, together with input from a variety of sources, including a literature search which produced the self-managing team concept, provided the direction for our organizational model. This was followed by contacting some of the proponents of sociotechnical management. As a result, it was recognized that to attain the desired outcomes and accomplish our mission, we had to move away from a hierarchically arranged, functional, and highly specialized structure that extensively used rules, records, reports, and precedents. Instead, we had to move toward a flat, full-service, self-managing, self-regulating service team concept that would move decision making closer to the transaction and to the customer. Management then created a tentative model of the new organization. This model was worked with all employees, using the nominal group process, in an attempt to get their input into potential pitfalls.

Once the organizational concept was finalized, the number of service teams needed to serve our customers was determined by modeling service activity by region. The goal was to have as many teams (i.e., customer face-offs) as could be supported by existing staff capabilities. We concluded that the "critical mass" of knowledge and skills currently available in the department could support 16 service teams. Managers were then selected to lead these teams.

Implementation. The next step was to develop an implementation plan. Implementation teams were named, again using a significant cross-section of employees. The charges to the implementation teams were to do everything necessary to ready the department for a physical move to the new organizational structure. In addition to continuing the EDP resource team, the physical resource team, and the celebration team, teams were formed around service functions of the "old" organization. They were to address the disbursement of the three functions of the insurance services: life, medical, and disability.

Employee Assignments. After decisions were reached on how the functions and staff should be disbursed and the timing of the moves was established, the new management team addressed the issue of employee assignments. After an initial "reallocation" of employees was agreed upon, employees were given the opportunity to request a change in tentative team assignment. However, because it was necessary to balance the existing knowledge among the teams, changes in assignments were not made unless exceptional reasons existed. This "assignment issue" was perhaps one of the biggest and least anticipated social issues of the renewal effort. Not since high school had adults had their social choices removed: choices of colleagues, work location, and work environment. As these new "groups" moved into the group formation stages of "forming, storming, norming, and performing," much time and energy was spent in the storming and norming phases.

Security. The impact of organizational change—including downsizing—caused this to be a trying time for many employees, even though all employees were guaranteed employment (not positions). It was especially so for supervisors and managers. The organizational redesign reduced supervisory positions from 62 to 22. By the end of 1987, a total of 57.5 full-time equivalent positions were eliminated. To reduce the stress created by this downsizing and the impact of overall change, stress management sessions were made available to all employees through the medical department. Several hundred employees took advantage of this opportunity. A course on managing change was also made available to management through a local technical institute. A career counseling service was offered to employees whose jobs were eliminated. And finally, an existing corporate "Employee Placement Program" was strengthened to help employees cope with the loss of positions (not employment) as a result of the total corporate renewal effort.

The Move. The physical move from a functional structure to one centered around self-managing teams was made in August 1987. This move was one of the first opportunities to demonstrate the power of "team problem solving." Our building services and space management units provided estimates of three to five months to move the 484 employees and associated equipment. Obviously IPS management could not live with that kind of time frame. The physical resources implementation team, led by their advisor, a newly appointed and creative regional manager, together with the building services people, synergistically arrived at an alternative that was to move people but not workstations. This required employees to accept the inadequacies of their new workstations until they could be modified at a later date. Our space management folks also had to accept something less than a "clean" move. The only change in equipment was to provide computer terminals on workstations where they had not been required earlier. Employees moved themselves by packing their belongings in boxes, putting boxes on their chairs, and wheeling both to their new workstations. This was something never before done. An incentive was provided. The move began at noon on a Friday. As soon as the unit was moved, employees were given the rest of the day off. The move was completed in less than two hours. Terminals caught up the following Tuesday.

Self-Managing Work Teams at IPS

Teams within Teams. There are four significant aspects of the IPS organizational team design:

1. It's a regional organization with each region providing all services to their designated customers. (These service regions paralleled the existing field distribution and management regions.)

2. Each region has four service teams, with each service team providing almost all services to a specific group of agencies. A few services were handled by such a small staff that it was difficult to spread them to service teams in the early stages of restructuring. The number of employees sufficient to constitute adequate "critical mass" to permit disbursement was a major point of discussion. Management tended to be more risk-oriented than staff in this area.

3. Each service team was initially structured to have three self-managing work teams within it, one around the underwriting and issue functions; another around "service" functions such as loans, terminations, dividends, pre-authorized check handling, etc.; and the third around the claims functions.

4. Our goal is to move to more wholistic self-managing teams by encouraging the integration of the three functional teams. Finally, IPS had a cadre of functional specialists with responsibility for establishing functional policy and for monitoring the appropriate administration of policy across regions and teams. These functional specialists are currently organized by line of business and report to the regional managers.

Self-Managed Teams Defined. The focal point of our current organization is clearly the self-managing work team. The self-managing work team concept, as found in our literature search and adopted by AAL, is as follows:

- Self-managing work teams are semi-autonomous groups of workers who share the responsibility for carrying out a significant piece of work and who run their own operations with almost no supervision. The group has the authority and the technical, interpersonal, and managerial skills to make decisions about how the work should be done.

- The team is accountable as a group for processing all work for which it's responsible. Members plan, do, and control their work. The team decides who will do what work and assigns members to tasks. The group has control over scheduling and coordinating its own work, formulating vacation schedules, monitoring quality, solving technical problems, and improving work methods. Employees have both responsibility and accountability for quantity, quality, and costs. The team meets regularly to discuss goals; to identify, analyze, and solve work-related problems; and/or to provide improvement ideas.

- Employees typically possess a variety of skills and are encouraged to develop new skills to increase their flexibility. Workers typically learn second and third jobs. The team is responsible for motivating, training, coaching, and developing its members. The team trains one another or arranges for their own training.

- The team is also responsible for employee evaluation and discipline. The group, as a whole, reviews overall team performance, conducts peer evaluation of individual members, and handles problems such as absenteeism and poor performance. Teams need to be skilled in handling the social system as well. This means being able to celebrate their success, recognize one another's efforts, thank one another for help, and in general reinforce positive behavior. As teams mature they hire new members or do final selection of new team members.

- Reward systems typically reward teamwork as well as the individual acquisition of skills and the individual's performance. For example, the team's results may determine the size of the compensation resource pool available to be distributed as increases and/or bonuses to individual members of the team. Team members then determine how the team's allocation is distributed to individual team members.

There are some aspects of the self-managing work team concept that have not been implemented at AAL. For example, peer appraisal is achieved by anonymous input and not by direct input and significant performance problems continue to be turned over to managers for disciplinary measures.

Benefits of the Self-Managing Team Concept

The benefits of the self-managing team concept to both management and employees are perhaps obvious. Nevertheless, we'll state a few of them. Fred Emery has identified six intrinsic factors that are motivators:

1. Variety and challenge
2. Elbow room for decision making
3. Feedback and learning
4. Mutual support and respect
5. Wholeness and meaning
6. Room to grow; a bright future

With respect to these motivators, Marvin Weisbord, in his book *Productive Workplaces*, comments that "the first three must be optimal—not too much, which adds to stress and anxiety, nor too little, which produces stultifying tedium. The second trio are open ended. No one can have too much respect, growing room, or 'wholeness'—meaning a view of both the origin and the customer's use of your work." All of this assumes that in place are "satisfiers" identified by Emery and Trist, a list of six conditions of employment: fair and adequate pay, job security, benefits, safety, health, and due process. As Weisbord comments, "Only in workplaces embodying both lists can the century-old dreams of labor-management cooperation ever come true."

It is our contention that the six motivational factors can be met far more effectively through the self-managing team structure as described above than through the traditional one person/one task, multi-level hierarchical management structure.

Joseph Boyett and Henry Conn suggest in their book *Maximum Performance Management*, that excellence is a function of the knowledge and skills, motives, and abilities of employees. However, they also suggest that we cannot directly change them and thus we are stuck with the internal traits and characteristics employees bring to the job. They further suggest that we can, however, adjust the work environment to compensate for weaknesses in knowledge and skills, motives, and/or abilities. The three leverages they propose for doing this are:

1. Information   Shared Values and Business Strategies
                  Linked Missions and Goals
                  Measures and Feedback
                  Identification of Critical Behaviors
2. Consequences   Social Reinforcement
                  Contingent Awards
                  Pay-for-Performance (Variable portion up to 40% of
                    total compensation)
3. Involvement   Non-Voluntary
                  Management Directed Teams
                  Cross-Functional Task Forces

We'd suggest that AAL's self-managing team approach supported by our pay-for-performance compensation system, which is anchored to team measures and results, takes full advantage of these areas of leverage far better and with far less effort than can be done in a traditional hierarchical structure.

Manager's Role in Self-Managing Team Environment

The move to self-managing teams required a redefinition of the role of the team manager. The manager is still responsible and accountable for the bottom line results of the team, but these results are attained differently. In the new work environment, the creative abilities of all team members are used, not just those of the manager.

The redefined role requires managers to:

- set direction by creating and focusing the team's efforts toward a common vision;
- to coach and counsel, to ensure and support the development of team members;
- to lead the team in problem solving;
- to make sure the team has needed information and resources; and
- to encourage the team to make its own decisions on operating problems.

The new role requires managers to manage through use of "boundaries" or "parameters" rather than by directive. Key challenges are the need to create a motivating work environment and to remove barriers for team members. The latter is accomplished by managing relationships among teams and between the team and other areas of the organization.

Although the role of the manager in a self-managing team environment differs from the role of a manager in the traditional environment, research has shown that the profile of outstanding managers is very similar regardless of the environment. They are visionaries, use a participative management style, and can deal with ambiguity and lack of structure. They share information and responsibility with employees and are committed both to the work and to the individuals on their team. And they deliver results!

Key Support Systems

Pay-for-Applied-Services for Individuals and Teams. Pay-for-Applied-Services (PAS) is the name selected for the compensation systems designed to support self-managing work teams. It offers maximum flexibility in order to support the unique job design needs of each team.

One of our more significant challenges during the development of PAS was to integrate it into a corporate culture firmly entrenched in the Hay system of job evaluation. Nevertheless, the task was uniquely and creatively accomplished by a team including individuals from the service areas and corporate compensation services.

Within IPS, individual position descriptions have been replaced by a team job description and individual personal assignments. The personal assignment is a listing of the services an individual performs to support the needs of the team and their own career interests. Employees have identified approximately 165 services that are being performed within the department.

Compensation is delivered through four components. The first is a "valued services" component. As new services are learned and applied, the value of the services learned and applied is added to the employee's ongoing compensation. The value of individual services is determined using the know-how portion of the Hay system. A matrix has been constructed using Hay know-how values. One axis of the matrix is absolute values representing the minimum AAL is willing to pay for a service if it were a stand-alone service. The other axis of the matrix is incremental values. The more an individual learns with the same base know-how value, the less additional learning is worth.

The second component of pay delivery is the team incentive. Incentive dollars are tied to productivity measures. Allocation is based on a team's contribution to productivity. Distribution to individuals within the team is based on an individual's support of the team. Incentive dollars are distributed quarterly.

The third component is a market adjustment feature. In order to remain competitive within the market place and with comparable jobs within the organization, market adjustments are considered annually. These adjustments may be made to either the matrix or the incentive "pot." When made to the matrix, a recalculation of the value of individual personal assignments will result. Where appropriate, immediate adjustments are made to pay.

The fourth component is an individual-incentive program. IPS has added an incentive component that recognizes outstanding achievement by individual employees. This lump-sum incentive is paid once a year only to those employees who are already paid at market value. This incentive is worth as much as 6 percent of an individual's compensation.

This new compensation system encourages cross-training, enhances team flexibility, and encourages team performance but, very importantly, still permits compensation dollars to be managed and controlled. It was implemented on April 1, 1989, and underwent a degree of modification in 1991 to bring it into closer synchronization with a new incentive compensation plan introduced to the rest of the organization in 1991.

Training for Self-Managing Work Teams. A comprehensive training program continues to be developed for all employees working in a sociotechnical management environment within the organization. The entire program design and delivery to all employees was completed in 1990. Some of the topics covered include:

- Team self-management roles. Typical supervisory responsibilities that teams may take on in their own self-management includes:
  Planning and scheduling own time schedules
  Securing and allocating resources
  Scheduling and coordinating work in team
  Setting standards, rotating assignments
  Providing performance data
  Recruiting, selecting, and fixing
  Disciplining and rewarding
  Celebrating successes
  Motivating/training
  Coaching/developing
  Problem solving and conflict resolution

Management allocates these tasks to team members as the team is ready for them. A part of the preparation for this passing of responsibilities includes training and development activities relevant to each team's needs.

- Team manager's role. Service team managers must play a stronger coaching and counseling role than the traditional manager. They find themselves in the role of facilitator, empowerer, and consultant, responsible for "managing the culture." Therefore, the training program developed for managers pays special attention to the development of these skills.

Performance appraisal

- Peer (individual) appraisal. Self-managing work teams require a new concept in performance appraisals. Members of the team use an anonymous peer appraisal concept. In addition, teams "certify" their members' skill levels.
- Group (team) appraisal. Teams are expected to function as teams and not just groups of individuals. Team members receive training in the skill areas required to enable groups of individuals to function as a team. The individual's ability to function as a team member is evaluated as part of the training process. However, managers assess the team's actual behavior in this area. Teams are able to assess their own progress against the standards and goals that contribute to bonus results.

Successes and Challenges of Change and Self-Managed Teams at IPS

External Visibility

The self-managing work team concept initially found only a modest level of credibility within the rest of the organization because, in the minds of many, it still had to be proven. The attention given our efforts helped support the validity of the work team concept. Examples include an article about our efforts by John Hoerr in the July 10, 1989 issue of *Business Week*; several references by Tom Peters in his syndicated newspaper column; several other references in other national and local publications; requests for and subsequent site visits by many organizations; and invitations to make presentations about our team concept by organizations such as the Association for Quality and Participation and the Work in America Institute. Subsequently, demonstrated improvements in productivity and customer satisfaction made it more difficult to criticize the concept. However, the one soft spot that plagued us for some time was overall employee satisfaction. Employee satisfaction was probably impacted most significantly by the introduction of an incentive compensation system with pay at risk during a time when the rest of the organization remained on the traditional merit system.

Employee Successes and Challenges

Employee reactions to the redesigned organization are monitored by a number of approaches. First, monthly employee "feedback" sessions are sponsored and hosted by the department head. Employees are randomly selected from throughout the department and offered the opportunity to air their concerns, ask questions, and suggest changes. This approach is also used by regional managers.

In addition, a survey instrument was introduced in July 1987, to monitor employee attitude as IPS moved through implementation of the redesigned organization. The survey continues to be used on a periodic basis. Results are evaluated on a regional and service team level as well as on a departmental level. Employee attitude goals are established for service teams and actual results against goals are used in evaluating managers' overall performance. The first reading was taken in July 1987, just prior to the physical move. A second was taken in October 1987, shortly after the physical move, followed by a third in May 1988, a fourth in September 1989 following the introduction of the Pay-for-Applied-Services compensation system, and the last in August of 1990. A few comparative readings from the old organization were available from several years before. Some results are shown in Exhibit 1.

The significant impact of change can be noted in the overall satisfaction of employees. A very stable "comfortably staffed" functional organization in 1983 resulted in a relatively high level of overall satisfaction. Surprisingly, the design phase and, not so surprisingly, the implementation phase of the new design resulted in a significant deterioration in overall employee satisfaction even though employees were heavily involved in developing and implementing the new design. However, it should be pointed out that employees, for the most part, still respond that they would not want to go back to the old structure and organization, even though there are some things about the new they dislike.

The Tough Spots. Two specific "problem" areas identified by the survey were (1) lack of advance training for the new roles and duties employees were being asked to assume and (2) the employees' inability to measure how well they were doing in their new roles.

First, the training issue was an enormous challenge for both management and employees. Enlarging jobs put a tremendous strain on training capabilities during the early stages of transformation. That, together with not having a compensation system in place to support the cross-training concept, may have negatively impacted employee morale by not having adequate incentives in place. It's understandable that employees did not feel very good about this aspect of the renewal effort. Second, moving from individual standards to measuring and rewarding individuals on the basis of team results is a difficult change for some to accept in a culture in which "individuality" has been lauded and many prefer to be "fully" in control of their own destinies.

In addition, as previously mentioned, the approach used to assign employees to new work teams had a significant negative impact on the existing "social system." This was

EXHIBIT 1
Percent Agreeing

	1983	7/87	10/87	5/88	9/89	8/90	8/91
Overall satisfaction	70%	56%	47%	41%	51%	58%	65%
Encouraged to innovate		58%	73%	69%	66%	70%	69%
Adequate training		60%	49%	51%	57%	58%	58%
Permitted to use judgment		81%	90%	88%	89%	89%	88%
Good communication between field and HO	30%	58%	66%	58%	54%	66%	68%
Familiar with measures for for doing good job		64%	38%	42%	45%	52%	57%

further compounded in January 1989 when the department moved from a five-region structure to a four-region structure to parallel a similar move in the field distribution system. The other major impact on employee satisfaction was the installation of a new compensation system that has the effect of putting a part of their compensation "at risk" based on performance. The aggregation of all of this change has had a negative impact on employees' overall satisfaction level. It's doubtful that the negative impact of change can be avoided, but what could be avoided is drawing it out over an extended period of time. In our case, we began the design in January 1987, and implemented the last piece, the compensation program, in 1989 and 1991. This is probably an excessive time frame.

Nevertheless, there are some really positive results. For example, communications between the employee and our customers has improved. The employee now feels challenged to innovate. And employees feel free to use their own rather than a supervisor's judgment. We also have a very large number of employees who favor the new compensation system because of the positive impact it has had on their ability to influence their earnings.

One of the most noteworthy results is the gain in productivity that has been accomplished and which will be addressed later. An additional "nice to see" is the rapidity with which the organization is moving from the concept of three functional self-managing work teams within a service team to a more integrated, functionally inclusive, self-managing team. The latter was a longer range design goal but it is coming to realization much more quickly than anticipated.

Customer Successes and Challenges

Perhaps the most visible success thus far is the favorable impact the new self-managed design is having on IPS's customers—the field staff. Input gathered from them, as part of a field renewal effort and reported in March 1988, indicated that the field staff felt the new IPS organization was one of the four best things about AAL.

A survey instrument was implemented to measure the satisfaction of the field staff. The results are shown in Exhibit 2.

The improvement in customer attitude between August 1985 and March 1988 is probably primarily related to (1) the promise of "better" service, (2) the "face off" of specific service teams with specific customers (agencies), (3) field visits where members of service teams would attend agency meetings, and (4) an experimental "partnership program" in which specific IPS employees would "partner" with specific agents. The slight deterioration in October 1988 is probably somewhat related to the establishment of higher expectations and to field renewal activity that was taking place. Speed, for example, shows a fairly significant deterioration in level of satisfaction when, in fact, we've been providing better service than earlier in the renewal process. Other "anecdotal evidences" of customer satisfaction are numerous letters and other communications about how pleased individuals are with the support they're getting from their home office service team; flowers, candy, and other "treats" received by service teams from their field customers; and customer-hosted "celebrations" in conjunction with successful sales results.

Looking at the results of the survey instrument from the perspective of ignoring the "neutral" responses and focusing only on the "disagrees," would suggest even better results. For example:

	PERCENT DISAGREEING		
	9/89	9/90	10/91
IPS understands field	19%	12%	13%
IPS wants to help field	2%	2%	2%
IPS will respond	4%	5%	2%
Satisfactory speed	14%	8%	13%
Accuracy	6%	2%	4%

Productivity Successes and Challenges

Very tangible productivity gains have been realized. As previously indicated, the department was initially "right-sized" by 59 positions (12 percent) resulting in a savings of over

EXHIBIT 2
Percent Agreeing

	8/85	9/87	10/88	9/89	9/90	10/91
IPS understands field	27%	47%	45%	48%	57%	60%
IPS wants to help field		83%	78%	79%	84%	89%
IPS will respond	*	84%	82%	85%	85%	89%
Satisfactory speed	61%	68%	61%	65%	77%	73%
Accuracy	76%	79%	74%	77%	85%	84%

*No survey data, but focus of high level of complaints from field.

one million dollars of salaries and benefits. Additional reallocation of employee resources has since occurred. On the other hand, business processed has continued to increase. A "macro" productivity model developed to monitor our progress shows a cumulative productivity increase of approximately 29 percent through 1990. This means that if we were operating at the same standard of productivity as we were in 1985 and 1986, we would require about 120 more positions than we had at the end of 1990.

We anticipate additional productivity gains as cross-training progresses and teams mature. However, the amount of time and energy it takes to cross-train while continuing to process business should not be underestimated. It is a significant commitment of time and resources.

Future Design Changes

The first phases of the sociotechnical design were implemented in IPS in August 1987. A review of the original design decisions, in view of the knowledge gained from a little over a year of operation, took place in December 1988. As a consequence, we implemented several modifications to the organization in March 1989 and introduced the individual-incentive modification to the compensation system (PAS) in 1991.

First, we've moved from a five-region to a four-region design to face off with a similar change that was made in the alignment of our field distribution organization effective January 1989. Second, we moved the reporting relationship of "specialists" from service team managers to the regional managers. This was done to recognize that specialists have a departmental role, not a service team role, and thus are a part of the departmental management team. We later reorganized the specialists by line of business with each regional manager taking responsibility for one of the major areas. Third, we moved from 16 service team managers to 15, further broadening the span of control of the managers. This was possible because of the progress made in the self-managing capabilities of employees.

It should be pointed out that this "fine-tuning" of the organization resulted in employee reassignments and as a result was followed by some deterioration in the morale of employees who were looking for stability.

And finally, as previously mentioned, a modification of the compensation system was implemented in 1991.

CEO Diagnostic Intervention

We contracted with the Center for Effective Organizations (CEO), University of Southern California, in October 1992, to learn how to better understand the effect of IPS structure and support systems on team performance and employee satisfaction. We felt we needed to understand the employee concerns voiced in the November 1991 corporate employee survey, and we needed to respond by addressing these concerns. Also it was five years since IPS had been reorganized into teams and the timing would indicate that it was time to reassess our direction. We selected CEO to do the research because they would be a neutral third party, carried the prestige of being an internationally known organization in the study of teams and team work, and employed some of the leading thinkers on compensation, particularly skill-based pay.

As we began our research in the fall of 1992, we had four key objectives:

1. Assess the current status and design of the team-based IPS organization.

2.   Specifically address the issue of why improvements in employee morale lagged improvements in productivity and customer satisfaction.

3.   Suggest possible innovations in our team-based design, which could be implemented and tested for their impact on the effectiveness of teams and the department as a whole.

4.   Assist with the design, implementation, and assessment of innovations related to new ways of doing business that were planned for at least some of the work teams.

Here's what we learned from a year of intensive self-scrutiny:

1.   Despite our hypothesis that employee quality of work life (QWL) lagged improvements in productivity and customer satisfaction, QWL for IPS employees was in fact above average compared to other organizations.

2.   Our efforts at empowerment were effective, but room for continued progress remained.

3.   Employee quality of work life was not strongly related to either productivity or customer satisfaction.

     In other words, changes in employee quality of work life were not likely to have major effects on either productivity or customer satisfaction. This was a surprising finding, but is consistent with findings from other CEO research into the relationship of QWL to organizational performance. It does not mean QWL is unimportant, but that we can't predict how changes in employee QWL might affect other business results.

4.   The need for communication is strong.

5.   Overall satisfaction with pay was high, but not all employees agreed with AAL's compensation system or the philosophy behind it. Most employees demonstrated a good understanding of the PAS compensation system (base pay, team incentives, individual incentives) and the corporate Success Share incentive program. However, they indicated some dissatisfaction with non-annuitized incentive compensation (they would prefer annual base salary increases over annual bonuses), and felt that the compensation system does not effectively reward good performers.

6.   Service team director visibility was low; the supervisory style of the manager is not related to the team's performance.

     Most employees reported that they did not see their managers frequently and would appreciate more contact. A second learning was that there was no correlation between management style and team results in employee QWL, productivity, or customer satisfaction.

These findings led us to convene the department management team (regional managers, service team directors, and lead specialists) so we could communicate the issues to them and involve them in developing a work plan for addressing areas for improvement. The work of "fine-tuning" the organization based on the CEO findings was begun in August 1993.

Summary

In summary, the primary driving forces for the redesign of IPS were a desire to get closer to the customer, a desire to enlarge jobs and empower employees, and a need to "right-size" staff levels. The organizational concept utilized to accomplish our task was the self-managing work team. Although early results indicate customers are more satisfied and corporate productivity goals are being met, employee satisfaction goals are not being fully achieved. If there is one point to really emphasize, it's that the transition from traditional hierarchical management to sociotechnical management has not been without a lot of "pain" for all involved. Thus, IPS management would be the first to emphasize that we are still heavily into change even though it's been going on for several years.

Some of the more significant conclusions we've reached may be worth sharing. The greatest value of restructuring is probably derived from the process of organizational diagnosis, establishing a vision, and participatively discovering the answer to the gap between the results of the diagnosis and the vision and creating the organizational response. We also feel that "unfreezing" needs to occur to give permission for change (creating positive dissatisfaction is healthy), preferably led by top management example. In AAL's case, this took place through the corporate change that preceded the IPS effort. We'd suggest that it's impossible to over-communicate to employees as the process unfolds, that participation by impacted employees is a must, and that the impact of change on employees cannot be underestimated. It's helpful if support systems are implemented concurrently with the renewal efforts and if at all possible, it's probably best to implement all aspects of the change at one time to avoid prolonged "organizational instability" and the associated negative impact on employee morale.

Thus we'd suggest that some of the keys for success would include:

- Participation: Employee involvement at all levels will help ensure buy-in and the best results. The more "brain power" applied to the problem, the better chance the emerging solution will be successful.
- Vision: A clear energizing vision must be created to gain the commitment of staff and to motivate them through times of "pain."
- Commitment: Commitment of top management and support of other key corporate staff, such as human resource management, is critical. Employees have to know their efforts are part of a larger strategy.
- Patience: If the focus is on short-term results, the effort will probably not achieve the ultimate vision. If the goal is to avoid all "pain" in the organization, it's probably unachievable. Change brings pain, but pain disappears with newfound stability.
- Time: Implementation and cultural change take time. Although some immediate benefits will occur, the ultimate payoff may not be realized for several years.

If the above conditions are not present, success is unlikely.

Endnotes

1. Scherreik, S. "Off the Beaten Path in the Insurance Field," *New York Times* (December 25, 1993): LA5.
2. Hoerr, J. "Work Teams Can Rev-Up Paper-Pushers, Too," *Business Week* (November 28, 1988): 64–72.

3. This vision statement later became the organization's mission statement.

References

1. Boyett, J.H., and Henry P. Conn. *Maximum Performance Management.* Glenbridge Publishing Ltd., 1988.
2. Caudron, S. "Team Staffing Requires New HR Role," *Personnel Journal* (May 1994): 88–94.
3. Hoerr, J. "The Payoff from Teamwork," *Business Week* (July 10, 1989): 56–62.

4. Weisbord, M.R. *Productive Workplaces.* Jossey-Bass, Inc., 1987.
5. Wellins, R.S., W.C. Byham, and J.M. Wilson. *Empowered Teams.* Jossey-Bass, Inc., 1991.

BULLER | SCHULER

Managing Organizations and People

A Resource for Cases in Management, Organizational Behavior, and Human Resource Management

Abstract

The general manager of the production division of a Latin American export company is considering what to do about cross-functional teams and the quality council, both central to the implementation of total quality management (TQM). The company is the Tropical Export Company that produces LITEP—an acronym that refers to the labor intensive tropical export product grown in Playa Negra and exported by the company. The company is a U.S.-based multinational corporation with extensive production operations in Latin America that produces LITEP for industrialized markets, mainly North America and Europe. Several production divisions are located in the Central American country of Morazan. Each employs approximately 5,500 to 6,500 employees of whom around 500 to 550 are salaried; the rest are union members. The divisions are focused on exported volume of high quality LITEP. Quality is vital to the customer and volume is the key to lowering costs and increasing productivity.

Using Leadership to Promote TQM

Case Setting

The Tropical Export Company is a U.S.-based multinational corporation with extensive production operations in Latin America that produce LITEP—an acronym for the labor-intensive tropical export product grown and exported by the company—for industrialized markets, mainly North America and Europe. The company is one of the 3–4 major players in the industry. Several production divisions are located in the Central American country of Morazan. Each employs approximately 5,500 to 6,500 employees of whom around 500 to 550 are salaried; the rest are union members. The divisions are focused on exported volume of high-quality LITEP. Quality is vital to the customer and export volume is the key to lowering costs and increasing productivity.

The village-like, relatively closed, company towns created social situations where the distinction between one's work and social roles was blurred. The company was very figural in the gestalt of workers' lives in Playa Negra, the production division where the case occurred.

Adoption of TQM

Playa Negra was one of the first sites within the company where TQM was implemented, beginning with a training program. The objectives of the training program were to understand how to work within a TQM culture and learn the basic steps in beginning a TQM program to shift attention from inspecting the final product to analyzing the processes used to produce and ship LITEP. The transition from traditional quality inspection of the final product to TQM's continuous improvement of work processes involved the following changes:

1. include the internal customers in the analysis and revision of work processes;
2. focus on the prevention of quality problems rather than inspection;
3. manage the process rather than the results; managers were to work with subordinates in problem solving;
4. develop participative employees rather than passive subordinates;
5. provide basic analytical tools (e.g., Pareto charts, "fishbone" or cause-effect diagrams, control charts, histograms, and flow charts) to teams of subordinates who would analyze problems and make presentations to managers committed to listening rather than deciding based on intuition; and
6. assure continuous improvement of work processes that should ultimately be reflected in higher quality scores and customer satisfaction in the market rather than relying on a commodity–low cost producer approach.

There was no connection established between the TQM program and compensation; it was viewed as part of the participants' duties. However, executives did have bonuses tied to the achievement of TQM objectives.

The TQM process was housed in a structure parallel to the hierarchy and consisted of the following:

1. a quality council, made up of department heads and supervisors;
2. a full-time TQM coordinator who had fairly extensive experience within operations; he had worked for the company in purchasing, the controller's office, and operational roles for six years; and
3. the quality action—also called continuous improvement—teams, made up of a variety of people with particular expertise or involvement in a specific process that was designated for improvement by the quality council.

Such a parallel structure was necessary because the TQM process was not perceived as a replacement for the regular machine bureaucracy that had relentlessly met production targets for decades.

In Playa Negra, in addition to the introductory seminars given by the TQM coordinator, dozens of employees attended workshops conducted by external consultants. Topics covered included facilitation skills, leadership in participative workplaces, and statistical process control.

The General Manager's Questions

Armando, the general manager of Playa Negra, sat wondering how to proceed. He understood that TQM doctrine emphasized the importance of a relatively autonomous quality council and the need for cross-functional teams. Yet he was puzzled how to proceed in a culturally appropriate fashion. The dilemma was to strike a balance that would allow TQM to flourish while preserving enough continuity to maintain an organizational foundation that members found satisfying and consistent with their culturally determined expectations of the organization.

The quality council was to provide leadership to the TQM process. However, the council had done next to nothing for 18 months. Armando, the general manager, had quietly sat through the meetings as an observer. The controller, a relatively young expatriate, had led the council meetings.

Everyone, including Armando, was frustrated with the lack of progress. As Armando saw it, he had three alternatives:

1. He could continue within the council as he had for the past 18 months, basically an observer, in the hopes that the council would eventually coalesce around some high-priority project.
2. He could aggressively push his TQM agenda within the council. A colleague in another production division, Karl, had done this and was pleased that the quality coun-

cil was pursuing the projects that were high on his list of priorities. The general manager's control over the organization was extreme due to the power Latin society gives to heads of organizations and the role the company had carved out for the position in its century of neocolonialist domination of the Latino workforce. Karl, a European with long family links to the company and extensive production experience and competence, observed that even if he asked a question, the Latino council members would try to infer what his desires were and would try to please him. Karl's view was that it would take too long for the council to become truly autonomous and he had decided to use the culturally acceptable role of strong leadership to use the council as a vehicle to achieve his ends. He once confided to Armando that the council was a "manager's council." Both Armando and Karl, as general managers in a very competitive industry, were pressured by their superiors to complete numerous specific projects. Their annual bonuses, of up to 30% of their base pay, depended on achievement of these objectives. Thus, it was understandable why Karl would feel compelled to do what he was doing. Plus, the general manager's role is so powerful that using it to achieve the ends of TQM seemed better to Karl than "sitting around" through endless meetings.

3. A subsidiary, Packing, Inc., that provided plastic and cardboard packaging materials to Playa Negra, had a different approach. The assistant manager, who reported to the general manager and was second-in-command, assumed leadership of the quality council. The general manager was only allowed to attend when the council had completed analyzing an issue and wanted to present their recommendations to him. The assistant manager found that when the general manager observed, the other executives were preoccupied with what they thought he might want rather than analyzing a problem independent of the general manager. Armando wondered if he would get too distant from the process with this method. He was accustomed to assuming strong leadership.

Based on the advice of both the external and the corporate TQM consultants and his internal TQM coordinator, Armando had attempted to establish quality action teams with members from various functions who were to collaboratively problem solve and thereby improve interdepartmental communication. However, the department heads had resorted to "turf" conscious behaviors and were not allowing their subordinates, who were on the quality action teams, to cooperate with other departments without passing things up the hierarchy for review, thereby slowing the process down and involving the more turf conscious department heads. Armando saw three alternatives:

1. He knew he could order the department heads to do as he told them. In the past, when he led change efforts, he aggressively pursued what he wanted to accomplish by bringing his immediate subordinates along and disseminating the information associated with the change throughout the organization. He followed up with consistent monitoring and encouragement. However, if he aggressively pushed the concept of cross-functional teams, he was worried that if he was to be transferred, the department heads would abandon TQM as they would not have a sense of ownership of the process because they would not have internalized the TQM philosophy.

2. He could allow the department heads to revert back to functional teams and then later attempt to convince them of the utility of cross-functional teams and functional interdependence between departments.

3. He was also considering naming respected middle managers to head the teams who would then choose the members of the quality action teams from their own departments and other departments, based on the team leader's relationship with the prospective members and their perceived competence relating to the problem addressed.

The corporate TQM consultant, Bob, who had encouraged Armando to push the cross-functional teams and also to keep the quality council on track, was doing a training program that day. Armando invited him and the internal TQM coordinator, Francisco, to play a round of golf after work and discuss how they should proceed with the TQM process.

The Golf Game

Armando sat on the verandah of the club and watched Francisco and Bob walk toward him. Though they were not very good golfers, he enjoyed playing with them because it was a more relaxed way to discuss things with them. He had developed confidence in their ability to provide him with assistance but felt that they were mistaken by following TQM as though it were an ideology or an off-the-shelf recipe for the latest potion of managerial self-help. Armando had grown leery of such rigidity as he knew the extremely strong organizational culture of a 70-year-old LITEP production division and the uniqueness of Latino culture forced him to modify managerial interventions developed in the U.S. Armando greeted them, "Well, are you ready to wager a few pesos on the game? I'll give you 2-to-1 odds and bet 300 pesos."

Francisco and Bob looked at one another and shrugged assent. They knew they would lose but were also familiar with the custom of wagering and losing to the general manager.

They played a few holes and exchanged small talk about families and politics. Armando began the discussion, "I read your report, Bob. I understand that I have the power and authority to kick the council in the rear and get it moving, or the TQM budget might be at risk given the austerity campaign our financial wizards have imposed on us due to the falling P/E ratio. I also agree that I could force the department heads to adopt the cross-functional approach we've discussed for the quality action teams. I know that you believe such teams are essential due to the need for interdependent groups and cross-functional communication. But, I worry about jamming things down their throats because I could be transferred at any time to another production division and my successor might simply throw out the whole process if it's not strongly entrenched and supported by the department heads and supervisors."

Bob responded, "Your position is such a powerful one that I think you can get away with it and I think there's enough support in corporate to lean on the incoming general manager to follow the playbook we've laid out."

Francisco and Armando exchanged furtive glances and smiles. They were continually amazed that the U.S. corporate offices believed they could simply order the Latin American production divisions to follow some policy. If they followed everything corporate said there would be no production. They would either be paralyzed by strikes or have on-going conflict with the local government. Armando understood how the company's neocolonialist past had fostered the arrogance that confused decision making but also understood that sometimes he had to be cautious in aggressively pushing things that didn't seem to fit with the peculiar culture of the LITEP production divisions.

Armando mused about Bob's reference to the power given the role of the general manager. "From a cultural standpoint, I know my Central American compatriots would accept my autocratic authority. I understand that the 'in-group,' as you call my department heads and supervisors, will do as I say. However, this same bond also works within departments and creates a powerful 'in-group' feeling that works against cross-functional teams."

As Armando prepared to drive, Bob thought how struck he had been by the loyalty, commitment, and obedience that characterized the organizational culture. He had likened it to the military. People did as they were told. They hesitated to contradict their superiors. They expressed high levels of commitment to the company. Turnover was practically nonexistent; people spent their lives working for LITEP, Inc.

Bob was also aware that the general managers, including Armando, enjoyed great power and respect because they had passed all the tests laid before them in their careers and deserved their designation as general manager. They had mastered various jobs and tasks over the 15 years or more that it usually took to become a general manager. When they attained the level of general manager, they were generally recognized as competent production and operations specialists who also had soundly developed managerial and political skills.

Armando drove within 25 yards of the hole. While walking up the fairway they continued chatting. Armando said, "We can't spell out everything. You seem to want to follow a recipe or some doctrine you heard from Deming, Juran, or one of the other TQM gurus. It doesn't work that way. Aside from our culture being very different than where you saw TQM work in the U.S., things are in such an upheaval now that conditions are too unpredictable to spell every step out." Armando understood that this uncertainty allowed the general manager great power as there were no established rules and procedures to solve such nonroutine problems.

Francisco listened and thought about Armando. He believed that Armando had highly developed political skills and charismatic leadership qualities. As a large fit man, he struck an imposing image. During meetings, he frequently stood and walked around the room speaking with a thundering voice and waved his arms to emphasize a point. He combined an engaging manner with total authority; one could speak frankly with him and challenge him with solid arguments, yet one was always aware of his authority. Francisco asked Armando, "What is it about TQM that you like?"

Armando thought for a few moments and replied, "I enjoy getting a large organization to do what I want it to do. I see TQM as an opportunity to try something new. You learn from your bosses but you want to do more. TQM gave me that opportunity. I have nothing to fear from more employee participation or the involvement that comes with TQM. If you know the business, you can help people problem solve in a manner that enables them to develop. By giving people authority, they will come to you and seek your input. This gives me more power than I would have had if I simply had told a passive work force what to do. I want a proactive group seeking answers. But I never submit anything to a group for their input when I already know the answer. You don't have to tell people you're in charge—they know it."

Francisco thought of all the conversations he had had with company colleagues about the power of the general manager. In one club in another LITEP producing country Francisco had visited, he saw a photo of a former American general manager (who later became the regional vice president) wearing two six-shooters, prominently displayed as part of the club's memorabilia. He also recalled the Spanish businessman who had said that many years ago he bought the first car owned by a "civilian" (i.e., non-company)a geographically isolated division. When it was delivered on the company train, the general manager initially refused to allow it to be unloaded saying he hadn't given his authorization.

As though he sensed what Francisco was thinking about, Armando continued, "If you think I'm autocratic you should have seen the first American general manager I worked for. He had a boat called 'Solo Mio' ("only mine") that nobody touched, except to keep it ready for his personal and exclusive use. This was how company employees grew to feel a general manager should behave."

Armando continued, "You must recall that our employees are not professionally educated specialists with strong ties outside Playa Negra. Sure, there are professional engineers, accountants, and some college educated production specialists, but most of the supervisors do not have much education. Instead they learned their jobs within the company. This made them heavily socialized within Playa Negra—an army of enlisted men, if you will. And I'm their general."

Bob thought about how power was most evident within hierarchical interaction with subordinates. He recalled how the need to dominate subordinates was commonly expressed by superiors. Once a subordinate threatened to quit if he did not receive a raise in his salary to increase it to a level comparable to that of others. His manager swore Bob to secrecy and said, "Julian is very good." Bob believed that the correct inference was that subordinates should not be told by their superiors how valuable they were because such knowledge would give them power.

Bob thought also of how for one department head, hierarchy was more than simple power associated with a senior position. It had a raw element to it wherein his authority could not be questioned. He expressed the explicit desire that his subordinates fear him. His preference for primitive domination was extreme but such a desire for control over subordinates was not unusual in traditional LITEP culture. He actually asked Bob to do a survey feedback of his department to find out if his subordinates held a sufficient degree of fear for him.

They continued playing. Bob and Francisco were soundly beaten. They paid the obligatory "round fee" to Armando. As Armando walked to his car, Francisco said to Bob, "He'll do what he wants but I think he has a point about not pushing the council too hard. If he's replaced, the new general manager could throw everything out the window.

Also, I'm having a devil of a time getting the department heads to support the cross-functional teams."

Bob countered, "Yes, but we know Armando could make things happen if he wanted to and also I strongly believe that the corporate offices won't allow any new general manager, in the event Armando is transferred, to regress to the bad old days and drop his support of TQM."

BULLER | SCHULER

Managing Organizations and People

A Resource for Cases in Management, Organizational Behavior, and Human Resource Management

Abstract

This case raises the question of how an organization can "change the fabric" of its work force in order to take advantage of new opportunities that it sees in the business environment. How can this change be accomplished with minimal dysfunctional effects on the individual and the organization? This is the overall problem with which John Moore, Human Resource Manager, is faced. The problem is two-fold; where can he begin . . . how should he begin? The Company wishes to present a new image to its customers and to the business community. An essential precondition for this new image is a change in the "type" of individual who it feels can best help the Company meet its new objectives.

Peoples Trust Company

The Peoples Trust Company first opened its doors to the public on June 1, 1875, with a total salaried staff of eight members: a treasurer, a secretary, and six assistants (three of whom held the positions of day watchman, night watchman, and messenger). Located in a large, midwestern city, the original company had occupied the basement floor of a new five-story office building with an electric-bell system, steam heat, and steam-driven elevator.

During its early years, the Trust Company had concentrated its activities on providing vault services to its customers for the safekeeping of tangible items and securities. Management had been able to develop the reputation of being a highly conservative trust company that concentrated on a relatively small and select market of wealthy individuals from the local area. In the years following, the vault service had been retained as an accommodation to its customers, but the company's emphasis had slowly shifted from vault service to a wider range of banking and trust services.

Until the early 1900s, banking services had overshadowed trust services in terms of assets volume. Following the turn of the century, trust assets had begun to grow at an increasing rate. Over the years, the company had been able to achieve an impressive record

■ This case was prepared by Hrach Bedrosian, New York University. It is adapted here by Paul Buller and Randall Schuler and used with the permission of Hrach Bedrosian.

of sound and steady growth. According to a story often told in banking circles: "Peoples Trust was so conservative that they prospered even during the Depression!"

In 1973, with the appointment of a new president, a new era began for Peoples Trust Company. Between 1973 and 1988, trust assets under supervision rose by $145 million, while deposits increased by more than $20 million. The company entered 1993 with about $2 billion in trust assets and $90 million in savings deposits.

Accompanying this recent growth has been the company's desire to fashion a new image for itself. In 1989, Mr. Robert Toller assumed the presidency of Peoples Trust. In 1992, he remarked, ". . . it should be said that the old concept of a trust involving merely the regular payment of income and preservation of capital is largely obsolete." Accordingly, the Investment Division of the company had been expanded and strengthened. Similar changes had been effected in the Trust and Estate Administrative Group and other customer services. Among these were the improvement of accounting methods and procedures, the installation of electronic data processing systems, and complete renovation of the company's eight-floor building and facilities. Most recently, the company has extended its services into the field of management consulting. This had been acknowledged as a "pioneer" step for a banking institution. The president recently characterized the company as "an organization in the fiduciary business."

At the time these data were gathered, the company had a total of 602 employees. Of this number, 109 were in what is considered the "officer-group"[1] positions of the company. The company's relations with its employees over the years have been satisfactory. The Peoples Trust is generally recognized by city residents and those in suburban areas as a good place to work. The company hires most of its employees from the local area.

In the period before 1990, Peoples Trust had provided satisfactory advancement opportunities for its employees, and it had been possible for a young, high-school graduate who showed promise on the job to work his/her way up gradually to officer status. Graduates of banking institutions were also sought for employment with the company. Ordinarily individuals were considered eligible for promotion to the jobs above them after they had thoroughly mastered the details of their present positions.

Prior to 1990, the total staff of the company was small enough so that there was no need to prepare official organization charts or job descriptions. Virtually all of the employees knew each other on a first-name basis, and they were generally familiar with each other's area of job responsibility. New employees were rapidly able to learn "whom you had to go to for what."

In 1990, the company management called in an outside consultant to appraise its organizational structure and operations and to confer on the rapid expansion and diversification of banking services that the company had planned. The presence of the consultants and the subsequent preparation of organization charts and job descriptions reportedly "shook up a lot of people"—many feared loss of their jobs or, at least, substantial changes in the nature of work and assignments. However, there was little overt reaction among the officer-level employees in terms of turnover and/or other indices of unrest.

Over the years it had been the policy of the company to pay wages that were at least average or a little above the average paid by comparable banking organizations in the area. This, combined with favorable employee relations and the stable and prestigious nature of the work, resulted in a low turnover of personnel. The bulk of employee turnover occurred among the younger employees who filled clerical positions throughout the company's various departments.

Since 1990, the staffing picture at Peoples Trust has been shifting. Several changes have taken place in the top management of the company. By adding several new customer services, the company has altered the very nature of its business. This has resulted in a trend toward "professionalism" of many of the officer-level positions in that these positions now require individuals with higher levels of education and broader abilities. The impact of these changes on current employees has been a matter of concern to several executives in the company, particularly to Mr. John Moore, Manager of the Organization Planning and Human Resources Department. Mr. Moore described his picture of the situation to the researcher as follows.[2]

**Interview
with John
Moore—V.P.,
Organization
Planning and
Human
Resources**

Our problem here is one of a changing image and along with it the changing of people. As a trust company, we had no other ties with an individual's financial needs . . . we could only talk in terms of death. We wanted to be able to talk in terms of life—we got active in the investment-advisory business.

The old wealth around here is pretty well locked up, so we wanted to provide services to new and growing organizations and to individuals who are accumulating wealth. Our problem is one of reorientation. We used to provide one service for one customer. We now want to enter new ventures, offer new services, and attract new customers. The problem has become one of how to make the change . . . do we have the talent and the people to make the change?

We have a "band" of people (see Exhibits 1 and 2) in our organization . . . in the 35 to 50 age group who came in under the old hiring practices and ground rules. Given the new directions in which our company is moving and the changing job requirements, it's clear that, considering their current qualifications and capabilities, these individuals have nowhere to go. Some have been able to accept this, and this acceptance includes watching others move past them. Others have difficulty accepting it . . . a few have left . . . and we haven't discouraged anyone from leaving. For those who can't accept it, there is the problem of integrating their career strategy with ours. We've articulated our objectives clearly; now individuals need clarification of their own strategies.

As I see it, change caught up with these individuals. They had on-the-job training in their own areas, but that doesn't help them much to cope with the new demands. New functional areas are being melded on top of old ones. For example, marketing is new; so is information systems. They both require qualities that our existing employee staff didn't have.

To date, we have not approached any of these people in an individual way to discuss their problems with them. Our objectives are to further develop these people, but we'll first have to get the support of the department managers who supervise them.

We want to find ways to further develop human resources of the kind represented by this group through a variety of approaches. I am thinking here not only of formal job training in management development, but also of management techniques that would help individuals identify new kinds of qualifications or possible new standards of performance they must take into consideration in planning their own personal growth.

We also have to find ways to provide more opportunities for minorities and women in the organization, particularly at the officer level. Although Peoples Trust is not a federal contractor, we would like to be seen as and be an affirmative action employer and an organization where everyone has an equal chance for employment and promotion.

We have to change the conditioning of old times throughout the company. A recently hired MBA is now an officer. Years ago that couldn't have happened so rapidly. And not everyone here is in agreement that the appointment I just mentioned should have happened the way it did. We have to develop support in our company for the new recruiting image.

There are two things which really concern me most about this whole problem:

1. We have a problem in under-utilization of resources.
2. There is a problem that is presented to the growth and development of the company in having some of the individuals I have been discussing settled into key spots.

The company really bears the responsibility for the current situation as I described it. In addition, what this all means to me is that our human resource function may change considerably over the coming year.

After this interview with Mr. Moore, the researcher talked with other company executives to learn their views of the problems outlined by Mr. Moore. The findings from these interviews are presented below.

**Interview with
Fred Bellows—
Human
Resource
Planning**

Historically, we have been conservatively managed . . . you might say "ultra-conservatively." But now we want to change that image. Several years ago there was a revolution in top management. In 1989, Mr. Toller took over and brought in young people, many not from the banking field but from other types of business and consulting organizations. Our employment philosophy may be stated as follows: "We want above-

EXHIBIT 1
Peoples Trust
Company

Name	Age	Education	Date of Hire	Positions Held
Linda Horn	37	Two-year technical institute of business administration	1985	Messenger Clearance clerk Accounting clerk Unit head (working supervisor) Section head (supervisor)
Richard Gaul*	30	Two-year junior college program in 1977 in business administration	1987	Business machines operator Section head (supervisor) Operations officer
Fred James	35	B.A. degree, local university American Institute of Banking	1986	Loan clerk Teller Accounting unit head (working supervisor)
Fran Wilson*	35	One year at a local university	1991	Methods analyst Operations unit head (working supervisor) Systems programmer Property accounting department head
Martin Pfieffer*	32	Prep school	1987	Messenger Accounting clerk Section head (supervisor) Department head
James Klinger	38	B.A. degree from local university 1972	1982	Messenger Accounting clerk Records clerk Unit head (working supervisor) Administrative specialist
Karen Kissler*	35	B.A. degree from local university 1974 co-op program	1984	Messenger Real property specialist Assistant estate officer
Charles Ferris	42	Two-year junior college program in business administration American Institute of Banking	1972	Messenger Deposit accounting section Head (supervisor) Unit head (working supervisor)
William Jagger	54	High school	1959	Messenger Trust liaison clerk Accounting clerk Bookkeeping section head
Thomas Geoghigan*	42	Two-year junior college program in business administration	1979	Messenger Securities accountant Property custodian Office manager Assistant operations officer

*Officer

**EXHIBIT 2
Peoples Trust
Company
Organization Chart
(June 1993)**

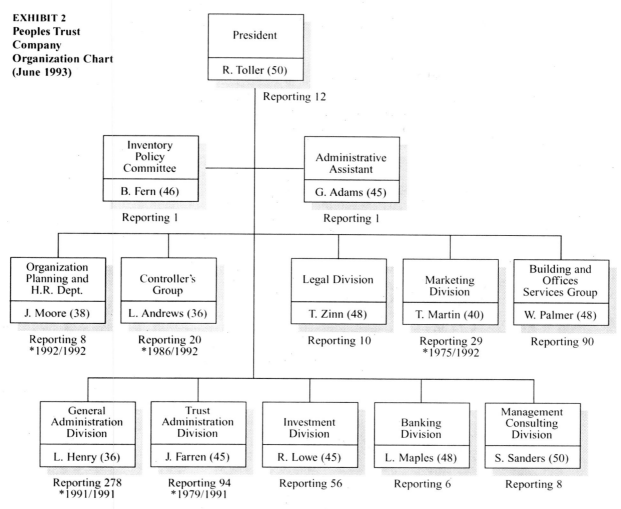

Note: Numbers in parentheses indicate manager's age. These are included for planning purposes only. Numbers below each position indicate number of subordinates.

*Indicates year in which manager joined the Company and year in which he/she assumed current position. For example, Mr. Larry Andrews joined Peoples Trust Company in 1986 and became Controller in 1992.

average people . . . for above-average pay . . . and we want to give them a chance to learn and grow and move with the organization." This applies mainly to those in whom we see management-level potential.

They are told in their employment interview that if they don't see opportunity with us, then they should leave. This is in contrast to the old philosophy that this is a secure place to work, that you can stay here by keeping your nose clean, and that you can sit and wait for pot luck to become a trust officer.

Many people are caught in this changing philosophy. A case in the Trust Administration Division is a good example. There we have an employee in a Grade 10 job who has been with the bank eight years. We just hired a new person out of college who we put in that same Grade 10. Now they're both at the same level, but they're entirely different people in terms of education, social background, etc.

Now the Head of our Trust Division bucks this sort of thing. She argues that we don't need all "stars" in the company. Yet, the president wants young, dynamic individuals who can develop and be developed. So I'm trying to get the Trust Division to define: What does the job really require?

We have a number of people with two years of accounting training who have been with the company anywhere from six to nine years. Under our old system they'd be okay, but under the new system they're not. They're not realistic about their future. Our problem is that we're being honest, but few are getting the message.

We bring in a new individual . . . ask others to train that person . . . and then promote that person over their heads. We have people whose jobs we could get done for a lot less money. When, if ever, do we tell them to go elsewhere?

Interview with Larry Andrews— Controller

There is no question but that there has been a complete revolution around here. In the past, we were in business to serve the community; to handle small accounts, and to help the small investor who needed investment service. Our motto was "help anyone who needs help." Our employees were geared to this kind of work orientation and felt at home with it. They could easily identify themselves with this sort of approach to doing business. Most people were quite comfortable; their personal goals coincided with the company goal.

But we found that we couldn't make money conducting this kind of business. So, we've had to extend our services to attract people who have money and can afford our service. Now the company goal has changed. For example, the Trust Department is now concerned with the management of property in general. The "dead man's bank" has become the "live people's service organization." So we've had to create a kind of snob appeal that too many of our people can't identify with or don't believe in.

Many problems have emerged from these changes. Before, individuals' knowledge of the details of their jobs was their greatest asset. They worked to develop that knowledge and protected it. Now—and I'm speaking of supervisory jobs—the important factor is to have some familiarity with the work but to be able to work with people; to get others to do the detail. Too many of our people still don't understand this. . . .

The route to the top is no longer clear. Over a five-year period this organization has changed. There have been reorganizations, new functions created, and some realignment of existing functions. Many who felt they had a clear line to something higher in the organization now find that that "something" isn't there anymore.

We've had lots of hiring-in at higher levels. Many old-timers have been bypassed. In some cases, the new, outside hirees came into jobs that never existed before, or were hired into a job that had previously existed, but which is now a "cut" above what it was before. What used to be a top job is now a second or third spot.

What we need now are people who are "professional managers"—by that I mean a supervisor versus a technical specialist. Years ago supervision could be concentrated in a few key individuals . . . but in the past five years we've grown 20 percent to 30 percent and have a management hierarchy. A person used to be able to grow up as a technical specialist and develop managerial skills secondarily.

To a small extent it's a matter of personality too. We have a new president, and what is acceptable to him differs from what was acceptable to his predecessor. There's a new mix of personal favoritism that goes along with the new vogue. Technical specialists are "low need" as far as the company is concerned. I estimate we now have about 30 people in this category in officer-level jobs.

Interview with Tom Martin— Marketing Division Head

There have been many changes over the past six years. Mr. Toller took a look at the organization . . . and then hired a consultant to do an organization study. It was sort of an outside stamp of approval.

His hope was to move some of the dead wood . . . the senior people who were past their peak and didn't represent what the company wanted anymore in its managerial and officer staff. Few of these individuals have the capacity to change, and for others it may already be too late to change. Many had leveled off in their development long before these changes came about, and the changes just made it more apparent. Early retirement has been given to some of those over sixty. Others remained as titular head of their departments, but in essence report to a younger person who is really running the department.

Banking used to be a soft industry . . . you were hired and never fired. If you were a poor performer, you were given a lousy job that you could stay at. No one was ever called in and told to shape up. The pay was so poor it attracted people who wanted to work in a sheltered area, and they were satisfied to try and build a career in that area. So it was a job with low pay, high prestige, and some opportunity.

Our biggest problem is to convince people that they are not technicians anymore, that they are to supervise their people and work to develop them. Apparently, for many older individuals, and younger ones too, this is an impossible assignment. They can do the jobs themselves, but having anyone else do it in any other way runs against their grain.

If our rate of growth in staffing over the next 10 years is as fast as the previous 10 years, I'm afraid we can only absorb about 50 percent of our most promising people.

Interview with Jane Farren—Trust Administration Division Head

We have several people for whom there is very little opportunity anymore. We just don't see any potential in these people. There are about 15 of them who are in their 40s and are really not capable of making any independent decisions. We're trying to get them to see other opportunities . . . both inside and outside the company. For example, our Real Estate group was big in the 1960s and 1970s. We're trying to make it important again, and there may be some opportunities in that area.

To give you an idea of the problem we're faced with: One individual is really a personality problem. He's an attorney but he can't get along with others. He wants people to come to him, he focuses on detail too much, and he has great difficulty in telling others what to do and how to do it. He has to do the job all by himself.

Another individual: We gave him a section to supervise but he really hasn't measured up. But, he was the president's pet. I suppose we'll let him continue on . . . he's 57 . . . and then retire him early.

Interview with Mr. L. Henry—General Administration Division

The company has been undergoing basic change. In the past, if people demonstrated technical competence they were promoted, and that was fine while the company was a small, stable group, and everyone knew what the other was thinking. But then, many in the senior group began to retire. With this "changing of the guard" and the growth of the company, many of us have lost communication with our counterparts. Many of us are new in this field, new to this company, and, of course, new to each other. But we recognize this, so half the communication problem is solved. In a sense, we're not constrained by "how it was done before."

Endnotes

1. Membership in the officer group is determined by an employee's being legally empowered to represent the company in a transaction.
2. Mr. Moore drew from his files a list of 10 individuals who he felt were representative of the group whose lack of appropriate experience or qualifications created a road block to their future development and advancement with the company. These individuals are described in Exhibit 1.

BULLER | SCHULER

Managing Organizations and People

A Resource for Cases in Management, Organizational Behavior, and Human Resource Management

Abstract

Forest Products Company (FPC), of Weyerhaueser Company, is faced with increased domestic and global competition. Competitors are becoming more specialized and flexible in meeting the needs of their customers. Charley Bingham, CEO, and the top management team of FPC have decided that a massive reorganization is needed in the company. However, implementation of this reorganization is hampered due to resistance and lack of skills on the part of many middle managers. Horace Parker, director of executive development at FPC, suggests that the successful transformation of the company will depend on how well the company supports the reorganization with changes in its culture, skill base, team orientation, and leadership style.

Seeing the Forest and the Trees

The changing face of competition, both domestic and global, was looking directly into the window of the headquarters of the Forest Products Company (FPC) of the Weyerhaeuser Corporation in Seattle. It was a face that reflected the trend away from the large firm, commodity lumber business and toward the small mills that tailor-made products to meet the demands of their customers. Interestingly, these small mills owed their existence, in large part, to the sale of machinery by the larger firms when they were faced with the depressed housing market in the early 1980s. As a consequence of being able to buy this machinery at depressed prices, these small, nonunion, owner-operated, entrepreneurial, customer-oriented mills were able to not only be the most market-oriented but also the lowest cost operations.

Deciding that going out of business was not an alternative, Charley Bingham, the CEO of FPC, suggested that something needed to he done, preferably sooner than later. Together, the top dozen managers decided that a massive reorganization was called for, accompanied by a radical change in strategy. According to Bingham, the change in strategy went something like this:

Approximately 80 percent of our sales dollars in 1982 represented products sold as commodities. By 1995 we resolved that we must reverse the proportions.

1

The massive reorganization mirrored that being done by the headquarters. The headquarters decided to decentralize dramatically. The three operating units, of which FPC was one, were given free reign on how to do their business. Given this scenario, Bingham and his top team decided it needed to create an organization capable of acting and responding just like their competitors. Thus, they created 200 profit centers with each center being largely responsible for its own bottom line.

This restructuring soon proved to be only a step in the right direction. The ability of the organization to implement its new strategy was being undermined by the pervasive poor morale. In addition, many middle managers, those needed to actually carry out the change, were pessimistic about the possibility of sustained future success. Silently, they even questioned their own ability to operate the profit centers.

With insights from Horace Parker, director of executive development at FPC, the rest of the top team came to realize that there would have to be a total transformation of the organization: the corporate culture, knowledge base, skill levels, style of leadership, and team orientation would all have to change, for all employees. With 18,000 employees across the U.S., Parker wasn't sure where to start. The others said they would help, but Horace had to tell them what to do. Horace, of course, is waiting to hear what you have to tell him.

Discussion Questions for "Seeing the Forest and the Trees"

In responding to this case, it would help students to refer to the reading, R.S. Schuler, "Strategic Human Resource Management: Linking the People with the Strategic Needs of the Business," *Organizational Dynamics* (Summer 1992): 18–32. To narrow down your analysis, focus on those aspects most closely related to management and executive development.

1. What are the business objectives here that Horace must use to focus his activities?
2. What are his new management and executive development objectives?
3. How should he go about addressing the implications of these objectives for management and executive development?
4. In addition to management and executive development, what other organizational changes are needed to support this transformation?

BULLER | SCHULER

Managing Organizations and People

A Resource for Cases in Management, Organizational Behavior,
and Human Resource Management

Abstract

This case highlights the strategic importance of including the best people from around the world in a multinational corporation's senior leadership. The setting is Bestfoods International, one of the largest global food companies. The case describes the philosophy and approach of the CEO, Dick Shoemate, and of Laura Brody, a senior HR manager who strongly believes in the strategic function of Human Resources. Along with her bosses, Dick Bergeman, the senior VP of HR, and Shoemate, Brody is faced with the challenge of increasing business competitiveness by increasing the number of women in leadership positions around the world and making headway on an issue that is perceived differently in various parts of the world. Brody frames this challenge as an organizational change effort and is herself a skillful change agent.

Women and Global Leadership at Bestfoods

Laura Brody had just finished analyzing the progress she'd made in her first two years as Director of Diversity and Development for Bestfoods International, formerly known as CPC. Brody is a stylish woman in her forties, possessed of a droll sense of humor. She had begun working for Bestfoods ten years earlier in Management Development. The position provided Brody the opportunity to meet and develop good relationships with many of the managers who were identified as having senior management potential and who were now in senior executive positions. Brody spent eight years coordinating the company's well-respected annual Senior Management Development Program. The program, taught by world-famous professors, was for managers who had been tapped to become leaders. She also had helped organize Bestfood's global action-learning programs (where knowledgeable people were brought together from all parts of the company to tackle strategic, systemwide issues). These programs were often held at Arrowwood, an off-site corporate conference center just outside New York City.

Brody came to Bestfoods in 1988 and was surprised to find that the company seemed to be far behind most leading companies in promoting diversity, particularly in the company's proportion of women and minorities. She found herself revisiting what it was like

■ By Joyce S. Osland, San Jose State University, and Nancy J. Adler, McGill University. The development of this case was funded by the CIBER program at the University of Washington under a grant from the U.S. Department of Education.

1

to work with senior men who had limited experience working alongside high-level professional women. Corporate efforts to date had been limited primarily to diversity awareness training. When Brody was asked to take over the diversity function in 1995, she wanted to be sure that real, substantive change was possible. Brody explained to her prospective boss, Dick Bergeman, Senior Vice President of Human Resources, that she needed to be assured of the company's sincerity and willingness to support progress and changes in this area. Bergeman is an engaging, well-respected 22-year veteran with Bestfoods who spearheaded the transformation of Human Resources from an administrative function to an integral part of the global strategy team. He replied, "I can't tell you I will automatically agree to everything you propose, but I will agree that it is your job to make change happen. And if I say 'no' the first time, then it is your job to figure out a different way to approach it or structure it and come back at me again and again and again." Since Brody was not expecting "carte blanche" up front, she was sufficiently reassured by his response and took the job. Brody's diagnosis of her new job was that the company supported diversity, but there were few specific strategies in place for her to implement. She saw her position as "a double-edged sword."

It was a wonderful opportunity to stand out on my own, set an agenda and implement it. As this was a senior position, I was expected to establish the goals and strategies for the company-wide diversity function. If I was successful, I could be well positioned for future career progress. If not, like my two predecessors, I might have to look for future career growth elsewhere.

Bestfoods has had a diversity function since 1989. It evolved from traditional EEO[1] compliance reporting and had two previous directors, a male Hispanic and a male African American. Unlike Brody, both were disadvantaged by not having an established network throughout the organization, since one was brought in from outside the company and the other had experience only in the U.S. division in labor relations. Brody suspected that the climate had not really been ripe for change in the area of diversity until the last few years. Another advantage Brody enjoyed was the fit between her personality and the challenges of this particular job. In the early years of her career, she had received feedback that she was too direct and not easily deterred from pursuing a certain path. Brody was counseled to "go along to get along." Characteristics that had formerly been seen as weaknesses, however, were now perceived as her strengths.

In my current job, I am expected to be the conscience of the organization. Like an Old Testament prophet, I am frequently expected to preach fire and brimstone, nudging the company in a certain direction even though they may not want to go that way. For once my style and the type of person I am fit exactly with what my job demands and what my boss expects me to do. I love my job! As I told Dick Bergeman, "I can't believe you pay me to make trouble—I would have done that for free!"

Company Background

Bestfoods is among the largest global food companies, with annual sales in 1998 of $8.4 billion. Their most well-known brands include: *Hellmann's* and *Best Foods* condiments and dressings; *Mazola* corn oil and margarine; *Knorr* soups, sauces, and bouillon; *Skippy* peanut butter; *Thomas'* English muffins; and *Entenmanns's* baked goods. Bestfoods also has a catering division that is known as *Caterplan* in most global markets. Bestfoods has operations in more than 60 countries and markets products in 110 countries. The 93-year-old company is well positioned internationally with over 90 years of operating experience in Europe, 70 years in Latin America, and more than 68 years in Asia. Although headquartered in the United States, the company earns 60 percent of its revenues from non-U.S. sources. The company projects future growth to continue to come primarily from outside the mature markets of North America and Western Europe. Africa, Asia, Eastern Europe, the Middle East, Latin America, and the countries of the former Soviet Union are projected to lead increases in twenty-first century revenue. At present the company has four geographic divisions: Europe, North America, Asia, and Latin America.

Bestfoods has a highly decentralized structure, which gives general managers and local management the autonomy to adapt and modify changes suggested by corporate headquarters. One of the company's strengths is its global strategic vision combined with a consistent local focus and decision making. CEO Dick Shoemate appreciates the difficult balance between giving the local divisions power to make their own decisions and integrating these units into a coherent whole. "It's our strength, but it's also a challenge when we try to make changes."

The company's vision (see Appendix A) is to be the best international food company in the world by building on the organization's core businesses, values, and strengths. Bestfoods has three global *core businesses*: savory products (e.g., soups, bouillon, sauces), dressings, and catering. The company's *core values* are:

- *Growing* (financial success, business growth, people development, and diversity)
- *Caring* (adherence to the law and highest moral and ethical standards, respect for individual worth and ability, satisfying customer and consumer needs, safe workplaces, and protecting the environment)
- *Sharing* (valuing teamwork, internal and external partnering, learning from experience, and transferring learning with pride)
- *Daring* (courage, candor, conviction, pioneering and leadership, quick decision making, and aggressiveness in seizing new markets)

The company's identified *core strengths* are:

- A unique culture combining global strategic vision with local focus, decision making, and action; and
- A proven ability to transfer and use products, skills, technology, and people from all parts of the world.

To best link employee actions with the company's vision, Bestfoods uses a strategic performance measurement system called the Balanced Scorecard. "The Balanced Scorecard provides a framework that helps shape our activities and measure our performance in four critically important areas (customer satisfaction, people development, business practices, and innovation and learning) which together result in a fifth critical area, financial performance, the ultimate measure of the best."[2] Instead of one uniform global measurement system, each division, affiliate, department, and functional group within the company creates its own Balanced Scorecard that identifies the key activities, or "strategic drivers," that will move its particular business closer to the company's goals. Nevertheless, the CEO may announce specific new goals to add to the Corporate Balanced Scorecard at WorldTeam Meetings, which the company holds about every three years. At the World-Team meetings, approximately 150 of the most senior executives from around the world spend several days together focusing on strategic issues, sharing innovative implementation plans, and learning together. The WorldTeam meetings are another way to coordinate the far-flung global company.

Dick Shoemate is chairman, president, and chief executive officer of Bestfoods. He joined the company in 1962 and held positions in manufacturing, finance, and business management in the consumer foods and corn refining businesses. Shoemate was president of the Corn Refining division before assuming the corporate presidency in 1988. Unlike many CEOs, Shoemate is not only bright but unassuming and down to earth. He is both approachable and an excellent listener. Shoemate is equally impressive and comfortable dealing with board members as with the 60 children of employees he addressed on "Take Your Child to Work Day." Shoemate, in his late 50s, wants one of the marks he leaves on Bestfoods to be increased diversity worldwide and at the most senior levels.

Diversity at Bestfoods

Of the corporation's 44,000 employees, two-thirds currently work outside of the United States. In the U.S. division, Bestfoods has 10 to 15 percent more minorities than the industry norm, but 5 to 10 percent fewer women. Although Bestfoods has been known as a company where people spent most of their career, Brody found that, like at many companies, a disproportionate number of women and minorities leave Bestfoods within their first 3 to 5 years. Historically, women at Bestfoods tended to hit the "glass ceiling" at the middle-management level. Women have succeeded primarily in staff positions, such as the corporate legal department, which has the highest representation of women. There are numerous entry-to-midlevel women in Human Resources, but the division-level executives are all male. There are women in marketing who have attained midlevel jobs and some who have been promoted into senior-level positions, but only one woman has successfully made the leap from marketing to a general manager position. The usual career path that men followed in Bestfoods to become senior executives has gone from general manager positions to operating division presidents to corporate officers. Women have remained a small percentage of the candidate pool for senior executive jobs, because they tended to be scarce in the usual career pipelines to the top-line positions and high-level positions outside the United States.

Not surprisingly, the 1997 employee survey in the United States showed that minorities and women perceived less opportunity for advancement and career development than did whites or men. Similarly, they perceived their performance to be less linked to compensation than did whites or men. It surprised many at the company, however, that men ranked "workload and pace interfere with work/life balance" as the #1 issue among the five diversity-related issues they would like the company to address. Although women ranked this issue last at #5, the work/life integration issue cut across gender and hierarchy. For example, while female administrative staff might worry about making it to a day care center by 5 or 6 P.M., some senior men grumbled that their wives were "threatening to divorce them" if they missed one more family event.

Retention analyses revealed that at every management level, women and minorities had more turnover than males and whites. As a result of these findings, Brody's objective within the United States was to have better retention and development of both women and minorities.

When Brody and her staff did a global analysis of female employees, they discovered that 15 percent of the employees who had been designated as "high potential" were women. They also found that there were more U.S. women in management positions when compared to other regions, although Europe appointed the first woman as a country general manager. Among the approximately 264 participants who attended the Senior Management Development Programs from 1988 to 1998, the company sent only 15 female managers. It wasn't until 1998 that a senior female manager attended who was not an American. Brody knew that attitudes towards promoting women varied widely throughout the company, from extremely supportive to indifferent—or even chauvinistic in a few cases. For the most part, she believed that although managers were well intentioned, they were uncertain about how and what improvements could be made regarding career advancement for women. Texaco's former CEO was sitting on Bestfood's Board of Directors when Texaco was fined $176 million for racial discrimination in 1996. Not only was Bestfoods aware that it never wanted to find itself in a similar position, the company was committed to advancing diversity as a key competitive element in its overall business strategy.

Bestfoods has a diverse Board of Directors. Of their 14 Directors, 2 are female CEOs, 1 is an African American CEO, 7 are white U.S. American male CEOs, and 4 are male CEOs from other countries. Bestfoods has 3 female corporate officers, 1 each from manufacturing, marketing, and public relations. By 1997, 14 percent of the members of the Board of Directors, 15 percent of the corporate officers, and 13 percent of directors and vice-presidents were women.

The Reasons Behind the Figures

When Brody and her staff ponder the barriers that women face at Bestfoods, she thinks some attitudes and behaviors may be due to generational rather than gender issues. For example, most of the corporate officers are in their late fifties and early sixties and have stay-at-home wives. They have never watched their wives struggle to climb the corporate ladder or juggle the competing demands of work and home life. Nor have their own careers been affected by the demands of a dual-career marriage. As a result, Brody wonders how well some of the senior male executives really understand the barriers or challenges today's women often face.

For example, a common complaint among women is that men have the luxury of coming to work early and staying late if they want to attempt to impress the boss in this fashion. Because many women are responsible for dropping off and picking up children at school or day care and then supervising them at home while preparing dinner, they have to work more regular hours. This does not mean the women work fewer hours or less hard. However, to the extent that the corporate culture values time spent in the office (rather than actual time spent working and achieving results) as an indicator of loyalty and promotability, working mothers (and some fathers) are at a disadvantage. One division manager has the night watchman keep track of the time employees leave at the end of the day; accurately or not, his employees interpret this as a clear signal that, "If you want to get ahead, you must work late."

Another factor that could be hindering development and ultimately retention is that the company has few women at high enough levels to be selected for senior management development opportunities. The corporation's senior-level management training programs are offered to senior managers who the company has already promoted up the hierarchy. Few women attain that level and therefore receive little in the way of company-sponsored, formal management and career development opportunities, or the executive-level exposure and visibility that such opportunities provide.

Diversity as a Strategic Issue

While the number of senior women, corporate officers, and board members at Bestfoods is respectable when compared to many companies, neither Brody nor Shoemate think it is adequate to support the future they envision for Bestfoods. Consumer foods, not unlike many other industries, has become increasingly competitive; only the companies with top talent and top brands survive. Moreover, whereas many consumer foods companies used to be able to operate as loose confederations of fairly autonomous country operations, global competition is now forcing all members of the industry to more closely coordinate their worldwide operations.

To succeed in such an environment, Bestfoods needs to attract and retain the best talent available globally and have local employees from each country in which they operate reflect the consumer base. With women making more than 80 percent of purchasing decisions for Bestfoods' products, the company will suffer if it fails to understand women's perspectives, needs, and decision-making criteria. Shoemate sees promoting women into senior management positions not primarily as a matter of diversity but rather as an issue of strategic competitive advantage. On numerous occasions, he has explicitly expressed his commitment to developing the most highly talented women and men from around the world.

We believe that one of Bestfoods' unique competitive strengths is a management team that delivers outstanding performance in the local marketplace and also works together to build the "Best International Food Company in the World." . . . We actively seek to identify and to develop high performing Bestfoods' managers throughout the company, including men and women from all countries and ethnic backgrounds.

Shoemate knows, however, that words are not enough to change an organization. He personally appointed all three of Bestfoods' female corporate officers during his tenure as CEO. Nevertheless, he wants to see more rapid progress on the goal of including more women in senior management and leadership. He made a note to himself to discuss with Brody what form this change should take at Bestfoods.

Managing Change at Bestfoods

No CEO can simply mandate change in a highly decentralized multinational that values local autonomy. Focusing on diversity further complicates change efforts because it is sometimes viewed as a "U.S. issue." Within some cultures, equity among women and men is not a well-publicized concern, and diversity is locally defined to refer to other groupings within the population. Therefore, for companies headquartered in the United States, the leadership has to tread carefully. Both within the food industry and within Bestfoods, employees tend to work their way up, and executives brought in from the outside often do not adjust to the informal norms and values of the company. This practice has the advantage of providing continuity and a strong organizational culture, but the downside is less new blood and fewer innovations. Bestfoods' U.S. employees tend to reflect "Middle

America,"—conservative, traditional people with "old-fashioned American values." Brody affectionately describes the company as a Norman Rockwell painting. While the pace and pressure has picked up in recent years, it is neither an industry nor a company with a prior reputation for being "fast-paced." Brody describes Bestfoods' culture as traditional, conservative, polite, "gentlemanly," and non-confrontational. While the politeness contributes to the pleasant relations Bestfoods is noted for, it also makes face-to-face confrontations rare; criticism and dissent tend to go underground. The emphasis upon tradition makes change slow and risky. Some executives are leery of being blamed if changes they initiate don't work. As a result, some managers use the "drip method" of change— small changes over time that eventually add up to progress.

While individuals may approach change somewhat cautiously, Bestfoods has developed a very effective group method for taking advantage of opportunities and resolving problems that affect all divisions. When the global action-learning task forces come together, they analyze situations and, towards the end of the meeting, present their recommendations to top management. The CEO and his direct reports immediately consider each recommendation and respond to the task force before the meeting ends.

As a result of all these factors, Brody's strategy has been to focus on getting the decision makers "on board" and then making incremental changes. Her style is to plant the seeds of ideas and provide information and options to the executive team so they can begin thinking about diversity more broadly and from different perspectives.

Brody's Philosophy on Human Resource Development

Brody has a very clear idea of the role of Human Resources, as seen in the following description of her job.

As an HR executive, I do not see myself as merely an ombudsperson for employees. I have always seen HR as a critical management responsibility. There are several aspects of HR in which one is required to be the conscience of the organization. I spent many of my formative years as a consultant working with clients on diagnostic and implementation issues to help make organizations more effective. So my focus is more proactive and action-oriented, trying to create programs that lead to long-term change rather than compliance. My goal has always been to "make a difference" at work. I've learned that everything has to be linked to the business. Line management has to have an itch they want to scratch, and it's my responsibility to make them feel that itch—whether they know it or not. So I don't see HR as an administrative staff function, but as an organization development function that needs to work with line managers. Although people like me are sometimes seen as mavericks, I think you have to understand the needs of the business, create effective relationships with line management, and bend rules to solve problems. Traditionally, HR has a reputation for writing the policies and then telling people why they can't *do things.*

Brody went on to explain that the traditional HR roles are switched at Bestfoods. In most companies, corporate HR establishes policy and procedures and then administers them, while the operating divisions creatively try to bend the rules to meet the needs of local line managers. At Bestfoods, HR policies are frequently developed and implemented at the divisional level, while the corporate group often has more freedom to experiment and be innovative.

Laying the Groundwork for Change

Bestfoods already had a Diversity Advisory Council (DAC) when Brody took over. It continues today and is composed of 14 members—senior executives in the U.S. business, corporate staff, and the vice-presidents of Human Resources from each unit. The Council is chaired by the CEO and facilitated by Brody. Her predecessor met with the Council a few times a year, and their primary achievement was coming to consensus on a common diversity training program for senior managers throughout North America. By contrast, Brody adopted a team-building approach with the Council. She knew they had to establish a common vision, so Brody spent almost her entire first year working with them to craft a vision and to agree upon a definition of diversity. Brody worked to ensure that Bestfoods defined diversity very broadly (see Appendix B) for two reasons: (1) to avoid excluding white males and (2) so that other countries would not see diversity only in light of U.S. EEO requirements. The Council also developed a Balanced Scorecard for diversity that mirrors the Corporate Balanced Scorecard (see Appendix B). As Brody states,

In corporate life, you only make progress on things you measure, and you only measure things that are important—such as operating income, profitability, ROI, ROA, and market share. These things are all measured and tracked very, very frequently. So in terms of making progress on diversity, the measurable goal was increased career opportunity— promotions, salary levels, and representation at senior management levels—and not the "nice-to-haves," like calendars with every ethnic holiday posted or "feeling included"; it was in fact about being included. I preached that you could not have an effective diversity function without, at a minimum, having effective equal employment policies and actions in place.

Brody and the Council also linked diversity to the corporate vision.

It's very simple. We could not be the best food company in the world if we weren't recruiting and retaining the talented women and minorities who make up large proportions of current MBA programs and who bring different perspectives and experiences from those of whites and men. Since the number of minorities we have is fairly good, one of the first things I did was to focus on the representation of women, an area in which our numbers were not so good. I had industry measures to justify doing this. I also had my own personal experience in the organization and the frustration at seeing a lot of diversity awareness training going on but not seeing many tangible results coming out of it.

Consistent with the CEO's perspective, Brody sees diversity as a business issue and insists on promoting it as such. She does not see her job as reengineering society or changing societal attitudes; her primary focus is on behaviors and practices that will benefit the company. Brody's team building with the Diversity Advisory Council paid off. After about two years, the Council wanted to raise the bar on diversity and chose to go forward in a proactive way. To learn what leading companies were doing about leveraging workforce inclusion to increase their business competitiveness, Brody invited outside practitioners who were involved in best-practice efforts to make presentations to the Council. She also gathered a variety of benchmarking and best-practice studies and reports for Council members.

In addition to the groundwork Brody was laying with the Diversity Advisory Council, she established a program called Cultural Connections, an employee-driven education and awareness program, and a peer coaching and mentoring program for new hires called SOS, "Sponsoring Our Success." Brody's new initiatives complemented Bestfoods' long history of involvement with INROADS (Bergeman is on the Board of Directors for the northern New Jersey chapter). INROADS is an internship program for high school and college-age minority students that had proven successful for the company in recruiting top talent, as many interns later joined Bestfoods. Brody's department, which consisted of one other professional and a secretary, coordinated entry-level diversity awareness training, sexual harassment prevention training, and diversity training for the most senior 300 managers and executives in the company. At her suggestion, Shoemate sent out an open letter to all employees in 1997 regarding the company's diversity initiative (see Appendix B) and another "state of diversity" letter to U.S. employees in 1998 (see Appendix C). Brody's job is made easier by both Shoemate's and Bergeman's sincere belief in the strategic importance of diversity.

While these efforts have been successful, Brody knows that still more has to be done, and she too would like to pick up the pace of change. Among others, she has been considering three alternatives that might have an even larger impact.

1. Conduct a survey that would compare the differences in perception between women and men regarding development and retention in the company and more clearly identify the unique barriers women face.
2. Hold a meeting modeled after the global action-learning programs, to tackle the problem of retaining and promoting women.
3. Offer a leadership development program for midlevel women managers.

One day Brody was in Shoemate's office getting his signature on some letters. He was in the midst of reviewing the 1997 employee survey data and said, "Laura, if you could do one thing to improve things for women in this company, what would it be?" Brody knew this was a big opportunity. The mental rolodex in her head started spinning as she quickly considered a variety of options she'd been pondering. Brody took a deep breath and pitched her best idea.

I really cannot speak for all women. But if I were the CEO, what I would want to do is to engage a significant number of women in this dialogue. What about sponsoring a global forum for high potential and senior women representing all the businesses from around the world and bringing them to Arrowwood? They could help us better understand the environment and culture in the company and how it impacts women. We could do what we always do with a business issue that needs to be driven from the center—have an action-learning program with outside experts to design and facilitate it. We could receive both information and recommendations from participants on how to proceed and make progress, and we could also do some leadership training at the same time.

Shoemate asked a few probing questions and suggested she flesh it out with Bergeman. Brody and Bergeman prepared a position paper that Bergeman discussed with the Corporate Strategy Council (CSC) at its next meeting in April. The CSC is composed of the six most senior corporate officers who are responsible for the four geographic divisions, the baking business, and the corporate staff. The CSC immediately approved the forum idea. Shoemate requested that it take place no later than the end of July. That meant Brody had only 90 days to organize her company's first-ever Women's Global Leadership Forum.

Brody and her staff dove into preparations, and the plans began to fall into place. The question that continued to nag Brody was how to ensure that the Forum resulted in real organizational change. She worried that participants might leave feeling good, with raised expectations about what the company would do for women, only to be disillusioned if the recommended changes didn't materialize afterwards. As it turned out, senior management shared Brody's concern about unrealistically heightened expectations. Some of them also wondered how they could participate and interact with the attendees so that neither group would feel threatened.

Forum Invitations and Reactions

To create a comprehensive list of senior and high potential women, Brody solicited nominations from all division presidents, which she personally reviewed along with the corporate high-potential lists and succession plans. Next, the CEO sent a letter to all six members of the Corporate Strategy Council describing the Forum and requesting that they rank order their nominees. As Bestfoods does with its Senior Management Development Program, the company allocated spaces at the Women's Global Leadership Forum according to the relative size of each division and geographical area to ensure balanced representation. Brody's goal was to invite 50 participants, of which at least half were to come from outside the United States. As an early indication of the high level of support, every division requested additional spaces. Brody responded by increasing the number of participants to 60 and choosing 10 of these as facilitators for small group sessions. Shoemate personally sent a letter of invitation to each participant. Fifty-five women from 25 countries were able to accept the invitation.

Brody knew that merely asking the division presidents to identity their high potential women, thereby adding them to the recognized and visible talent pool for the company's future leadership, was a significant intervention in and of itself. "Even if we'd never held the Forum, it was a good exercise for the senior executives to stop and consider how many highly talented women managers they had and where they were in the company. One president promoted a woman a few months earlier than he had planned to as a result of thinking about whom he wanted to nominate for the Forum!"

The reactions to the Forum announcement were, for the most part, very positive. Several people commented that this was one of the most exciting and forward-looking initiatives the company had ever tackled. Many women were gratified to be identified as participants. Not all women, however, reacted positively. Some senior women, primarily Americans, worried that attending an all-women forum might encourage others to think their success was owed primarily to their status as women rather than to their competence; they had no desire to be at the forefront of women's issues. Some women who were not invited, from secretaries to Directors, felt excluded from yet another "private club." Some invitees were also concerned about the potentially negative reactions from their male colleagues and bosses, including worrying about the likelihood of a male backlash.

There were sporadic dismissive and skeptical comments by both men and women who doubted that the Forum would result in anything more than a "bitch session." One senior male manager told his female subordinate, "Have a good time at the koffee-klatch" as she left for the Forum. Some men complained of discrimination because they were not invited. However, other men thought the Forum was long overdue and emphasized their support. Brody kept Shoemate and Bergeman informed of the resistance she encountered so there would not be any surprises regarding this controversial program among the senior managers. At one point, Brody sent Shoemate a note saying, "You know how women get crabby and lose their sense of humor when they're left out? Well, guess what—it seems that men also get crabby and lose their sense of humor when they are excluded!" Given her strict deadline, Brody didn't feel she had enough time to deal with the backlash in depth, other than being aware of it and trying to deflect it with humor and an ongoing reiteration of the CEO's rationale and goals for championing the forum.

Planning the Forum

As far as Brody was aware, no other company had ever held a global meeting for its most senior and high-potential women with the intent of opening a dialogue on global leadership and organizational change. There were no models to follow, so she began searching for an outside consultant to help design the Forum. After some difficulty finding someone with expertise on both women's leadership and international issues, she hired Dr. Nancy J. Adler, an international management professor and consultant. To get a feel for the organization, Adler interviewed Shoemate, Bergeman, all corporate officers including the three female corporate officers, and one of the female board members. She and Brody began designing a program to fit Bestfoods' needs and to meet the Forum's goals:

- Increase the global competitiveness of Bestfoods;
- Develop the global leadership skills of Bestfoods' most highly talented and senior women;
- Create an internal network among Bestfoods' women leaders to facilitate their global effectiveness; and
- Develop both global and local recommendations for enhancing Bestfoods' ability to support the career advancement and success of an increasing number of highly talented and senior women.

Adler suggested hiring another consultant to conduct cross-cultural training for the group facilitators and to present an organization change and leadership framework at the Forum itself. Brody hired Dr. Joyce Osland, a management professor and long-term expatriate with extensive experience in organization development consulting and designing leadership workshops for female executives in Latin America. Brody wanted consultants with expatriate experience and knowledge for two reasons. First, companies frequently identify a lack of international experience as a reason for not promoting women to senior positions. Second, given the increasing global competition in the industry, Brody was convinced that senior women would be much better positioned if they had more "cross-border" and international experience.

Early in the process, Brody warned Bergeman that the cost of the program would be higher than the original estimate. His response was, "Spend whatever you need to put on an outstanding program." Bergeman was aware that some people who were ambivalent about the program might try to find reasons for it to fail. He therefore insisted that everything about the program be first rate. While Bergeman remained available when Brody wanted his support or advice, he allowed her to take full responsibility for the program.

Pre-Forum Survey

Brody's team carried out a survey-feedback process aimed at producing data that would serve as a baseline and cause people to reexamine their thinking about the opportunities and barriers for women's career advancement. Brody was especially interested in surveying both senior women and men, so both groups' views would be visible at the Forum. She developed a survey modeled after the Catalyst[3] report, "Women in Corporate Leadership: Progress & Prospects."[4] A primary purpose of the survey was to determine whether there were significant differences of opinion between the views of women and men in Bestfoods regarding individual and corporate strategies that would most benefit women, common reasons preventing women from advancing, beliefs about women, and personal experiences in the company. Brody sent the survey to all corporate officers, the 125 most senior executives who were being invited to this year's WorldTeam meeting, and the 60 women who had been invited to the Forum. The response rate for the survey was 70 percent. Brody understood quite clearly that for any significant organizational change to occur, the senior levels of management, almost exclusively male, had to be part of a coalition for change. For that to happen, they had to be included on the front end as part of the overall organizational change process. Brody sent the survey results to all the survey participants after the Forum.

The survey data revealed the following key points:

1. Although women and men agreed on most of the barriers perceived to be inhibiting women's career advancement (women's lack of mobility for international assignments and lack of both general management and line experience), the women reported a number of barriers that appear to have been invisible to the men:
   - Senior men's discomfort with ambitious women;
   - Senior men's negative stereotyping and preconceptions of women; and
   - Senior men's difficulty in reporting to a woman.
2. While women and men agreed on the three most important strategies for women's career success at Bestfoods (consistently exceeding performance expectations, gaining line management experience, and seeking difficult and high visibility assignments), they disagreed on other key strategies.
   - The majority of women believed that they had to "develop a style that men are comfortable with" in order to succeed, whereas men ranked this strategy next to last in terms of importance.
   - Women were more likely than men to believe they had to develop a relationship with an influential mentor in order to succeed.
   - More men than women stressed the importance of gaining international experience.
   - None of the men stated that they would consider changing companies to get ahead while 14 percent of the women stated that they would consider leaving Bestfoods for another company.
3. Men and women agreed on the five most important corporate strategies that would benefit women (more assignments managing people; include more women on divisional and global strategic task forces; include more women in the Senior Management Development Program; hold managers more accountable for identifying, developing, and advancing high potential women; and include a higher percentage of women in succession plans). However, women placed greater importance on each of these corporate strategies than did their male colleagues.
4. It was noteworthy that both women and men perceived the barriers facing women to be greater than the reality of what women actually experience. For example, while some men hold stereotypical assumptions about women in general, they reported that these assumptions usually disappear when they actually work with or for a women manager. However, the specific women they know and work with are typically viewed as "exceptions" to the rule.

Brody and her team worked long hours to analyze the extensive survey data and present it in such a way that both women and men in the company would be able to understand each other's different views of reality. She hoped the survey results would trigger more in-depth discussion at the Forum, so more people would be motivated to eliminate the gap in perceptions and find new ways for women and men to work together.

The Women's Global Leadership Forum

Brody and the consultants wanted to ensure that the Forum was more than just an effective leadership training seminar for women that developed recommendations for organizational change. They had confidence that the participants would develop recommendations that were appropriate for Bestfoods, but what would happen afterwards? Much depended upon the continued support of senior executives and their reaction to the Forum. To encourage their growing support, the majority of Bestfoods' most senior executives (CEO, Corporate Strategy Council, Diversity Advisory Council, corporate officers, and a Board member) joined the women participants at the welcome dinner, as well as at other sessions (at which their presence would not be inhibitive), and at the all-important presentation of recommendations on the final morning of the 4$^{1}/_{2}$ day Women's Global Leadership Forum. The senior executives' inclusion allowed them to see the women participants in action, hear their opinions firsthand, and learn for themselves what the company needed to do, and to avoid doing, in order to succeed.

The design of the Forum tried to enhance the women's preparation for proactive roles in the company's future leadership. The Forum design included three types of sessions: (1) individual professional development sessions focusing on global leadership skills; (2) organization development sessions aimed at gathering information and making recommendations to the company on women's retention, development, and advancement; and (3) sessions facilitating the formation of a women's network. At the participants' request, the design was modified to allow more time in small groups to formulate recommendations for presentation to the senior executives at the final session. Leadership development activities included "herstories" about significant women who influenced the values and leadership styles of the participants, skill assessment, skill building and coaching, experiential exercises, a panel of female CEOs and Bestfoods' highest ranking women, another panel of Bestfoods' senior male executives who gave career advice, and Brody's presentation of the survey results.

As predicted, the Forum had some intense and challenging moments as the widely diverse group of 55 women with differing goals, opinions, experiences, and communication and behavior styles met and discussed key corporate and personal challenges. Nevertheless, the participants judged the Forum to be a resounding success.

Forum Recommendations and Executive Response

A highlight of the Forum was the participants' presentation to the CEO, Corporate Strategy Council, and the Diversity Advisory Council on the last day. The women stayed up late the night before, working in teams on the various recommendations. In an offer that reflected their skills as mentors and coaches, the senior American women graciously suggested that younger women from outside the United States do the actual presenting so that they could benefit more directly from the high visibility. Before the presentations began, Shoemate requested that the participants be candid and assured them that they could be totally honest in their feedback. All participants were visibly pulling for the presenters. At one point, a highly articulate and self-assured Chinese woman in her late twenties brought down the house when she assured Shoemate that "There's no need to feel threatened by us—we don't want your job. We want to be CEOs of bigger, better companies than Bestfoods!" Their specific recommendations, found in Appendix D, focused on three key areas: Career Development (enhancing career opportunities), Diversity (increasing representation of women in senior and high-level positions), and Work/Life Balance (enabling women to perform to their highest capabilities while recognizing their multiple roles). In addition to recommending what the company should do, the participants also identified what they themselves should do to enhance their own career opportunities.

While the women participated in a final small group session, Shoemate and the senior executives discussed the recommendations and planned their response. Shoemate suggested separating the recommendations into three categories:

- Current company initiatives—recommendations the company is already doing but which need to be accelerated and better communicated to employees;
- New corporate-wide recommendations, which the Corporate Strategy Council could consider at its next meeting;
- New "local" recommendations best addressed within specific countries, regions, or divisions.

When the women rejoined the executives, Shoemate responded to each recommendation, some of which he immediately accepted. He was very open to feedback and did not argue with or become defensive about any points the women raised. He promised to look into existing programs and policies that were not consistently working to the benefit of women's development and retention. Shoemate eloquently referred to his belief that the company's strength lies in its local decision making and explained why he hesitates to mandate most policies from corporate headquarters. However, he also clarified what he could do as CEO to make change happen and assured the women that he would communicate to them the outcome of each recommendation as soon as possible. Shoemate's obvious sincerity and thoughtfulness made a positive impression, as did the response of other CSC members. Shoemate closed the session with an inspirational story about his first experience as a very young manager whose orders were obeyed because, like the women at the Forum, he had the backing and utter confidence of his boss. Shoemate and Bergeman then led a standing ovation for Brody and her staff.

Two hours later, after bidding goodbye to participants about to jet off to all corners of the globe, Brody gratefully collapsed on a lawn chair on Arrowwood's manicured grounds. She was delighted that the Forum had ended on such a positive note. The immediate feedback at least seemed to indicate that it had indeed been the catalyst she was hoping for. Nevertheless, Brody still had that nagging question, "What next steps have to take place so that real change in the company and its leadership occurs and becomes institutionalized?"

Appendix A   **The Bestfoods Vision**

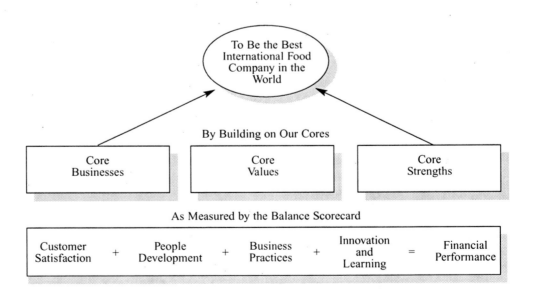

Appendix B

cpc
International

CPC INTERNATIONAL INC., INTERNATIONAL PLAZA,
ENGLEWOOD CLIFFS, NEW JERSEY 07632

C.R. SHOEMATE
CHAIRMAN AND PRESIDENT   January 10, 1997

An open letter to all CPC Employees . . .

Subject: CPC's Diversity Initiative

CPC's strong culture and proud traditions are deeply rooted in our core values of honesty, integrity, fairness, and respect. They are also the best foundation on which to build our future. Our values have not changed over time but the way we demonstrate them continues to change. Our customers and consumers, business partners and investors, our own workforce and managers reflect a more diverse society in the growing globaleconomy. Our World Team vision, To Become the Best International Food Company in The World, our core values and company policies challenge every one of us to help in our drive toward becoming the best. That is only possible when every one of us truly believes we will have the opportunity to fulfill our potential at CPC.

Our diversity initiative is an ongoing process that affects everyone in the company. In order to ensure a more inclusive environment that values the contributions of all, we need to engage every person in this effort. The diversity vision that follows highlights the business rationale for increasing and leveraging our diversity, so that CPC employees can develop a shared understanding of why this is a strategic imperative.

The diagram that depicts elements of diversity in the workplace clearly demonstrates our commitment to a broad spectrum of differences that go far beyond equal opportunity programs, which are often limited to race and gender.

The Diversity Advisory Council has embraced four long-term objectives for CPC: Preferred Employer, Balanced Workforce, Equitable Workplace, and Enhanced Business Results. The Balanced Scorecard that follows identifies the drivers and measures to which Corporate Staff, Corn Refining North America, Best Foods and the Baking Business are committed. Division Presidents will be reviewing their progress with me every year.

But progress throughout CPC is everyone's responsibility. Increase your own awareness of people who are different from you and understand how your own assumptions affect the way you treat others. Support our Diversity initiative by following and reinforcing equal treatment and respect for all. Challenge others and speak up if you see inappropriate behavior or hear derogatory comments or jokes and talk to other people about your concerns and suggestions.

On the back cover of this brochure are additional questions and answers about our progress in this important area.

I hope you join me in continued learning and self improvement to reach our vision for the future.

C R Shoemate

Our Diversity Vision for the Future

We will value, leverage, and increase variety and difference in our workforce so that our diversity is the perpetual stimulant of innovation, creativity, and effective problem solving, providing us with a sustainable competitive advantage that helps us reach the highest levels of quality, productivity and profitability in achieving CPC's vision to become the best international food company in the world.

We envision a workplace where diversity is fully integrated into the organization to create an environment that encourages, values, and respects the uniqueness of the individual; fosters achievement; and optimizes business opportunities.

Elements of Diversity Recognized in the Workplace

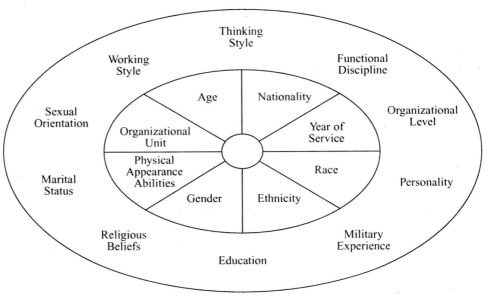

A myriad of characteristics make us who we are. The whole person contributes to the diversity of CPC International and to our success as a company.

Long-Term Objectives

Preferred Employer	Establish best practice standards of excellence that earn the corporation internal recognition by employees and external recognition by the marketplace for being the preferred employer to all segments of the population.
Balanced Workforce	Ensure every CPC organization's workforce reflects variety and difference at all levels.
Equitable Workplace	Ensure an equitable workplace in which opportunities and rewards are supported by policies and practices based on achievement, fairness, and equity. Our core values demand that we treat one another with respect and dignity at all times, taking individual responsibility for development and performance in an environment free from bias and discrimination.
Enhanced Business Results	Ensure that variety and difference in the CPC World Team is leveraged to reach the highest levels of innovation, creativity, effective problem solving, and performance for the benefit of our customers, consumers, employees, and shareholders.

Diversity Balanced Scorecard

Objectives	Drivers	Measures
Preferred Employer	Recognition by employees	Employee survey results
	Recognition by external employment candidates	Turnover/retention rates
		Recruiting results
Balanced Workforce	Representative of consumer base and workplace availability	Trends in consumer and workforce demographics
	Reflective of customer base	Customer demographics
	Inclusive of WorldTeam	Variety and difference reflected in all organization levels
	Workforce diversity plan by each operating unit based on people development challenges for the year 2000	People development component of the balanced scorecard
Equitable Workplace	Freedom from bias and discrimination as recognized by local employment law and our employees	Employee survey results (i.e. employee satisfaction with career development components of the performance enhancement process)
	Effective policies and practices	Legal claims filed and (litigated) results
Enhanced Business Results	Business Growth	Shareholder return, net sales and earnings

Selected Questions and Answers

Q: Why is CPC interested in diversity?

A: A highly competent and motivated workforce that is characterized by variety and fully qualified to advance in the CPC WorldTeam is a critical element of realizing our vision, "TO BECOME THE BEST INTERNATIONAL FOOD COMPANY IN THE WORLD."

Q: A new members of our department recently transferred from another unit of CPC. He is standoffish and makes me uncomfortable. Another team leader told me to join in making him feel more welcome, that this is part of diversity. I thought diversity referred to race and gender.

A: People are unique individuals and "diversity" encompasses a wide range of things that make us different from others. Organization unit can be one of them. Share your department's "informal" rules with a newcomer. Make an extra effort to include a new employee in your lunch plans. Learning and growing is a two-way street. Ask about the unit he came from and what he sees as some differences. Take the opportunity to broaden your horizons by learning from him.

Q: Sometimes at staff meetings my peers repeat ethnic jokes they've heard recently. I am uncomfortable with this type of humor. What can I do?

A: Part of supporting diversity is challenging others when they make ethnic, cultural, gender-related, or sexually derogatory jokes. But sometimes we are hesitant to speak up in a group because we think we are the only one with that concern. Often that is not the case. If you find something offensive, chances are others do too. You are not "off the hook" because you didn't tell the joke. Creating an inclusive environment at CPC means each of us has the responsibility to help educate others when certain behavior is objectionable.

Q: Who can I talk to to find out more about our diversity efforts?

A: Many people at CPC are actively involved and committed to these initiatives. A good place to start is with your immediate manager or your local Human Resources department. You can also contact the Workforce Diversity and Development Unit at Englewood Cliffs.

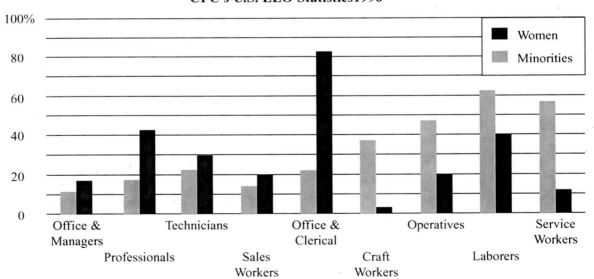

CPC's U.S. EEO Statistics 1996

Appendix C BESTFOODS

January 12, 1998

An open letter to all Bestfoods North American Salaried Employees . . .

Last year at this time, I introduced our Diversity Initiative and our diversity vision for the future. The Diversity Advisory Council, of which I am Chairman, defined a global diversity strategy. Our goal is to establish a workplace where diversity is fully integrated into the organization creating an environment and culture that encourages, values, and respects the uniqueness of the individual; fosters achievement; and optimizes business opportunities.

Our long-term objectives have four components: Preferred Employer, Balances Workforce, Equitable Workplace, Enhanced Business Results. Each of our business units, as well as the corporate staff, has been engaged in specific actions this past year to ensure that Bestfoods benefits fully from the contributions, creativity, energy, and commitment of the broadest range of men and women representing different cultures, religions, ages, abilities, ethnic and racial backgrounds, and points of view. This is a competitive asset that every one of us must wholeheartedly embrace and actively foster if we are to achieve the outstanding growth that we seek. What are some of the specific accomplishments from this past year?

In order to measure our progress as **preferred employer**, we have committed to our second employee survey. Once again, there are a group of core questions that will be asked around the world. Several questions relate specifically to the amount of respect, inclusiveness, and fair treatment accorded to every Bestfoods employee.

We intensified our efforts to make faster progress in establishing a **balanced workforce** with more variety and difference reflected in all organization levels. We have begun breaking down glass ceilings and walls across the company. As a result of opening up our posting program globally for senior management positions, we have created more cross functional, cross divisional, and international moves than ever before.

We have made great strides in enhancing our career development practices resulting in a more **equitable workplace**. Our Performance Enhancement Process is being used worldwide. Every employee participating now has an individual development plan linked to our Bestfoods Leadership Competencies. And our WorldTeam Development Process, which drives our succession planning, has been revitalized.

All of these efforts are helping to reenergize the organization and are contributing to our **enhanced business results**. At a time when we must achieve more, often with fewer available resources, we are still meeting our financial targets. This was confirmed last year by Wall Street and our shareholders when our stock-price went above 100 for the first time ever!

Our Diversity Initiative is more that a training program, it is the way we do business and live our core values. It is hard work and sometimes frustrating. It requires full participation. Each one of us must be willing to act as a diversity change agent. This means acting as a role model and it often takes personal courage to do so.

In the past I have asked you to join me in continued learning and self-awareness. We are making progress and moving in the right direction. I now ask you to join me in becoming a change agent for the future.

C R Shoemate

Bestfoods Diversity Initiative

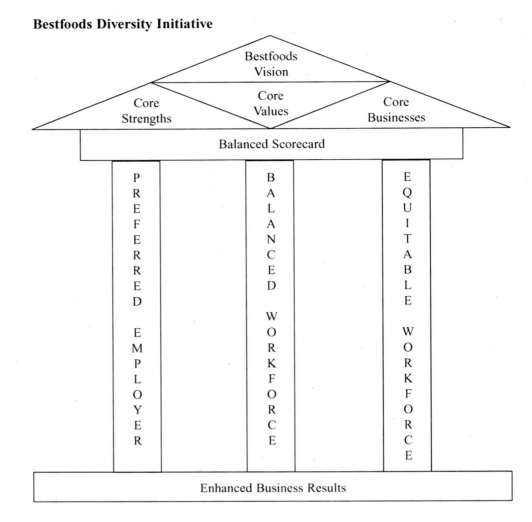

1997 Divisional Progress
Corporate
- Sponsoring Our Success
- Cultural Connections
- Revised EEO and Sexual Harassment Policies

Bestfoods North America
- Analysis and focus on recruiting/development gaps in Operations and Sales
- Enhanced INROADS participation
- Awareness and skill training for managers

Baking Business
- Mentoring Program
- Enhanced entry-level college recruiting and career development: Mfg; Sales; Fin; Mktg.
- 1st time INROADS participation: five interns

Bestfoods U.S. EEO Statistics*

1996 versus 1997

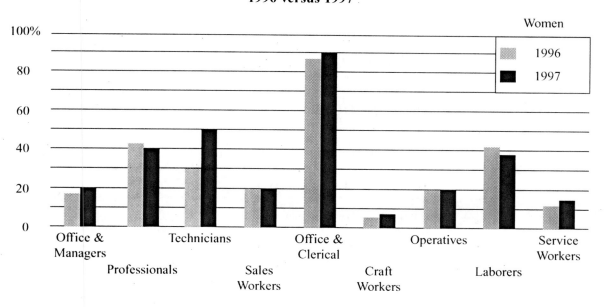

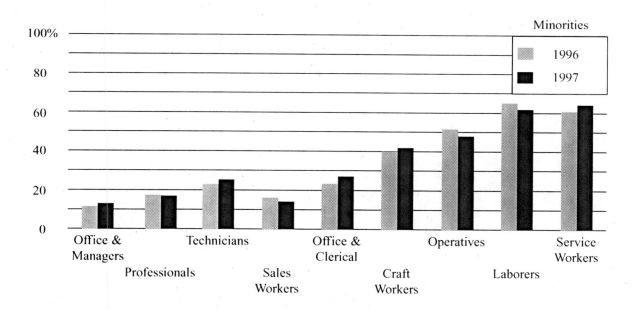

*These numbers include Corn Products North America.

Selected Questions and Answers

Q: What are the critical factors that we need to address in order to be successful with our Diversity Initiative?

A: The Conference Board recently conducted a survey with leading edge organizations in diversity. The companies identifying the greatest progress with diversity efforts had two things in common: active support and involvement by their CEO and integrating diversity efforts into business and organizational objectives.

Q: How do we compare to other companies that are implementing diversity programs?

A: Although our Corporate initiative is fairly recent, Dick Shoemate's leadership on this issue has helped Bestfoods rapidly catch up with "best practice" companies. We have made great strides in integrating diversity into many of our business practices. Some of the key areas where this is occurring include: ongoing management and employee communications, employee awareness, education and involvement, management accountability measured by the balanced scorecard, the Performance Enhancement and Career Development Planning Process, community involvement and outreach, and divisional diversity action plans.

Q: What impact has the recent restructuring had on minority representation in our workforce?

A: There has been virtually no negative impact on minority representation despite a difficult year. In fact, we exceed the industry average for minority white collar workers by 5 percent and for blue collar by 10 percent.

Q: Does Bestfoods think diversity is only an issue in the United States?

A: We are deeply committed to extending our Diversity Initiative beyond the United States. Our definition of workforce diversity includes nationality, religion, age, and gender. These are just some of the elements of diversity that often resonate outside the United States. While legislation is increasing in many countries, our own U.S. heritage of equality and democracy tends to put emphasis on these issues here. However, the drivers of diversity are clearly universal. Ranked in order of importance they are customers and markets, global diversity, productivity, external workforce demographic trends, and internal workforce demographics.

Q: How many international employees are there in Bestfoods? How many are women?

A: Bestfoods has approximately 130 employees on international assignments represent 34 nationalities. China, Hong Kong, Spain, and Colombia each have a female expatriate on assignment. We expect this number to continue to grow. Of our global posting applicants, 17 percent were women.

Q: Has Bestfoods ever had a class-action suit filed?

A: We have never had a class-action suit filed against us in our 90-year history. In fact, the number of discrimination charges filed by our 17,000 U.S. employees is very small. Year-to-date, we have only had 10 charges of discrimination filed with the EEOC, three of which have been dismissed for "no reasonable cause."

Equal Employment Opportunity

Bestfoods is committed to prohibiting discrimination in all employment practices including recruiting, hiring, pay, training, promotion, discipline, and termination on the basis of race, color, sex, age, religion, national origin, sexual orientation, disability, or veteran status. The Company prohibits harassment, including sexual harassment of its employees, in any form. The Company is also committed to an affirmation action policy, which will promote and ensure equal opportunity for minorities, women, individuals with disabilities, and covered veterans.

Appendix D   **Women's Global Leadership Forum Recommendations**

Career Development

To Enhance Career Opportunities

- Increase participation in high visibility projects/assignments
    - Senior management development program
    - Task force assignments via posting and self-nomination
- Create flexible international assignments
    - Include assignment not involving relocation
    - Shorter-term assignment (6 months–1 year)
    - Job swapping/exchange
- Clarify career path and development opportunities
    - Provide honest, clear, consistent feedback
    - Full and consistent use of PEP (employee development program)
    - Management accountability for implementing action plans (PEP + employee interest)
- Take same level of risk with women as with men in promoting people
- Post all eligible job openings consistently

Diversity

To increase representation of women in high-level positions:

- Have CEO communicate expectations to *all* global managers
- Create ombudspersons
- Appoint global representation on Corporate Diversity Advisory Council
- Share full results of Women's Global Leadership Forum survey with all divisions
- Benchmark with other companies and recognized experts
- Insure appropriate measures in Balanced Scorecard

Work/Life Balance

To enable women to perform to their highest capabilities. Provide options for:

- Telecommuting
- Flexible work schedule, including maternity leave
- Job sharing
- Part-time opportunities

Personal Responsibilities for Career Development

- To take responsibility for your own personal career development:
    - Identify goals
    - Communicate personal willingness for high-risk, challenging assignments
    - Self-nominate for those assignments as available
- Learn how to better develop personal networks to facilitate access to career opportunities
- To prepare for future opportunities:
    - Develop leadership skills
    - Increase cultural sensitivities
    - Develop language skills
    - Maintain open-minded attitudes
    - Support, nurture, and develop career growth opportunities for those we manage

Personal Responsibilities for Work/Life Balance

- Communicate personal needs and offer alternatives to meet those needs
- Set priorities and recognize the need for tradeoffs
- Be sensitive to the needs of individuals we manage

Women's Global Leadership Forum Group Responsibilities

- Support diversity initiatives and share Forum results
- Network on the basis of relationships developed at the Forum
- Borrow with pride
- Share best practice local learnings with other Forum participants

Women and Global Leadership At Bestfoods Discussion Questions

1. Should the headquarters of the U.S.-based multinationals promote diversity initiatives in their worldwide subsidiaries? If so, what's the best way to accomplish this?
2. Do you agree with Brody's idea to hold the forum? Why or why not? Can you suggest an alternative that would accomplish the same purpose or be even more effective?
3. What challenges and problems do Brody and Shoemate face in getting their diversity strategy implemented?
4. Prior to the opening session of the forum, what steps have Brody and her HR colleagues taken to promote diversity efforts throughout the company?
5. What actions or factors contributed to making this a successful change effort?
6. What else should Brody and Bestfoods do to institutionalize the changes begun at the Women's Global Leadership Forum?

Endnotes

1. Equal Employment Opportunity (EEO) laws, under the provisions of TITLE VII of the Civil Rights Act of 1964, were created in the United States to ensure work environments free from illegal discrimination on the grounds of race, color, religion, disability, age, national origin, or sex.
2. 1998 Vision and Policies pamphlet.
3. Catalyst, located in New York City, is a well-respected research and education institute that focuses on corporate women in senior leadership and management positions.
4. Sheila W. Wellington. (1996) "Women in Corporate Leadership: Progress and Prospects." New York: Catalyst.

Managing Organizations and People: Cases in Management, Organizational Behavior, and Human Resource Management, 7e (Modular Edition)
(Edited by Paul F. Buller & Randall S. Schuler)

Please indicate the readings you would like to include in your custom reader with a check mark. Then indicate the sequence you would like your readings to appear, starting with 1. Fax this completed form, along with your contact information, to your Custom Consultant at 800.270.3310, or call Customer Service at 800.355.9983 for assistance.

✔	Seq.	Module/Title	Price	✔	Seq.	Module/Title	Price
		Module I—Management and Leadership			29.	The Tall Pines Hotel and Conference Center	$1.50
		(0-324-31472-8)	**$7.25**		30.	A Broader View Seizes More Opportunities	1.50
	1.	Custom Chip, Inc.	1.50		31.	Moon Over ER	1.50
	2.	Dick Spencer	1.50		32.	Heartland State Bank (A)	1.50
	3.	The Marketing Campaign at ChemCorp	1.50		33.	Heartland State Bank (B)	1.50
	4.	Traveler Import Cars, Inc.	1.50			**Module VI—Managing Diversity (0-324-31477-9)**	**7.25**
	5.	The Prominent Dr. Rombach	1.50		34.	Managing Workforce Diversity: People Related Issues	
	6.	The United Way and the Boy Scouts: Controversy				at the Barden Corporation	1.50
		in Portland, Oregon	1.50		35.	Propmore Corporation	1.50
		Module II—Strategy, Planning, and Organizational			36.	Promotion to Police Sergeant	1.50
		Culture (0-324-31473-6)	**7.25**		37.	Propco, Inc.	1.50
	7.	American Express	1.50		38.	The Business of Culture at Acoma Pueblo	1.50
	8.	XEL Communications Inc.	1.50		39.	Personnel Selection Procedures in Latin America	1.50
	9.	XEL Communications "C"	1.50			**Module VII—Motivation and Performance**	
	10.	Europska Databanka	1.50			**(0-324-31478-7)**	**7.25**
	11.	The Boston YWCA: 1991	1.50		40.	How to Motivate Fred Maiorino?	1.50
	12.	BCH Telecommunications	1.50		41.	The Kriendler Executive Dining Room	1.50
	13.	Riding the Rollercoaster of Entrepreneurship	1.50		42.	Nordstorm	1.50
		Module III—Organizational Structure and Design			43.	Southwest Airlines: Can Luv Rule the World?	1.50
		(0-324-31474-4)	**7.25**		44.	Lincoln Electric Company	1.50
	14.	The Plaza Inn	1.50		45.	An American in Paris	1.50
	15.	Dowling Flexible Metals	1.50			**Module VIII—Communication and Group Dynamics**	
	16.	Microsoft: Adapting to New Challenges	1.50			**(0-324-31479-5)**	**7.25**
	17.	Sunday at Al Tech	1.50		46.	Motor Parts Corporation	1.50
	18.	The ZX Software Development Group: Santa Cruz	1.50		47.	Contract Negotiations in Western Africa	1.50
	19.	The Wreck of Amtrack's Sunset Limited	1.50		48.	Does This Milkshake Taste Funny?	1.50
		Module IV—Organizational Control, Power, and Conflict			49.	Insubordination or Unclear Loyalties?	1.50
		(0-324-31475-2)	**7.25**		50.	The Luggers Versus the Butchers	1.50
	20.	Pearl Jam's Dispute with Ticketmaster	1.50		51.	Donor Services Department	1.50
	21.	Suntory	1.50			**Module IX—Organizational Change and Transformation**	
	22.	Baksheesh	1.50			**(0-324-31480-9)**	**7.25**
	23.	Conflict Management	1.50		52.	Transformation at Harley Davidson	1.50
	24.	Iroquois Container Corporation: Flagstone Operations	1.50		53.	Organizational Change: Planning and Implementing	
	25.	Astrotech Fuel Systems (A)	1.50			Teams at AAL and IPS	1.50
	26.	Unsavory Problems at Tasty's: A Case Exercise about			54.	Using Leadership to Promote TQM	1.50
		Whistleblowing	1.50		55.	Peoples Trust Company	1.50
		Module V—Human Resource Management			56.	Seeing the Forest and the Trees	1.50
		(0-324-31476-0)	**7.25**		57.	Women and Global Leadership at Bestfoods	1.50
	27.	Precision Measurement of Japan	1.50				
	28.	Bringing HR into the Business	1.50				

Cengage Learning Custom Publishing
5191 Natorp Boulevard
Mason, OH 45040
800.355.9983
Fax: 800.270.3310

Custom Module Order Form

Managing Organizations and People: Cases in Management, Organizational Behavior, and Human Resource Managment, 7e (Modular Edition) (Edited by Paul F. Buller & Randall S. Schuler)

TO:	FROM:
COMPANY:	DATE:
FAX NUMBER:	TOTAL PAGES INCLUDING COVER:
PHONE NUMBER:	SENDER'S TELEPHONE NUMBER:
RE:	SENDER'S EMAIL ADDRESS:

ATTENTION ADOPTING INSTRUCTOR:

To ensure that your Case Module readers arrive in time for the start of your course, please submit your selections at least six weeks prior to the start of your course in one of the following ways:

1. Fax: Complete this form and fax it to the Database Order Coordinator at 800.270.3310

2. Mail: Complete this form and mail it to the following address:
Database Order Coordinator
Cengage Learning Custom Publishing
5191 Natorp Boulevard
Mason, OH 45040

INSTRUCTOR:

DEPARTMENT:

SCHOOL:

CITY, STATE, ZIP:

COURSE NUMBER & TITLE:

QUANTITY:

COURSE START DATE:	TODAY'S DATE:

We will print desk copies when we print your order. Desk copies will be sent to the address above. If you would like them sent elsewhere, contact your Cengage Learning Representative or call your Custom Consultant at 800.355.9983.

Managing Organizations and People: Cases in Management, Organizational Behavior, and Human Resource Management, 7e (Modular Edition)
(Edited by Paul F. Buller & Randall S. Schuler)

Please indicate the readings you would like to include in your custom reader with a check mark. Then indicate the sequence you would like your readings to appear, starting with 1. Fax this completed form, along with your contact information, to your Custom Consultant at 800.270.3310, or call Customer Service at 800.355.9983 for assistance.

✔	Seq.	Module/Title	Price	✔	Seq.	Module/Title	Price
		Module I—Management and Leadership				29. The Tall Pines Hotel and Conference Center	$1.50
		(0-324-31472-8)	$7.25			30. A Broader View Seizes More Opportunities	1.50
		1. Custom Chip, Inc.	1.50			31. Moon Over ER	1.50
		2. Dick Spencer	1.50			32. Heartland State Bank (A)	1.50
		3. The Marketing Campaign at ChemCorp	1.50			33. Heartland State Bank (B)	1.50
		4. Traveler Import Cars, Inc.	1.50			**Module VI—Managing Diversity (0-324-31477-9)**	7.25
		5. The Prominent Dr. Rombach	1.50			34. Managing Workforce Diversity: People Related Issues	
		6. The United Way and the Boy Scouts: Controversy				at the Barden Corporation	1.50
		in Portland, Oregon	1.50			35. Propmore Corporation	1.50
		Module II—Strategy, Planning, and Organizational				36. Promotion to Police Sergeant	1.50
		Culture (0-324-31473-6)	7.25			37. Propco, Inc.	1.50
		7. American Express	1.50			38. The Business of Culture at Acoma Pueblo	1.50
		8. XEL Communications Inc.	1.50			39. Personnel Selection Procedures in Latin America	1.50
		9. XEL Communications "C"	1.50			**Module VII—Motivation and Performance**	
		10. Europska Databanka	1.50			(0-324-31478-7)	7.25
		11. The Boston YWCA: 1991	1.50			40. How to Motivate Fred Maiorino?	1.50
		12. BCH Telecommunications	1.50			41. The Kriendler Executive Dining Room	1.50
		13. Riding the Rollercoaster of Entrepreneurship	1.50			42. Nordstorm	1.50
		Module III—Organizational Structure and Design				43. Southwest Airlines: Can Luv Rule the World?	1.50
		(0-324-31474-4)	7.25			44. Lincoln Electric Company	1.50
		14. The Plaza Inn	1.50			45. An American in Paris	1.50
		15. Dowling Flexible Metals	1.50			**Module VIII—Communication and Group Dynamics**	
		16. Microsoft: Adapting to New Challenges	1.50			(0-324-31479-5)	7.25
		17. Sunday at Al Tech	1.50			46. Motor Parts Corporation	1.50
		18. The ZX Software Development Group: Santa Cruz	1.50			47. Contract Negotiations in Western Africa	1.50
		19. The Wreck of Amtrack's Sunset Limited	1.50			48. Does This Milkshake Taste Funny?	1.50
		Module IV—Organizational Control, Power, and Conflict				49. Insubordination or Unclear Loyalties?	1.50
		(0-324-31475-2)	7.25			50. The Luggers Versus the Butchers	1.50
		20. Pearl Jam's Dispute with Ticketmaster	1.50			51. Donor Services Department	1.50
		21. Suntory	1.50			**Module IX—Organizational Change and Transformation**	
		22. Baksheesh	1.50			(0-324-31480-9)	7.25
		23. Conflict Management	1.50			52. Transformation at Harley Davidson	1.50
		24. Iroquois Container Corporation: Flagstone Operations	1.50			53. Organizational Change: Planning and Implementing	
		25. Astrotech Fuel Systems (A)	1.50			Teams at AAL and IPS	1.50
		26. Unsavory Problems at Tasty's: A Case Exercise about				54. Using Leadership to Promote TQM	1.50
		Whistleblowing	1.50			55. Peoples Trust Company	1.50
		Module V—Human Resource Management				56. Seeing the Forest and the Trees	1.50
		(0-324-31476-0)	7.25			57. Women and Global Leadership at Bestfoods	1.50
		27. Precision Measurement of Japan	1.50				
		28. Bringing HR into the Business	1.50				

Cengage Learning Custom Publishing
5191 Natorp Boulevard
Mason, OH 45040
800.355.9983
Fax: 800.270.3310

Custom Module Order Form

Managing Organizations and People: Cases in Management, Organizational Behavior, and Human Resource Managment, 7e (Modular Edition) (Edited by Paul F. Buller & Randall S. Schuler)

TO:

COMPANY:

FAX NUMBER:

PHONE NUMBER:

RE:

FROM:

DATE:

TOTAL PAGES INCLUDING COVER:

SENDER'S TELEPHONE NUMBER:

SENDER'S EMAIL ADDRESS:

ATTENTION ADOPTING INSTRUCTOR:

To ensure that your Case Module readers arrive in time for the start of your course, please submit your selections at least six weeks prior to the start of your course in one of the following ways:

1. Fax: Complete this form and fax it to the Database Order Coordinator at 800.270.3310

2. Mail: Complete this form and mail it to the following address:
    Database Order Coordinator
    Cengage Learning Custom Publishing
    5191 Natorp Boulevard
    Mason, OH 45040

INSTRUCTOR:

DEPARTMENT:

SCHOOL:

CITY, STATE, ZIP:

COURSE NUMBER & TITLE:

QUANTITY:

COURSE START DATE:

TODAY'S DATE:

We will print desk copies when we print your order. Desk copies will be sent to the address above. If you would like them sent elsewhere, contact your Cengage Learning Representative or call your Custom Consultant at 800.355.9983.

Managing Organizations and People: Cases in Management, Organizational Behavior, and Human Resource Management, 7e (Modular Edition)
(Edited by Paul F. Buller & Randall S. Schuler)

Please indicate the readings you would like to include in your custom reader with a check mark. Then indicate the sequence you would like your readings to appear, starting with 1. Fax this completed form, along with your contact information, to your Custom Consultant at 800.270.3310, or call Customer Service at 800.355.9983 for assistance.

✔	Seq.	Module/Title	Price	✔	Seq.	Module/Title	Price
		Module I—Management and Leadership				29. The Tall Pines Hotel and Conference Center	$1.50
		(0-324-31472-8)	**$7.25**			30. A Broader View Seizes More Opportunities	1.50
		1. Custom Chip, Inc.	1.50			31. Moon Over ER	1.50
		2. Dick Spencer	1.50			32. Heartland State Bank (A)	1.50
		3. The Marketing Campaign at ChemCorp	1.50			33. Heartland State Bank (B)	1.50
		4. Traveler Import Cars, Inc.	1.50			**Module VI—Managing Diversity (0-324-31477-9)**	**7.25**
		5. The Prominent Dr. Rombach	1.50			34. Managing Workforce Diversity: People Related Issues	
		6. The United Way and the Boy Scouts: Controversy				at the Barden Corporation	1.50
		in Portland, Oregon	1.50			35. Propmore Corporation	1.50
		Module II—Strategy, Planning, and Organizational				36. Promotion to Police Sergeant	1.50
		Culture (0-324-31473-6)	**7.25**			37. Propco, Inc.	1.50
		7. American Express	1.50			38. The Business of Culture at Acoma Pueblo	1.50
		8. XEL Communications Inc.	1.50			39. Personnel Selection Procedures in Latin America	1.50
		9. XEL Communications "C"	1.50			**Module VII—Motivation and Performance**	
		10. Europska Databanka	1.50			**(0-324-31478-7)**	**7.25**
		11. The Boston YWCA: 1991	1.50			40. How to Motivate Fred Maiorino?	1.50
		12. BCH Telecommunications	1.50			41. The Kriendler Executive Dining Room	1.50
		13. Riding the Rollercoaster of Entrepreneurship	1.50			42. Nordstorm	1.50
		Module III—Organizational Structure and Design				43. Southwest Airlines: Can Luv Rule the World?	1.50
		(0-324-31474-4)	**7.25**			44. Lincoln Electric Company	1.50
		14. The Plaza Inn	1.50			45. An American in Paris	1.50
		15. Dowling Flexible Metals	1.50			**Module VIII—Communication and Group Dynamics**	
		16. Microsoft: Adapting to New Challenges	1.50			**(0-324-31479-5)**	**7.25**
		17. Sunday at Al Tech	1.50			46. Motor Parts Corporation	1.50
		18. The ZX Software Development Group: Santa Cruz	1.50			47. Contract Negotiations in Western Africa	1.50
		19. The Wreck of Amtrack's Sunset Limited	1.50			48. Does This Milkshake Taste Funny?	1.50
		Module IV—Organizational Control, Power, and Conflict				49. Insubordination or Unclear Loyalties?	1.50
		(0-324-31475-2)	**7.25**			50. The Luggers Versus the Butchers	1.50
		20. Pearl Jam's Dispute with Ticketmaster	1.50			51. Donor Services Department	1.50
		21. Suntory	1.50			**Module IX—Organizational Change and Transformation**	
		22. Baksheesh	1.50			**(0-324-31480-9)**	**7.25**
		23. Conflict Management	1.50			52. Transformation at Harley Davidson	1.50
		24. Iroquois Container Corporation: Flagstone Operations	1.50			53. Organizational Change: Planning and Implementing	
		25. Astrotech Fuel Systems (A)	1.50			Teams at AAL and IPS	1.50
		26. Unsavory Problems at Tasty's: A Case Exercise about				54. Using Leadership to Promote TQM	1.50
		Whistleblowing	1.50			55. Peoples Trust Company	1.50
		Module V—Human Resource Management				56. Seeing the Forest and the Trees	1.50
		(0-324-31476-0)	**7.25**			57. Women and Global Leadership at Bestfoods	1.50
		27. Precision Measurement of Japan	1.50				
		28. Bringing HR into the Business	1.50				

Cengage Learning Custom Publishing
5191 Natorp Boulevard
Mason, OH 45040
800.355.9983
Fax: 800.270.3310

Custom Module Order Form

Managing Organizations and People: Cases in Management, Organizational Behavior, and Human Resource Managment, 7e (Modular Edition) (Edited by Paul F. Buller & Randall S. Schuler)

TO:	FROM:
COMPANY:	DATE:
FAX NUMBER:	TOTAL PAGES INCLUDING COVER:
PHONE NUMBER:	SENDER'S TELEPHONE NUMBER:
RE:	SENDER'S EMAIL ADDRESS:

ATTENTION ADOPTING INSTRUCTOR:

To ensure that your Case Module readers arrive in time for the start of your course, please submit your selections at least six weeks prior to the start of your course in one of the following ways:

1. Fax: Complete this form and fax it to the Database Order Coordinator at 800.270.3310

2. Mail: Complete this form and mail it to the following address:
Database Order Coordinator
Cengage Learning Custom Publishing
5191 Natorp Boulevard
Mason, OH 45040

INSTRUCTOR:

DEPARTMENT:

SCHOOL:

CITY, STATE, ZIP:

COURSE NUMBER & TITLE:

QUANTITY:

COURSE START DATE: TODAY'S DATE:

We will print desk copies when we print your order. Desk copies will be sent to the address above. If you would like them sent elsewhere, contact your Cengage Learning Representative or call your Custom Consultant at 800.355.9983.

Managing Organizations and People: Cases in Management, Organizational Behavior, and Human Resource Management, 7e (Modular Edition)
(Edited by Paul F. Buller & Randall S. Schuler)

Please indicate the readings you would like to include in your custom reader with a check mark. Then indicate the sequence you would like your readings to appear, starting with 1. Fax this completed form, along with your contact information, to your Custom Consultant at 800.270.3310, or call Customer Service at 800.355.9983 for assistance.

✔	Seq.	Module/Title	Price	✔	Seq.	Module/Title	Price
		Module I—Management and Leadership				29. The Tall Pines Hotel and Conference Center	$1.50
		(0-324-31472-8)	**$7.25**			30. A Broader View Seizes More Opportunities	1.50
		1. Custom Chip, Inc.	1.50			31. Moon Over ER	1.50
		2. Dick Spencer	1.50			32. Heartland State Bank (A)	1.50
		3. The Marketing Campaign at ChemCorp	1.50			33. Heartland State Bank (B)	1.50
		4. Traveler Import Cars, Inc.	1.50			**Module VI—Managing Diversity (0-324-31477-9)**	**7.25**
		5. The Prominent Dr. Rombach	1.50			34. Managing Workforce Diversity: People Related Issues	
		6. The United Way and the Boy Scouts: Controversy				at the Barden Corporation	1.50
		in Portland, Oregon	1.50			35. Propmore Corporation	1.50
		Module II—Strategy, Planning, and Organizational				36. Promotion to Police Sergeant	1.50
		Culture (0-324-31473-6)	**7.25**			37. Propco, Inc.	1.50
		7. American Express	1.50			38. The Business of Culture at Acoma Pueblo	1.50
		8. XEL Communications Inc.	1.50			39. Personnel Selection Procedures in Latin America	1.50
		9. XEL Communications "C"	1.50			**Module VII—Motivation and Performance**	
		10. Europska Databanka	1.50			(0-324-31478-7)	**7.25**
		11. The Boston YWCA: 1991	1.50			40. How to Motivate Fred Maiorino?	1.50
		12. BCH Telecommunications	1.50			41. The Kriendler Executive Dining Room	1.50
		13. Riding the Rollercoaster of Entrepreneurship	1.50			42. Nordstorm	1.50
		Module III—Organizational Structure and Design				43. Southwest Airlines: Can Luv Rule the World?	1.50
		(0-324-31474-4)	**7.25**			44. Lincoln Electric Company	1.50
		14. The Plaza Inn	1.50			45. An American in Paris	1.50
		15. Dowling Flexible Metals	1.50			**Module VIII—Communication and Group Dynamics**	
		16. Microsoft: Adapting to New Challenges	1.50			(0-324-31479-5)	**7.25**
		17. Sunday at Al Tech	1.50			46. Motor Parts Corporation	1.50
		18. The ZX Software Development Group: Santa Cruz	1.50			47. Contract Negotiations in Western Africa	1.50
		19. The Wreck of Amtrack's Sunset Limited	1.50			48. Does This Milkshake Taste Funny?	1.50
		Module IV—Organizational Control, Power, and Conflict				49. Insubordination or Unclear Loyalties?	1.50
		(0-324-31475-2)	**7.25**			50. The Luggers Versus the Butchers	1.50
		20. Pearl Jam's Dispute with Ticketmaster	1.50			51. Donor Services Department	1.50
		21. Suntory	1.50			**Module IX—Organizational Change and Transformation**	
		22. Baksheesh	1.50			(0-324-31480-9)	**7.25**
		23. Conflict Management	1.50			52. Transformation at Harley Davidson	1.50
		24. Iroquois Container Corporation: Flagstone Operations	1.50			53. Organizational Change: Planning and Implementing	
		25. Astrotech Fuel Systems (A)	1.50			Teams at AAL and IPS	1.50
		26. Unsavory Problems at Tasty's: A Case Exercise about				54. Using Leadership to Promote TQM	1.50
		Whistleblowing	1.50			55. Peoples Trust Company	1.50
		Module V—Human Resource Management				56. Seeing the Forest and the Trees	1.50
		(0-324-31476-0)	**7.25**			57. Women and Global Leadership at Bestfoods	1.50
		27. Precision Measurement of Japan	1.50				
		28. Bringing HR into the Business	1.50				

Cengage Learning Custom Publishing
5191 Natorp Boulevard
Mason, OH 45040
800.355.9983
Fax: 800.270.3310

Custom Module Order Form

Managing Organizations and People: Cases in Management, Organizational Behavior, and Human Resource Managment, 7e (Modular Edition) (Edited by Paul F. Buller & Randall S. Schuler)

TO:	FROM:
COMPANY:	DATE:
FAX NUMBER:	TOTAL PAGES INCLUDING COVER:
PHONE NUMBER:	SENDER'S TELEPHONE NUMBER:
RE:	SENDER'S EMAIL ADDRESS:

ATTENTION ADOPTING INSTRUCTOR:

To ensure that your Case Module readers arrive in time for the start of your course, please submit your selections at least six weeks prior to the start of your course in one of the following ways:

1. Fax: Complete this form and fax it to the Database Order Coordinator at 800.270.3310

2. Mail: Complete this form and mail it to the following address:
Database Order Coordinator
Cengage Learning Custom Publishing
5191 Natorp Boulevard
Mason, OH 45040

INSTRUCTOR:

DEPARTMENT:

SCHOOL:

CITY, STATE, ZIP:

COURSE NUMBER & TITLE:

QUANTITY:

COURSE START DATE:

TODAY'S DATE:

We will print desk copies when we print your order. Desk copies will be sent to the address above. If you would like them sent elsewhere, contact your Cengage Learning Representative or call your Custom Consultant at 800.355.9983.

Managing Organizations and People: Cases in Management, Organizational Behavior, and Human Resource Management, 7e (Modular Edition)
(Edited by Paul F. Buller & Randall S. Schuler)

Please indicate the readings you would like to include in your custom reader with a check mark. Then indicate the sequence you would like your readings to appear, starting with 1. Fax this completed form, along with your contact information, to your Custom Consultant at 800.270.3310, or call Customer Service at 800.355.9983 for assistance.

✔	Seq.	Module/Title	Price	✔	Seq.	Module/Title	Price
		Module I—Management and Leadership				29. The Tall Pines Hotel and Conference Center	$1.50
		(0-324-31472-8)	**$7.25**			30. A Broader View Seizes More Opportunities	1.50
		1. Custom Chip, Inc.	1.50			31. Moon Over ER	1.50
		2. Dick Spencer	1.50			32. Heartland State Bank (A)	1.50
		3. The Marketing Campaign at ChemCorp	1.50			33. Heartland State Bank (B)	1.50
		4. Traveler Import Cars, Inc.	1.50			**Module VI—Managing Diversity (0-324-31477-9)**	**7.25**
		5. The Prominent Dr. Rombach	1.50			34. Managing Workforce Diversity: People Related Issues	
		6. The United Way and the Boy Scouts: Controversy				at the Barden Corporation	1.50
		in Portland, Oregon	1.50			35. Propmore Corporation	1.50
		Module II—Strategy, Planning, and Organizational				36. Promotion to Police Sergeant	1.50
		Culture (0-324-31473-6)	**7.25**			37. Propco, Inc.	1.50
		7. American Express	1.50			38. The Business of Culture at Acoma Pueblo	1.50
		8. XEL Communications Inc.	1.50			39. Personnel Selection Procedures in Latin America	1.50
		9. XEL Communications "C"	1.50			**Module VII—Motivation and Performance**	
		10. Europska Databanka	1.50			**(0-324-31478-7)**	**7.25**
		11. The Boston YWCA: 1991	1.50			40. How to Motivate Fred Maiorino?	1.50
		12. BCH Telecommunications	1.50			41. The Kriendler Executive Dining Room	1.50
		13. Riding the Rollercoaster of Entrepreneurship	1.50			42. Nordstorm	1.50
		Module III—Organizational Structure and Design				43. Southwest Airlines: Can Luv Rule the World?	1.50
		(0-324-31474-4)	**7.25**			44. Lincoln Electric Company	1.50
		14. The Plaza Inn	1.50			45. An American in Paris	1.50
		15. Dowling Flexible Metals	1.50			**Module VIII—Communication and Group Dynamics**	
		16. Microsoft: Adapting to New Challenges	1.50			**(0-324-31479-5)**	**7.25**
		17. Sunday at Al Tech	1.50			46. Motor Parts Corporation	1.50
		18. The ZX Software Development Group: Santa Cruz	1.50			47. Contract Negotiations in Western Africa	1.50
		19. The Wreck of Amtrack's Sunset Limited	1.50			48. Does This Milkshake Taste Funny?	1.50
		Module IV—Organizational Control, Power, and Conflict				49. Insubordination or Unclear Loyalties?	1.50
		(0-324-31475-2)	**7.25**			50. The Luggers Versus the Butchers	1.50
		20. Pearl Jam's Dispute with Ticketmaster	1.50			51. Donor Services Department	1.50
		21. Suntory	1.50			**Module IX—Organizational Change and Transformation**	
		22. Baksheesh	1.50			**(0-324-31480-9)**	**7.25**
		23. Conflict Management	1.50			52. Transformation at Harley Davidson	1.50
		24. Iroquois Container Corporation: Flagstone Operations	1.50			53. Organizational Change: Planning and Implementing	
		25. Astrotech Fuel Systems (A)	1.50			Teams at AAL and IPS	1.50
		26. Unsavory Problems at Tasty's: A Case Exercise about				54. Using Leadership to Promote TQM	1.50
		Whistleblowing	1.50			55. Peoples Trust Company	1.50
		Module V—Human Resource Management				56. Seeing the Forest and the Trees	1.50
		(0-324-31476-0)	**7.25**			57. Women and Global Leadership at Bestfoods	1.50
		27. Precision Measurement of Japan	1.50				
		28. Bringing HR into the Business	1.50				

Cengage Learning Custom Publishing
5191 Natorp Boulevard
Mason, OH 45040
800.355.9983
Fax: 800.270.3310

Custom Module Order Form

Managing Organizations and People: Cases in Management, Organizational Behavior, and Human Resource Managment, 7e (Modular Edition) (Edited by Paul F. Buller & Randall S. Schuler)

TO:	FROM:
COMPANY:	DATE:
FAX NUMBER:	TOTAL PAGES INCLUDING COVER:
PHONE NUMBER:	SENDER'S TELEPHONE NUMBER:
RE:	SENDER'S EMAIL ADDRESS:

ATTENTION ADOPTING INSTRUCTOR:

To ensure that your Case Module readers arrive in time for the start of your course, please submit your selections at least six weeks prior to the start of your course in one of the following ways:

1. Fax: Complete this form and fax it to the Database Order Coordinator at 800.270.3310

2. Mail: Complete this form and mail it to the following address:
Database Order Coordinator
Cengage Learning Custom Publishing
5191 Natorp Boulevard
Mason, OH 45040

INSTRUCTOR:

DEPARTMENT:

SCHOOL:

CITY, STATE, ZIP:

COURSE NUMBER & TITLE:

QUANTITY:

COURSE START DATE: | TODAY'S DATE:

We will print desk copies when we print your order. Desk copies will be sent to the address above. If you would like them sent elsewhere, contact your Cengage Learning Representative or call your Custom Consultant at 800.355.9983.

Managing Organizations and People: Cases in Management, Organizational Behavior, and Human Resource Management, 7e (Modular Edition)
(Edited by Paul F. Buller & Randall S. Schuler)

Please indicate the readings you would like to include in your custom reader with a check mark. Then indicate the sequence you would like your readings to appear, starting with 1. Fax this completed form, along with your contact information, to your Custom Consultant at 800.270.3310, or call Customer Service at 800.355.9983 for assistance.

✔	Seq.	Module/Title	Price	✔	Seq.	Module/Title	Price
		Module I—Management and Leadership				29. The Tall Pines Hotel and Conference Center	$1.50
		(0-324-31472-8)	**$7.25**			30. A Broader View Seizes More Opportunities	1.50
		1. Custom Chip, Inc.	1.50			31. Moon Over ER	1.50
		2. Dick Spencer	1.50			32. Heartland State Bank (A)	1.50
		3. The Marketing Campaign at ChemCorp	1.50			33. Heartland State Bank (B)	1.50
		4. Traveler Import Cars, Inc.	1.50			**Module VI—Managing Diversity (0-324-31477-9)**	**7.25**
		5. The Prominent Dr. Rombach	1.50			34. Managing Workforce Diversity: People Related Issues	
		6. The United Way and the Boy Scouts: Controversy				at the Barden Corporation	1.50
		in Portland, Oregon	1.50			35. Propmore Corporation	1.50
		Module II—Strategy, Planning, and Organizational				36. Promotion to Police Sergeant	1.50
		Culture (0-324-31473-6)	**7.25**			37. Propco, Inc.	1.50
		7. American Express	1.50			38. The Business of Culture at Acoma Pueblo	1.50
		8. XEL Communications Inc.	1.50			39. Personnel Selection Procedures in Latin America	1.50
		9. XEL Communications "C"	1.50			**Module VII—Motivation and Performance**	
		10. Europska Databanka	1.50			**(0-324-31478-7)**	**7.25**
		11. The Boston YWCA: 1991	1.50			40. How to Motivate Fred Maiorino?	1.50
		12. BCH Telecommunications	1.50			41. The Kriendler Executive Dining Room	1.50
		13. Riding the Rollercoaster of Entrepreneurship	1.50			42. Nordstorm	1.50
		Module III—Organizational Structure and Design				43. Southwest Airlines: Can Luv Rule the World?	1.50
		(0-324-31474-4)	**7.25**			44. Lincoln Electric Company	1.50
		14. The Plaza Inn	1.50			45. An American in Paris	1.50
		15. Dowling Flexible Metals	1.50			**Module VIII—Communication and Group Dynamics**	
		16. Microsoft: Adapting to New Challenges	1.50			**(0-324-31479-5)**	**7.25**
		17. Sunday at Al Tech	1.50			46. Motor Parts Corporation	1.50
		18. The ZX Software Development Group: Santa Cruz	1.50			47. Contract Negotiations in Western Africa	1.50
		19. The Wreck of Amtrack's Sunset Limited	1.50			48. Does This Milkshake Taste Funny?	1.50
		Module IV—Organizational Control, Power, and Conflict				49. Insubordination or Unclear Loyalties?	1.50
		(0-324-31475-2)	**7.25**			50. The Luggers Versus the Butchers	1.50
		20. Pearl Jam's Dispute with Ticketmaster	1.50			51. Donor Services Department	1.50
		21. Suntory	1.50			**Module IX—Organizational Change and Transformation**	
		22. Baksheesh	1.50			**(0-324-31480-9)**	**7.25**
		23. Conflict Management	1.50			52. Transformation at Harley Davidson	1.50
		24. Iroquois Container Corporation: Flagstone Operations	1.50			53. Organizational Change: Planning and Implementing	
		25. Astrotech Fuel Systems (A)	1.50			Teams at AAL and IPS	1.50
		26. Unsavory Problems at Tasty's: A Case Exercise about				54. Using Leadership to Promote TQM	1.50
		Whistleblowing	1.50			55. Peoples Trust Company	1.50
		Module V—Human Resource Management				56. Seeing the Forest and the Trees	1.50
		(0-324-31476-0)	**7.25**			57. Women and Global Leadership at Bestfoods	1.50
		27. Precision Measurement of Japan	1.50				
		28. Bringing HR into the Business	1.50				

Cengage Learning Custom Publishing
5191 Natorp Boulevard
Mason, OH 45040
800.355.9983
Fax: 800.270.3310

Custom Module Order Form

Managing Organizations and People: Cases in Management, Organizational Behavior, and Human Resource
Managment, 7e (Modular Edition) (Edited by Paul F. Buller & Randall S. Schuler)

TO:	FROM:
COMPANY:	DATE:
FAX NUMBER:	TOTAL PAGES INCLUDING COVER:
PHONE NUMBER:	SENDER'S TELEPHONE NUMBER:
RE:	SENDER'S EMAIL ADDRESS:

ATTENTION ADOPTING INSTRUCTOR:

To ensure that your Case Module readers arrive in time for the start of your course, please submit your selections at least six weeks prior to the start of your course in one of the following ways:

1. Fax: Complete this form and fax it to the Database Order Coordinator at 800.270.3310

2. Mail: Complete this form and mail it to the following address:
Database Order Coordinator
Cengage Learning Custom Publishing
5191 Natorp Boulevard
Mason, OH 45040

INSTRUCTOR:

DEPARTMENT:

SCHOOL:

CITY, STATE, ZIP:

COURSE NUMBER & TITLE:

QUANTITY:

COURSE START DATE:	TODAY'S DATE:

We will print desk copies when we print your order. Desk copies will be sent to the address above. If you would like them sent elsewhere, contact your Cengage Learning Representative or call your Custom Consultant at 800.355.9983.

Managing Organizations and People: Cases in Management, Organizational Behavior, and Human Resource Management, 7e (Modular Edition)
(Edited by Paul F. Buller & Randall S. Schuler)

Please indicate the readings you would like to include in your custom reader with a check mark. Then indicate the sequence you would like your readings to appear, starting with 1. Fax this completed form, along with your contact information, to your Custom Consultant at 800.270.3310, or call Customer Service at 800.355.9983 for assistance.

✔	Seq.	Module/Title	Price	✔	Seq.	Module/Title	Price
		Module I—Management and Leadership				29. The Tall Pines Hotel and Conference Center	$1.50
		(0-324-31472-8)	**$7.25**			30. A Broader View Seizes More Opportunities	1.50
		1. Custom Chip, Inc.	1.50			31. Moon Over ER	1.50
		2. Dick Spencer	1.50			32. Heartland State Bank (A)	1.50
		3. The Marketing Campaign at ChemCorp	1.50			33. Heartland State Bank (B)	1.50
		4. Traveler Import Cars, Inc.	1.50			**Module VI—Managing Diversity (0-324-31477-9)**	**7.25**
		5. The Prominent Dr. Rombach	1.50			34. Managing Workforce Diversity: People Related Issues	
		6. The United Way and the Boy Scouts: Controversy				at the Barden Corporation	1.50
		in Portland, Oregon	1.50			35. Propmore Corporation	1.50
		Module II—Strategy, Planning, and Organizational				36. Promotion to Police Sergeant	1.50
		Culture (0-324-31473-6)	**7.25**			37. Propco, Inc.	1.50
		7. American Express	1.50			38. The Business of Culture at Acoma Pueblo	1.50
		8. XEL Communications Inc.	1.50			39. Personnel Selection Procedures in Latin America	1.50
		9. XEL Communications "C"	1.50			**Module VII—Motivation and Performance**	
		10. Europska Databanka	1.50			**(0-324-31478-7)**	**7.25**
		11. The Boston YWCA: 1991	1.50			40. How to Motivate Fred Maiorino?	1.50
		12. BCH Telecommunications	1.50			41. The Kriendler Executive Dining Room	1.50
		13. Riding the Rollercoaster of Entrepreneurship	1.50			42. Nordstorm	1.50
		Module III—Organizational Structure and Design				43. Southwest Airlines: Can Luv Rule the World?	1.50
		(0-324-31474-4)	**7.25**			44. Lincoln Electric Company	1.50
		14. The Plaza Inn	1.50			45. An American in Paris	1.50
		15. Dowling Flexible Metals	1.50			**Module VIII—Communication and Group Dynamics**	
		16. Microsoft: Adapting to New Challenges	1.50			**(0-324-31479-5)**	**7.25**
		17. Sunday at Al Tech	1.50			46. Motor Parts Corporation	1.50
		18. The ZX Software Development Group: Santa Cruz	1.50			47. Contract Negotiations in Western Africa	1.50
		19. The Wreck of Amtrack's Sunset Limited	1.50			48. Does This Milkshake Taste Funny?	1.50
		Module IV—Organizational Control, Power, and Conflict				49. Insubordination or Unclear Loyalties?	1.50
		(0-324-31475-2)	**7.25**			50. The Luggers Versus the Butchers	1.50
		20. Pearl Jam's Dispute with Ticketmaster	1.50			51. Donor Services Department	1.50
		21. Suntory	1.50			**Module IX—Organizational Change and Transformation**	
		22. Baksheesh	1.50			**(0-324-31480-9)**	**7.25**
		23. Conflict Management	1.50			52. Transformation at Harley Davidson	1.50
		24. Iroquois Container Corporation: Flagstone Operations	1.50			53. Organizational Change: Planning and Implementing	
		25. Astrotech Fuel Systems (A)	1.50			Teams at AAL and IPS	1.50
		26. Unsavory Problems at Tasty's: A Case Exercise about				54. Using Leadership to Promote TQM	1.50
		Whistleblowing	1.50			55. Peoples Trust Company	1.50
		Module V—Human Resource Management				56. Seeing the Forest and the Trees	1.50
		(0-324-31476-0)	**7.25**			57. Women and Global Leadership at Bestfoods	1.50
		27. Precision Measurement of Japan	1.50				
		28. Bringing HR into the Business	1.50				

Cengage Learning Custom Publishing
5191 Natorp Boulevard
Mason, OH 45040
800.355.9983
Fax: 800.270.3310

Custom Module Order Form

Managing Organizations and People: Cases in Management, Organizational Behavior, and Human Resource Managment, 7e (Modular Edition) (Edited by Paul F. Buller & Randall S. Schuler)

TO:	FROM:
COMPANY:	DATE:
FAX NUMBER:	TOTAL PAGES INCLUDING COVER:
PHONE NUMBER:	SENDER'S TELEPHONE NUMBER:
RE:	SENDER'S EMAIL ADDRESS:

ATTENTION ADOPTING INSTRUCTOR:

To ensure that your Case Module readers arrive in time for the start of your course, please submit your selections at least six weeks prior to the start of your course in one of the following ways:

1. Fax: Complete this form and fax it to the Database Order Coordinator at 800.270.3310

2. Mail: Complete this form and mail it to the following address:
Database Order Coordinator
Cengage Learning Custom Publishing
5191 Natorp Boulevard
Mason, OH 45040

INSTRUCTOR:

DEPARTMENT:

SCHOOL:

CITY, STATE, ZIP:

COURSE NUMBER & TITLE:

QUANTITY:

COURSE START DATE: TODAY'S DATE:

We will print desk copies when we print your order. Desk copies will be sent to the address above. If you would like them sent elsewhere, contact your Cengage Learning Representative or call your Custom Consultant at 800.355.9983.